GRIMMS' TALES
FOR YOUNG AND OLD

GRIMMS' TALES FOR YOUNG AND OLD

THE COMPLETE STORIES

❧ Translated by Ralph Manheim ❧

DOUBLEDAY & COMPANY, INC., GARDEN CITY, NEW YORK

3120830   12/09

Translated from the Winkler-Verlag (Munich) edition
of the Complete Kinder- und and Hausmärchen
(Tales for Young and Old) by Jakob and Wilhelm Grimm,
as first published in 1819.

Designed by Laurence Alexander

Library of Congress Cataloging in Publication Data

Grimm, Jakob Ludwig Karl, 1785–1863.
  Grimms' tales for young and old.

  Translation of Kinder- und Hausmärchen by
J. L. K. Grimm and W. K. Grimm.
  Includes index.
  SUMMARY: A new and modern translation of the entire
collection of folk and fairy tales written by the
Brothers Grimm.
  1. Fairy tales. [1. Fairy tales. 2. Folklore—
Germany] I. Grimm, Wilhelm Karl, 1786–1859, joint
author. II. Manheim, Ralph, 1907–   III. Title.
PT921.G62 1977   398.2′1′0943
         ISBN 0-385-11005-7
Library of Congress Catalog Card Number 76–56318

CONTENTS

Legends for Children

GRIMMS' TALES
FOR YOUNG AND OLD

Translator's Preface

Some students of folklore have found fault with the Grimm brothers for "improving" on the tales they collected. The Grimms themselves claimed to have taken down the stories faithfully. Of course they improved on the spoken word; some storytellers are fluent, others hem and haw, and from the storytelling point of view there would seem to be no point in recording their hemming and hawing. But at the same time the Grimms *were* astonishingly faithful, undeterred by the irrational or unseemly. To appreciate their fidelity, one need only look at most English translations, where the puzzling "Hans My Hedgehog" becomes "Hans the Hedgehog," where the donkey, instead of "emitting" goldpieces from both ends, merely spits them out, and the Devil's grandmother, instead of "lousing" him, picking the lice out of his hair, merely strokes his head. More important—and this, I believe, is the greatest mark of their genius— they make us hear the voices of the individual storytellers, and much more clearly I am sure than if they had been two tape recorders. In the German text the human voice takes on a wide variety of tones—mysterious, elegiac, hushed-and-frightened, poetic, whimsical, rowdy, solemnly or mock-solemnly moralizing, and so on. But everywhere—or almost—it is a natural human voice, speaking as someone might speak, and seldom if ever do we hear anything resembling the never-never, good-nursery, fairy-tale style prevalent in the English translations of these and other folk tales.

Why, in English, were they called fairy tales in the first place? For, despite a considerable population of devils, witches, goblins, and elves, there are, strictly speaking, no fairies in these stories, but only "wise women," good or bad, of indeterminate age, not remarkable for their looks, and rarely equipped with wands, while the German word *Märchen* means only a fantastic tale and is translated into virtually every other language by an equivalent of "tale" or "story."

The reason is that when the tales first arrived in England, such "absurdities" were thought to be fit only for children, who were distinctly second-class citizens at the time. The adults of the reading classes were much too busy making money, Empire-building, and finding scientific explanations for the sun and everything under it, to bother with village idiots who get to be kings, tables that set themselves, or stupid peasant women with identity crises. And since the tales were addressed to children, they were termed fairy tales and, by and large, gift-wrapped in a fairy-tale style that was supposed to appeal to children.

In the present century, however, and especially in the last few decades, the *Tales for Young and Old* (a title much closer to the German *Kinder- und Hausmärchen* than *Fairy Tales*) have, with no change on their part, become more and more modern. Modern psychology has taught us that the human mind, like the folk tale, is a jumble of rational and irrational elements. Modern art and literature have broken down the barriers between genres and shown us the depth and beauty of the incongruous. And, as part of this general movement of desegregation, parents have moved closer to their children, the smaller ones at least.

Since the times had caught up with the *Tales*, since there was no longer any reason to rationalize or bowdlerize them, and since they are such wonderful stories, I thought the time had come to attempt a new translation that would be faithful to the Grimm brothers' faithfulness. I have tried to use a simple, natural language, though when the original waxes literary (as in the story of "A Sparrow and His Four Sons") I wax with it. I have tried to capture the tones of the various narrators. And, by no means least, I have paid close attention to descriptive detail, because the tellers of these stories were close observers and even their wildest fantasies, not to mention their comedies of village life, are set in houses, streets, and landscapes with which they were thoroughly familiar.

Especially in connection with such detail, but also in many other matters, I am deeply indebted to my friend Wolfgang Sauerlander for his help and advice.

R.M.

1

The Frog King or
Iron Heinrich

IN OLDEN TIMES, when wishing still helped, there lived a king, whose daughters were all beautiful, but the youngest was so beautiful that even the sun, who had seen many things, was filled with wonder every time he shone upon her face. Not far from the king's palace there was a great, dark forest, and under an old lime tree in the forest there was a spring. When the weather was very hot, the princess went out to the forest and sat near the edge of the cool spring. And when the time hung heavy on her hands, she took a golden ball, threw it into the air and caught it. It was her favorite plaything.

One day it so happened that when she held out her little hand to catch the golden ball, the ball passed it by, fell to the ground, and rolled straight into the water. The princess followed the ball with her eyes, but it disappeared, and the spring was deep, so deep that you couldn't see the bottom. She began to cry; she cried louder and louder, she was inconsolable. As she was lamenting, someone called out to her: "What's the matter, princess? Why, to hear you wailing, a stone would take pity." She looked to see where the voice came from and saw a frog sticking his big ugly head out of the water. "Oh, it's you, you old splasher," she said. "I'm crying because my ball has fallen into the spring." "Stop crying," said the frog. "I believe I can help you, but what will you give me if I bring you your plaything?" "Anything you like, dear frog," she said. "My clothes, my beads, my jewels, even the golden crown I'm wearing." The frog replied: "I don't want your clothes, your beads and jewels, or your golden crown. But if you will love me, if you will let me be your companion and playmate, and sit at your table and eat from your golden plate and drink from your golden cup and sleep in your bed, if you promise me that, I'll go down and fetch you your golden ball." "Oh yes," she said, "I promise you anything you want, if only you'll bring me my ball." But she thought: "What nonsense that silly frog talks; he lives in the water with other frogs and croaks; how can he be a companion to anybody?"

Once the frog had her promise, he put his head down and dived, and in a little while he came swimming back to the surface. He had her golden ball in his mouth and he tossed it onto the grass. When she saw her beautiful plaything, the princess was very happy. She picked it up and ran off with it. "Wait, wait," cried the frog. "Take me with you, I can't run like you." He croaked and he croaked at the top of his lungs, but it did him no good. The princess didn't listen. She hurried home and soon forgot the poor frog. There was nothing he could do but go back down into his spring.

The next day, when she had sat down to table with the king and all his courtiers and was eating from her golden plate, something came hopping *plip plop, plip plop,* up the marble steps. When it reached the top, it knocked at the door and cried out: "Princess, youngest princess, let me in." She ran to see who was there, and when she opened the door, she saw the frog. She closed the door as fast as she could and went back to the table. She was frightened to death. The king saw that her heart was going pit-a-pat and said: "What are you afraid of, my child? Is there a giant outside come to take you away?" "Oh no," she said. "It's not a giant, but only a nasty frog." "What does the frog want of you?" "O father dear, yesterday when I was playing beside the spring in the forest, my golden ball fell in the water. And because I was crying so, the frog got it for me, and because he insisted, I promised he could be my companion. I never thought he'd get out of his spring. And now he's outside and he wants to come in after me." Then the frog knocked a second time and cried out:

> "Princess, youngest princess,
> Let me in.
> Don't you remember what
> You promised yesterday
> By the cool spring?
> Princess, youngest princess,
> Let me in."

Then the king said: "When you make a promise, you must keep it; just go and let him in." She went and opened the door; the frog hopped in and followed close at her heels. There he sat and cried

out: "Lift me up beside you." She didn't know what to do, but the
king ordered her to obey. Once the frog was on the chair, he wanted
to be on the table, and once he was on the table, he said: "Now push
your golden plate up closer to me, so we can eat together." She did as
he asked, but anyone could see she wasn't happy about it. The frog enjoyed his meal, but almost every bite stuck in the princess's throat.
Finally he said: "I've had enough to eat and now I'm tired, so carry
me to your room and prepare your silken bed. Then we'll lie down
and sleep." The princess began to cry. She was afraid of the cold
frog; she didn't dare touch him and now he wanted to sleep in her
lovely clean bed. But the king grew angry and said: "He helped you
when you were in trouble and you mustn't despise him now." Then
she picked him up between thumb and forefinger, carried him upstairs, and put him down in a corner. But when she lay down in the
bed, he came crawling over and said: "I'm tired. I want to sleep as
much as you do; pick me up or I'll tell your father." At that she grew
very angry, picked him up and dashed him against the wall with all
her might. "Now you'll get your rest, you nasty frog."

But when he fell to the floor, he wasn't a frog any longer; he was a
king's son with beautiful smiling eyes. At her father's bidding, he became her dear companion and husband. He told her that a wicked
witch had put a spell on him and that no one but she alone could have
freed him from the spring, and that they would go to his kingdom together the next day. Then they fell asleep and in the morning when
the sun woke them a carriage drove up, drawn by eight white horses
in golden harness, with white ostrich plumes on their heads, and
behind it stood the young king's servant, the faithful Heinrich.
Faithful Heinrich had been so sad when his master was turned into a
frog that he had had three iron bands forged around his heart, to keep
it from bursting with grief and sadness. The carriage had come to
take the young king back to his kingdom. Faithful Heinrich lifted the
two of them in and sat down again in back, overjoyed that his master
had been set free. When they had gone a bit of the way, the prince
heard a cracking sound behind him, as though something had broken.
He turned around and cried out:

> "Heinrich, the carriage is falling apart."
> "No, master, it's only an iron ring.
> I had it forged around my heart

For fear that it would break in two
When, struck by cruel magic, you
Were turned to a frog in a forest spring."

Once again and yet once again, the cracking was heard, and each time the king's son thought the carriage was falling to pieces, but it was only the bands snapping and falling away from faithful Heinrich's heart, because his master had been set free and was happy.

2

The Cat and the Mouse Set Up Housekeeping

A CAT MADE THE ACQUAINTANCE of a mouse and went on at such length about her feelings of love and friendship that the mouse finally consented to set up housekeeping with her. "But," said the cat, "we shall have to provide for the winter if we're not to go hungry. It would be risky for a little mouse like you to go foraging. You'd be sure to end up in a trap." The mouse agreed that this was excellent advice and they bought a pot of fat. But they didn't know where to put it. Finally, after long deliberation, the cat said: "I can't think of a safer place than the church, because no one would dare to take anything in a church. We'll put it under the altar and we won't touch it until we need it." So the pot was hidden away, but it wasn't long before the cat felt a craving for it and said to the mouse: "By the way, friend mouse, I've been invited to a christening. My cousin has given birth to a baby boy, white with brown spots, and I'm to be the godmother. Let me go out today and you do the housework by yourself." "Yes, of course," said the mouse. "Go, by all means, and if they give you something nice to eat, think of me. I only wish I could have a taste of that sweet red childbed wine." But it wasn't true, the cat had no cousin and hadn't been invited to any christening. She went straight to the church, crept over to the fat and licked off the top. Then she went for a stroll on the rooftops, looking for opportunities. After that she stretched out in the sun and wiped her whiskers every time she thought of the fat. It was evening when she finally got home. "Well," said the mouse, "there you are again. I'll bet you've had an enjoyable day." "Not bad," said the cat. "What name did they give the baby?" the mouse asked. "Top-off," said the cat very dryly. "Top-off!" the mouse exclaimed. "That's a strange and unusual name. Is it customary in your family?" "What's so strange about it?" said the cat. "It's no worse than Crumb-thief, as your godchildren are called."

It wasn't long before the cat had another craving. She said to the mouse: "You'll have to do me a favor and attend to the housekeeping by yourself. I've been asked to another christening, and I can't refuse, because the child has a white ring around its neck." The good mouse consented, and the cat crept along the town wall to the church and ate up half the fat. "Nothing tastes better than what you yourself eat," she said, and was very pleased with her day's work. When she came home, the mouse asked: "What did they christen the child?" "Half-gone," the cat replied. "Half-gone! You don't say so! Never in all my life have I heard that name. I bet it's not in the calendar of saints."

Soon the cat's mouth watered again for the delicacy. "All good things come in threes," she said to the mouse. "I'm to stand godmother again. The child is all black with white paws; otherwise, it hasn't a single white hair on its whole body. That only happens once in several years. You'll let me go out again, won't you?" "Top-off! Half-gone!" the mouse replied. "Those names are so peculiar, they give me dark thoughts." "All day long you sit home in your fuzzy dark-gray coat and your long pig-tail," said the cat. "It makes you moody. That's what comes of not going out in the daytime." During the cat's absence, the mouse washed the dishes and put the house in order, and meanwhile the greedy cat emptied the pot of fat. "Now that it's gone," said the cat to herself, "there's nothing more to worry about." Her belly was full, and it was night when she waddled contentedly home. The moment she came in, the mouse asked her what name had been given the third child. "You won't like it any better than the others," said the cat. "The name is All-gone." "All-gone!" cried the mouse. "That's the most dubious name I ever heard. I've never seen it in print. All-gone! What can it mean?" She shook her head, rolled up in a ball and went to sleep.

After that no one invited the cat to any more christenings, but when winter came and there was nothing more to be found out of doors, the mouse remembered their treasure and said: "Come on, cat, let's go out to the pot of fat we've been saving. We'll enjoy it." "Oh yes," said the cat. "You'll enjoy it as much as if you stuck your dainty little tongue out the window." Off they went, and when they got there, the pot was still in its place, but it was empty. "Ah," said the mouse. "Now I see what has happened. Now the light dawns. Some friend you turned out to be! You ate it all up when you went to stand godmother. First top off, then half gone, then . . ." "Be still!" cried the cat. "One more word and I'll eat you up." "All gone" was already on the mouse's tongue. No sooner was it out than the cat took a leap, grabbed the mouse and gobbled her up. You see how it is? That's the way of the world.

3

Mary's Child

A WOODCUTTER AND HIS WIFE lived at the edge of a large forest. They had only one child, a little girl of three. But they were so poor they no longer had their daily bread and they didn't know what they would give her to eat. One day the woodcutter, heavy with care, went out into the forest to work, and suddenly, while he was cutting wood, a tall, beautiful woman stood before him. On her head she wore a crown of shining stars, and she said to him: "I am the Virgin Mary, the Christ child's mother. You are poor and needy. Bring me your child, I shall take her with me and be her mother and care for her." The woodcutter did her bidding. He went and got his child and entrusted her to the Virgin Mary, who took her up to heaven with her. There the child lived well; she ate cakes and drank sweet milk, her clothes were of gold, and the angel children played with her. One day, when she was fourteen, the Virgin Mary called her and said: "Dear child, I'm going on a long journey. Here: I'm giving you the thirteen keys to the thirteen doors of the kingdom of heaven for safekeeping. You may open twelve of them and look at the wonders inside, but the thirteenth, which this little key unlocks, is forbidden you. Take care not to open it; if you do, you will be unhappy." The girl promised to obey, and when the Virgin Mary had gone, she began to inspect the rooms of the kingdom of heaven. Each day she opened one of them, until she had opened all twelve. In each one sat an Apostle, surrounded by great splendor. She delighted in all the glory and magnificence, and so did the little angel children who always went with her. Now only the forbidden door was left, and she was ever so eager to know what was hidden behind it. She said to the angel children: "I won't open it all the way and I won't go in. I'll just barely open it, so we can see a little something through the crack." "Oh no," said the angel children, "that would be a sin, the Virgin Mary forbade it, and something terrible might happen." Then she said nothing more, but the desire in her heart refused to be still. It pecked and gnawed, and left her no peace. One day when the angel children had all gone out, she thought: "Now I'm all alone, I could take a look; no one will know if I do." She picked out the key, and when she had it in her hand, she put it in the lock, and when she had put it in, she turned it. The door sprang open and there sat the Holy Trinity in fire and radiance. She stood there for a while, marveling at what she saw, and then she touched her finger ever so slightly to the light. And her whole finger turned golden. Seized with a great fear, she slammed the door and ran away. No matter what she did, her fear wouldn't stop, and her heart pounded and pounded and wouldn't calm down. She washed and she scrubbed, but the gold stuck to her finger and wouldn't go away.

It wasn't long before the Virgin Mary came back from her journey. She called the girl and asked her to give back the keys of heaven. As the girl handed her the keys, the Virgin Mary looked into her eyes and asked: "Did you open the thirteenth door?" "No," she said. The Virgin Mary laid her hand on the girl's heart and felt how it was pounding and pounding, and then she knew she had disobeyed her command and opened the door. She asked again: "You really didn't?" "No," said the girl for the second time. Then the Virgin Mary saw her finger, which had been turned golden when it touched the heavenly fire. She knew the girl had sinned, and asked a third time: "You didn't?" "No," said the girl for the third time. Then the

Virgin Mary said: "You've disobeyed me, and what's more, you've lied. You are no longer worthy to be in heaven."

Then the girl sank into a deep sleep, and when she awoke she was back on earth, lying in a clearing in the woods. She wanted to cry out, but she couldn't make a sound. She jumped up and wanted to run away, but whichever way she turned the way was blocked by dense thorny thickets, and she couldn't break through. In the clearing where she was imprisoned there was an old hollow tree, and that was where she had to make her home. When night came, she crawled inside and slept, and when it rained and stormed, she found shelter there. But it was a wretched life, and when she remembered how lovely it had been in heaven and how the angel children had played with her, she wept bitterly. Roots and wild berries were her only food and she went looking for them as far as she could go. In the autumn she gathered fallen nuts and leaves and brought them to her hollow tree. The nuts were her winter food, and when the snow and ice came she crawled into the leaves like a poor little animal, to keep from freezing. Soon her clothes were torn and fell off her body piece by piece. As soon as the sun shone warm again, she went out and sat beside the tree, and her long hair covered her all around like a coat. Year after year she sat there and felt the hardship and misery of the world.

One day when the leaves were fresh and green again, the king of the country went hunting in the forest. He was chasing a deer, and because the deer had fled into the thicket surrounding the clearing, he got down off his horse, parted the brambles and hacked out a path for himself with his sword. When at last he made his way through, he saw a beautiful girl sitting under the tree, covered to the tips of her toes by her golden hair. He stopped and looked at her with amazement. And then he spoke to her, saying: "Who are you? Why are you sitting here in the wilderness?" But she didn't answer, for she couldn't open her mouth. The king spoke again: "Will you come with me to my palace?" At that she nodded her head a little. The king picked her up in his arms, carried her to his horse, and rode home with her. And when they came to the royal palace, he saw to it that she was dressed in beautiful clothes and given plenty of everything. And though she couldn't speak, she was so winsome and beautiful that he fell in love with her and soon they were married.

When close to a year had passed, the queen brought a son into the world. That night, as she lay alone in her bed, the Virgin Mary appeared to her and said: "If you tell me the truth and admit that you opened the forbidden door, I shall loose your tongue and give you back your speech; but if you persist in your sin and stubbornly deny it, I shall take your newborn child away with me." Then it was given the queen to answer, but she was still obstinate. "No," she said, "I didn't open the forbidden door," and the Virgin Mary picked up the newborn child in her arms and disappeared with him. Next morning, when the child was nowhere to be found, the courtiers began to mutter that the queen was an ogress and had killed her own child. She heard what they were saying and she couldn't reply, but the king refused to believe it, because he loved her so.

A year later the queen gave birth to another son. That night the Virgin Mary came to her again and said: "If you admit that you opened the forbidden door, I shall give you back your child and loose your tongue; but if you persist in your sin and deny it, I shall take this newborn babe away with me too." And again the queen said: "No, I didn't open the forbidden door," and the Virgin took the child from her arms and carried him up to heaven. In the morning, when this child too had disappeared, the courtiers said aloud that the queen had devoured it, and the king's councilors demanded that she be brought to trial. But the king loved her so that he refused to believe it and forbade his councilors to speak of it, on pain of death.

The next year the queen gave birth to a beautiful baby girl. For the third time the Virgin Mary appeared to her during the night and said: "Follow me." She took her by the hand and led her up to heaven, and showed her her two eldest children, who were laughing and playing with the globe. When the queen showed how happy she was, the Virgin Mary asked: "Has your heart softened now? If you admit that you opened the forbidden door, I shall give you back your two sons." But the queen answered for the third time: "No, I didn't open the forbidden door." At that, the Virgin made her sink down to the earth again and took away her third child with the others.

The next morning, when it became known, all the courtiers cried aloud: "The queen is an ogress; she must be condemned." This time the king could not disregard his councilors. She was brought to trial, and since she couldn't answer and couldn't defend herself, she was condemned to be burned at the stake. The wood was piled up, and when she was bound to the stake and the fire began to burn all around her, the hard ice of pride melted, her heart was moved with remorse, and she thought: "If only I could confess before I die that I opened the door." Then her voice came back to her and she cried aloud: "Yes, Mary, I did it!" At that moment, the heavens sent rain that put out the flames. Above her a light flared up, and the Virgin Mary came down with both little boys at her sides and the newborn daughter in her arms. She spoke kindly to her: "All those who repent and who confess—their sin will be forgiven." And she handed her the three children, loosed her tongue, and gave her happiness for all the rest of her life.

4

The Boy Who Left Home to Find Out About the Shivers

A FATHER HAD TWO SONS; the elder was bright and clever, able to deal with anything that came his way, but the younger was so stupid that he understood nothing and could learn nothing. Everyone who saw him said: "His father will have his troubles with that one!" If there was anything to be done, it was always the elder who had to do it. But if his father asked the elder son to get something at dusk, let alone at night, and if his way would have taken him through the graveyard or some other spooky place, he would say: "Oh, no, father, I won't go. It gives me the shivers." Or in the evening, when stories that made your flesh creep were told around the fire, the listeners would sometimes say: "Oh, it gives me the shivers." The younger son sat in the corner and listened, but he didn't understand. "They keep saying: 'It gives me the shivers, it gives me the shivers!' It doesn't give *me* the shivers: it must be another one of those tricks that I just can't learn."

One day his father said to him: "Listen, you over there in the corner, you're getting to be big and strong. You'll have to learn something to make a living by. Your brother is always working, but you're useless." "Oh yes, father," he answered. "I'd be glad to learn something; if possible, I'd like to learn how to get the shivers; that's something I just don't understand." When he heard that, the elder son laughed and thought to himself: "My goodness, what a blockhead my brother is. He'll never come to any good. As the twig is bent, so the tree will lean." The father sighed and answered: "It won't hurt you to find out about the shivers, but it won't get you a living."

A few days later the sexton dropped in for a visit. The father unburdened himself and told him how ignorant his younger son was, how he knew nothing and learned nothing. "Just imagine, when I asked him what he wanted to do for a living, he said he wanted to learn how to get the shivers." "If that's all he wants," said the sexton, "I'll teach him; give him to me, I'll lick him into shape." The father liked the idea, because he thought: "The boy is bound to get something out of it." So the sexton took him to stay at his house, and gave him the job of ringing the church bell. A few days later, he woke him at midnight and told him to climb up into the belfry and ring the bell. "Now you'll learn what the shivers are," he thought, and secretly went up ahead of him. When the boy came to the top and turned around to grab the bellrope, he saw a white figure on the stairs, across from the sound hole. "Who's there?" he cried, but the figure didn't answer and didn't move. "Answer me," the boy cried out, "or go away. You've no business here in the middle of the night." But the sexton stood there without moving, to make the boy think he was a ghost. The boy cried out a second time: "What are you doing here? Answer me if you're an honest man, or I'll throw you down the stairs." "He wouldn't do that," the sexton thought. And he didn't utter a sound and he stood there like a stone. The boy called out a third time, and when that didn't help, he braced himself and pushed the ghost down the stairs, and the ghost tumbled down ten steps and lay still in a corner. Then the boy rang the bell, went home, and lay down without saying a word. The sexton's wife waited a long time for her husband, but he didn't come back. Finally she got worried, woke the boy, and asked: "Do you know what's become of my husband? He went up into the belfry ahead of you."

"No," the boy answered. "But somebody was standing on the stairs across from the sound hole, and when he wouldn't answer and wouldn't go away, I thought he was up to no good, so I pushed him down the stairs. Go take a look. You'll see if it was him. I'd be very sorry." The wife went to the belfry and found her husband lying in the corner groaning. He had broken a leg.

She carried him home and ran screaming and ranting to the boy's father. "Your boy has done something terrible!" she cried. "He's thrown my husband down the stairs and broken his leg. Get the good-for-nothing out of our house." The father was horrified; he went to the sexton's house and gave the boy a piece of his mind. "What godless thing have you done now? The Devil must have put you up to it." "Father," he said, "just listen. I'm perfectly innocent. He was standing there in the night like someone that's up to no good. I didn't know who he was, and I warned him three times to say something or go away." "Heavens above," said the father. "With you I'll never have anything but trouble. Get out of my sight, I don't want to see you any more." "Yes, father, gladly, just wait till it's light and I'll go away and learn to get the shivers. Then at least I'll know something to earn a living by." "Learn whatever you like," said the father. "It's all the same to me. Here are fifty talers, take them and go out into the wide world, but never tell a soul where you come from or who your father is, because I'm ashamed of you." "Yes, father, as you please. If that's all you ask of me, it won't be hard to remember."

When the day dawned, the boy put his fifty talers in his pocket and went out on the high road, and all the while he mumbled to himself: "If I could only get the shivers! If I could only get the shivers!" Then a man overtook him and heard the conversation the boy was having with himself. When they had gone on a little way and the gallows came in sight he said: "Look, there's a tree where seven have celebrated their marriage to the ropemaker's daughter, and now they're learning to fly. Sit down under it and wait till night comes, then you'll get the shivers all right." "If that's all there is to it," said the boy, "it will be easy. If I learn to get the shivers as quickly as all that, I'll give you my fifty talers; come back in the morning." Then the boy went to the gallows, sat down under it and waited for night to fall. Since he was cold, he made a fire, but by midnight the wind was blowing so cold that in spite of the fire he couldn't get warm.

And when the wind buffeted the hanged men so that they knocked together and swung back and forth, he thought: "If I'm freezing down here by the fire, imagine what it must be like for them up there." Being a kindhearted boy, he took a ladder, climbed up, untied them one by one, and brought them down, all seven. Then he stirred up the fire and blew on it, and sat them all around it to warm themselves. But they sat motionless, and the fire took hold of their clothes. "Be careful," he said, "or I'll hang you up again." But the dead men didn't hear him, they didn't say a word, and they just let their rags burn. That made him angry and he said: "If you won't be careful I can't help you. Next thing you know, you'll set me on fire." And he hung them up again one by one. Then he sat down beside his fire and fell asleep. In the morning the man came back for his fifty talers. "Well," he said, "now do you know what the shivers are?" "No," he replied. "How could I? Those fellows up there didn't open their mouths. They're so stupid they let the few rags they have on their backs catch fire and burn." The man saw he wouldn't be getting any fifty talers that day. As he was going away, he said: "I never saw anybody like that before."

The boy started off too, and again he talked to himself. "Oh, if I could only get the shivers! Oh, if I could only get the shivers!" A carter who was walking along behind him heard him and asked: "Who are you?" "I don't know," said the boy. "Where are you from?" "I don't know." "Who's your father?" "I mustn't say." "What is it that you keep mumbling the whole time?" "Oh," said the boy, "I wish I could get the shivers, but no one can teach me how." "That's a lot of nonsense," said the carter. "Forget it. Come with me and I'll get you a place to stay." The boy went with the carter, and in the evening they came to an inn, where they decided to spend the night. As they stepped into the hall, he said it again in a loud voice: "If I could only get the shivers! If I could only get the shivers!" The innkeeper heard him and laughed. "If that's what you want," he said, "I believe it can be arranged." "Don't say such things," said the innkeeper's wife. "Think of all the foolhardy fellows who have lost their lives; what a shame if those pretty eyes were never to see the light of day again." But the boy said: "I don't care how hard it is, I want to learn, that's what I left home for." And he gave the innkeeper no peace until he told him about a haunted castle nearby, where a man could easily learn all about the shivers if he was willing to spend three nights there. The king had promised his daughter in marriage to the man who could do it, and she was the most beautiful maiden under the sun. Besides, there were great treasures in the castle, guarded by evil spirits; those treasures would be set free and could make a poor man very rich. Many had already gone in, but none had come out again. The next morning the boy went to the king and said: "If you let me, I'd like to spend three nights in the haunted castle." The king looked at him, and because he liked him he said: "You can ask for three things to take with you into the castle, but they must be lifeless things." He replied: "Then give me fire, a lathe, and a wood carver's bench and knife."

The king had these taken to the castle during the day. At nightfall the boy went in, made a bright fire in one of the rooms, set up the wood carver's bench with the knife beside it, and sat down on the lathe. "Oh, if I could only get the shivers!" he said. "But I won't learn in this place either." Toward midnight he thought he'd stir up the fire. As he was blowing on it, he suddenly heard voices from the corner. "Miaow, miaow, we're so cold!" "Fools!" he cried. "What's the good of screaming? If you're cold, come sit by the fire and warm yourselves." No sooner had he spoken than two big black cats took a great leap to where he was sitting, sat down on either side of him, and looked at him with their wild fiery eyes. After a while, when they had warmed themselves, they said: "Friend, how about a game of cards?" "Why not?" he replied, "but first show me your paws." Then they stretched out their claws. "My goodness!" he said. "What long nails you have! Wait, I'll have to cut them before we begin." With that he seized them by the scruffs of their necks, lifted them up on the wood carver's bench and made their paws fast in the vise. "Now that I've seen your fingers," he said, "I don't feel like playing cards any more." Then he killed them and threw them out into the pond. But when he had got rid of those two and was sitting down by his fire again, black cats and black dogs on red-hot chains came rushing out of every nook and cranny, more and more of them until there was no place for him to escape to. They yelped and screamed horribly, trampled his fire, tore it apart, and tried to put it out. He looked on calmly for a while, but then when he had had enough, he seized his knife, shouted: "Get out, you no-goods," and lashed out at them. Some ran away, but he killed the rest and threw them into the pond. When he came back, he blew up his fire from the sparks and warmed himself. As he was sitting there, he could hardly keep his eyes open, and he wanted to sleep. He looked around and saw a big bed in the corner. "That's just what I need," he said, and lay down. But as he was closing his eyes, the bed began to roll of its own accord, and went rolling all around the castle. "Perfect," he said. "Better and better." And on it rolled, as though drawn by six horses, through doorways and up and down stairs. All of a sudden, one-two-three, it turned upside down, and lay on top of him like a mountain. But he threw off the blankets and pillows, climbed out, and said: "Now if you've a mind to, go right on rolling." Then he lay down by his fire and slept until daylight. In the morning the king came in. When he saw him lying on the floor, he thought the ghosts had killed him and he was dead. "What a pity!" he said. "Such a handsome boy!" The boy heard him, sat up and said: "Not so fast." The king was amazed, but he was glad too, and asked how he had made out. "Pretty well," he said. "One night has passed, the two others will pass too." When he turned up at the inn, the innkeeper's eyes nearly popped out of his head. "I never expected to see you alive again," he said. "Have you found out what it is to have the shivers?" "No," he said. "It's hopeless. If only someone could tell me!"

On the second night he went back to the old castle, sat down by the fire, and started talking to himself, the old lament: "If I could only get the shivers!" At the approach of midnight, a din and a hubbub were heard, first softly, then louder and louder. Then it was still for a while, and then, with loud screams, half a man came down the chimney and fell in front of him. "Hey!" cried the boy, "that's not enough. Where's the other half?" Then the noise started up again, howling and raging, and the other half fell down. "Wait," said the boy. "I'll stir up the fire for you." When he had stirred up the fire, he looked around. The two halves had put themselves together, and a horrible man was sitting in his place. "That wasn't our bargain," said the boy, "the bench is mine." The man tried to push him away, but the boy wouldn't let him; he shoved him with all his might and sat down in his place again. Then more men came tumbling down the chimney, one after another. They produced nine dead men's thigh-bones and two skulls and started playing ninepins. The boy felt like playing and asked: "Hey, can I join you?" "Sure, if you've got money." "Plenty of money," he said, "but those balls aren't really round." So he took the skulls, sat down at the lathe, and turned them till they were round. "There," he said. "Now we'll be able to bowl right. Whee! What a game we'll have!" He played and lost some of his money, but then the clock struck twelve, and they all disappeared. Then he lay down and fell into a peaceful sleep. The next morning the king came in to inquire. "How did you make out this time?" he asked. "I played ninepins and lost a few coppers." "Didn't you get the shivers?" "Go on!" he said. "I just enjoyed myself. If only I knew what the shivers were!"

On the third night he sat down on his bench again and said sadly: "If I could only get the shivers!" When it grew late, six big men came in, carrying a coffin. "Ha ha," he said, "that must be my cousin who died a few days ago." He beckoned with his finger and cried out: "Come out, cousin, come out." They set the coffin down on the floor, and he went over and took the lid off. There was a dead man lying inside. The boy felt his face, but it was as cold as ice. "Wait," he said. "I'll warm you a little." He went to the fire, warmed his hand and put it on the dead man's face, but it stayed cold. Then he took him out, sat down by the fire, put the dead man's head on his lap, and rubbed his arms to start the blood moving. When that didn't help, he remembered that "when two lie in bed together, they warm each other," so he put him into the bed, covered him up and got in with him. After a while the dead man warmed up and began to move. Then the boy said: "See, cousin, I've warmed you, haven't I?" But the dead man shouted: "Now I'm going to strangle you." "What!" cried the boy. "Is that my thanks? Back you go into your coffin." At that he picked him up, tossed him in, and closed the lid. Then the six men came and carried the coffin away. "I just can't get the shivers," said the boy, "I'll never learn how in this place, not if I live to be a hundred."

Then a man came in; he was bigger than all the others and terrifying to look at. But he was old and had a long white beard. "You little scamp," he cried out. "Now you'll find out about the shivers, because you're going to die." "Not so fast," said the boy. "If you want to kill me, you'll have to catch me." "I'll catch you all right," said the monster. "Take it easy and stop bragging, I'm as strong as you, probably

stronger." "We'll see about that," said the old man. "If you're
stronger than I am, I'll let you go; come on, we'll give it a try." Then
he led him through dark passages to a smithy, picked up an ax and
with one blow drove one anvil into the ground. "I can do better than
that," said the boy and went to the other anvil. The old man came up
beside him to watch, and his white beard hung down. The boy seized
the ax, split the anvil at one stroke and crammed the old man's beard
in the crack. "Now I've got you," he said. "Now who's going to die?"
And he picked up an iron rod and rained blows on the old man until
he whimpered and begged him to stop and promised to give him
great riches. The boy pulled out the ax and let the old man go.
Whereupon the old man led him back to the castle and there in a
cellar showed him three chests full of gold. "One part is for the
poor," he said, "one part is for the king, and the third is for you."
At that the clock struck twelve, the ghost disappeared, and the boy
was standing in the dark. "Never mind," he said, "I'll find my way
out." He groped until he found his room, and then he went to sleep
beside his fire. In the morning the king came in and said: "This time I
bet you've learned what the shivers are." "No," he replied. "What
can they be? My dead cousin was here, and then an old man with a
beard turned up; he showed me a lot of money down in the cellar,
but nobody told me what the shivers are." Then the king said:
"You've set the castle free and you shall marry my daughter."
"That's all very well and good," he replied, "but I still don't know
what the shivers are."

The gold was brought up and the wedding was celebrated, but
much as the young king loved his wife and happy as he was, he kept
saying: "If I could only get the shivers. If I could only get the
shivers." In the end it got on her nerves. "Never mind," said her
lady's maid. "Leave it to me. I'll give him the shivers." She went out
to the brook that ran through the garden and had them bring her a
whole pail full of minnows. That night when the young king was
sleeping, his wife pulled off the blanket and emptied the pail full of
cold water and minnows on top of him. The little fishes flipped and
wriggled all over him. He woke up and cried out: "Oh, dear wife,
I'm shivering, I'm shivering! Now at last I know what the shivers
are!"

5

The Wolf and the Seven Young Kids

ONCE THERE WAS a goat who had seven young kids, and she loved them as a mother loves her children. One day she thought she'd go to the forest for food, so she gathered all seven around her and said: "Dear children, I'm going to the forest. Watch out for the wolf, for if he gets in, he'll gobble you up, bones and all. The scoundrel often disguises himself, but you'll recognize him by his gruff voice and his black feet." The kids said: "Dear mother, we'll be careful. You needn't worry about leaving us." The mother bleated and started off with an easy mind.

It wasn't long before someone knocked at the door and called out: "Open up, dear children, your mother is here, and she's brought something for each one of you." But the kids recognized the wolf by his gruff voice. "We won't open," they cried. "You're not our mother. She has a lovely, delicate voice, and your voice is gruff. You're the wolf." Then the wolf went to the store and bought a big piece of chalk. He ate the chalk and it made his voice smooth. Then he went back, knocked at the door, and called out: "Open up, dear children. You mother is here and she's brought something for each one of you." But the wolf had put his black paw on the window ledge. The kids saw it and cried: "We won't open. Our mother hasn't got black feet like you; you're the wolf." Then the wolf went to the baker and said: "I've bruised my foot; coat it with dough." After the baker had coated his paw with dough, he went to the miller and said: "Sprinkle white flour on my paw." The miller thought: "The wolf wants to trick somebody," and refused. But the wolf said: "If you won't do it, I'll eat you up." Then the miller was afraid and made his paw white. Yes, that's the way people are.

The villain went to the door for the third time, knocked, and said:

"Open up, children, your dear mother has come home, and she's brought something for each one of you from the forest." The kids cried out: "First show us your paw; then we'll see if you're our dear mother." He put his paw on the window ledge, and when they saw it was white, they thought he'd been telling the truth and opened the door. But who should come in but the wolf. They were scared to death and tried to hide. One jumped under the table, the second into the bed, the third into the stove, the fourth into the kitchen, the fifth into the cupboard, the sixth under the washbasin, the seventh into the grandfather clock. But the wolf found them all and made short shrift of them; one after another, he gobbled them up. The only one he didn't find was the youngest in the clock. When the wolf had satisfied his greed, he waddled away, lay down under a tree on the green meadow outside, and fell asleep.

A little later the goat came home from the woods. Oh, what a sight met her eyes! The door was wide open. Table, chairs, and benches were overturned, the washbasin was smashed to pieces, blanket and pillows had been torn off the bed. She looked for her children, but they were nowhere to be found. She called them by their names, one after another, but no one answered. Finally, when she got to the youngest, a thin voice cried out: "Mother dear, I'm in the clock." She brought him out and he told her how the wolf had come and gobbled up all the others. You can imagine how she wept over her poor children.

Finally, still weeping and wailing, she went out, and the youngest kid went with her. When they came to the meadow, the wolf was lying there under the tree, snoring so hard the branches trembled. She looked at him from all sides, and saw that something was jumping and wriggling in his full belly. "Gracious," she thought, "could my poor children that he gobbled up for his supper still be alive?" She sent the kid running home for scissors, needle and thread. Then she cut the monster's belly open, and no sooner had she made the first cut than a kid stuck his head out, and as she went on cutting all six jumped out, one after the other. They were all alive and hadn't even been hurt, because in his greed the monster had swallowed them whole. How happy they all were! They snuggled up to their mother and each hopped about like a tailor at his wedding. Then the mother goat said: "Now go find me some stones; we'll fill this godless beast's belly with them while he's still asleep." So the kids picked up stones as fast as they could and stuffed them into the wolf's belly until it was full. Then the mother goat sewed him up so deftly that he didn't notice a thing and didn't even move.

When the wolf finally had his sleep out, he stood up. The stones made him very thirsty, so he thought he'd go to the well and drink. But when he started to walk and to move from side to side, the stones clattered and rattled in his belly. He cried out:

> "What's rumbling and bumbling
> Around in my belly?
> I thought it was six little kids,
> But it's only a lot of stones."

And when he came to the well and bent over the water to drink, the heavy stones pulled him in and he drowned. When the seven kids saw that, they came running and cried aloud: "The wolf is dead! The wolf is dead!" And they and their mother went dancing round and round the well for joy.

6
Faithful Johannes

ONCE THERE WAS an old king who fell sick and thought: "Most likely I am lying on my deathbed." And he said: "Send me Faithful Johannes." Faithful Johannes was his favorite servant, so called because he had always been so faithful. When he came to the bedside, the king said: "Dear, faithful Johannes, I feel that my end is near. Only one thing weighs on my mind: my son is still at an age when he doesn't know what's best for him. I won't be able to close my eyes in peace unless you promise to teach him everything he needs to know and to be a foster father to him." Faithful Johannes replied: "I'll never desert him; I'll serve him faithfully, even at the cost of my life." The old king said: "Now my mind is at rest and I can die in peace." And he went on: "After my death you must show him the whole palace, every room and hall and vault and all the treasures in them. But you mustn't show him the last room on the long corridor, where the portrait of the Princess of the Golden Roof is hidden. If he sees that portrait, he will be overcome with love for her. He will fall into a faint and later on he will face great perils for her sake; you must protect him from that." When Faithful Johannes had given the king his hand and repeated his promise, the king fell silent, laid his head on his pillow, and died.

After the old king was buried, Faithful Johannes told the young king what he had promised his father on his deathbed and said: "That promise I will keep. I will be faithful to you as I was to him, though it cost me my life." When the days of mourning had passed, Faithful Johannes said to the young king: "Now it is time for you to see your patrimony. The palace is yours now, and I will show it to you." Whereupon he led him all over, upstairs and down, and showed him all the treasures and magnificent rooms. The one door he did not open was the door to the room where the dangerous portrait was hidden. The portrait was placed in such a way that it was the first thing you saw when the door opened, and it was so wonderfully wrought that you couldn't help thinking it lived and breathed, and that nothing in the world could be more gracious and beautiful. Of course the young king noticed that Faithful Johannes always passed one door by, and he said: "Why don't you ever open that door?" "There's something inside that would frighten you," he answered. The king said: "I've seen the whole palace, and now I want to know what's in that room." He went to the door and tried to open it by force, but Faithful Johannes held him back, saying: "I promised your father on his deathbed that I wouldn't let you see what's in that room. It could bring dire misfortune both to you and to me." "I don't believe it," said the young king. "And if I don't go in, I'm sure it will be the end of me. Day and night I shall have no peace until I've seen it. And now I mean to stand here until you open that door."

Faithful Johannes saw there was no help for it. His heart was heavy, and he sighed mournfully as he took the key from the big bunch. He opened the door and went in first, thinking he would cover the portrait with his body so the king wouldn't see it. Much good it did him! The king stood up on tiptoes and looked over his shoulder. When he saw the portrait of the maiden, so beautiful and so resplendent with gold and jewels, he fell to the ground in a faint.

Faithful Johannes lifted him up and carried him to his bed. "Now it has happened. Good God, what will be the end of it?" Then he restored the young king with wine and soon he was himself again. The first words he spoke were: "Ah, what a beautiful portrait! Who is it?" "It's the Princess of the Golden Roof," said Faithful Johannes. And the king said: "My love for her is so great that if all the leaves on the trees were tongues they couldn't describe it. I'll stake my life to win her. You are my dear, faithful Johannes, you must help me."

For a long while the faithful servant pondered: how should they go about it? For even to approach the princess was no easy matter. When at last he had thought of a way, he said to the king: "All her chairs, tables, bowls, cups, and dishes, everything she keeps around her, is gold. There are five casks of gold in your treasure house. Have the goldsmiths of the kingdom work one of them into all manner of vessels and implements, into birds, beasts, and miraculous creatures. Such things will please her. We shall sail to her country and try our luck with them." The king sent for all the goldsmiths and they had to work day and night until at last the marvelous things were ready. When they had all been loaded on board a ship, Faithful Johannes dressed up as a merchant, and the king had to do likewise, so as to make himself unrecognizable. Then they put out to sea and sailed until they reached the city where the Princess of the Golden Roof lived.

Faithful Johannes told the king to stay on board and wait for him. "Maybe I'll bring the princess back with me," he said. "So take care to put everything in order. Have them set out the golden vessels and adorn the whole ship with them." Then he gathered all manner of golden things into his apron and went straight to the royal palace. When he entered the courtyard, a beautiful girl was standing by the well; she had two golden buckets and she was drawing water. As she turned and made ready to carry the glittering water away, she saw the stranger and asked him who he was. "I'm a merchant," he replied. And he opened his apron and let her look. "My, what beautiful things!" She put down her buckets, examined them one by one, and said: "The princess must see them; she's so fond of gold work I'm sure she'll buy them all." She took him by the hand and led him into the palace, for she was the princess's maid-in-waiting. When the princess saw the things, she was delighted and said: "They're so

beautifully made; I'd like to buy them all." But faithful Johannes
said: "I'm only the servant of a rich merchant: what I have here is
nothing to what my master has on his ship. Nothing more artful and
charming has ever been made of gold." She wanted him to have it all
brought to her, but he said: "There's so much it would take days to
move it, and there aren't enough rooms in your palace to show it in."
Her curiosity and eagerness grew so great that she finally said: "Take
me to the ship; I'll go there myself to see your master's treasures."

Faithful Johannes led her to the ship. He was very happy. When
the king caught sight of her, he saw that she was even more beautiful
than her portrait, and he thought his heart would burst. She went
aboard and the king led her inside the ship; but Faithful Johannes
remained on deck and told the helmsman to cast off. "Unfurl the
sails, make the ship fly like a bird in the air." Meanwhile the king
showed her the golden vessels one by one, the bowls and cups and
dishes, the birds and beasts and fantastic animals. Hours passed while
she was looking at them from all sides, and in her joy she didn't notice that the ship was moving. After examining the last piece, she
thanked the merchant and decided to go home, but when she stepped
out on deck she saw that the ship was far from shore, speeding over
the high seas with all sails unfurled. "Oh," she cried in horror. "I've
been deceived and carried away. I've fallen into the hands of a merchant. I'd sooner die!" But the king took her by the hand and said:
"I'm not a merchant; I'm a king, every bit as well born as you. If I've
carried you off by treachery, it's because I was overpowered by love.
When first I saw your portrait, I fell to the ground in a faint." At
that the Princess of the Golden Roof was comforted; her heart spoke
in his favor and she gladly consented to become his wife.

But while they were on the high seas it so happened that Faithful
Johannes, who was sitting in the bow of the ship playing a tune,
saw three ravens come flying through the air. He stopped playing
and listened to their conversation, for he knew their language. One of
them cried out: "Look, he's taking the Princess of the Golden Roof
home with him." "So he is," said the second, "but he hasn't got her
yet." "What do you mean he hasn't got her?" cried the third. "He's
got her right here in his ship." The first spoke again and said: "A lot
of good that will do him! When they go ashore, a chestnut horse will
come running toward him. He'll want to jump on its back, and if he

does, it will fly away with him and he'll never see his princess again."
The second spoke: "Is there no way of saving him?" "Oh yes, if
someone else jumps on quickly, grabs the pistol that's sure to be in
the saddle holster, and shoots the horse dead. Then the young king
will be saved. But who knows that? And if anyone knows and tells
him, he'll be turned to stone from the tips of his toes to his knees."
Then the second raven said: "I know still more. Even if the horse is
killed, the young king won't be able to keep his bride. When they
reach the palace together, he will see a bridal robe laid out in a basin;
it will seem to be woven of gold and silver, but it will really be made
of sulfur and pitch, and if he puts it on, it will burn him to the mar-
row." The third asked: "Is there no way of saving him?" "Oh yes,"
said the second. "If someone picks up the robe with gloves and
throws it in the fire and burns it up, then the king will be saved. But
what's the good of that! If anyone knows and tells him, half his body
will be turned to stone, from his knees to his heart." Then the third
said: "I know still more. Even if the bridal robe is burned, the young
king won't keep his bride. After the wedding there will be a ball.
While the young queen is dancing, she will suddenly turn pale and
fall down as though dead. Unless someone lifts her up and sucks three
drops of blood from her right breast and spits them out, she will die.
But if someone knows it and tells, his whole body from the top of his
head to the tips of his toes will turn to stone." When the ravens had
said all that, they flew away. Faithful Johannes had understood every
word. From that time on, he was silent and sad, because if he didn't
tell his master what he had heard, his master would come to grief,
and if he did tell him, he would be forfeiting his own life. In the end
he said to himself: "I will save my master, even if I have to die for
it."

When they went ashore, it so happened that what the ravens had
predicted came true. A magnificent chestnut horse came galloping toward the king. "Look!" cried the king. "This horse shall carry me to
my palace." He was about to mount the horse, but Faithful Johannes
was too quick for him; he swung himself into the saddle, drew the
pistol from the holster, and shot the horse dead. The king's other servants, who bore Faithful Johannes no love, cried out: "What a shame
to kill that beautiful beast, which was going to carry the king to his
palace!" But the king said: "Be still and let him go. He is my dear,

faithful Johannes. Who knows what good may come of it?" When they went into the palace, there was a basin in the hall, and in it lay the bridal robe, looking as if it were made of gold and silver. The young king went over and was going to take hold of it, but Faithful Johannes pushed him away, picked it up with gloves, hurried to the fire and burned it. Again the other servants began to grumble, saying: "What do you think of that? Now he's gone and burned the king's bridal robe." But the young king said: "Who knows what good may come of it? Leave him alone, he's my dear, faithful Johannes." The king and the princess were married. The dancing began and the bride joined in. Faithful Johannes was watchful and kept looking at her face. Suddenly she turned pale and fell to the floor as though dead. He leaped to the spot, picked her up, and carried her to the bedchamber. As she lay on the bed, he knelt down, sucked the three drops of blood from her right breast and spat them out. Before you knew it, she began to breathe and come to herself. But the young king had seen what had happened and he was angry, because he didn't know why Faithful Johannes had done it. "Throw him into prison!" he cried. The next morning Faithful Johannes was condemned to death and taken to the gallows. As he stood there on the scaffold, he said: "Every condemned man is allowed to speak up before he dies. Shall I too be granted that right?" "Yes," said the king. "It is granted." Then Faithful Johannes said: "I have been condemned unjustly. I have always been faithful to you." And he told the story: how he had heard the conversation of the ravens on the high seas and had had to do all those things to save his master. At that the king cried: "Oh, my dear, faithful Johannes, forgive me! Forgive me! Bring him down." But no sooner had Faithful Johannes said his last word than he fell lifeless and turned to stone.

The king and the queen were very sad, and the king said: "Alas, how faithful he was and how ill I rewarded him!" And he gave orders that the stone statue should be carried to his bedchamber and placed beside his bed. Every time he looked at it he wept and said: "Oh, if only I could bring you back to life, my dear, faithful Johannes." Time passed, and the queen gave birth to twin sons, who throve and were a great joy to her. Once when the queen was at church and the two children were playing with their father, he looked at the stone statue and his heart was full of grief. He sighed and cried out: "Oh, if only I could bring you back to life, my dear, faithful Johannes!" The stone began to speak and said: "You *can* bring me back to life, but you must sacrifice what you love most in all the world." The king cried out: "For you I will give everything I have." The stone spoke again: "If with your own hand you cut both your children's heads off and daub me with their blood, I shall come back to life." The king was horrified when he heard that he would have to kill his beloved children, but remembering how Faithful Johannes had been and how he had died for him, he drew his sword and cut the children's heads off with his own hand. When he had daubed the stone with blood, it came back to life and Faithful Johannes stood before him, hale and hearty. He said to the king: "Your fidelity shall not go unrewarded." He took the children's heads, set them in place, and daubed the wounds with their blood. In an instant they were whole again, jumping about and playing as though nothing had happened to them. The king was overjoyed. When he saw the queen coming, he hid Faithful Johannes and the two children in a big cupboard. As she entered the room, he said to her: "Did you pray when you were in church?" "Yes," she said, "but I kept thinking of Faithful Johannes and the terrible misfortune that came to him on our account." He replied: "Dear wife, we can bring him back to life, but it will cost us our two sons; we shall have to sacrifice them." The queen grew pale and horror gripped her heart, but she said: "We owe it to him for being so faithful." Delighted to hear that she felt the same as he had, he went and opened the cupboard. Out stepped the children and Faithful Johannes, and the king said: "God be praised, he is saved, and we have our sons again too." And he told her how it had all come about. After that they lived happily to the end of their lives.

7

A Good Stroke of Business

A PEASANT TOOK HIS COW to market and sold it for seven talers. On the way home he had to pass a pond, and before he even got near it he heard the frogs croaking: "Ek, ek, ek, ek." "Bless me," he said to himself. "They don't know what they're talking about. It was seven talers I made, not eight." When he got to the water, he called out to them: "What stupid animals you are! Don't you know any better than that? It was seven talers, not eight." But the frogs stuck to their "ek, ek, ek, ek." "If you won't believe me," he said, "I can count them out for you." He took the money from his pocket and counted out the seven talers, twenty-four groschen to each one. But the frogs paid no attention to his reckoning and went right on with their "ek, ek, ek, ek." Now the peasant was really angry. "All right," he cried. "If you think you're so smart, count them yourself," and with that he threw all his money into the water. Then he stood still and waited, for he thought that when they finished counting his money they'd bring it back. But the frogs were stubborn; they kept on croaking "ek, ek, ek, ek" and they didn't return his money either. He waited a long while, until night began to fall and he had to go home. Then he gave the frogs a good piece of his mind: "You splashing, bug-eyed block-heads!" he cried. "Big-mouths, that's what you are. You can shout until my ears ache, but you can't count seven talers. Do you expect me to wait here all night?" So he went away, but the frogs kept croaking "ek, ek, ek, ek" after him, and he was in a very bad humor when he got home.

After a while he bought another cow and butchered it. He figured that if he got a good price for the meat he'd be making as much as the two cows were worth and still have the hide left over. When he got to town with the meat, a pack of dogs were gathered outside the gate, with a big greyhound in the lead who danced around the meat, sniffing and barking: "Arf, arf, arf, arf." When he wouldn't stop, the peasant said to him: "I understand. You're saying 'half, half,' because you want half the meat, but where would I be if I gave it to you?" The dog's only reply was "arf, arf." "Will you promise not to eat it up, and can you vouch for your friends here?" "Arf, arf," said the dog. "Well, all right, since you insist, I'll let you have all of it. I know you and I know who you work for, but let me tell you this: I want my money within three days or you'll hear from me. Just bring it out to my place." With that he unloaded the meat and turned back. The dogs pounced on it and barked: "Arf, arf." The peasant heard them from far off and said to himself: "Would you listen to that! Now they all want half. But the big one will have to answer to me."

When the third day came, the peasant thought: "Tonight I'll have my money." He was as happy as could be. But no one came and no one brought him any money. "There's no relying on anyone these days," he said. In the end he lost patience, went to town and asked the butcher for his money. The butcher thought he was joking, but the peasant said: "Why would I be joking? I want my money. Didn't your big dog deliver the meat three days ago from the cow I'd just killed?" That made the butcher angry; he picked up a broomstick and chased him away. "Just wait," said the peasant. "There's still some justice left in the world." So he went to the royal palace and asked for an audience. They took him to the king, who was sitting there with his daughter, and the king asked him what his trouble was. "Trouble enough," he said. "The frogs and the dogs have robbed me, and the butcher has paid me with a stick." Then he told the king at great length what had happened. The king's daughter laughed loudly, and the king said: "I can't say you're in the right, but you shall marry my daughter. Never in all her life has she laughed like this, and I've promised her hand to the man who could make her laugh. You can thank God for your good fortune." "Never mind," said the peasant, "I don't want her. I've only got one wife, and even that's too many for me. Whenever I come home, it's as if there were one standing in every corner." At that the king grew angry and said: "You're nothing but an unmannerly lout." "Oh, Your Majesty," said the peasant, "what can you expect from a pig but pork?" "Look," said the king. "You shall have another reward. Go now, but come back in three days and you shall have five hundred."

When the peasant came out of the palace, the sentry said: "You made the king's daughter laugh. I'll bet you've been nicely rewarded." "I should say so," said the peasant. "I'm getting five hundred." "Then share it with me," said the soldier; "What can you do with all that money?" "Because it's you," said the peasant, "I'll let you have two hundred. Go to the king in three days, and they'll count it out for you." A Jew was standing nearby and heard the conversation. He ran after the peasant, grabbed him by the coattails, and said: "God's wonders, what a lucky man you are! Let me change it for you; I'll give it to you in small coins. What would you do with hard talers?" "All right," said the peasant. "You can have three hundred. Give them to me in coins right now. Go see the king in three days and you'll be repaid." The Jew was delighted with the profit he was making and paid out the sum in bad groschen, three of which are worth as much as two good ones. When the three days had passed, the peasant went to the king as the king had ordered. "Take off his coat," said the king. "He shall have his five hundred." "Oh no!" said the peasant, "they don't belong to me any more. I've given the sentry two hundred, and the Jew changed three hundred for me. I've got nothing coming to me at all." Just then the soldier and the Jew came in. They demanded what they had got out of the peasant, and both were given their just measure of lashes. The soldier bore it bravely, he'd been whipped before, but the Jew cried pitifully: "Oh oh oh! Are these my hard talers?" The king couldn't help laughing at what the peasant had done. His anger had boiled down and he said: "You lost your reward before you even got it, so I'll make it up to you. Go to my treasure room and take as much money as you please." The peasant didn't wait to be asked twice. He stuffed his big pockets with as much as they would hold. Then he went to the tavern and counted his money. The Jew, who had crept in after him, heard him muttering to himself: "That rascally king has put one over on me. Why didn't he give me the money himself? Then I'd know how much I've got. How can I know if it's right when I picked it up without looking?" "God help us," said the Jew to himself. "This man's speaking disrespectfully of our king. I'll go and denounce him. I'll get a reward and, better still, he'll be punished." When the king heard what the peasant had said, he flew into a rage and told the Jew to go and bring the offender. The Jew ran to the peasant. "You must come to the king this minute." "Don't tell me," said the peasant. "I know what's right. First I'm going to have a new coat made. Do you think a man with so much money in his pockets can go to the king in a ragged old coat like this?" The Jew saw that the peasant wouldn't budge without a new coat and he was afraid that if the king's anger had time to blow over he would lose his reward and the peasant his punishment. So he said: "I'll lend you a fine coat for a little while just to do you a good turn. What won't a man do out of kindness!" The peasant accepted, put on the Jew's coat and went to the king. The king reproached the peasant for the wicked words the Jew had reported. "Nonsense," said the peasant. "Anything a Jew says is a lie; you'll never hear a word of truth coming out of *his* mouth. Why, I wouldn't put it past him to claim that I'm wearing his coat." "What's this!" cried the Jew. "You say it's not my coat? Didn't I lend it to you to do you a good turn, so you could come and see the king?" When the king heard that, he said: "This Jew must have deceived somebody, either me or the peasant," and had the peasant paid a little more in hard talers. The peasant went home in the good coat, with the good money in his pocket, and said: "I got it right this time."

8

A Miraculous Fiddler

ONCE THERE WAS a miraculous fiddler who was going through the woods all by himself, thinking of this and thinking of that, and when he was good and sick of thinking he said to himself: "The time hangs heavy on my hands out here in the woods. What I need is a good companion." Then he took his fiddle from his back and played a tune that went ringing through the trees. It wasn't long before a wolf came trotting through the thicket. "Ah, here comes a wolf," said the fiddler. "That's not what I want." But the wolf came closer and spoke to him: "Oh, my dear fiddler, how beautifully you play! I wish I could learn to play like that." "It's easy," said the fiddler. "You just have to do everything I say." "O fiddler," said the wolf, "I shall obey you as a pupil obeys his teacher." The fiddler bade him come along, and after a while they came to an old oak tree that was hollow inside and split down the middle. "Here we are," said the fiddler. "If you want to learn how to play, put your forepaws into this crack." When the wolf complied, the fiddler quickly picked up a stone and with one blow wedged the wolf's paws in so tight that he was held fast like a prisoner. "Wait here till I get back," he said, and went his way.

A little while later he said to himself again: "The time hangs heavy on my hands out here in the woods; I'll get myself another companion." He took his fiddle and again the music went ringing through the woods. It wasn't long before a fox came slinking through the trees. "Ah, here comes a fox," said the fiddler. "That's not what I want." The fox came up to him and said: "Oh, my dear fiddler, how beautifully you play! I wish I could learn to play like that." "It's easy," said the fiddler. "You just have to do everything I say." "O fiddler," said the fox, "I shall obey you as a pupil obeys his teacher." "Follow me," said the fiddler. After a while they came to a path with high bushes on either side. The fiddler stopped, took hold of a hazel tree, bent it down to the ground from one side, and stepped on the tip. Then he bent another tree down from the other side and said: "Very well, friend fox, if you want to learn something, give me your left forepaw." The fox obeyed and he tied it to the lefthand tree. "Friend fox," he said, "now give me your right forepaw," and he tied it to the righthand tree. When he had made sure the knots were tight enough, he let go. The bushes sprang back, lifting the fox up with them, and he found himself wriggling in midair. "Wait here till I get back," said the fiddler, and went his way.

Once again he said to himself: "The time hangs heavy on my hands out here in the woods; I'll get myself another companion." He took his fiddle and the music rang through the woods. Then a hare came bounding through the trees. "Ah, here comes a hare," said the fiddler. "That's not what I want." "Oh, my dear fiddler," said the hare, "how beautifully you play! I wish I could learn to play like that." "It's easy," said the fiddler. "You just have to do everything I say." "O fiddler," said the hare, "I shall obey you as a pupil obeys his teacher." After a while they came to a clearing with an aspen tree in it. The fiddler tied a long string around the hare's neck and fastened the other end to the tree. "And now, friend hare, step lively. i want you to run around this tree twenty times." The hare obeyed, and when he had finished, the string had wound itself around the tree trunk twenty times and he was caught. He struggled and tugged, but it only drove the string deeper into the soft skin of his throat. "Wait here till I get back," said the fiddler and went his way.

In the meantime the wolf had tugged and pulled and bitten on the stone, and finally freed his paws from the crack. Seething with rage, he ran after the fiddler, ready to tear him to pieces. When the fox saw him running, he wailed and whimpered for all he was worth: "Brother wolf, help me. The fiddler deceived me." The wolf pulled the trees down, cut the strings with his teeth and freed the fox, who went along with him to get even with the fiddler. They found the bound hare and set him free, and all three went in search of their enemy.

The fiddler had played once again, and this time he was luckier. His music reached the ears of a poor woodcutter, who instantly, without thinking twice, stopped work and with his ax under his arm came to listen to the music. "Here comes the right companion at last," said the fiddler. "It's a person I wanted, not wild animals." And he played so sweetly and beautifully that the poor man stood as though spellbound, and his heart leaped for joy. As he stood there, the wolf, the fox, and the hare came along, and he could see they were up to no good. So he lifted his flashing ax and stood in front of the fiddler, as if to say: "Anyone who wants to hurt my friend here will have me to deal with." At that the animals took fright and ran off into the woods. Out of gratitude the fiddler played one more tune for the woodcutter. Then he went his way.

9

The Twelve Brothers

THERE WERE ONCE a king and a queen who lived together peaceably and had twelve children, who were all boys. One day the king said to his wife: "If the thirteenth child you are about to bear is a girl, the twelve boys must die, so that her wealth may be great and that she alone may inherit the kingdom." He had twelve coffins made and filled with wood shavings, and in each one there was a little pillow. He had them taken to a locked room, gave the queen the key, and told her not to speak of them to anyone.

The mother sat all day and grieved, and her youngest son, who was always with her and whom she called Benjamin, after the Bible, said to her: "Mother dear, why are you so sad?" "Dearest child," she said, "I'm not allowed to tell you." But he gave her no peace until she unlocked the room and showed him the twelve coffins full of wood shavings. Then she said: "Dearest Benjamin, your father has had these coffins made for you and your eleven brothers, for if I give birth to a girl you are all to be killed and buried in them." She wept as she spoke, and her son comforted her, saying: "Don't cry, mother dear, we can take care of ourselves. We'll run away." And she said: "Go to the forest with your eleven brothers. Let each of you by turns climb the highest tree you can find and keep watch. If I give birth to a boy, I shall raise a white flag on this tower, and then you may come back. But if I give birth to a girl, I shall raise a red flag. Then you must escape as fast as you can, and God keep you. Every night I shall get up and pray for you; in the winter I shall pray that you find fire to warm yourselves, and in the summer that you're not wilting in the heat."

When she had given them her blessing, her sons went out into the forest. They took turns watching the tower from the top of the tallest oak tree. When eleven days had passed and it was Benjamin's turn, he saw a flag going up, and it was not the white one but the blood-red one, proclaiming that they should all die. When the brothers heard that, they grew angry and said: "Are we to die on a girl's account? We swear to avenge ourselves. Whenever we meet a girl, her red blood will flow."

Then they went deeper into the forest, and right in the middle where it was darkest they found an enchanted hut that no one was living in. "We will live here," they said, "and you, Benjamin, because you're the youngest and weakest, will stay home and keep house. The rest of us will go out and get food." So they went into the forest and shot hares and deer and birds and pigeons, anything that was good to eat. They brought their kill to Benjamin, who dressed and cooked the meat, and in that way they stilled their hunger. They lived in the hut for ten years, and the time didn't seem long to them.

By then the queen's daughter had grown to be a little girl. She was good of heart and fair of face, and she had a gold star on her forehead. Once when a big washing had been done, she saw twelve men's shirts and asked her mother: "Whom do these shirts belong to? They're much too small for father." Her mother answered with a heavy heart: "Dear child, they belong to your twelve brothers." The little girl said: "Where are my twelve brothers? This is the first I've heard of them." "God only knows where they are," said the queen. "They're out in the world, wandering." Then she took the little girl and unlocked the room and showed her the twelve coffins with the wood shavings and the little pillows in them. "These coffins," she said, "were meant for your brothers, but they secretly went away before you were born." She told her how it had all come about, and the little girl said: "Mother dear, please don't cry. I shall go and look for my brothers."

So she took the twelve shirts and went straight into the big forest. All day she walked and in the evening she came to the enchanted hut. She went in and saw a young boy, who asked her: "Where have you come from and where are you going?" He was amazed to find her so beautiful, dressed like a queen, and with a gold star on her forehead. She answered: "I'm a king's daughter and I'm looking for my twelve brothers, and I shall go on as far as the sky is blue until I find them." And she showed him the twelve shirts that belonged to them. Then Benjamin knew she was his sister and said: "I'm Benjamin, your youngest brother." She wept for joy, and so did Benjamin, and they hugged and kissed each other ever so lovingly. But then he said: "Dear sister, there's still a hitch. Long ago we swore that any girl who crossed our path must die, because we had to leave our kingdom on a girl's account." And she said: "I'll gladly die if that will save my twelve brothers." "No," he said. "I don't want you to die. Sit here under this tub until my eleven brothers come home. I'm sure I can win them over." She did as he had said, and at nightfall the others came home from the hunt. Their supper was ready, and as they sat at the table eating, they asked: "What's new?" "Haven't you heard?" said Benjamin. "No," they replied. "Well," he said, "you've been out in the woods, and I've stayed home; yet I know more than you."

"Tell us!" they cried. "Do you promise," he said, "not to kill the first girl who crosses our path?" "Yes!" they all cried. "We shall spare her. Now tell us." Then he said: "Our sister is here!" He lifted up the tub and out came the king's daughter dressed like a queen; she had a gold star on her forehead and was ever so beautiful. They were all overjoyed. They hugged her and kissed her, and loved her with all their hearts.

From then on she stayed in the hut with Benjamin and helped him with his work. The eleven went out into the forest and caught game and deer and birds and pigeons for them to eat, and their sister and Benjamin prepared their meals. She gathered firewood and wild plants and put the pots on the fire, so that supper was always ready when the eleven came home. And she kept the house in order, and made the beds up white and clean, and her brothers were always contented and they lived together in perfect harmony.

One day the two of them prepared a fine meal. When the others came home, they all sat down to eat and drink, and they were full of joy. Now there was a little garden behind the enchanted hut, and in it there were twelve lilies. She wanted to give her brothers pleasure, and so she broke off the flowers, meaning to give one to each of her brothers at supper. But no sooner had she broken off the flowers than her twelve brothers were turned into twelve ravens that flew away over the forest, and in the same moment the hut and garden vanished. The poor girl was left alone in the wilderness, and when she looked around an old woman was standing beside her, who said: "My child, what have you done? Why didn't you leave those twelve flowers alone? They were your brothers, and now they've been turned into ravens forever." The girl wept and said: "Is there no way of saving them?" "No," said the old woman. "In all the world there's only one way and it's so hard that you can't hope to succeed, for you would have to keep silent for seven years, without speaking and without laughing, and if you said a single word or if a single hour were wanting from the seven years, all your trouble would be in vain, and that one word would kill your brothers."

Then the girl said in her heart: "I know for sure that I'll save my brothers." She picked out a tall tree and climbed up in it, and there she sat spinning, and she neither spoke nor laughed. Now it so happened that a king went hunting in that forest. He had a big greyhound who ran to the tree where the girl was sitting, and he jumped up, yapping and barking. That brought the king to the foot of the tree. He saw the beautiful princess with the gold star on her forehead, and he was so enchanted with her beauty that he called out and asked her if she would like to be his wife. In reply, she said nothing, but she nodded her head a little. So he climbed the tree in person, carried her down, put her on his horse, and took her home. The wedding was celebrated with great splendor and joy, but the bride neither spoke nor laughed. After they had lived happily together for a few years, the king's mother, who was a wicked woman, began to slander the young queen. She said to the king: "That woman you brought home is no better than a beggar. Who knows what godless tricks she's up to! Even if she's dumb and can't speak, she could laugh once in a while. Anybody who doesn't laugh has a guilty conscience." At first the king refused to believe her, but the old woman kept it up so long and accused her of so many wicked things that the king finally let himself be convinced and condemned her to death.

They made a big fire in the courtyard, and they were going to burn her in it. The king stood at a window and looked down with tears in his eyes, for he still loved her. She was already tied to the stake and the fire was licking at her clothes with red tongues when the last moment of the seven years passed. A whirring was heard, twelve ravens came flying through the air and swooped down. And the moment they touched the ground they became her twelve brothers, for she had saved them. They broke up the fire, put out the flames, set their dear sister free, and hugged her and kissed her. And now that she was able to open her mouth and speak, she told the king why she had kept silent and never laughed. The king was glad to hear she was innocent and they all lived happily together until they died. The wicked stepmother was tried and sentenced and put in a barrel filled with boiling oil and poisonous snakes, and she died a cruel death.

10

A Pack of No-goods

THE ROOSTER SAID to the hen: "The nuts are getting ripe. Let's you and me go up on the hill and have a good feed before the squirrel carts them all away." "Oh yes," said the hen. "Come on. We'll have a lovely time together." So they climbed the hill, and because of the fine weather they stayed all day. Now I don't know if it was because they were feeling uppity, but they didn't like the idea of walking home, so Rooster built a little carriage out of nut shells. When it was finished, Hen sat down in the back and said: "It looks like you'll have to harness yourself." "Don't make me laugh," said Rooster. "I'd sooner walk home. That wasn't our agreement. I'm willing to sit on the box and drive, but pull between the shafts?—oh no! Nothing doing."

As they were arguing, a duck came along. "You thieves!" she quacked. "Who told you to come up here on my nut hill? Just wait! I'll make you pay for this!" And opening her bill as wide as she could, she leaped at the rooster. But Rooster wasn't behindhand. He fought back with a will and finally belabored the duck so hard with one of his spurs that she begged for mercy and gladly agreed to being harnessed to the carriage for punishment. Rooster sat down on the box. He was the coachman, and he shouted as they sped away: "Run, duck, as fast as you can!" When they had gone a little way, they met two pedestrians, a pin and a needle, who cried out: "Stop! Stop! It will soon be pitch dark"—they said—"too dark for us to go another step. And the road is so filthy and we'd be so much obliged for a lift. You see, we've been to the tailors' tavern outside the town gate and we lingered too long over our beer." Seeing they were skinny and wouldn't take up too much room, Rooster told them to hop in, but they had to promise not to step on his feet or on Hen's. Late that night they came to an inn. They didn't want to go any farther in the darkness and, besides, the duck was footsore and wobbly, so they decided to stop. At first the landlord said his house was full, and hemmed and hawed about taking them in. He probably thought they didn't look like the better class of people. But they spoke so sweetly, promising to give him the egg Hen had laid on the road and to let him keep the duck who laid one very day, that in the end he said they could stay the night. They sat down to table, ordering the very best, and spent the evening carousing. In the gray of dawn, when the whole house was still asleep, Rooster woke Hen, took her egg and pecked it open. The two of them gobbled it up and threw the shells on the hearth. Then they went to the needle, who was still asleep, took him by the head and stuck him in the cushion of the landlord's chair; next they stuck the pin in his towel, and then, without so much as a by-your-leave, they flew away. The duck, who had stayed in the yard because she preferred to sleep out of doors, heard them swishing over the heath and roused herself. As soon as she could find a brook, she swam away, which was quicker than pulling a carriage. A few hours later, the landlord dragged himself out of bed, washed, and picked up the towel to dry himself. The pin scraped across his face and made a red line from ear to ear. Then he went to the kitchen and thought he'd light his pipe, but when he leaned over the hearth the egg shells flew into his eyes. "Everything has it in for my face this morning," he said, and sank dejectedly into the grandfather chair. But a second later he bellowed, "Ouch!" and jumped up, because the needle had stuck him even worse, and not in the face. Now he was very angry and suspected the guests who had arrived so late at night. But when he went looking for them, they were gone. Thereupon he swore that he would never again take in a pack of no-goods, who eat all they want, pay nothing, and, to top it all, thank you with mean tricks.

11

Little Brother and Little Sister

LITTLE BROTHER TOOK his little sister by the hand and said: "Since our mother died, we haven't had a happy hour. Our stepmother beats us every day, and when we go to see her, she kicks us and drives us away. We get hard breadcrusts to eat, and the dog under the table is better off, for now and then she throws him something good. The pity of it! Oh, if our poor mother knew! Come, let's go out into the wide world together." All day they walked, over meadows, fields, and rocks, and when it rained, Little Sister said: "God and our hearts are weeping together!" At nightfall they came to a large forest, and they were so worn out with misery, hunger, and their long journey that they crawled into a hollow tree and fell asleep.

When they woke up the next morning, the sun was high in the sky and shone straight on the hollow tree. Little Brother said: "Little Sister, I'm thirsty. If there were a spring, I'd go and drink. I think I hear one now." Little Brother stood up and took Little Sister by the hand and they went looking for the spring. But their wicked stepmother was a witch. She had seen the children go away and had crept after them stealthily, as witches do, and had put a spell on all the springs in the forest. When they found a spring that leaped glittering over the stones, Little Brother wanted to drink, but Little Sister heard the spring speak as it gurgled and flowed: "If you drink of me, you'll be turned into a tiger; if you drink of me, you'll be turned into a tiger." And Little Sister cried out: "I beg you, Little Brother, don't drink. If you do, you'll be turned into a ferocious tiger, and you'll tear me to pieces." Little Brother didn't drink, though he was very thirsty, and he said: "I'll wait till the next spring." When they came to the next spring, it spoke too, and Little Sister heard it. "If you drink of me," it said, "you'll be turned into a wolf; if you drink of me, you'll be turned into a wolf." Little Sister cried: "Little Brother, I beg you, don't drink. If you do, you'll be turned into a wolf and you'll eat me up." Little Brother didn't drink and said: "I'll wait till the next spring, but then I'll have to drink, whatever you say. I'm just too thirsty." When they came to the third spring, Little Sister heard it speak as it gurgled and flowed. "If you drink of me, you'll be turned into a deer; if you drink of me, you'll be turned into a deer." Little Sister said: "Oh, Little Brother, I beg you, don't drink. If you do you'll be turned into a deer and run away from me." But Little Brother had already knelt down and leaned over and taken a drink of water, and no sooner had the first drops touched his lips than he turned into a fawn.

Little Sister wept over her poor bewitched little brother, and the fawn wept too and was very sad. Finally the little girl said: "Don't cry, dear fawn, I shall never leave you." She undid her golden garter and tied it around the fawn's neck, and she gathered reeds and plaited them into a soft rope. She fastened the rope to the garter and led the fawn by it, and they went deeper and deeper into the forest. When they had gone a long, long way, they came to a hut, and she looked in. It was empty and she thought: "Here we can stop and live." With leaves and moss she made a soft bed for the fawn, and every morning she went out and gathered roots and berries and nuts, and for the fawn she brought tender grass. He ate it out of her hand and gamboled merrily about. At night when Little Sister was tired and had said her prayers, she laid her head on the fawn's back. That was her pillow and she fell into a sweet sleep. If Little Brother had only had his human shape, it would have been a glorious life.

For a time they were all alone in the forest. But it so happened that the king of the country held a great hunt. The forest rang with the sound of horns, the barking of dogs, and the joyous cries of the hunters. The fawn heard the sounds of the hunt and longed to join in. "Oh, please," he said to Little Sister, "let me go. I can't bear it any longer." And he pleaded and pleaded until she finally gave in. "But be sure to come home at nightfall," she said. "I shall lock my door against the cruel hunters. You must knock and say: 'Little Sister, let me in'; then I'll know who it is. If you don't say that, I won't open my door." Then the fawn ran off into the forest, and he was so glad to be out in the open that he bounded with joy. The king and his huntsmen saw the beautiful beast and chased him, but they couldn't catch him, and when they thought they had him for sure he darted into a thicket and vanished. At nightfall he ran to the hut, knocked, and said: "Little Sister, let me in." The door was opened, in he leaped, and he slept all night on his soft bed. Next morning the hunt started in again, and when the fawn heard the horn and the hunters' halloo, he couldn't keep still, and he said: "Open the door, Little Sister. I shall die if I don't go." Little Sister opened the door and said: "But tonight you must come back again and say the same words." When the king and his huntsmen saw the fawn with the golden collar again, they all chased him, but he was too quick and nimble for them. It went on all day, but by nightfall the huntsmen had finally surrounded him and one of them wounded him slightly in the foot, so that he limped and couldn't run very fast. One hunstman crept after him to the hut and heard him say: "Little Sister, let me in," and saw how the door was opened for him and immediately closed again. The huntsman took it all in, went to the king and told him what he had seen and heard. And the king said: "We shall hunt again tomorrow."

Little Sister was dismayed when she saw that her fawn was wounded. She washed off the blood, sprinkled herbs on the wound, and said: "Now lie down, dear fawn. Lie down and get well." The wound was so slight that by morning the fawn didn't feel it anymore. And when he heard the sounds of the hunt, he said: "I can't bear it, I've got to join in. They'll never catch me." Little Sister wept and said: "They'll kill you, and here I shall be in the forest, all alone and forsaken. No, I won't let you out." "Then I shall die of misery right here," said the fawn. "When I hear the hunting horn, I can't keep still!" What was Little Sister to do? With a heavy heart she opened the door and the fawn bounded happily into the woods. When the king saw him, he said to his huntsmen: "Hunt him all day until nightfall, but let no one harm him." And as soon as the sun had set, he said to the huntsman: "Come now and show me the hut." When the king came to the door, he knocked and called out: "Dear little sister, let me in." The door opened, the king went in, and there stood a girl more beautiful than any he had ever seen. She was frightened when she saw that it wasn't the fawn but a man with a golden crown on his head. But the king looked at her tenderly, held out his hand, and said: "Will you come to my palace with me and be my wife?" "Oh yes,"

she said, "but the fawn must come with me. I won't ever leave him."
The king said: "He shall stay with you as long as you live and want
for nothing." Just then the fawn came bounding in. Little Sister tied
the plaited rope to his collar, took hold of the rope, and led him out
of the hut.

The king took the beautiful girl on his horse with him and they
rode to his palace, where the wedding was celebrated with great
splendor. Now she was a queen, and for a long time they lived happily together. The fawn was given the best of care and played about
in the palace gardens. But the wicked stepmother, who had driven
the children out into the world, thought Little Sister had been torn
to pieces by wild beasts and that Little Brother, after being turned
into a fawn, had been killed by hunters. When she heard they were
happy and prospering, envy and jealousy settled in her heart and
gave her no peace. She had only one thought: how was she to bring
misfortune on the two of them after all? Her own daughter, who was
as ugly as the night and had only one eye, kept grumbling and
finding fault: "And now she's a queen! Some people have all the
luck. It should have been me!" "Never mind," said the old woman,
and bade her take comfort. "When the time comes, I'll know what to
do." The time came and the queen gave birth to a beautiful little boy
when the king was out hunting. The old witch disguised herself as a
chambermaid, went to the room where the queen was lying, and
said: "Come, your bath is ready; it will do you good and give you
new strength. Quick, before it gets cold." The daughter was there
too. They carried the feeble queen into the bathroom, put her in the
tub, locked the door, and ran away. They had made such a furious
fire in the bathroom that the beautiful young queen was soon
smothered.

When that was done, the old woman covered her daughter's head
with a nightcap and put her into bed in the queen's place. She also
gave her the queen's face and appearance, but she couldn't replace
the missing eye. To keep the king from noticing it, she had to lie on
the side where she had no eye. When he got home that night and
heard that a son had been born to him, he was very happy. He
wanted to go to his wife's bedside to see how she was getting along,
but the old woman cried out: "Don't! Don't open the curtains! It's

too soon for the queen to look at the light, and she needs rest." The king stepped back and didn't find out that a false queen was lying in the bed.

At midnight everyone was asleep except for the nurse, who was sitting beside the cradle in the nursery. She saw the door open and she saw the real queen come in. She took the baby out of the cradle, put it to her breast and suckled it. Then she plumped up the pillow, laid the child down again, and covered it up with its little quilt. And she didn't forget the fawn. She went to the corner where he was lying and stroked his back. Then without a word she left the room. In the morning the nurse asked the guards if anyone had come into the palace during the night, and they said: "No, we haven't seen a soul." After that the queen came many nights, and never said a word; the nurse always saw her but didn't dare mention it to anyone.

After a certain time had passed, the queen began to speak when she came, saying:

> "How is my child? And how is my fawn?
> I shall come twice more, then never again."

The nurse didn't answer, but when the queen had vanished, she went to the king and told him everything. "Dear God," said the king, "how can this be? I'll stay with the child tonight and keep watch." So that evening he went to the nursery. At midnight the queen appeared again and said:

> "How is my child? And how is my fawn?
> I shall come once more, then never again."

And she suckled the child as usual and vanished. The king didn't dare speak to her, but he kept watch again the next night. Again she spoke:

> "How is my child? And how is my fawn?
> I've come this last time, then never again."

Then the king couldn't hold back. He crossed the room at one bound and said: "You can't be anyone but my dear wife." "Yes," she replied, "I am your dear wife," and in that moment, by the grace of God, life was restored to her, and the roses came back to her cheeks. Then she told the king what the wicked witch and her daughter had done to her. The king had them brought to trial and they were sentenced. The daughter was taken to the forest, where she was torn to pieces by wild beasts, and the witch was thrown into the fire and miserably burned. When the witch had burned to ashes, the fawn was freed from the spell and given his human form again. And Little Sister and Little Brother lived happily together to the end of their days.

12
Rapunzel

ONCE AFTER A MAN AND WIFE had long wished in vain for a child, the wife had reason to hope that God would grant them their wish. In the back of their house there was a little window that looked out over a wonderful garden, full of beautiful flowers and vegetables. But there was a high wall around the garden, and no one dared enter it because it belonged to a witch, who was very powerful and everyone was afraid of her. One day the wife stood at this window, looking down into the garden, and her eyes lit on a bed of the finest rapunzel, which is a kind of lettuce. And it looked so fresh and green that she longed for it and her mouth watered. Her craving for it grew from day to day, and she began to waste away because she knew she would never get any. Seeing her so pale and wretched, her husband took fright and asked: "What's the matter with you, dear wife?" "Oh," she said, "I shall die unless I get some rapunzel to eat from the garden behind our house." Her husband, who loved her, thought: "Sooner than let my wife die, I shall get her some of that rapunzel, cost what it may." As night was falling, he climbed the wall into the witch's garden, took a handful of rapunzel, and brought it to his wife. She made it into a salad right away and ate it hungrily. But it tasted so good, so very good, that the next day her craving for it was three times as great. Her husband could see she would know no peace unless he paid another visit to the garden. So at nightfall he climbed the wall again, but when he came down on the other side he had an awful fright, for there was the witch right in front of him. "How dare you!" she said with an angry look. "How dare you sneak into my garden like a thief and steal my rapunzel! I'll make you pay dearly for this." "Oh, please," he said, "please temper justice with mercy. I only did it because I had to. My wife was looking out of the window, and when she saw your rapunzel she felt such a craving for it that she would have died if I hadn't got her some." At that the witch's anger died down and she said: "If that's how it is, you may take as much rapunzel as you wish, but on one condition: that you give me the child your wife will bear. It will have a good life and I shall care for it like a mother." In his fright, the man agreed to everything, and the moment his wife was delivered, the witch appeared, gave the child the name of Rapunzel, and took her away.

Rapunzel grew to be the loveliest child under the sun. When she was twelve years old, the witch took her to the middle of the forest and shut her up in a tower that had neither stairs nor door, but only a little window at the very top. When the witch wanted to come in, she stood down below and called out:

> "Rapunzel, Rapunzel,
> Let down your hair for me."

Rapunzel had beautiful long hair, as fine as spun gold. When she heard the witch's voice, she undid her braids and fastened them to the window latch. They fell to the ground twenty ells down, and the witch climbed up on them.

A few years later it so happened that the king's son was passing through the forest. When he came to the tower, he heard someone singing, and the singing was so lovely that he stopped and listened. It was Rapunzel, who in her loneliness was singing to pass the time. The prince wanted to go up to her and he looked for a door but found none. He rode away home, but the singing had so touched his heart that he went out into the forest every day and listened. Once as he was standing behind a tree, he saw a witch come to the foot of the tower and heard her call out:

> "Rapunzel, Rapunzel,
> Let down your hair."

Whereupon Rapunzel let down her braids, and the witch climbed up to her. "Aha," he thought, "if that's the ladder that goes up to her, then I'll try my luck too." And next day, when it was beginning to get dark, he went to the tower and called out:

> "Rapunzel, Rapunzel,
> Let down your hair."

A moment later her hair fell to the ground and the prince climbed up.

At first Rapunzel was dreadfully frightened, for she had never seen a man before, but the prince spoke gently to her and told her how he had been so moved by her singing that he couldn't rest easy until he had seen her. At that Rapunzel lost her fear, and when he asked if she would have him as her husband and she saw he was young and handsome, she thought: "He will love me better than my old godmother." So she said yes and put her hand in his hand. "I'd gladly go with you," she said, "but how will I ever get down? Every time you come, bring a skein of silk and I'll make a ladder with it. When it's finished, I'll climb down, and you will carry me home on your horse." They agreed that in the meantime he would come every evening, because the old witch came during the day. The witch noticed nothing until one day Rapunzel said to her: "Tell me, Godmother, how is it that you're so much harder to pull up than the young prince? With him it hardly takes a minute." "Wicked child!" cried the witch. "What did you say? I thought I had shut you away from the world, but you've deceived me." In her fury she seized Rapunzel's beautiful hair, wound it several times around her left hand and picked up a pair of scissors in her right hand. Snippety-snap went the scissors, and the lovely braids fell to the floor. Then the heartless witch sent poor Rapunzel to a desert place, where she lived in misery and want.

At dusk on the day she had sent Rapunzel away, she fastened the severed braids to the window latch, and when the prince came and called:

> "Rapunzel, Rapunzel,
> Let down your hair,"

she let the hair down. The prince climbed up, but instead of his dearest Rapunzel, the witch was waiting for him with angry, poisonous looks. "Aha!" she cried. "You've come to take your darling wife away, but the bird is gone from the nest, she won't be singing any more; the cat has taken her away and before she's done she'll scratch your eyes out too. You've lost Rapunzel, you'll never see her again." The prince was beside himself with grief, and in his despair he jumped from the tower. It didn't kill him, but the brambles he fell into scratched his eyes out and he was blind. He wandered through the forest, living on roots and berries and weeping and wailing over the loss of his dearest wife. For several years he wandered wretchedly, until at last he came to the desert place where Rapunzel was living in misery with the twins she had borne—a boy and a girl. He heard a voice that seemed familiar, and when he approached Rapunzel recognized him, fell on his neck and wept. Two of her tears dropped on his eyes, which were made clear again, so that he could see as well as ever. He took her to his kingdom, where she was welcomed with rejoicing, and they lived happy and contented for many years to come.

13

The Three Little Men in the Woods

THERE WAS ONCE a man whose wife died and a woman whose husband died, and the man had a daughter and the woman also had a daughter. The girls knew each other and went for a walk together and then they went to the woman's house. And the woman said to the man's daughter: "Listen to me. Go and tell your father I want to marry him. Then you will wash in milk every morning and drink wine, but my daughter will wash in water and drink water." The girl went home and told her father what the woman had said. The man said: "What should I do? Marriage is a joy, but it's also torture." Finally, when he couldn't make up his mind, he took off his boot and said: "See this boot? There's a hole in it. Take it up to the attic, hang it on a nail, and pour water into it. If the water stays, I'll take a wife; if it runs out, I won't." The girl did as she was bidden. The water pulled the sides of the hole together and the boot stayed brimful. She told her father what had happened. Then he went up to the attic to see for himself, and when he saw it was true, he went to the widow and courted her, and the wedding was celebrated.

Next morning, when the two girls got up, the husband's daughter had milk to wash in and wine to drink, and the wife's daughter had water to wash in and water to drink. On the second morning, the husband's daughter as well as the wife's daughter had water to wash in and water to drink. On the third morning, the husband's daughter had water to wash in and water to drink, and the wife's daughter had milk to wash in and wine to drink. And that's how it was from then on. The wife hated her stepdaughter like poison and racked her brains looking for ways to make things worse for her from day to day. For one thing, she was envious, because her stepdaughter was beautiful and sweet-tempered, while her own daughter was ugly and horrid.

One winter day, when the ground was frozen solid and hill and dale were covered with snow, the wife made a dress out of paper, called the girl and said: "Put on this dress and go out into the woods. I want you to bring me a little basket full of strawberries. I have a craving for them." "My goodness!" said the girl. "Strawberries don't grow in the wintertime; the ground is frozen and everything is covered with snow. And why do you want me to go out in this paper dress?—it's so cold your breath freezes. The wind will blow through it and the brambles will tear it off me." "Don't you dare talk back to me!" cried the stepmother. "Get a move on and don't show your face again until that basket is full of strawberries." Then she gave her a piece of stale bread. "This will do you for the day," she said. And she thought: "She'll die of cold and hunger out there, and I'll never see her again."

Obediently the stepdaughter put on the paper dress and went out with the little basket. As far as the eye could see, there was nothing but snow, and not the slightest blade of green. When she got to the woods, she saw a hut. Three dwarfs were peering out of it. She bade them good morning and knocked shyly at the door. "Come in!" they cried. She went in and sat down on the bench by the stove to warm herself and eat her breakfast. The dwarfs said: "Give us some." "Gladly," she said, and broke her piece of bread in two and gave them half. "What are you doing out here in the woods in that thin dress in the dead of winter?" they asked. "I've been sent to look for strawberries," she said. "And I'm not to go home until I've picked a basketful." When she had eaten her bread, they gave her a broom and said: "Sweep the snow away from the back door." While she was outside, the three little men talked it over: "What should we give her for being so good and kind and sharing her bread with us?" The first said: "My gift is that she shall become more beautiful every day." The second said: "My gift is that whenever she says a word a gold piece shall fall out of her mouth." The third said: "My gift is that a king shall come and take her for his wife."

The girl did as the dwarfs had bidden her. She took the broom and swept the snow from behind the hut, and what do you think she found? Ripe strawberries, every one of them dark red, coming up from under the snow. In her joy she picked until her basket was full, thanked the little men, gave each of them her hand, and ran home to bring her stepmother what she had asked for. When she went in and said, "Good evening," a gold piece fell from her mouth. Then she told them what had happened in the woods, and as she spoke the gold pieces kept falling out of her mouth, so that the floor was soon covered with them. "Of all the arrogance!" said her stepsister. "Throwing money around like that!" But in her heart she envied her, and wanted to go out into the woods and look for strawberries. Her mother said: "No, no, my darling daughter, it's too cold, you'd freeze to death." But the daughter gave her no peace, and in the end she let her go. She made her a beautiful fur coat to wear, and gave her sandwiches and cake to take with her.

The girl went to the woods and headed straight for the hut. Again the three dwarfs were peering out, but she didn't say good morning or honor them with so much as a glance. Without a word of greeting she stomped into the hut, sat down by the stove, and began to eat her sandwiches and cake. "Give us some!" the little men cried out, but she replied: "How can I when I haven't enough for myself?" When she had finished eating, they said: "Here's a broom, go and sweep around the back door." "Pooh! Go do your own sweeping," she said. "I'm not your maid." When she saw they weren't going to give her anything, she went outside. The little men talked it over. "What shall we give her for being so horrid and having a wicked, envious heart, and never giving anything away." The first said: "My gift is that she shall become uglier every day." The second said: "My gift is that whenever she says a word a toad shall jump out of her mouth." The third said: "My gift is that she shall die a cruel death." The girl looked for strawberries outside the hut, and when she didn't find any she went peevishly home. And when she opened her mouth to tell her mother what had happened, a toad jumped out at every word, and everyone thought she was disgusting.

The stepmother was angrier than ever. All she could think of was how to bring sorrow to her husband's daughter, who was growing more beautiful every day. In the end, she took a kettle, put it on the fire, and boiled yarn in it. When the yarn was boiled, she threw it over the poor girl's shoulder, gave her an ax, and told her to go out to the frozen river, cut a hole in the ice and rinse the yarn. Obediently she went to the river and began to chop a hole in the ice. While she was chopping, a marvelous carriage came along and a king was sitting in it. The carriage stopped and the king asked: "Who are you, my child, and what are you doing here?" "I'm a poor girl and I'm rinsing yarn." The king felt sorry for her, and when he saw how beautiful she was, he said: "Would you like to ride away with me?" "Oh yes, with all my heart," she said, for she was glad to get away from her mother and sister.

So she got into the carriage and rode away with the king, and when they got to his palace their wedding was celebrated with great splendor, and that was the little men's gift to the girl. A year later the young queen gave birth to a son, and when her stepmother heard of her great good fortune, she and her daughter came to the palace as if to pay her a visit. Then one day when the king had gone out and no one else was there, the wicked woman grabbed the queen by the head and her daughter grabbed her by the feet, and they picked her up from her bed and threw her out of the window into the river. Then the ugly daughter lay down in the bed, and the old woman pulled the blankets up over her head. When the king came home and wanted to speak to his wife, the old woman cried: "Hush, hush, not now. She's all in a sweat, you must let her rest." The king thought no harm and didn't come back until the next morning. Then he spoke to his wife and she answered, and at every word a toad jumped out of her mouth, when up until then it had always been a gold piece. He asked what was wrong with her, but the old woman said it came of the bad sweat she'd been in, and the trouble would soon go away.

That night the kitchen boy saw a duck swimming in the drainage runnel, and the duck said:

> "What are you doing, king?
> Are you awake, or slumbering?"

When he didn't answer, the duck said:

> "What are my guests about?"

And the kitchen boy answered:

> "They're sound asleep, no doubt."

Then the duck asked:

> "And what of my baby sweet?"

And he answered:

> "He's in his cradle asleep."

Then the duck took the form of the queen and went up and suckled the child and plumped up his bed and covered him up. Then she turned into a duck again and swam away in the runnel. Next night she did the same thing, and on the third she said to the kitchen boy: "Go and tell the king to take his sword and stand on the threshold and swing it over me three times." The kitchen boy ran to the king and told him, and he came with his sword and swung it three times over the ghost. The third time his wife stood before him alive and well and as lovely as ever.

The king was very happy, but he kept the queen hidden in a bedchamber until the Sunday when the child was to be christened. After the christening, the king said: "What should be done to a person who drags someone out of bed and throws him into the water?" The old woman answered: "The villain should be shut up in a barrel studded with nails and rolled down the hill into the water." The king said: "You've pronounced your own sentence." He sent for just such a barrel, and the old woman and her daughter were put into it, and the lid was hammered tight, and it was rolled down the hill into the river.

14

The Three Spinners

ONCE THERE WAS a lazy girl who didn't want to spin, and nothing her mother could say did a bit of good. In the end the mother became so angry and impatient that she beat her, and the daughter began to cry. The queen happened to be riding past. When she heard the girl's cries, she stopped her carriage, went into the house, and asked the mother why she was beating her daughter so hard that her screams could be heard out on the road. The woman was ashamed to say that her daughter was lazy, so she said: "I can't make her stop spinning; all she wants to do is spin and spin, but I'm poor and I can't afford all that flax." The queen replied: "There's nothing I like more than the sound of spinning, and I'm never happier than when I hear the wheels whir. Let me take your daughter home with me to my palace. I've got plenty of flax, and I'll let her spin to her heart's content." The mother was delighted, and the queen took the girl away with her. When they got to the palace, she took her upstairs and showed her three rooms that were full of the finest flax, from floor to ceiling. "Just spin this flax," she said. "If you succeed, you shall have my eldest son for a hubsand. You may be poor, but what does it matter? You're a good hard worker, and that's all the dowry you need." The girl was frightened to death, for she couldn't have spun all that flax if she lived to be three hundred and sat there from morning to night. When she was left alone, she began to cry and she cried for three days without lifting a finger. On the third day the queen came in. She was surprised to see that none of the flax had been spun, but the girl explained that she hadn't been able to begin because leaving her mother had made her too sad. The queen accepted her excuse, but said as she was leaving: "I expect you to start working tomorrow."

When the girl was alone again, she didn't know what to do. In her distress she stood at the window, looking out, and she saw three women coming down the road. The first had a broad, flat foot; the second had a lower lip so big that it hung down over her chin; and the third had a broad thumb. They stopped outside the window, looked up, and asked her what the matter was. She told them about the trouble she was in, and they offered to help her. "We'll spin all your flax for you, and quickly too," they said, "if only you'll invite us to your wedding and not be ashamed of us and introduce us as your cousins and let us sit at your table." "With all my heart," she said. "Come in. You can start work right away." So she let the three queer women in, and made a space in the first room for them to sit in and start spinning. The first drew the thread and plied the treadle, the second moistened the thread, the third twisted it and struck the table with her finger, and each time she struck the table a skein of yarn fell to the floor, and it was spun ever so finely. The girl hid the three spinners from the queen and showed her such a quantity of spun yarn every time she came in that she couldn't praise her enough. When the first room was empty, they started on the second, and then on the third, and it too was soon emptied. Then the three women took their leave and said to the girl: "Don't forget your promise. It will be your good fortune."

When the queen saw the empty rooms and the enormous pile of yarn, she arranged for the wedding. The bridegroom was glad to be getting such a clever hard-working wife and praised her mightily. "I have three cousins," the girl said. "They've been very good to me, and it wouldn't be right to forget them now, in my happiness. Would you let me invite them to the wedding and ask them to sit at my table?" The queen and the bridegroom said: "Why on earth wouldn't we let you?" When the festivities began, the three old maids appeared in outlandish costumes, and the bride said: "Welcome, dear cousins." "Good Lord!" said the bridegroom. "How did you ever come by such ungainly looking cousins?" He went over to the one with the broad, flat foot, and asked: "How did you get such a broad foot?" "By treading," she replied. "By treading." The bridegroom went over to the second and asked: "How did you ever get that hanging lip?" "By licking," she replied. "By licking." And he asked the third: "How did you get that broad thumb?" "By twisting thread," she replied. "By twisting thread." The prince was horrified. "In that case," he said, "my beautiful bride shall never touch a spinning wheel again." From then on there was no further question of her having to spin that horrid flax.

15

Hansel and Gretel

AT THE EDGE of a large forest there lived a poor woodcutter with his wife and two children. The little boy's name was Hansel, and the little girl's was Gretel. There was never much to eat in the house, and once, in time of famine, there wasn't even enough bread to go around. One night the woodcutter lay in bed thinking, tossing and turning with worry. All at once he sighed and said to his wife: "What's to become of us? How can we feed our poor children when we haven't even got enough for ourselves?" His wife answered: "Husband, listen to me. Tomorrow at daybreak we'll take the children out to the thickest part of the forest and make a fire for them and give them each a piece of bread. Then we'll leave them and go about our work. They'll never find the way home again and that way we'll be rid of them." "No, Wife," said the man. "I won't do it. How can I bring myself to leave my children alone in the woods? The wild beasts will come and tear them to pieces." "You fool!" she said. "Then all four of us will starve. You may as well start planing the boards for our coffins." And she gave him no peace until he consented. "But I still feel badly about the poor children," he said.

The children were too hungry to sleep, and they heard what their stepmother said to their father. Gretel wept bitter tears and said: "Oh, Hansel, we're lost." "Hush, Gretel," said Hansel. "Don't worry. I'll find a way." When the old people had fallen asleep, he got up, put on his little jacket, opened the bottom half of the Dutch door, and crept outside. The moon was shining bright, and the pebbles around the house glittered like silver coins. Hansel crouched down and stuffed his pocket full of them. Then he went back and said to Gretel: "Don't worry, little sister. Just go to sleep, God won't forsake us," and went back to bed.

At daybreak, before the sun had risen, the woman came and woke the two children. "Get up, you lazybones. We're going to the forest for wood." Then she gave each a piece of bread and said: "This is for your noonday meal. Don't eat it too soon, because there won't be any more." Gretel put the bread under her apron, because Hansel had the pebbles in his pocket. Then they all started out for the forest together. When they had gone a little way, Hansel stopped still and looked back in the direction of their house, and every so often he did it again. His father said: "Hansel, why do you keep looking back and lagging behind? Wake up and don't forget what your legs are for." "Oh, father," said Hansel, "I'm looking at my white kitten; he's sitting on the roof, trying to bid me good-bye." The woman said: "You fool, that's not your white kitten. It's the morning sun shining on the chimney." But Hansel hadn't been looking at his kitten. Each time, he had taken a shiny pebble from his pocket and dropped it on the ground.

When they came to the middle of the forest, the father said: "Start gathering wood, children, and I'll make a fire to keep you warm." Hansel and Gretel gathered brushwood till they had a little pile of it. The brushwood was kindled and when the flames were high enough the woman said: "Now, children, lie down by the fire and rest. We're going into the forest to cut wood. When we're done, we'll come back and get you."

Hansel and Gretel sat by the fire, and at midday they both ate their pieces of bread. They heard the strokes of an ax and thought their father was nearby. But it wasn't an ax, it was a branch he had tied to a withered tree, and the wind was shaking it to and fro. After sitting there for some time, they became so tired that their eyes closed and they fell into a deep sleep. When at last they awoke, it was dark night. Gretel began to cry and said: "How will we ever get out of this forest?" But Hansel comforted her: "Just wait a little while. As soon as the moon rises, we'll find the way." And when the full moon had risen, Hansel took his little sister by the hand and followed the pebbles, which glistened like newly minted silver pieces and showed them the way. They walked all night and reached their father's house just as day was breaking. They knocked at the door, and when the woman opened it and saw Hansel and Gretel, she said: "Wicked children! Why did you sleep so long in the forest? We thought you'd never get home." But their father was glad, for he had been very unhappy about deserting them.

A while later the whole country was again stricken with famine, and the children heard their mother talking to their father in bed at night: "Everything has been eaten up. We still have half a loaf of bread, and when that's gone there will be no more. The children must go. We'll take them still deeper into the forest, and this time they won't find their way home; it's our only hope." The husband was heavy-hearted, and he thought: "It would be better if I shared the last bite with my children." But the woman wouldn't listen to anything he said; she only scolded and found fault. Once you've said yes, it's hard to say no, and so it was that the woodcutter gave in again.

But the children were awake; they had heard the conversation. When the old people had fallen asleep, Hansel got up again. He wanted to pick up some more pebbles, but the woman had locked the door and he couldn't get out. But he comforted his little sister and said: "Don't cry, Gretel. Just go to sleep, God will help us."

Early in the morning the woman came and got the children out of bed. She gave them their pieces of bread, but they were smaller than the last time. On the way to the forest, Hansel crumbled his bread in his pocket. From time to time he stopped and dropped a few crumbs on the ground. "Hansel," said his father, "why are you always stopping and looking back? Keep moving." "I'm looking at my little pigeon," said Hansel. "He's sitting on the roof, trying to bid me goodbye." "Fool," said the woman. "That's not your little pigeon, it's the morning sun shining on the chimney." But little by little Hansel strewed all his bread on the ground.

The woman led the children still deeper into the forest, to a place where they had never been in all their lives. Again a big fire was made, and the mother said: "Just sit here, children. If you get tired, you can sleep awhile. We're going into the forest to cut wood, and this evening when we've finished we'll come and get you." At midday Gretel shared her bread with Hansel, who had strewn his on the ground. Then they fell asleep and the afternoon passed, but no one came for the poor children. It was dark night when they woke up, and Hansel comforted his little sister. "Gretel," he said, "just wait till the moon rises; then we'll see the breadcrumbs I strewed and they'll show us the way home." When the moon rose, they started out, but they didn't find any breadcrumbs, because the thousands of birds that fly around in the forests and fields had eaten them all up. Hansel said to Gretel: "Don't worry, we'll find the way," but they didn't find it. They walked all night and then all day from morning to night, but they were still in the forest, and they were very hungry, for they had nothing to eat but the few berries they could pick from the bushes. And when they were so tired their legs could carry them no farther, they lay down under a tree and fell asleep.

It was already the third morning since they had left their father's house. They started out again, but they were getting deeper and deeper into the forest, and unless help came soon, they were sure to die of hunger and weariness. At midday, they saw a lovely snow-white bird sitting on a branch. It sang so beautifully that they stood still and listened. When it had done singing, it flapped its wings and flew on ahead, and they followed until the bird came to a little house and perched on the roof. When they came closer, they saw that the house was made of bread, and the roof was made of cake and the windows of sparkling sugar. "Let's eat," said Hansel, "and the Lord bless our food. I'll take a piece of the roof. You, Gretel, had better take some of the window; it's sweet." Hansel reached up and broke off a bit of the roof to see how it tasted, and Gretel pressed against the windowpanes and nibbled at them. And then a soft voice called from inside:

> "Nibble nibble, little mouse,
> Who's that nibbling at my house?"

The children answered:

> "The wind so wild,
> The heavenly child,"

and went right on eating. Hansel liked the taste of the roof, so he tore off a big chunk, and Gretel broke out a whole round windowpane and sat down on the ground to enjoy it. All at once the door opened, and an old, old woman with a crutch came hobbling out. Hansel and Gretel were so frightened they dropped what they were eating. But the old woman wagged her head and said: "Oh, what dear children! However did you get here? Don't be afraid, come in and stay with me. You will come to no harm." She took them by the hand and led them into her house. A fine meal of milk and pancakes, sugar, apples, and nuts was set before them. And then two little beds were made up clean and white, and Hansel and Gretel got into them and thought they were in heaven.

But the old woman had only pretended to be so kind. Actually she was a wicked witch, who waylaid children and had built her house out of bread to entice them. She killed, cooked, and ate any child who fell into her hands, and that to her was a feast day. Witches have red eyes and can't see very far, but they have a keen sense of smell like animals, so they know when humans are coming. As Hansel and Gretel approached, she laughed her wicked laugh and said with a jeer: "Here come two who will never get away from me." Early in the morning, when the children were still asleep, she got up, and when she saw them resting so sweetly with their plump red cheeks, she muttered to herself: "What tasty morsels they will be!" She grabbed Hansel with her scrawny hand, carried him to a little shed, and closed the iron-barred door behind him. He screamed for all he was worth, but much good it did him. Then she went back to Gretel, shook her awake, and cried: "Get up, lazybones. You must draw water and cook something nice for your brother. He's out in the shed and we've got to fatten him up. When he's nice and fat, I'm going to eat him." Gretel wept bitterly, but in vain; she had to do what the wicked witch told her.

The best of food was cooked for poor Hansel, but Gretel got nothing but crayfish shells. Every morning the old witch crept to the shed and said: "Hansel, hold out your finger. I want to see if you're getting fat." But Hansel held out a bone. The old woman had weak eyes and couldn't see it; she thought it was Hansel's finger and wondered why he wasn't getting fat. When four weeks had gone by and Hansel was still as skinny as ever, her impatience got the better of her and she decided not to wait any longer. "Ho there, Gretel," she cried out. "Go and draw water and don't dawdle. Skinny or fat, I'm going to butcher Hansel tomorrow and cook him." Oh, how the little girl wailed at having to carry the water, and how the tears flowed down her cheeks! "Dear God," she cried, "oh, won't you help us? If only the wild beasts had eaten us in the forest, at least we'd have died together." "Stop that blubbering," said the witch. "It won't do you a bit of good."

Early in the morning Gretel had to fill the kettle with water and light the fire. "First we'll bake," said the old witch. "I've heated the oven and kneaded the dough." And she drove poor Gretel out to the oven, which by now was spitting flames. "Crawl in," said the witch, "and see if it's hot enough for the bread." Once Gretel was inside, she meant to close the door and roast her, so as to eat her too. But Gretel saw what she had in mind and said: "I don't know how. How do I get in?" "Silly goose," said the old woman. "The opening is big enough. Look. Even I can get in." She crept to the opening and stuck her head in, whereupon Gretel gave her a push that sent her sprawling, closed the iron door and fastened the bolt. Eek! How horribly she screeched! But Gretel ran away and the wicked witch burned miserably to death.

Gretel ran straight to Hansel, opened the door of the shed, and cried: "Hansel, we're saved! The old witch is dead." Hansel hopped out like a bird when someone opens the door of its cage. How happy they were! They hugged and kissed each other and danced around. And now that there was nothing to be afraid of, they went into the witch's house and in every corner there were boxes full of pearls and precious stones. Hansel stuffed his pockets full of them and said: "These will be much better than pebbles," and Gretel said: "I'll take some home too," and filled her apron with them. "We'd better leave now," said Hansel, "and get out of this bewitched forest." When they had walked a few hours, they came to a big body of water. "How will we ever get across?" said Hansel. "I don't see any bridge." "And there's no boat, either," said Gretel, "but over there I see a white duck. She'll help us across if I ask her." And she cried out:

> "Duckling, duckling, here is Gretel,
> Duckling, duckling, here is Hansel.
> No bridge or ferry far and wide—
> Duckling, come and give us a ride."

Sure enough, the duck came over to them and Hansel sat down on her back and told his sister to sit beside him. "No," said Gretel, "that would be too much for the poor thing; let her carry us one at a time." And that's just what the good little duck did. And when they were safely across and had walked a little while, the forest began to look more and more familiar, and finally they saw their father's house in the distance. They began to run, and they flew into the house and threw themselves into their father's arms. The poor man hadn't had a happy hour since he had left the children in the forest, and in the meantime his wife had died. Gretel opened out her little apron, the pearls and precious stones went bouncing around the room, and Hansel reached into his pockets and tossed out handful after handful. All their worries were over, and they lived together in pure happiness. My story is done, see the mouse run; if you catch it, you may make yourself a great big fur cap out of it.

16

The Three Snake Leaves

THERE WAS ONCE a poor man who couldn't support his only son any longer. One day the son said: "Dear father, you're having such a bad time of it and I'm only a burden to you. I'd better leave home and see if I can earn my own living." Then the father gave him his blessing and they parted in great sorrow. At that time a powerful king was waging war. The boy entered his service, joined in the campaign, and reached the enemy lines just as a battle was being fought. The danger was great, the bullets flew thick and fast, and his comrades fell on all sides. When the captain was killed, the men were going to take flight, but the boy stepped forward, bade them take courage, and said: "We won't let our country go under!" The men followed him, and he pressed forward and defeated the enemy. When the king heard that he had him alone to thank for the victory, he raised him up above all others, gave him great treasures, and made him the first in his kingdom.

The king had a daughter, who was very beautiful, but also very strange. She had sworn an oath not to take any man for her lord and master unless he promised that if she died first he would let himself be buried alive with her. "If he really loves me," she said, "why would he want to go on living?" And she said she would do likewise and let herself be buried with him if he should die first. So far her strange oath had frightened all her suitors away, but the boy was so taken with her beauty that nothing could discourage him and he asked her father for her hand. "Do you know what you must promise?" the king asked. "Oh yes," he said. "I shall have to let myself be buried with her if I outlive her. But my love is so great that I care nothing for the risk." Then the king consented and the marriage was celebrated with great splendor.

For a while they lived happily together, but then it so happened that the young queen fell gravely ill and no doctor could help her. When she lay dead, the young king remembered the promise he had been obliged to make, and he shuddered at the thought of being buried alive, but there was nothing he could do, for the king had stationed sentries at all the gates, and he could not escape his fate. When the day came for the body to be buried, he was taken down to the royal vault along with it, and the door was locked and bolted.

Beside the coffin there was a table, and on it there were four candles, four loaves of bread, and four bottles of wine. When these provisions were gone, he would starve. There he sat in grief and anguish. Each day he ate only one bite of bread and drank only one mouthful of wine; yet he knew that death was coming closer and closer. As he sat staring, he saw a snake crawl from one corner of the vault and approach the corpse. Thinking it had come to nibble at the body, he drew his sword and said: "While I live, you will not touch that body!" and he cut the snake into three pieces. In a little while a second snake came crawling out of the corner. When it saw the first snake lying there dead and in pieces, it went away, but soon came back with three green leaves in its mouth. It took the three pieces of the dead snake, put them together as they belonged, and laid a leaf on each wound. Instantly what had been parted was made one, the snake stirred and came to life again, and the two snakes hurried away together. The leaves were still lying on the floor, and it occurred to the unhappy young king who had witnessed the whole scene that the miraculous power of the leaves, which had brought a snake back to life, might help a human being as well. So he picked up the leaves and laid one on the dead woman's mouth and the two others on her two eyes. No sooner had he done this than the blood stirred in her veins and the color came back into her pale face. Then she drew breath, opened her eyes, and said: "Heavens! Where am I?" "You are with me, my dear wife," he replied, and told her exactly what had happened and how he had brought her back to life. Then he gave her some bread and wine, and when her strength had revived she stood up. They went to the door and knocked and shouted so loud that the sentries heard them and told the king. The king himself came down and opened the door. He found them both alive and well, and they all rejoiced that their sorrow was over. The young king took the three snake leaves, gave them to a servant, and said: "Take good care of them, and carry them with you wherever you go. Who knows what use we may make of them in time of trouble!"

But a change took place in the wife after she was brought back to life. All her love for her husband seemed to have gone out of her heart. Some time later he decided to go on a sea voyage to visit his old father, and on shipboard she forgot the great love and devotion he had shown her and conceived a guilty passion for the sea captain. Once when the young king lay asleep she called the captain. Then she took the sleeper by the head and the captain took him by the feet, and they threw him into the sea. After the shameful deed was done, she said to the captain: "Now we will go back home and say he died at sea, and I will sing your praises to my father and he will betroth me to you and make you the heir to his crown." But the faithful servant, who had seen what they had done, secretly untied a boat from the ship, got into it and went in search of his master, letting the villains go their way. He fished the body out of the sea, put the three snake leaves, which he carried with him, on the young king's eyes and mouth, and brought him back to life.

The two of them rowed with all their might. Day and night they rowed, and their boat flew over the waves so fast that they reached the old king before the others. He was surprised to see them coming back alone, and asked them what had happened. When he heard of his daughter's treachery, he said: "I can't believe she would do such a terrible thing, but the truth will soon come to light." And he bade them go into a hidden room and not let anyone know they were there. Soon the big ship arrived and the wicked woman appeared before her father with a mournful face. "Why have you come back alone?" he asked her. "Where is your husband?" "Oh, father dear," she replied, "I've come home in deep mourning. My husband suddenly fell sick and died at sea, and if this good sea captain hadn't helped me, I don't know what I'd have done. He was there when my husband died, so he can tell you all about it." The king said: "I'm going to bring the dead man back to life," and he opened the door and bade the two to come out. When the woman saw her husband, she was thunderstruck; she fell on her knees and begged for mercy. The king said: "Don't speak to me of mercy. He was ready to die with you and he gave you back your life, but you killed him in his sleep and shall be punished as you deserve." She and her accomplice were put on board a ship with holes drilled in it, and sent out over the stormy sea, where they soon sank.

17
The White Snake

LONG AGO THERE LIVED a king who was famed far and wide for his wisdom. Nothing remained hidden from him, and it was as though knowledge of the most secret things came to him through the air. But he had a strange custom. When the noonday meal had been cleared away and there was no one else at the table, a trusted servant had to bring him one more dish. This dish was covered; the servant himself didn't know what was in it, and neither did anyone else, for the king didn't take the cover off and eat until he was all alone. One day after this had been going on for some time the servant was overpowered by curiosity while removing the dish. He took it secretly to his room, and when he had carefully locked the door, he raised the lid and saw that a white snake was inside. Once he had seen it, he couldn't help wanting to taste it, so he cut off a little piece and put it in his mouth. And no sooner had it touched his tongue, than he heard strange sweet whisperings outside his window. When he went over and listened it turned out that the whispering voices were those of sparrows, who were having a chat, telling each other about all sorts of things they had seen in the woods and fields. Tasting the snake had given him the power to understand the language of the birds and beasts.

Now it so happened that just that day the queen's best ring disappeared and the trusted servant, who was free to go where he pleased in the palace, was suspected of stealing it. The king summoned him and spoke angrily, saying that unless he named the thief by the following day he would be pronounced guilty and beheaded. It did him no good to protest his innocence; the king dismissed him without a word of comfort.

In his fear and distress he went down into the courtyard and racked his brains for a way out of his difficulty. Some ducks were sitting quietly by a brook, taking it easy, preening themselves and having a private chat. The servant stopped and listened. They told each other about all the places where they had been waddling about that morning and all the good food they had found, and one of them said dejectedly: "There's something weighing on my stomach. I was eating so fast that I swallowed a ring that was lying on the ground below the queen's window." The servant seized her by the neck, carried her straight to the kitchen, and said to the cook: "Here's a well-fed duck. I'd kill her if I were you." "Yes indeed," said the cook, hefting the duck in his hand, "she has worked hard at putting on weight and it's high time she was roasted." He cut her throat, and when she was being cleaned the queen's ring was found in her stomach. The servant had no further trouble convincing the king of his innocence. Wanting to make amends for the injustice he had done him, the king asked him if there was anything he desired and offered him any post he might wish for at court.

The servant declined all honors and asked only for a horse and a bit of money to keep him, for he longed to see the world and to travel for a while. This the king granted, and the servant started out. One day as he was passing a pond, he noticed three fishes who were caught in the rushes and gasping for water. Though fish are said to be mute, he heard them bewailing the miserable death they were facing. Being a kindhearted man, he got down off his horse and put the three captives back into the water. Wriggling with joy, they stuck out their heads and called: "We shall remember this and reward you for saving us." He rode on, and after a while he thought he heard a voice in the sand at his feet. He listened and heard an ant king complaining: "If humans would only keep their clumsy beasts away from us! This stupid horse is mercilessly trampling my people with his big heavy hooves!" At that the servant turned into a side path and the ant king called out: "We shall remember this and reward you." The path led into a forest, and there the servant saw a father and mother raven throwing their chicks out of the nest: "Away with you, you gallows birds!" they cried. "We can't fill your bellies any more; you're big enough to find your own food." The poor chicks flapped their wings helplessly and couldn't get off the ground. "We're only helpless children," they screamed. "How can we find our own food when we can't fly yet? You're leaving us here to starve to death." At that the kindly young man alighted, killed his horse with his sword, and gave it to the young ravens to feed on. They came hopping over, ate their fill, and cried out: "We shall remember this and reward you."

From then on he had to use his own legs, and after walking a long way he came to a big city. The streets were full of noise and bustle, and a horseman came along, announcing that the king's daughter was looking for a husband, but that anyone wishing to bid for her hand must perform a difficult task, and that if he failed in it he would lose his life. Many had tried, but had risked their lives to no purpose. When the young man saw the king's daughter, he was so dazzled by her beauty that he forgot the danger, went to the king and presented himself as a suitor.

He was led straight to the sea, and before his eyes a gold ring was thrown into the water. Then the king bade him retrieve the ring from the bottom, and added: "If you come up without it, you will be thrown back in and so on again and again until you perish in the waves." The courtiers all grieved for the handsome young man, and then they left him alone on the shore. As he stood there wondering what to do, he suddenly saw three fishes swimming toward him, and they were none other than those whose lives he had saved. The middle one had a shell in its mouth. He put it down on the shore at the young man's feet, and when he picked it up and opened it, the gold ring was inside. Full of joy, he brought it to the king, expecting him to grant the promised reward. But when the haughty princess heard that he was not her equal in birth, she scorned him and said he would have to perform a second task. She went down into the garden and strewed ten sacks full of millet in the grass. "You must pick it all up before the sun rises tomorrow morning," she said, "and there mustn't be a single grain missing." The boy sat down in the garden and searched his mind for a way of performing this task, but nothing occurred to him, and there he sat as sad as sad can be, expecting to be led to his death at daybreak. But when the first rays of sun fell on the garden, he saw the ten sacks standing in a row, all filled to the brim, and not a single grain was missing. The ant king had come during the night with his thousands and thousands of ants, and the grateful creatures had gathered the millet grain by grain and packed it into the sacks. The king's daughter, her very own self, came down into the garden and was amazed to see that the task had been done. But her haughty heart still refused to be subdued, and she said: "He has indeed performed the two tasks, but he shall not become my husband until he has brought me an apple from the tree of life." The young man didn't know where the tree of life was. He started off, resolved to keep going as long as his legs would carry him, but he had no hope of finding it. One evening after searching three kingdoms, he came to a forest. He sat down under a tree and was just falling asleep when he heard a sound in the branches and a golden apple fell into his hands. At the same time three ravens flew down, perched on his knees, and said: "We are the three young ravens you saved from starvation. When we grew up and heard you were looking for the golden apple, we flew across the sea to the end of the world, where the tree of life grows, and took the apple." Full of joy, the young man started back home. He brought the beautiful princess the golden apple, and after that she had no excuse left. They divided the apple of life and ate it together. Then her heart was filled with love for him and they lived to a ripe old age in perfect happiness.

18

The Straw, the Coal, and the Bean

THERE WAS ONCE a poor old woman who lived in a village. She had come by a mess of beans and was getting ready to cook them. So she laid a fire on her hearth, and to make it take faster she kindled it with a handful of straw. As she was pouring the beans into the pot, one of them escaped unnoticed and fell to the floor, where it landed beside a wisp of straw. A little while later a glowing coal jumped from the hearth and landed not far from the other two. The straw spoke up and said: "Dear friends, where have you come from?" The coal replied: "Luckily for me I jumped out of the fire; it took a great effort, but if I hadn't done it, death would have been certain; I'd have burned to ashes." The bean said: "I've come off with a whole skin too, but if the old woman had got me into the pot, I'd have been mercilessly cooked like my friends." "Would I have had a better fate?" said the straw. "The old woman has sent all my brothers up in fire and smoke; she seized sixty at one stroke and did them to death. Luckily I slipped through her fingers." "But what are we to do now?" asked the coal. "Considering that we've been lucky enough to escape death," said the bean, "I think we should band together like good comrades and set out for foreign parts before some new calamity overtakes us."

The suggestion appealed to the others and they started out together. Soon they came to a brook. There was no bridge and there seemed to be no way of getting to the other side. The straw had a good idea and said: "I'll lie down across it, and you'll walk over me as if I were a bridge." So the straw stretched out from bank to bank, and the still-glowing coal, who was an impetuous sort, danced boldly onto the newly built bridge. But when he got to the middle and heard the water gurgling below, he took fright and didn't dare go any farther. The straw caught fire, broke in the middle, and fell into the brook. The coal slid in after him, hissed as he hit the water, and gave up the ghost. The bean, who was cautious by nature, had stayed on the bank. He couldn't help laughing when he saw what had happened. He laughed and laughed until finally he burst. It would have been all up with him as well if a traveling tailor hadn't stopped to rest by the brook. The tailor, who was softhearted, took out needle and thread and sewed the bean up. The bean thanked him kindly, but as the tailor had used black thread, beans have had a black seam ever since.

19

The Fisherman and His Wife

THERE WAS ONCE a fisherman who lived with his wife in a pigsty not far from the sea, and every day the fisherman went fishing. And he fished and he fished.

One day he was sitting with his line, looking into the smooth water. And he sat and he sat.

His line sank to the bottom, deep deep down, and when he pulled it up there was a big flounder on it. And the flounder said: "Look here, fisherman. Why not let me live? I'm not a real flounder, I'm an enchanted prince. What good would it do you to kill me? I wouldn't be much good to eat. Put me back in the water and let me go." "Save your breath," said the fisherman. "Do you think I'd keep a talking flounder?" So he put him back in the smooth water, and the flounder swam down to the bottom, leaving a long trail of blood behind him. Whereupon the fisherman got up and went home to his wife in the pigsty.

"Husband," said the wife, "haven't you caught anything today?" "No," said the fisherman. "I caught a flounder who said he was an enchanted prince, so I let him go." "Didn't you make a wish?" the wife asked. "No," he said. "What should I wish for?" "That's easy," said the wife. "It's so dreadful having to live in this pigsty. It stinks, it's disgusting: you could have wished for a little cottage. Go back and tell him we want a little cottage. He's sure to give us one." "How can I go back again?" said the husband. "Didn't you catch him and let him go?" said the wife. "He's bound to do it. Go right this minute." The husband didn't really want to go, but neither did he want to cross his wife, so he went to the shore.

When he got there, the sea was all green and yellow and not nearly as smooth as before. He stood there and said:

> "Little man, whoever you be,
> Flounder, flounder in the sea,

> My wife, her name is Ilsebil,
> Has sent me here against my will."

The flounder came swimming and asked: "Well, what does she want?" "It's like this," said the fisherman. "I caught you, didn't I, and now my wife says I should have wished for something. She's sick of living in a pigsty. She wants a cottage." "Just go home," said the flounder. "She's already got it."

The fisherman went home and his wife wasn't sitting in their pigsty any more. She was sitting on a bench outside a little cottage. She took him by the hand and said: "Come on in; look, it's much nicer." They went in, and there was a little hallway and a lovely little parlor and a bedroom with a bed for each of them, and a kitchen and a pantry, all with the best of furnishings and utensils, tinware and brassware, and everything that was needed. And behind the cottage there was a small barnyard with chickens and ducks in it and a little garden full of vegetables and fruit. "See," said the wife. "Isn't it nice?" "Yes indeed," said the husband. "If only it lasts, we shall live happy and contented." "We'll see about that," said the wife. Then they had something to eat and went to bed.

All went well for a week or two. Then the wife said: "Listen to me, husband. This cottage is too cramped and the garden and barnyard are too small. The flounder could have given us a bigger house. I'd like to live in a big stone castle. Go to the flounder and tell him to give us a castle." "Wife, wife," said the husband, "this cottage is plenty good enough. Why would we want to live in a castle?" "Don't argue," said the wife. "Just get going. The flounder can do that for us." "No, wife," said the husband. "The flounder has just given us a cottage, I don't think I ought to go back so soon, he might not like it." "Get going," said the wife. "It's no trouble at all to him and he'll be glad to do it." The husband's heart was heavy; he didn't want to go. He said to himself: "It's not right." But he went.

When he got to the sea, the water wasn't green and yellow any more, it was purple and dark-blue and gray and murky, but still calm. He stood there and said:

> "Little man, whoever you be,
> Flounder, flounder in the sea,
> My wife, her name is Ilsebil,
> Has sent me here against my will."

"Well, what does she want?" said the flounder. "Dear me!" said the fisherman in distress. "Now she wants to live in a big stone castle." "Just go home," said the flounder. "She's standing at the gate."

So the man started off and thought he was going home, but when he got there he found a big stone castle, and his wife was standing at the top of the staircase ready to go in. She took him by the hand and said: "Come on in." He went in with her and inside there was a great hall with a marble floor and lots of servants, who flung the big doors open, and the walls were all bright and covered with beautiful tapestries, and in the rooms all the tables and chairs were of gold. Crystal chandeliers hung from the ceiling, and all the halls and bedchambers had carpets, and the tables were so weighed down with victuals and the very best of wine that you'd have thought they'd collapse. And behind the house there was a big yard with barns and stables, and the very best of carriages, and there was also a wonderful big garden with the loveliest flowers and fruit trees, and a park that must have been half a mile long, with stags and deer and hares in it and everything you could possibly wish for. "Well," said the wife. "Isn't it nice?" "Yes, indeed," said the husband. "If only it lasts! We will live in this beautiful castle and be contented." "We'll see about that," said the wife. "We'll sleep on it." And with that they went to bed.

Next morning the wife woke up first. It was just daybreak, and from her bed she could see the beautiful countryside around her. Her husband was still stretching when she poked him in the side with her elbow and said: "Husband, get up and look out of the window. See here. Couldn't we be king over all that country? Go to the flounder and tell him we want to be king." "Wife, wife," said the husband. "What do we want to be king for? I don't want to be king." "Well," said the wife, "if you don't want to be king, then I'll be king. Go to the flounder. I want to be king." "But wife," said the fisherman, "why do you want to be king? I can't tell him that!" "Why not?" asked the wife. "Get going this minute. I must be king." Then the husband went, and he was very unhappy because of his wife wanting to be king. "It's not right, it's not right at all," he thought. And he didn't want to go, but he went.

When he got to the sea, it was all gray-black, and the water came churning up from the depths and it had a foul smell. And he stood there and said:

> "Little man, whoever you be,
> Flounder, flounder in the sea,
> My wife, her name is Ilsebil,
> Has sent me here against my will."

"Well, what does she want?" said the flounder. "Dear me," said the man. "She wants to be king." "Just go home," said the flounder, "she is already."

So the man went home, and when he got there the castle was much larger and had a big tower with marvelous ornaments. A sentry was standing at the gate, and there were lots of soldiers and drums and trumpets. And when the fisherman went inside, everything was made of pure marble and gold, with velvet covers and big golden tassels. The doors of the great hall opened, and there was the whole royal household, and his wife was sitting on a high throne of gold and diamonds, wearing a big golden crown and holding a scepter made of pure gold and precious stones, and on both sides of her ladies-in-waiting were standing in rows, each a head shorter than the last. He went and stood there and said: "My goodness, wife! So now you're king?" "That's right," said his wife. "Now I'm king." So he stood there and looked at her and after he'd looked awhile he said: "Now that you're king, suppose we let well enough alone. Let's stop wishing." "No, husband," she said, and she looked very upset. "Already the time is hanging heavy on my hands. I can't stand it any more. Go to the flounder. I'm king, but I've got to be emperor too." "Wife, wife," said the man, "why do you want to be emperor?" "Husband," she said, "go to the flounder. I want to be emperor." "Good Lord, woman," said the fisherman, "he can't make you emperor. I can't tell the flounder that! There's only one emperor in the empire. The flounder can't make you emperor, he just can't." "Fiddlesticks," said the woman. "I'm the king and you're only my husband, so do as you're told. If he can make a king he can also make an emperor. I want to be emperor and that's that. Get going." So he had to go. But on the way he was frightened, and he thought to himself: "This won't end well. Emperor is too much of a good thing. The flounder must be getting sick of all this."

When he got to the sea, it was all black and murky, the water came churning up from the depths and throwing up bubbles, and the wind was so strong that the sea frothed and foamed. The fisherman was filled with dread. And he stood there and said:

> "Little man, whoever you may be,
> Flounder, flounder in the sea,
> My wife, her name is Ilsebil,
> Has sent me here against my will."

"Well, what does she want?" said the flounder. "Oh, flounder," he said, "my wife wants to be emperor." "Just go home," said the flounder. "She is already."

So the fisherman went home, and when he got there, the whole palace was made of polished marble with alabaster figures and golden ornaments. Soldiers were marching and blowing trumpets and beating drums outside, and inside the building barons and counts and dukes were going about the duties of servants. They opened the doors for him and the doors were pure gold. When he went in, his wife was sitting on a throne which was all one block of gold and at least two miles high; and on her head she was wearing a big golden crown that was three ells high and studded with diamonds and rubies. In one hand she was holding the scepter and in the other the Imperial Orb, and on either side of her stood a row of lifeguards, each shorter than the one before him, from the most enormous giant, who was two miles high, to the tiniest dwarf, who was no bigger than my little finger. And before her stood a crowd of princes and dukes. Her husband went and stood among them and said: "Well, wife. It looks like you're emperor now." "That's right," she said. "I'm emperor." He stood there and took a good look at her, and when he'd been looking for a while, he said: "Well, wife, now that you're emperor, suppose we let well enough alone." "Husband," she said, "what are you standing there for? Yes, yes, I'm emperor, but now I want to be pope too, so go to the flounder." "Woman, woman," said the husband, "what won't you be asking next! You can't get to be pope, there's only one pope in all Christendom. He can't make you pope." "Husband," she said, "I want to be pope, so do as you're told. I insist on being pope before the day is out." "No, wife," said the husband, "I can't tell him that, it's too much; the flounder can't make you pope." "Husband," said the woman. "That's poppycock. If he can make an emperor, he can make a pope. Do as you're told. I'm the emperor and you're only my husband, so you'd better get going." At that he was afraid and went, but he felt faint. He shivered and shook and he was wobbly at the knees. A strong wind was blowing, the clouds were flying fast, and toward evening the sky darkened. The leaves were blowing from the trees, the water roared and foamed as if it were boiling, and the waves pounded against the shore. In the distance he saw ships that were bobbing and bounding in the waves, and firing guns in distress. There was still a bit of blue in the middle of the sky, but there was red all around it as in a terrible storm. He stood there in fear and despair and said:

> "Little man, whoever you be,
> Flounder, flounder in the sea,
> My wife, her name is Ilsebil,
> Has sent me here against my will."

"Well, what does she want?" said the flounder. "Dear me!" said the fisherman. "She wants to be pope." "Just go home," said the flounder, "she is already."

So he went home, and when he got there, he found a big church with palaces all around it. He pushed through the crowd. Inside, the whole place was lighted with thousands and thousands of candles, and his wife, dressed in pure gold, was sitting on a throne that was even higher, much higher, and she was wearing three big golden crowns. All around her were church dignitaries, and on both sides of her there were rows of candles, from the biggest, which was as tall and thick as the biggest tower, down to the smallest kitchen candle. And all the emperors and kings were down on their knees to her, kissing her slipper. "Well, wife," said the fisherman, watching her closely, "so now you're pope?" "That's right," she said. "I'm pope." He stood there looking at her, and he felt as if he were looking into the bright sun. Then, after he'd been looking at her for a while, he said: "Well, wife, now that you're pope, suppose we let well enough alone!" But she sat there as stiff as a board, she didn't stir and she didn't move. "Wife," he said to her, "you'd better be satisfied now. You can't get to be anything better than pope." "I'll see about that," said the wife, and then they both went to bed. But she wasn't satisfied, her ambition wouldn't let her sleep, and she kept wondering what more she could get to be.

The fisherman slept soundly, for he had covered a lot of ground that day, but his wife couldn't get to sleep. All night she tossed and turned, wondering what more she could get to be, but she couldn't think of a single thing. Then the sun began to rise, and when she saw the red glow, she sat up in bed and looked out of the window. And when saw the sun rising, she thought: "Ha! Why couldn't I make the sun and the moon rise? Husband!" she cried, poking him in the ribs. "Wake up. Go and see the flounder. I want to be like God." The fisherman was still half-asleep, but her words gave him such a start that he fell out of bed. He thought he'd heard wrong and he rubbed his eyes. "Wife, wife!" he cried out, "what did you say?" "Husband," she said, "if I can't make the sun and moon rise it will be more than I can bear. If I can't make them rise I'll never have another moment's peace." She gave him a grisly look that sent the cold shivers down his spine and cried: "Get going now. I want to be like God." "Wife, wife!" he cried, falling down on his knees, "the flounder can't do that. He can make an emperor and a pope, but please, please, think it over and just go on being pope." At that she grew angry, her hair flew wildly around her head. She tore her nightgown to shreds, and gave him a kick. "I won't stand for it!" she cried. "I won't stand for it another minute. *Will* you get a move on?" Then he pulled on his trousers and ran out like a madman.

A storm was raging. The wind was blowing so hard he could hardly keep his feet. Trees and houses were falling, the mountains were trembling, great boulders were tumbling into the sea, the sky was as black as pitch, the thunder roared, the lightning flashed, the sea was rising up in great black waves as big as mountains and church towers, and each one had a crown of foam on top. He couldn't hear his own words, but he shouted:

> "Little man, whoever you be,
> Flounder, flounder in the sea,
> My wife, her name is Ilsebil,
> Has sent me here against my will."

"Well, what does she want?" asked the flounder. "Dear me," he said, "she wants to be like God." "Just go home, she's back in the old pigsty already."

And there they are living to this day.

20

The Brave Little Tailor

ONE SUMMER MORNING a little tailor was sitting on his table near the window. He was in high good humor and sewed with all his might. A peasant woman came down the street, crying out: "Good jam— cheap! Good jam—cheap!" That sounded sweet to the tailor's ears. He stuck his shapely little head out of the window and cried: "Up here, my good woman, you'll find a buyer." The woman hauled her heavy baskets up the three flights of stairs to the tailor's, and he made her unpack every single pot. He examined them all, lifted them up, sniffed at them, and finally said: "This looks like good jam to me; weigh me out three ounces, my good woman, and if it comes to a quarter of a pound you won't find me complaining." The woman, who had hoped to make a good sale, gave him what he asked for, and went away grumbling and very much out of sorts. "God bless this jam and give me health and strength," cried the little tailor. Where- upon he took bread from the cupboard, cut a slice straight across the loaf, and spread it with jam. "I bet this won't taste bitter," he said, "but before biting into it I'm going to finish my jacket." He put the bread down beside him and went on with his sewing, taking bigger and bigger stitches in his joy. Meanwhile, the flies that had been sit- ting on the wall, enticed by the sweet smell, came swarming down on the jam. "Hey, who invited you?" cried the little tailor and shooed the unbidden guests away. But the flies, who didn't understand his language, refused to be dismissed and kept coming in greater and greater numbers. Finally, at the end of his patience, the tailor took a rag from the catchall under his table. "Just wait! I'll show you!" he cried, and struck out at them unmercifully. When he stopped and counted, no less than seven flies lay dead with their legs in the air. He couldn't help admiring his bravery. "What a man I am!" he cried. "The whole town must hear of this." And one two three, he cut out a belt for himself, stitched it up, and embroidered on it in big letters:

"Seven at one blow!" Then he said: "Town, my foot! The whole
world must hear of it!" And for joy his heart wagged like a lamb's
tail.

The tailor put on his belt and decided to go out into the world, for
clearly his shop was too small for such valor. Before leaving, he ran-
sacked the house for something to take with him, but all he could
find was an old cheese, so he put that in his pocket. Just outside the
door, he caught sight of a bird that had got itself caught in the
bushes, and the bird joined the cheese in his pocket. Ever so bravely
he took to the road, and because he was light and nimble, he never
seemed to get tired. Up into the mountains he went, and when he
reached the highest peak he found an enormous giant sitting there
taking it easy and enjoying the view. The little tailor went right up
to him; he wasn't the least bit afraid. "Greetings, friend," he said.
"Looking out at the great world, are you? Well, that's just where I'm
headed for, to try my luck. Would you care to go with me?" The
giant looked at the tailor contemptuously and said: "You little
pipsqueak! You miserable nobody!" "Is that so?" said the little tailor,
unbuttoning his coat and showing the giant his belt. "Read that!
That'll show you the kind of man I am!" When he had read what
was written—"Seven at one blow!"—the giant thought somewhat better of the little man. All the same, he decided to put him to the test,
so he picked up a stone and squeezed it until drops of water appeared.
"Do that," he said, "if you've got the strength." "That?" said the tailor. "Why, that's child's play for a man like me." Whereupon he
reached into his pocket, took out the soft cheese, and squeezed it
until the whey ran out. "What do you think of that?" he cried. "Not
so bad, eh?" The giant didn't know what to say; he couldn't believe
the little man was so strong. So he picked up a stone and threw it so
high that the eye could hardly keep up with it: "All right, you little
runt, let's see you do that." "Nice throw," said the tailor, "but it fell
to the ground in the end. Watch me throw one that won't ever come
back." Whereupon he reached into his pocket, took out the bird, and
tossed it into the air. Glad to be free, the bird flew up and away and
didn't come back. "Well," said the tailor. "What do you think of
that?" "I've got to admit you can throw," said the giant, "but now
let's see what you can carry." Pointing at a big oak tree that lay
felled on the ground, he said: "If you're strong enough, help me

carry this tree out of the forest." "Glad to," said the little man. "You take the trunk over your shoulder, and I'll carry the branches; they're the heaviest part." The giant took the trunk over his shoulder, and the tailor sat down on a branch, so that the giant, who couldn't look around, had to carry the whole tree and the tailor to boot. The tailor felt so chipper in his comfortable back seat that he began to whistle "Three Tailors Went a-Riding," as though hauling trees were child's play to a man of his strength. After carrying the heavy load for quite some distance, the giant was exhausted. "Hey!" he cried out, "I've got to drop it." The tailor jumped nimbly down, put his arms around the tree as if he'd been carrying it, and said to the giant: "I wouldn't have thought a tiny tree would be too much for a big man like you."

They went on together until they came to a cherry tree. The giant grabbed the crown where the cherries ripen soonest, pulled it down, handed it to the tailor, and bade him eat. But the tailor was much too light to hold the tree down. When the giant let go, the crown snapped back into place and the tailor was whisked high into the air. When he had fallen to the ground without hurting himself, the giant cried out: "What's the matter? You mean you're not strong enough to hold that bit of a sapling?" "Not strong enough? How can you say such a thing about a man who did for seven at one blow? I jumped over that tree because the hunters down there were shooting into the thicket. Now you try. See if you can do it." The giant tried, but he couldn't get over the tree and got stuck in the upper branches. Once again the little tailor had won out.

"All right," said the giant. "If you're so brave, let me take you to our cave to spend the night with us." The little tailor was willing and went along with him. When they got to the cave, the other giants were sitting around the fire. Each one was holding a roasted sheep in his hands and eating it. The little tailor looked around and thought: "This place is a good deal roomier than my workshop." The giant showed him a bed and told him to lie down and sleep. But the bed was too big for the little tailor, so instead of getting into it, he crept into a corner. At midnight, when the giant thought the tailor must be sound asleep, he got up, took a big iron bar and split the bed in two with one stroke. That will settle the little runt's hash, he thought. At the crack of dawn the giants started into the forest. They had forgot-

ten all about the little tailor. All at once he came striding along as
chipper and bold as you please. The giants were terrified. They
thought he would kill them all, and ran away as fast as their legs
would carry them.

The little tailor went his way. After following his nose for many
days he came to the grounds of a king's palace. Feeling tired, he lay
down in the grass and went to sleep, and while he was sleeping some
courtiers came along. They examined him from all sides and read the
inscription on his belt: "Seven at one blow!" "Goodness," they said,
"what can a great war hero like this be doing here in peacetime? He
must be some great lord." They went and told the king. "If war
should break out," they said, "a man like that would come in very
handy. Don't let him leave on any account." This struck the king as
good advice, and he sent one of his courtiers to offer the tailor a post
in his army. The courtier went back to the sleeper, waited until he
stretched his limbs and opened his eyes, and made his offer. "That's
just what I came here for," said the tailor. "I'll be glad to enter the
king's service." So he was received with honor and given apartments
of his own.

But the soldiers, who were taken in by the little tailor, wished him
a thousand miles away. "What will become of us?" they asked. "If
we quarrel with him and he strikes, seven of us will fall at one blow.
We won't last long at that rate." So they took counsel together, went
to the king and asked to be released from his service. Because, they
said, "we can't hope to keep up with a man who does for seven at one
blow." The king was sad to be losing all his faithful servants because
of one and wished he had never laid eyes on him. He'd have been
glad to get rid of him, but he didn't dare dismiss him for fear the
great hero might strike him and all his people dead and seize the
throne for himself. He thought and thought, and at last he hit on an
idea. He sent word to the little tailor that since he was such a great
hero he wanted to make him an offer. There were two giants living
in a certain forest, and they were murdering, looting, burning, and
laying the country waste. No one dared go near them for fear of his
life. If the hero should conquer and kill these two giants, the king
would give him his only daughter to wife, with half his kingdom as
her dowry. And, moreover, the king would send a hundred knights
to back him up. "Sounds like just the thing for me," thought the little

tailor. "It's not every day that somebody offers you a beautiful princess and half a kingdom." "It's a deal," he replied. "I'll take care of those giants, and I won't need the hundred knights. You can't expect a man who does for seven at one blow to be afraid of two."

The little tailor started out with the hundred knights at his heels. When they got to the edge of the forest, he said to his companions: "Stay here. I'll attend to the giants by myself." Then he bounded into the woods, peering to the right and to the left. After a while he caught sight of the two giants, who were lying under a tree asleep, snoring so hard that the branches rose and fell. Quick as a flash the little tailor picked up stones, filled both his pockets with them, and climbed the tree. Halfway up, he slid along a branch until he was right over the sleeping giants. Then he picked out one of the giants and dropped stone after stone on his chest. For a long while the giant didn't notice, but in the end he woke up, gave his companion a poke, and said: "Why are you hitting me?" "You're dreaming," said the other. "I'm not hitting you." When they had lain down to sleep again, the tailor dropped a stone on the second giant. "What is this?" he cried. "Why are you pelting me?" "I'm not pelting you!" the first grumbled. They argued awhile, but they were too tired to keep it up and finally their eyes closed again. Then the little tailor took his biggest stone and threw it with all his might at the first giant's chest. "This is too much!" cried the giant, and jumping up like a madman he pushed his companion so hard against the tree that it shook. The other repaid him in kind and they both flew into such a rage that they started pulling up trees and belaboring each other until they both lay dead on the ground. The little tailor jumped down. "Lucky they didn't pull up the tree I was sitting in," he said to himself. "I'd have had to jump into another like a squirrel. But then we tailors are quick." He drew his sword, gave them both good thrusts in the chest, and went back to the knights. "The job is done," he said. "I've settled their hash. But it was a hard fight. They were so desperate they pulled up trees to fight with, but how could that help them against a man who does for seven at one blow!" "Aren't you even wounded?" the knights asked. "I should say not!" said the tailor. "Not so much as a scratch." The knights wouldn't believe him, so they rode into the forest, where they found the giants lying in pools of blood, with uprooted trees all around them.

The little tailor went to the king and demanded the promised reward, but the king regretted his promise and thought up another way to get rid of the hero. "Before I give you my daughter and half my kingdom," he said, "you will have to perform one more task. There's a unicorn loose in the forest and he's doing a good deal of damage. You will have to catch him first." "If the two giants didn't scare me, why would I worry about a unicorn? Seven at one blow is my meat." Taking a rope and an ax, he went into the forest, and again told the knights who had been sent with him to wait on the fringe. He didn't have long to look. In a short while the unicorn came along and rushed at the tailor, meaning to run him straight through with his horn. "Not so fast!" said the tailor. "It's not as easy as all that." He stood still, waited until the unicorn was quite near him, and then jumped nimbly behind a tree. The unicorn charged full force and rammed into the tree. His horn went in and stuck so fast that he hadn't the strength to pull it out. He was caught. "I've got him," said the tailor. He came out from behind the tree, put the rope around the unicorn's neck, and, taking his ax, chopped the wood away from the horn. When that was done, he led the beast to the king.

But the king was still unwilling to grant him the promised reward and made a third demand. Before the wedding he wanted the tailor to capture a wild boar which had been ravaging the forest, and said the royal huntsmen would help him. "Gladly," said the little tailor. "It's child's play." He didn't take the huntsmen into the forest with him, and they were just as pleased, for several times the boar had given them such a reception that they had no desire to seek him out. When the boar caught sight of the tailor, he gnashed his teeth, foamed at the mouth, made a dash at him, and would have lain him out flat if the nimble hero hadn't escaped into a nearby chapel. The boar ran in after him, but the tailor jumped out of the window, ran around the chapel and slammed the door. The infuriated beast was much too heavy and clumsy to jump out of the window, and so he was caught. The little tailor ran back to the huntsmen and told them to go and see the captive with their own eyes. He himself went to the king, who had to keep his promise this time, like it or not, and give him his daughter and half the kingdom. If he had known that, far from being a war hero, the bridegroom was only a little tailor, he would have been even unhappier than he was. And so the wedding was celebrated with great splendor and little joy, and a tailor became a king.

One night the young queen heard her husband talking in his sleep. "Boy," he said, "hurry up with that jerkin you're making and get those breeches mended or I'll break my yardstick over your head." Then she knew how he had got his start in life. Next morning she went to her father, told him her tale of woe, and begged him to help her get rid of a husband who had turned out to be a common tailor. The king bade her take comfort and said: "Leave the door of your bedroom unlocked tonight. My servants will be waiting outside. Once he's asleep they'll go in, tie him up, and put him aboard a ship bound for the end of the world." The young queen was pleased, but the armor-bearer, who was devoted to the hero, heard the whole conversation and told him all about the plot. "They won't get away with that!" said the little tailor. That night he went to bed with his wife at the usual hour. When she thought he was asleep, she got up, opened the door, and lay down again. The little tailor, who was only pretending to be asleep, cried out in a loud voice: "Boy, hurry up with that jerkin you're making and get those breeches mended or I'll break my yardstick over your head. I've done for seven at one blow, killed two giants, brought home a unicorn, and captured a wild boar. And now I'm expected to be afraid of these scoundrels at my door." When they heard that, the servants were terrified. Not one of them dared lay hands on him and they ran as if the hosts of hell had been chasing them. And so the little tailor went on being a king for the rest of his days.

21

Ashputtle

A RICH MAN'S WIFE fell sick and, feeling that her end was near, she called her only daughter to her bedside and said: "Dear child, be good and say your prayers; God will help you, and I shall look down on you from heaven and always be with you." With that she closed her eyes and died. Every day the little girl went out to her mother's grave and wept, and she went on being good and saying her prayers. When winter came, the snow spread a white cloth over the grave, and when spring took it off, the man remarried.

His new wife brought two daughters into the house. Their faces were beautiful and lily-white, but their hearts were ugly and black. That was the beginning of a bad time for the poor stepchild. "Why should this silly goose sit in the parlor with us?" they said. "People who want to eat bread must earn it. Get into the kitchen where you belong!" They took away her fine clothes and gave her an old gray dress and wooden shoes to wear. "Look at the haughty princess in her finery!" they cried and, laughing, led her to the kitchen. From then on she had to do all the work, getting up before daybreak, carrying water, lighting fires, cooking and washing. In addition the sisters did everything they could to plague her. They jeered at her and poured peas and lentils into the ashes, so that she had to sit there picking them out. At night, when she was tired out with work, she had no bed to sleep in but had to lie in the ashes by the hearth. And they took to calling her Ashputtle because she always looked dusty and dirty.

One day when her father was going to the fair, he asked his two stepdaughters what he should bring them. "Beautiful dresses," said one. "Diamonds and pearls," said the other. "And you, Ashputtle. What would you like?" "Father," she said, "break off the first branch that brushes against your hat on your way home, and bring it to me." So he bought beautiful dresses, diamonds and pearls for his two stepdaughters, and on the way home, as he was riding through a copse, a hazel branch brushed against him and knocked off his hat. So he broke off the branch and took it home with him. When he got home, he gave the stepdaughters what they had asked for, and gave Ashputtle the branch. After thanking him, she went to her mother's grave and planted the hazel sprig over it and cried so hard that her tears fell on the sprig and watered it. It grew and became a beautiful tree. Three times a day Ashputtle went and sat under it and wept and prayed. Each time a little white bird came and perched on the tree, and when Ashputtle made a wish the little bird threw down what she had wished for.

Now it so happened that the king arranged for a celebration. It was to go on for three days and all the beautiful girls in the kingdom were invited, in order that his son might choose a bride. When the two stepsisters heard they had been asked, they were delighted. They called Ashputtle and said: "Comb our hair, brush our shoes, and fasten our buckles. We're going to the wedding at the king's palace." Ashputtle obeyed, but she wept, for she too would have liked to go dancing, and she begged her stepmother to let her go. "You little sloven!" said the stepmother. "How can you go to a wedding when you're all dusty and dirty? How can you go dancing when you have neither dress nor shoes?" But when Ashputtle begged and begged, the stepmother finally said: "Here, I've dumped a bowlful of lentils in the ashes. If you can pick them out in two hours, you may go." The girl went out the back door to the garden and cried out: "O tame little doves, O turtledoves, and all the birds under heaven, come and help me put

> the good ones in the pot,
> the bad ones in your crop."

Two little white doves came flying through the kitchen window, and then came the turtledoves, and finally all the birds under heaven came flapping and fluttering and settled down by the ashes. The doves nodded their little heads and started in, peck peck peck peck, and all the others started in, peck peck peck peck, and they sorted out all the good lentils and put them in the bowl. Hardly an hour had passed before they finished and flew away. Then the girl brought the bowl to her stepmother, and she was happy, for she thought she'd be allowed to go to the wedding. But the stepmother said: "No, Ashputtle. You have nothing to wear and you don't know how to dance; the people would only laugh at you." When Ashputtle began to cry, the stepmother said: "If you can pick two bowlfuls of lentils out of the ashes in an hour, you may come." And she thought: "She'll never be able to do it." When she had dumped the two bowlfuls of lentils in the ashes, Ashputtle went out the back door to the garden and cried out: "O tame little doves, O turtledoves, and all the birds under heaven, come and help me put

> the good ones in the pot,
> the bad ones in your crop."

Then two little white doves came flying through the kitchen window, and then came the turtledoves, and finally all the birds under heaven came flapping and fluttering and settled down by the ashes. The doves nodded their little heads and started in, peck peck peck peck, and all the others started in, peck peck peck peck, and they sorted out all the good lentils and put them in the bowls. Before half an hour had passed, they had finished and they all flew away. Then the girl brought the bowls to her stepmother, and she was happy, for she thought she'd be allowed to go to the wedding. But her stepmother said: "It's no use. You can't come, because you have nothing to wear and you don't know how to dance. We'd only be ashamed of you." Then she turned her back and hurried away with her two proud daughters.

When they had all gone out, Ashputtle went to her mother's grave. She stood under the hazel tree and cried:

> "Shake your branches, little tree,
> Throw gold and silver down on me."

Whereupon the bird tossed down a gold and silver dress and slippers embroidered with silk and silver. Ashputtle slipped into the dress as fast as she could and went to the wedding. Her sisters and stepmother didn't recognize her. She was so beautiful in her golden dress that they thought she must be the daughter of some foreign king. They never dreamed it could be Ashputtle, for they thought she was sitting at home in her filthy rags, picking lentils out of the ashes. The king's son came up to her, took her by the hand and danced with her. He wouldn't dance with anyone else and he never let go her hand. When someone else asked for a dance, he said: "She is my partner."

She danced until evening, and then she wanted to go home. The king's son said: "I'll go with you, I'll see you home," for he wanted to find out whom the beautiful girl belonged to. But she got away from him and slipped into the dovecote. The king's son waited until her father arrived, and told him the strange girl had slipped into the dovecote. The old man thought: "Could it be Ashputtle?" and he sent for an ax and a pick and broke into the dovecote, but there was no one inside. When they went indoors, Ashputtle was lying in the ashes in her filthy clothes and a dim oil lamp was burning on the chimney piece, for Ashputtle had slipped out the back end of the dovecote and run to the hazel tree. There she had taken off her fine clothes and put them on the grave, and the bird had taken them away. Then she had put her gray dress on again, crept into the kitchen and lain down in the ashes.

Next day when the festivities started in again and her parents and stepsisters had gone, Ashputtle went to the hazel tree and said:

> "Shake your branches, little tree,
> Throw gold and silver down on me."

Whereupon the bird threw down a dress that was even more dazzling than the first one. And when she appeared at the wedding, everyone marveled at her beauty. The king's son was waiting for her. He took her by the hand and danced with no one but her. When others came and asked her for a dance, he said: "She is my partner." When evening came, she said she was going home. The king's son followed her, wishing to see which house she went into, but she ran away and disappeared into the garden behind the house, where there was a big beautiful tree with the most wonderful pears growing on it. She climbed among the branches as nimbly as a squirrel and the king's son didn't know what had become of her. He waited until her father arrived and said to him: "The strange girl has got away from me and I think she has climbed up in the pear tree." Her father thought: "Could it be Ashputtle?" He sent for an ax and chopped the tree down, but there was no one in it. When they went into the kitchen, Ashputtle was lying there in the ashes as usual, for she had jumped down on the other side of the tree, brought her fine clothes back to the bird in the hazel tree, and put on her filthy gray dress.

On the third day, after her parents and sisters had gone, Ashputtle went back to her mother's grave and said to the tree:

> "Shake your branches, little tree,
> Throw gold and silver down on me."

Whereupon the bird threw down a dress that was more radiant than either of the others, and the slippers were all gold. When she appeared at the wedding, the people were too amazed to speak. The king's son danced with no one but her, and when someone else asked her for a dance, he said: "She is my partner."

When evening came, Ashputtle wanted to go home, and the king's son said he'd go with her, but she slipped away so quickly that he couldn't follow. But he had thought up a trick. He had arranged to have the whole staircase brushed with pitch, and as she was running down it the pitch pulled her left slipper off. The king's son picked it up, and it was tiny and delicate and all gold. Next morning he went to the father and said: "No girl shall be my wife but the one this golden shoe fits." The sisters were overjoyed, for they had beautiful feet. The eldest took the shoe to her room to try it on and her mother went with her. But the shoe was too small and she couldn't get her big toe in. So her mother handed her a knife and said: "Cut your toe off. Once you're queen you won't have to walk any more." The girl cut her toe off, forced her foot into the shoe, gritted her teeth against the pain, and went out to the king's son. He accepted her as his bride-to-be, lifted her up on his horse, and rode away with her. But they had to pass the grave. The two doves were sitting in the hazel tree and they cried out:

> "Roocoo, roocoo,
> There's blood in the shoe.
> The foot's too long, the foot's too wide,
> That's not the proper bride."

He looked down at her foot and saw the blood spurting. At that he turned his horse around and took the false bride home again. "No," he said, "this isn't the right girl; let her sister try the shoe on." The sister went to her room and managed to get her toes into the shoe, but her heel was too big. So her mother handed her a knife and said: "Cut off a chunk of your heel. Once you're queen you won't have to walk any more." The girl cut off a chunk of her heel, forced her foot into the shoe, gritted her teeth against the pain, and went out to the king's son. He accepted her as his bride-to-be, lifted her up on his horse, and rode away with her. As they passed the hazel tree, the two doves were sitting there, and they cried out:

> "Roocoo, roocoo,
> There's blood in the shoe.
> The foot's too long, the foot's too wide,
> That's not the proper bride."

He looked down at her foot and saw that blood was spurting from her shoe and staining her white stocking all red. He turned his horse around and took the false bride home again. "This isn't the right girl, either," he said. "Haven't you got another daughter?" "No," said the man, "there's only a puny little kitchen drudge that my dead wife left me. She couldn't possibly be the bride." "Send her up," said the king's son, but the mother said: "Oh no, she's much too dirty to be seen." But he insisted and they had to call her. First she washed her face and hands, and when they were clean, she went upstairs and curtseyed to the king's son. He handed her the golden slipper and sat down on a footstool, took her foot out of her heavy wooden shoe, and put it into the slipper. It fitted perfectly. And when she stood up and the king's son looked into her face, he recognized the beautiful girl he had danced with and cried out: "This is my true bride!" The stepmother and the two sisters went pale with fear and rage. But he lifted Ashputtle up on his horse and rode away with her. As they passed the hazel tree, the two white doves called out:

> "Roocoo, roocoo,
> No blood in the shoe.
> Her foot is neither long nor wide,
> This one is the proper bride."

Then they flew down and alighted on Ashputtle's shoulders, one on the right and one on the left, and there they sat.

On the day of Ashputtle's wedding, the two stepsisters came and tried to ingratiate themselves and share in her happiness. On the way to church the elder was on the right side of the bridal couple and the younger on the left. The doves came along and pecked out one of the elder sister's eyes and one of the younger sister's eyes. Afterward, on the way out, the elder was on the left side and the younger on the right, and the doves pecked out both the remaining eyes. So both sisters were punished with blindness to the end of their days for being so wicked and false.

22

The Riddle

THERE WAS ONCE a king's son who longed to travel, so he started out, taking no one with him but a faithful servant. Once as night was falling he found himself in the midst of a big forest and had no idea where to look for shelter. Then he saw a hut and a girl walking toward it, and when he came closer he saw she was young and beautiful. He spoke to her and said: "Dear child, may my servant and I stop for the night in this hut?" "Oh yes," she said in a sad voice. "Of course you may, but I wouldn't advise you to. Don't go in!" "Why not?" the king's son asked. The girl sighed and said: "My stepmother practices evil arts, and she has it in for travelers." Then he knew he had come to a witch's house, but he couldn't go any farther in the darkness and besides he wasn't afraid, so he went in. The old woman was sitting in an armchair by the fire. "Good evening," she croaked, as friendly as you please, looking at the stranger with her red eyes. "Sit down and make yourselves at home." She was cooking something in a little pot, and she blew up the coals under it. Her daughter warned the strangers to be careful and not to take food or drink, because the old woman concocted evil potions. They slept peacefully until early in the morning.

When they were getting ready to leave and the king's son had already mounted his horse, the old woman said: "Wait. Let me offer you a farewell drink." While she was getting it, the king's son rode away, and only the servant, who still had to tighten his saddle girths, was there when the witch came out with the drink. "Bring this to your master," she said. But at that same moment the glass burst and the poison fell on the horse, and it was so potent that the beast fell down dead on the spot. The servant ran after his master and told him what had happened. But he didn't want to abandon his saddle and went back for it. When he reached the dead horse, a raven was sitting there, eating its flesh. The servant killed the raven and took it along, saying: "Who knows if we'll find anything better today?" All day they journeyed through the forest and they couldn't seem to find their way out of it. At nightfall they came to an inn. The servant handed the raven to the landlord and bade him prepare it for their dinner. But they had fallen on a den of murderers and when it was dark twelve murderers came in to kill and rob the strangers. But before getting to work they sat down to table. The landlord and the witch sat down with the murderers, and all together they ate a bowl of soup in which the chopped meat of the raven had been cooked. No sooner had they taken a few bites than they all fell dead, for some of the poison from the horse's flesh had gone into the raven. Now there was no one left in the house but the landlord's daughter, who was a good girl and had taken no part in the godless goings-on. She opened all the doors and showed the king's son great piles of treasure. But he said he wanted none of it, told her to keep it for herself, and rode away with his servant.

After wandering about for a long while, they came to a city where there was a beautiful but arrogant princess, who had let it be known that she would marry the man who gave her a riddle she couldn't solve, but that if she did solve his riddle his head would be cut off. She allowed herself three days' thinking time, but she was so clever she always guessed the answer sooner. Nine suitors had already lost their heads before the king's son got there, but dazzled by her great beauty, he resolved to stake his life. Introduced into her presence, he said: "Here is my riddle: One killed none, yet killed twelve. What is it?" She didn't know. She thought and thought, but she couldn't find the answer. She looked into all her books of riddles, but it wasn't there. This riddle, in short, was too much for her. When she could think of nothing else to do, she called her chambermaid and bade her creep into the prince's bedchamber and listen to his dreams, for she thought that in his sleep he might give his riddle away. But the clever servant had lain down in his master's bed, and when the chambermaid came in he tore off her mantle, and drove her away with rods. The second night the princess sent her maid-in-waiting to see if she could eavesdrop more successfully, but again the servant tore off her mantle and chased her away with rods. After that the prince thought the third night would be safe, and lay down in his own bed. This time it was the princess herself who came, wearing a mist-gray mantle. She sat down beside him, and when she thought he was asleep and dreaming, she spoke to him, hoping he would answer in his sleep as people often do. But he was awake and well aware of what was going on. "One killed none," she said. "What is it?" He replied: "A raven who ate the flesh of a poisoned horse and died of it." "And yet killed twelve," she said. "What is it?" "Twelve murderers who ate the raven and died of it." When she knew the answer to the riddle, she wanted to creep away, but he held on to her mantle and she had to leave it behind. Next morning the princess announced that she had guessed the riddle, sent for the twelve judges and gave the answer in their presence. But the king's son asked to be heard and said: "She crept into my room during the night and questioned me. She would never have guessed it otherwise." The judges said: "Bring us a proof." Then the servant brought the three mantles, and when the judges saw the mist-gray one, which the princess often wore, they said: "Have this mantle embroidered with gold and silver, for it will be your wedding mantle."

23

The Mouse, the Bird, and the Sausage

ONCE A MOUSE, a bird, and a sausage joined forces. They set up housekeeping, lived together for years in peace and happiness, and increased their worldly goods most remarkably. The bird's job was to fly to the forest every day and bring wood, the mouse had to carry water, make the fire, and set the table, and the sausage did the cooking.

Too much well-being makes for discontent. One day the bird met another bird, and boasted of his unusual good fortune. But the other bird made fun of him and called him a poor fool, who did all the hard work while his companions were taking it easy at home. When the mouse had laid the fire and carried the water, he went to his little room and rested until he was told to set the table. As for the sausage, all he did was to sit by the pot, lifting the lid now and then to make sure it was boiling, and then just before mealtime he would slither himself through the soup or vegetables once or twice for flavoring, and that was all there was to it. By the time the bird got home and put down his burden, they were sitting at the table, and when they had finished eating they slept like logs until next morning. In short, they lived like the gods.

The bird mulled over what the other bird had said, and next morning he refused to go to the forest. He said he'd been their slave long enough; they'd made a fool of him, but now they'd have to change around and try a different arrangement. The mouse and the sausage disagreed; they argued tooth and nail, but the bird got his way and they had to give his idea a try. They drew lots, and the way it fell out the sausage had to get wood, the mouse became the cook, and the bird had to carry water.

What happened? The sausage went out for wood, the bird made the fire, the mouse put the pot on, and they waited for the sausage to come home with the wood for the next day. But the sausage was gone so long that the others began to worry and the bird went out to see what was wrong. He hadn't gone far when he caught sight of a dog, who had taken the poor sausage for fair game, attacked him, and laid him low. The bird was indignant; he charged the dog with criminal assault, but that didn't help, because the dog claimed to have found forged letters on the sausage, and that of course was a capital offense.

Sadly the bird picked up the wood, flew home, and told the mouse what he had seen and heard. Despite their bitter grief, they agreed that they had best stay together. The bird set the table and the mouse did the cooking. When the vegetables were done, he thought he'd hop into the pot and slither through them for flavor as the sausage used to do, but he was stopped short before he even got to the middle, and there he left his hair, hide, and life.

When the bird got ready to serve the meal, the cook was gone. In consternation the bird rummaged through the wood, searched and called, but the cook was nowhere to be found. What with the bird's carelessness the wood caught fire and the whole place went up in flames. The bird hurried out for water, but the bucket slipped and fell into the well. The bird fell with it and couldn't stop himself, so he drowned.

24

Mother Holle

A WIDOW HAD TWO DAUGHTERS, the one beautiful and hard-working, the other ugly and lazy. But she was much fonder of the ugly, lazy one, because she was her own daughter, and the other was the household drudge who had to do all the work. Every day the poor girl had to sit near a well by the roadside and spin until her fingers bled. Now it so happened that once when her spindle was covered with blood she bent over the well and dipped it in the water to wash it off. But the spindle slipped from her hands and fell to the bottom. She burst into tears, ran home to her stepmother, and told her what had happened. The stepmother scolded her unmercifully. "You let it fall in," she cried. "So you can just get it out again." The poor girl went back to the well and she didn't know what to do. In the end she was so frightened that she jumped into the well in the hope of retrieving the spindle. Then she lost consciousness, and when she awoke she was in a beautiful meadow. The sun was shining and there were thousands of lovely flowers.

She started walking across the meadow, and after a while she came to a baker's oven. It was full of bread, and the bread cried out: "Oh, take me out, take me out, or I'll burn; I was done long ago." So the girl found a baker's shovel and took all the loaves out, one by one. Then she went on and came to a tree that was full of apples and it cried to her: "Oh, shake me, shake me; all of us apples are ripe." She shook the tree, the apples fell like rain, until none were left on the tree, and after piling them up she went on.

Finally she came to a little house. An old woman was looking out of the window, and she had such big teeth that the girl was afraid and started to run away. But the old woman called out to her: "What are you afraid of, dear child? Stay with me; if you do my housework and do it properly, you won't regret it. Just so you take care to make my bed nicely and shake it till the feathers fly, for then it will snow on

earth. I'm Mother Holle."* The old woman spoke so kindly that the
girl took heart and agreed to work for her. And she did her work to
Mother Holle's satisfaction, and always shook the bed so hard that
the feathers flew about like snowflakes. In return she had a good life,
never a harsh word, and every day there was boiled meat or roast
meat. But after she had been with Mother Holle for some time she
grew sad. At first she herself didn't know what was wrong, but then
she knew it was homesickness. Though she was a thousand times better off than she had ever been at home, she longed to be back. In the
end she said to Mother Holle: "I'm homesick. I know how well off I
am down here, but I can't stay any longer, I must go back to my
family." Mother Holle said: "It pleases me that you should long for
home, and because you've served me so faithfully I'll take you back
myself." So she took her by the hand and led her to a big door. The
door opened, and just as the girl was going through, gold came rain-
ing down from above and clung to her, so that she was soon covered
with gold from head to toe. "That's your reward for working so
hard," said Mother Holle. And then she gave the girl the spindle that
had fallen into the well. The door closed and the girl was up in the
world again, not far from her mother's house. When she went into
the yard, the rooster was standing on the rim of the well, and he
crowed:

> "Cock-a-doodle-doo,
> Our golden girl is home anew."

Then she went into the house, and her mother and sister made a great
fuss over her because she was covered with gold.

She told them everything that had happened, and when the mother
heard how she had come by her great riches, she wanted the same
good fortune for her ugly, lazy daughter, so she told her to sit by the
well and spin. To make her spindle bloody, she pricked her fingers
and put her hand in a bramblebush, and then she threw the spindle in
the well and jumped in after it. She woke up on the same beautiful
meadow as her sister, and walked the same way. When she got to the
oven, the bread cried out again: "Oh, take me out, take me out, or I'll
burn. I was done long ago." But the lazy girl answered: "Do you

---

* When it snows in Hessen, the people say: "Mother Holle is making her bed."

think I want to get all dirty?" and went on. Soon she came to the apple tree, which cried: "Oh, shake me, shake me, all of us apples are ripe." But she answered: "Wouldn't you like that! Suppose one of you fell on my head!" And she went on. When she got to Mother Holle's house, she wasn't afraid, because she had heard about her big teeth, and she agreed right away to work for her. The first day she forced herself to work hard and do as Mother Holle told her, for she was thinking of all the money she would give her. But the second day she began to take it easy, and on the third day it was even worse, for she didn't even want to get up in the morning. And she didn't make Mother Holle's bed properly, and didn't shake it till the feathers flew. Mother Holle soon had enough of her slovenly ways and dismissed her. The lazy girl was glad because now, she thought, it was time for the golden rain. And true enough, Mother Holle took her to the door, but as she was passing through, it wasn't gold that poured down on her, but a big caldron full of pitch. "That's your reward for your services," said Mother Holle, and closed the door. So then the lazy girl went home, but she was all covered with pitch and when the rooster on the rim of the well saw her he crowed:

> "Cock-a-doodle-doo,
> Our dirty girl is home anew."

And the pitch refused to come off, and it stuck to her as long as she lived.

25

The Seven Ravens

A MAN HAD SEVEN SONS and no daughter, though he longed very much for one. At last his wife gave him hope of another child, and when the child was born it was a girl. There was great joy, but the infant was sickly and puny, so weak that she had to be christened at home. In great haste the father sent one of the boys to the well for water, and the other six went along. They all wanted to be the first to draw water, and in the scramble the pitcher fell into the well. There they stood. They were all afraid to go home and they didn't know what to do. When they didn't come back, the father grew impatient and said: "Those wicked boys have forgotten. They must be playing some game again." He was afraid the little girl might die unchristened and in his anger he cried out: "I wish they'd all turn into ravens." No sooner were the words spoken than he heard a whirring over his head, and when he looked up he saw seven coal-black ravens flying away.

The parents could not undo the curse, and sad as they were over the loss of their seven sons, they were partly comforted by their little daughter, who soon grew strong and healthy and became more beautiful with every day that passed. Her parents were careful not to mention her brothers, and for a long time she didn't even know she had any. But one day she heard some people talking about her, saying, oh yes, she was indeed a lovely child, but on the other hand she was to blame for the misfortune that had befallen her seven brothers. That made her very sad, and she went to her father and mother and asked if she had had brothers and what had become of them. After that her parents could keep silent no longer, but they said her brothers' misfortune had been God's will and that her birth could not be held to blame. But day after day her conscience plagued her, and she felt she had to save her brothers at all costs. She knew neither rest nor peace until one day she stole away from home and went out into the wide world in the hope of finding them somewhere. All she took with her was a ring in remembrance of her parents, a loaf of bread and a jug of water for when she was hungry and thirsty, and a little chair for when she was tired.

On and on she went, farther and farther, until she reached the end of the world. She went to the sun, but it was too hot and terrible and it ate little children. So she ran away and went to the moon, but the moon was too cold and creepy and wicked, and when it saw the child it said: "I smell, I smell human flesh." So she hurried on and she didn't stop till she came to the stars. They were friendly and kind to her. Each one was sitting on its own little chair, and the morning star stood up and gave her a chicken's leg and said: "Without this chicken's leg you'll never get into the glass mountain, and that's where your brothers are."

The girl took the chicken's leg, wrapped it carefully in a cloth, and went on until she came to the glass mountain. The gate was locked and she wanted to take out the chicken's leg, but when she unfolded the cloth it was empty. She had lost the gift of the kindly stars. What was she to do now? She was determined to save her brothers, but she had no key to the glass mountain. So the good little sister took a knife, cut off one of her fingers, and put it into the lock. The gate opened. She went in, and a dwarf came up to her and said: "What are you looking for, child?" "I'm looking for my brothers, the seven ravens." The dwarf replied: "The lord ravens aren't home, but if you care to wait for them, come in." Then the dwarf brought in the ravens' food on seven little plates, and their drink in seven little cups, and the little sister ate a bite from each plate and drank a sip from each cup. And into the last cup she dropped the ring she had brought with her.

Suddenly she heard a whirring of wings, and the dwarf said: "Here come the lord ravens." The ravens were hungry and thirsty and they went straight to their plates and cups. And one after another of them said: "Who has eaten from my plate? Who has drunk from my cup? A human mouth has been here." And when the seventh got to the bottom of his cup, the ring rolled out. He looked at it, recognized it as his parents' ring, and said: "God grant that our sister may be here. Then we are saved." The girl was standing behind the door. When she heard that wish, she came out and all the ravens took on human form again. Then they hugged and kissed each other and went happily home.

26

Little Red Cap

ONCE THERE WAS a dear little girl whom everyone loved. Her grandmother loved her most of all and didn't know what to give the child next. Once she gave her a little red velvet cap, which was so becoming to her that she never wanted to wear anything else, and that was why everyone called her Little Red Cap. One day her mother said:

"Look, Little Red Cap, here's a piece of cake and a bottle of wine. Take them to grandmother. She is sick and weak, and they will make her feel better. You'd better start now before it gets too hot; walk properly like a good little girl, and don't leave the path or you'll fall down and break the bottle and there won't be anything for grandmother. And when you get to her house, don't forget to say good morning, and don't go looking in all the corners."

"I'll do everything right," Little Red Cap promised her mother. Her grandmother lived in the wood, half an hour's walk from the village. No sooner had Little Red Cap set foot in the wood than she met the wolf. But Little Red Cap didn't know what a wicked beast he was, so she wasn't afraid of him. "Good morning, Little Red Cap," he said. "Thank you kindly, wolf." "Where are you going so early, Little Red Cap?" "To my grandmother's." "And what's that you've got under your apron?" "Cake and wine. We baked yesterday, and we want my grandmother, who's sick and weak, to have something nice that will make her feel better." "Where does your grandmother live, Little Red Cap?" "In the wood, fifteen or twenty minutes' walk from here, under the three big oak trees. That's where the house is. It has hazel hedges around it. You must know the place." "How young and tender she is!" thought the wolf. "Why, she'll be even tastier than the old woman. Maybe if I'm crafty enough I can get them both." So, after walking along for a short while beside Little Red Cap, he said: "Little Red Cap, open your eyes. What lovely flowers! Why don't you look around you? I don't believe you even hear how sweetly the birds are singing. It's so gay out here in the wood, yet you trudge along as solemnly as if you were going to school."

Little Red Cap looked up, and when she saw the sunbeams dancing this way and that between the trees and the beautiful flowers all around her, she thought: "Grandmother will be pleased if I bring her a bunch of nice fresh flowers. It's so early now that I'm sure to be there in plenty of time." So she left the path and went into the wood to pick flowers. And when she had picked one, she thought there must be a more beautiful one farther on, so she went deeper and deeper into the wood. As for the wolf, he went straight to the grandmother's house and knocked at the door. "Who's there?" "Little Red Cap, bringing cake and wine. Open the door." "Just raise the latch," cried the grandmother, "I'm too weak to get out of bed." The wolf raised the latch and the door swung open. Without saying a single word he went straight to the grandmother's bed and gobbled her up. Then he put on her clothes and her nightcap, lay down in the bed, and drew the curtains.

Meanwhile Little Red Cap had been running about picking flowers, and when she had as many as she could carry she remembered her grandmother and started off again. She was surprised to find the door open, and when she stepped into the house she had such a strange feeling that she said to herself: "My goodness, I'm usually so glad to see grandmother. Why am I frightened today?" "Good morning," she cried out, but there was no answer. Then she went to the bed and opened the curtains. The grandmother had her cap pulled way down over her face, and looked very very strange.

"Oh, grandmother, what big ears you have!"

"The better to hear you with."

"Oh, grandmother, what big eyes you have!"

"The better to see you with."

"Oh, grandmother, what big hands you have!"

"The better to grab you with."

"But, grandmother, what a dreadful big mouth you have!"

"The better to eat you with."

And no sooner had the wolf spoken than he bounded out of bed and gobbled up poor Little Red Cap.

When the wolf had stilled his hunger, he got back into bed, fell asleep, and began to snore very very loud. A hunter was just passing, and he thought: "How the old woman is snoring! I'd better go and see what's wrong." So he stepped into the house and went over to the bed and saw the wolf was in it. "You old sinner!" he said, "I've found you at last. It's been a long time." He leveled his musket and was just about to fire when it occurred to him that the wolf might have swallowed the grandmother and that there might still be a chance of saving her. So instead of firing, he took a pair of scissors and started cutting the sleeping wolf's belly open. After two snips, he saw the little red cap, and after another few snips the little girl jumped out, crying: "Oh, I've been so afraid! It was so dark inside the wolf!" And then the old grandmother came out, and she too was still alive, though she could hardly breathe. Little Red Cap ran outside and brought big stones, and they filled the wolf's belly with them. When he woke up, he wanted to run away, but the stones were so heavy that his legs wouldn't carry him and he fell dead.

All three were happy; the hunter skinned the wolf and went home with the skin, the grandmother ate the cake and drank the wine Little Red Cap had brought her and soon got well; and as for Little Red Cap, she said to herself: "Never again will I leave the path and run off into the wood when my mother tells me not to."

Another story they tell is that when Little Red Cap was taking another cake to her old grandmother another wolf spoke to her and tried to make her leave the path. But Little Red Cap was on her guard. She kept on going, and when she got to her grandmother's she told her how she had met a wolf who had bidden her good day but given her such a wicked look that "if it hadn't been on the open road he'd have gobbled me right up." "Well then," said the grandmother, "we'll just lock the door and he won't be able to get in." In a little while the wolf knocked and called out: "Open the door, grandmother, it's Little Red Cap. I've brought you some cake." But they didn't say a word and they didn't open the door. So Grayhead circled the house once or twice and finally jumped on the roof. His plan was to wait until evening when Little Red Cap would go home, and then he'd creep after her and gobble her up in the darkness. But the grandmother guessed what he had in mind. There was a big stone trough in front of the house, and she said to the child: "Here's a bucket, Little Red Cap. I cooked some sausages yesterday. Take the water I cooked them in and empty it into the trough." Little Red Cap carried water until the big trough was full. The smell of the sausages rose up to the wolf's nostrils. He sniffed and looked down, and in the end he stuck his neck out so far that he couldn't keep his footing and began to slide. And he slid off the roof and slid straight into the big trough and was drowned. And Little Red Cap went happily home, and no one harmed her.

27

The Musicians of Bremen

A MAN HAD A DONKEY, who for years had been hauling sacks of grain to the mill without a word of complaint, but his strength was failing and he was becoming more and more unfit for work. His master was beginning to think of doing away with him, but the donkey saw that trouble was in the air, so he ran away and started out for Bremen, thinking he might be able to join the town band. When he had gone a little way, he saw a hound lying beside the path, panting like someone who had walked until he was ready to drop. "Hey there, Towzer," said the donkey. "Why are you panting so?" "Alas," said the dog, "because I'm old and getting weaker every day, and I can't hunt any more. My master wanted to kill me, so I ran away, but what will I do for my daily bread?" "Listen to me," said the donkey. "I'm on my way to Bremen to join the town band. Come along, you can join too. I'll play the lute and you'll play the drum." The dog liked the idea and they went on together.

It wasn't long before they saw a cat sitting by the wayside, making a face a mile long. "Well, Mr. Whiskers," said the donkey, "what's wrong with you?" "How," said the cat, "can anyone be cheerful when his life is hanging by a thread? Just because I'm getting old and my teeth aren't as sharp as they used to be and I'd sooner sit by the fire and spin than chase mice, my mistress wanted to drown me. Yes, yes, I escaped, but now I'm at my wits' end—where am I to go?" "Come to Bremen with us. You're good at serenading, you can join the band too." That appealed to the cat, and he went along.

Soon the three fugitives passed a farm. The cock was standing on the roof over the gate, crowing for all he was worth. "Why," asked the donkey, "are you screaming like that? It's bloodcurdling." "I'm predicting good weather," said the cock, "because it's the day Our Lady washes out the Christ Child's little shirts and hangs them up to dry, but tomorrow's Sunday. We're having company, and the farmer's wife is heartless. I heard her tell the cook she wanted to eat me tomorrow in the soup, and I'm to have my head cut off this evening. So now I'm screeching while the screeching's good." "Redcomb," said the donkey, "don't be a fool. Why not come with us instead? We're on our way to Bremen. Whatever happens, it's sure to be better than death. You've got a fine voice, and if we all sing together, we're sure to be a hit." The cock liked the proposal, and all four went on together.

But they couldn't get to Bremen in one day, and that evening they came to a forest and decided to stop for the night. The donkey and the dog lay down under a big tree, the cat climbed up on a branch, and the cock flew to the very top of the tree, where he felt safest. Before going to sleep, he looked around in all directions. He thought he saw a spark in the distance, and he told his companions there must be a house nearby, for he'd seen a light. "In that case," said the donkey, "let's be moving on, for this is a most uncomfortable spot." The dog thought there might be a few bones with a bit of meat on them. And so they started off in the direction of the light, and it grew brighter and brighter and bigger and bigger, until at last they came to a brightly lit house where some robbers were living. The donkey, who was the tallest, went to the window and looked in. "What do you see, Old Gray?" asked the cock. "What do I see?" the donkey replied. "I see a table covered with good things to eat and drink, and I see some robbers feasting." "Just the thing for us," said the cock. "No doubt about that," said the donkey. "If we could only get in." How were they to drive the robbers away? The animals talked it over and at last they hit on a plan. The donkey stood up on his hind legs and put his forefeet on the window ledge; the dog jumped up on the donkey's back, the cat climbed on the dog, and finally the cock flew up in the air and perched on the cat's head. At a certain signal they all struck up their music: the donkey brayed, the dog barked, the cat miaowed, and the cock crowed. Then they leaped through the window and burst into the room in a shower of glass. The robbers, who thought a ghost had attacked them, jumped up with blood-curdling yells and fled to the woods. Whereupon the friends sat down at the table, glad to take potluck, and ate as if they expected to get nothing more for a month.

When the four musicians had finished eating, they put out the light and found themselves places to sleep, each according to his nature and convenience. The donkey lay down on the dung heap in the yard, the dog behind the door, the cat in the warm ashes on the hearth, while the cock made himself at home on a jutting roof beam. Tired as they were from their travels, they soon fell asleep. After midnight the robbers saw from the distance that there was no light in the house and that everything seemed quiet. "We shouldn't have let ourselves be scared so easily," said the captain of the band, and ordered one of the robbers to go back and investigate. The scout found nothing to alarm him and went into the kitchen to strike a light. He mistook the cat's fiery eyes for live coals and held up a match to them, thinking it would take fire. But the cat, who didn't think it was funny, sprang at the robber's face, spitting and scratching. Scared out of his wits, the robber ran to the back door, but the dog jumped up and bit him in the leg. And out in the yard, as he was running past the dung heap, the donkey gave him a good kick with his hind legs. Then the cock, who had been disturbed by the noise and was wide awake, called from his perch: "Cock-a-doodle-doo!" At that the robber ran back to his captain as fast as his legs would carry him, and said: "There's a horrible witch in the house. She spat at me and scratched my face with her long fingers. Behind the door there's a man with a knife and he stabbed me in the leg. In the yard there's a black monster who hit me with a wooden club, and up on the roof sits the judge. 'Bring the rascal here to me!' he shouted. So I ran." After that the robbers didn't dare return to the house, and the four Bremen musicians liked it so well that they never left it. And the mouth of the person who last told this story is still warm.

28

The Singing Bone

A CERTAIN COUNTRY was full of weeping and wailing, because of a wild boar that was ravaging the peasants' fields, killing their cattle, and tearing people to pieces with its tusks. The king promised a rich reward to anyone who would rid the country of this plague, but the beast was so big and strong that no one dared go near the forest where it lived. At last the king let it be known that the man who captured or killed the wild boar should have his daughter for his wife.

Now there were two brothers living in that country, a poor man's sons. They came forward and offered to brave the danger. The elder, who was clever and crafty, was moved by ambition, and the younger, who was simple and innocent, by goodness of heart. The king said: "To make sure of finding the beast, you will enter the forest from opposite sides." So the elder went in from the west and the younger from the east. When the younger had gone a short way, a little man with a black spear came up to him and said: "I will give you this spear because your heart is pure and innocent. With it you can attack the wild boar without fear; he will do you no harm." He thanked the little man, shouldered the spear, and went on unafraid. In a short while, he caught sight of the boar. He held out the spear and in its blind fury the boar ran against it with such force that its heart was cut in two. Whereupon the young man flung the beast over his shoulder and started homeward, meaning to bring it to the king.

On the opposite edge of the forest, there was a tavern where people were making merry and drinking wine. His elder brother had stopped there, thinking that the boar wouldn't run away and that he might as well have a few glasses of wine to give him courage. When he saw his younger brother coming out of the forest with the boar over his shoulder, his wicked, envious heart gave him no peace, and he called out: "Come in, dear brother, rest awhile and refresh yourself with a glass of wine." The younger brother, who suspected no evil, went in and told him how the little man had given him a spear and how he had killed the boar with it. The elder brother kept him there until nightfall, and they left together. It was dark when they came to the bridge across the stream. The elder brother let the younger go ahead, and when he had gone halfway struck him so hard from behind that he fell dead. He buried him under the bridge, took the boar and brought it to the king, claiming to have killed it himself, whereupon the king gave him his daughter for his wife. When his younger brother failed to reappear, he said: "The boar must have torn him to pieces," and everyone believed him.

But nothing remains hidden from God, and in due time the

brother's evil deed came to light. Years later a shepherd was driving his flock across the bridge. He caught sight of a snow-white bone in the sand down below and thought it would make a good mouthpiece for his horn. He went down, picked it up, and carved a mouthpiece from it. Much to the shepherd's amazement, the bone began to sing of its own accord the moment he set it to his lips:

"Oh dear shepherd, that's my bone
That you are playing on.
My very own brother struck me down
And took the boar I'd killed.
He buried me beside the water,
And married the king's daughter."

"What an amazing horn to sing by itself!" said the shepherd. "I must take it to the king." When he stood before the king, the horn sang the same song, and the king understood. He gave orders for the ground under the bridge to be dug up and the murdered man's skeleton was found. The wicked brother, who couldn't deny his crime, was sewn up in a sack and drowned, while the bones of the murdered man were laid to rest in a beautiful grave in the churchyard.

29

The Devil with the Three Golden Hairs

THERE WAS ONCE a poor woman who bore a son, and because he had a caul when he came into the world, a fortuneteller prophesied that in his fourteenth year he would marry the king's daughter. Not long afterward the king came to the village, and no one knew he was the king. When he asked the villagers what was new, they answered: "A few days ago a child was born with a caul. That means he'll succeed in everything he undertakes, and what's more, the fortuneteller said he would marry the king's daughter in his fourteenth year." The king was wicked at heart, and the prophecy made him angry. He went to the parents, put on a friendly face, and said: "You poor

souls, if you entrust your child to me, I shall take good care of him."
At first they refused, but when the stranger offered a great deal of
gold, they thought: "It's sure to turn out all right for him, because
he's a luck child." So in the end they consented.

The king put the child in a box and rode until he came to a deep
river. Then he threw the box in the water and said to himself: "I've
saved my daughter from an unwanted suitor." But instead of sinking,
the box drifted like a boat, and not a single drop of water got into it.
It drifted to within two miles of the king's palace, and there it caught
in a mill dam. The miller's man, who luckily happened to be standing
there, saw it and pulled it out with a hook, thinking he had found a
great treasure. But when he opened it, there was a pretty little boy
inside, as fresh and rosy as you please. He brought the child to the
miller and his wife, who, having no children of their own, were
delighted and said: "He is God's gift to us." They took good care of
the foundling, and brought him up to be good and true.

It so happened that one day when the king was caught in a storm
he took shelter in the mill. He asked the miller and his wife if the big
boy were their son. "No," they replied. "He's a foundling. Fourteen
years ago he floated down to the mill dam in a box, and our man
fished him out of the water." Well aware that the boy was none
other than the luck child he had thrown into the water, the king said:
"My good people, would you let the boy carry a letter to the queen?
I shall reward him with two gold pieces." "As Your Majesty commands," they replied, and told the boy to get ready. The king wrote
the queen a letter, saying: "As soon as the boy bearing this letter ar-
rives, I want him to be killed and buried. It must be done before my
return."

The boy started out with the letter, but he lost his way and at
nightfall found himself in a large forest. Seeing a light in the darkness, he headed for it and came to a hut. When he went in, an old
woman was sitting all alone by the fire. She started at the sight of the
boy and asked: "Where have you come from and where are you
going?" "I've come from the mill," he replied, "and I'm on my way
to the queen with a letter. But I got lost in the woods and now I'd
like to spend the night here." "You poor boy," said the old woman.
"You've walked into a den of thieves. When they come home they'll
kill you." "Let them come," said the boy. "I'm not afraid, and I'm

too tired to go on." With that he stretched out on the bench and fell asleep. A little later the thieves came in and asked angrily: "Who is that boy lying there?" "Oh," said the old woman, "it's only an innocent child. He was lost in the forest, so I took pity on him and let him stay. He's taking a letter to the queen." The thieves opened the letter and read it, and it said the boy should be killed the minute he got there. The hardhearted thieves were moved to pity. The leader tore up the letter and wrote another, saying the boy should be married to the queen's daughter the minute he got there. They let him lie peacefully on the bench until morning, and when he woke up they gave him the letter and showed him the right way. When the queen received the letter and read it, she did what it said, and ordered a magnificent wedding feast. So the king's daughter was married to the luck child. And since the boy was both handsome and charming, she was happy and content to live with him.

After a while the king returned to his palace and saw that the prophecy had been fulfilled and that the luck child was married to his daughter. "How could such a thing have happened?" he asked. "I gave entirely different orders in my letter." The queen showed him the letter and bade him see for himself. The king read the letter and saw it had been exchanged for the one he had written. So he asked the boy what had happened to the letter that had been entrusted to him and why he had delivered a different one. "I don't know," said the boy. "They must have exchanged it when I spent the night in the forest." The king was very angry. "Did you really think you could get off so easily?" he said. "If you want my daughter, you will have to go down to hell and get me three golden hairs from the Devil's head; if you do that, you can keep my daughter." With this task the king hoped to be rid of him forever. But the luck child replied: "Don't worry. I'll bring you the three golden hairs. I'm not afraid of the Devil." Whereupon he took his leave and started on his travels.

He came to a large city, where the watchman at the gate asked him what trade he plied and what he knew. "I know everything," he said. "In that case," said the watchman, "you can do us a favor and tell us why the fountain in our marketplace, that used to flow with wine, has gone dry and doesn't even give water anymore." "That I will tell you," said the luck child. "Just wait till I get back." He went his way and when he came to another city, the watchman at the gate asked him again what trade he plied and what he knew. "I know every-thing," he said. "Then you can do us a favor and tell us why a tree in our city that used to bear golden apples doesn't even grow leaves any-more." "That I will tell you," he replied. "Just wait till I get back." He went his way and came to a big stream. The ferryman asked him what trade he plied and what he knew. "I know everything," he said. "Then," said the ferryman, "you can do me a favor and tell me why I keep having to cross back and forth and no one ever relieves me." "That I will tell you," he said. "Just wait till I get back."

After crossing the river, he found the entrance to hell. It was black and sooty inside, and the Devil wasn't at home, but his grandmother was sitting there in a big armchair. "What do you want?" she asked. She didn't look very fierce. "I need three golden hairs from the Devil's head," he replied, "or I won't be able to keep my wife." "That's a good deal to ask," she said. "If the Devil finds you here, you'll wish he hadn't. But I feel sorry for you, so I'll see what I can do to help you." Thereupon she turned him into an ant and said: "Crawl into the folds of my skirt. There you'll be safe." "Thank you," he said, "that's fine, but in addition there are three things I'd like to know: why a fountain that used to flow with wine has dried up and doesn't even give water anymore, why a tree that used to bear golden apples doesn't even grow leaves anymore, and why a ferryman keeps having to cross back and forth and no one relieves him." "Those are very hard questions," she said, "but just keep very quiet and listen to what the Devil says when I pull out the three golden hairs."

At nightfall the Devil came home. The moment he entered he no-ticed that something was amiss. "I smell, I smell human flesh," he said. "Something is wrong around here." He looked in every corner but he found nothing. The grandmother scolded him: "The place has just been swept and put in order," she cried, "and now look at the mess you've made. You've got human flesh on the brain. Just sit down and eat your supper." When he had eaten, he felt tired. He laid his head in his grandmother's lap and told her to louse him a little. Be-fore long he was fast asleep, wheezing and snoring. The old woman took hold of one golden hair, pulled it out and set it down beside her. "Ouch!" cried the Devil. "What are you doing?" "I had a bad dream," said the grandmother, "so I grabbed hold of your hair."

"What did you dream?" the Devil asked. "I dreamed that a fountain which used to flow with wine had dried up and didn't even give water anymore. Why do you think that is?" "Aha," said the Devil, "if they only knew! There's a toad sitting under a stone in the fountain. If they kill it, the wine will flow again."

The grandmother loused him again until he fell asleep and snored so loud the windowpanes rattled. Then she pulled out the second hair. "Hey!" cried the Devil in a rage. "What are you doing?" "Don't get angry," she said. "I was dreaming." "What did you dream this time?" he asked. "I dreamed there was an apple tree in a certain kingdom that always used to bear golden apples and now it doesn't even grow leaves. Why do you think that is?" "Aha!" the Devil replied. "If they only knew! There's a mouse gnawing at the root. If they kill it, it will bear golden apples again, but if it keeps on gnawing the tree will wither away entirely. Now stop bothering me with your dreams. If you wake me up again, I'll slap your ears down."

His grandmother said soothing words and loused him again until he fell asleep and began to snore. Then she took hold of the third golden hair and pulled it out. The Devil started up and was going to treat her roughly, but she smoothed him down again and said: "No one can help his bad dreams." He was curious in spite of himself and asked: "What did you dream?" "I dreamed of a ferryman who complained that he kept having to cross back and forth and that no one relieved him. Why do you think that is?" "Ho ho, the blockhead!" the Devil replied. "When someone comes and wants to cross over, let him just put the pole in his hands; then the other fellow will have to take over, and he will be free." Now that the grandmother had pulled the three golden hairs and the three questions had been answered, she left the old serpent in peace and he slept until daybreak.

When the Devil went out again, the old woman took the ant from the fold in her skirt and gave the luck child back his human form. "Here you have the three golden hairs," she said, "and I'm sure you heard the Devil's answers to your three questions." "I heard them all right," he said, "and I won't forget them." "Then you've got what you wanted," she said, "and now you can go your way." He thanked the old woman for helping him in his need and left hell in the best of spirits, delighted that everything had gone so well. When he came to the ferry, the ferryman asked him for the promised answer. "First take me across," said the luck child, "then I'll tell you how you can be set free." When they got to the opposite shore, he gave him the Devil's advice: "The next time someone wants to be ferried across, just put the pole in his hand." On he went, and when he came to the city where the barren tree was growing, he was asked again for an answer. And he told the watchman what he had heard from the Devil: "Kill the mouse that's gnawing at its root and it will bear golden apples again." The watchman thanked him and as a reward gave him two donkeys laden with gold, and the donkeys followed him. Last he came to the city where the fountain had gone dry. And he repeated to the watchman what the Devil had said: "A toad is sitting under a stone in the fountain. You must find it and kill it, then the fountain will give plenty of wine again." The watchman thanked him and he too gave him two donkeys laden with gold.

At last the luck child got home to his wife, who was overjoyed to see him again and hear how well everything had gone. He gave the king what he had asked for, the Devil's three golden hairs, and when the king saw the four donkeys laden with gold he was really delighted. "Now you've met all the conditions," he said, "and you can keep my daughter. But dear son-in-law, tell me this: Where did you get all this gold? That's an enormous treasure." "I crossed a river," he said, "and that's where I found it. The whole bank was made of gold instead of sand." The king was devoured with greed. "Could I get some too?" he asked. "All you want," the luck child replied. "There's a ferryman on the river. Get him to take you across; once you're on the other side, you'll be able to fill your sacks." The greedy king started out as fast as he could, and when he got to the river he signaled to the ferryman to take him across. The ferryman came and bade him get on board, and when they got to the other side he put the pole in his hand and jumped off. From then on the king had to ferry people across the stream as a punishment for his sins.

"Is he still at it?" "Why not? It's not likely that anyone has taken the pole away from him."

30

The Louse and the Flea

A LOUSE AND A FLEA kept house together. They brewed their beer in an eggshell, and one day the louse fell in and got scalded. The flea began to scream at the top of his lungs. "Why are you screaming so?" asked the door. "Because Louse has got scalded." At that the door began to creak. A broom in the corner spoke up: "Why are you creaking, Door?" "Haven't I cause enough to creak?

> Louse has got scalded
> Flea is crying."

At that the broom began to sweep furiously. A cart came along and said: "Why are you sweeping, Broom?" "Haven't I cause enough to sweep?

> Louse has got scalded
> Flea is crying,
> Door is creaking."

"In that case, I'm going to run," said the cart, and he began to run furiously. He ran past the rubbish heap, and the rubbish heap said: "Why are you running, Cart?" "Haven't I cause enough to run?

> Louse has got scalded,
> Flea is crying,
> Door is creaking,
> Broom is sweeping."

"In that case I'm going to burn like mad," said the rubbish heap, and burst into a blaze. A tree, which was growing beside the rubbish heap, said: "Why are you burning, Rubbish Heap?" "Haven't I cause enough to burn?

> Louse has got scalded,
> Flea is crying,
> Door is creaking,
> Broom is sweeping,
> Cart is running."

"In that case I'm going to shake myself," said the tree, and shook himself so hard that all his leaves fell off. A girl who came out with her water pitcher saw him do it and said: "Tree, why are you shaking yourself?" "Haven't I cause enough to shake myself?

> Louse has got scalded,
> Flea is crying,
> Door is creaking,
> Broom is sweeping,
> Cart is running,
> Rubbish Heap is burning."

"In that case I'm going to smash my water pitcher," said the girl, and smashed her water pitcher. "Girl, why are you smashing your pitcher?" said the spring the water came from. "Haven't I cause enough to smash my pitcher?

> Louse has got scalded,
> Flea is crying,
> Door is creaking,
> Broom is sweeping,
> Cart is running,
> Rubbish Heap is burning,
> Tree is shaking himself."

"Goodness gracious," said the spring. "In that case I'm going to gush." And he began to gush furiously. And they were all drowned in the gushing water, the girl, the tree, the rubbish heap, the cart, the broom, the door, the flea, and the louse, the whole lot of them.

31

The Girl Without Hands

A MILLER HAD FALLEN on hard times, and all he had left was his mill and the big apple tree behind it. One day when he went to the forest for wood, an old man whom he had never seen before came up to him and said: "Why wear yourself out chopping wood? I will make you rich if you promise to give me what is standing behind your mill." "What can that be but the apple tree?" thought the miller, and agreed to the bargain. "In three years I shall come and take what is mine," said the stranger with a sneer, and went his way.

When the miller got home, his wife came out to meet him and said: "Tell me, miller, where has all this treasure come from all of a sudden? Every chest and box is full of it. No one brought it, and I don't understand." The miller replied: "It comes from a stranger I met in the forest. He promised to make me rich, and in return I agreed to let him have what is standing behind the mill. The big apple tree isn't too much to give for all this." The miller's wife was horrified. "Oh, husband," she said, "that was the Devil. He wasn't thinking of the apple tree; he was thinking of our daughter, who was standing behind the mill, sweeping the yard."

The miller's daughter was beautiful and God-fearing; all through the three years she lived in piety, without sin. When the three years had passed and the Evil One was to come for her, she washed herself clean and drew a circle around herself with chalk. The Devil appeared bright and early, but he couldn't get near her. He was very angry. "Keep her away from water," he said to the miller. "If you let her wash, I shall have no power over her." The miller obeyed, for he feared the Devil. Next morning the Devil came again, but she had shed tears on her hands, and they were clean and pure. Again he was unable to get near her, and in his rage he said to the miller: "Chop her hands off; otherwise I shall have no power over her." The miller was horrified. "How can I chop my own child's hands off?" he said. But the Devil threatened him, saying: "If you don't do as I say, you will belong to me, and I'll come and take you away." The miller was so frightened that he promised to obey. He went to his daughter and said: "My child, the Devil will take me away unless I chop your hands off, and in my fear I promised I'd do it. Help me in my affliction and forgive me the injury I am going to do you." "Dear father," she replied. "Do what you will with me. I am your child." Thereupon she held out her hands and let him chop them off. The Devil came a third time, but she had wept so long and so abundantly on the stumps that they were clean and pure in spite of everything. So he had to give up; he had lost all rights over her.

The miller said to her: "I have gained so much treasure, thanks to you, that I shall always care for you most tenderly." But she replied: "I cannot stay here. I am going away. Kindly people will provide for my needs." She bade them tie her maimed arms to her back, and at sunrise she started out. All day she walked and at nightfall she came to the king's orchard. In the moonlight she saw trees full of wonderful fruit, but she couldn't get into the orchard because there was water all around it. She was very hungry, for she had traveled all day without a bite to eat. "Oh," she thought, "if only I could get in and eat some of that fruit; I shall die if I don't." Whereupon she knelt down and prayed to God. Then suddenly an angel appeared and closed a sluice in the stream, so that the moat went dry and she was able to cross. She went into the garden and the angel went with her. She saw a tree full of fine pears, but they had all been counted. She went up to the tree, took just one pear off it with her mouth and ate it to still her hunger. The gardener saw what she had done, but because the angel was there too he was afraid and thought the girl must be a spirit, so he didn't dare cry out or say anything to the spirit. When she had eaten the pear, her hunger was stilled, so she went and hid in the thicket. Next morning the king who owned the orchard came and counted the pears. He saw that one was missing and asked the gardener what had become of it, since it was neither on the tree nor under it. The gardener replied: "Last night a spirit without hands came into the orchard and took off one pear with its mouth." "How did this spirit cross the moat?" the king asked. "And where did it go after eating the pear?" The gardener replied: "Someone in white came down from the sky and closed the sluice and stopped the water so the spirit could cross the moat. I was afraid because it must have been an angel. That's why I didn't call out or ask any questions. Then, after eating the pear, the spirit crossed back over." The king said: "If what you say is true, I shall watch with you tonight."

At nightfall the king went to the orchard, taking a priest with him to speak to the spirit. The three of them sat down under the tree and watched. At midnight the girl came creeping out of the thicket, went up to the tree, and once again took a pear off with her mouth. And beside her stood the angel in white. The priest stepped forward and said: "Hast thou come from God, or art thou of the world? Art thou a spirit or a human being?" She replied: "I am not a spirit, but only a poor girl, forsaken by all except God." The king said: "Though you may be forsaken by the whole world, I will not forsake you." He took her with him to his royal palace and because she was so beautiful

ful and good he loved her with all his heart, had silver hands made for her, and took her as his wife.

A year later the king had to go to war. He confided the young queen to his mother's care and said: "If she is brought to bed, take good care of her, and write me a letter at once to let me know." In due time she gave birth to a fine little boy, and his old mother wrote him a letter with the good news. But the messenger stopped to rest beside a brook and, tired by his long ride, fell asleep. Whereupon the Devil, who was still bent on harming the pious queen, came and exchanged the letter for another, announcing that the queen had given birth to a changeling. When the king read the letter, he was horrified and greatly distressed, but he wrote back saying that they should take good care of the queen until his return. On his way back with the letter, the messenger stopped to rest in the same place and fell asleep again. And again the Devil came and substituted a letter, telling them to kill the queen and her child. The king's old mother was horrified when she read the letter. She couldn't believe it and wrote again to the king, but the answer was always the same, because the Devil kept substituting forged letters. And the last letter of all added that they should keep the queen's tongue and eyes as proof that they had done the king's bidding.

The old mother wept at the thought of shedding such innocent blood. During the night she sent for a doe, cut out its tongue and eyes, and kept them. Then she said to the queen: "I can't have you killed as the king commands, but you mustn't stay here any longer. Go out into the wide world with your child and never return." She tied the child to the young queen's back, and the poor queen went away in tears. She came to a great wild forest, and there she fell on her knees and prayed to God. The angel of the Lord appeared to her and led her to a little house with a sign over the door, saying: "All are welcome." Out of the house came a snow-white maiden, who said: "Welcome, Your Majesty," and led her in. The angel untied the little boy from the queen's back, held him up to her breast to suckle, and afterward put him into a lovely white bed. "How did you know I was a queen?" the poor woman asked. The snow-white maiden answered: "I am an angel, sent by God to care for you and your child." So she lived in the little house for seven years and was well cared for, and because of her piety her hands grew again by the grace of God.

At last the king came home from the wars, and his first wish was to see his wife and child. His old mother burst into tears. "You wicked man," she said. "Why did you write and tell me to take two innocent lives?" And after showing him the two letters the Devil had forged, she went on to say: "I obeyed your commands." And she showed him the tongue and the eyes. At that the king wept so bitterly over his poor wife and his baby boy that his old mother took pity on him and said: "Console yourself. She is alive. I secretly had a doe killed and kept the tongue and eyes. Then I tied your child to your wife's back and told her to go out into the wide world and I made her promise never to return, because you were so angry." The king said: "I will go as far as the sky is blue and take neither food nor drink until I find my dear wife and child, if they have not been killed or died of hunger in the meantime."

The king wandered almost seven years. He searched every cleft and cavern, but he didn't find her, and he thought she must have perished. In all that time he took neither food nor drink, but God kept him. At last he came to a great forest and there he found the little house with the sign saying: "All are welcome." The snow-white maiden came out and took him by the hand and led him in. "Welcome, Your Majesty," she said, and asked him where he came from. He replied: "I have been wandering for almost seven years, looking for my wife and child, and I cannot find them." The angel offered him food and drink, but he declined and only asked leave to rest a little. Then he lay down and covered his face with a handkerchief.

The angel went into the room where the queen was sitting with her son, whom she usually called "Sorrowful," and said to her: "Take your child and come out; your husband is here." She went to where he was lying and the handkerchief slipped from his face. "Sorrowful," she said, "pick up your father's handkerchief and cover his face with it." The child picked it up and put it over the king's face. The king heard all this in his sleep and purposely made the handkerchief fall again. The little boy grew impatient and said: "Mother dear, how can I cover my father's face? I have no father on earth. You've taught me to pray to our father which art in heaven, and you've told me that my father was in heaven and that he was God. Why should I recognize this wild man? He's not my father." When the king heard that, he sat up and asked her who she was. "I am your wife," she answered, "and this is your son, Sorrowful." He saw her living hands and said: "My wife had silver hands." She replied: "God in His mercy made my natural hands grow again." The angel went into the bedchamber, brought out the silver hands, and showed them to the king. Then he knew for sure that this was his dear wife and his dear child, and he kissed them both and was glad, and said: "A heavy load has fallen from my heart." The angel of God gave them one last meal, and after that they went home to the king's old mother. There was rejoicing throughout the land, and the king and queen had another wedding, and lived happily ever after.

32

Clever Hans

"WHERE ARE YOU GOING, HANS?" asks Hans's mother. "To see Gretel," says Hans. "Good luck, Hans." "Sure thing. 'Bye, mother." " 'Bye, Hans."

Hans goes to Gretel's. "Afternoon, Gretel." "Afternoon, Hans. What have you brought me?" "Brought nothing. You give something." Gretel gives Hans a needle. Hans says: " 'Bye, Gretel." " 'Bye, Hans."

Hans takes the needle, sticks it in a hay wagon, and walks home behind the wagon. "Evening, mother." "Evening, Hans. Where have you been?" "Been to see Gretel." "What did you bring her?" "Brought nothing. She gave." "What did Gretel give you?" "Gave a needle." "What did you do with the needle, Hans?" "Stuck it in hay wagon." "That was foolish, Hans. You should have stuck it in your sleeve." "Don't worry. Better luck next time."

"Where are you going, Hans?" "To see Gretel, mother." "Good luck, Hans." "Sure thing. 'Bye, mother." " 'Bye, Hans."

Hans goes to Gretel's. "Afternoon, Gretel." "Afternoon, Hans. What have you brought me?" "Brought nothing. You give something." Gretel gives Hans a knife. " 'Bye, Gretel." " 'Bye, Hans."

Hans takes the knife, sticks it in his sleeve and goes home. "Evening, mother." "Evening, Hans. Where have you been?" "Been to see Gretel." "What did you bring her?" "Brought nothing. She gave." "What did Gretel give you?" "Gave knife." "What did you do with the knife, Hans?" "Stuck it in sleeve." "That was foolish, Hans. You should have put it in your pocket." "Don't worry. Better luck next time."

"Where are you going, Hans?" "To see Gretel, mother." "Good luck, Hans." "Sure thing. 'Bye, mother." " 'Bye, Hans."

Hans goes to Gretel's. "Afternoon, Gretel." "Afternoon, Hans. What have you brought me?" "Brought nothing. You give something." Gretel gives Hans a young goat. " 'Bye, Gretel." " 'Bye, Hans."

Hans takes the goat, ties her legs, and puts her in his pocket. By the time he gets home the goat has smothered. "Evening, mother." "Evening, Hans. Where have you been?" "Been to see Gretel." "What did you bring her?" "Brought nothing. She gave." "What did Gretel give you?" "Gave goat." "What have you done with the goat, Hans?" "Put her in pocket." "That was foolish, Hans. You should have put a rope around the goat's neck and led her home." "Don't worry. Better luck next time."

"Where are you going, Hans?" "To see Gretel, mother." "Good luck, Hans." "Sure thing. 'Bye, mother." " 'Bye, Hans."

Hans goes to Gretel's. "Afternoon, Gretel." "Afternoon, Hans. What have you brought me?" "Brought nothing. You give something." Gretel gives Hans a piece of bacon. " 'Bye, Gretel." " 'Bye, Hans."

Hans takes the bacon, ties a rope around it, and drags it behind him. Dogs come and eat the bacon. When he gets home, he has the rope in his hand but there's nothing on it. "Evening, mother." "Evening, Hans. Where have you been?" "Been to see Gretel." "What did you bring her?" "Brought nothing. She gave." "What did Gretel give you?" "Gave piece of bacon." "What have you done with the bacon, Hans?" "Tied a rope around it, dragged home, dogs took away." "That was foolish, Hans. You should have carried the bacon on your head." "Don't worry. Better luck next time."

"Where are you going, Hans?" "To see Gretel, mother." "Good luck, Hans." "Sure thing. 'Bye, mother." " 'Bye, Hans."

Hans goes to Gretel's. "Afternoon, Gretel." "Afternoon, Hans.

What have you brought me?" "Brought nothing. You give something." Gretel gives Hans a calf. " 'Bye, Gretel." " 'Bye, Hans."

Hans takes the calf and puts it on his head. The calf kicks him in the face. "Evening, mother." "Evening, Hans. Where have you been?" "Been to see Gretel." "What did you bring her?" "Brought nothing. She gave." "What did Gretel give you?" "Gave calf." "What have you done with the calf, Hans?" "Put it on head, kicked face." "That was foolish, Hans. You should have put a rope around the calf's neck and led it to the feed rack." "Don't worry. Better luck next time."

"Where are you going, Hans?" "To see Gretel, mother." "Good luck, Hans." "Sure thing. 'Bye, mother." " 'Bye, Hans."

Hans goes to Gretel's. "Afternoon, Gretel." "Afternoon, Hans. What have you brought me?" "Brought nothing. You give something." Gretel says to Hans: "I'll go along with you."

Hans takes Gretel, puts a rope around her neck, leads her to the feed rack, and ties her fast. Then Hans goes to his mother. "Evening, mother." "Evening, Hans. Where have you been?" "Been to see Gretel." "What did you bring her?" "Brought nothing." "What did Gretel give you?" "Gave nothing. Came along." "Where did you leave Gretel?" "Put rope around her neck, tied her to feed rack, and threw her some grass." "That was foolish, Hans. You should have cast sheep's eyes at her." "Don't worry. I will."

Hans goes to the barn, cuts the eyes out of all the sheep, and throws them in Gretel's face. At that Gretel gets angry, tears herself loose, and runs away. She's not engaged to Hans anymore.

33

The Three Languages

IN SWITZERLAND there was once an old count. He had an only son, who was stupid and couldn't learn a thing. The father said: "Listen, my son. I've tried and tried, but I can't drum anything into your head. You will have to go away. I'm sending you to a famous teacher; let him see what he can do with you." The boy was sent to a strange city, and spent a whole year with the teacher. Then he returned home, and his father asked him: "Well, my son, what have you learned?" "Father," he replied, "I've learned what dogs say when they bark." "Heaven help us!" the father cried. "Is that all you've learned? In that case I'll send you to another teacher in another city." The boy was brought to the second teacher, and again he stayed a whole year. When he returned home, his father asked him for the second time: "Well, my son, what have you learned?" "Father, I've learned what the birds say." The father flew into a rage. "Oh, you good-for-nothing!" he cried, "wasting all that precious time and learning nothing. Aren't you ashamed of yourself? Now I'm going to send you to a third teacher, but if you don't learn something this time, I won't be your father any more." The son spent a year with the third teacher, and when he returned home his father asked him: "My son, what have you learned?" He replied: "Dear father, this year I've learned what the frogs say when they croak." The father grew angrier than ever, jumped up, called all his servants, and said: "This dolt is no longer my son. I disown him. Take him out into the forest and kill him." They took him out into the forest, but when it came time to kill him they felt sorry for him and let him go. Then they cut a deer's eyes and tongue out and took them to the old count as proof that they had done his bidding.

The boy wandered from place to place. After a while he came to a castle and asked for a night's lodging. "Very well," said the lord of the castle. "If you are willing to spend the night in the old dungeon, you may stay, but I warn you, you will be facing great danger, for the place is full of wild dogs that bark and howl night and day. At certain hours a human must be brought in to them, and they devour him on the spot." Because of this the whole region lived in grief and sorrow, but no one knew what to do. The boy, however, was fearless. "Just give me some food for your barking dogs," he said, "and take me down to them. They won't hurt me." Since he himself insisted, they gave him food for the wild dogs and led him down into the dungeon. Instead of barking at him when he went in, the dogs gathered around him wagging their tails, ate what he set before them, and didn't harm a hair of his head. The next morning, to everyone's amazement, he came up safe and sound and said to the lord of the castle: "The dogs have told me in their language why they are living down there and bringing evil upon the country. They are under a spell and forced to guard a great treasure that is in the dungeon. They will know no peace until someone digs it up, and I have learned by listening to them how it can be done." All those who heard him were overjoyed, and the lord of the castle promised to adopt him as his son if he performed the task. Down he went again, and since he knew what had to be done he was able to do it. He brought up a chest full of gold, and from that time on the howling of the wild dogs was never heard again. They had vanished, and the country was rid of them.

Some time later he took it into his head to go to Rome. On the way he rode past a marsh where some frogs sat croaking. He pricked up his ears, and when he heard what they were saying he grew thoughtful and sad. At length he arrived in Rome. The pope had just died, and the cardinals couldn't make up their minds whom to choose as his successor. In the end they agreed to wait until God sent a sign. Just as this decision was announced—at that very moment—the young count entered the church, and suddenly two snow-white doves flew down on his shoulders and perched there. In this the cardinals saw a sign from heaven and asked him on the spot if he wanted to be pope. At first he was undecided, for he didn't know if he was worthy, but the doves advised him to accept and at length he said, "Yes." He was anointed and consecrated, and thus was borne out the prophecy of the frogs that had upset him so in the course of his journey; namely, that he would become His Holiness, the Pope. Then he had to say a Mass. He didn't know a single word of it, but the two doves, who were still perched on his shoulders, whispered it all into his ears.

34

Clever Else

A MAN ONCE HAD a daughter who was known as Clever Else. When she grew up, her father said: "It's time to marry her." "Yes, indeed," said her mother. "If only someone comes along who will have her!" At last someone came from far away. His name was Hans, and he courted her, but he set one condition: Clever Else must turn out to be really intelligent. "Never fear," said her father, "she's as bright as a button." And the mother said: "Why, she's so smart she sees the wind coming down the street and hears the flies coughing." "That's good," said Hans. "She's got to be really intelligent, or I won't take her."

As they were sitting at the table after dinner, the mother said: "Else, go down to the cellar and get some beer." Clever Else took the pitcher from the wall and went down to the cellar. On the way she passed the time by lifting the pitcher lid and clapping it down again. When she got to the cellar, she took a chair and set it beside the barrel, because she was afraid that stooping might give her a backache or do her some other injury. Then she put the pitcher down and opened the tap. To keep her eyes busy while the beer was flowing, she studied the wall and after looking this way and that for some time she caught sight, right over her head, of a pickax the masons had left there by mistake. At that, Clever Else began to cry and said: "If I get Hans and we get a child and he gets big and we send him down to the cellar to draw beer, the pickax will fall on his head and kill him." There she sat weeping and wailing for all she was worth over the impending calamity.

Upstairs they were waiting for the beer, but no sign of Clever Else. The mother said to the maid: "Go down to the cellar and see what's become of Else." The maid went down and found her sitting by the barrel, weeping and wailing. "Else," said the maid, "why are you crying?" "My goodness," she replied, "how can I help it? If I get Hans and we get a child and he gets big and he comes down here to

draw beer, maybe that pickax will fall on his head and kill him."
"My, what a clever Else we've got!" said the maid. Whereupon she
sat down beside her and she too began to cry over the impending calamity.

After a while, when the maid didn't come back, Else's father said
to the hired man: "You'd better go down to the cellar and see what's
become of Else and the maid." The hired man went down, and there
sat Clever Else and the maid, weeping together. "What are you crying about?" he asked. "My goodness," Else replied, "how can I help
it? If I get Hans and we get a child and he gets big and comes down
here to draw beer, this pickax will fall on his head and kill him." "My,
what a clever Else we've got!" said the hired man, and sat down beside her and began to bawl.

Upstairs they were waiting for the hired man. When he didn't
come back, the husband said to the wife: "You'd better go down to
the cellar and see what's become of Else." The wife went down and
found all three of them lamenting, and when she asked why, Else told
her the same story: that her future child would probably be killed
when he got big and came down to draw beer and the pickax fell on
his head. "My, what a clever Else we've got!" said the mother in her
turn, and sat down and joined in the weeping.

Upstairs the husband waited another short while, but when his
wife didn't come back and his thirst grew greater and greater, he
said: "I'd better go down to the cellar myself and see what's become
of Else." But when he got there and found them all weeping, and
heard it was because the child Else might some day bear might be
killed by the pickax if he happened to be under it drawing beer at the
exact time when it fell, he cried out: "My, what a clever Else!" and
sat down and joined in the weeping.

For a long time the suitor sat upstairs alone. When no one came
back, he thought: "They must be waiting for me down there; I'd
better go and see what they're up to." When he arrived in the cellar,
all five of them were screaming and yelling pitifully, one worse than
the next. "What terrible thing has happened?" he asked. "Oh, dear
Hans," said Else, "if we marry and have a child and he gets big and
we send him down here to draw beer, that pickax somebody left up
there by mistake might smash his skull and kill him if it happened to
fall. Haven't we reason enough to cry?" "My word," said Hans,

"that's as much intelligence as I can use in *my* household. I'll marry you because you're such a clever Else." With that, he took her by the hand, led her upstairs, and married her.

One day, after Hans had had her for a while, he said: "Wife, I'm going to the village to work and make us some money. You go out to the field and cut rye for our bread." "Yes, my dear Hans, I will." When Hans had gone, she made a good thick porridge and took it out into the field with her. When she got there she said to herself: "What shall I do? Cut first? Or eat first? Bless my soul! I'll eat first." When she had eaten her potful of porridge and was full to bursting, she spoke to herself again: "What shall I do? Cut first? Or sleep first? Bless my soul! I'll sleep first." So she lay down in the rye and fell asleep.

Hans had been home for hours, but no sign of Else. He said to himself: "What a clever Else I've got! She's such a hard worker she doesn't even come home to eat." But when the sun began to set and there was still no sign of her he went to see what she had cut. But nothing was cut, and she was lying in the rye asleep. Hans ran home and came back with a fowler's net with little bells on it. He threw it over her and she went right on sleeping. Then he went home, locked the door, and sat down to work. Finally, long after dark, Clever Else woke up. When she rose to her feet, there was a jingling all around her and the bells tinkled at every step she took. She was scared to death and so bewildered she didn't know whether she was Clever Else or not. "Am I," she asked herself, "or aren't I?" But she couldn't answer and for a while she just stood there. Finally she thought: "I'll go home and ask if it's me or not; they'll be sure to know." She ran home but the door was locked. Then she knocked at the window and cried out: "Hans, is Else in there?" "Oh yes," said Hans, "she's here." At that she was terrified and cried: "Oh my God, then I'm not me." She went to another house, but when the people heard the bells, they didn't want to open and no one would let her in. So she ran straight out of the village, and no one has seen her since.

35

The Tailor in Heaven

IT SO HAPPENED that one fine day the Lord went for a stroll in the heavenly gardens. He took all the apostles and saints with him and no one was left in heaven but St. Peter, who had received orders not to admit a soul during the Lord's absence. So St. Peter stood by the gate and kept watch. Pretty soon someone knocked. St. Peter asked who was there and what he wanted. "It's an honest little tailor asking to come in," came a thin voice. "As honest as a thief on the gallows," said St. Peter. "You've been light-fingered, you've filched snippets of cloth. You can't come in, the Lord forbade me to admit anyone while he's out." "Have mercy," said the tailor, "it's not stealing to take wee little scraps that fall off the table all by themselves. And look how I'm limping, my feet are covered with blisters from the long journey; I can't possibly turn back. Just let me in and I'll do all the dirty work. I'll carry the babies, wash their clothes, mend them when they're torn, and scrub the benches they've played on." St. Peter let himself be moved by pity and opened the gate of heaven just wide enough for the lame tailor, who was very skinny, to slip through. Then he told him to sit in a corner behind the door and not to move or make any noise, because if the Lord noticed him when he got back he'd be very angry.

The tailor did as he was bidden, but after a while when St. Peter stepped outside for a moment, his curiosity got the better of him and he stood up and went prowling about, looking into every corner of heaven. At last he came to a place where there were lots of costly and beautiful chairs, and in the middle an armchair that was all of gold, set with glittering jewels. It was much taller than the other chairs and there was a golden footstool in front of it. This was the chair the Lord sat in when he was at home, and when he sat in it he could see everything that happened on earth. The tailor stood still and looked at the chair for quite some time, for it took his fancy more than anything else he had seen. Finally his eagerness got the better of him: he climbed up and sat down on it. Now he could see everything that was happening on earth, and he saw an ugly old woman, who was washing clothes by the side of a brook, secretly putting two veils to one side. The sight threw him into such a rage that he seized the golden footstool and hurled it through the sky at the thieving old woman on earth. And then when he couldn't retrieve the footstool, he quietly left the chair, crept back to his old place behind the door, and pretended he hadn't stirred from the spot.

When the Lord and master came back with his heavenly train, he didn't notice the tailor behind the door. But when he sat down in his armchair, he saw that his footstool was missing. He asked St. Peter what had become of it, and St. Peter didn't know. Then the Lord asked him if he had let anyone in. "I can't think of anyone but a lame tailor," said St. Peter. "He's still sitting behind the door." The Lord told the tailor to come forward and asked him if he had taken the footstool and what he had done with it. "O Lord," the tailor answered joyfully, "I saw an old woman down on earth steal two veils while washing clothes, and in my wrath I hurled the footstool at her." "You scoundrel!" said the Lord. "If I were to judge like you, what do you suppose would have happened to *you* long ago? And besides, all my chairs, benches, tables, even my fire tongs, would be gone; I'd have thrown them all at sinners. We can't keep you in heaven. It's out through the gate with you, then you can go where you please. There's only one judge here in heaven, and that's me, the Lord."

St. Peter had to see the tailor out through the gate. And because his shoes were torn and his feet covered with blisters, he picked up a walking stick and went to Waitawhile, where the God-fearing soldiers sit making merry.

36

The Magic Table, the Gold Donkey, and the Cudgel in the Sack

LONG AGO THERE WAS a tailor who had three sons and only one goat. Since the goat supplied them with milk, they had to give her good fodder and take her out to graze every day. This the sons did by turns. Once the eldest son took her to the churchyard, where the tenderest grass grew, and let her browse and gambol. Late in the day, when it was time to go home, he asked her: "Goat, have you had enough to eat?" And the goat replied:

> "I'm just so stuffed,
> I couldn't eat another tuft: meh meh!"

"Then let's go home," said the boy, took her by the rope, led her back to her stall, and tied her up. "Well," said the old tailor, "has the goat had enough to eat?" "Oh yes," said the son, "she's just so stuffed she couldn't eat another tuft." But the father wanted to see for himself, so he went to the stall, stroked the precious beast, and asked: "Goat, have you really had enough to eat?" The goat replied:

> "Enough to eat? Don't make me laugh.
> I've just been jumping over ditches,
> I didn't find a single leaf: meh meh!"

"What's this!" cried the tailor and ran upstairs to his son. "You miserable liar!" he said. "Telling me the goat has had enough to eat when you've been starving her!" And in his rage he took his yardstick from the wall and drove the boy out of the house.

Next day it was the second son's turn. He found a place along the garden hedge where only the best shoots grew, and the goat nibbled them right down to the ground. Late in the day, when he wanted to go home, the boy asked the goat: "Goat, have you had enough to eat?" And the goat replied:

"I'm just so stuffed,
I couldn't eat another tuft: meh meh!"

"Then let's go home," said the boy, and took her home and tied her up in her stall. "Well," said the old tailor, "has the goat had enough to eat?" "Oh yes," said the boy, "she's just so stuffed she couldn't eat another tuft." But the tailor wasn't satisfied. He went to the stall and asked: "Goat, have you really had enough to eat?" The goat replied:

"Enough to eat? Don't make me laugh.
I've just been jumping over ditches,
I didn't find a single leaf: meh!"

"The godless wretch!" cried the tailor, "letting such a good creature go hungry!" Whereupon he ran upstairs and chased the boy out of the house with his yardstick.

Next it was the third son's turn. Resolved to do things right, he sought out bushes with the finest leaves and let the goat eat them. Late in the day, when he wanted to go home, the boy asked the goat: "Goat, have you had enough to eat?" The goat replied:

"I'm just so stuffed,
I couldn't eat another tuft: meh meh!"

"Then let's go home," said the boy, led her to her stall, and tied her up. "Well," said the old tailor, "has the goat had enough to eat?" "Oh yes," said the son, "she's just so stuffed she couldn't eat another tuft." But the father didn't trust him. He went downstairs and asked: "Goat, have you really had enough to eat?" The wicked animal replied:

"Enough to eat? Don't make me laugh.
I've just been jumping over ditches,
I didn't find a single leaf: meh meh!"

"Oh, you pack of liars!" cried the tailor. "One as godless and wicked as the next! You won't make a fool of me any more!" And in his rage he jumped up and gave the poor boy such a tanning with his yardstick that he ran out of the house.

Now the old tailor was alone with his goat. Next morning he went down to the stall, carressed the goat and said: "Come, my pet, I'll take you out to graze myself." He picked up her rope and led her to green hedges and clumps of milfoil, and everything else that goats like to eat. "Now for once you can eat to your heart's content," he said, and let her graze until late in the day. Then he asked: "Goat, have you had enough to eat?" And she replied:

"I'm just so stuffed,
I couldn't eat another tuft: meh meh!"

"Then let's go home," said the tailor, led her to the stall, and tied her up. As he was leaving, he turned around once again and asked: "Have you really had enough to eat for once?" But the goat treated him no better and cried out:

"Enough to eat? Don't make me laugh.
I've just been jumping over ditches,
I didn't find a single leaf: meh meh!"

When he heard that, the tailor was flabbergasted. Now he realized that he had driven his sons away for no cause. "You ungrateful wretch!" he cried. "Wait. It's not enough to throw you out. I'm going to mark you so you won't dare show your face among self-respecting tailors." He ran up the stairs, took his razor, lathered the goat's head, and shaved it as smooth as the palm of his hand. Then he picked up his whip, because the yardstick seemed too good for her, and gave her such a beating that she leaped and ran for dear life.

Now the tailor was all alone in the house, and he grew very sad. He longed to have his sons back again, but no one knew where they had gone. The eldest had apprenticed himself to a carpenter. He worked hard and learned well, and when the time came for him to start on his travels, the carpenter gave him a little table. It was made of ordinary wood and there was nothing special about its appearance, but it had one excellent quality. If you put it down and said: "Table, set yourself," instantly a tablecloth would appear on the good little table, and on the tablecloth there would be a plate with a knife and fork beside it, and as many platters of roast meat and stewed meat as there was room for, and a big glass of the kind of red wine that rejoices the heart. The young journeyman thought: "That will keep me to my dying day," and from then on he wandered about in high good spirits. He never stopped to ask whether an inn was good or bad or whether you could get anything to eat there or not. When he felt like eating, he didn't bother with inns, but took his table down off his back in a field, in a forest, on a meadow, or wherever he pleased. "Set yourself," he would say, and everything his heart desired would be right there.

At last he decided to go home to his father, thinking that by then his father's anger must have died away and that the old man would be glad to see him with his magic table. One evening on his way home he stopped at an inn. A large party of travelers had arrived before him. They welcomed him and invited him to share their meal, for otherwise, they said, he would probably get nothing to eat. "No," said the carpenter, "I won't take the crumbs out of your mouths. You be my guests instead." They laughed, for they thought he was joking. But he put his little wooden table down in the middle of the room and said: "Table, set yourself." Before you knew it, the table was covered with better food than the landlord could have provided, and the aroma rose to the guests' nostrils. "Help yourselves, dear friends," said the carpenter. When the guests saw he meant it, they didn't wait to be asked twice, pulled out their knives and fell to. What amazed them was that the second one dish was empty another took its place. The innkeeper stood in a corner, looking on. He didn't say a word, but he thought: "I could use a cook like that in my inn." The carpenter and his company feasted until late into the night. Finally they went to sleep. The young journeyman went to bed, and put his magic table against the wall. The innkeeper's thoughts gave him no peace. He remembered a little old table in his storeroom that looked just like this one. He crept in, took it and substituted it for the magic table. Next morning the carpenter paid for his bed, loaded his table on his back, never dreaming that it was the wrong one, and went his way.

At midday he arrived home, and his father welcomed him with joy. "Well, my dear boy, what trade have you learned?" "I've become a carpenter, father." "A good trade," said the old man, "but what have you brought back from your travels?" "Father, the best thing I've brought back is this little table." The tailor examined it from all sides and said: "It's no masterpiece you've made there; it's just an ugly old table." "But it's a magic table," said the son. "When I put it down and tell it to set itself, the most wonderful dishes appear, along with a wine that rejoices the heart. Invite all our friends and relatives. For once let them eat and drink their fill; my little table will give them all they can hold." When the guests were all there, he put his table down in the middle of the room and said: "Table, set yourself." But the table didn't lift a finger; it was just as bare as any common table that doesn't understand when it's spoken to. The poor journeyman realized that his table had been exchanged for another, and blushed to be standing there looking like a liar. The relatives had a good laugh at his expense and went home as hungry and thirsty as they had come. The father took out his old shreds and patches and went on tailoring, and the son went to work for a master carpenter.

The second son had apprenticed himself to a miller. When his time was up, the miller said to him: "Because you've worked so faithfully and well, I will give you a donkey of a very special kind; he will neither draw a cart nor carry sacks." "Then what is he good for?" asked the young journeyman. "He spits gold," said the miller. "If you put him on a cloth and say, 'Bricklebrit,' the good creature will spit gold pieces both in front and behind." "That's wonderful," said the journeyman, thanked the miller, and went out into the world. When he needed money, he had only to say, "Bricklebrit," and his donkey rained gold pieces; all he had to do was to pick them up. Where he went, the best was not too good for him; the more expensive the better, for his purse was always full.

After wandering about for a while, he thought: "I must go and see my father; if I arrive with a gold donkey, he's sure to forget his anger and welcome me with open arms." It so happened that he came to the same inn where his brother's little table had been exchanged. He was leading his donkey by the bridle. The innkeeper wanted to take the beast and tie him up, but the young journeyman said: "Don't bother. I'll take my gray to the stable and tie him up myself. You see, I have to know where he is." This struck the innkeeper as odd, and he figured that a man who had to look after his own donkey couldn't have much money to spend. But when the stranger reached into his pocket, brought out two gold pieces, and told him to buy something good, the innkeeper couldn't get over it and hastened to provide the best fare he could find. After dinner the guest asked how much he owed. The innkeeper thought he might as well overcharge him and said he still owed several gold pieces. The journeyman reached into his pocket, but he had used up all his gold. "If you'll wait a moment," he said, "I'll go and get some gold." And he left the room, taking the tablecloth with him. The innkeeper didn't know what to make of it, and his curiosity was aroused. He crept after him and when the guest barred the stable door, he looked in through a knothole. The stranger

spread out the tablecloth under the donkey and said: "Bricklebrit."
Instantly the animal began to rain gold pieces from both ends. "My
word!" said the inkeeper. "That's a quick way to mint ducats! An
excellent moneybag." The guest paid up and went to bed. During the
night the innkeeper crept down to the stable, led the money machine
away, and left another donkey in its place. Early next morning the
journeyman left the inn with the new animal, thinking it was his gold
donkey.

At midday he reached home. His father was glad to see him again
and welcomed him with open arms. "Well, my son," the old man
asked, "what have you made of yourself?" "A miller, dear father," he
replied. "And what have you brought back from your travels?" "Just
a donkey." "There are plenty of donkeys here," said the father. "A
good goat would have been more to my liking." "Yes, but this is no
ordinary donkey," said the son. "It's a gold donkey. When I say,
'Bricklebrit,' the good creature spits out a whole cloth full of gold
pieces. Just send for our relatives and I'll make them all rich." "Suits
me," said the tailor. "I won't plague myself with the needle any
more." And he ran off to invite the relatives. When they were all
there, the miller told them to make room, spread out his cloth, and
brought the donkey into the parlor. "Now watch," he said, and cried
out: "Bricklebrit!" But what fell wasn't gold pieces, and it was plain
that this animal knew nothing of the art of minting, for not every ass
can make money. The poor miller made a long face. He saw he had
been cheated and apologized to the relatives, who went home as poor
as they had come. There was no help for it. The old man had to go
back to his needle, and the young journeyman went to work for a
miller.

The third brother had apprenticed himself to a turner, and his apprenticeship was the longest because the turner's trade demands a
good deal of skill. His brothers wrote him a letter telling how badly
they had fared and how in the last night before their homecoming
the innkeeper had cheated them out of their wonderful magic gifts.
When the turner had completed his apprenticeship and was about to
set out on his travels, the master turner, considering that he had
worked well and faithfully, gave him a sack and said: "There's a
cudgel in it." "I can sling the sack over my shoulder, and it will come
in handy," said the boy. "But what's the use of a cudgel? It will only

make the sack heavy." "I'll tell you," said the master. "If anyone harms you, you have only to say: 'Cudgel, come out of the sack,' and the cudgel will jump out and dance such a jig on their backs that they won't be able to move for a week; and it won't stop until you say: 'Cudgel, get back in the sack.'" The journeyman thanked him and slung the sack over his shoulder. If anyone stepped on his toes or threatened him, he would say: "Cudgel, come out of the sack." Instantly the cudgel would jump out and dust the fellow's coat or jacket right on his back, without waiting for him to take it off, and did it so quickly that before the next in line knew what was going on it was his turn.

At nightfall the young turner arrived at the inn where his brothers had been cheated. He put his sack down on the table and began telling the innkeeper about all the wonderful things he had seen in the world. "Yes, yes," he said. "Some people find magic tables and gold donkeys and such-like; fine things, I grant you, and I don't despise them, but small beer compared to the treasure I've got in my sack." The innkeeper pricked up his ears: "What on earth can that be?" he wondered. "His sack must be full of jewels. I ought to be able to get that too, because all good things comes in threes." At bedtime the turner stretched out on the bench, using his sack for a pillow. When the innkeeper thought the guest was fast asleep, he went over and tugged very gently and carefully at the sack, meaning to take it away and put another in its place. But that was exactly what the turner had been waiting for. Just as the innkeeper was getting ready for a good hard tug, he cried: "Cudgel, come out of the sack!" In a flash the cudgel jumped out, attacked the innkeeper, and gave him a sound thrashing. The innkeeper screamed pitifully, but the louder he screamed the harder the cudgel beat time on his back, until at last he fell exhausted. Then the turner said: "Give me the magic table and the gold donkey, or the dance will start in again." "Oh no!" said the innkeeper as meekly as you please. "I'll give you anything you say, if only you'll make that goblin crawl back into his sack." "I will put mercy before justice," said the journeyman, "but watch your step next time!" Then he cried out: "Cudgel, get back in the sack," and gave it a rest.

Next morning the turner rode home to his father with the magic table and the gold donkey. The tailor was glad to see him again and asked him what he had learned in foreign parts. "Dear father," he replied, "I've become a turner." "A difficult craft," said the father. "And what have you brought back from your travels?" "A wonderful thing, dear father," said the son, "a cudgel in a sack." "What!" cried the father. "A cudgel! What's the good of that? You can cut one from any tree." "Not like this one, dear father. When I say: 'Cudgel, come out of the sack,' it jumps out and dances a jig on anyone who wants to harm me, until he's lying on the ground begging for mercy. With this cudgel I've recovered the magic table and the gold donkey the thieving innkeeper took from my brothers. Send for them now and invite all our relations; I'll feast them and fill their pockets with gold." The old tailor wasn't fully convinced, but he sent for the relatives all the same. The turner spread a cloth on the floor, led in the gold donkey, and said to his brother: "Now, dear brother, you talk to him." The miller said, "Bricklebrit," and before you knew it, the gold pieces came tumbling down on the carpet like a spring shower, and the donkey didn't stop until they all had so much they couldn't have carried any more. (I can see by the look on your face that you wish you had been there.) Then the turner brought in the table and said: "Dear brother, you talk to it." And no sooner had the carpenter said: "Table, set yourself," than the table was set and covered with the finest dishes. A banquet, the like of which had never been seen in the good old tailor's house, was served up, the relatives stayed until late into the night, and they were all happy and gay. The tailor locked up his needle and thread, his yardstick and flatiron, in a cupboard, and lived in joy and luxury with his sons.

But what became of the goat who had made the tailor drive his sons away? I'll tell you. She was ashamed of her bald head, so she ran to a fox's hole and crawled in. When the fox came home, a pair of big eyes flashed at him out of the darkness, and he was so frightened that he ran away. He met the bear, and seeing the frantic look on the fox's face, the bear asked him: "What's the matter, brother fox? Why are you making such a face?" "Oh!" said Redcoat, "there's a ferocious beast in my hole, and he glared at me with fiery eyes." "We'll soon get rid of him," said the bear, and went to the burrow and looked in. But when he saw the fiery eyes, he too was stricken with terror and ran away, for he wanted no truck with such a ferocious creature. He met the bee, and when the bee saw his disgruntled look, she said:

"Bear, that's a mighty sour face you're making. Where's your good humor?" "It's easy for you to talk," said the bear. "There's a ferocious beast with glaring eyes in Redcoat's house, and we can't drive it out." The bee said: "Bear, you've touched my heart. I'm only a poor weak creature you don't deign to look at, but I think I can help you." She flew into the fox's hole, sat down on the goat's smooth-shaven head, and stung her so fiercely that she jumped up, bleating, "Meh meh!" and ran out like a madwoman. And to this day no one knows where she ran to.

37

Thumbling

THERE WAS ONCE a poor peasant who sat by the stove one evening and poked the fire while his wife was spinning. "Isn't it sad," he said, "that we have no children? Other people's houses are noisy and gay, and here it's so quiet." "Yes, indeed," said his wife with a sigh, "even if there were only one, and even if he were no bigger than my thumb, I'd be satisfied. Oh, how dearly we would love him!" It so happened that the wife began to ail, and seven months later she gave birth to a child, who though perfectly shaped was no bigger than a thumb. "It's just what we wished for," they said, "and he shall be our dear child." Because of his size they called him Thumbling. Though they gave him all the food he could eat, he didn't grow and never got any bigger than he had been on the day he was born. But his eyes sparkled with intelligence, and he soon proved to be a clever, nimble little fellow, who succeeded in everything he undertook.

One day his father was getting ready to go out and cut wood, and he mumbled to himself: "If only there were someone who could drive the wagon out after me." "Oh, father," Thumbling cried, "I'll bring the wagon; you can count on me. It will be in the forest when you need it." The man laughed and said: "How can that be? You're much too small to hold the reins." "Never mind. If mother will just harness the horse, I'll sit in his ear and tell him which way to go."

"All right," said the father. "We'll give it a try." When the time came, the mother harnessed the horse and put Thumbling in his ear. The little fellow shouted, "Gee up!" and "Whoa!" and told the horse which way to go. All went well; it was as if a coachman had been driving, and the horse took the right way to the forest. As the wagon was rounding a bend the little fellow cried out, "Gee up!" and it so happened that just then two strange men came along. "Bless my soul!" cried one of them. "What's this? Here comes a wagon, and a driver is telling the horse what to do, but there isn't any driver." "There's something fishy about it," said the other. "Let's follow the wagon and see where it stops." The wagon went deep into the forest, straight to the place where the wood was being cut. When Thumbling saw his father, he cried out: "You see, father. Here I am with the wagon. Just lift me down." His father held the horse with his left hand and with his right hand lifted his little son down from the horse's ear. Then Thumbling, as spry as you please, sat down on a blade of straw.

At the sight of him, the two strange men were speechless with amazement. They went off to one side, and one of them said: "Listen to me. That little fellow will make our fortune if we take him to a big city and charge admission for seeing him. Let's buy him." They went to the peasant and said: "Sell us the little man. We'll treat him well." "No," said the father. "He's the apple of my eye, and I wouldn't sell him for all the money in the world." But when Thumbling heard the offer, he climbed up along the folds of his father's coat, stood on his shoulder and whispered in his ear: "Father, let them take me. Don't worry, I'll soon be back." So the father sold him to the men for a tidy sum of money. "Where do you want to sit?" they asked him. "Oh, just put me on the brim of your hat; then I can stroll around and look at the country. I won't fall." They let him have his way and when Thumbling had taken leave of his father, off they went with him. They walked until dusk, and then the little fellow said: "Put me down for a moment. I have to go." "Just stay where you are," said the man on whose hat he was riding, "I don't mind. It gets splattered by the birds now and then." "No," said Thumbling. "I know what's right and proper; just put me down for a moment." The man took off his hat and put the little fellow down in a field by the wayside. For a while he jumped from clod to clod and crawled about; then he slipped into a mouse hole he had spied. "Good-bye, gentlemen," he cried out. And he taunted them: "Just run along home without me." They came running and poked sticks into the mouse hole, but in vain, for Thumbling crawled in deeper and deeper. Soon it was pitch dark and there was nothing they could do but go their way with bad tempers and empty purses.

When Thumbling saw they were gone, he crawled out of the underground passage. "It's dangerous walking in the fields after dark," he said. "A neck or a leg is easily broken." Luckily he came across an empty snail shell. "Thank goodness," he said. "Here's a safe place to spend the night." And he settled down in it. Just as he was falling asleep, he heard two men passing, and one of them said to the other: "How are we going to get hold of the rich priest's gold and silver?" "I can tell you!" cried Thumbling. "What was that?" asked one of the thieves in a fright. "I heard someone speak." They stopped walking and listened, and Thumbling spoke again. "Take me with you and I'll help you." "Who are you?" "Just feel the ground," he replied, "and listen where the voice comes from." After a while the thieves found him and picked him up. "You little rascal," they said. "How can you help us?" "It's easy," he said. "I'll crawl between the iron bars. Then, once I'm in the priest's room, you'll tell me what you want and I'll hand it out to you." "All right," they said. "We'll see what you can do." When they got to the presbytery, Thumbling crawled into the priest's room, but as soon as he was inside he began to shout: "Do you want everything that's here?" The thieves were frightened and said: "Speak softly, will you? You'll wake everybody up." But Thumbling pretended not to understand and shouted: "What do you want? Do you want everything that's here?" The cook, who was sleeping in the next room, heard him. She sat up in the bed and listened. The thieves, who had started to run away in their fright, took courage and thought: "The little fellow is teasing us." So they came back and whispered to him: "Now get to work and hand us something." And Thumbling shouted as loud as he could: "I'll give you anything you want. Just stick your hands in." The cook, who was listening, heard him clearly. She jumped out of bed and came stumbling in, while the thieves ran as if they had had the Wild Hunter at their heels. The cook, who couldn't see a thing, went and lit a candle. When she came back with it, Thumbling slipped out unseen and made for the barn. She looked into every nook and cranny. When she found nothing she went back to bed and imagined she had dreamt the whole thing.

Thumbling scrambled about in the hay and found himself a nice place to sleep. He thought he would stay there until daybreak, and then go home to his parents. But something very different awaited him. Yes, indeed; this world is full of misery and trouble. In the gray of dawn, the cook got up to feed the cows. She went to the barn and picked up an armful of hay, which happened to be the exact same armful where poor Thumbling lay sleeping. He was so sound asleep he didn't notice, and he didn't wake up until he was between the jaws of the cow, who had picked him up with the hay. "Good God!" he cried. "How did I get into this fulling mill!" But he soon realized where he was. He was careful to keep away from the teeth that would have crushed him, but he couldn't help sliding down into the stomach with the hay. "There's not much sunshine in this place," he said to himself. "They forgot to put in windows, and I don't see anyone bringing candles." In short, the place was not at all to his liking, and the worst of it was that more and more hay was coming through the door, which left less and less room for him. That frightened him so that he finally shouted with all his might: "No more feed! No more feed!" At that moment the cook was milking the cow. When she heard someone speaking though there was no one in sight and it was the same voice she had heard during the night, she was so frightened she fell off her stool and spilled the milk. She ran to her master as fast as her legs would carry her and cried out: "Good gracious, father, the cow has been talking." "You're out of your mind," said the priest, but all the same he went to the barn to see for himself.

No sooner had he stepped in than Thumbling cried out: "No more feed! No more feed!" The priest was frightened too, for he thought an evil spirit had got into the cow, and he ordered the cow to be slaughtered. Slaughtered she was, and the stomach, where Thumbling was sitting, was thrown on the rubbish pile. Thumbling had a hard time working his way through. He finally reached the surface and was just going to stick his head out when another misfortune struck. A hungry wolf came running and swallowed the whole stomach at one gulp. But Thumbling didn't lose heart. "Maybe this wolf can be reasoned with," he thought. So he shouted up to it from the depths of its belly: "Dear wolf, I know where you can find a wonderful feed." "Where's that?" asked the wolf. "In such and such a house. You'll have to crawl in through the drain, and you'll find all the cake, bacon, and sausages you can eat." And he gave him an exact description of his father's house.

The idea appealed to the wolf. That night he squeezed into the larder through the drain and gobbled to his heart's content. When he had eaten his fill, he wanted to leave, but he had grown so fat that he couldn't get out the same way. Thumbling, who had counted on just that, began to scream and yell in the wolf's belly, and to make as much noise as he could. "Be still!" said the wolf. "You'll wake everybody up." "Nonsense," said Thumbling. "You've had a good feed, now I'm going to have some fun too," and he began to shout at the top of his lungs. Finally his father and mother woke up, ran to the larder, opened the door by a crack and looked in. At the sight of the wolf, they ran away, and when they came back, the man had an ax and his wife had the scythe. "Stand behind me," said the man. "If my first blow doesn't kill him, you swing your scythe and cut him in two." Thumbling heard his father's voice and cried out: "Father dear, I'm here. I'm in the wolf's belly." The father was overjoyed. "Thank the Lord!" he cried. "Our dear child is found again." Telling his wife to put down the scythe for fear of hurting Thumbling, he lifted his ax and struck the wolf such a blow on the head that he fell dead. Then they brought a knife and a pair of scissors, cut open the belly, and took the little fellow out. "Dear me," said the father, "how worried we've been on your account!" "Oh, father, what travels I've had! And how good it is to breathe fresh air again!" "But where have you been?" "Oh, father, I've been in a mouse hole, a cow's stomach, and a wolf's belly. But now I'm going to stay home with you." "And we won't sell you again for all the money in the world," said the parents, and hugged and kissed their dear Thumbling. They gave him food and drink, and had new clothes made for him, because the old ones had been spoiled in the course of his adventures.

38
Mrs. Fox's Wedding

FIRST STORY

THERE WAS ONCE an old fox with nine tails, who thought his wife was unfaithful and wanted to put her to the test. He stretched out under the bench, and there he lay as still as a mouse, pretending to be stone dead. Mrs. Fox shut herself up in her room and her maid, Mistress Cat, stood by the fire cooking. When it became known that the old fox was dead, suitors began coming. The maid heard a knock at the door. When she opened, a young fox was standing there, and he said:

> "What are you doing, Mistress Kitten?
> Are you sewing, are you knitting?"

She replied:

> "Since you ask me what I'm doing,
> I must tell you that I'm brewing
> The loveliest hot buttered beer.
> Would you care to have some, sir?"

"Thank you kindly," said the fox. "But what is Mrs. Fox doing?" The maid replied:

> "She is sitting in her room
> Deep in grief and deep in gloom,
> Weeping till her eyes are red,
> Because old Mr. Fox is dead."

"Be so good as to tell her a young fox is here and asks leave to court her." "I will indeed, young sir."

> Trippety trip, the cat went up,
> Clippety clap, the door was shut.
> "Mrs. Fox, are you at home?"
> "Why ask, dear Kitten? Has someone come?"
> "Oh yes, a suitor, Mrs. Fox."
> "Then tell me how the fellow looks.

Has he nine lovely tails like the late Mr. Fox?" "Oh no," said the cat. "He has only one." "Then I won't have him."

Mistress Cat went down and sent the suitor away. Soon another knock was heard, and another fox was at the door, come to court Mrs. Fox; he had two tails, but he fared no better than the first. Then still others came, each with one tail more than the last, and they were all rejected, until finally one who had nine tails like old Mr. Fox presented himself. When the widow heard that, she was delighted and said to the cat:

> "Then open gate and portal wide,
> And sweep old Mr. Fox outside."

But just as the wedding was about to begin, old Mr. Fox came out from under the bench, beat the whole company black and blue, and drove them all, including Mrs. Fox, out of the house.

SECOND STORY

After old Mr. Fox had passed away, the wolf came courting. He knocked at the door, and the cat, who was Mrs. Fox's maid, opened it. The wolf greeted her and said:

> "Good day, Dame Cat of Marrowbone,
> Why are you sitting all alone,
> And what is that you're making?"

The cat replied:

> "I'm making milk with crumbled bun.
> Would you care to sample some?"

"No, thank you, Dame Cat," said the wolf. "Is Mrs. Fox at home?" The cat said:

> "She's sitting upstairs in her room,
> Deep in grief and deep in gloom.
> Many a bitter tear she's shed,
> Because old Mr. Fox is dead."

The wolf replied:

> "If she wants another spouse,
> Tell her I am in the house."
> Swishing her tail, the kitten ran
> Up to announce the gentleman.
> With her five gold rings she knocks:
> "Are you receiving, Mrs. Fox?
> If you want another spouse,
> We have a suitor in the house."

Mrs. Fox asked: "Is the gentleman wearing red breeches, and has he a pointed muzzle?" "No," said the cat. "Then he won't do for me."

After the wolf was sent away, a dog came, and then a stag, a hare, a bear, a lion, and one after another all the beasts of the forest. But each of the suitors lacked one of old Mr. Fox's sterling qualities, and the cat had to send them all away. At last a young fox appeared. And Mrs. Fox asked: "Is the gentleman wearing red breeches, and has he a pointed muzzle?" "Yes," said the cat, "he has." "Then send him up," said Mrs. Fox, and told the maid to prepare the wedding feast.

> "Cat, it's time to sweep the house.
> Out the window with my old spouse.
> He brought home many a luscious mouse,
> But he ate them all alone
> And gave me nary a one."

So she married young Mr. Fox, and they all danced and made merry at the wedding, and if they haven't stopped dancing they're still at it.

39

The Elves

FIRST STORY

A SHOEMAKER, through no fault of his own, had become so poor that all he had left was enough leather for a single pair of shoes. In the evening, he cut out the shoes, meaning to start work on them the next day. Then, as his conscience was clear, he went calmly to bed, commended himself to God, and fell asleep. In the morning he said his prayers and was sitting down to work when he saw the shoes lying all finished on his workbench. He was so surprised that he didn't know what to think. He picked the shoes up and looked at them more closely. Not a single stitch was awry, the workmanship was as perfect as if the shoes had been made by a master craftsman. Better still, a customer soon came in, and he liked the shoes so well that he paid more than usual for them. With the money the shoemaker was able to buy leather for two pairs of shoes. He cut them out in the evening, meaning to start work with new courage in the morning, but there was no need to, for when he got up the shoes were already finished. And they too found buyers, who gave him enough money to buy leather for four pairs of shoes. In the morning he found the four pairs of shoes all finished. And so it went on: the shoes he cut out in the evening were always finished by morning, so that he was soon making a good living and in the course of time became wealthy. One night shortly before Christmas, after the man had cut the leather and just as they were getting ready for bed, the man said to his wife: "Suppose we stay up tonight to see who has been helping us." His wife was pleased with the idea and lit the lamp. Then they hid behind some clothes that were hanging in the corner, and waited. At midnight two cunning little naked men came in, sat down at the workbench, took the pieces that had been cut out, and began to punch, sew, and hammer so nimbly and quickly with their little fingers that the shoemaker could only stare in amazement. They worked without a moment's rest until all the shoes lay finished on the bench, and then they ran away.

Next morning the woman said: "Those little men have made us rich; we ought to show our gratitude. They must be cold running around like that with nothing on. Do you know what? I'm going to make them shirts and coats and vests and breeches, and knit a pair of stockings for each of them. You can be making two pairs of shoes." "Good idea," said the shoemaker, and that evening, when everything was finished, they put their presents on the workbench instead of the cut-out leather. Then they hid to see what the little men would do. At midnight they came bounding in, ready for work. At first they were puzzled to see wee little clothes instead of cut-out leather, but then they leaped for joy. As quick as a flash they slipped into their pretty little clothes, smoothed them down, and sang:

> "See what pretty boys we are!
> We will work on shoes no more."

They hopped and danced, jumped over chairs and benches, and finally danced out the door. After that they never came back, but the shoemaker prospered till the end of his days, and succeeded in everything he set his hand to.

SECOND STORY

There was a once a poor servant girl, who worked hard and was neat and clean. Every day she swept the house and threw the rubbish on a big heap outside the door. One morning as she was about to start work, she found a letter on the rubbish heap. Since she couldn't read, she put her broom down in the corner and took the letter to her mistress. It was an invitation from the elves, asking the girl to stand godmother to one of their children. The girl didn't know what to do. Finally, when the people of the house had talked to her for some time and assured her that this sort of invitation can't be turned down, she accepted. Three elves came and took her to the hollow mountain where the little folk lived. Everything there was tiny, but delicate and beautiful beyond description. The child's mother was lying in a bed of black ebony with pearl bed knobs; the blankets were embroidered in gold, the cradle was ivory, and the bath was pure gold. After the christening the girl wanted to go home again, but the elves begged her to spend three days with them, and so she did. The hours passed in joy and happiness, and the little folk did everything they could to please her. When she finally insisted on leaving, they filled her pockets with gold and led her out of the mountain. As soon as she got home, she wanted to start work again, picked up the broom that was still standing in the corner, and began to sweep. But some strange people came out of the house and asked her who she was and what she was doing there. It wasn't three days she had spent with the little folk in the mountain, as she thought, but seven years, and her old masters had died in the meantime.

THIRD STORY

The elves had taken a mother's child out of the cradle and in his place left a changeling with a big head and staring eyes, who couldn't do anything but eat and drink. In her distress the mother went to the neighbor woman for advice. The neighbor woman told her to take the changeling into the kitchen, put him down on the stove, light a fire, and boil water in two eggshells. That would make the changeling laugh, and if he laughed that would be the end of him. The mother did everything the neighbor woman had told her. When she put the eggshells filled with water on the fire, the blockhead said:

"I am as old
As the Westerwold,
And I've never seen anyone cooking in an eggshell."

And he began to laugh. And as he was laughing, a big crowd of elves came in, bringing back the right child. They put him down on the stove and took the changeling away with them.

40

The Robber Bridegroom

THERE WAS ONCE a miller who had a beautiful daughter, and when she grew up he wanted to see her well married and provided for. He thought: "If the right kind of suitor comes along and asks for her hand, I'll let him have her." A suitor soon turned up. He seemed to be very rich, and since the miller could see nothing wrong with the man, he promised him his daughter. But the girl didn't love him as a girl should love her betrothed, and she didn't trust him. Whenever she looked at him or thought about him, her heart shrank with horror. Once he said to her: "You're engaged to me, but you never come to see me." The girl replied: "I don't know where you live." Her betrothed said: "My house is in the dark forest." She tried to get out of it by saying she couldn't find the way. The bridegroom said: "I expect you to visit me there next Sunday. I've already invited the guests, and I'll strew ashes in the forest to help you find the way." When Sunday came and the girl was ready to set out, she was terrified, though she herself didn't know why, and she filled both her pockets with peas and lentils to mark the path. At the entrance to the forest she found the trail of ashes and followed it, but at every step she threw a few peas on the ground to the right and left of her. She walked almost all day until she came to the darkest part of the forest. There she saw a house standing all by itself, and she didn't like it because it looked so dark and forbidding. She went in but there was no one to be seen and the place was deadly silent. Suddenly a voice cried out:

"Go home, young bride, go home,
To a murderer's house you've come."

She looked up and saw that the voice came from a bird in a cage that was hanging on the wall. Again it cried out:

"Go home, young bride, go home,
To a murderer's house you've come."

The girl went from room to room until she had seen the whole house, but all the rooms were empty and there wasn't a living soul to be seen. Finally she went down to the cellar. An old, old woman was sitting there wagging her head. "Can you tell me if my betrothed lives here?" the girl asked. "Oh, you poor child," said the old woman. "What a place you've come to! This is a den of murderers. You expect to be wedded soon, but it's death you're going to wed. Look. They've made me put this big kettle on to boil. If they lay hands on you, they'll chop you to pieces without mercy, and they'll cook you and eat you, because they're ogres. You'd be lost if I didn't take pity on you and save you."

The old woman hid her behind a big barrel, where she couldn't be seen. "Be as still as a mouse," she said. "Don't budge or it will be the end of you. Tonight when the robbers are asleep, we'll run away. I've been waiting a long time for this chance." No sooner had she spoken than the wicked robbers came home, dragging another young girl. They were drunk and paid no attention to her screams and moans. They gave her wine to drink, three glasses full, one white, one red, one yellow, and her heart burst in two. Then they tore off her fine clothes, put her on a table, chopped her beautiful body into pieces, and sprinkled them with salt. The poor bride behind the barrel shuddered and trembled, for now she saw what the robbers had in mind for her. One of them caught sight of a gold ring on the murdered girl's little finger and when it wouldn't come off easily he took an ax and chopped off the finger. But the finger jumped over the barrel and fell straight into the bride's lap. The robber took a candle and went looking for it, but he couldn't find it. Another of the robbers asked him: "Have you looked behind the big barrel?" But the old woman cried: "Come and eat! You can look for it tomorrow. The finger won't run away."

"The old woman is right," said the robbers. They stopped looking and sat down to eat. The old woman poured a sleeping potion in their wine, and it wasn't long before they lay down, fell asleep, and began to snore. When the bride heard them, she came out from behind the barrel. The sleepers were lying on the ground in rows. She had to walk over them, and she was very much afraid of waking one of them, but God guided her steps. The old woman went upstairs with her and opened the door, and they hurried away from the den of murderers as fast as they could go. The wind had carried away the ashes, but the peas and lentils had sprouted and showed the way in the moonlight. They walked all night. In the morning they came to the mill and the girl told her father everything that had happened.

When the wedding day came, the bridegroom appeared, and the miller had invited all his friends and relatives. As they sat down at the table, each guest was asked to tell a story. When the bride sat silent and didn't open her mouth, the bridegroom said to her: "Can't you think of anything, my love? You too must tell us a story." "Very well," she replied. "I will tell you a dream. I was walking through a forest alone. At last I came to a house. When I went in, there wasn't a soul to be seen, but on the wall there was a bird in a cage, and it cried out:

'Go home, young bride, go home,
To a murderer's house you've come.'

And then it said the same thing again. My darling, it was only a dream. Then I went from room to room, and all the rooms were empty, and everything was strange and forbidding. Finally I went down to the cellar. And there sat an old, old woman, wagging her head. I asked her: 'Does my betrothed live here?' And she answered: 'Oh, you poor child. You've come to a den of murderers. Your betrothed does live here, but he's going to chop you up and kill you, and then he'll cook you and eat you.' My darling, it was only a dream. But the old woman hid me behind a big barrel, and no sooner was I hidden than the robbers came in, dragging a young girl. They gave her three kinds of wine, white, red, and yellow, and her heart burst in two. My darling, it was only a dream. They pulled off her fine clothes, chopped her beautiful body into pieces, and sprinkled them with salt. My darling, it was only a dream. One of the robbers saw there was still a ring on her little finger, and when it didn't come off easily he took an ax and chopped it off, but the finger jumped up and flew over the big barrel and fell in my lap. And here is the finger with the ring on it!" With these words she took it out and showed it to the company.

The robber, who had turned as white as a sheet during her story, jumped up and tried to run away, but the guests held him fast and handed him over to the authorities. And he and his whole band were executed for their crimes.

41

Mr. Korbis

A HEN AND A ROOSTER once decided to take a trip together. The rooster built a beautiful carriage with four red wheels and harnessed four mice to it. The hen and the rooster sat down inside, and away they drove. Soon they met a cat, who said: "Where are you going?" Rooster replied:

> "Come what may,
> We're on our way
> To Mr. Korbis's house."

"Take me with you," said the cat. Rooster replied: "Gladly. Climb on behind. We wouldn't want you to fall off in front.

> "Be careful not to soil
> My wheels that look so nice.
> Roll, carriage, roll,
> And pipe, little mice.
> Come what may,
> We're on our way
> To Mr. Korbis's house."

Then came a millstone, then an egg, then a duck, then a pin, and finally a needle, and they all climbed into the carriage and went along. When they got to Mr. Korbis's house, Mr. Korbis wasn't home. The mice pulled the carriage into the barn, the rooster flew up on a perch with the hen, the cat settled on the hearth, the duck sat down on the well sweep, the egg wrapped itself up in the towel, the pin stuck itself into the easy chair, the needle jumped up on the bed and straight into the pillow, and the millstone lay down over the door. When Mr. Korbis came home, he went to the hearth and started to make a fire, but the cat threw ashes all over his face. He ran to the kitchen and started to wash, but the duck squirted water at him. He started to dry himself with the towel, but the egg came rolling out at him, broke, and plastered his eyes closed. He sat down in the chair to rest, but the pin stuck him. That made him angry and he flung himself on the bed, but when he laid his head on the pillow, the needle stuck him so hard that he yelled and ran out of the house in a rage. But when he got to the door, the millstone jumped down and knocked him dead. Mr. Korbis must have been a very wicked man.

42
The Godfather

A POOR MAN HAD so many children that he had already asked everyone to be godfather, and when still another child was born to him, there was no one left to ask. He didn't know what to do, and in his distress he lay down and fell asleep. In a dream he was told to go out into the country and ask the first person he met to be godfather, and when he woke up, he decided to do as his dream had told him. He went out into the country and asked the first person he met to be godfather. The stranger gave him a little bottle of water and said: "This is miraculous water; with it you can heal the sick. But you must be careful to notice where Death is standing. If he is standing by the patient's head, give the patient some of the water and he will get well; but if he is standing by the patient's feet, there is nothing you can do, for the patient must die." From that time on the man always knew whether a sick person could be saved or not. He became famous for his skill and he made a great deal of money. Once he was called to the sickbed of the king's child. When he entered the room, he saw death standing by the child's head and cured the child with the water. The same thing happened a second time, but the third time Death was standing by the child's feet and the child had to die.

The man thought he would like to visit the godfather and tell him how he had fared with the water. But when he went into the house, he found strange goings-on. On the first floor a shovel and a broom were fighting, giving each other terrible blows. "Where does the godfather live?" he asked them. The broom replied: "One flight up." When he got to the second floor, he saw dead fingers lying all about. "Where does the godfather live?" he asked. One of the fingers replied: "One flight up." On the third floor there was a pile of skulls, which directed him: "One flight up." On the fourth floor he saw some fish sizzling in a pan, frying themselves. They too said: "One flight up." On the fifth floor, he came to a door and looked through the keyhole. The godfather was inside, and he had a pair of long horns. When the man opened the door and went in, the godfather jumped into the bed and covered himself up. The man said: "Godfather, what are these strange goings-on in your house? When I got to the first floor, a shovel and a broom were fighting, giving each other terrible blows." "How can you be so simple-minded?" said the godfather. "That was the hired man and the maid having a chat." "And on the second floor I saw dead fingers lying around." "My word, what a fool you are! Those were salsify roots." "On the third floor I saw a pile of skulls." "You fool, those were cabbages." "On the fourth floor I saw fishes sizzling in a pan, frying themselves." No sooner had he said this than the fishes came in and dished themselves up. "And when I got to the fifth floor, I looked through the keyhole and saw you, godfather, and you had long horns." "Damn you, that's not true!" Then the man was afraid and ran away. The Lord knows what the godfather would have done to him otherwise.

43

Frau Trude

ONCE THERE WAS a little girl who was stubborn and insolent, and disobeyed her parents. How could she possibly have kept out of trouble? One day she said to her parents: "I've heard so much about Frau Trude. I think I'll go and see her one of these days. They say her house is so strange, with such unusual things in it, and I'm ever so curious." Her parents forbade her to go. "Frau Trude is a wicked woman," they said. "She does godless things. If you go and see her you're not our child any more." But the child paid no attention to what her parents said and went to see Frau Trude all the same. When she came in, Frau Trude asked her: "Why are you so pale?" "Oh," she answered, shaking all over. "I saw something that gave me a scare." "What did you see?" "I saw a black man on your stairs." "That was a charcoal burner." "Then I saw a green man." "He was a hunter." "After that I saw a blood-red man." "He was a butcher." "Oh, Frau Trude, I was so afraid. I looked through the window and I didn't see you, but I saw the Devil with a fiery head." "Oho!" she said. "You saw the witch in her true headdress. I've long been waiting for you and asking for you. You shall burn bright for me." Then she turned the girl into a block of wood and threw it into the fire. And when it blazed, she sat down beside it, warmed herself, and said: "It is indeed burning bright."

44

Godfather Death

A POOR MAN HAD twelve children and he had to work day and night to provide them even with bread. When a thirteenth came into the world, the man was so distressed that he didn't know what to do. Finally he ran out into the high road, resolved to ask the first person he met to stand godfather. The first person he met was God, who already knew what was on his mind and said to him: "You poor man, I feel sorry for you; I will hold your child over the font, and take care of him and make him happy on earth." The man asked: "Who are you?" "I am God." "Then," said the man, "I don't want you for a godfather, because you give to the rich and let the poor go hungry." He said that because he didn't know how wisely God distributes wealth and poverty. And he turned away from the Lord, and went on. Then the Devil came up to him and said: "What are you looking for? If you take me as godfather to your child, I will give him mounds of gold and all the pleasures in the world." The man asked: "Who are you?" "I'm the Devil." "Then," said the man, "I don't want you for a godfather, because you deceive people and lead them astray." When he had left the Devil, dry-boned Death came striding toward him and said: "Take me as godfather." The man asked: "Who are you?" "I am Death. I make all people equal." The man said: "You're the right one for me, you take rich and poor alike; you shall stand godfather to my child." Death replied: "I shall make him rich and famous, for the man who has me for a friend will want for nothing." "The christening is next Sunday," said the man. "Don't be late." Death came as he had promised and stood godfather very nicely.

One day when the boy was grown, his godfather came to him and said: "Follow me." He led him into the forest, showed him an herb that grew there, and said: "The time has come to give you your christening present. It will make you a famous physician. Always, when you are called to a patient's bedside, I will appear to you. If I stand by the patient's head, you may speak boldly and promise to cure him, and then if you give him some of this herb he will recover; but if I stand by his feet, then the patient belongs to me, and you must say that all efforts would be in vain and that no doctor in the world can save him. Take care not to use the herb against my will, or you may find yourself in trouble."

Soon the young man was the most famous physician in the world. It was said of him: "He need only look at a patient and he knows what to expect, whether he will get well or die." People came from far and wide, brought him to the bedsides of the sick, and gave him so much money that he was soon a rich man. Now it so happened that the king fell ill. The physician was summoned and asked if recovery was possible. But when he approached the bed, Death was standing by the king's feet, so that no herb on earth could save him. "If only I could outwit Death for once," thought the physician. "Of course he won't like it, but since I'm his godson he may be willing to stretch a point. I'll risk it." Thereupon he took hold of the patient and turned him around the other way, so that Death was standing by his head. Then he gave him some of the herb, and the king got well.

But Death came to the physician and was looking very dark and angry. He shook his finger at him and said: "You've put one over on me. I'll forgive you this once, because you're my godson, but don't you dare do it again, or it will be all up with you. Then I'll take *you* away with me."

Soon the king's daughter fell gravely ill. She was his only child. He wept day and night until his eyes clouded over, and he let it be known that the man who saved her from death should become her husband and inherit the crown. When the physician came to the sick girl's bedside, he saw Death standing at her feet. He should have remembered his godfather's warning, but the great beauty of the king's daughter and the hope of becoming her husband drove every other thought out of his head. Death cast angry glances at him, raised his hand and threatened with his bony fist, but the physician didn't see him. He lifted the patient up, put her head where her feet had been, and gave her the herb. Instantly her cheeks flushed red and she came to life again.

When Death saw he had been cheated out of his property for the second time, he strode up to the physician and said: "It's all up with you; your turn has come." And he gripped him so firmly in his ice-cold hand that he couldn't resist, and dragged him to an underground cave. There he saw thousands and thousands of candles burning in endless rows, some large, some medium-sized, others small. At every moment some went out and others flared up, so that the flames seemed to leap this way and that and to be always changing. "You see," said Death, "these candles are human lives. The big ones belong to children, the medium-sized ones to married people in their prime, and the small ones to the aged. But sometimes even children and young people have only small candles." "Show me my life candle," said the physican, thinking it would be quite a big one. Death pointed to a tiny little candle-end that was threatening to go out, and said: "See, there it is." "Oh, dear godfather," said the terrified physician, "light me a new one. Do it for my sake, so I can enjoy my life and become king and marry the king's beautiful daughter." "I can't do it," said Death. "One must go out before a new one can be kindled." "Then," the physician pleaded, "put the old one on top of a new one that will start burning the moment the old one goes out." Pretending to do as he was asked, Death took hold of a big new candle. But he purposely made a false move because he wanted his revenge. The stub toppled over and went out, and instantly the physician fell to the ground. He had fallen into the hands of Death.

45

Thumbling's Travels

A TAILOR HAD A SON who was small, no bigger than a thumb, and for that reason he was called Thumbling. But the boy had plenty of spunk, and he said to his father: "Father, I want to see the world, and no one can stop me." "Very well, my son," said the old man, and he took a long darning needle, held it over the candle and made a knob of sealing wax on it. "Here," he said, "is a sword to take with you." The little tailor wanted to have one more meal with his parents, and he bounded into the kitchen to see what his mother had been cooking. The stew had just been ladled out, and the serving dish was on the stove. "Mother," he asked, "what is there to eat?" "See for yourself," said his mother. Thumbling jumped up on the stove and looked into the dish. But he stuck his neck out too far. The steam from the dish caught him and carried him up the chimney and out into the air. For a while he floated about on the steam, then finally he glided down to the ground. Once the little tailor was out in the wide world, he wandered from place to place and even went to work for a master tailor, but the food wasn't good enough for him. He said to the master's wife: "If you don't give us better food, I'll leave here first thing in the morning. I'll take a piece of chalk, and here's what I'll write on the door: Too much potatoes and not enough meat, good-bye, you penny-pinching cheat." That made the master's wife angry. "You wretched grasshopper!" she cried, and picked up a rag and tried to hit him with it. But the little tailor slipped deftly under the thimble, peered out from underneath and stuck out his tongue at her. She picked up the thimble and tried to grab him, but Thumbling jumped into the rag, and when she unfolded it and looked for him he slipped into a crack in the table. "Ho ho!" he cried, sticking out his head, and when she tried to strike him he jumped down into the drawer. But in the end she caught him and chased him out of the house.

Thumbling walked until he came to a big forest. There he met a band of robbers who were planning to rob the king's treasure. When they saw the little tailor, they thought: "A little fellow like that can crawl through a keyhole; he's as good as a picklock." And one of them cried out: "Hey, you giant Goliath! We're on our way to the king's treasure room. Do you want to come along? You can crawl in and toss out the money." Thumbling thought it over and finally said, "Yes." They went to the treasure room and he examined the door from top to bottom, looking for a crack. Soon he found one that was wide enough to let him in. He started to slip through, but one of the two guards who were standing by the door noticed him and said to the other: "Would you look at that ugly spider! I'm going to squash it." "What has the poor creature done to you?" said the other. "Leave it alone." Then Thumbling slipped through the crack into the treasure room, opened the window above where the robbers were standing, and threw taler after taler out to them. Thumbling was hard at work when he heard the king coming to inspect his treasure room, and he crawled into the first hiding place he could find. The king noticed that a good many talers were missing, but he couldn't see how anyone could have stolen them, for the locks and bolts were in good condition and everything seemed secure. On his way out, he said to the two guards: "Keep your eyes open. Someone is making off with my money." When Thumbling started work again, they heard the coins inside moving and jingling clinkety-clink. They moved quickly and tried to catch the thief, but the little tailor heard them coming and he was even quicker. He jumped into a corner, covered himself with a taler, and jeered at the guards: "Hey, here I am!" The guards ran to the corner, but before they got there he had hopped under a taler in another corner, crying: "Hey, here I am!" Again the guards came running, but long before they got to him, Thumbling was in a third corner crying out: "Hey, here I am!" So he made fools of them and led them a merry chase around the treasure room until they were worn out. After they had given up and left, he got back to work and little by little tossed out all the talers. When he came to the last taler he threw it with all his might, then hopped nimbly aboard it, and rode out through the window on it. The robbers were full of praise. "You are a mighty hero!" they said. "Would you like to be our captain?" But Thumbling declined, saying he wanted to see the world first. Then they divided the spoils, but the little tailor asked only for one kreuzer, because that was all he could carry.

He buckled on his sword, bade the robbers good-bye, and went his way. He apprenticed himself to several masters, but that kind of thing didn't suit him, and in the end he went to work as a hired man at an inn. The maids hated him, for without being seen he could watch all their secret doings, and then he would tell the innkeeper what they had filched from the platters and what they had helped themselves to in the cellar. "You just wait," they muttered. "We'll show you." And they arranged to play a little trick on him. A few days later, when one of the maids was mowing the meadow, she saw Thumbling leaping about and crawling up and down the blades of grass. Quick as a flash, she mowed him along with the grass, bundled up everything she had mown in a cloth, and secretly gave it to the cows. Among the cows was a big black one, who swallowed Thumbling without hurting him. But down below he didn't like it at all, for it was pitch dark, with no sign of a candle. While the cow was being milked, he cried out:

> "Strip, strap, strull,
> Will the pail soon be full?"

But what with the sound of the milking, he wasn't understood. A little later the farmer came into the barn and said: "That cow is to be slaughtered tomorrow." Thumbling was so frightened that he sang out: "Let me out first! I'm inside her." The farmer heard him but didn't know where the voice came from. "Where are you?" he called. "In the black one," he replied, but the farmer didn't know what he meant, and left the barn.

Next morning the cow was slaughtered. Luckily, when the carcass was dismembered and cut up, not a single blow struck Thumbling, but he ended up in the sausage meat. When the butcher arrived and set to work, Thumbling shouted at the top of his lungs: "Don't cut too deep, don't cut too deep, I'm underneath." But the cleavers were making so much noise that nobody heard him. Thumbling was in a fine fix, but danger makes one spry, and he jumped about so deftly between the cleavers that neither of them touched him and he came off unharmed. But there was no way of escaping, and in the end he had to let himself be stuffed into a blood sausage along with the scraps of bacon. It was very close in there, and to make matters worse, he was hung up to smoke in the chimney, where the time dragged on and on, and he became terribly bored. Finally winter came and he was taken down, because the sausage was to be set before a guest. The innkeeper's wife began to slice the sausage and Thumbling was careful not to stick his head out too far for fear she would cut it off. Finally he saw his chance, made an opening for himself, and jumped out.

The little tailor resumed his travels at once, for he had no desire to stay in the house where he had fared so badly. But his freedom was short-lived. In the open country he met a fox who absent-mindedly snapped him up. "Hey, Mr. Fox," the little tailor cried. "It's me, and I'm halfway down your throat. Let me go." "Sure thing!" said the fox. "You're no good to me at all. I'll let you go if you promise me the chickens in your father's barnyard." "With all my heart," said Thumbling. "You shall have every last one of them, I promise you." So the fox let him go and even carried him home. When the father saw his beloved son again, he gladly gave the fox every chicken he owned. "But to make up for it I'm bringing you a tidy sum of money," said Thumbling, and handed his father the kreuzer he had earned on his travels.

"But why did the fox get the poor chickens to eat?" "You little dunce. Wouldn't *your* father care more for his child than for the chickens in his barnyard?"

46

Fowler's Fowl

THERE WAS ONCE a wizard who used to disguise himself as a poor man and go begging outside people's houses and catch pretty girls. Nobody knew where he took them, because they were never seen again. One day he came to the door of a man who had three beautiful daughters. He looked like a poor, frail beggar, and he had a basket on his back, supposedly for the things people gave him. He asked for something to eat, and when the eldest daughter came and held out a piece of bread, he barely touched her and she jumped into his basket —she couldn't stop herself. Then he hurried away with long strides and carried her to his house in the middle of a dark forest. The house was very grand. He gave her everything she could wish for, and said: "My darling, I'm sure you'll be happy with me, you have everything your heart desires." After a few days he said: "I'm going away and I'll have to leave you for a little while. Here are the keys. Look around; you may go wherever you like, except into the one room that this little key opens. That is forbidden on pain of death." He also gave her an egg and said: "Take good care of this egg. Carry it with you, because if it's lost something terrible will happen." She took the keys and the egg and promised to do just as he had said. When he had gone, she went through the house from cellar to attic, and took a good look at everything. The rooms glittered with gold and silver, and she thought she had never seen anything so magnificent. Finally she came to the forbidden door. She wanted to pass it by, but her curiosity gave her no peace. She examined the key, and it looked just like the others. She put it into the lock and turned it a little. The door sprang open. But what did she see when she went in! In the middle of the room there was a big basin full of blood, and in it there were dead bodies that had been chopped in pieces. Beside the basin there was a block of wood with a gleaming ax on it. She was so frightened that the egg she was holding slipped out of her hand and fell into the basin. She took it out and wiped the blood off, but it didn't help, a second later the stain was back again. She wiped and scraped, but she couldn't get it off.

It wasn't long before the man came home from his trip, and the first thing he asked for were the key and the egg. She gave them to him, but she was trembling, and when he saw the red spots he knew right away that she had been in the bloody room. "You've gone into that room against my wishes," he said. "Well, now you'll have to go in against yours. Your life is over." He threw her down, dragged her in by the hair, and cut off her head on the block. Her blood ran down over the floor. Then he chopped her up and threw her into the basin with the others.

"Now I'll go and get the second," said the wizard, and again he went to the house disguised as a poor man and begged. When the second daughter brought him a piece of bread, he caught her like the first just by touching her, and carried her away. She fared no better than her sister. Her curiosity got the better of her; she opened the bloody room, looked in, and paid for it with her life when he came home. Then he went back and took the third, but she was clever and sly. The first thing she did after he had given her the keys and the egg and had gone away was to put the egg in a safe place. Then she explored the house, and last she went into the forbidden room. And what did she see! Both her dear sisters lay there in the basin, foully murdered and chopped in pieces. But she got to work and gathered the pieces and put them in their right place, head and body and arms and legs. When nothing was missing, the pieces began to move and knit together, and the two girls opened their eyes and came alive again. They hugged and kissed and were all very happy. When the man came home, he asked for the key and the egg, and when he couldn't find the least trace of blood, he said: "You've stood the test; you shall be my wife." After that he lost his power over her and had to do her bidding. "Very well," she said. "But first you must take my father and mother a basket full of gold and I want you to carry it on your own back. In the meantime I'll make ready for the wedding." She ran to her sisters, whom she had hidden in a little room, and said: "The time has come. I can save you now. The villain himself will carry you home. But the moment you get there, you must send me help." She put them both in a basket and covered them up with gold until not a bit of them could be seen. Then she called in the wizard and said: "You can take the basket now, but don't let me catch you stopping to rest on the way; I'll be watching you from my little window."

The wizard heaved the basket onto his back and started out, but it weighed on him so heavily that the sweat ran over his face. He sat down and thought he'd rest awhile, but one of the girls in the basket cried out: "I'm looking out of my little window, and I can see you resting. Get a move on!" He thought it was his bride calling and started off. After a while he thought he'd sit down again, but again the cry came: "I'm looking out of my little window, and I can see you resting. Get a move on!" Every time he tried to sit down the cry came and he had to start off again, until finally, groaning and breathless, he carried the basket with the gold and the two girls in it into their parents' house.

Meanwhile the bride made ready for the wedding and invited all the wizard's friends. Then she took a grinning skull, decked it with jewels and a wreath of flowers, carried it upstairs and set it down in the attic window, looking out. When everything was ready, she plunged herself in a barrel of honey, cut open a featherbed and rolled in the feathers. Then, looking like a strange bird that no one could have recognized, she left the house. On the way she met some of the wedding guests, and they asked her:

"Oh Fowler's fowl, where from, where from?"
"From Fitz the Fowler's house I've come."
"Then tell us what the young bride's doing."
"From cellar to garret she's swept the house.
Now she's up at the window looking out."

Then finally she met the bridegroom, who was walking back very slowly. And he too asked:

"Oh Fowler's fowl, where from, where from?"
"From Fitz the Fowler's house I've come."
"Then tell me what the young bride's doing."
"From cellar to garret she's swept the house.
Now she's up at the window looking out."

The bridegroom looked up and saw the decorated skull. He thought it was his bride and nodded and waved. But when he and his guests had gone into the house, the bride's brothers and cousins who had been sent to rescue her arrived. They locked all the doors so no one could get out and set fire to the house, and the wizard and all his crew were burned alive.

47

The Juniper Tree

A LONG TIME AGO, at least two thousand years, there was a rich man who had a good and beautiful wife, and they loved each other dearly, but much as they longed for children, they had none. Day and night the woman prayed, but no children came. Outside the house there was a garden, and in the garden there was a juniper tree. One winter's day the wife stood under the tree, peeling herself an apple, and as she was peeling the apple she cut her finger and her blood fell on the snow. She looked at the blood and it made her very sad. "Ah!" she sighed. "Ah! If only I had a child as red as blood and as white as snow." When she had said that, she was happy; she had a feeling that something would come of it. Then she went back into the house. A month went by and the snow with it; two months, and the world was green; three months and flowers came out of the ground; four months and the trees of the forest pressed together and the green branches mingled; the woods resounded with the singing of birds and the blossoms fell from the trees. The fifth month passed and she stood under the juniper tree. It smelled so sweet that her heart leaped for joy, and she was so happy she fell down on her knees. When the sixth month had passed, the fruit was big and firm, and she became very still. After the seventh month she snatched at the juniper berries and ate so greedily that she grew sad and sickened. When the eighth month had passed, she called her husband and wept and said: "If I die, bury me under the juniper tree." With that she took comfort and she was happy until the next month had passed. Then she bore a child as white as snow and as red as blood, and when she saw the child she was so happy that she died.

Her husband buried her under the juniper tree and he wept and wept. After a while he felt a little better. Though he still wept now and then, he could bear it, and after another while he took a second wife.

By this second wife he had a daughter. The first wife's child was a little boy, and he was as red as blood and as white as snow. When the woman looked at her daughter, she loved her dearly, but when she looked at the little boy she was sick at heart. It seemed to her that he would always be a thorn in her side, and she kept wondering how she might get the whole fortune for her daughter. The Devil got into her and drove her to hate the little boy and slap him and pinch him and make him stand in the corner. The poor child lived in terror and when he came home from school, there wasn't a quiet nook he could call his own.

One day the woman went up to the pantry. Her little daughter came in and said: "Mother, give me an apple." "Yes, my child," said the woman, and gave her a fine apple out of the chest. Now this chest had a big heavy lid with a big sharp iron lock. "Mother," said the little daughter, "won't you give my brother one too?" That vexed the woman, but she said: "Oh yes, as soon as he gets home from school." When she looked out of the window and saw he was coming, it was as if the Devil had got into her. She snatched the apple away from her daughter and said: "You shan't have one before your brother." Then she threw the apple into the chest and shut the lid. When the little boy came in, the Devil drove her to say as sweetly as could be: "Would you care for an apple, my son?" But her eyes were full of hate. "Mother," said the little boy, "how grisly you look! Yes, give me an apple." Something made her feel she had to press him. "Come with me," she said, and then she raised the lid. "Now pick out a nice apple." When the little boy bent down, the Devil prompted her and bam! she brought the lid down so hard that his head came off and fell in with the red apples. She was overcome with fear and she thought: "If only I could turn away the blame!" She went up to her room and took a white cloth from her drawer. She put the head back on the neck, tied the cloth around it so that nothing could be seen, sat him down in a chair in front of the door, and put an apple in his hand.

Later on Marleenken went to the kitchen. Her mother was standing by the fire, stirring a pot of hot water round and round. "Mother," said Marleenken, "my brother is sitting by the door. He's as white as a sheet and he's holding an apple. I asked him to give me the apple but he didn't answer. It was scary." "Go back," said her mother, "and if he doesn't answer, slap him in the face." So Marleenken went back and said: "Brother, give me the apple." But he didn't say a word, so she slapped him in the face and his head fell off. She was so frightened she began to scream and cry. She ran to her mother and said: "Oh, mother, I've knocked my brother's head off," and she wept and wept and couldn't be comforted. "Marleenken," said her mother, "what a dreadful thing to have done! But don't breathe a word, we won't tell a soul, it can't be undone now. We'll cook him up into stew." The mother took the little boy and chopped him up and put the pieces into the pot and cooked him up into a stew. Marleenken stood there and wept and wept. Her tears fell into the pot and there was no need of salt.

When the father came home, he sat down to table and said: "Where is my son?" The mother served up a big bowl of stew, and Marleenken wept and couldn't stop. The father asked again: "Where is my son?" "Oh," said the mother, "he's gone away to visit his mother's great-uncle; he'll be gone for a little while." "What will he do there? Why, he didn't even say good-bye to me." "Well, he wanted to go, and he asked me if he could stay six weeks. He'll be well taken care of." "It makes me very sad," said the man. "It's not right what he's done, he should have said good-bye to me." Then he began to eat and said: "Marleenken, why are you crying? Your brother will be back soon." And then he said: "Oh, wife, this stew is so good! Give me some more." The more he ate, the more he wanted. "Give me more," he said. "You shan't have any. I have a feeling it all belongs to me." He ate and ate until he had eaten it all up, and he threw all the bones under the table. Marleenken went to her room and got her best silk kerchief. She picked up all the bones from under the table, tied them in the silk kerchief, and took them outside. Weeping bitterly, she put them down in the green grass under the juniper tree. When she had put them down she suddenly felt light at heart and stopped crying. Then the juniper tree moved; its branches parted and came together as though it were clapping its hands for joy. A mist went up from the tree, in the middle of the mist there was a flame, and out of the flame rose a beautiful bird that sang gloriously and flew high into the air. When it was gone, the juniper tree became as it was before, but the kerchief with the bones was gone. And Marleenken felt as light and gay as if her brother were still alive. She went merrily back to the table and ate.

Meanwhile the bird flew off and lighted on the roof of a goldsmith's house and sang:

> "My mother killed me,
> My father ate me,
> My sister Marleenken
> Gathered up my bones,
> Tied them in a silken kerchief,
> And put them under the juniper tree.
> Keewitt, keewitt, what a fine bird am I!"

The goldsmith was sitting in his workshop, making a gold chain. He heard the bird singing on his roof and thought: Isn't that beautiful! He stood up and as he was stepping over the threshold one of his slippers fell off. But he went right out into the middle of the street with only one slipper on. He was wearing his apron; in one hand he was holding the gold chain, in the other his pincers, and the sun was shining brightly on the street. He stopped still and looked up at the bird and said: "Bird, you're a wonderful singer! Sing me that song again." "No," said the bird. "I don't sing twice for nothing. Give me that gold chain and I'll sing it again." "Here," said the goldsmith. "Here's the gold chain. Now sing it again." The bird came flying down. Taking the gold chain in his right claw, he settled in front of the goldsmith and sang:

> "My mother killed me,
> My father ate me,
> My sister Marleenken
> Gathered up my bones,
> Tied them in a silken kerchief,
> And put them under the juniper tree.
> Keewitt, keewitt, what a fine bird am I!"

Then the bird flew off to a shoemaker's house, lighted on the roof and sang:

> "My mother killed me,
> My father ate me,
> My sister Marleenken
> Gathered up my bones,
> Tied them in a silken kerchief,
> And put them under the juniper tree.
> Keewitt, keewitt, what a fine bird am I!"

When the shoemaker heard the song, he ran out in front of his house in his shirtsleeves and looked up at his roof. He had to shade his eyes with his hand to keep the sun from blinding him. "Bird," he said, "you're a wonderful singer!" And he called in through the door: "Wife! Come out here a minute, there's a bird up there. See him? He's a wonderful singer!" Then he called his daughter and his other children and his apprentices, and his hired man and his maid, and they all came out into the street and looked at the bird, and saw how beautiful he was: he had red and green feathers and a ring like pure gold around his neck, and the eyes in his head glistened like stars. "Bird," said the shoemaker, "sing me that song again." "No," said the bird. "I don't sing twice for nothing. You must give me something." "Wife," said the shoemaker, "go up to the attic. On the top shelf you'll find a pair of red shoes. Bring them down." The woman went and brought the shoes. "There you are, bird," said the man. "Now sing the song again." The bird flew down, took the shoes in his left claw, flew back on the roof, and sang:

> "My mother killed me,
> My father ate me,
> My sister Marleenken
> Gathered up my bones,
> Tied them in a silken kerchief,
> And put them under the juniper tree.
> Keewitt, keewitt, what a fine bird am I!"

When he had finished singing he flew away. He had the chain in his right claw and the shoes in his left claw, and he flew far away to a mill, and the mill was turning, clippety clap, clippety clap, clippety clap. And inside the mill sat twenty miller's men, hewing a stone, hick hack hick hack hick hack, and the mill went clippety clap, clippety clap, clippety clap. The bird lighted on a lime tree outside the mill and sang:

> "My mother killed me"—

and one stopped working,

> "My father ate me"—

and two more stopped working and listened,

> "My sister Marleenken"—

and four stopped,

> "Gathered up my bones,
> Tied them in a silken kerchief"—

and only eight were still hewing,

> "And put them under"—

only five

> "the juniper tree"—

and only one.

> "Keewitt, keewitt, what a fine bird am I!"

The last stopped just in time to hear the end. "Bird," he said, "you're a wonderful singer. I want to hear that too. Sing it again for me." "No," said the bird. "I don't sing twice for nothing. Give me the millstone and I'll sing it again." "If it were only mine," said the miller's man, "I wouldn't hesitate." "It's all right," said the others, "if he sings again he can have it." The bird flew down and the millers, all twenty of them, set to work with a beam and hoisted the stone, heave-ho, heave-ho, heave-ho. The bird stuck his head through the hole and, wearing the stone like a collar, flew back to the tree and sang:

> "My mother killed me,
> My father ate me,
> My sister Marleenken
> Gathered up my bones,
> Tied them in a silken kerchief,
> And put them under the juniper tree.
> Keewitt, keewitt, what a fine bird am I!"

When he had finished his song, he spread his wings, and in his right claw he had the chain and in his left claw he had the shoes, and round his neck he had the millstone, and he flew far away to his father's house.

His father and mother and Marleenken were sitting at the table, and the father said: "I suddenly feel so lighthearted, so happy." "I don't," said the mother. "I feel frightened, as if a big storm were coming on." As for Marleenken, she sat there weeping. The bird came flying, and as he lighted on the roof the father said: "Oh, I'm so happy, the sun's shining so bright outside, and I feel as if I were going to see an old friend again." "I don't," said the woman. "I'm so afraid, my teeth are chattering and it's as if I had fire in my veins." And she tore open her bodice. Marleenken sat in her corner and wept. She held her apron up to her eyes and she wept till the apron was sopping wet. Then the bird lighted on the juniper tree and sang:

> "My mother killed me"—

At that the mother stopped her ears and closed her eyes; she wanted neither to see nor to hear, but the roaring in her ears was like the loudest storm, and her eyes burned and flashed like lightning.

> "My father ate me"—

"Oh, mother," said the man, "there's a beautiful bird out there. He's singing so gloriously, and the sunshine is so warm, the air smells like cinnamon."

> "My sister Marleenken"—

Marleenken buried her head in her lap and wept and wept. But the man said: "I'm going out. I've got to see that bird close to." "Oh, don't go," said his wife. "I feel as if the whole house were quaking and going up in flames." But the man went out and looked at the bird.

> "Gathered up my bones,
>   Tied them in a silken kerchief,
>   And put them under the juniper tree.
>   Keewitt, keewitt, what a fine bird am I!"

With that the bird dropped the gold chain, and it fell right around the man's neck and fitted perfectly. He went inside and said: "See what a fine bird that is. He gave me this splendid gold chain, and he's so beautiful." But his wife was so terrified she fell flat on the floor and her cap fell off her head. And the bird sang again:

> "My mother killed me"—

"Oh, if only I were a thousand feet under the ground and couldn't hear it!"

> "My father ate me"—

And again the woman fell down as though dead.

> "My sister Marleenken"—

"I think I'll go out too," said Marleenken, "and see if the bird will give me something." And out she went.

> "Gathered up my bones,
>   Tied them up in a silken kerchief"—

Here he threw down the shoes.

"And put them under the juniper tree.
Keewitt, keewitt, what a fine bird am I!"

All at once she felt light and gay. She put on the new red shoes and danced and bounded into the house. "Oh," she said, "I was so sad when I went out, and now my heart is so light. What a wonderful bird! He gave me a pair of red shoes." The woman jumped to her feet and her hair shot up like tongues of flame. "I feel as if the world were coming to an end. Maybe I'll feel better if I go outside too." As she stepped out of the door, bam! the bird dropped the millstone on her head and squashed it. The father and Marleenken heard the noise and went out. Steam and fire and flame were rising up, and when they were gone little brother was standing there. He took his father and Marleenken by the hand, and they were all very happy, and they went into the house and sat down at the table and ate.

48

Old Sultan

A PEASANT HAD a faithful dog called Sultan, who had grown so old that he had lost all his teeth and couldn't hold on to anything. One day as the peasant was standing outside the door with his wife, he said: "I'm going to shoot Sultan tomorrow, he's no use to us any more." His wife, who felt sorry for the faithful beast, replied: "He has served us so many years and always done his best. Couldn't we just feed him out of kindness?" "Nonsense," said the husband. "You don't know what you're talking about. He hasn't a tooth left in his head; no thief would be afraid of him. It's time for him to go. He has served us well, I won't deny it, but he's been very well fed for his pains."

The poor dog, who was lying in the sun nearby, was sad to hear that the next day was to be his last. He had a good friend—the wolf— and at nightfall he crept out to the woods and told him what they were planning to do. "Listen to me, old friend," said the wolf, "there's nothing to worry about. I can help you. Here's my plan. Tomorrow bright and early your master and his wife will go out to make hay. They'll take their baby along because there won't be anyone left in the house. While they're at work, they always leave the child in the shade behind the hedge. Lie down beside him as if you were guarding him. I'll come out of the woods and grab the baby; then you must chase after me, as if to get him away from me. I'll drop him and you'll take him back to his parents. They'll think you've rescued their baby and they'll be much too grateful to dream of harming you; far from it, you'll be their favorite and want for nothing."

The plan appealed to the dog and they carried it out. The father screamed when he saw the wolf running across the fields with his baby, but when old Sultan brought the infant back, he was happy. He fondled the dog and said: "No one will touch a hair of your head; you shall be fed all the rest of your life." And to his wife he said: "Go home now and make old Sultan some bread soup, he won't need to chew that, and give him the pillow off my bed as a present from me." From then on old Sultan was so well off he could have wished for nothing better. After a while the wolf came to see him and told him how glad he was that everything had succeeded so well. "But now, old friend," he said, "I hope you'll look the other way if I make off with one of your master's fat sheep now and then. You know what hard times we've been having." "Certainly not!" said the dog. "I shall always be faithful to my master. I can't let you do a thing like that." The wolf didn't think he meant it, and that night he crept in, meaning to carry away a sheep. But the peasant, whom faithful Sultan had informed of the wolf's intentions, was waiting for him and gave him a good going-over with his flail. The wolf had to run for it, but as he was leaving he called out to the dog: "Some friend you turned out to be! Just wait. You'll pay for this."

Next morning the wolf sent the wild boar as his second and challenged the dog to a duel out in the woods. The only second old Sultan could find was a three-legged cat. As they made their way together, the cat limped and the pain made him hold his tail up in the air. The wolf and his second were already on the spot, but when they saw their adversary coming, they thought he was carrying a saber because that was what the cat's upraised tail looked like to them. And seeing the poor animal hobbling along on three legs, they thought he was picking up stones to throw at them. They were both so frightened that the boar crept away into the thicket and the wolf climbed a tree. When the dog and the cat arrived, they were surprised to see no one. But the boar hadn't been able to hide completely in the thicket; his ear stuck out. While the cat was looking suspiciously around, the boar's ear twitched and, thinking a mouse was stirring in the leaves, the cat jumped on it and took a hard bite. The boar jumped up with a roar and ran away shouting: "The guilty party is up there in the tree." The dog and cat looked up and saw the wolf, who was ashamed of having been cowardly, and agreed to make peace with the dog.

49

The Six Swans

A KING ONCE WENT HUNTING in a large forest and pursued a stag so furiously that none of his men could keep up with him. Toward nightfall, he stopped and looked around, and saw that he was lost. He searched for a way out of the forest but found none. Then he saw an old woman and her head wagged from side to side as she came toward him; she was a witch. "Good woman," he said to her, "can you show me the way out of this forest?" "Yes, indeed, Your Highness," she replied. "That I can, but on one condition, and if you don't meet it you'll never get out of the forest and you'll die of hunger." "What is the condition?" the king asked. "I have a daughter," said the old woman, "who is so beautiful you won't find her equal in the whole world. She is worthy to be your wife, and if you make her your queen I'll show you the way out of the forest." In fear and dread the king consented, and the old woman led him to her hut. Her daughter, who was sitting by the fire, welcomed the king as if she had been expecting him. He saw that she was indeed very beautiful, but he didn't like her and he couldn't look at her without a secret shudder. When he picked the girl up and put her in front of him on his horse, the old woman showed him the way. He returned to his royal palace and the wedding was celebrated.

The king had been married once before and had seven children by his first wife, six boys and a girl, whom he loved more than anything in the world. Fearing that their stepmother might mistreat or even harm them, he took them to a solitary castle deep in the forest. It was so well hidden and the way was so hard to find that he himself couldn't have found it if a wise woman hadn't given him a ball of magic yarn. When he tossed the ball before him, the yarn unwound itself and showed him the way. The king went out so often to see his beloved children that the queen noticed his absence. She was curious and wondered what he did out there in the forest all alone. She gave his servants a lot of money and they told her the secret. They also told her about the ball of yarn, which alone could show the way, and she had no peace until she had found out where the king kept it. Then she made little white silk shirts, and sewed a magic spell into them, for she had learned witchcraft from her mother. One day when the king had gone hunting she took the little shirts and went out into the forest, and the ball of yarn showed her the way. When the children saw someone coming in the distance, they thought it was their father and ran happily to meet him. She threw a shirt over each of them, and the moment the shirts touched them they turned into swans and flew away over the trees. The queen went home delighted, thinking she was rid of her stepchildren, but the king's daughter hadn't run out with her brothers, and the queen didn't know she existed. Next day the king went to see his children, but he found only the girl. "Where are your brothers?" he asked. "Oh, father dear," she said, "they've gone away and left me all alone." And she told him how she had stood at her window and seen her brothers turn into swans and fly away over the trees, and she showed him the feathers which they had dropped in the courtyard and which she had picked up. The king grieved but he didn't think the queen had done this wicked thing and, fearing the girl would also be stolen from him, he decided to take her home with him. But she was afraid of her stepmother and asked him to let her spend one last night in the castle.

The poor girl thought to herself: "I can't stay here any longer; I must go and look for my brothers." When night came, she slipped away and went straight into the forest. She walked all night and the

next day as well, until she was too tired to go on. Then she caught
sight of a hut and when she opened the door she saw a room with six
little beds in it. She didn't dare lie down on any of the beds, but
crawled under one of them, stretched out on the hard ground and
thought she'd spend the night there. But just before sundown she
heard a flapping of wings and saw six swans come flying in the window. They settled on the ground and blew at each other and blew off
all their feathers, and their swan skins came off like shirts. The girl
looked at them and recognized her brothers. She was overjoyed to see
them and crawled out from under the bed. The brothers were just as
happy to see their little sister, but their joy was short-lived. "You
can't stay here," they said. "This is a robbers' den. If they come
home and find you, they'll murder you." "Can't you protect me?"
she asked. "No," they said, "because we can only take our swan skins
off for a quarter of an hour every evening, and then we're turned
back into swans." The sister wept and said: "But can't you be set
free?" "Oh no," they said. "There is a way, but it's too hard. You'd
have to go without speaking or laughing for six years, and during
that time you'd have to sew us six little shirts out of starflowers. If a
single word crossed your lips, all your pains would be wasted."
When the brothers had finished speaking, the quarter of an hour was
over. They were turned back into swans and flew out of the window.

The girl decided to set her brothers free, even if it cost her her life.
She left the hut, went out into the middle of the forest, climbed a tree
and spent the night there. Next morning she climbed down, gathered
starflowers and began to sew. There was no one to talk to and she
was in no mood for laughing; she just sat there, attending to her
work. One day, after she had been there a long time, the king of the
country went hunting in the forest and his huntsmen came to the tree
where she was sitting. They called out to her and said: "Who are
you?" But she didn't answer. "Come down," they said. "We won't
hurt you." But she only shook her head. When they kept pressing
her with questions, she tossed down her gold necklace, thinking that
would satisfy them. When they persisted, she threw down her girdle,
and when that did no good her garters and little by little everything
she was wearing, until she had nothing on but her shift. But the
hunters refused to be put off; they climbed up, carried her down and
took her to the king. The king asked her: "Who are you? What

were you doing in that tree?" But she didn't answer. And though he asked her in all the languages he knew, she remained as silent as a fish. But she was so beautiful that the king's heart was moved, and he was filled with a great love for her. He threw his cloak over her, picked her up on his horse and carried her to his palace. There he had her dressed in rich garments and her beauty was as radiant as the day, but not a single word could be coaxed out of her. He seated her next to him at the table, and her gentle, demure ways were so much to his liking that he said: "This is the girl I want for my wife and none other in all the world," and a few days later they were married.

But the king had a wicked mother, who was displeased at this marriage and spoke ill of the young queen. "This slut who can't talk!" she said. "Who knows where she comes from? She's not worthy of a king." And a year later when the queen brought her first child into the world, the old woman took it away and daubed the queen's mouth with blood as she slept. Then she went to the king and accused the queen of eating her baby. The king refused to believe it and wouldn't let anyone harm her. As for the queen, she spent her days over her sewing and paid no attention to anything else. Her second child was a handsome boy and the wicked mother-in-law practiced the same deception, but the king couldn't bring himself to believe her. "She is much too good and pious to do such a thing," he said. "If she could speak and defend herself, her innocence would be plain." But when the old woman stole the newborn child for the third time and accused the queen and the queen didn't say a single word in self-defense, the king couldn't help himself. He had to let justice take its course, and the judges sentenced her to death by fire.

When the day came for the sentence to be carried out, it was also the last day of the six years during which she could neither speak nor laugh, and she had set her dear brothers free from the magic spell. The six shirts were finished, except for one that still lacked its left sleeve. When she was led to the stake, she carried the shirts over her arm. As she stood there and they were just coming to light the fire, she looked up and saw six swans come flying through the air. She knew she would soon be saved and her heart swelled for joy. The swans flew down and came so close that she was able to throw their shirts over them. The moment the shirts touched them their swan skins fell off, and there stood her brothers, strong and handsome.

Only the youngest lacked his left arm and had a swan's wing in place of it. They hugged and kissed, and the queen went to the king, who was utterly bewildered. She opened her mouth and said: "Dearest husband, now I can speak and tell you that I am innocent and falsely accused." Then she told him about the old woman's deception, and how she had taken away her three children and hidden them. To the king's great joy the three children were produced and for her punishment the wicked mother-in-law was tied to the stake and burned to ashes. And the king and the queen and her six brothers lived for many years in peace and happiness.

50

Brier Rose

LONG, LONG AGO there lived a king and a queen, who said day after day: "Ah, if only we had a child!" but none ever came. Then one day when the queen was sitting in her bath a frog crawled out of the water and said to her: "You will get your wish; before a year goes by, you will bring a daughter into the world." The frog's prediction came true. The queen gave birth to a baby girl who was so beautiful that the king couldn't get over his joy and he decided to give a great feast. He invited not only his relatives, friends, and acquaintances, but also the Wise Women, for he wanted them to feel friendly toward his child. There were thirteen Wise Women in his kingdom, but he had only twelve golden plates for them to eat from, so one of them had to stay home. The feast was celebrated with great splendor, and when it was over the Wise Women gave the child their magic gifts: one gave virtue, the second beauty, the third wealth, and so on, until they had given everything a person could wish for in this world. When eleven had spoken, the thirteenth suddenly stepped in. She had come to avenge herself for not having been invited, and without a word of greeting, without so much as looking at anyone, she cried out in a loud voice: "When she is fifteen, the princess will prick her finger on a spindle and fall down dead." Then without another word she turned around and left the hall. Everyone was horror-stricken. But the twelfth Wise Woman, who still had her wish to make, stepped forward, and since she couldn't undo the evil spell but only soften it, she said: "The princess will not die, but only fall into a deep hundred-year sleep."

The king, who wanted to guard his beloved child against such a calamity, sent out an order that every spindle in the whole kingdom should be destroyed. All the Wise Women's wishes for the child came true: she grew to be so beautiful, so modest, so sweet-tempered and wise that no one who saw her could help loving her. The day she turned fifteen the king and the queen happened to be away from home and she was left alone. She went all over the castle, examining room after room, and finally she came to an old tower. She climbed a narrow winding staircase, which led to a little door with a rusty key in the lock. She turned the key, the door sprang open, and there in a small room sat an old woman with a spindle, busily spinning her flax. "Good day, old woman," said the princess. "What are you doing?" "I'm spinning," said the old woman, nodding her head. "And what's that thing that twirls around so gaily?" the princess asked. With that she took hold of the spindle and tried to spin, but no sooner had she touched it than the magic spell took effect and she pricked her finger.

The moment she felt the prick she fell down on the bed that was in the room and a deep sleep came over her. And her sleep spread to the entire palace. The king and the queen had just come home, and when they entered the great hall they fell asleep and the whole court with them. The horses fell asleep in the stables, the dogs in the courtyard, the pigeons on the roof, and the flies on the wall. Even the fire on the hearth stopped flaming and fell asleep, and the roast stopped crackling, and the cook, who was about to pull the kitchen boy's hair because he had done something wrong, let go and fell asleep. And the wind died down, and not a leaf stirred on the trees outside the castle.

All around the castle a brier hedge began to grow. Each year it grew higher until in the end it surrounded and covered the whole castle and there was no trace of a castle to be seen, not even the flag on the roof. The story of Brier Rose, as people called the beautiful sleeping princess, came to be told far and wide, and from time to time

a prince tried to pass through the hedge into the castle. But none succeeded, for the brier bushes clung together as though they had hands,
so the young men were caught and couldn't break loose and died a
pitiful death. After many years another prince came to the country
and heard an old man telling about the brier hedge that was said to
conceal a castle, where a beautiful princess named Brier Rose had
been sleeping for a hundred years, along with the king and the queen
and their whole court. The old man had also heard from his grandfather that a number of princes had tried to pass through the brier
hedge but had got caught in it and died a pitiful death. Then the
young man said: "I'm not afraid. I will go and see the beautiful Brier
Rose." The good old man did his best to dissuade him, but the prince
wouldn't listen.

It so happened that the hundred years had passed and the day had
come for Brier Rose to wake up. As the king's son approached the
brier hedge, the briers turned into big beautiful flowers, which
opened of their own accord and let him through, then closed behind
him to form a hedge again. In the courtyard he saw the horses and
mottled hounds lying asleep, and on the roof pigeons were roosting
with their heads under their wings. When he went into the castle, the
flies were asleep on the wall, the cook in the kitchen was still holding
out his hand as though to grab the kitchen boy, and the maid was sitting at the table with a black hen in front of her that needed plucking. Going farther, he saw the whole court asleep in the great hall,
and on the dais beside the throne lay the king and the queen. On he
went, and everything was so still that he could hear himself breathe.
At last he came to the tower and opened the door to the little room
where Brier Rose was sleeping. There she lay, so beautiful that he
couldn't stop looking at her, and he bent down and kissed her. No
sooner had his lips touched hers than Brier Rose opened her eyes,
woke up, and smiled sweetly. They went downstairs together, and
then the king and the queen and the whole court woke up, and they
all looked at each other in amazement. The horses in the courtyard
stood up and shook themselves; the hounds jumped to their feet and
wagged their tails; the pigeons on the roof took their heads from
under their wings, looked around and flew off into the fields; the flies
on the wall started crawling, the fire in the kitchen flamed up and

cooked the meal; the roast began to crackle again, the cook boxed the kitchen boy's ear so hard that he howled, and the maid plucked the chicken. The prince and Brier Rose were married in splendor, and they lived happily to the end of their lives.

51
Fledgling

ONCE THERE WAS a forester who went out hunting, and in the middle of the forest he heard a sound like a child crying. He followed the sound and finally came to a tall tree and in the treetop he saw a child. The mother had fallen asleep under the tree, and an eagle, seeing the child in her arms, had flown down, picked him up in its beak, and carried him to the top of the tree.

The forester climbed the tree, brought the child down, and thought to himself: "I'll take him home and bring him up with my little Lenchen." So he took the child home and the two children grew up together. The boy who had been found in the tree was called Fledgling, because he had been carried off by a bird. Fledgling and Lenchen loved each other so dearly that one grew sad when the other was out of sight.

Now the forester had an old cook. One night she took two buckets and began to haul water. She went out to the well not once but many times. Lenchen saw her and said: "What's going on, old Sanna, why are you hauling so much water?" "I'll tell you why if you promise not to tell a soul." Lenchen promised not to tell a soul and the cook said: "Tomorrow morning when the forester goes hunting, I'm going to put on a pot of water and when it boils I'm going to throw Fledgling in and cook him."

Bright and early next morning the forester got up and went hunting, and the two children were still in bed when he left. Lenchen said to Fledgling: "If you won't leave me, I won't leave you." And Fledgling said: "I will never never leave you." "Then I'll tell you something," said Lenchen. "Last night old Sanna hauled so much water that I asked her what it was for. She said she'd tell me if I promised not to tell a soul, so I promised, and she told me that when my father went hunting this morning she was going to boil water in the kettle and throw you in and cook you. So let's get up and dress as fast as we can and go away together."

The two children got up and dressed quickly and went away. When the water in the kettle came to a boil, the cook went into the bedroom, meaning to take Fledgling and throw him in. But when she went over to the beds, both children were gone. A great fear came over her and she said to herself: "What will I say when the forester comes home and sees the children are gone? Quick, we must follow them and get them back again."

So the cook told three servants to run and catch the children. But the children had sat down at the edge of the forest, and when they saw the servants coming in the distance, Lenchen said to Fledgling: "If you won't leave me, I won't leave you." Fledgling answered: "I will never, never leave you." "Then turn into a rosebush," said Lenchen, "and I'll be the rose on it." When the three servants came to the edge of the forest, they saw nothing but a rosebush with a rose on it, and no sign of the children. "There's nothing we can do here," they said, and went home and told the cook they hadn't seen a thing except for a rosebush with one rose on it. The old cook scolded them. "You simpletons," she said, "you should have cut the rosebush in two and broken off the rose and brought it home. Hurry back and do it now." So back they went, but the children saw them coming in the distance, and Lenchen said: "Fledgling, if you won't leave me, I won't leave you." And Fledgling said: "I will never never leave you." "Then turn into a church," said Lenchen, "and I'll be the crown in it." So when the three servants arrived, they saw nothing but a church with a crown in it. They said to one another: "What can we do here? Let's go home." When they got home, the cook asked them if they had found anything. No, they said, all they had found was a church with a crown in it. "You fools," the cook scolded. "Why didn't you smash the church and bring the crown home with you?" This time the old cook bestirred herself and went out with the three servants to look for the children. But the children saw the three servants in the distance and the cook waddling after them. Lenchen said: "Fledgling, if you won't leave me, I won't leave you." And Fledgling said: "I will never, never leave you." "Then turn into a pond," said Lenchen, "and I'll be the duck on it." The cook came along and when she saw the pond she lay down beside it and thought she would drink it up. But the duck came swimming, took her head in its beak and dragged her into the water. The old witch drowned and the children went home together. They were very happy, and if they haven't died they're still alive.

52

King Thrushbeard

A KING HAD A DAUGHTER who was unequaled for beauty, but she was so proud and thought so much of herself that no suitor was good enough for her. She rejected one after another and to make matters worse poked fun at them. Once the king gave a great feast and invited all the marriageable young men from far and near. They were all lined up in the order of their rank: first came the kings, then the dukes, princes, counts, and barons, and last of all the knights. The king's daughter was led down the line, but to each suitor she had some objection. One was too fat and she called him a "wine barrel." The next was too tall: "Tall and skinny, that's a ninny." The third was short: "Short and thick won't do the trick." The fourth was too pale: "As pale as death." The fifth too red: "A turkey cock." The sixth wasn't straight enough: "Green wood, dried behind the stove." She found some fault with every one of them, but she made the most fun of a kindly king who was standing at the head of the line, and whose chin was slightly crooked. "Heavens above!" she cried. "He's got a chin like a thrush's bill!" And from then on he was known as "Thrushbeard."

When the old king saw that his daughter did nothing but make fun of people and rejected all the suitors who had come to the feast, he flew into a rage and swore to make her marry the first beggar who came to his door. A few days later a wandering minstrel came and sang under the window in the hope of earning a few coins. When the

king heard him, he said: "Send him up." The minstrel appeared in his
ragged, dirty clothes, sang for the king and his daughter, and asked
for a gift when he had finished. The king said: "Your singing has
pleased me so well that I'll give you my daughter for your wife."
The princess was horrified, but the king said: "I swore I'd give you
to the first beggar who came by, and I'm going to abide by my oath."
All her pleading was in vain, the priest was called, and she was married to the minstrel then and there. After the ceremony the king said:
"Now that you're a beggar woman, I can't have you living in my
palace. You can just go away with your husband."

The beggar took her by the hand and led her out of the palace, and
she had to go with him on foot. They came to a large forest, and she
asked:

> "Who does that lovely forest belong to?"
> "That forest belongs to King Thrushbeard.
> If you'd taken him, you could call it your own."
> "Alas, poor me, if I'd only known,
> If only I'd taken King Thrushbeard!"

Next they came to a meadow, and she asked:

> "Who does that lovely green meadow belong to?"
> "That meadow belongs to King Thrushbeard.
> If you'd taken him, you could call it your own."
> "Alas, poor me, if I'd only known,
> If only I'd taken King Thrushbeard!"

Then they passed through a big city, and she asked:

> "Who does this beautiful city belong to?"
> "This city belongs to King Thrushbeard.
> If you'd taken him, you could call it your own."
> "Alas, poor me, if only I'd known,
> If only I'd taken King Thrushbeard!"

"You give me a pain," said the minstrel, "always wishing for another
husband. I suppose I'm not good enough for you!" At last they came
to a tiny little house, and she said:

> "Good God, this shack is a disgrace!
> Who could own such a wretched place?"

The minstrel answered: "It's my house and yours, where we shall
live together." The king's daughter had to bend down to get through
the low doorway. "Where are the servants?" she asked. "Servants,
my foot!" answered the beggar. "If you want something done, you'll

have to do it for yourself. And now make a fire and put on water for my supper because I'm dead tired." But the king's daughter didn't know the first thing about fires or cooking, and the beggar had to help her or he wouldn't have had any supper at all. When they had eaten what little there was, they went to bed. But bright and early the next morning he made her get up and clean the house. They worried along for a few days, but then their provisions were gone, and the man said: "Wife, we can't go on like this, eating and drinking and earning nothing. You'll have to weave baskets." He went out and cut willow withes and brought them home. She began to weave but the hard withes bruised her tender hands. "I see that won't do," said the man. "Try spinning, maybe you'll be better at it." She sat down and tried to spin, but the hard thread soon cut her soft fingers and drew blood. "Well, well!" said the man. "You're no good for any work. I've made a bad bargain. But now I think I'll buy up some earthenware pots and dishes. All you'll have to do is sit in the market-place and sell them." "Goodness gracious!" she thought, "if some-body from my father's kingdom goes to the marketplace and sees me sitting there selling pots, how they'll laugh at me!" But there was no help for it, she had to give in or they would have starved. The first day all went well; people were glad to buy her wares because she was beautiful; they paid whatever she asked, and some didn't even trouble to take the pots they had paid for. The two of them lived on the proceeds as long as the stock held out, and then the husband bought up a fresh supply of crockery. She took a place at the edge of the market, set out her wares around her and offered them for sale. All of a sudden a drunken hussar came galloping through, upset her pots and smashed them all into a thousand pieces. She began to cry, she was worried sick. "Oh!" she wailed, "what will become of me? What will my husband say!" She ran home and told him what had happened. "What did you expect?" he said. "Setting out earthenware pots at the edge of the market! But stop crying. I can see you're no good for any sensible work. Today I was at our king's palace. I asked if they could use a kitchen maid, and they said they'd take you. They'll give you your meals."

So the king's daughter became a kitchen maid and had to help the cook and do the most disagreeable work. She carried little jars in both her pockets to take home the leftovers they gave her, and that's what she and her husband lived on. It so happened that the marriage of the king's eldest son was about to be celebrated. The poor woman went upstairs and stood in the doorway of the great hall, looking on. When the candles were lit and the courtiers began coming in, each more magnificent than the last and everything was so bright and full of splendor, she was sad at heart. She thought of her miserable life and cursed the pride and arrogance that had brought her so low and made her so poor. Succulent dishes were being carried in and out and the smell drifted over to her. Now and then a servant tossed her a few scraps, and she put them into her little jars to take home. And then the king's son appeared; he was dressed in silk and velvet and had gold chains round his neck. When he saw the beautiful woman in the doorway, he took her by the hand and asked her to dance with him, but she refused. She was terrified, for she saw it was King Thrushbeard, who had courted her and whom she had laughed at and rejected. She tried to resist, but he drew her into the hall. Then the string that kept her pockets in place snapped, the jars fell to the floor, the soup spilled and the scraps came tumbling out. The courtiers all began to laugh and jeer, and she would sooner have been a hundred fathoms under the earth. She bounded through the door and tried to escape, but on the stairs a man caught her and brought her back, and when she looked at him she saw it was King Thrushbeard again. He spoke kindly to her and said: "Don't be afraid. I am the minstrel you've been living with in that wretched shack; I disguised myself for love of you, and I was also the hussar who rode in and smashed your crockery. I did all that to humble your pride and punish you for the insolent way you laughed at me." Then she wept bitterly and said: "I've been very wicked and I'm not worthy to be your wife." But he said: "Don't cry, the hard days are over; now we shall celebrate our wedding." The maids came and dressed her magnificently, her father arrived with his whole court and congratulated her on her marriage to King Thrushbeard, and it was then that the feast became really joyful. I wish you and I had been there.

53

Snow White

ONCE IN MIDWINTER when the snowflakes were falling from the sky like feathers, a queen sat sewing at a window, with an ebony frame. And as she was sewing and looking out at the snowflakes, she pricked her finger with her needle and three drops of blood fell on the snow. The red looked so beautiful on the white snow that she thought to herself: "If only I had a child as white as snow and as red as blood and as black as the wood of my window frame." A little while later she gave birth to a daughter, who was as white as snow and as red as blood, and her hair was as black as ebony. They called her Snow White, and when she was born, the queen died.

A year later the king took a second wife. She was beautiful, but she was proud and overbearing, and she couldn't bear the thought that anyone might be more beautiful than she. She had a magic mirror, and when she went up to it and looked at herself, she said:

"Mirror, Mirror, here I stand.
    Who is the fairest in the land?"

and the mirror answered:

"You, O Queen, are the fairest in the land."

That set her mind at rest, for she knew the mirror told the truth.

But as Snow White grew, she became more and more beautiful, and by the time she was seven years old she was as beautiful as the day and more beautiful than the queen herself. One day when the queen said to her mirror:

"Mirror, Mirror, here I stand.
    Who is the fairest in the land?"—

the mirror replied:

"You, O Queen, are the fairest here,
    But Snow White is a thousand times more fair."

The queen gasped, and turned yellow and green with envy. Every time she laid eyes on Snow White after that she hated her so much that her heart turned over in her bosom. Envy and pride grew like weeds in her heart, until she knew no peace by day or by night. Finally she sent for a huntsman and said: "Get that child out of my sight. Take her into the forest and kill her and bring me her lungs and her liver to prove you've done it." The huntsman obeyed. He took the child out into the forest, but when he drew his hunting knife and prepared to pierce Snow White's innocent heart, she began to cry and said: "Oh, dear huntsman, let me live. I'll run off through the wild woods and never come home again." Because of her beauty the huntsman took pity on her and said: "All right, you poor child. Run away." To himself, he thought: "The wild beasts will soon eat her," but not having to kill her was a great weight off his mind all the same. Just then a young boar came bounding out of the thicket. The huntsman thrust his knife into it, took the lungs and liver and brought them to the queen as proof that he had done her bidding. The cook was ordered to salt and stew them, and the godless woman ate them, thinking she was eating Snow White's lungs and liver.

Meanwhile the poor child was all alone in the great forest. She was so afraid that she looked at all the leaves on the trees and didn't know what to do. She began to run, she ran over sharp stones and through brambles, and the wild beasts passed by without harming her. She ran as long as her legs would carry her and then, just before nightfall, she saw a little house and went in to rest. Inside the house everything was tiny, but wonderfully neat and clean. There was a table spread with a white cloth, and on the table there were seven little plates, each with its own knife, fork, and spoon, and seven little cups. Over against the wall there were seven little beds all in a row, covered with spotless white sheets. Snow White was very hungry and thirsty, but she didn't want to eat up anyone's entire meal, so she ate a bit of bread and vegetables from each plate and drank a sip of wine from each cup. Then she was so tired that she lay down on one of the beds, but none of the beds quite suited her; some were too long and some were too short, but the seventh was just right. There she stayed and when she had said her prayers she fell asleep.

When it was quite dark, the owners of the little house came home. They were seven dwarfs who went off to the mountains every day with their picks and shovels, to mine silver. They lit their seven little candles, and when the light went up they saw someone had been there, because certain things had been moved. The first said: "Who has been sitting in my chair?" The second: "Who has been eating off my plate?" The third: "Who has taken a bite of my bread?" The fourth: "Who has been eating some of my vegetables?" The fifth: "Who has been using my fork?" The sixth: "Who has been cutting with my knife?" And the seventh: "Who has been drinking out of my cup?" Then the first looked around, saw a little hollow in his bed and said: "Who has been lying in my bed?" The others came running, and cried out: "Somebody has been lying in my bed too." But when the seventh looked at his bed, he saw Snow White lying there asleep. He called the others, who came running. They cried out in amazement, went to get their seven little candles, and held them over Snow White: "Heavens above!" they cried. "Heavens above! What a beautiful child!" They were so delighted they didn't wake her but let her go on sleeping in the little bed. The seventh dwarf slept with his comrades, an hour with each one, and then the night was over.

Next morning Snow White woke up, and when she saw the seven dwarfs she was frightened. But they were friendly and asked: "What's your name," "My name is Snow White," she said. "How did you get to our house?" the dwarfs asked. And she told them how her stepmother had wanted to kill her, how the huntsman had spared her life, and how she had walked all day until at last she found their little house. The dwarfs said: "If you will keep house for us, and do the cooking and make the beds and wash and sew and knit, and keep everything neat and clean, you can stay with us and you'll want for nothing." "Oh yes," said Snow White. "I'd love to." So she stayed and kept the house in order, and in the morning they went off to the mountains to look for silver and gold, and in the evening they came home again and dinner had to be ready. But all day Snow White was alone, and the kindly dwarfs warned her, saying: "Watch out for your stepmother. She'll soon find out you're here. Don't let anyone in."

After eating Snow White's lungs and liver, the queen felt sure she was again the most beautiful of all. She went to her mirror and said:

"Mirror, Mirror, here I stand.
Who is the fairest in the land?"

And the mirror replied:

> "You, O Queen, are the fairest here,
> But Snow White, who has gone to stay
> With the seven dwarfs far, far away,
> Is a thousand times more fair."

The queen gasped. She knew the mirror told no lies and she realized that the huntsman had deceived her and that Snow White was still alive. She racked her brains for a way to kill her, because she simply had to be the fairest in the land, or envy would leave her no peace. At last she thought up a plan. She stained her face and dressed like an old peddler woman, so that no one could have recognized her. In this disguise she made her way across the seven mountains to the house of the seven dwarfs, knocked at the door and cried out: "Pretty things for sale! For sale!" Snow White looked out of the window and said: "Good day, old woman, what have you got to sell?" "Nice things, nice things!" She replied. "Laces, all colors," and she took out a lace woven of bright-colored silk. "This woman looks so honest," thought Snow White. "It must be all right to let her in." So she unbolted the door and bought the pretty lace. "Child!" said the old woman, "you look a fright. Come, let me lace you up properly." Suspecting nothing, Snow White stepped up and let the old woman put in the new lace. But she did it so quickly and pulled the lace so tight that Snow White's breath was cut off and she fell down as though dead. "Well, well," said the queen, "you're not the fairest in the land now." And she hurried away.

A little while later, at nightfall, the seven dwarfs came home. How horrified they were to see their beloved Snow White lying on the floor! She lay so still they thought she was dead. They lifted her up, and when they saw she was laced too tightly, they cut the lace. She breathed just a little, and then little by little she came to life. When the dwarfs heard what had happened, they said: "That old peddler woman was the wicked queen and no one else. You've got to be careful and never let anyone in when we're away."

When the wicked woman got home, she went to her mirror and asked:

> "Mirror, Mirror, here I stand,
> Who is the fairest in the land?"

And the mirror answered as usual:

"You, O Queen, are the fairest here,
But Snow White, who has gone to stay
With the seven dwarfs far, far away,
Is a thousand times more fair."

When she heard that, it gave her such a pang that the blood rushed to her heart, for she realized that Snow White had revived. "Never mind," she said. "I'll think up something now that will really destroy you," and with the help of some magic spells she knew she made a poisoned comb. Then she disguised herself and took the form of another old woman. And again she made her way over the seven mountains to the house of the seven dwarfs, knocked at the door and said: "Pretty things for sale! For sale!" Snow White looked out and said: "Go away. I can't let anyone in." "You can look, can't you?" said the old woman, taking out the poisoned comb and holding it up. The child liked it so well that she forgot everything else and opened the door. When they had agreed on the price, the old woman said: "Now I'll give your hair a proper combing." Suspecting nothing, poor Snow White stood still for the old woman, but no sooner had the comb touched her hair than the poison took effect and she fell into a dead faint. "There, my beauty," said the wicked woman. "It's all up with you now." And she went away. But luckily it wasn't long till nightfall. When the seven dwarfs came home and found Snow White lying on the floor as though dead, they immediately suspected the stepmother. They examined Snow White and found the poisoned comb, and no sooner had they pulled it out than she woke up and told them what had happened. Again they warned her to be on her guard and not to open the door to anyone.

When the queen got home she went to her mirror and said:

"Mirror, Mirror, here I stand.
Who is the fairest in the land?"

And the mirror answered as before:

"You, O Queen, are the fairest here,
But Snow White, who has gone to stay
With the seven dwarfs far, far away,
Is a thousand times more fair."

When she heard the mirror say that, she trembled and shook with rage. "Snow White must die!" she cried out. "Even if it costs me my own life." Then she went to a secret room that no one else knew

about and made a very poisonous apple. It looked so nice on the outside, white with red cheeks, that anyone who saw it would want it;
but anyone who ate even the tiniest bit of it would die. When the
apple was ready, she stained her face and disguised herself as a peasant woman. And again she made her way across the seven mountains
to the house of the seven dwarfs. She knocked at the door and Snow
White put her head out of the window. "I can't let anyone in," she
said. "The seven dwarfs won't let me." "It doesn't matter," said the
peasant woman. "I only want to get rid of these apples. Here. I'll
make you a present of one." "No," said Snow White. "I'm not allowed to take anything." "Are you afraid of poison?" said the old
woman. "Look, I'm cutting it in half. You eat the red cheek and I'll
eat the white cheek." But the apple had been so cleverly made that
only the red cheek was poisoned. Snow White longed for the lovely
apple, and when she saw the peasant woman taking a bite out of it she
couldn't resist. She held out her hand and took the poisonous half.
And no sooner had she taken a bite than she fell to the floor dead.
The queen gave her a cruel look, laughed a terrible laugh, and said:
"White as snow, red as blood, black as ebony. The dwarfs won't
revive you this time." And when she got home and questioned the
mirror:

> "Mirror, Mirror, here I stand,
> Who is the fairest in the land?"

the mirror answered at last:

> "You, O Queen, are the fairest in the land."

Then her envious heart was at peace, insofar as an envious heart can
be at peace.

When the dwarfs came home at nightfall, they found Snow White
lying on the floor. No breath came out of her mouth and she was really dead. They lifted her up, looked to see if they could find anything poisonous, unlaced her, combed her hair, washed her in water
and wine, but nothing helped; the dear child was dead, and dead she
remained. They laid her on a bier, and all seven sat down beside it
and mourned, and they wept for three whole days. Then they were
going to bury her, but she still looked fresh and alive, and she still
had her beautiful red cheeks. "We can't lower her into the black

earth," they said, and they had a coffin made out of glass, so that she could be seen from all sides, and they put her into it and wrote her name in gold letters on the coffin, adding that she was a king's daughter. Then they put the coffin on the hilltop, and one of them always stayed there to guard it. And the birds came and wept for Snow White, first an owl, then a raven, and then a dove.

Snow White lay in her coffin for years and years. She didn't rot, but continued to look as if she were asleep, for she was still as white as snow, as red as blood, and as black as ebony. Then one day a prince came to that forest and stopped for the night at the dwarfs' house. He saw the coffin on the hilltop, he saw lovely Snow White inside it, and he read the gold letters on the coffin. He said to the dwarfs: "Let me have the coffin, I'll pay you as much as you like for it." But the dwarfs replied: "We wouldn't part with it for all the money in the world." "Then give it to me," he said, "for I can't go on living unless I look at Show White. I will honor and cherish her forever." Then the dwarfs took pity on him and gave him the coffin. The prince's servants hoisted it up on their shoulders and as they were carrying it away they stumbled over a root. The jolt shook the poisoned core, which Snow White had bitten off, out of her throat, and soon she opened her eyes, lifted the coffin lid, sat up, and was alive again. "Oh!" she cried. "Where am I?" "With me!" the prince answered joyfully. Then he told her what had happened and said: "I love you more than anything in the world; come with me to my father's castle and be my wife." Snow White loved him and went with him, and arrangements were made for a splendid wedding feast.

Show White's wicked stepmother was among those invited to the wedding. When she had put on her fine clothes, she went to her mirror and said:

> "Mirror, Mirror, here I stand,
> Who is the fairest in the land?"

And the mirror answered:

> "You, O Queen, are the fairest here,
> But the young queen is a thousand times more fair."

At that the wicked woman spat out a curse. She was so horror-stricken she didn't know what to do. At first she didn't want to go to the wedding, but then she couldn't resist; she just had to go and see the young queen. The moment she entered the hall she recognized Snow White, and she was so terrified that she just stood there and couldn't move. But two iron slippers had already been put into glowing coals. Someone took them out with a pair of tongs and set them down in front of her. She was forced to step into the red-hot shoes and dance till she fell to the floor dead.

54

The Knapsack, the Hat, and the Horn

ONCE THERE WERE three brothers who grew poorer and poorer until in the end they were starving and had nothing at all to eat. "We can't go on like this," they said. "We'd better go out into the world and try our luck." They started off and they walked and they walked; they trampled a good many blades of grass, but no luck came their way. Then one day they found themselves in a great forest. In the middle of the forest there was a mountain, and when they went closer they saw that the mountain was all of silver. The eldest said: "This is the good luck I've been looking for, I ask for no more." Whereupon he took as much of the silver as he could carry, turned back and went home again. But the other two said: "We expect our luck to give us something more than silver," and they went their way without so much as touching the silver. When they had traveled another few days, they came to a mountain of pure gold. The second brother stood and pondered, for he was undecided. "What should I do?" he asked himself. "Should I take enough gold to last me the rest of my life, or should I go on?" At last he made up his mind, filled his pockets, said good-bye to his brother, and went home.

But the third said: "Silver and gold mean nothing to me. I'll keep on trying my luck; maybe there's something better in store for me." He went on, and when he had traveled three days he came to a forest that was even bigger than the others. It seemed to have no end and, finding nothing to eat or drink, he was faint with hunger. He climbed a tall tree to look for the end of the forest, but as far as he could see there was nothing but treetops. He started to climb down, but hunger nagged him and he thought: "If I could only fill my belly once again!" When he reached the ground, he was amazed to see a table covered with bowls of food that steamed up at him. "For once my wish has come true," he said to himself. "And in the nick of time." Without asking where the food had come from or who had cooked it, he went over to the table and ate heartily until he had had enough. When he had finished, he said: "It would be a shame to let this fine tablecloth rot out here in the woods," so he folded it neatly, and put it in his pocket. Then he went his way and in the evening, when he felt hungry again, he decided to put his tablecloth to the test. He spread it out on the ground and said: "I wish you to be covered again with good things to eat." No sooner had his wish crossed his lips than the tablecloth was covered with as many dishes full of the choicest food as there was room for. "Now I see in whose kitchen my food is cooked," he said. "And I'll treasure you more than mountains of silver and gold." For he saw it was a magic table-cloth. But he felt that he couldn't very well go home with nothing more to show than a tablecloth, so he decided to travel some more and keep on trying his luck.

One evening in a lonely forest he met a grimy black charcoal burner, who was cooking potatoes for his supper. "Good evening, blackbird," he said. "What's it like out here in the wilds?" "One day like another," said the charcoal burner, "and every evening potatoes. Would you like to be my guest?" "Many thanks," said the traveler. "I wouldn't want to take the food out of your mouth. You weren't expecting company, but if you'll put up with me, you can be *my* guest." "Where is this meal to come from?" asked the charcoal burner. "I can see you're not carrying anything, and there's no one for miles around with any food to give us." "Leave it to me," said the traveler. "I promise you the best food you've ever tasted." He took the tablecloth out of his knapsack, spread it out on the ground, and said: "Tablecloth, set yourself." In a flash the cloth was served with roast meat and stewed meat, and they were as hot as if they had just come from the kitchen. The charcoal burner gaped, but he didn't wait to be asked twice. He helped himself and stuffed bigger and bigger pieces into his black mouth. When they had finished eating, the charcoal burner chuckled and said: "That tablecloth of yours is all right. It would be just the thing for me out here in the woods with no one to cook for me. What would you say to a trade? There's a soldier's knapsack hanging in the corner. It's old and it's not much to look at, but it has magic powers. Still, I don't need it any more and I'll let you have it in exchange for your tablecloth." "First," he replied, "I've got to know what these magic powers are." "I'm coming to that," said the charcoal burner. "Every time you slap it, a corporal pops up with six men, all armed to the teeth, and whatever you command them to do they'll do it." "All right," said the traveler. "If that's the story, let's trade."

He gave the charcoal burner the tablecloth, took the knapsack off its hook, slung it over his shoulder, and started out. When he had gone a little way, he thought he'd test the knapsack's magic powers, and gave it a slap. In half a second seven battle-hardened soldiers were standing there, and the corporal said: "What does my lord and master command?" "Go back to that charcoal burner on the double and tell him I want my tablecloth." They left about-faced and in no time at all they were back with the tablecloth; they hadn't asked the charcoal burner, they'd just taken it. He dismissed them and went on, hoping that even better luck would come his way.

At sunset he came across another charcoal burner, who was cooking his supper over the fire. "If you'd care to join me in a dish of dry salted potatoes, come and sit down," said Mr. Coaldust. "No," said the traveler. "You be *my* guest this time." He spread the tablecloth, and in a flash it was covered with the finest dishes. They ate and drank and enjoyed themselves, and when they had finished their meal, the charcoal burner said: "Up there on the shelf there's a shabby old hat that has strange powers. If you put it on and turn it around, a battery of field guns starts firing, ten or twelve of them. They shatter everything in sight, nothing can withstand them. The hat's no use to me, I'd gladly exchange it for your tablecloth." "It's a deal," said the traveler, taking the hat and putting it on. He left the tablecloth behind, but when he'd gone a little way he slapped his knapsack and his soldiers got it back for him. "Luck makes for luck!" he thought to himself. "Something tells me there's more to come." His thoughts had not deceived him.

After another day's journey he came across a third charcoal burner, who just like the others asked him to share a mess of dry potatoes. Again the traveler invited the charcoal burner to a meal provided by the magic tablecloth, and the charcoal burner liked it so well that in exchange for it he offered a horn that had very different powers from those of the hat. When you blew it, first the walls and fortifications, then the towns and villages collapsed. Again he gave the charcoal burner his tablecloth, and again his soldiers got it back. So now he had the knapsack, the hat, and the horn, all three. "That does it," he said to himself. "I'm a made man, and it's high time I went home to see how my brothers are getting along."

When he got there, he found that his brothers had built a splendid house with their silver and gold and were living in style. He went in, but seeing that his coat was in tatters, that his hat was shabby, and that he was carrying a wretched old knapsack, they refused to recognize him as their brother. They jeered at him and said: "How can you claim to be our brother, who despised silver and gold and held out for still better luck? When he turns up, he won't be a beggar, he'll be a king with a coach and four." With that they threw him out of the house. He was very angry. He kept slapping his knapsack until a hundred and fifty men were lined up in front of him. First he gave them orders to surround his brothers' house; then two of the soldiers were to take hazel switches and tan his haughty brothers' hides until they knew who he was. There was a terrible hubbub; the townspeople came running and tried to help the two brothers in their distress, but the soldiers were too much for them. The king finally got wind of it. He flew into a rage and ordered a captain to march his company to the town and drive the troublemaker out. But the man with the knapsack raised a larger army, which put the captain and his men to flight. The king said: "We'll have to teach that upstart a lesson," and next day he sent out a whole battalion, but they accomplished even less. The man with the knapsack raised even more soldiers, and wanting to get the war over with as quickly as possible, he turned his hat around on his head several times. The heavy guns went into play, and the king's men were routed. "So far so good," said the man with the knapsack, "but I won't make peace until the king gives me his daughter for my wife and lets me rule the whole kingdom in his name." When the king was told of his terms, he said to his daughter: "It's a bitter pill, but what can I do? If I want peace and want to keep my crown on my head, I'll have to give him what he asks."

So the marriage was celebrated, but the king's daughter didn't like one bit being married to a commoner with a shabby hat and an old knapsack. She wanted to get rid of him and racked her brains day and night for a way to do it. She said to herself: "Could it be his knapsack that gives him his magic powers?" Then she dissembled, fondled him until his heart was soft, and said: "If you'd only take off that ugly knapsack; it's so unbecoming it makes me ashamed of you." "Dear child," he said. "This knapsack is my greatest treasure. As long as I have it, I don't have to be afraid of anyone in the world." And he told her about its miraculous power. She threw her arms around him as though to kiss him, but deftly slipped the knapsack off his shoulders and ran away. As soon as she was alone, she slapped it and commanded the soldiers to arrest their former commander and escort him out of the palace. When they had obeyed, the false wife sent still more soldiers with orders to drive him out of the country. He'd have been lost if it hadn't been for his hat. No sooner were his hands free than he gave it a few turns. Instantly the guns began to thunder and to smash everything in sight and the king's daughter herself had to go and beg for mercy. She promised to mend her ways and pleaded so pathetically that he let himself be persuaded to make peace. After that she was all smiles and pretended to love him, and before long she had him so bamboozled that he confided in her and explained that even if someone got hold of the knapsack they wouldn't be able to hurt him as long as he had his old hat. Once she knew the secret, she waited until he had fallen asleep, took his hat, and had him thrown out into the street. But he still had his horn, and in his fury he blew it with all his might. Instantly everything collapsed—walls and fortifications, towns and villages—and the king and his daughter were crushed to death. If he had blown the horn a little longer instead of putting it down, everything would have been destroyed and not one stone would have been left standing on another. After that no one resisted him and he got to be king over the whole country.

55

Rumpelstiltskin

ONCE THERE WAS a miller who was poor but had a beautiful daughter. One day he happened to be talking with the king, and wanting to impress him he said: "I've got a daughter who can spin straw into gold." The king said to the miller: "That's just the kind of talent that appeals to me. If your daughter is as clever as you say, bring her to my palace tomorrow and I'll see what she can do." When the girl arrived, he took her to a room that was full of straw, gave her a spinning wheel, and said: "Now get to work. You have the whole night ahead of you, but if you haven't spun this straw into gold by tomorrow morning, you will die." Then he locked the room with his own hands and she was left all alone.

The poor miller's daughter sat there, and for the life of her she didn't know what to do. She hadn't the faintest idea how to spin straw into gold, and she was so frightened that in the end she began to cry. Then suddenly the door opened and in stepped a little man. "Good evening, Mistress Miller," he said. "Why are you crying so?" "Oh," she said. "I'm supposed to spin straw into gold, and I don't know how." The little man asked: "What will you give me if I spin it for you?" "My necklace," said the girl. The little man took the necklace, sat down at the spinning wheel, and whirr, whirr, whirr, three turns, and the spool was full. Then he put on another, and whirr, whirr, whirr, three turns, and the second spool was full. All night he spun, and by sun-up all the straw was spun and all the spools were full of gold.

First thing in the morning the king stepped in. He was amazed and delighted when he saw the gold, but the greed for gold grew in his heart. He had the miller's daughter taken to a larger room full of straw and told her to spin this too into gold if she valued her life. She had no idea what to do and she was crying when the door opened. Again the little man appeared and said: "What will you give

me if I spin this straw into gold for you?" "The ring off my finger."
The little man took the ring and started the wheel whirring again,
and by morning he had spun all the straw into glittering gold. The
king was overjoyed at the sight, but his appetite for gold wasn't
satisfied yet. He had the miller's daughter taken into a still larger
room full of straw and said: "You'll have to spin this into gold tonight, but if you succeed, you shall be my wife." "I know she's only
a miller's daughter," he said to himself, "but I'll never find a richer
woman anywhere."

When the girl was alone, the little man came for the third time and
said: "What will you give me if I spin the straw into gold for you
this time?" "I have nothing more to give you," said the girl. "Then
promise to give me your first child if you get to be queen." "Who
knows what the future will bring?" thought the miller's daughter.
Besides, she had no choice. She gave the required promise, and again
the little man spun the straw into gold. When the king arrived in the
morning and found everything as he had wished, he married her, and
the beautiful miller's daughter became a queen.

A year later she brought a beautiful child into the world. She had
forgotten all about the little man. Suddenly he stepped into her room
and said: "Now give me what you promised." The queen was horrified; she promised him all the riches in the kingdom if only he
let her keep her child, but the little man said: "No. I'd sooner have a
living thing than all the treasures in the world." Then the queen
began to weep and wail so heart-rendingly that the little man took
pity on her: "I'll give you three days' time," he said. "If by then you
know my name, you can keep your child."

The queen racked her brains all night; she went over all the names
she had ever heard, and she sent out a messenger to inquire all over
the country what other names there might be. When the little man
came next day, she started with Caspar, Melchior, and Balthazar, and
reeled off all the names she knew, but at each one the little man said:
"That is not my name." The second day she sent servants around the
district to ask about names, and she tried the strangest and most unusual of them on the little man: "Could your name be Ribcage or
Muttonchop or Lacelegs?" But each time he replied: "That is not my
name."

The third day the messenger returned and said: "I haven't discovered a single new name, but as I was walking along the edge of the forest, I rounded a bend and found myself at the foot of a high hill, the kind of place where fox and hare bid each other good night. There I saw a hut, and outside the hut a fire was burning, and a ridiculous little man was dancing around the fire and hopping on one foot and bellowing:

> 'Brew today, tomorrow bake,
> After that the child I'll take,
> And sad the queen will be to lose it.
> Rumpelstiltskin is my name
> But luckily nobody knows it.' "

You can imagine how happy the queen was to hear that name. It wasn't long before the little man turned up and asked her: "Well, Your Majesty, what's my name?" She started by asking: "Is it Tom?" "No." "Is it Dick?" "No." "Is it Harry?" "No."

"Could it be Rumpelstiltskin?"

"The Devil told you that! The Devil told you that!" the little man screamed, and in his rage he stamped his right foot so hard that it went into the ground up to his waist. Then in his fury he took his left foot in both hands and tore himself in two.

56

Darling Roland

THERE WAS ONCE a woman who was a genuine witch and she had two daughters, an ugly, wicked one whom she loved because she was her own, and a beautiful, good one, whom she hated because she was her stepdaughter. At one time the stepdaughter had a pretty apron. The other daughter liked it so much that she grew envious and said to her mother: "I must and will have that apron." "Hush, my child," said the old woman. "Have it you will. Your stepsister deserved to die long ago. Tonight when she's asleep I'll go and chop her head off. Just take care to lie on the inside of the bed and push her to the outside." The poor girl would have been lost if she hadn't been standing in the corner and heard every word they said. They didn't let her out of the house all day, and when it came time to go to bed the witch's daughter got in first so as to be on the inside. But when she had fallen asleep, her stepsister pushed her gently to the outer edge and took her place by the wall. In the dead of night the old woman came creeping in. In her right hand she held an ax and with her left hand she groped to make sure someone was lying on the outside. Then she gripped the ax in both hands and chopped her own child's head off.

When she had gone away, the girl got up and went to the house of her sweetheart, whose name was Roland, and knocked at the door. When he came out, she said: "Darling Roland, we must run away; my stepmother tried to kill me, but she killed her own daughter instead. When the sun comes up and she sees what she's done, we'll be lost." "All right," said Roland, "but you'd better take her magic wand first. Without it we'll never get away if she follows us." After taking the magic wand, she picked up her stepsister's head and let three drops of blood fall to the floor, one by the bed, one in the kitchen, and one on the stairs. Then she hurried away with her darling.

In the morning when the old witch got up, she wanted to give her daughter the apron and called her, but she didn't come. "Where are you?" the old woman called. "Here on the stairs. I'm sweeping," said the first drop of blood. The old woman went out, saw no one on the stairs, and called again: "Where are you?" "Here in the kitchen. I'm warming myself," said the second drop of blood. She went into the kitchen, but found no one and called once more: "Where are you?" "Here in bed. I'm sleeping," cried the third drop of blood. She went to the room and approached the bed. What did she see? Her own child bathed in blood; and she herself had cut her head off!

The witch flew into a rage and leaped to the window. She had the gift of seeing far into the distance and she saw her stepdaughter hurrying away with her darling Roland. "A lot of good that will do you!" she cried out. "You've gone a long way, but I'll catch you." She put on her seven-league boots that covered an hour's journey at each step, and overtook them in no time. But when the girl saw the old woman striding up, she took the magic wand and turned her darling Roland into a lake and herself into a duck swimming in the middle of the lake. The witch stood on the bank, tossed in crusts of bread, and did everything she could think of to lure the duck. But the duck didn't let herself be lured, and at nightfall the old woman had to give up and go home.

The girl and her darling Roland took back their natural forms and walked all night until daybreak. Then the girl turned herself into a beautiful flower growing in the middle of a bramblebush, and turned her darling Roland into a fiddler. In a little while the witch came striding up and said to the fiddler: "Dear fiddler, may I pick that lovely flower?" "Yes, of course," he replied. "And while you're doing it I'll play for you." She knew perfectly well who the flower was, and as she hurried into the bush in her eagerness to pick the flower, he began to play. Like it or not, she had to dance, for it was a magic tune. The faster he played the more she had to jump. The brambles ripped her clothes off, and cut and scratched her till she was all covered with blood. But he kept right on playing and she had to dance till she fell to the ground dead.

Once they were saved, Roland said: "Now I'll go home to my father and arrange for our wedding." "I'll stay here and wait for you," said the girl. "And to keep from being recognized I'll turn myself into a red stone." So Roland went away and the girl, who had turned herself into a red stone, stood in the field, waiting for her darling. When Roland got home, he fell into the clutches of another woman and forgot his sweetheart. The poor girl stood there for a long, long time, but when he didn't come back, she grew sad, turned herself into a flower, and said to herself, "If only someone would come along and trample me to death."

But it so happened that a shepherd who was minding his sheep in the field saw the flower. He thought it was so beautiful that he plucked it and took it home and put it in his cupboard. Then weird things started happening in the shepherd's hut. By the time he got up in the morning, all the housework had been done; the floor had been swept, the tables and benches dusted, a fire made in the hearth, and the water brought in; and when he came home at midday the table was set and a good meal was ready. All this puzzled him, for he never saw a living soul, and the hut was too small for anyone to hide in. Of course he was glad to be so well served, but after a while he began to feel frightened and went to a Wise Woman for advice. The Wise Woman said: "There's magic at the bottom of this. Look sharp when you wake up in the morning. If you see anything moving, no matter what, throw a white cloth over it. That will break the magic." The shepherd did as she had said, and the next morning, just as day was breaking, he saw the cupboard open and the flower come out. Quick as a flash he jumped out of bed and threw a white cloth over it. That broke the magic, and there stood a beautiful girl, who confessed that she had been the flower and kept house for him. Then she told him her story, and as he liked her he asked her to marry him, but she said no, because even if her darling Roland had forsaken her she meant to be faithful to him. But she promised to stay with the shepherd and go on keeping house for him.

The time came for Roland to be married, and in that country it was the custom that all the girls for miles around should attend the wedding and sing in honor of the bridal couple. When the faithful girl heard the news, she was so sad she thought her heart would break. She didn't want to go, but the others came and took her along. Every time she was supposed to sing, she kept stepping back, but in the end she was the only one left and she couldn't help herself. When she started her song and Roland heard her, he jumped up and said: "I know that voice. That's my true bride, I don't want the other." Everything he had forgotten, everything he had lost sight of, suddenly flowed back into his heart. The faithful girl was wedded to her darling Roland, her sorrow was ended, and her joy began.

57

The Golden Bird

LONG, LONG AGO there was a king who had a beautiful garden behind his castle, and in the garden there was a tree that bore golden apples. When the apples ripened, they were counted, and the very next morning one was missing. This was reported to the king and he gave orders that someone should keep watch every night under the tree. He had three sons, and at nightfall he sent the eldest to the garden, but at midnight he was overcome by sleep and in the morning another apple was gone. The next night the second son had to keep watch, but he fared no better; when the clock struck twelve he fell asleep, and in the morning still another apple was gone.

Then it was the third son's turn to keep watch, and he was willing, but the king didn't think much of him and felt sure he'd make out even worse than his brothers. But in the end he gave his permission. The boy lay down under the tree, kept watch, and fought off his sleepiness. When the clock struck twelve, something came whishing through the air, and in the moonlight he saw a bird with feathers all of gold. The bird alighted on the tree and had already plucked off an apple when the boy shot an arrow at it. The bird flew away, but the arrow had grazed it, and one of its golden feathers fell to the ground. The boy picked it up, brought it to the king next day, and told him what he had seen during the night. The king summoned his council, and all the councilors agreed that a feather like that was worth more than the whole kingdom. "If this feather is so valuable," said the king, "I can't be satisfied with one; I must and will have the whole bird."

The eldest son set out; he thought himself very clever, and was sure he would find the golden bird. When he had gone a little way, he saw a fox sitting at the edge of a forest, raised his gun and took aim. The fox cried out: "Don't shoot, and I'll give you some good advice. You're looking for the golden bird. This evening you'll come to a village with two inns on opposite sides of the road. One will be brightly lit and full of revelry, but don't stop there; stop at the other, even if you don't like the looks of it." "How can a stupid animal like that give me sensible advice?" thought the king's son and pulled the trigger, but he missed the fox, who stretched out his tail and sped away into the forest. The king's son went on, and in the evening he came to the village where the two inns were; in the one there was singing and dancing, and the other looked gloomy and run-down. "I'd be a fool," he thought, "to stop at that gloomy old inn and pass the fine one by." So he went to the cheerful inn, stayed there carousing, and forgot the bird, his father, and everything he had ever learned.

After a while when the eldest son didn't come home, the second set out to look for the golden bird. Like the eldest, he met the fox, who gave him good advice that he disregarded. He came to the two inns; from the one came sounds of revelry and his brother stood at the window, calling out to him. He couldn't resist, but went in and from that moment on thought of nothing but pleasure.

More time went by, and the youngest son wanted to go out and try his luck, but his father wouldn't let him. "What would be the sense of it?" he said to himself. "He's even less likely than his brothers to find the golden bird, and if he gets into trouble he won't know how to help himself, because he's not quite right in the head." But finally, when the boy gave him no peace, he let him go. Again the fox was sitting at the edge of the forest. Again he pleaded for his life and offered his advice. The third son was a good-natured boy. "Don't be afraid, friend fox," he said. "I'm not going to hurt you." "You won't regret it," said the fox. "And now climb onto my tail, you'll get there quicker." No sooner had he sat down than the fox began to run, and away he went over bush and brake, so fast that the wind whistled through the boy's hair. When they came to the village, the boy alighted, took the fox's advice, and without so much as looking around, went to the shabby inn, where he spent a quiet night. Next morning as he left the village, there was the fox again. "Now," he said. "I'm going to tell you what you must do from now on. Keep going straight ahead. In the end you'll come to a castle. A whole company of soldiers will be lying outside it, but don't let them worry you, they'll all be sound asleep and snoring; go right through their ranks and straight into the castle. Pass through all the rooms; in the last one you'll find a golden bird sitting in a wooden cage. Beside it there's an empty gold cage for show. Whatever you do, don't take the bird out of the plain cage and put it in the golden one; you'd only be making trouble for yourself." With these words the fox stretched out his tail again and the king's son sat down on it. Again he ran over bush and brake, so fast that the wind whistled through the boy's hair. When he reached the castle, he found everything just as the fox had said. He got to the last room and there was the golden bird sitting in a wooden cage, and a golden cage hung beside it. The three golden apples were lying around on the floor. Thinking it would be ridiculous to leave the beautiful bird in such a plain, ugly cage, he opened the door, took hold of the bird and put it in the golden cage. At that same moment the bird let out a piercing scream. The soldiers woke up, rushed in, and carried him off to prison. The next morning he was taken to court, where he confessed everything and was sentenced to death. But the king promised to spare his life on one condition, namely, if he brought him the golden horse who ran faster than the wind. And if he succeeded he could have the golden bird as well.

The king's son started out, but he sighed mournfully, for where was he to find the golden horse? But then he saw his old friend the fox sitting beside the path. "You see," said the fox, "this happened because you didn't take my advice. Never mind, I'll help you and tell you how to get to the golden horse. Go straight ahead till you come to a castle. There in the stable you'll find the horse. The grooms will be sound asleep and snoring, and you won't have any trouble in leading the golden horse out. Just remember one thing: put on the plain wood-and-leather saddle and not the gold one that's hanging beside it, or you'll only be making trouble for yourself." Then the fox stretched out his tail, the king's son sat down on it, and off he ran over bush and brake, so fast that the wind whistled through the boy's hair. Everything happened as the fox had said. He went to the stable where the golden horse was standing. Just as he was picking up the plain saddle, he thought: "A beautiful animal like this deserves a beautiful saddle. It would be sacrilege to use the other one." But no sooner had the golden saddle touched the horse than he began to neigh loudly. The grooms woke up, seized the boy, and threw him into prison. Next morning the king promised to spare his life and give him the golden horse as well if he brought the beautiful princess from the golden castle.

The boy started out with a heavy heart, but luckily for him he soon met the faithful fox. "I really should leave you to your troubles," said the fox, "but I feel sorry for you and I'll help you again, just this once. This path will lead you straight to the golden castle. You'll be there this evening. At night when everyone's asleep, the beautiful princess goes to the bathhouse to bathe. As she goes in, run up to her and kiss her. She'll follow you and you'll be able to take her away with you. But don't let her say good-bye to her parents, or you'll only be making trouble for yourself." Then the fox held out his tail, the king's son sat down on it, and away they went over bush and brake, so fast that the wind whistled through the boy's hair. When he got to the golden castle, it was just as the fox had said. He waited until midnight when everyone was fast asleep and the beautiful princess went to the bathhouse. Then he ran up to her and kissed her. She said she'd be glad to go with him, but wept and implored him to let her say good-bye to her parents. At first he refused, but finally, when she wept more and more and fell on her knees, he gave in. And no sooner had the princess approached her father's bed than he and everyone else in the castle woke up, and the boy was seized and put in prison.

Next morning the king said to him: "You have forfeited your life. You will be pardoned only if you can take away the mountain that blocks the view from my window. You'll have to do it within eight days, but if you succeed, you shall have my daughter as your reward." The king's son set to work. He dug and he shoveled without a moment's rest, but at the end of seven days, when he saw how little he had done and had to admit that with all his work he had hardly made a dent in the mountain, he fell into deep gloom and gave up hope. But that evening the fox appeared and said: "I don't know why I bother with you, you don't deserve it, but just lie down and sleep, and I'll do the job for you." Next morning, when he woke up and looked out of the window, the mountain had disappeared. The boy ran happily to the king and told him the mountain was gone. Like it or not, the king had to keep his word and gave him his daughter.

The two of them started out together, and it wasn't long before they met the faithful fox. "You've got the best prize right there," said the fox. "But the golden horse goes with the princess from the golden castle." "How am I to get him?" asked the boy. "I'll tell you," said the fox. "First bring the beautiful princess to the king who sent you to the golden castle. They'll be overjoyed and they'll gladly give you the golden horse and bring him out to you. Mount him right away, bid them good-bye and shake hands with each one of them. Last of all, take the beautiful princess by the hand, lift her up on the horse's back with one swing, and gallop away. No one will be able to catch you, because that horse runs faster than the wind."

It all went off smoothly, and the king's son carried the beautiful princess away on the golden horse. The fox went with them and said to the boy: "Now I'll help you get the golden bird too. When you come near the castle where the bird is, let the princess down and I'll look after her. Then ride the golden horse into the courtyard of the castle. They'll be overjoyed to see him, and they'll bring out the golden bird. The moment you have the cage in your hand, gallop back to us and get the princess." When this too had gone off smoothly, the king's son prepared to ride home with his treasures. "Wait," said the fox. "Now you must reward me for my help." "What reward would you like?" the boy asked. "When we get to that forest you see, shoot me dead and chop off my head and paws." "Fine gratitude that would be!" said the king's son. "I couldn't possibly do that." The fox said: "If you won't do it, then I must leave you; but one last piece of advice before I go. Be on your guard against two things: don't buy any gallows meat, and don't sit on the rim of a well." With that he ran off into the forest.

The boy thought: "What a strange animal! What weird ideas! Who would want to buy gallows meat? And when has it ever entered my head to sit on the rim of a well?" He rode on with the beautiful princess and came to the village where his two brothers had stayed. There was great hubbub and to-do, and when he asked what was going on he was told that two men were going to be hanged. When he went closer, he saw it was his two brothers, who had been up to all sorts of wickedness and run through all their money. He asked if there wasn't some way of saving them. "If you want to buy them free—" he was told. "But why waste your money on those good-for-nothings?" Without a moment's thought he paid up, the brothers were set free and they all continued the journey together.

After a while they came to the forest where they had first met the fox. Since the forest was cool and pleasant and it was hot in the sun, the two brothers said: "Let's rest here by the well, and eat and drink." He consented, and while they were talking he forgot the fox's advice and, suspecting nothing, sat down on the rim of the well. His two brothers pushed him backward into the well, took the princess, the horse, and the bird, and went home to their father. "Look what we've got," they said. "Not just the golden bird, but also the golden horse and the princess from the golden castle." There was great rejoicing at the news, but the horse didn't eat, the bird didn't sing, and the princess sat and wept.

But the youngest brother wasn't dead. Luckily the well was dry. He fell on dead moss and wasn't hurt, but he couldn't get out. Again the faithful fox stood by him in his trouble. He leaped into the well and scolded him for forgetting his advice. "But I can't help myself," said the fox. "I'll get you out of this." And he told him to grab his tail and hold on tight, and pulled him out. "But you're still in danger," he said. "Your brothers weren't sure you were dead, so they've stationed guards all over the forest with orders to kill you on sight." A poor man was sitting by the path. The boy changed clothes with him and thus disguised made his way to the king's palace. No one recognized him, but the bird began to sing, the horse began to eat, and the beautiful princess stopped crying. The king was amazed. "What can this mean?" he asked. The princess replied: "I don't know, but I was so sad and now I'm so happy. I feel as if my true betrothed were here." And she told him everything that had happened, though the two brothers had threatened to kill her if she breathed a word. The king ordered everyone in the palace to be brought before him. The boy came too in his rags, disguised as a poor man, but the princess recognized him right away and fell on his neck. The wicked brothers were seized and executed, while the boy married the beautiful princess and was appointed heir to the king.

But what became of the poor fox? One day much later the king's son went walking in the forest and met the fox. The fox said: "Now you have everything you could desire and I'm as wretched as ever, though it's in your power to set me free." And again he implored him to shoot him dead and cut off his head and paws. This time he did it, and no sooner was it done than the fox turned into a man, who was none other than the young princess's brother, freed at last from a magic spell that had been put on him. Now nothing more was wanting to their happiness, as long as they lived.

58

The Dog and the Sparrow

A SHEEP DOG HAD a mean master, who let him go hungry. When he couldn't stand it any more, he left home, and he was very sad. On the road he met a sparrow, who said: "Brother dog, why are you so sad?" The dog replied: "I'm hungry and I have nothing to eat." The sparrow said: "Come to town with me, I'll get you plenty to eat." So they went to town together, and when they came to a butcher shop, the sparrow said to the dog: "Stand here, I'll get you a piece of meat." He flew up on the counter and glanced around to make sure no one was looking. Then he pecked, tugged, and pulled at a piece of meat that was lying near the edge until it fell down. The dog grabbed it, ran into a corner and ate it. The sparrow said: "Now we'll go to another butcher shop. I'll get you another piece of meat, then you'll be full." When the dog had eaten the second piece of meat, the sparrow asked: "Have you had enough, brother dog?" "Oh yes," he said. "I've had enough meat, but I haven't had any bread." The sparrow said: "You shall have bread too. Come along." He led him to a bakery and pecked at some rolls until they fell down. Then the dog wanted still more, so he took him to another bakery and knocked down some more bread. When the dog had eaten that up, the sparrow asked: "Brother dog, have you had enough?" "Yes," he said. "Now let's go for a little stroll in the country."

So they went out on the highway. It was a warm day, and when they had gone a little way, the dog said: "I'm tired, I think I'll take a little nap." "Yes, do," said the sparrow. "Meanwhile I'll sit on a branch." The dog lay down in the road and fell fast asleep. As he lay there sleeping, a wagoner came along in his wagon. He had a team of three horses, and he was hauling two barrels of wine. The sparrow saw he was keeping to the middle of the road where the dog was lying and that he had no intention of turning aside. "Wagoner," he cried out, "don't do it or I'll make you poor." But the wagoner growled: "How can you make me poor?" cracked his whip, drove the wagon right over the dog, and killed him. The sparrow cried out: "You've killed my brother the dog. That's going to cost you your wagon and your horses." "Wagon and horses indeed! That's something I'd like to see," said the wagoner, and drove on. The sparrow crawled under the canvas wagon cover and pecked at one of the barrel bungs until it came out. The wagoner didn't notice the wine flowing behind him, but when he happened to look back he saw the wagon was dripping wet. He examined the barrels and found that one was empty. "Alas, poor me!" he cried. "Not poor enough yet," said the sparrow, and flew down onto the head of one of the horses, and pecked his eyes out. When the wagoner saw that, he took out his ax and tried to strike the sparrow, but the sparrow flew up into the air, the wagoner struck his horse's head, and the horse fell dead. "Alas, poor me!" he cried. "Not poor enough yet," said the sparrow, and when the wagoner drove on with his two remaining horses, the sparrow crawled under the canvas cover again and pecked the bung from the second barrel, so that all the wine flowed out. When the wagoner saw what had happened, he cried once more: "Alas, poor me!" The sparrow answered: "Not poor enough yet," flew down on the second horse's head, and pecked his eyes out. The wagoner came running and took a swing with his ax, but the sparrow flew up into the air and the blow struck the horse, who fell dead. "Alas, poor me!" "Not poor enough yet," said the sparrow, flew down on the third horse's head, and pecked at his eyes. In his rage the wagoner swung his ax at the sparrow without looking, and struck his third horse dead. "Alas, poor me!" he cried. "Not poor enough yet," answered the sparrow. "Now I'm going to make you poor in your own home."

The wagoner left his wagon where it was and went home in a raging fury. "Alas!" he said to his wife. "Terrible things have happened! My wine has run out and all three of my horses are dead." "Oh, husband," she said, "what a wicked bird has come into the house! He's collected all the birds in the whole world and now they're in the loft eating up all our wheat." He went upstairs, and there were thousands and thousands of birds on the floor. They had eaten all the wheat, and the sparrow was right there in the middle. "Alas, poor me!" the wagoner cried. "Not poor enough yet," said the sparrow. "Wagoner, it's going to cost you your life," and out he flew.

The wagoner was ruined. He went down into the parlor and sat by the stove in a poisonous rage. The sparrow settled on the window ledge and cried: "Wagoner, it's going to cost you your life." The wagoner picked up his ax and threw it at the sparrow, but it missed the bird and only smashed the windowpane. The sparrow hopped in, perched on the stove, and cried: "Wagoner, it's going to cost you your life." Crazed and blinded with fury, the wagoner demolished the stove and then, as the sparrow hopped from place to place, smashed all his furniture, mirror, table, benches, and last the walls of the house, and each time he missed the sparrow. But in the end he caught him in his hand. "Should I knock him dead?" his wife asked. "No!" he cried. "That would be too easy a death. This bird needs to suffer. I'm going to swallow him." With that he put the sparrow in his mouth and swallowed him whole. But the bird began to flutter in his stomach, and fluttered up into the man's mouth, and stuck his head out and cried: "Wagoner, it's going to cost you your life." The wagoner handed his wife the ax and said: "Wife, knock this bird in my mouth dead." The wife swung the ax but missed the bird and hit the wagoner square on the head. The wagoner dropped dead and the sparrow flew away.

59

Frederick and Liza-Kate

THERE WAS ONCE a young man named Frederick and a young woman named Liza-Kate, who got married and set up housekeeping. One day Frederick said: "I'm going out to the field now, Liza-Kate; when I get back I want to see some cooked meat on the table for my hunger and a cool drink for my thirst." "Don't worry, Frederick dear," said Liza-Kate. "Don't worry, I'll have everything ready for you." When it was almost time for the meal, she took a sausage out of the chimney, put it in a frying pan with some butter, and set it on the fire. As the sausage began to fry and sizzle, Liza-Kate stood holding the handle of the frying pan and thinking to herself. Suddenly she had an idea: "While the sausage is cooking I could go down to the cellar and draw the beer." So she set the frying pan down firmly, took a mug, went down to the cellar and opened the beer tap. The beer ran into the mug, Liza-Kate watched it flow, and then she had an idea: "Dear me! The dog isn't tied. What's to stop him from taking the sausage out of the pan? That's all I need." She was up the stairs in a jiffy, but the spitz already had the sausage between his teeth and was dragging it across the floor. Liza-Kate wasted no time. She followed him and chased him out into the field, but the dog was too quick; he held on to the sausage and went bounding over the furrows with it. "What's done is done!" she said. Then she turned back, walking very slowly because she was tired from running and needed to cool off. Meanwhile the beer was flowing out of the keg, for she hadn't shut the tap, and when the mug was full the beer overflowed into the cellar and didn't stop until the whole keg was empty. Liza-Kate saw the disaster from the top of the stairs. "How dreadful!" she cried. "What will I do now to keep Frederick from noticing?" She thought awhile, and then she had an idea. They had bought some fine wheat flour at the last fair, and there was still a sack of it left. She would bring it down from the loft and strew it on the spilt beer. "That's the ticket," she said to herself. "Save your flour for a needy hour." She went up to the loft, carried the sack down, and threw it straight at the mug of beer, upsetting the mug and adding the contents to the flood. "That's fine," she said. "The more the merrier." She strewed flour all over the cellar, and when she had finished, she was delighted with her handiwork. "How neat and clean it all looks!" she cried.

At midday Frederick came home. "Well, wife, what have you got for me?" "Oh, Frederick dear, I was frying you a sausage, but while I was drawing the beer to go with it the dog took it out of the pan, and while I was running after the dog the beer ran out of the keg and when I threw the flour on the beer to dry it up, I upset your mug, but don't fret, the cellar is bone-dry again." Frederick said: "Liza-Kate, Liza-Kate, you shouldn't have done that. The idea! Letting the dog run off with the sausage and the beer run out of the keg, and to top it all wasting our fine flour!" "How right you are, Frederick dear, I didn't know all that. You should have told me."

The man thought: "If that's the kind of wife I've got, I'll have to be more careful." Over the years he had taken in a tidy sum in talers. He exchanged them for gold and said to Liza-Kate: "Look. Here are some yellow counters. I'm going to put them in a pot and bury them in the barn under the cow's manger, but don't go near them or you'll wish you hadn't." "No, Frederick, dear. Of course I won't." While Frederick was out, some peddlers came to the village selling earthenware pots. They asked the young woman if she wanted to buy anything. "Oh, kind friends," said Liza-Kate, "I haven't any money and I can't buy anything, but if you can use some yellow counters, I'll be glad to trade." "Yellow counters? Why not? Let's have a look." "Just go to the barn and dig under the cow's manger and you'll find the yellow counters. I'm not allowed to go near them." The good-for-nothings went to the place and dug. When they found the pure gold, they picked it up and ran, leaving their pots behind. Liza-Kate thought she ought to put the new pots to some use, but her kitchen was fully equipped, so she knocked the bottoms out of all the new ones and hung them on the fence poles around the house as ornaments. When Frederick came home and saw the new ornaments, he said: "Liza-Kate, what have you done?" "I bought them with the yellow counters under the cow's manger; I didn't go anywhere near them myself, the peddlers had to dig them up." "Wife, wife!" said Frederick. "What have you done! Those weren't counters, they were pure gold, all our savings. You shouldn't have done that." "How right you are, Frederick dear," she said. "I didn't know. You should have told me."

For a while Liza-Kate stood thinking. Then she said: "Listen to me, Frederick dear. We can get the gold back. Let's run after the thieves." "All right," said Frederick. "We'll try. But in case we get hungry on the way, bring some butter and cheese." "Oh yes, Frederick dear, of course I will." They started out, and Liza-Kate fell behind because Frederick was a faster walker. "I'm better off this way," she thought, "because if we turn back I'll have a head start." They came to a hill, and there were deep wagon ruts in the road. "My, how they've gouged and torn the poor earth!" said Liza-Kate to herself. "She'll never get well as long as she lives." So out of the kindness of her heart she took her butter and rubbed the ruts on both sides of the road, so the wheels wouldn't hurt them so. As she was bending over in her labor of mercy, a cheese fell out of her pocket and rolled down the hill. She said to herself: "I've dragged myself up this hill and I'm blessed if I'll go down again; another cheese can go and get it." So she took a second cheese and rolled it down. When the cheeses didn't come back, she said to herself: "Maybe they're lonesome all by themselves, maybe they're waiting for company," and she sent a third to join them. When all three failed to come back, she thought: "I don't know what to make of it! Hmm. Maybe the third has got lost, I'll send a fourth to call them." But the fourth was no more successful than the third. At the end of her patience, Liza-Kate threw the fifth and sixth cheeses down the hill, and they were the last she had. She stood there awhile, looking down to see if they were coming, but when they didn't come back, she said: "You'd be the right ones to send looking for death, because you certainly take your time. Do you expect me to wait here all day? Not I, I'm going on ahead, you can run after me, you have younger legs than I." Liza-Kate went on and soon caught up with Frederick, who had stopped to wait for her because he was hungry. "Let's have some of that food you brought," he said. She handed him the dry bread. "What about the butter and cheese?" he asked. "Oh, Frederick dear," she said. "I rubbed the ruts in the road with the butter, but the cheeses will be here soon. One of them ran away, so I sent the others after it." "You shouldn't have done that, Liza-Kate," said Frederick. "It was silly of you to rub the butter into the road and to let the cheeses roll down the hill." "How right you are, Frederick dear. You should have told me."

They ate the dry bread together, and Frederick said: "Liza-Kate, did you lock up our house before you left?" "No, Frederick dear, you should have told me." "Then go back home before we go any farther, lock the house, and bring us something else to eat. I'll wait for you here." Liza-Kate went back home and thought: "If Frederick asked for something else to eat, I suppose it's because he doesn't care for butter and cheese, so I'll tie up some dried pears in a towel and bring him a pitcher of vinegar." She bolted the top half of the Dutch door but lifted the lower half off the hinges and hoisted it up on her back, because she thought that if the door were safe the house would be safe too. She took her time going back and said to herself: "This way Frederick will be able to take a good rest." When she finally got there, she said: "Here, Frederick dear, I've brought the door. This way you'll be able to watch it yourself." "Lordy!" he said. "What a clever wife I've got! She takes off the bottom half of the door so anybody that feels like it can go in, and bolts the top half. It's too late for you to go back home again, but as long as you've brought the door, you can keep on carrying it." "I don't mind the door, Frederick dear, but the pears and the vinegar are getting too heavy for me. I think I'll hang them on the door and let the door carry them."

They went into the forest and looked for the thieves but didn't find them. In the end it got dark, so they climbed a tree and decided to spend the night there. But no sooner had they made themselves comfortable in the tree than who should come along but those scamps who make off with things that don't want to go, and find things that haven't been lost. They stopped right under the tree where Frederick and Liza-Kate had settled, and after making a fire, they began to share their spoils. Frederick climbed down the other side of the tree and picked up some big stones; then he climbed back up again. His idea was to hit the thieves with the stones and kill them. But he missed, and the thieves cried out: "It will soon be morning. The wind is blowing the pine cones down." Liza-Kate still had the door on her back. It felt so heavy she thought the dried pears must be to blame, so she said: "Frederick dear, I think I'll have to drop the pears." "No, Liza-Kate, not now," he answered. "They might give us away." "Oh, Frederick dear, I have to, they're just too heavy." "Then drop them for God's sake." The pears fell between the branches and the thieves down below said: "The birds are dropping their droppings." After a while when the door still weighed on her, Liza-Kate said: "Oh, Frederick dear, I think I'll have to pour out the vinegar." "No, Liza-Kate, you mustn't. It might give us away." "Oh, Frederick dear, I have to, it's just too heavy." "Then do it, for God's sake!" She poured out the vinegar, it came down on the thieves, and they said to one another: "The dew is beginning to fall." Finally Liza-Kate thought: "Could it be the door that feels so heavy?" And she said: "Oh, Frederick dear, I think I'll have to throw the door down." "No, Liza-Kate, not now. It might give us away." "Oh, Frederick dear, I have to. It's just too heavy." "No, Liza-Kate, don't you dare." "Oh, Frederick dear, I'm dropping it." "All right," he said angrily. "Then drop it, for God's sake." It fell with a terrible crash and the thieves down below cried out: "The Devil's coming down from the tree!" And they ran away, leaving everything behind them. In the morning when the two of them climbed down, they found all their gold and took it home.

When they were home again, Frederick said: "Now, Liza-Kate, you must get to work and no nonsense." "Yes, Frederick dear, I will; I'll go right out to the field and reap." When Liza-Kate got to the field, she said to herself: "Should I sleep before I reap or eat before I reap? I've got it, I'll eat!" So eat she did, and eating made her sleepy. She was half-asleep when she picked up the scythe, and she cut all her clothes to pieces, her apron, her skirt, and her shift. When she woke up after a long sleep, she was standing there half-naked and she said to herself: "Is it me? Or isn't it me? No, it can't be me!" In the meantime night had fallen. Liza-Kate ran to the village, knocked at her husband's window, and cried out: "Frederick dear." "What is it?" "I'd just like to know if Liza-Kate's there." "Oh yes," he said. "She must be asleep in the other room." "That's good," she said. "Then I must be home already." And she ran away.

Outside the village she met some thieves who had come there to steal. She went up to them and said: "Let me help you steal." The thieves agreed, because they thought she must know her way around the village. Liza-Kate stopped in front of a house and cried: "Folks! Have you got something we can steal?" The thieves said to themselves: "A big help she is!" and decided they'd better get rid of Liza-Kate. "Just outside the village," they said to her, "there's a turnip field belonging to the priest. Go pull some turnips for us." Liza-Kate went to the field and started pulling turnips, but she was so lazy that she crouched and never stood up. A man came by, saw someone rooting around in the turnips and thought it must be the Devil. He ran back to the village and went to the priest's house. "Father," he said, "the Devil's got into your field, and he's pulling up your turnips. "Heavens above!" said the priest. "I've got a game leg or I'd go and drive him away." "I'll carry you on my back," said the man, and he picked him up on his back and carried him out to the field. Just as they got there, Liza-Kate stood up and stretched. "Oh, it's the Devil!" cried the priest, and they both ran away. The priest was so frightened that he ran even faster with his game leg than the man who had carried him with his two sound legs.

60

The Two Brothers

THERE WERE ONCE two brothers, the one rich and the other poor. The rich one was a goldsmith, and he was wicked through and through; the poor one earned his living making brooms, and he was good and upright. The poor one had two children, twin boys who looked as much alike as two drops of water. They went to the rich man's house now and then, and were sometimes given leavings to eat.

One day when the broommaker went to the forest for birch twigs he saw a bird that was all of a golden color and more beautiful than any he had ever seen. He picked up a stone, threw it, and hit the bird, but only a single golden feather fell to the ground, and the bird flew away. The man picked up the feather and took it to his brother, who looked at it and said: "It's pure gold," and gave him a great deal of money for it.

The next day the broommaker climbed a birch tree, meaning to lop off a few branches, and the same bird came flying out. When the man looked about he found a nest with an egg in it, and the egg was gold. He took it home with him and brought it to his brother, who said again: "It's pure gold," and gave him as much as it was worth.

Finally the goldsmith said: "I'd like to have the bird itself." The broommaker went to the woods for the third time. Again he saw the golden bird, this time perched on a branch, and brought it down with a stone. He took it to his brother, who gave him a great deal of money for it. "Now I'll be able to manage," thought the broommaker and went contentedly home.

The goldsmith was crafty and full of knowledge. He knew what sort of bird it was. He called his wife and said: "Roast this bird for me and be careful not to lose one bit of it. I mean to eat it all by myself." This, you see, was no ordinary bird. The wonderful thing about it was that whoever ate its heart and liver would find a gold piece under his pillow every morning. The wife cleaned the bird and put it on a spit to roast. While it was roasting she had to leave the kitchen because of some other work, and just then the broommaker's children came running in. They stopped beside the spit and turned it a few times, and when two little pieces dropped into the pan, one of the boys said: "Let's eat these two little bits; I'm so hungry, and no one will notice." So they popped the two little pieces into their mouths. When the woman came back, she saw they had been eating something and asked: "What have you been eating?" "Some little bits that fell out of the bird," they said. "That was the heart and the liver!" the woman cried in dismay, and not wanting her husband to miss them and get angry, she quickly killed a young cock, took out the heart and liver and put them into the golden bird. When the bird was done, she served it to the goldsmith, who ate every bit of it all by himself. But next morning when he reached under his pillow, expecting to find a gold piece, there was no more gold piece than any other day.

The two children knew nothing of their good fortune. When they got up the next morning, something fell to the floor with a ringing sound, and when they looked, it was two gold pieces. They brought them to their father, who was amazed and said: "How can this be?" But when they found two more the following morning and so on every day, he went to his brother and told him the strange story. The goldsmith saw at once what had happened and knew the children had eaten the golden bird's heart and liver. He was an envious, hardhearted man, and to avenge himself, he said to the father: "Your children are in league with the Devil. Don't take that gold and don't keep them in your house any longer, because he's got them in his power, and if you let him he'll destroy you too." The father was afraid of the Devil. Much as he hated to do it, he took the twins out into the forest and, with a heavy heart, left them there.

The children roamed about looking for the way home, but they couldn't find it and only got more and more lost. Finally they met a hunter, who asked: "Who are you, and where do you come from?" "We're the poor broommaker's children," they replied, and they told him how their father hadn't wanted to keep them at home any longer because there were two gold pieces under their pillow every morning. "There's no great harm in that," said the hunter, "if you go on being good and upright and don't get lazy." The good man took a liking to the children. He had none of his own, so he took them home with him and said: "I shall be your father and bring you up." So he brought them up and taught them how to hunt. They continued to find gold pieces when they got up in the morning, and he kept their gold for them in case they should need it some time in the future.

One day when they were grown to manhood their foster father took them into the forest with him and said: "Today I am going to test your marksmanship; if you pass the test, I shall release you from your apprenticeship and declare you master hunters." They all went to the raised blind and waited a long while, but no game appeared. Then the hunter looked up and saw a flock of wild geese flying in a triangle and said to one of the boys: "Shoot one down from each corner." He did so and passed his test. Soon another flock came along, flying in the form of a figure two. The hunter bade the other brother bring one down from each corner, and he too passed the test. Thereupon the foster father said: "Well done! You are now master hunters." Then the two brothers went to the forest together, took counsel, and agreed on a plan. At dinner that night, they said to their foster father: "We won't touch a single mouthful of food until you grant us a favor." "What is your favor?" he asked. "We have learned our trade," they replied, "and now we must prove ourselves. Let us go out into the world." The old man said happily: "You speak like true hunters; that is just what I was hoping. Go, and I'm sure you will prosper." And then they ate and drank joyfully together.

When the day they had decided on came, the foster father gave each of them a good gun and a dog, and told them to take as many of the saved-up gold pieces as they wished. He went a bit of the way with them and in leave-taking gave them a knife with a shiny bright blade. "If you ever separate," he said, "thrust this knife into a tree at the crossroads. Then if one of you comes back, he will be able to see how his absent brother has fared, for the side facing the way he went will rust when he dies; but as long as he is alive it will remain bright." The two brothers went farther and farther and came to a forest so large they couldn't possibly get through it in a single day. They stopped for the night and ate what they had put in their hunting pouches; then they walked all the second day, and there was still no end to the forest. They had nothing more to eat, and one of the brothers said: "We shall have to kill some game or go hungry." He loaded his gun and looked around. When an old hare came along, he took aim, but the hare cried out:

> "Hunter, hunter, let me live,
> Two little ones to you I'll give,"

and ran off into the thicket and came back with two young hares. They frisked so merrily and were so winsome that the hunters hadn't the heart to kill them. So they kept them and the little hares followed at their heels. Soon a fox crept by. They were going to shoot, but the fox cried out:

> "Hunter, hunter, let me live,
> Two little ones to you I'll give,"

and sure enough, he brought them two young foxes. Again the hunters hadn't the heart to kill them and said they could keep the hares company. It wasn't long before a wolf stepped out of the thicket. The hunters took aim, but the wolf cried:

"Hunter, hunter, let me live,
Two little ones to you I'll give."

The hunters put the two young wolves with the other animals, and they all followed after them. Then came a bear, who wanted to go trotting around a while longer. He cried out:

"Hunter, hunter, let me live,
Two little ones to you I'll give."

The two bears were made to join the others, and now there were eight animals. And who came last of all? A lion appeared, shaking his mane. But that didn't frighten the hunters; they took aim, but just as the others had done, the lion said:

"Hunter, hunter, let me live,
Two little ones to you I'll give."

He too brought his two young ones, and now the hunters had two lions, two bears, two wolves, two foxes, and two hares, who followed them and served them. But that didn't appease their hunger, so they said to the foxes: "Hey, you slyboots, get us something to eat; everyone knows how crafty and cunning you are." They answered: "Not far from here there's a village where we've helped ourselves to a chicken or two. We'll show you the way." So they went to the village, bought themselves something to eat, fed their animals as well, and continued their journey. The foxes knew the region well, for they had spied out all the hen houses, and were always able to tell the hunters which way to go.

They wandered about for a while, but found no employment that would have kept them together. In the end they said: "There's nothing for it. We'll have to separate." After dividing the animals, so that each had a lion, a bear, a wolf, a fox, and a hare, they said good-bye, promised to love each other like true brothers unto death, and thrust the knife their foster father had given them into a tree. Then the one set off eastward, the other westward.

Followed by his animals, the younger brother came to a town that was all hung with black crepe. He went to an inn and asked the innkeeper where he could lodge his animals. The innkeeper put them in a barn with a hole in the wall. The hare crawled out and got himself a cabbage, the fox got himself a hen and when he had eaten it took a cock as well. The wolf, the bear, and the lion were too big for the hole, so the innkeeper had them brought to a place where there was a cow lying in the grass and they ate their fill. Finally, when the animals were all taken care of, the hunter asked the landlord why the whole town was hung with crepe. The innkeeper said: "Because our king's only daughter must die tomorrow." "Is she so very sick?" the hunter asked. "No," said the innkeeper, "she's in the best of health, but she must die all the same." "How can that be?" the hunter asked.

"Not far from the town there's a mountain. A dragon lives there, and every year he must have a spotless maiden, or else he lays the whole country waste. The maidens have all been given to the dragon and only the king's daughter is left, so king's daughter or not, she can't be spared, they're handing her over to the dragon tomorrow." "But why doesn't someone kill this dragon?" the hunter asked. "It's a sad story," said the innkeeper. "A great many knights have tried, and they've all lost their lives. The king has promised his daughter's hand to the man who kills the dragon, and he'll inherit the kingdom as well when the old king dies."

The hunter said nothing more about it, but next morning he took his animals and climbed the dragon's mountain. There was a little church at the top and on the altar there were three goblets filled to the brim, and beside them there was an inscription saying: "He who drains these goblets will become the strongest man on earth. He will wield the sword that is buried outside the door." The hunter did not drink. He went out and found the buried sword, but he couldn't move it. Then he went back in and drained the goblets. Now he was strong enough to pull the sword out of the ground and wield it with ease. When the time came for the maiden to be handed over to the dragon, the king, the marshal, and all the courtiers came with her. From the distance she caught sight of the hunter on the dragon's mountain and thought it was the dragon waiting for her. She didn't want to go up, but the whole town would have been lost, and in the end she resigned herself to her bitter journey. Grieving, the king and the courtiers returned home, but the marshal stayed, for his instructions were to look on from a distance.

When the king's daughter reached the top of the mountain, it wasn't the dragon standing there but the young hunter, who comforted her and promised to save her. Then he took her to the church and locked her in. In a little while the seven-headed dragon swooped down with a powerful roar. He was surprised when he saw the hunter and asked: "What are you doing up here on my hill?" The hunter replied: "I've come to fight you." The dragon said: "Quite a few knights have died up here, and I'll make short shrift of you too." With that he spewed flame from all his seven gullets. The idea was to set the dry grass on fire so the hunter would suffocate in the heat and smoke, but the animals came running up and trampled out the fire. Next the dragon charged, but the hunter swung his sword so swiftly that it sang in the air and cut off three of the monster's heads. Now the dragon was really angry; he rose up in the air, spewing fiery flames, and was just about to swoop down on the hunter when again he swung his sword and cut off three more heads. The dragon sank to the ground, but then, in spite of his weakness, attacked again. With his last strength the hunter cut the monster's tail off, but after that he couldn't fight any more, so he called his animals, who tore the dragon to pieces. Once the battle was over, the hunter opened the church door.

The king's daughter was lying on the floor, for during the fight she had fainted dead away with fear. He carried her out, and when she revived and opened her eyes, he showed her the dismembered dragon and told her she was saved. She was very happy and said: "Then you will be my dearest husband, for my father promised my hand to the man who killed the dragon." To reward the animals she took off her coral necklace and divided it among them. The lion got the golden clasp. To the hunter she gave her handkerchief with her name embroidered on it. The hunter cut the seven tongues out of the dragon's seven heads, wrapped them in the handkerchief, and put them carefully away.

After that he felt quite exhausted with the heat and the fighting, so he said to the king's daughter: "We're both so tired and faint; let's sleep awhile." When she agreed, they lay down on the ground and the hunter said to the lion: "Keep watch. Don't let anyone attack us in our sleep." And they both fell asleep. The lion lay down beside them to keep watch, but he too was tired after the fight, so he called the bear and said: "Lie down beside me, I need to sleep a little. Wake me if anything happens." The bear lay down beside him, but he too was tired, so he called the wolf and said: "Lie down beside me, I need to sleep a little. Wake me if anything happens." The wolf lay down beside him, but he too was tired, so he called the fox and said: "Lie down beside me, I need to sleep a little. Wake me if anything happens." The fox lay down beside him, but he too was tired, so he called the hare and said: "Lie down beside me, I need to sleep a little. Wake me if anything happens." The hare sat down beside him, but the poor hare was tired too and though there was no one he could fall back on, he too fell asleep. So now the king's daughter, the hunter, the lion, the bear, the wolf, the fox, and the hare were all sound asleep.

When the marshal, who had been instructed to look on from a distance, didn't see the dragon fly away with the king's daughter and all was quiet on the hill, he took heart and went up. There lay the dragon torn to pieces, and not far away he saw the king's daughter and a hunter with all his animals, all sound asleep. Being a wicked, godless man, he took his sword, cut the hunter's head off, picked the king's daughter up in his arms, and carried her down the hill. At the bottom she woke with a start and the marshal said: "I've got you in my power. You're to say it was I who killed the dragon." "I can't say that," she replied. "It was a hunter with his animals." At this he drew his sword and made her promise by threatening to kill her if she didn't. Then he took her to the king, who thought the dragon had torn his beloved child to pieces and couldn't get over his joy at seeing her alive. The marshal said: "I killed the dragon and saved your daughter and the whole kingdom. She must therefore be my wife, as you promised." The king asked his daughter: "Is what he says true?" "Oh yes," she said. "I suppose it must be true, but the marriage must not be celebrated for a year and a day." You see, she thought there might be news of her beloved hunter in the meantime.

On the dragon's mountain the animals were still lying asleep beside their dead master. A bumblebee came along and settled on the hare's nose, but the hare brushed it off with his paw and went on sleeping. The bumblebee came back, and again the hare brushed it off and went on sleeping. But then it came back a third time and stung him on the nose and that woke him up. The moment the hare woke up, he

woke the fox and the fox woke the wolf and the wolf woke the bear
and the bear woke the lion. And when the lion woke up and saw that
the king's daughter was gone and his master was dead, he let out a
thundering roar and cried: "Who did this? Bear, why didn't you
wake me?" The bear asked the wolf: "Why didn't you wake me?"
The wolf asked the fox: "Why didn't you wake me?" And the fox
asked the hare: "Why didn't you wake me?" Only the poor hare had
no excuse, and he got all the blame. They were going to pounce on
him, but he pleaded and said: "Don't kill me; I'll bring our master
back to life. I know of a mountain where a root grows, and if you
put that root into anyone's mouth it will cure him of any sickness or
wound. But it takes two hundred hours to get to that mountain." The
lion said: "We expect you back with the root in twenty-four hours."
The hare darted away, and in twenty-four hours he was back with
the root. The lion set the hunter's head in place, the hare put the root
in his mouth, and instantly the parts knitted together, the heart began
to beat, and life returned.

When the hunter woke up, he was dismayed to see that the maiden
was gone. "She must have wanted to get rid of me," he thought. "So
she slipped away while I was asleep." The lion had been in such a
hurry that he put his master's head on back to front, but the hunter
was so busy with his sorrowful thoughts about the king's daughter
that he didn't notice. It was only at midday, when he wanted to eat,
that he noticed his head was facing in the wrong direction. That
puzzled him and he asked the animals what had happened to him in
his sleep. The lion told him how they had all been so tired and fallen
asleep, how on waking they had found him dead with his head cut
off, how the hare had brought the life root, how he, the lion, had put
the head on backward because he had been in too much of a hurry,
but would now correct his mistake. With that he ripped the hunter's
head off again and turned it around, whereupon the hare fastened it
on and healed the wound with the root.

Sadly the hunter wandered from place to place, making his animals
dance for people. When exactly a year had passed, he came to the
same town where he had saved the king's daughter from the dragon,
and this time the whole place was hung with scarlet. "What does this
mean?" he asked the innkeeper. "A year ago the town was hung with
crepe; why is it hung with scarlet now?" The innkeeper replied: "A

year ago our king's daughter was to be handed over to the dragon, but the marshal fought the dragon and killed him, and tomorrow is to be their wedding day. That is why the town was hung with crepe in mourning and that is why it is hung with scarlet today in rejoicing."

At noon on the day appointed for the wedding, the hunter said to the innkeeper: "Would you believe, sir, that I shall eat bread from the king's table right here in your house before the day is out?" The innkeeper replied: "I'll bet a hundred gold pieces that you'll do nothing of the kind." The hunter took the bet and put up a pouch with exactly that many gold pieces in it. Then he called the hare and said: "My dear Lightfoot, go and get me some bread such as the king eats." The hare was the least of the animals, there was no one he could pass the order on to, so he himself had to go. "Oh, oh!" he thought. "If I go running through the streets all by myself, the butcher dogs will all come chasing after me." He had thought right: the dogs came bounding after him with every intention of making holes in his skin. But he gave a jump—did you see him?—and slipped into a sentry box. The soldier didn't even know he was there. The dogs came and tried to get him out, but that wasn't to the soldier's liking and he went after them with the butt of his gun till they ran away howling and yapping. When the hare saw the coast was clear, he raced into the palace, went straight to the king's daughter, sat down under her chair and scratched her foot. She thought it was her dog and said: "Will you go away!" The hare scratched her foot a second time, and again she thought it was her dog and said: "Will you go away!" But the hare was not to be discouraged. When he scratched a third time, she looked down and recognized him by the coral on his neck. She picked him up on her lap, carried him to her room, and said: "Dear hare, what can I do for you?" He replied: "My master who killed the dragon is here. He has sent me to ask you for a loaf of bread such as the king eats." When she heard that, she was delighted. She sent for the baker and ordered him to bring a loaf of bread such as the king ate. "But," said the hare, "the baker must also carry it for me. Then the butcher dogs won't hurt me." The baker carried the bread to the door of the inn. Then the hare stood up on his hind legs, took the loaf in his forepaws, and brought it to his master. The hunter said to the innkeeper: "You see, sir, the hundred gold pieces are mine."

The innkeeper was amazed, but the hunter went on: "Yes, sir, I've got the bread, but now I want to eat some of the king's roast!" The innkeeper said: "That's something I'd like to see," but this time he didn't offer to bet. The hunter called the fox and said: "Foxy, go and get me some roast such as the king eats." The fox knew all the tricks, he slunk along the walls and fences, so the dogs didn't even see him. When he got to the palace he sat down under the king's daughter's chair and scratched her foot. She looked down, recognized the fox by the coral on his neck, and said: "Dear fox, what can I do for you?" He replied: "My master who killed the dragon is here. He sent me to ask for a roast such as the king eats." Thereupon she sent for the cook, and he had to prepare a roast such as the king ate and carry it to the door of the inn. Then the fox took the platter, swished his tail to shoo away the flies that had settled on the roast, and brought it to his master.

The hunter said to the innkeeper: "You see, sir, here I have bread and meat, but now I want trimmings such as the king eats." He called the wolf and said: "Dear wolf, go and get me some trimmings such as the king eats." The wolf went straight to the palace, for he feared no one, and when he got to the king's daughter he plucked at the back of her dress, so she had to look around. She recognized him by the coral on his neck, took him to her room and said: "Dear wolf, what can I do for you?" He replied: "My master who killed the dragon is here. He has sent me to ask for trimmings such as the king eats." So she sent for the cook, who had to prepare trimmings such as the king ate and carry them as far as the door of the inn, where the wolf took the dish from him and brought it to his master.

The hunter said to the innkeeper: "You see, sir, now I have bread, meat, and trimmings, but I also want some pastry such as the king eats." Whereupon he called the bear and said: "Dear bear, you have a sweet tooth. Go and get me some pastry such as the king eats." The bear trotted off to the palace and everybody got out of his way. But when he came to the gate the sentries threatened him with their muskets and wouldn't let him pass. He stood up on his hind legs and boxed their ears with his paws, left and right, so that all the sentries fell flat. Then he went straight to the king's daughter, stood behind her, and gave a soft growl. She looked back, recognized the bear, bade him follow her to her room, and said: "Dear bear, what can I do for you?" He replied: "My master who killed the dragon is here. He sent me to ask for some pastry such as the king eats." She sent for the pastry cook and he had to bake some pastry such as the king ate and carry it to the door. First the bear licked up the sugar plums that had rolled off, then he stood up on his hind legs, took the dish and brought it to his master.

The hunter said to the innkeeper: "You see, sir. Now I have bread, meat, trimmings, and pastry, but now I want wine such as the king drinks." He called the lion and said: "Dear lion, you like to get drunk now and then. Go and get me some wine such as the king drinks." The lion strode down the street, and the people scattered. When he came to the palace guard they tried to bar the way, but he let out one roar and they all ran. He went to the royal apartments and knocked on the door with his tail. The king's daughter opened the door and gave a start when she saw the lion, but then she recognized him by the golden clasp of her necklace, bade him follow her to her room, and said: "Dear lion, what can I do for you?" He replied: "My master who killed the dragon is here. He sent me to ask for wine such as the king drinks." Thereupon she sent for the cupbearer and ordered him to give the lion some wine such as the king drank. The lion said: "I'd better go along to make sure I get the right kind." He went down to the cellar with the cupbearer, and when they got there the cupbearer wanted to draw some of the common wine such as the king's servants drank, but the lion said: "Wait! Let me taste that wine." He drew half a measure and downed it at one gulp. "No," he said. "That's not the right kind." The cupbearer glared at him and went to another barrel that was reserved for the king's marshal. The lion said: "Wait! Let me taste that wine first." He drew half a measure, drank it up, and said: "This is better, but it's still not right." That infuriated the cupbearer and he said: "How can a stupid animal claim to know anything about wine!" The lion struck him a blow behind the ears that made him sit down with a bump, and when he'd picked himself up he didn't say one word but led the lion to a special little cellar where the king's wine, that no one else ever touched, was kept. The lion drew half a measure and tasted it. "This may be the right kind," he said, and told the cupbearer to fill half a dozen bottles, after which they went back up the stairs. When the lion stepped out into the open, he was slightly tipsy and swayed from side to side. The cupbearer had to carry the wine to the door, where the lion took the handle of the basket between his teeth and brought the wine to his master.

The hunter said to the innkeeper: "You see, sir, I have bread, meat, trimmings, pastry, and wine, such as the king has, and now I shall dine with my animals." He sat down and ate and drank, sharing both food and drink with the hare, the fox, the wolf, the bear, and the lion. He was happy, for he saw that the king's daughter still loved him. When the meal was over, he said to the innkeeper: "As you see, sir, I've eaten and drunk as the king eats and drinks; now I shall go to the king's palace and marry the king's daughter." The innkeeper asked: "How can that be, since she already has a betrothed and this is her wedding day!" The hunter took out the handkerchief the king's daughter had given him on the dragon's hill, and the monster's seven tongues were still wrapped in it. "I'll do it," he said, "with the help of what I have here in my hand." The innkeeper looked at the handkerchief. "I'm ready to believe anything," he said, "but not that, and I'll stake my inn on it." The hunter took out a pouch containing a thousand gold pieces, put it on the table, and said: "I'll stake this against your inn."

Meanwhile the king and his daughter were sitting at the royal table. "What did all those animals want of you that kept running in and out of my palace?" he asked her. She replied: "I'm forbidden to say, but you would do well to send for the master of those animals." The king sent a servant to the inn to invite the stranger to the palace, and the servant arrived just after the hunter had made his bet with the innkeeper. The hunter said to the innkeeper: "You see, sir, the king has sent his servant to invite me, but I won't go like this." And to the servant he said: "Kindly ask the king to send me kingly garments and a carriage with six horses and servants to attend me." When the king heard the answer, he said to his daughter: "What shall I do?" She said: "You would do well to send for him, as he asks." So the king sent kingly garments, a carriage with six horses, and servants to attend him. When the hunter saw them coming, he said to the innkeeper: "You see, sir, they've sent for me just as I asked." And he put on the kingly garments, took the handkerchief with the dragon's tongues in it, and rode to the palace. When the king saw him coming, he asked his daughter: "How should I receive

him?" She replied: "You would do well to go out and meet him."
The king went out and met him and led him in and the animals followed. The king showed him to a place on one side of himself and his
daughter. The marshal, as the bridegroom, sat on the other side, but
he didn't recognize the hunter. The dragon's seven heads were
brought in and displayed, and the king said: "The marshal cut these
seven heads off the dragon. I am therefore giving him my daughter to
wife." At that the hunter stood up, opened the seven mouths, and
asked: "What has become of the dragon's seven tongues?" The marshal turned pale with fright and couldn't think of a word to say. Finally in his terror he said: "Dragons have no tongues."

The hunter said: "It would be better if liars had none. Dragon's
tongues are the badges of the dragon-killer." He opened the handkerchief, and there they were, all seven. He put each tongue into the
mouth to which it belonged, and they all fitted perfectly. Then he
took the handkerchief that had the name of the king's daughter
embroidered on it, showed it to her, and asked whom she had given it
to. She replied: "To the man who killed the dragon." He called the
animals, took their strings of coral and the lion's golden clasp, showed
them to the king's daughter and asked whom they belonged to. She
replied: "The necklace and the golden clasp were mine. I divided
them among the animals who had helped to kill the dragon." And the
hunter said: "When I was tired and lay down to rest after the fight,
the marshal came and cut my head off in my sleep. Then he carried
the king's daughter away and claimed he had killed the dragon. That
was a lie and I've proved it with the tongues, the handkerchief, and
the necklace." And then he told his story: how his animals had healed
him with a miraculous root, how he had wandered about with them
for a year, and how, when at last he returned to this same town, he
had learned of the marshal's deception from the innkeeper. The king
asked his daughter: "Is it true that this young hunter killed the
dragon?" "Yes," she replied, "it's true. Now I may speak of the marshal's crime, for it has come to light through none of my doing. You
see, he made me promise to keep silent. That was why I insisted that
the marriage shouldn't be celebrated for a year and a day."

The king summoned twelve councilors and bade them pronounce
judgment on the marshal. Their judgment was that he should be torn
apart by four oxen. So the marshal was executed, and the king gave

his daughter to the hunter and appointed him regent over the whole kingdom. The marriage was celebrated with great rejoicing, the young king sent for his father and his foster father and overwhelmed them with presents. Nor did he forget the innkeeper, but sent for him and said: "You see, sir, I've married the king's daughter, and your inn is mine." The innkeeper replied: "Yes, by right it is." The young king said: "But we shall put mercy before right. Keep your inn. And I also make you a present of the thousand gold pieces."

Now all was well with the young king and queen and they lived happily together. He often went hunting, because he loved it, and his faithful animals went with him. Now not far from the palace there was a forest that was said to be enchanted. The story was that once you went into it you had a hard time getting out. But the young king wanted very much to hunt there and left the old king no peace until he gave him permission. Then he rode out with a large retinue. When he got to the forest, he saw a white doe and said to his men: "Stay here till I get back, I'm going to chase that beautiful doe." So he rode off into the forest and only his animals followed him. His men waited until nightfall. Then when he didn't come back they rode home and said to the young queen: "The young king went off after a white doe in the enchanted forest, and he didn't come back." When she heard that, she was very worried. He, in the meantime, had chased the beautiful doe, but hadn't been able to overtake her. She would seem to be within gunshot, a moment later he would see her bounding away in the distance, and in the end she disappeared altogether.

Seeing that he was deep in the forest, he took his horn and blew it, but there was no answer, for his men didn't hear him. At nightfall he realized that he couldn't return home that day, so he got down from his horse, made a fire under a tree, and prepared to spend the night there. As he was sitting by the fire with his animals, who had lain down beside him, he thought he heard a human voice. He looked around but he couldn't see a thing. Then he heard a moaning that seemed to come from above him, and looking up he saw an old woman sitting in the tree. "Oh, oh, oh," she kept wailing. "I'm so cold!" "Come down and warm yourself if you're cold," he cried out. "No, no," she said. "Your animals would bite me." "Don't worry, grandma," he said. "They won't hurt you. Come on down." But she was a witch and she said: "I'll break off a switch and throw it down.

If you hit them over their backs with it, they won't hurt me." She threw down a switch. He hit them with it, and in an instant they were still, turned to stone. Once the animals were out of the way, the witch jumped down and touched the hunter with the switch, whereupon he too was turned to stone. Then with a peal of laughter she dragged him and the animals to a ditch where there were already quite a few similar stones.

When the young king didn't come home, the queen's worry and fear became greater and greater. Now it so happened that at that very time the other brother, who had gone east when they separated, arrived in the kingdom. After looking in vain for employment, he had wandered from place to place, making his animals dance for people. After a while he thought of the knife they had thrust into a tree trunk when they separated, and decided to go and see how his brother was getting along. When he got to the tree, his brother's side of the blade was half-rusty and half-bright. "That's bad," he thought. "Something must have happened to my brother, but maybe I can still save him, because half the blade is bright." He went westward with his animals and when he reached the town gate a sentry came out and asked him whether he should announce his coming to his wife, the young queen, for she had been dreadfully worried, fearing he had died in the enchanted forest. The young king and his brother, you see, looked so much alike that the sentry mistook the one for the other, and besides the brother also had wild animals running after him. He understood the sentry's mistake and thought: "I'd better pretend to be him; that will make it easier to save him." So he let the sentry take him to the palace, where he was welcomed with great joy. His young wife thought he was her husband and asked why he had stayed away so long. He replied: "I was lost in a forest and I couldn't find my way out." That night he was taken to the royal bed, but he put a two-edged sword between himself and the young queen. She didn't know what to make of it, but she was afraid to ask questions.

He stayed for a few days, finding out all he could about the enchanted forest. Then he said: "I must go hunting there again." The king and the young queen tried to dissuade him but he insisted and rode out with a large retinue. When he came to the forest the same thing happened to him as had happened to his brother. He saw a white doe and said to his men: "Stay here till I get back. I'm going to chase that beautiful doe." He rode into the forest, followed by his animals. But he couldn't overtake the doe and found himself so deep in the forest that he had to spend the night there. Then when he had made a fire, he heard someone moaning above him: "Oh, oh, oh, I'm so cold!" He looked up, saw the same witch in the tree, and said: "Come down and warm yourself if you're so cold." "No, no!" she cried. "Your animals would bite me." And he said: "Don't worry, grandma. They won't hurt you." And she cried: "I'll break off a switch and throw it down. If you hit them with it, they won't hurt me." When the hunter heard that, he didn't trust the old woman. "I won't hit my animals," he said. "Come on down or I'll climb up and get you." "Don't make me laugh!" she said. "You can't do a thing to me." And he answered: "If you won't come down, I'll shoot you down." "Go ahead and shoot," she said. "I'm not afraid of your bullets." He took aim and fired, but the witch was proof against lead bullets. She laughed aloud and cried out: "You can't hit me!"

But the hunter knew what was what. He tore three silver buttons off his jacket and loaded his gun with them, for against silver her magic was powerless, and the moment he pulled the trigger she came hurtling down with a scream. He put his foot on her and said: "You old witch, if you don't tell me this minute where my brother is I'll pick you up in both hands and throw you into the fire." She was so terrified that she begged for mercy and said: "He and his animals are lying in a ditch. They have been turned to stone." He made her take him to the ditch and threatened her. "You old baboon!" he said. "You just bring my brother and all the other creatures lying here back to life, or it's into the fire with you!" She took a switch and touched the stones. His brother and the animals came to life. And many others as well, merchants, craftsmen, shepherds, stood up, thanked the hunter for setting them free, and went home. The twin brothers hugged and kissed in their joy at seeing each other again. They seized the witch, tied her and put her on the fire. When she had burned, the forest opened of its own accord and the royal palace could be seen in the distance, perhaps four or five miles away.

The two brothers went back together and told each other their stories on the way. When the younger said he was regent over the whole country, the other said: "So I found out, for when I arrived at the palace and was mistaken for you, royal honors were shown me. The young queen took me for her husband, and I had to sit beside her at table and sleep in your bed." When the young king heard that, he became so jealous and angry that he drew his sword and cut his brother's head off. But when his brother lay there dead and he saw the red blood flowing, he was overcome with regret. "My brother saved me," he cried out, "and this is how I've rewarded him." He wept and wailed, but then his hare came up to him and offered to get some of the life root. He darted away and brought it back in time. The dead brother was brought back to life and wasn't even aware of the scar.

Then they walked on, and the younger brother said: "You look like me, you have kingly garments like me, and the animals follow you as they do me. Let's go in by the two opposite gates and appear before the old king at the same time from opposite directions." So they separated, and at the same moment two sentries, one from each gate, came to the old king and announced that the young king with the animals had returned from the hunt. The old king said: "That's impossible, the two gates are an hour's walk apart." But just then the two brothers entered the courtyard from two opposite directions, and both climbed the stairs at the same time. The king said to his daughter: "Tell me which is your husband. They look exactly alike, and I don't know." She couldn't say and she was quite bewildered, but in the end she remembered the necklace she had given the animals. She looked them over and soon found her golden clasp on one of the lions. "The one this lion follows is my right husband," she cried happily. The young king laughed and said: "Yes, he is indeed the right one." They sat down to table together and ate and drank and made merry. That night when the young king went to bed, his wife asked: "Why did you put a double-edged sword into the bed these last few nights? I thought you were going to kill me." Then he knew how faithful his brother had been.

61
Farmer Little

THERE WAS A VILLAGE where all the farmers were rich and there was only one poor one, whom they called Farmer Little. He didn't even own a cow, much less the money to buy one with, though he and his wife were dying to have one. One day he said to her: "Listen, wife, I have a good idea. You know your cousin the carpenter? We'll get him to make us a wooden calf and paint it brown, so it looks like any other calf. It's sure to grow up sooner or later, and then we'll have a cow." The idea appealed to his wife, so their cousin the carpenter sawed and planed till the calf was finished, and painted it just right. He'd made it to stand with its head down, as if it were grazing.

When the cows were driven out to pasture the next morning, Farmer Little called the cowherd and said: "Look, I've got a calf here, but he's small and needs to be carried." "All right," said the cowherd, whereupon he picked the calf up in his arms, carried it out to the pasture, and set it down in the grass. The little calf stood there the whole time as if it were grazing, and the cowherd said: "That calf will be running around soon. Lord, how it eats even now!" That evening before driving the herd home again, he said to the calf: "If you're strong enough to stand here filling your belly, you're strong enough to go back on your own four legs. You won't catch me carrying you." Now Farmer Little was standing outside his house waiting for his calf. When the cowherd drove the cows through the village and the calf was missing, he asked what had become of him. The cowherd replied: "He's still out there, grazing. He didn't want to stop and come home with the rest of us." "That won't do," said Farmer Little. "I want my calf back." They went out to the pasture together, but someone had stolen the little calf, and it was gone. "It must have gone astray," said the cowherd. But Farmer Little said: "Don't give me that!" And he took the cowherd to the mayor who, to punish him for his negligence, ordered him to give Farmer Little a cow in place of the calf that had run away.

Now Farmer Little and his wife had the cow they'd been wanting so long. They were ever so happy, but they had no feed and couldn't give her anything to eat, so they had to have her slaughtered. They salted the meat, and Farmer Little set out for town, thinking he'd sell the hide and buy a new calf with the proceeds. On his way he passed a mill, and there sat a raven with broken wings. Feeling sorry for the bird, Farmer Little picked it up and wrapped it in the hide. Then a storm blew up, the wind howled and the rain came down in buckets. He couldn't go on, so he went into the mill and asked for shelter. The miller's wife was alone in the house. She said to Farmer Little: "Lie down in the straw over there," and she gave him bread and cheese. Farmer Little ate his bread and cheese and lay down with the hide beside him. "He was tired," the woman thought, "he must be asleep by now." Just then the priest arrived, and the miller's wife was very glad to see him. "My husband is out," she said, "so we can have a feast." Farmer Little pricked up his ears. When he heard the word "feast" he was furious with her for fobbing him off with bread and cheese. She proceeded to serve four things: roast meat, salad, cake, and wine.

Just as they were sitting down to eat, there was a knock at the door. "Heavens!" cried the woman. "There comes my husband!" Quick, she hid the roast meat in the oven, the wine under the pillow, the salad on the bed, the cake under the bed, and the priest in the hall cupboard. Then she let her husband in and said: "Thank the Lord you're back. What a terrible storm! You'd think the world was coming to an end!" The miller saw Farmer Little lying in the straw and asked: "What's he doing here?" "Oh," said his wife, "the poor devil came in the pouring rain and asked for shelter, so I gave him some bread and cheese and told him he could lie in the straw." "No harm in that," said the miller, "but quick, get me something to eat." "There's nothing but bread and cheese," she said. "Anything you've got will suit me," said the miller. "Bread and cheese will be fine."

Then he looked at Farmer Little and said: "Get up. Have another bite to eat with me." Farmer Little didn't have to be asked twice. He got up and ate. After a while the miller saw the hide with the raven in it lying on the ground and asked: "What have you got

there?" Farmer Little replied: "I've got a fortuneteller in there."
"Could he prophesy something for me?" the miller asked. "Why
not?" said Farmer Little. "But he only tells four things, he keeps the
fifth to himself." The miller was curious and said: "Get him to prophesy." Farmer Little squeezed the raven's head till he croaked and
went *"krr krr."* "What did he say?" the miller asked. "In the first
place he says there's wine under the pillow." "Bless my soul!" said the
miller, and went over to the pillow and found the wine. "What's
next?" he asked. Farmer Little made the raven croak again and said:
"In the second place, he says there's roast meat in the oven." "Bless my
soul!" said the miller, and went over to the oven and found the roast
meat. Farmer Little made the raven prophesy again: "In the third
place, he says there's salad on the bed." "Bless my soul!" said the
miller, and went over and found the salad. Farmer Little squeezed the
raven once more, made him croak, and said: "In the fourth place, he
says there's cake under the bed." "Bless my soul!" cried the miller,
looked under the bed, and found the cake.

The two of them sat down at the table together. The miller's wife,
who was frightened to death, went to bed and took all the keys with
her. The miller wanted to hear about the fifth thing, but Farmer Little said: "First let's quietly eat the other four, because the fifth is
something bad." When they had finished eating, they bargained over
the price the miller would pay for the fifth prophecy and finally
agreed on three hundred talers. Farmer Little squeezed the raven's
head again, and he gave a loud croak. "What did he say?" the miller
asked. Farmer Little replied: "He said the Devil's got into the hall
cupboard." "Well," said the miller, "I won't have the Devil staying
in my cupboard," and he unbolted the back door. His wife had to
hand over the key and Farmer Little opened the cupboard. The priest
ran out as fast as he could, and the miller said: "The raven was right,
I saw the black villain with my own eyes." Next morning at daybreak Farmer Little slipped away with the three hundred talers.

Back home Farmer Little gradually began to spread out. He built
himself a fine house and the other farmers said: "Farmer Little seems
to have been where the golden snow falls and people take money
home by the shovelful." Farmer Little was haled before the mayor
and asked where his wealth came from. He replied: "I took my cow's
hide to town and sold it for three hundred talers." When the farmers

heard that, they thought it was a golden opportunity and they all jumped at it. They ran home, killed their cows, skinned them, and hurried to town in their eagerness to sell their hides at such a splendid profit. The mayor said: "My maid must go first." When she got to town she went to see the merchant, but he gave her only three talers for a hide; and when the others came in, he didn't even give them that much. "What do you expect me to do with all these hides?" he said.

The farmers were furious with Farmer Little for hoodwinking them, and denounced him to the mayor as a swindler. Unanimously the village council sentenced the innocent Farmer Little to die by being rolled into the water in a leaky barrel. Farmer Little was led away and a priest was brought to say a mass for his soul. The others left them alone, and when Farmer Little looked at the man, he recognized the priest who had been with the miller's wife and said: "I got you out of that cupboard, so you get me out of this barrel." The shepherd was just passing with a flock of sheep and Farmer Little happened to know that the shepherd had a great longing to be mayor. So he shouted at the top of his lungs: "No, I won't do it! The whole world can ask me, but I won't do it!" When he heard that, the shepherd went over to him and asked: "What's this all about? What won't you do?" Farmer Little replied: "They promise to make me mayor if I get into this barrel, but I won't do it." The shepherd said: "If that's all it takes to be mayor, I'll gladly get into the barrel." "Good," said Farmer Little. "Just get in, and they'll make you mayor." The shepherd was delighted and got into the barrel. Farmer Little put the lid on, took the shepherd's flock and drove it away. The priest went to the village council and told them the mass had been said. Whereupon they all came and rolled the barrel toward the water. As it began to roll, the shepherd cried out: "I'll be glad to be mayor." They thought it was Farmer Little shouting and said: "We don't doubt it. But first you'll take a look around down there." And they rolled the barrel into the water.

Then the farmers started for home. When they got to the village, who should come along but Farmer Little, cheerfully driving a flock of sheep. The farmers were amazed. "Farmer Little!" they cried. "Where have you come from? Have you come out of the water?" "That's right," said Farmer Little. "I sank deeper and deeper until I got to the bottom. Then I kicked the barrel open and crawled out. Beautiful meadows down there, with lots of lambs grazing on them, so I brought a flock of them back with me." "Are there any left?" the farmers asked. "Plenty," said Farmer Little, "more than you have any use for." The farmers decided to go after the sheep; each of them would bring back a flock. "I'll go first," said the mayor, and they all went down to the water together. Just then the blue sky happened to be full of the little fleecy clouds known as lambkins, and they were reflected in the water. "Look!" cried the farmers. "Look at the sheep on the bottom!" The mayor elbowed his way to the front and said: "I'll go down first and look around; if it's promising, I'll call you." He jumped in with a splash. They heard a gurgle from the water and thought he was calling, "Come!" whereupon the whole lot of them rushed in after him. After that there was no one left in the village. Farmer Little inherited everything and became a rich man.

62

The Queen Bee

TWO KING'S SONS once went in search of adventure, fell into a wild, dissolute way of life, and never came home again. Their youngest brother, who was known as Blockhead, went looking for them, but when at last he found them, they scoffed at him for supposing that a simpleton like him could make his way in the world, when they, who were so much more intelligent, had failed completely. The three of them went on together and after a while they came to an anthill. The two eldest wanted to crush it and watch the little ants scurry about in terror and carry their eggs away, but Blockhead said: "Leave them alone. I won't let you molest them." A little farther on they came to a lake with a great many ducks swimming on it. The two elder brothers wanted to catch some and roast them, but Blockhead stopped them. "Leave those ducks alone," he said. "I won't let you kill them." Finally they came to a beehive with so much honey in it that it ran down the tree trunk. The two elder brothers wanted to smother the bees by making a fire at the foot of the tree, and take the honey. But again Blockhead stopped them, saying: "Leave those bees alone, I won't let you hurt them."

Later on the three brothers came to a castle. When they went in, there were stone horses in the stables and there wasn't a human being to be seen. They passed through all the rooms until at the very end they came to a door with three locks, and in the middle of the door there was a little window. In this room they saw a little gray man sitting at a table. They called out to him, once, twice, but he didn't hear them. When they called a third time, he got up, unlocked the door and came out. He didn't say one word, but led them to a richly spread table, and then, when they had eaten and drunk, he showed each of them to a separate bedroom. Next morning the little gray man came to the eldest, beckoned, and led him to a stone tablet with an inscription listing three tasks that had to be performed if the castle was to be freed from the spell. The first was that the king's daughter's pearls, a thousand of them, were lying in the moss in the woods, and they had to be gathered up before sunset, and if a single one was missing, the seeker would be turned to stone. The eldest brother went and searched all day, but when the day was over he had found only a hundred, and, just as the tablet said, he was turned to stone. The next day the second brother tried his hand at it; but he fared hardly better than the first: he found only two hundred pearls, and was turned to stone.

Then at last it was Blockhead's turn. He searched in the moss, but the work of finding the pearls was too hard, and it went too slowly. He sat down on a stone and began to cry. While he was sitting there, the king of the ants whose lives he had saved came along with five thousand ants, and it wasn't long before the little creatures had found all the pearls and piled them up in one place.

The second task was to fish the key to the king's daughter's bedroom out of the sea. When Blockhead got to the shore, the ducks he had saved came swimming, dived down, and brought up the key. The third task was the hardest, to pick out the youngest and nicest of the king's three daughters, who were lying asleep. All three were exactly alike, the only difference was that before falling asleep they had eaten three different kinds of sweets—the eldest a lump of sugar, the second a drop or two of syrup, and the youngest a spoonful of honey. The queen of the bees that Blockhead had saved from fire came along, tasted the lips of all three, and finally stopped at the mouth that had eaten honey. That showed the king's son which was the right one. With that the magic spell was broken, all the people in the castle were wakened from their sleep, and the ones who had been turned to stone regained their human form. Blockhead married the youngest and nicest daughter and became king after her father's death. His two brothers married her two sisters.

63

The Three Feathers

THERE WAS ONCE A KING who had three sons. Two were clever, but the third was called Blockhead because he was simple and hardly opened his mouth. When the king became old and feeble and thought his end was near, he didn't know which of his sons to leave his kingdom to. So he called them together and said: "Go out and search, and the one who brings me the finest carpet shall be king after my death." And to make sure there would be no quarrel among them, he led them to a place outside the castle, blew three feathers into the air, and said: "Go as they fly." One feather flew east and another west, while the third flew straight ahead but not far, and soon fell to the ground. The first brother went right, the second brother went left, and they scoffed at Blockhead who had to stop where the third feather had fallen.

Blockhead sat down. He was very sad. Suddenly he caught sight of a trap door not far from the feather. He lifted it up, found a stairway and went down. At the bottom there was another door. He knocked, and heard someone inside calling:

> "Little green maid
> Perched on a log,
> Hobgoblin's dog,
> Wobblin' goblin,
> Quick, go and see
> What that knocking can be."

The door opened and there sat a big fat toad, surrounded by a crowd of little toads. The fat toad asked him what he wanted, and he replied: "I'm looking for the finest and most beautiful carpet in all the world." Whereupon she called one of the young toads and said:

> "Little green maid
> Perched on a log,
> Hobgoblin's dog,
> Wobblin' goblin,
> That box you see,
> Bring it here to me."

The young toad brought the box, the fat toad opened it, took out a carpet so fine that nothing like it could have been woven on the earth above, and gave it to Blockhead. He thanked her and went back up the stairs.

The two elder brothers had thought the youngest was much too stupid to find anything, much less bring it back. "Why," they said, "should we go to the trouble of searching?" So they stopped the first shepherdess they met, took the crude shawl she had on, and brought it back to the king. Blockhead had just arrived with his beautiful carpet. The king was amazed when he saw it and said: "By right the kingdom should go to the youngest." But the two others gave their father no peace. They said it just wouldn't do for Blockhead, who was a fool in every respect, to be king, and begged their father to set another task. At length he said: "The one who brings me the most beautiful ring shall inherit the kingdom." Again he took them outside, blew three feathers into the air, and bade them follow the feathers. Again the two eldest went east and west. Blockhead's feather flew straight ahead and fell near the trap door. Again he went down to the fat toad, and this time he told her he needed the most beautiful ring on earth. She called for her big box, took out a ring which was set with glittering gems and was so beautiful that no goldsmith on earth could have made it, and gave it to Blockhead. The two elder brothers laughed at the thought of Blockhead looking for a golden ring. They went to no trouble at all but just hammered the nails out of the rim of an old cartwheel and brought it to the king. When Blockhead produced his gold ring, his father said again: "The kingdom goes to him." But the two elder brothers kept nagging at their father until he set a third task. The kingdom, he said, would go to the one who brought back the most beautiful maiden. Again he blew the three feathers into the air and again they flew as they had before.

Blockhead went straight to the fat toad and said: "I need the most beautiful maiden in the world." "Well, well!" said the toad. "The most beautiful maiden in the world isn't here right now, but you shall have her all the same." Whereupon she gave him a hollowed-out carrot with six mice harnessed to it. Blockhead asked her sadly: "What good will this do me?" The toad replied: "Just take one of my little toads and put her inside." He picked one out at random and put her into the carriage, and no sooner was she in it than she turned into a beautiful maiden, the carrot turned into a carriage, and the six mice turned into horses. Whereupon he kissed her, lashed the horses into a gallop, and brought her to the king. His brothers turned up a little later. They hadn't bothered to look for a beautiful maiden, but had taken the first peasant wenches they came across. When the king saw them, he said: "The kingdom will go to the youngest after my death." But again the two eldest fussed and fumed. "We can't let Blockhead be king!" they cried, and insisted that the brother whose wife could jump through a ring that was hanging in the middle of the hall should be chosen. They thought: "These peasant women are strong enough to do it; the sensitive damsel will only kill herself if she tries." Again the old king consented. When the two peasant women jumped, they managed to get through the ring, but they were so clumsy they fell and broke their big, thick arms and legs. Then the fair lady Blockhead had brought home jumped, and she glided through the ring as lightly and easily as a deer. After that there was nothing the brothers could say. The crown went to Blockhead, and he reigned wisely for many years.

64

The Golden Goose

THERE WAS ONCE a man who had three sons, and the youngest, who was called Blockhead, was despised, scoffed at, and put down on every occasion. One day the eldest son decided to go into the forest and cut wood, and before he went his mother gave him a fine pancake and a bottle of wine to stave off his hunger and thirst. When he got to the forest, he met a little old gray man, who bade him good day and said: "I'm so hungry and thirsty. Give me a piece of that pancake you have in your pocket, and a drink of your wine." The clever son said: "If I give you my cake and wine, I won't have any for myself. Don't bother me." And left the little man standing there. He started to chop a tree down, and a moment later he missed his aim, his ax hit him in the arm, and he had to go home and get bandaged. That was the little gray man's doing.

Next the second son went into the forest, and his mother gave him a pancake and a bottle of wine, as she had the eldest. He too met the little old gray man, who asked him for a piece of his pancake and a drink of his wine. But the second son too replied cleverly: "What I give you I won't have for myself. Don't bother me." And left the little man standing there. He didn't have long to wait for his punishment. After the first few strokes at the tree he hit himself in the leg and had to be carried home.

Then Blockhead said: "Father, let me go out and cut wood." His father replied: "Your brothers have tried it and hurt themselves, you'd better leave it alone, you don't know the first thing about wood cutting." But Blockhead begged and pleaded until finally the father said: "All right, go ahead, if you get hurt it will teach you to know better." His mother gave him a pancake made of water and ashes and a bottle of sour beer. When he got to the forest, he too met the little old gray man, who greeted him and said: "I'm so hungry and thirsty. Give me a piece of your pancake and a drink out of your bottle." Blockhead replied: "All I've got is an ash cake and some sour beer; if that suits you, come sit down and have some." They sat down, and when Blockhead brought out his ash cake, it was a fine pancake and the sour beer was good wine. They ate and drank, and when they had finished the little man said: "Because you have a good heart and cheerfully share what's yours, I'll give you good luck. See that old tree over there? Cut it down and you'll find something in the roots." Then the little man left him.

Blockhead cut the tree down, and when it fell there was a goose in the roots with feathers of pure gold. He picked the goose up in his arms and went to an inn for the night. The innkeeper had three daughters, and when they saw the goose they were curious to know more about the strange bird. They all coveted the golden feathers, and the eldest thought: "I'll surely get a chance to pluck one of them." When Blockhead went off to bed, she grabbed the goose's wing, but her finger and hand stuck fast. A little later the second came along, and her only thought was to pluck a golden feather. But no sooner had she touched her sister than she stuck fast. Finally, the third came in with the same purpose. The two others cried out: "Keep away, for heaven's sake, keep away!" But she didn't see why she should keep away. "Why shouldn't I go where they are?" she thought, and ran over to them, touched her sister and stuck fast. So they all had to spend the night with the goose.

Next morning Blockhead picked the goose up in his arms and started off. He paid no attention to the three girls who were hanging on to it, and they had to keep running after him, now left, now right, whichever way he happened to go. As they were trotting down a country lane, the parson came along. When he saw the procession he said: "Horrid girls, you ought to be ashamed! Why are you chasing this young fellow? Do you think it's nice?" With that he grabbed the youngest by the hand and tried to pull her back, but the moment he touched her, he too stuck fast and had to run along with the others. In a little while the sexton came by. When he saw the pastor running after the three girls, he cried out in amazement: "Hey, Reverend, where are you going so fast? Don't forget, we've got a christening today." He ran after him, took him by the sleeve, and stuck fast. As the five of them trotted along, they passed two peasants coming from the fields with their hoes. The parson called to the peasants for help, but no sooner had they touched the sexton than they stuck fast, and now there were seven running after Blockhead and his goose.

Later in the day he came to a city where there was a king whose daughter was so solemn that no one could make her laugh. He had decreed that the first man to make her laugh should have her for his wife. When Blockhead heard that, he went before the king's daughter with his goose and its retinue, and when she saw the seven of them running along in a chain, she burst out laughing, and it looked as if she'd never stop. So Blockhead claimed her as his wife, but the king didn't approve of him as a son-in-law and raised all sorts of objections. Finally he said that before Blockhead could marry his daughter he'd have to bring him a man who could drink up a whole cellar full of wine. Blockhead thought the little gray man might help him and went out into the forest. In the place where he had chopped the tree down he saw a very unhappy-looking man sitting on the ground. Blockhead asked him what the trouble was, and the man replied: "I've got such a thirst that I can't quench it. Cold water doesn't agree with me. I've just drunk up a whole barrel of wine, but that's only a drop in the bucket." "I can help you," said Blockhead. "Come with me and you'll get your fill." Thereupon he led him to the king's cellar, and the man set to work on the great hogsheads. He drank and drank till his sides ached, and before the day was out he had drained the whole cellar. Again Blockhead claimed his bride, but the king was so reluctant to let this dolt, whom everybody called Blockhead, marry his daughter, that he thought up a new condition: now he wanted a man who could eat a whole mountain of bread. Blockhead didn't have to think very long. He went out into the forest, and in the very same place found a man who was tightening a belt around his belly and making the most miserable face. "I've eaten a whole ovenful of bread," the man said, "but with a hunger like mine that's as good as nothing. My belly is as empty as ever and if I didn't strap it tight my hunger would kill me." Blockhead was glad to hear it. "Come with me," he said, "and you'll eat your fill." He took him to the courtyard of the king's palace. All the flour in the whole kingdom had been brought there and baked into a huge mountain of bread. But the man from the forest stepped right up and began to eat, and in a single day the whole mountain was gone.

Blockhead claimed his bride for the third time, but the king thought up still another condition. Now he wanted a ship that could sail both on land and on water. "But as soon as you bring me that ship you shall have my daughter," he said. Blockhead went straight into the forest, and there sat the little gray man he had given his pancake to. "I've drunk and I've eaten for you," he said, "and I'll give you your ship too. I'm doing all this because you were kind to me." So he gave him the ship that sailed both on land and on water. When the king saw it, he couldn't deny him his daughter any longer, and the marriage was celebrated. At the king's death Blockhead inherited the kingdom and lived happily with his wife for many years.

65
Thousandfurs

THERE WAS ONCE a king, whose wife had golden hair and was so beautiful that there was none on earth to compare with her. It so happened that she fell ill and when she felt she was about to die, she called the king and said: "If you decide to marry after my death, don't take anyone who isn't as beautiful as I am and who hasn't got golden hair like mine. You must promise me that." When the king had promised, she closed her eyes and died.

For a long while the king was inconsolable and had no thought of taking a second wife. At length his councilors said: "There's no help for it; the king must marry, for we must have a queen." Messengers were sent far and wide to look for a bride in every way as beautiful as the dead queen. But in the whole world there was none to be found, and even if one had been found she would not have had such golden hair. So they came back empty-handed.

Now the king had a daughter who was every bit as beautiful as her dead mother, and she had the same golden hair. One day when she had grown up, the king looked at her and saw that she resembled his dead wife in every way. He fell passionately in love with her and said to his councilors: "I am going to marry my daughter, for she is the living image of my dead wife, and I shall never find another like her."

When they heard that, the councilors were aghast. "A father cannot marry his daughter," they said. "God forbids it. No good can come of sin, and the whole kingdom would be dragged down to perdition with you." The daughter was even more horrified when she heard of her father's decision, but she still hoped to dissuade him. She said to him: "Before I consent to your wish I must have three dresses, one as golden as the sun, one as silvery as the moon, and one as glittering as the stars. In addition, you must give me a cloak made of a thousand kinds of fur, a snippet of which must be taken from every animal in your kingdom." "He can't possibly get me all that," she thought, "and maybe trying will distract him from his wicked plan." But the king was not to be discouraged. The most accomplished maidens in his kingdom were made to weave the dresses, one as golden as the sun, one as silvery as the moon, and one as glittering as the stars, and his hunters were sent out to capture all the animals in the kingdom and take a snippet of fur from each one. When the cloak of a thousand furs was ready, the king spread it out in front of her and said: "The wedding will be celebrated tomorrow."

When the king's daughter saw there was no hope of changing her father's mind, she decided to run away. That night when the whole palace was asleep, she got up and took three things from among her treasures: a gold ring, a little golden spinning wheel, and a golden bobbin. Then she put her three dresses—the sun dress, the moon dress, and the star dress—into a nutshell, wrapped herself in her cloak of a thousand furs, and blackened her face and hands with soot. After commending herself to God, she slipped out of the palace, and walked all night until she came to a large forest. By that time she was tired, so she crawled into a hollow tree and fell asleep.

The sun rose and she went on sleeping, and she was still asleep when the sun was high. Now it so happened that the king to whom this forest belonged was out hunting. When his dogs came to the tree they sniffed and ran around it and barked. The king said to his hunters: "Go and see what sort of animal is hiding there." The hunters did his bidding. After a while they came back and said: "There's a strange animal in that tree, we've never seen anything like it. It has a thousand different kinds of fur, and it's lying there fast asleep." The king said: "See if you can catch it alive, then tie it up, put it in the wagon, and we'll take it home with us." When the hunters grabbed hold of the girl, she woke up in terror and cried out: "I'm a poor child, abandoned by my father and mother. Have pity on me and take me home with you." "Thousandfurs," they said, "you'll be just right for the kitchen. Come with us, you can sweep up the ashes." And they put her into the wagon and drove her to the royal palace. There they settled her in a den under the stairs, where the daylight never entered, and said: "This will be your bedroom and living room, Thousandfurs." After that she was sent to the kitchen, where she was made to do all the nasty work, hauling wood and water, keeping up the fires, plucking fowls, cleaning vegetables, and sweeping up the ashes.

For a long while Thousandfurs led a wretched life. Ah, my fair princess, what's to become of you! But one day a ball was given at the palace, and she said to the cook: "Could I go up and watch for a little while? I'll stand outside the door." The cook replied: "Yes, why not? Just so you're back in half an hour to sweep up the ashes." She picked up her little oil lamp and went to her den, took off her fur cloak, and washed the soot from her face and hands, revealing her great beauty. Then she opened the nutshell and took out the dress that shone like the sun. As she walked up to the ballroom, all the courtiers stepped aside for her, for none of them recognized her and they thought she must be a king's daughter. The king came up to her, gave her his hand and danced with her, all the while thinking in his heart: "Never have my eyes beheld anyone so beautiful." When the dance was over, she curtseyed, and before the king knew it she had vanished, no one knew where. The guards who were posted outside the palace were called and questioned, but none had seen her.

She had run to her den, quickly taken her dress off, blackened her face and hands, and put on her fur cloak: she was Thousandfurs again. She went to the kitchen to do her work and sweep up the ashes, but the cook said: "Let that go until tomorrow, and make the king's soup instead, because I'd like to go up and look on for a while. But don't drop any hairs in it or you won't get any more to eat." The cook went upstairs and Thousandfurs made bread soup for the king as best she knew how. When it was done she brought her gold ring from her den and put it in the dish. When the ball was over the king sent for his soup, and it tasted so good that he thought he had never eaten better. When he got to the bottom of the tureen, he saw a gold ring and couldn't imagine how it had got there. He sent for the cook, who was terrified and said to Thousandfurs: "You must have dropped a hair in the soup; if you have, you'll be beaten!" When he appeared before the king, the king asked him who had made the soup. The cook replied: "I did." "That's not true," said the king, "because it wasn't made in the usual way and it was much better." The cook said: "I have to admit I didn't make it. Thousandfurs made it." "Send her to me," said the king.

When Thousandfurs appeared before the king, he asked: "Who are you?" "I'm a poor child who's lost her father and mother." "What is your work in my palace?" he asked, and she replied: "I'm good for nothing but having boots thrown at my head." "And where did you get the ring that was in my soup?" She replied: "I don't know anything about any ring." So the king got nothing out of her and had to send her back to the kitchen.

Some time later there was another ball. Again Thousandfurs asked the cook for leave to look on. He replied: "Yes, but be back in half an hour to make the king the bread soup he's so fond of." She ran to her den, washed herself quickly, took the dress that was as silvery as the moon out of the nutshell, and put it on. When she went upstairs, she looked like a king's daughter. The king came up to her and was glad to see her again. A dance was just starting, so they danced together. When it was over, she vanished again so quickly the king couldn't see where she went. She ran down to her den, made herself into a furry animal again, and went to the kitchen to make bread soup. When the cook went upstairs, she took the little golden spinning wheel and put it in the tureen, and the soup was poured over it. Then the soup was brought to the king and he ate it. He liked it as well as he had the first time and he sent for the cook, who had to admit once again that Thousandfurs had made it. Again she appeared before the king, but again she said she was good for nothing but having boots thrown at her head and didn't know anything about any golden spinning wheel.

When the king gave a ball for the third time, it was just the same as before. The cook said: "Thousandfurs, you must be a witch. You always put something in the soup that makes the king like it better than my soup." But when she begged and pleaded, he let her go for the usual length of time. She put on the dress that glittered like the stars and stepped into the hall. Again the king danced with the beautiful girl and thought she had never been so beautiful. While they were dancing he slipped a gold ring on her finger without her noticing. He had given orders that the dance should last a long time. When it was over, he tried to hold on to her hands, but she tore herself loose and ran off into the crowd so quickly that she vanished before his eyes. She ran as fast as she could to her den under the stairs, but as she had stayed too long, more than half an hour, she couldn't take off her beautiful dress. She just threw the fur cloak over it, and in her haste she didn't smear all her fingers with soot—one of them stayed white. She ran to the kitchen, made bread soup for the king, and when the cook went upstairs put the golden bobbin into it. When the king found the bobbin at the bottom, he sent for Thousandfurs. As she stood before him, he caught sight of her white finger and saw the ring he had slipped on it while they were dancing. Thereupon he seized her hand and held it fast. When she tried to tear herself away, her fur cloak opened a little, and he caught the glitter of her starry dress. He tore off her cloak, uncovering her golden hair, and there she stood in all her glory, unable to hide any longer. When she had washed the soot and ashes from her face, she was more beautiful than anyone who had ever been seen on earth. The king said: "You are my dearest bride. We shall never part." Then the wedding was celebrated and they lived happily until they died.

66

Bunny Rabbit's Bride

A WOMAN AND HER DAUGHTER had a lovely garden full of cabbages. During the winter a bunny rabbit came into the garden and ate up all the cabbages. The woman says to her daughter: "Go out in the garden and chase the bunny rabbit away." The little girl says to the bunny rabbit: "Shoo, shoo, bunny rabbit! You're eating up all our cabbages." Says the bunny rabbit: "Come, little girl, sit down on my bunny rabbit's tail and come with me to my bunny rabbit's hut." The little girl doesn't feel like it.

Next day the bunny rabbit comes again and eats some more cabbages and the woman says to her daughter: "Go out in the garden and chase the bunny rabbit away." The little girl says to the bunny rabbit: "Shoo, shoo, bunny rabbit! You're eating up all our cabbages." Says the bunny rabbit: "Come, little girl, sit down on my bunny rabbit's tail and come to my bunny rabbit's hut." The little girl doesn't feel like it.

On the third day the bunny rabbit comes again and eats some more cabbages. The woman says to her daughter: "Go out in the garden and chase the bunny rabbit away." The little girl says: "Shoo, shoo, bunny rabbit! You're eating up all our cabbages." Says the bunny rabbit: "Come, little girl, sit down on my bunny rabbit's tail and come with me to my bunny rabbit's hut." The little girl sits down on the bunny rabbit's tail, the bunny rabbit carries her far away to his hut, and says: "Now cook up some green cabbage and millet seed, while I go and invite the wedding guests." And all the wedding guests came flocking. (Who were these wedding guests? I can tell you that because someone has told me: they were all rabbits and the crow was the parson come to marry the bridal pair, and the fox was the sexton, and the altar was under the rainbow.)

But the little girl was sad, because she was all alone. Bunny Rabbit comes and says: "Serve up, serve up, the wedding guests are merry." The bride says nothing and weeps. Bunny Rabbit goes away, Bunny Rabbit comes back and says: "Serve up, serve up, the wedding guests are hungry." Again the bride says nothing and weeps. Bunny Rabbit goes away, Bunny Rabbit comes back and says: "Serve up, serve up, the wedding guests are waiting." The bride says nothing, Bunny Rabbit goes away, but then she makes a straw doll and dresses it in her clothes, puts a wooden spoon in its hand, sits it down by the millet pot, and goes back home to her mother. Bunny Rabbit comes back again and says: "Serve up, serve up!" When there's no answer, he goes in and hits the doll on the head. Her cap falls off and Bunny Rabbit sees it's not his bride. He goes away and he's very sad.

67

The Twelve Huntsmen

THERE WAS ONCE a king's son who was betrothed to a girl and loved her dearly. One day as they were sitting happily together, news came that his father was very sick and wished to see him before he died. He said to his sweetheart: "I must go away and leave you. Take this ring as a token of remembrance. When I am king, I shall come back and take you home with me." He rode away and when he got home, his father was on the point of death. "Dearest son," he said, "I wanted to see you once more before I died. Promise to marry in accordance with my wishes," and he named a certain king's daughter. The son was so grief-stricken that he didn't stop to think. He only said: "Yes, dear father, I will do as you wish." Whereupon the king closed his eyes and died.

When the son was proclaimed king and the days of mourning had passed, he had to keep his promise. He sent messengers to ask for the hand of the king's daughter, and it was granted. When his first betrothed heard the news, she was so unhappy about his infidelity that she almost pined away. Her father said to her: "Dearest child, why are you so sad? If there is anything you wish, you shall have it." She thought for a moment, then she said: "Dear father, I should like eleven girls exactly like myself in height, girth, and appearance." The king replied: "If it's possible, you shall have them," and he gave orders that his whole kingdom should be searched until eleven girls exactly like his daughter in height, girth, and appearance were found.

When they appeared before the king's daughter, she had twelve huntsmen's suits made, all alike. The eleven girls had to put them on, and she herself donned the twelfth suit. Thereupon she took leave of her father and rode away with them. They rode to the court of her faithless betrothed, whom she loved so dearly, and when they got there, she asked if he needed huntsmen. "Maybe you could hire all twelve of us," she suggested. The king looked at her and didn't recognize her, but because they were all so handsome, he said yes, he'd gladly engage them. So then they became the king's twelve huntsmen.

Now it so happened that the king had a lion, who was a most extraordinary animal, for he knew everything that was hidden and secret. One evening he said to the king: "You think you've got twelve huntsmen there?" The king replied: "Yes, indeed. Twelve huntsmen." "Wrong," said the lion, "they're twelve girls." Said the king: "That cannot be. I challenge you to prove it." "Very well," said the lion. "Just have the floor of your antechamber strewn with dried peas. You'll see. Men have a firm tread; when they walk over peas not a single pea budges, but girls trip and skitter and shuffle their feet, and that makes the peas roll." The king thought well of the lion's advice and had the floor strewn with peas.

But the king had a servant who was devoted to the huntsmen. When he heard they were to be put to the test he told them all about it and said: "The lion has been trying to tell the king that you're girls." The king's daughter thanked him and said to her companions: "Be on your guard. You must tread firmly on the peas." When the king sent for the twelve huntsmen the following morning and they passed through to the antechamber where the peas were, they trod so firmly and their step was so strong and steady that not a single pea moved or rolled. When they had left the king, he said to the lion: "You've lied to me. They walk like men." The lion replied: "They knew they were being put to the test and were on their guard. Have twelve spinning wheels put in the antechamber. They will go over to them and smile. No man would do that." The king thought well of the lion's advice and had the spinning wheels put in the antechamber.

But the servant who wished the huntsmen well went to them and exposed the trick. When the king's daughter was alone with her eleven girls, she said: "You must be on your guard and not turn to look at the spinning wheels." The following morning when the king sent for his twelve huntsmen, they went straight through the antechamber without even looking at the spinning wheels. Again the king said to the lion: "You've lied to me. They're men; they didn't even look at the spinning wheels." The lion replied: "They knew they were being put to the test, so they were on their guard." But the king had lost faith in his lion.

When the king went hunting, the twelve huntsmen always went with him, and as time passed he became fonder and fonder of them. One day when they were out hunting, news came that the king's betrothed was on her way. When his real betrothed heard that, it almost broke her heart and she fell to the ground in a faint. Thinking his beloved huntsman had had an accident, the king rushed to his help and pulled off his glove. Instantly he saw the ring he had given his first betrothed, and when he looked at her face he recognized her. His heart was so moved that he kissed her, and when she opened her eyes he said: "You are mine and I am yours. No one in all the world can change that." And he sent a messenger to the other betrothed, telling her to go back to her own kingdom, for he already had a wife, and letting it be known that a man who has found his old key doesn't need a new one. The wedding was celebrated and the lion restored to favor, for he had told the truth after all.

68

The Thief and His Master

JAN WANTS HIS SON to learn a trade, so he goes into the church and prays the Lord to tell him which trade would be best for him. The sexton, who's standing behind the altar, says: "Thieving, thieving." Jan goes home to his son and tells him he'll have to learn thieving, the Lord said so. Then they go looking for somebody who's good at thieving. After they've walked quite a ways, they come to a big forest, and in that forest, there's a little house with an old woman in it. Jan asks her: "Would you happen to know somebody who's good at thieving?" "You can learn that right here," says the woman. "My son's a master thief." He talks with the son and asks him if he's really good at thieving. The master thief says: "I'll teach your son all there is to know. Come back in a year's time, and if you recognize your son you won't have to pay me. If you don't recognize him, you'll owe me two hundred talers."

The father goes home and the son studies witchery and thieving.

When the year is out, the father starts worrying: how will he ever recognize his son? As he's walking along deep in worry, he meets a little man who says: "What are you worrying about, friend? You look so gloomy." "Oh," says Jan, "I apprenticed my son to a master thief a year ago. He told me to come back in a year's time, and if I didn't recognize my son I'd have to pay him two hundred talers, and if I did recognize him I wouldn't have to pay him anything. Now I'm afraid I won't recognize him and I don't know where I'm going to get the money from." The little man said: "Take a crust of bread with you and when you get there stand under the chimney hood. On the crossbeam there will be a cage with a bird peeping out of it. That's your son."

Jan goes to the house and puts the crust of black bread down beside the cage. A little bird peers out. "Howdy, son," says the father. "Is that you?" The son is glad to see his father, but the master thief says: "The Devil must have told you or you'd never have recognized him." "Let's be going, father," says the boy.

The father starts for home with his son. On the road a carriage comes toward them. The son says to the father: "I'm going to turn myself into a greyhound. You'll make a lot of money out of me." A gentleman calls from the carriage: "Ho, my good man. Do you want to sell your dog?" "Yes," says the father. "How much do you want for him?" "Thirty talers." "That's a lot of money, my good man, but seeing what a fine dog he is, I'll take him." The man takes him into the carriage, but after they've gone a little way the dog jumps out the window, and he's not a greyhound any more and he's back with his father.

They go home together. The next day is market day in the next village. The boy says to his father: "Now I'll turn myself into a fine horse. Sell me. But when you've sold me, you must take my bridle off, or I won't be able to turn myself into a man again." The father goes off to the market with the horse. The master thief comes along and buys him for a hundred talers, but the father forgets to take the bridle off. The master thief goes home with the horse and puts him in the stable. When the maid comes in the horse says: "Take my bridle off, take my bridle off." The maid stands there gaping: "Heavens above, you can talk!" She goes and takes his bridle off; the horse turns into a sparrow and flies out of the door. The wizard turns into a sparrow too and flies after him. They get together and play dice, the master loses, dives into the water and turns into a fish. The boy turns into a fish too, they play again, and the master loses. The master turns into a cock, the boy turns into a fox and bites the master's head off. So he died, and he's still dead.

69
Jorinda and Joringel

THERE WAS ONCE an old castle in a great dense forest; an old woman lived there all by herself and she was a wicked witch. In the daytime she turned herself into a cat or a night owl, but at night she resumed her human form. She had a way of luring birds and game, and when she had killed them, she would boil or roast them. If anyone came within a hundred steps of the castle, they froze in their tracks and couldn't stir from the spot until she said certain words that broke the spell. If an innocent girl went inside the circle, the witch turned her into a bird and shut her up in a wicker cage, which she carried to one of the rooms in her castle. She had about seven thousand of these rare birds, all in wicker cages.

Now there was once a girl named Jorinda, who was more beautiful than all the other girls in the world. She was betrothed to a handsome boy named Joringel. They were planning to marry soon and their greatest joy was in being together. One afternoon, wanting to be alone and undisturbed, they went into the forest. "Take care," said Joringel, "don't go too near the castle." It was a lovely evening; the sun shone between the tree trunks and lit up the dark green darkness of the forest, and the turtledoves sang mournfully in the old beech trees.

Now and then Jorinda wept. She sat down in the sun and sighed, and Joringel sighed too. They were as sad as if death had been near. They looked around in bewilderment, for they no longer knew the way home. The sun was still half above the hill and half below it. Joringel looked through the bushes and saw the old castle wall only a few steps away. He was overcome with horror and dread. Jorinda sang:

> "My little bird with the ring so red
>   sings sorrow, sorrow, sorrow;
> he sings that the turtledove is dead,
>   sings sorrow, sor— jug, jug, jug."

Joringel looked at Jorinda. She had been turned into a nightingale and was singing "jug jug jug." A night owl with fiery eyes flew around her three times and screeched three times: "To whoo, to whoo, to whoo." Joringel couldn't move, he stood as still as a stone, unable to weep, to speak, to move hand or foot. The sun had gone down; the owl flew into a bush; a moment later a gnarled old woman, yellow and scrawny, came out of it. She had big red eyes and a crooked nose, the end of which touched her chin. Muttering to herself, she caught the nightingale in her hands and carried it away. Joringel couldn't say a word or stir from the spot, and the nightingale was gone. At last the woman came back and said in a muffled voice: "Greetings, Zachiel! When the moon shines on the cage, let him go." And Joringel was free. He fell on his knees and begged the old woman to give him back his Jorinda, but she said he would never see her again and left him. He cried out, he wept, he moaned, but all in vain. "Oh! Oh! What's to become of me?" Joringel went away and came at last to a strange village, and stayed there a long time guarding the sheep. He often walked around the castle, but not too close. Then one night he dreamed he had found a blood-red flower with a fine large pearl in it. He plucked the flower and went to the castle with it. Everything he touched with the flower was freed from the spell. He also dreamed that the flower helped him get his Jorinda back again.

When he woke up the next morning, he began to search hill and dale for the flower; eight days he searched and early in the morning of the ninth he found the blood-red flower. In the middle there was a big dewdrop, as big as the finest pearl. Holding the flower, he journeyed day and night until he reached the castle. When he came to within a hundred paces of the castle, he was not held fast, but continued on to the gate. His heart leaped. He touched the gate with the flower, and it sprang open. He went in, passed through the courtyard, and listened for the sound of the birds. At length he heard

them. On and on he went till he found the room, and there was the
witch feeding the birds in the seven thousand cages. When she saw
Joringel, she was angry, very angry; she scolded, she spat poison and
gall at him, but she couldn't get near him, not within two paces. Pay-
ing no attention to her, he went up and down the room looking at the
birds in the cages, but there were hundreds of nightingales: how was
he ever to find his Jorinda? Suddenly, while he was watching the
birds, he saw the old witch taking a cage down on the sly and making
for the door with it. In a flash he jumped and touched the cage with
the flower. He also touched the old woman and she lost her power to
work magic. And there stood Jorinda with her arms around his neck,
as beautiful as ever. After turning all the other birds back into girls,
he went home with his Jorinda, and they lived happily together for
many years.

70

Born Lucky

A FATHER ONCE CALLED his three sons together and gave the first a
cock, the second a scythe, and the third a cat. "I'm old," he said. "I
haven't long to live, and I want to provide for you before I die. I
have no money, and I know these things I'm giving you don't look
like much. Everything depends on how intelligently you make use of
them. If you find a country where such things are still unknown,
your fortune is made."

After the father's death, the eldest started out with his cock, but
wherever he went cocks were already known. When he approached
a town, he would see them in the distance, turning with the wind on
the towers and steeples, and in every village he heard dozens of them
crowing. His own bird didn't startle anyone, and it didn't look as if
he'd ever make his fortune. But then finally he came to an island
where cocks were unknown and the people didn't even know how to
tell time. Of course they knew when it was morning and when it was
evening, but if they woke up during the night they had no idea what

time it was. "Look what a fine bird this is!" he said. "He has a ruby-
red crown on his head, and he wears spurs like a horseman. In the
course of the night he will crow three times for your benefit. What's
more, he will crow at regular intervals, and the last time he crows
you'll know it's just before sunrise. And another thing: if he crows in
broad daylight, the weather is sure to change, so be prepared." The
people were delighted. The next night no one slept. They all listened
gleefully as the cock, in a loud clear voice, announced the time, at
two o'clock, four o'clock, and six o'clock. Then they asked him if the
bird was for sale and how much he wanted for it. He replied: "Let's
say as much gold as a donkey can carry." "A trifle for so splendid a
bird!" they all cried, and gladly paid the price he had asked.

When he came home with his wealth, his brothers were amazed,
and the second said: "If that's how it is, I'll be on my way. I wonder
if I'll do so well with my scythe?" It didn't seem likely, for wherever
he went he saw peasants carrying scythes over their shoulders just as
he was doing. But in the end he too came to an island, and there the
people had never heard of scythes. When the grain was ripe in the
fields, they brought up cannon and shot it down. The result was uncertain. Some aimed too high and the cannon balls passed over the
grain; some missed the stalks, hit the ears and carried them away. Altogether, the waste was enormous, not to mention the villainous noise.
The boy stepped up with his scythe and mowed the grain so quickly
and quietly that the people stood gaping with amazement. They were
willing to give him whatever he asked for his scythe, and he went
home with a horse, on whose back they had loaded all the gold it
could carry.

Finally the third brother decided to try his luck with his cat. He
fared the same as the other two; as long as he stayed on the mainland,
he accomplished nothing, there were cats everywhere, so many that
people drowned the newborn kittens. In the end, he too went to an
island, where fortunately for him it turned out that cats were unknown and mice so plentiful that they danced about on the tables and
benches whether the master of the house was at home or not. The
people complained bitterly, and even the king in his palace didn't
know what to do. There were mice in every nook and cranny,
squeaking for all they were worth and gnawing at everything they
could get their teeth into. The cat set to work and before you knew

it she had cleared several rooms. The people implored the king to buy this wonderful beast for his kingdom. The king was only too glad to pay what was asked, which was a mule laden with gold, so that the third brother came home with the greatest treasure of all.

The cat had a fine time with the mice in the king's palace, and killed so many that no one could count them. In the end the work made her hot and thirsty. She stopped still, looked up into the air, and wailed: "Miaow! Miaow!" When the king and his courtiers heard the strange sound, they were so terrified that they all ran out of the palace. Outside, the king held a council and the councilors finally decided that the wisest course would be to send the cat a message asking her to leave the palace immediately, and threatening armed force if she didn't. The councilors said: "We'd rather be plagued by the mice, we're used to them, than be at the mercy of this monster." A page was sent up to ask the cat if she would leave the palace of her own free will. But the cat, who was thirstier than ever, only replied: "Miaow! Miaow!" The page understood: "Certainly not!" and that was the answer he brought back to the king. "In that case," said the councilors, "we shall have to resort to armed force." Cannon were brought up and the palace was bombarded till it went up in flames. When the fire reached the room where the cat was, she jumped out of the window. But the assailants kept up the bombardment until the whole palace was level with the ground.

71

Six Who Made Their Way in the World

THERE WAS ONCE a man who knew a thing or two. He served in the army and fought well and bravely, but when the war was over he was discharged with three pennies for travel money. "Wait a minute!" he said. "They can't do this to me. If only I can find the men I want, I'll make the king give me his whole treasury."

Bristling with rage, he went off into the forest, and there he saw a man pulling up trees, six of them, as if they were stalks of wheat. He said to the man: "Will you come with me and serve me?" "Yes," said the man, "but first let me take these few sticks home to my mother." He picked up one of the trees, wound it around the other five, put the bundle over his shoulder, and carried it away. Then he came back and went with his master, who said: "We two are sure to make our way in the world."

After a while they saw a hunter who was down on one knee, taking aim at something. The master said: "Hunter, what are you aiming at?" He replied: "There's a fly on the branch of an oak tree two miles from here; I'm going to shoot out its left eye." "Oh, come with me," said the man. "If we three band together, we're sure to make our way in the world." The hunter was willing and went along. They came to a place where the sails of seven windmills were whirling round and round, though there was no wind to the left or right, and not a leaf stirring. The master said: "I can't make out what's driving those windmills, there's not even a breeze." He went on with his two servants, and when they had gone two miles they saw a man perched on a tree. The man was holding one nostril closed and blowing out of the other. "Good God, man," said the master, "what are you doing up there?" The man replied: "Two miles from here there are seven windmills. Can't you see, I'm blowing at them to make them turn." "Oh, come with me," said the man. "If we four band together, we're sure to make our way in the world." So the blower climbed down and went along, and a little later they saw a man who was standing on one leg; he had unbuckled the other and laid it down beside him. The master said to him: "You've made yourself nice and comfortable, haven't you? Going to take a rest?" "I'm a runner," said the man. "I've unbuckled one leg to keep from running too fast. When I use both legs I go faster than a bird flies." "Oh, come with me. If we five band together, we're sure to make our way in the world." The runner joined them and before long they met a man who was wearing a hat, but it was all pulled down over one ear. The master said: "What's the matter with you? Why do you hang your hat on one ear, it makes you look like Tom Fool." "I have to," said the other, "because if I set it straight there will be such a deep frost that the birds will freeze in the air and fall to the ground dead."

"Oh, come with me," said the master, "if we six band together, we're sure to make our way in the world."

Soon the six of them came to a town where the king had made it known that anyone who ran a race with his daughter and won should become her husband, but that if he lost he would lose his head. The master went to him and said: "It's a deal, but my servant will run for me." The king replied: "In that case, you must stake his life as well; if he loses, both his head and yours will be forfeit." Once that was agreed on, the master buckled the runner's second leg on and said to him: "We're in this together. So don't dawdle." The contestants were to gather water from a spring that was a long way off, and the one who got back first would be the winner. The runner and the king's daughter were both given pitchers. They started running at the same time, but a minute later, when the king's daughter had gone only a little way, none of the onlookers could see the runner, it was as if a raging wind had passed. In next to no time he reached the spring, filled his pitcher with water, and turned back. But halfway back he suddenly felt tired, put the pitcher down, stretched out and fell asleep. He had found a horse's skull and was using it as a pillow, thinking the discomfort would prevent him from sleeping too long.

In the meantime the king's daughter, who was quite a remarkable runner for a common mortal, had reached the spring and was running back with her pitcher full of water. When she saw the runner lying there asleep, she was overjoyed. "The enemy is delivered into my hands," she said, emptied his pitcher, and ran on. All would have been lost if luckily the hunter hadn't been standing on the castle roof and seen it all with his sharp eyes. "The king's daughter shall not defeat us!" he cried, loaded his gun, took careful aim, and shot the horse's skull out from under the sleeper without hurting him. The runner awoke with a start and saw that his pitcher was empty and that the king's daughter was far ahead of him. But that didn't trouble him. He took his pitcher, ran back to the spring, filled it again with water, and reached the palace ten minutes before the king's daughter. "I was just beginning to move," he said. "What I was doing before can hardly be called running."

But the king didn't care one bit for the idea of a discharged soldier marrying his daughter, and she liked it still less. They cast about for a way of getting rid of him and his companions, and after a while the king said to her: "I've got it! Don't worry, they'll never see their homes again." And to the six he said: "Now I want you to eat, drink, and make merry together." Whereupon he led them to a room with an iron floor, and the doors were also of iron, and the window had thick iron bars. In the middle of the room there was a table set with choice dishes, and the king said to them: "Go in and enjoy yourselves." Once they were inside, he had the door locked and bolted. Then he sent for the cook and told him to make a fire under the room and stoke it until the iron was red-hot. The cook did as he was bidden, and pretty soon the six men in the room began to feel warm. At first they thought they were overheated from eating too much, but when it got hotter and hotter and they tried to go out but found the door and windows locked, they realized that the king was up to no good and wanted to burn them alive. "Never mind," said the man with the hat. "He won't succeed. I shall now create a frost that will make the fire slink away in shame." He set his hat straight, and instantly such a frost set in that the heat vanished and the food in the dishes began to freeze. When a few hours had passed and the king thought they must have perished in the heat, he had the door opened and looked in, wanting to see for himself how they were doing. But when the door opened, all six were standing there in the pink of health and said they appreciated the chance to come out and warm themselves, because the room was so cold the food had frozen solid in the dishes. The king in a rage went down and scolded the cook: "Why didn't you do as you were told?" The cook replied: "I made a beautiful fire. See for yourself." The king saw the raging flames under the iron room and realized that if he wanted to get the better of the six he'd have to think of something else.

Again the king cast about for a way to get rid of his unwelcome guests. Finally he sent for the master and said: "Would you relinquish your right to my daughter in exchange for gold? I'll give you as much as you ask for." He replied: "Oh yes, Your Majesty. If you give me as much as my servant can carry, I'll drop my claim to your daughter." That suited the king. "Very well, then," said the master. "I'll come for the gold in two weeks." Thereupon he called in all the tailors in the whole kingdom, and for two weeks they sat making a sack. When it was finished, the strong man, the one who pulled up trees, slung the sack over his shoulder and went to the king with it.

"Good Lord!" said the king. "The strength of the man! Why, that bolt of canvas he's carrying is as big as a house!" And in terror he thought: "What a lot of gold *he'll* carry away!" He sent for a barrel of gold. It took sixteen of the brawniest servants to carry it, but the strong man picked it up in one hand, tossed it into the sack, and said: "Better bring more next time, this hardly covers the bottom." Little by little, all the king's treasure was brought in. The strong man stuffed all the gold into his sack and it still wasn't half full. "Bring more!" he cried. "It takes more than a few crumbs to fill *this* sack!" In the end, seven thousand wagonloads of gold had to be brought in from all over the country, and the strong man tossed them right into the sack, oxen and all. "Why waste time sorting?" he said. "I'll take the stuff as it comes, so long as the sack gets full." When the sack had swallowed up all the wagons, there was still room for a lot more, but the strong man said: "Let's get this over with. There's no harm in tying up a sack that isn't quite full." So he tied it up, hoisted it onto his back and went away with his companions.

When the king saw that one solitary man was making off with the wealth of his whole kingdom, he was very angry and ordered his cavalry to mount their horses and follow the six and take the sack away from them. Two regiments soon overtook them and cried out: "You're prisoners. Put that sack of gold down or we'll cut you to pieces." "What's that?" said the blower. "Prisoners, you say? How would you all like to take a ride in the upper air?" Whereupon he held one nostril and blew through the other. Instantly the two regiments were wafted into the air and blown in all directions, one man here, another there, over the hills and far away. A sergeant begged for mercy, explaining that he was a self-respecting soldier with nine wounds and didn't deserve to be humiliated so. The blower let up for a moment and said to the sergeant who had come down unhurt: "Now go home and tell your king to send me another few regiments and I'll blow them all into the air." When the king received the message, he said: "Let the scoundrels go. They're too much for me." So the six brought their fortune home, divided it among them, and lived happily until they died.

72

The Wolf and the Man

ONE DAY THE FOX was telling the wolf about the strength of humankind, how they were too much for any animal, and an animal's only hope of resisting them lay in guile. The wolf replied: "If I ever get to see a human, I'll pounce on him all the same." "We'll see about that," said the fox. "Call for me tomorrow morning and I'll show you a human." The wolf turned up bright and early, and the fox led him to the path the hunter took every day.

First a discharged old soldier came along. "Is that a human?" the wolf asked. "No," said the fox. "He used to be one." Next came a little boy on his way to school. "Is that a human?" "No, but he will be some day." Finally the hunter appeared with his double-barreled gun slung over his shoulder and his hunting knife at his side. "Look," said the fox. "There comes a human. He's the one for you to pounce on. Meanwhile, I'll just mosey along to my hole." The wolf charged. When the hunter saw him coming, he said to himself: "Too bad I didn't load up with bullets." Nevertheless, he took aim and peppered the wolf's face with birdshot. The wolf winced and scowled, but it took more than that to scare him; he kept coming and the hunter emptied the other barrel in his face. The wolf fought down the pain and closed in on the hunter. The hunter drew his glistening knife and slashed him, right left, right left. The wolf howled and, bleeding all over, ran back to the fox. "Well, brother wolf," said the fox, "how did you make out with the human?" "My, oh my," said the wolf. "I never expected human strength to be like that. First he took a stick off his shoulder and blew into it and something flew in my face that tickled terribly. Then he blew into the stick again and I had hailstones and lightning flashes all over my nose, and when I got close to him he pulled a shiny rib out of his body and the way he lashed out at me he pretty near left me dead on the spot." "You see what a braggart you are!" said the fox. "It seems to me that your tongue overreached itself."

73

The Wolf and the Fox

THE WOLF HAD TAKEN the fox as his servant, and the fox was good and sick of his master, because the wolf was stronger, so the fox had to do everything he said. It so happened that the two of them were walking through the woods and the wolf said: "Red fox, get me something to eat, or I'll eat *you*." The fox replied: "I know of a farm where they've got two young lambs. If you like, we can go and get one." The idea appealed to the wolf and they went to the farm; the fox stole the lamb, brought it to the wolf, and went away. The wolf ate the lamb, but he wasn't satisfied, he wanted the other lamb as well. But he was so clumsy about getting it that the mother sheep heard him and started to bleat for all she was worth. The farmer and his wife came running, caught the wolf and beat him so cruelly that he went back to the fox limping and howling. "A fine mess you got me into," he said to the fox. "When I tried to take the other lamb, the farmer and his wife caught me and beat me to a pulp." The fox replied: "Why must you be such a glutton?"

The next day they went out again, and again the greedy wolf said: "Red fox, get me something to eat, or I'll eat *you*." "I know of a farm where the farmer's wife is making pancakes this afternoon. Suppose we go and get some." They went to the farm, and the fox crept around the house, peering and sniffing, until he located the dish. Then he took half a dozen pancakes and brought them to the wolf. "This ought to hold you for a while," said the fox, and went his way. The wolf gobbled down the pancakes in half a second and said: "That whets the appetite." Whereupon he went over and pulled the whole dish down. It broke with a crash, the farmer's wife came running, and when she saw the wolf she called the hired hands, who gave the wolf such a thrashing that he hobbled back to the fox on two lame legs, howling for all he was worth. "Look at the rotten mess you got me into!" he cried. "The hired hands caught me and tanned my hide." The fox replied: "Why must you be such a glutton?"

When they went out together on the third day, the wolf was still limping painfully. Again he said: "Red fox, get me something to eat, or I'll eat *you*. The fox replied: "I know of a man who has just slaughtered; he's got the salt meat in a barrel in the cellar. We'll go and get some." "But this time," said the wolf, "I'll go right in with you, so you can help me if I have trouble getting away." "Suits me," said the fox, and led him around corners and through passageways, until they finally got to the cellar. There was plenty of meat, and the wolf fell to. "No hurry," he thought. "I'll just stay here until this is finished." The fox helped himself too, but he kept looking round and running back to the hole they had come in by and testing to make sure he was still thin enough to get through. The wolf said: "Look here, fox, why do you keep running around and jumping in and out?" "I have to make sure no one's coming, don't I," said the sly fox. "My advice to you is, don't eat too much." Said the wolf: "I'm not leaving here until the barrel's empty." Just then the farmer, who had heard the fox jumping in and out, came into the cellar. The moment the fox saw him, he was out through the hole in one jump. The wolf tried to follow, but he had eaten so much he was too big for the hole and only got halfway through. The farmer picked up a club and struck him dead. As for the fox, he ran off into the woods, glad to be rid of the old glutton.

74

The Fox and His Cousin

DAME WOLF GAVE BIRTH to a cub and invited the fox to stand godfather. "After all, he's a close relation," she said. "He has a good head on his shoulders, and he's so clever with his paws; he'll help with my son's education and teach him to get on in the world." The fox appeared, behaved with great dignity, and said: "Dear Cousin, thank you for the honor you've shown me. I can assure you, you'll never regret it." At the banquet he ate his fill and made merry, and when it was over he said: "Dear Cousin Wolf, we are in duty bound to take

good care of this child. He will need good nourishing food to make
him big and strong. I know of a barn where we can easily get ourselves a nice sheep." An excellent idea, thought Dame Wolf, and followed the fox to the farm. He showed her the barn in the distance
and said: "You won't have any trouble crawling in there unseen—
meanwhile, I'll go around on the other side and see if I can't catch a
chicken." But he didn't do anything of the kind; he went to the edge
of the woods and lay down for a rest. Dame Wolf crept into the
barn, but there was a dog inside. The dog began to bark, the farmers
came running, caught Cousin Wolf and poured potash on her side. In
the end she got away and dragged herself to the woods, where the
fox was lying. The fox pretended to be in pain and said: "Oh, dear
Cousin Wolf, what a time I've had! The farmers attacked me and
broke all my bones. I'll just have to lie here and breathe my last, unless you carry me." Dame Wolf herself could hardly move, but she
was so worried about Cousin Fox, who had suffered no injury at all,
that she picked him up on her back and carried him all the way to
her house. There he had a good laugh at her expense and ran away,
crying: "Good-bye, dear cousin. Let's hope the scalding has done
you good."

75

The Fox and the Cat

ONE DAY THE CAT met Mr. Fox in the woods and said to herself:
"He's so clever, so experienced, so widely respected," and gave him a
friendly greeting. "Good day, dear Mr. Fox! How are you getting
along? How are you managing now that everything is so expensive?"
The fox was puffed up with pride; he looked the cat up and down,
and it took him quite some time to decide whether to answer or not.
Finally he said: "You wretched whisker-licker, you piebald jester,
you starveling mouse-hunter, who do you think you are? How dare
you ask me how I'm getting along? What have you ever learned?
What arts have you mastered?" "Only one," said the cat modestly.

"And what is that, pray?" "When dogs are after me, I can save my-self by climbing a tree." "Is that all?" said the fox. "I am the master of a hundred arts, and furthermore I have a whole bag of tricks. My heart bleeds for you. Come with me and I'll teach you how to get away from dogs." Just then a hunter came along with four dogs. The cat ran nimbly up a tree and settled in the crown, where the leaves and branches hid her completely. "Open up that bag, Mr. Fox, open up that bag," the cat cried out, but the dogs had already seized him and were holding him fast. "Too bad, Mr. Fox," the cat cried out. "Look at the jam you're in with your hundred arts. If you'd known how to climb up here like me, you'd have saved your life."

76

The Carnation

THERE WAS ONCE a queen who had no children because the Lord had shut her womb. Every morning she went into the garden and prayed to God for a son or a daughter. One day an angel came down from heaven and said: "Be of good cheer, you shall have a son gifted with magic powers. Whatever he wishes will come true." She went to the king and told him the good tidings, and when the time had come she bore a son and the king was very happy.

Every morning she went to the deer park with her child and bathed in a clear spring. Once when the child was a little older, the queen fell asleep as it lay in her arms, and the old cook, who knew that the child had magic thoughts, came and stole it away. He tore a chicken in pieces, and let the blood drip on the queen's apron and dress. Then he carried the child to a secret place, where it was suckled by a wet nurse, and accused the queen of letting wild animals steal her child. When the king saw the blood on the queen's apron, he believed the story and was so angry that he bade his masons build a high tower, into which neither the sun nor the moon ever shone. There his wife was immured and left to languish for seven years without food or drink. But God sent two angels from heaven in the form of white doves, and they brought her food twice a day, until the seven years were over.

Meanwhile the cook thought to himself: "If I stay here, the child might easily make trouble for me with his magic thoughts." So he slipped out of the palace and went to the boy, who by then was old enough to talk, and said: "Wish for a beautiful palace with a garden and everything that goes with it." No sooner were the words out of the boy's mouth than everything he had wished for was there. After a while the cook said: "It's not good for you to be all alone. Wish for a beautiful girl to keep you company." The king's son wished, and there she stood, so beautiful that no painter could have painted her picture. The two of them played together and loved each other dearly, and the old cook went hunting like a man of quality. But then it occurred to him that the king's son might wish to be with his father and then the cook would be in great danger. So he took the girl aside and said: "Tonight when the boy is asleep, go over to his bed and thrust this knife into his heart. Then bring me his heart and tongue. If you don't, you will lose your own life." He went away and when he came back next day, she hadn't done it. "Why," she asked, "should I take the life of an innocent boy who has never harmed a living soul?" The cook said: "If you don't, it will cost you your own life." When he had gone away, she had a little doe brought to her and killed. She took the heart and tongue and put them on a dish, and when she saw the old cook coming, she said to the boy: "Lie down on the bed and pull the blanket over you."

The villain came in and said: "Where are the boy's heart and tongue?" The girl handed him the dish, but the king's son threw off the blanket and said: "You old sinner, why were you going to kill me? Now let me tell you your punishment. You're to turn into a black poodle with a gold chain around your neck, and eat glowing coals and belch fire." No sooner had he spoken than the wicked old cook was turned into a poodle with a gold chain around his neck, and the kitchen helpers had to bring up live coals and he ate them and belched fire. The king's son stayed on in the palace for a short while, often thinking of his mother and wondering if she were still alive. Finally he said to the girl: "I'm going home to my own country. If you'll come with me, I'll take care of you." "Oh," she said, "it's such a long way, and what would I do in a foreign country where nobody

knows me?" Finally, since she was reluctant to go and they couldn't
bear to part, he made a wish that turned her into a beautiful carnation, and put her in his pocket.

When he set out, the poodle had to run after him, and so the king's
son returned to his own country. When he arrived, he went to the
tower where his mother was shut up, and the tower was so high that
he wished for a ladder. He climbed to the top, looked in, and cried:
"Dearest mother, Your Majesty, are you alive or dead?" "I'm not
hungry, I've just eaten," she replied, for she thought it was the angels. "I am your loving son," he said. "The wild beasts were supposed
to have stolen me out of your arms, but I'm still alive and I'll soon set
you free." Whereupon he climbed down, went to his father the king,
and had himself announced as a huntsman from foreign parts. When
he asked if the king would employ him, the king said yes, if he knew
his trade and could get him some venison, but added that no deer had
ever been seen in the entire region. The huntsman promised to bring
him as much venison as the royal table could bear. He called all the
king's huntsmen together and they followed him into the forest,
where he bade them form a circle but leave one end open. Then he
stepped inside the circle and started wishing. Before you knew it,
more than two hundred head of deer came running into the circle,
and the huntsmen shot them. The carcasses were loaded onto sixty
carts and brought to the king. At last, after many years of going
without, there was venison for the royal board.

The king was delighted and invited his court to banquet with him
the next day. When they were all assembled, he said to the huntsman: "Because you have hunted so well, you shall sit beside me." He
replied: "I can't do that, Your Majesty; I'm only a lowly hunter."
But the king kept saying: "You shall sit beside me," until he gave in.
As the king's son sat there, he thought of his dear mother and wished
that one of the councilors would speak of the queen and ask how she
was getting along in the tower, whether she was still alive or had
wasted away. No sooner had he wished it than the marshal spoke:
"Your Majesty, here we sit enjoying ourselves, but how is the queen
in the tower getting along?" The king replied: "Don't speak of her
to me! She let the wild beasts tear my beloved son to pieces." At that
the huntsman stood up and said: "Most gracious father, she is still
alive, and I am her son. The wild beasts didn't tear me to pieces, the

wicked old cook did it, he took me out of her arms while she was sleeping and let the blood of a chicken drip on her apron." Here he took the dog by its gold collar and said: "This is the villain!" He sent for glowing coals and, with the whole court looking on, the poodle had to eat them until he belched fire. Then the huntsman asked the king if he cared to see the villain in his true form, and wished him back into a cook. In a flash the cook was standing there in his white apron, with his knife at his side. When the king saw him, he was very angry and ordered him thrown into the deepest dungeon. Then the huntsman asked: "Father, would you like to see the girl who has been such an affectionate companion to me, who was told to kill me but refused to at the risk of her own life?" "Yes," said the king, "I would indeed like to see her." "Gracious father," said the son, "you shall see her in the form of a beautiful flower." He reached into his pocket, took out the carnation and set it on the royal table, and it was more beautiful than any the king had ever seen. Then the son said: "And now you shall see her in her true form." He wished, and once again she became a girl, so beautiful that no painter could have improved on her.

Thereupon the king sent two lady's maids and two manservants to the tower to get the queen and bring her to the royal table. But when they had brought her there, she ate nothing, and said: "God, who in His mercy sustained me in the tower, will soon set me free." After that she lived for three days and died happy. When she was buried, the two white doves who had brought her food in the tower, and who were really angels from heaven, looked on and perched on her grave. The old king had the cook torn into four pieces, but the king's heart was consumed with grief and he soon died. His son married the beautiful girl whom he had brought home in his pocket in the form of a flower, and whether or not they are still living is in the hand of God.

77

Clever Gretel

THERE WAS ONCE a cook by the name of Gretel, who wore shoes with red heels, and when she went out in them she wiggled and waggled happily, and said to herself: "My, what a pretty girl I am." And when she got home again, she'd be in such a good humor that she'd take a drink of wine, and then, as wine whets the appetite, she'd taste all the best parts of what she was cooking until she was full, and say: "A cook has to know how her cooking tastes."

One day her master said to her: "Gretel, I'm having a guest for dinner. I want you to make us two nice roast chickens." "Yes, master, I'll be glad to," said Gretel. She slit the chickens' throats, scalded, plucked, and spitted them, and toward evening put them over the fire to roast. The chickens began to brown and were almost done, but the guest hadn't arrived. Gretel called in to her master: "If your guest doesn't come soon, I'll have to take the chickens off the fire, but it would be a crying shame not to eat them now, while they're at their juiciest best." "In that case," said the master, "I'll go and get him myself." The moment his back was turned, she put the spit with the chickens on it to one side. "Standing over the fire so long makes a body sweat," she thought, "and sweating makes a body thirsty. How do I know when they'll get here? In the meantime I'll hop down to the cellar and have a little drink." Down she ran, filled a jug from the barrel, said: "God bless it to your use, Gretel," and took a healthy swig. "Wine goes with wine," she said, "and never should they part," and took a healthier swig. Then she went upstairs, put the chickens back on the fire, brushed them with butter, and gave the spit a few lively turns. But the chickens smelled so good that she thought: "Maybe they're not seasoned quite right, I'd better taste them." She touched her fingers to one, licked them, and cried out: "Oh, how delicious these chickens are! It's a crying shame not to eat them this minute!" She went to the window to see if the master and his guest were coming, but there was no one in sight. She went back to the chickens and thought: "That wing is burning. There's only one way to stop it." So she cut the wing off and ate it. It hit the spot, and when she had finished she thought: "I'll have to take the other one off too, or the master will see that something's missing." After doing away with the two wings, she went back to the window to look for her master. No master in sight, so then she had an idea. "How do I know? Maybe they're not coming. Maybe they've stopped at a tavern." She gave herself a poke: "Come on, Gretel. Don't be a spoilsport. One has been cut into; have another drink and finish it up. Once it's gone, you won't have anything to worry about. Why waste God's blessings?" Again she hopped down to the cellar, took a good stiff drink, and polished off the one chicken with joy in her heart. When one chicken was gone and there was still no sign of the master, Gretel looked at the other and said: "Where the one is, there the other should be. Chickens go in pairs, and what's good enough for one is good enough for the other. And besides, another drink won't hurt me any." Whereupon she took an enormous drink and started the second chicken on its way to rejoin the first.

She was still eating lustily when her master came along and called out: "Quick, Gretel. Our guest will be here in a minute." "Oh, yes, sir," said Gretel. "I'll serve you in a jiffy." The master looked in to make sure the table was properly set, took his big carving knife, and began to sharpen it in the pantry. The guest was a well-bred man. When he got to the house, he knocked softly. Gretel hurried to the door and looked out. When she saw the guest, she put her finger to her lips and said: "Sh-sh! Quick, go away! If my master catches you, you're done for. Do you know why he invited you to dinner? Because he wants to cut your ears off. Listen! That's him sharpening his knife!" The guest heard the master whetting his knife and ran down the steps as fast as his legs could carry him. But Gretel wasn't through yet. She ran screaming to her master: "A fine guest you brought into the house!" she cried. "Why, what's the matter, Gretel? What do you mean?" "I mean," she said, "that just as I was getting ready to serve up the chickens he grabbed them and ran away with them." "That's a fine way to behave," said the master, grieved at the loss of his fine chickens. "If he'd only left me one of them! Then at least I'd have something to eat." "Stop! Stop!" he shouted, but the guest pretended not to hear. So still holding his knife the master ran after him, crying out: "Just one! Just one!" meaning that the guest should leave him one chicken and not take both. But the guest thought the master had decided to content himself with one ear, and seeing that he wanted to take both his ears home with him, he ran as if someone had made a fire under his feet.

78

The Old Man and His Grandson

THERE WAS ONCE a very old man who was almost blind and deaf and whose knees trembled. When he sat at the table, he could hardly hold his spoon; he spilled soup on the tablecloth, and when he'd taken a spoonful some of it ran out of his mouth. His son and his son's wife thought it was disgusting and finally made the old man sit in a corner behind the stove. They brought him his food in an earthenware bowl and, worst of all, they didn't even give him enough. He looked sadly in the direction of the table, and his eyes filled with tears. One day his hands trembled so much that he dropped his bowl and it fell to the floor and broke. The young woman scolded him, but he said nothing and only sighed. She bought him a wooden bowl for a few kreuzers, and from then on he had to eat out of it. As they were sitting there one day, the little four-year-old grandson was on the floor playing with some pieces of wood. "What are you doing?" his father asked. The child replied: "I'm making a trough for father and mother to eat out of when I'm big." Husband and wife looked at each other for a while and burst into tears. After that they brought the old grandfather back to the table. He ate with them from then on, and even when he spilled a little something they said nothing.

hungry, so he said to St. Peter: "Look, this is a nice place. Let's stop
and cook the lamb and eat it." "All right with me," said St. Peter,
"but I don't know a thing about cooking. If you want to cook,
there's a pot. I'll be taking a little walk in the meantime. But don't
start eating till I get back. I won't be late." "Go ahead," said Brother
Scamp. "Cooking is right up my alley. I'll take care of it." When St.
Peter had gone, Brother Scamp butchered the lamb, made a fire,
threw the meat into the pot, and cooked it. After a while, the meat
was done, but the apostle wasn't back yet. Brother Scamp took the
meat out of the pot, cut it up, and found the heart. "That's supposed
to be the best part," he said to himself, tasted it, and little by little ate
it up. When St. Peter got back, he said: "You can have the whole
lamb for yourself. Just give me the heart, that's all I want." Brother
Scamp took knife and fork, pretended to look for the heart, and
finally gave up. "There isn't any," he said. "How is that possible?"
the apostle asked. "I have no idea," said Brother Scamp. "No, wait a
minute. What fools we are, looking for a lamb's heart! We both seem
to have forgotten that a lamb hasn't got a heart." "My word!" said
St. Peter. "That's news to me. All animals have hearts. Why
shouldn't a lamb have one?" "It just hasn't, brother. Think it over
carefully and you'll realize that a lamb really and truly has no heart."
"All right," said St. Peter. "Let it go. If there's no heart, I don't need
any of the lamb, you can have it all for yourself." "What I can't eat
I'll pack up in my knapsack," said Brother Scamp, ate half the lamb,
and put the rest in his knapsack.

They went their way, and St. Peter arranged for a broad stream to
bar their path. They had to cross it and St. Peter said: "You go first."
"No," said Brother Scamp. "You go first." "If the water's too deep
for him," he thought, "I'll stay here." St. Peter waded across, and the
water only came up to his knees. So Brother Scamp started off, but
the water got deeper and deeper till it was up to his neck. "Brother!"
he cried out. "Help me!" But St. Peter said: "Admit you ate the lamb's
heart." "No," he replied, "I didn't eat it." The water got still deeper,
till it was up to his mouth. "Brother!" he cried out. "Help me!"
Again St. Peter said: "Admit you ate the lamb's heart." "No," he
said. "I didn't eat it." All the same, St. Peter didn't want him to
drown, so he made the water go down and helped him across.

They went their way and came to a kingdom where they heard

that the king's daughter was deathly sick. "Hey, brother," said the soldier to St. Peter, "this looks like a good thing for us. If we can cure her, we'll be in clover for the rest of our lives." St. Peter agreed, but didn't move fast enough to suit him. "Shake a leg, brother," he said. "We want to get there before it's too late." But the more Brother Scamp pushed and prodded, the more St. Peter slowed down, and after a while they heard that the king's daughter was dead. "I knew it!" said Brother Scamp. "Now see what you've done with your shilly-shallying." "You talk too much," said St. Peter. "I can do more than heal the sick; I can also wake the dead." "In that case," said Brother Scamp, "I won't argue, but make sure you demand at least half the kingdom as our reward." When they got to the royal palace, everyone was in deep mourning. St. Peter went straight to the king and promised to bring his daughter back to life. They led him to her room, and he said: "Bring me a caldron full of water." When the water was brought, he told everyone to leave the room and only Brother Scamp was allowed to stay. St. Peter cut the dead girl's limbs off, threw them into the water, made a fire under the caldron and boiled them. When all the flesh had fallen off, he took the smooth white bones out of the water, put them on a table, and arranged them in their natural order. When they were ready, he stepped up to the table and said three times: "In the name of the most Holy Trinity, rise from the dead." The third time the king's daughter stood up, alive, healthy, and beautiful. The king was overjoyed. "Name your reward," he said to St. Peter. "Even if it should be half my kingdom, you shall have it." But St. Peter replied: "I want nothing." "Oh, you jughead!" thought Brother Scamp. He poked his comrade in the ribs and said: "Don't be a fool. You may not want anything, but I do." St. Peter still wanted nothing, but seeing the frame of mind his companion was in, the king bade his treasurer fill the soldier's knapsack with gold.

Again they went their way. When they came to a forest, St. Peter said to Brother Scamp: "Now we'll divide the gold." "Good idea!" said Brother Scamp. St. Peter divided the gold into three parts. "Now he's got some new bee in his bonnet," thought Brother Scamp. "Why is he dividing it into three parts when there are only two of us?" Said St. Peter: "I've divided it just right: one part for me, one for you, and one for whoever ate the lamb's heart." "That was me!" said

Brother Scamp, and swept up the gold in a twinkling. "You can take my word for it." "How is that possible?" said St. Peter. "When we know that a lamb has no heart." "How can you talk such nonsense, brother?" said the soldier. "A lamb has a heart just like any other animal. Why shouldn't it?" "All right," said St. Peter. "Keep the gold for yourself, but I've had enough of your company and I'm going on by myself." "Have it your way, brother," said the soldier. "Good-bye."

St. Peter turned off to one side and Brother Scamp thought: "I'm just as glad to see him go. What a queer customer he turned out to be!" He now had money enough, but he didn't know how to take care of it: he squandered it, he gave it away, and after a while he was penniless again. Soon he came to a country where he heard that the king's daughter had died, and he thought to himself: "Hey, there! There ought to be something in this for me! I'll bring her back to life and get myself paid good and proper." So he went to the king and offered to wake his daughter from the dead. The king had heard that a discharged soldier was going about bringing dead people back to life. He thought Brother Scamp might be this man, but he had his doubts, so he consulted his councilors, who said he might as well risk it since after all his daughter was dead. Brother Scamp asked for a caldron full of water and made everyone leave the room. Then he cut the dead girl's limbs off, threw them into the water, and made a fire underneath, just as he had seen St. Peter do. The water began to boil. When the flesh fell from the bones, he took them out and put them on the table, but he didn't know the right order, and he got them all mixed up. Nevertheless, he stepped up to the table and said: "In the name of the most Holy Trinity, rise from the dead." He said it three times but the bones didn't budge. He said it three more times, but all in vain. "Blasted girl!" he cried. "Get up, or I'll show you the reason why!" He had no sooner spoken than St. Peter came in through the window, once again disguised as a discharged soldier. "Godless man!" he said. "What are you doing there? How can the poor girl rise again when you've got her bones in such a muddle?" "Brother," said the soldier, "I've done the best I could." "I'll help you out this once," said St. Peter, "but if you ever attempt anything of this kind again, heaven help you, and another thing, you're not to ask for or accept any reward whatsoever from the king." Then St. Peter arranged the bones in their proper order and said three times: "In the name of the most Holy Trinity, rise from the dead." The king's daughter arose, as healthy and beautiful as before, and St. Peter left through the window. Brother Scamp was glad things had gone off so well, but annoyed at being forbidden to accept a reward. "The man's got a screw loose," he thought. "What he gives with one hand he takes back with the other. There's no sense in it." The king offered Brother Scamp any reward he chose. He declined as he had been told to, but with hints and dodges he got the king to fill his knapsack with gold, and off he went. St. Peter was at the palace gate. "Aren't you the limit!" he cried. "Didn't I forbid you to take anything? And here you are with your knapsack full of gold." "Can I help it if they force it on me?" said Brother Scamp. "Just don't try it a second time, or you'll wish you hadn't." "Of course not, brother, never fear. Why should I bother to wash bones when I've got all this gold?" "I can imagine how long your gold will last," said St. Peter. "But to keep you from going forbidden ways again, I'll give you the power to wish anything you please into your knapsack. Good-bye now, you won't be seeing me again." "So long," said Brother Scamp, and thought: "Glad to see you go, you queer bird! You won't catch me running after you!" And he gave no further thought to the miraculous power of his knapsack.

Brother Scamp wandered about with his money, and wasted it and squandered it the same as the first time. When he had only four kreuzers left, he came to a tavern. "I might as well spend them," he thought, and ordered three kreuzers' worth of wine and one of bread. As he sat drinking, the smell of roast goose came to his nostrils. He looked around and finally saw two geese that the tavern keeper was keeping in the oven. Suddenly he remembered that his comrade had told him he could wish anything he pleased into his knapsack. "Hey!" he thought. "Let's give it a try with the geese!" He went outside and said: "I wish those two roast geese would come out of the oven and into my knapsack." After saying these words, he unbuckled his knapsack and looked in, and there they were. "This is perfect!" he said. "Why, I'm a made man!" He sat down in a meadow and took out the geese. As he was busily eating, two journeymen came along and looked hungrily at the goose that hadn't been touched yet. Brother Scamp thought to himself: "One is enough for me," and called the two journeymen. "Here," he said, "take this goose and think of me as you eat it." They thanked him, went into the tavern, ordered a jug of wine and a loaf of bread, took out the goose Brother Scamp had given them, and started to eat. The tavern keeper's wife eyed them and said to her husband: "Those two over there are eating a goose. Go and see if it's not one of ours out of the oven." He went and looked, and the oven was empty. "Hey, you thieves," he said, "you think you're getting that goose pretty cheap, don't you? Pay up this minute or I'll tickle your hides with a hazel stick." "We're not thieves," they protested. "A discharged soldier gave us the goose out there in the meadow." "You can't pull the wool over my eyes," said the tavern keeper. "There was a soldier here, but he went out the door empty-handed; I was watching him. You're the thieves, and you'd better pay up." But they couldn't pay, so he took his stick and chased them out of the house.

Brother Scamp went his way and came to a place where there was a magnificent castle, and not far away a wretched inn. He went to the inn and asked to spend the night, but the innkeeper turned him away, saying: "There's no room. The house is full of noblemen." "That's funny," said Brother Scamp. "Why would they pick this place instead of that magnificent castle?" "Well, you see," said the innkeeper, "it's not so easy to spend a night in that castle. Some have tried, but none has ever come out alive." "If others have tried, so will I," said Brother Scamp. "Better not," said the innkeeper. "It will be the end of you." "Don't worry about me," said Brother Scamp. "Just give me the keys and something to eat and drink." The innkeeper gave him the keys and something to eat and drink. Brother Scamp went into the castle and enjoyed his meal. When he felt sleepy, he lay down on the floor, for there was no bed. He soon fell asleep, but in the middle of the night he was awakened by a frightful noise. When he opened his eyes, he saw nine ugly devils dancing around him in a circle. "Dance if you must," said Brother Scamp, "just so you don't get too near me." But the devils came closer and closer and almost stepped on his face with their nasty feet. "Quiet, you devil-spooks!" he cried, but the hubbub got worse and worse. Brother Scamp got very angry and shouted: "Quiet, I said!" He picked up a table leg and belabored them with it, but nine devils were too many for one soldier. While he was hitting the one in front of him, the ones behind him grabbed him by the hair and pulled cruelly. "Stinking devils!" he cried. "This is too much! But now you're going to see something. All nine of you into my knapsack!" Whish! In they went. He buckled the knapsack, tossed it into the corner, and suddenly all was still. Brother Scamp lay down again and slept until morning, when the innkeeper and the nobleman who owned the castle came to see what had become of him. They were amazed to find him alive and chipper and asked: "Haven't the ghosts hurt you?" "How could they hurt me? I've got them all in my knapsack. Now you can live in your castle again. The ghosts won't bother you any more." The nobleman thanked him, rewarded him generously, asked him to stay and enter his service, promising to provide for him as long as he lived. "No," said Brother Scamp. "I'm used to wandering around. I'll just hit the road." On his way, Brother Scamp stopped at a smithy, put the knapsack with the devils in it on the anvil, and asked the black-smith and his apprentices to pound it with all their might. The devils howled pitifully, and when he opened the knapsack eight were dead, but one, who had been in a fold, was still alive. That one slipped away and went back to hell.

Brother Scamp knocked about for a long time, and if anyone knew the story he'd have a long story to tell. But finally he grew old and thought of his death, so he went to a hermit who was known for his piety and said: "I'm tired of wandering, and now I want to see about getting into the kingdom of heaven." The hermit replied: "There are two roads. The one is broad and pleasant and leads to hell; the other is narrow and rough and leads to heaven." "I'd be a fool," thought Brother Scamp, "to take the rough and narrow way." So he took the broad, pleasant way and finally came to a big black gate. It was the gate of hell. He knocked, and the gatekeeper looked out to see who was there. When he saw Brother Scamp, he gave a start, for he just happened to be the ninth devil who had been in the knapsack with the others but had come off with only a black eye. Quick, he slammed the gate, bolted it, and ran to the head devil. "There's a man outside with a knapsack," he cried. "He wants to come in, but for goodness' sake don't let him, or he'll wish all hell into his knapsack. He had me in it and what a terrible pounding I got!" Brother Scamp was told he couldn't come in and should go away. "If they don't want me here," he thought, "I'll see if there's a place for me in heaven. I've got to stay somewhere." So he turned around and traveled until he came to the gate of heaven, and there again he knocked. St. Peter was on duty as gatekeeper, and Brother Scamp recognized him right off. "Well, if it isn't my old friend!" he thought. "He'll give me a better deal." But St. Peter said: "I can hardly believe it! You think you can get into heaven!" "Let me in, brother, I've got to go somewhere; if they'd taken me in hell, I wouldn't have come to you." "Nothing doing," said St. Peter, "you can't get in here." "Well," said Brother Scamp, "if you won't let me in, take back your knapsack, because I don't want to keep anything of yours." "Very well," said St. Peter. "Hand it over." He passed the knapsack through the bars, and St. Peter hung it up beside his chair. "Now," said Brother Scamp, "I wish myself into the knapsack." Whish! There he was in the knapsack, which was in heaven, and St. Peter had to let him stay there.

82

Hans the Gambler

THERE WAS ONCE a man who did nothing but gamble, so people called him Hans the Gambler, and he kept on gambling until he had lost his house and everything else. The day before his creditors were due to take his house, the Lord and St. Peter came and asked him to put them up for the night. Hans the Gambler said to them: "You're welcome to stay the night, but I can't give you a bed or anything to eat." The Lord said they'd buy their own food if only he'd put them up, and that was all right with Hans the Gambler. Then St. Peter gave him three groschen and told him to run over to the baker's for a loaf of bread. Hans started out, but he had to pass the house where the other no-good gamblers, who had won everything he owned, were playing cards, and they called out to him: "Hey, Hans, come on in!" "Oh no," he said. "You've cleaned me out, and now you're after my three groschen." But they wouldn't let him go. All this time St. Peter and the Lord had been waiting, and when he didn't come back, they went out to meet him. When he saw them coming down the street, he pretended he had dropped the money in a puddle and poked around as if he were looking for it, but the Lord knew he had gambled it away. St. Peter gave him three more groschen, but this time he didn't let himself be tempted and brought back the bread. The Lord asked him if he didn't have any wine, and he said: "No, sir, the barrels are all empty." But the Lord said: "Go down and look. The best wine is still there." At first he refused to believe it, but after a while he said: "All right, I'll go down, but I know there isn't any." He turned the tap and out came the very best wine. So he brought them the wine, and the two of them stayed the night. Early next morning, the Lord told Hans the Gambler to ask for three gifts. The Lord thought he'd ask to go to heaven, but Hans the Gambler asked for a deck of cards that would always win, dice that would always win, and a tree with all kinds of fruit growing on it. And another thing about this tree was that if somebody climbed it he wouldn't be able to come down until Hans told him to. The Lord gave him what he had wished for and went his way with St. Peter.

After that Hans the Gambler began to gamble in earnest and soon he was close to winning half the world. St. Peter said to the Lord: "Lord, this won't do. He'll end up by winning the whole world; we'll have to send Death to take him away." And so they did. When Death came to him, Hans was sitting at the gaming table. "Hans," said Death, "would you come outside with me for a minute?" But Hans said: "Just wait till this game is over. In the meantime, you could climb that tree out there and get us a little something to nibble on the way." So Death climbed the tree, but when he wanted to come down he couldn't. Hans the Gambler left him there for seven years, and in all that time nobody died.

Finally St. Peter said to the Lord: "Lord, this won't do. Nobody's dying any more. We'll have to see about this." So they went to see about it, and the Lord told Hans to let Death come down. Hans went to Death and said: "Come down!" Death grabbed him and strangled him, and away they went together to the other world. When they got there, Hans the Gambler went straight to the gate of heaven and knocked. "Who's there?" "Hans the Gambler." "We don't need you here. Go away." Then he went to the gate of purgatory and knocked again. "Who's there?" "Hans the Gambler." "No gambling here, we've got weeping and wailing enough already. Go away." So he went and knocked at the gate of hell, and there they let him in. But no one was home except old Lucifer and his lame devils, because all the straight-limbed ones had gone to earth on business, and the second he got there he sat down and started gambling again. Lucifer had nothing to stake but his lame devils, and Hans the Gambler won them all, because with his deck of cards he couldn't lose. He took the lame devils away with him, and they went to Hohenfurt, where they pulled up the hop poles. Then they went up to heaven and started to pry it loose. Heaven was beginning to crack, so St. Peter said: "'Lord, this won't do. We'll have to let him in, or he'll topple heaven over." So they let him in. But Hans the Gambler started right in gambling, and before you knew it there was such noise and confusion that no one could hear himself think. "Lord, this won't do," said St. Peter for the last time. "We'll have to throw him down, or he'll drive all heaven crazy." So they sent for him and threw him down. His soul was smashed and the splinters went into all the no-good gamblers that are living to this day.

83

Hans in Luck

AFTER SERVING HIS MASTER for seven years, Hans said to him: "Master, my time is up. I want to go back home to my mother, so give me my wages." His master replied: "You have served me honestly and faithfully, and I shall reward you likewise." Whereupon he gave Hans a lump of gold as big as his head. Hans pulled out his handkerchief, wrapped the gold in it, hoisted it up on his shoulder, and started for home. As he was plodding down the road, putting one foot in front of the other, he caught sight of a horseman riding along, as fresh and carefree as you please. "Ah," cried Hans, "what a lovely thing it is to ride! You're sitting as comfortably as in a chair, you don't stub your toes on any stones, you save shoe leather, and you move along without the slightest effort." The horseman, who had heard him, stopped and called out: "Then why are you walking, Hans?" "I have to," he said. "I've got this big lump to take home. True enough, it's gold, but it won't let me hold my head straight, and it weighs my shoulder down." "I'll tell you what," said the horseman. "Let's trade. I'll give you my horse, and you'll give me your lump of gold." "Gladly," said Hans, "but I'm warning you, it's very heavy, you're letting yourself in for something." The rider dismounted, took the gold, helped Hans into the saddle, put the reins firmly into his hands and said: "If you want to go really fast, you've got to click your tongue and shout, 'Gee up.'"

Hans was as happy as a lark to be sitting on the back of a horse, riding along so light and easy. After a while he thought it would be nice to go faster, so he clicked his tongue and shouted, "Gee up." The horse went into a brisk trot. Before Hans knew it, he'd been thrown and was lying in a ditch between the road and the fields. The horse would have run away if he hadn't been stopped by a peasant who happened to be coming along with a cow. Hans collected his limbs and scrambled to his feet. But he was out of sorts, and he said to the peasant: "Riding is no joke, especially when you get hold of a plug like this, that bucks and throws you. Why, I could have broken my neck. You'll never catch me riding again. Now your cow is a different story. You can amble along with her as slowly as you please, and in addition you're sure of having milk, butter, and cheese every day. What wouldn't I give for a cow like that!" "Well," said the peasant, "if it would make you happy, I'd be willing to trade my cow for your horse." Hans accepted with gladness in his heart, and the peasant mounted as fast as he could and galloped away.

Hans drove his cow quietly along, thinking about the fine bargain he had struck. "As long as I have a chunk of bread, and I can count on that, I'll always have butter and cheese to go with it. And if I'm thirsty, I'll just milk my cow. What more could I ask for?" When he came to a tavern, he stopped, joyfully ate all the food he had taken with him—his noonday meal and his supper—and invested his last few hellers in half a glass of beer. Then he went on with his cow, still in the direction of his mother's village. The heat became more and more crushing as the sun rose in the sky, and Hans was crossing a heath that looked as if it would take another hour to cross. He was so hot the thirst made his tongue stick to the roof of his mouth. "That's easily remedied," he thought. "I'll milk my cow and drink to my heart's content." He hitched the cow to a stump and, seeing as he had no pail, put his leather cap underneath. And he tried and he tried, but he couldn't get one drop of milk out of her. And besides, he was so clumsy about it that the cow finally lost patience and gave him such a kick in the head that he fell to the ground and for quite some time couldn't remember where he was. Luckily a butcher came along just then, carrying a young pig on a wheelbarrow. "Hey, what's going on here?" he cried, and helped our good Hans up. Hans told him what had happened. The butcher handed him his flask, saying: "Here, take a drink, it will make you feel better. That cow won't give any milk, she's too old. At the most she could pull a plow, or you could slaughter her." "Oh dear!" said Hans, running his fingers through his hair. "That is bad news. Of course it's a great thing to have an animal to butcher. All that meat! But I don't care much for cow meat, it's too dry. A young pig would be something else again, not to mention the sausages." "Listen to me, Hans," said the butcher. "As a personal favor, I'll trade you, the pig for the cow." "God bless you for your kindness," said Hans and gave the cow to the butcher, who untied the pig, removed him from the wheelbarrow, and pressed the lead rope into Hans's hand.

Hans went on, thinking how lucky he was; whenever there was any annoyance, it got straightened out before he knew it. After a while he found himself walking beside a young fellow with a fine white goose under his arm. They bade each other good day, and Hans began telling him about his luck and the trades he had made, always to his advantage. The young fellow told Hans he was taking the goose to a christening feast. "Feel the weight," he said, picking it up by the wings. "They've been fattening this bird for the last eight weeks. Anyone who takes a bite out of her will have to wipe the fat off both cheeks." "Yes, indeed," said Hans, hefting the goose in one hand. "It's a good weight, but my pig here is no slouch either." Meanwhile the young fellow was darting suspicious glances in all directions, and shaking his head from time to time. "Hmm," he said finally. "I don't know about that pig of yours. The mayor of the village I passed through a little while ago just had a pig stolen out of his barn. I'm afraid, very much afraid, it's the one you've got there. They've sent out some men, and I wouldn't want to be in your shoes if they catch you with that pig. At the very least, they'd throw you in the jug." Our good Hans was scared out of his wits. "Lordy!" he said. "Couldn't you help me out of this fix, you know your way around these parts better than I do. Take my pig and give me your goose." "It'll be risky for me too," said the young fellow. "But I wouldn't want you to get into trouble through any fault of mine." So he took the rope and hurried off into a bypath with the pig. Relieved of his worries, our good Hans resumed his homeward journey with the goose under his arm. "When you come right down to it," he said to himself, "I've gained by the trade: first, the beautiful roast goose I'll have, second, all the fat that will drip into the pan—why, I'll be able to butter my bread with goose fat for the next three months— and third, the lovely white feathers. No one will have to rock me to sleep once I've stuffed them into my pillow. How happy my mother will be!"

As he was passing through the last village, a scissors grinder was standing there with his grindstone. His wheel whirred, and he sang:

"Grinding scissors is my trade,
I grind whatever has a blade,
And as I grind I keep an eye
On everyone who passes by."

Hans stopped and watched, and after a while he went over to him. "Lucky man!" he said. "Grinding away so merrily." "Oh yes," said the scissors grinder. "Learn a trade and your living's made. A good scissors grinder is a man who can't put his hand in his pocket without finding money. But where did you buy that fine goose?" "I didn't buy it. I traded my pig for it." "And the pig?" "I traded a cow for it." "And the cow?" "I got it in exchange for a horse." "And the horse?" "I gave a lump of gold as big as my head for it." "And the gold?" "Oh, that was my wage for seven years' service." "You made a good thing of it every time," said the scissors grinder. "But your fortune will really be made when you arrange matters so as to hear the money jingling in your pocket every time you stand up." "How do I go about that?" Hans asked. "Become a scissors grinder like me. All you need is a grindstone, the rest will take care of itself. I've got one right here. It's not in very good condition, but I'll let it go cheap; just give me your goose. What do you say?" "How can you ask?" said Hans. "Why, I'll be the happiest man on earth. If I find money every time I put my hand in my pocket, I won't have a thing to worry about." With that he handed him the goose and took the grindstone. "And now," said the scissors grinder, picking up a common ordinary stone that was lying beside him on the ground, "I'll throw in this useful stone. It's good for hammering on, you'll be able to straighten your old nails. Take good care of it."

Hans took the stones and went his way with a happy heart. His eyes sparkled for joy. "I must have been born under a lucky star," he said. "Everything I wish for comes to me, it's just as if I were a Sunday's child." He had been on his feet since daybreak and was beginning to feel tired. He was also plagued by hunger, for in his joy at trading his horse for a cow he had eaten up all his provisions. In the end he was dragging himself painfully along, and had to stop every few minutes. Worst of all, the weight of the stones was killing him, and he couldn't help thinking how lovely it would be if he didn't have to carry them just then. Creeping along at a snail's pace, he finally came to a well, and there he decided to rest and have a nice refreshing drink of cold water. For fear of damaging the stones in sitting down, he first laid them carefully on the rim of the well. But when he leaned over to drink, he made a false move and grazed the stones. Both of them tumbled into the well. When he saw them sinking, Hans jumped for joy, knelt down and thanked God with tears in his eyes for showing him this great mercy after so many others, for relieving him of those heavy stones, his last burdens, and doing it in such a kindly way that he had no need to reproach himself. "No one under the sun is as lucky as I am!" he cried. And light of heart, without a care in the world, he ran home to his mother.

84

Hans Gets Married

THERE WAS ONCE a young peasant by the name of Hans whose cousin decided to get him a rich wife. So he made a good fire in the stove and set Hans down behind it. Then he brought in a bowl of milk and a lot of white bread, put a freshly minted coin in his hand, and said: "Hans, keep a good hold on this coin, break the bread into the milk, and stay right here until I get back." "All right," said Hans, "I'll do just as you say." The cousin put on a pair of patched old trousers and went to call on the daughter of a rich peasant in the next village. "What would you think of marrying my cousin Hans?" he asked. "You'll be getting a good sensible man. He'll make you happy." "How's he fixed for the wherewithal?" the grasping father asked. "Has he bread to break?" "My dear man," was the answer, "my young cousin isn't out in the cold. He's got a nice bit of money in hand, and plenty of bread to break. What's more, he's got as many patches (plots of land were then known as patches) as I have," and while speaking the cousin slapped his patched trousers. "Come with me if you like, and you'll see that I'm telling the truth." The grasping father thought the opportunity was too good to miss. "If that's how it is," he said, "I have no objection to the marriage."

So they were married on the day set, and when the young wife asked to go out and see her husband's land, Hans took off his Sunday clothes and put on his old patched smock, saying: "I wouldn't want to spoil my good clothes." They went out together, and wherever a patch of vineyard, field, or meadow was marked off, Hans would point his finger at it, at the same time tapping one of the big or little patches on his smock. "That patch is mine," he would say, "and so's that one, my dear, just look"—meaning that his wife shouldn't gape at the fields but look at his smock, which really did belong to him.

"Were you at the wedding?" "Oh yes, I was there, in all my finery. My headdress was of snow, but then the sun came out and it melted. My gown was of cobwebs, I walked through brambles and they tore it off me. My slippers were glass, and when I bumped into a stone they said, "Clink!" and broke into pieces.

85
The Golden Children

THERE WERE ONCE a poor man and a poor woman, who had nothing but a small hut, and they fished for a living and lived from hand to mouth. One day as the man was sitting by the shore casting his net, he pulled in a fish that was all of gold. And while he was gaping in amazement, the fish began to speak and said: "Listen to me, fisherman. If you let me go, I'll turn your hut into a magnificent palace." The fisherman replied: "What good will a palace be to me when I have nothing to eat?" "That will be taken care of," said the golden fish. "There will be a cupboard in the palace, and when you open it, you will find platters full of wonderful things to eat, the best you could possibly wish for." "In that case," said the fisherman, "I'll be glad to oblige." "Good," said the fish. "But there's one condition. You mustn't tell anyone, not a living soul, where your good fortune came from. If you breathe a single word, it will all be over."

The man threw the miraculous fish back into the water and went home. Where his hut had been there was now a huge palace. For a moment he stood and stared, but then he went in and found his wife dressed like a queen and sitting in a magnificent room. She was very happy. "Husband!" she said, "look what's happened all of a sudden! I like it." "So do I," said the man, "but I'm famished. Get me something to eat." "I haven't got anything," said the wife, "and I can't find a thing in this new house." "Don't let that worry you," said the husband. "See that big cupboard over there? Just open it." When she opened the cupboard, she found cake, meat, fruit, and wine, a heartwarming sight, and called out joyfully: "Oh, my dearest! What more could anyone wish for?" So they sat down and ate and drank together. When they had had enough, the wife said: "But tell me, husband, where did all this splendor come from?" "Don't ask me that," he said. "I'm not allowed to tell you. If I were to tell anyone, it would be all up with our good fortune." "Very well," she said. "If

I'm not supposed to know, then I don't want to know." But she didn't mean it. Day and night she could think of nothing else, and she kept pestering her husband until he lost patience and blurted out that it all came from a miraculous golden fish he had caught and thrown back into the sea. And no sooner had he spoken than the beautiful palace vanished, cupboard and all, and there they were, in the same old fisherman's hut.

The man had to go back to his fishing. But as luck would have it, he pulled up the golden fish again. "Listen to me," said the fish. "If you let me go, I'll give you back the palace with its cupboard full of boiled meats and roast meats. But be firm, and for goodness' sake don't tell anyone whom you got it from, or you'll lose it again." "I certainly won't," said the fisherman, and threw the fish back into the water. When he got home, there was the palace in all its splendor, and his wife was overjoyed at their good fortune. But her curiosity kept nagging at her and a few days later she started asking questions again: How had it come about? How had he managed it? For a while the fisherman kept silent, but in the end she had him so riled that he exploded and out came the secret. Instantly the palace vanished and they were back in their old hut. "Now you've done it!" said the fisherman. "Now we can go hungry again." "Well," said his wife, "if I don't know where my riches come from, I'd rather not have them. It makes me nervous."

The man went fishing again, and after a while he pulled in the golden fish for the third time. "Listen to me," said the fish. "I see I'm doomed to keep falling into your hands. Take me home and cut me into six pieces. Give two to your wife to eat, give two to your horse, and bury two in the ground. It will bring you good fortune." The man took the fish home and did as he had been told. From the two pieces he buried in the ground grew two golden lilies, the horse had two golden foals, and the fisherman's wife gave birth to two little boys, who were all of gold.

The boys grew up to be tall and handsome, and the lilies and horses grew along with them. One day the boys said: "Father, we would like to ride out into the world on our golden horses." He replied sadly: "How shall I bear it when you're gone and I don't know how you're getting along?" They answered: "The two golden lilies will stay here, and you'll be able to tell by looking at them. If they stay fresh, we shall be in good health; if they fade, we shall be sick; if they topple over, we shall be dead." They rode away and came to a tavern full of people. When the people saw the two golden children they laughed at them and mocked them. Hearing the mockery, one brother was overcome with shame and didn't want to go out into the world any more, so he went back home to his father. But the other rode on and came to a great forest. As he was riding into it, the people said: "Better stay out of that forest, it's full of robbers. They're sure to attack you, and when they see that you and your horse are made of gold, they'll kill you." But he knew no fear and said: "I must and will go through it." Thereupon he took bearskins and covered himself and his horse with them, so that nothing could be seen of the gold, and rode calmly into the forest. When he had gone a little way, he heard a rustling in the bushes, and then voices. From one side a voice called out: "Here comes somebody now," and from the other, "let him go. It's a bearskinner (a tramp), he's sure to be as poor as a churchmouse. What can we get out of him?" So the golden child rode straight through the forest, and nothing happened to him.

One day he came to a village, and there he saw a girl who was so beautiful he thought there could be none more beautiful on earth. His love for her was so great that he went to her and said: "I love you with all my heart. Will you be my wife?" The girl liked him so well in return that she consented, saying: "Yes, I will be your wife and remain faithful to you as long as I live." The wedding was held, and just as their rejoicing was at its height the bride's father came home and was surprised to see that his daughter was having her wedding celebration. "Where is the bridegroom?" he asked. They pointed out the golden child, but he was still wrapped up in his bearskins. The father said angrily: "No bearskinner can marry my daughter," and was going to murder him. The bride begged and pleaded, saying: "But he's my husband, I love him with all my heart," and in the end her father calmed down. But his daughter's husband was still on his mind, and the next morning he got up early to take a good look at him and see if he was really a common tramp. When he went in, he saw a beautiful golden man in the bed and the cast-off bearskins were lying on the floor. So he went back to his own room and thought: "Lucky I kept my temper, I might have committed a terrible crime."

That night the golden child dreamed he was hunting a magnificent stag, and when he woke up in the morning he said to his bride: "I'm going hunting." She was worried and begged him to stay home, saying: "I'm afraid something terrible will happen to you." But he replied: "I must and will go." He got up and went out into the forest, and it wasn't long before a noble stag stopped him just as in his dream. He raised his gun and was going to shoot, but the stag bounded away. All day he chased the stag through thickets and over ditches, and never got tired. At dusk he lost sight of the beast, and when he stopped to look around there was a little house not far off. It was a witch's house. When he knocked, an old crone came out and said: "What are you doing in this big forest so late in the day?" "Have you seen a stag?" he asked. "Oh yes," she said, "I know that stag well." A little dog, which had come out of the house with her, barked at him ferociously. He said to the dog: "Quiet, you wicked toad, or I'll shoot you dead." The witch cried out angrily: "What's this? Threatening to kill my little dog?" That same second she turned him into a stone, and there he lay. His bride waited in vain for him to come home and said: "The thing I was so afraid of, that weighed so heavily on my heart, must have happened."

Back home the other brother was looking at the golden lilies when suddenly one of them toppled over. "Good God!" he cried. "Something terrible has happened to my brother! I must go and find him. Maybe I can save him." His father said: "Don't go. What will become of me if I lose you too?" But he replied: "I must and will go." Away he rode on his golden horse and came at last to the big forest where his brother was lying, turned to stone. The old witch came out of her house and called out to him. She was going to turn him to stone, but instead of going near her he said: "Bring my brother back to life or I'll shoot you." She couldn't help herself; she touched the stone with her finger, and in a flash it came to life. The two golden children were overjoyed to see each other again. They hugged and kissed and rode out of the forest together, the one to his bride, the other home to his father. The father said: "I knew you had saved your brother, because suddenly the golden lily stood up as fresh and blooming as before." After that, they lived happily and everything went well with them until they died.

86

The Fox and the Geese

ONCE THE FOX CAME to a meadow and saw a flock of fine fat geese. He laughed and said: "What luck to find you all together! I'll be able to eat you one by one without wasting time." The geese cackled in terror, wept and wailed and begged for their lives. But the fox was unmoved, and said: "There will be no mercy. You must die." Finally one of them summoned up the courage to speak. "If we poor geese must lose our innocent young lives," she said, "grant us but one kindness: give us time to say one last prayer lest we die in sin. Then we shall all line up in a row so you can pick out the fattest every time. "Very well," said the fox, "that is a proper and pious wish. Go ahead and pray, I'll wait till you're finished." The first began a long-drawn-out prayer that went "Ga! ga! ga! ga!" over and over again. And since she went on and on, the second, instead of waiting her turn, started in with her "Ga! ga!" The third and fourth followed, and soon they were all cackling together. (Our story will resume when they have finished praying, but for the present they are still at it.)

87

The Poor Man and
the Rich Man

ONCE LONG, LONG AGO, when the Lord still walked the earth and rubbed shoulders with men, it so happened that he was tired at the end of the day, and night overtook him before he could find an inn. He came to two houses on opposite sides of the road, the one large and splendid, the other small and run-down. The big one belonged to a rich man and the small one to a poor man. The Lord said to himself: "I won't be a burden to the rich man if I spend the night at his house." When the rich man heard someone knocking at the door, he opened the window and asked the stranger what he wanted. The Lord answered: "Could you put me up for the night?" The rich man examined the stranger from top to toe, and seeing he was simply dressed and didn't look as if he had much money in his pocket, he shook his head, saying: "I can't take you in. I have herbs and seeds spread out to dry in every room, and besides, if I were to lodge everyone who knocked at my door, I'd soon have to go begging myself. Try somewhere else." Whereupon he shut the window and left the Lord standing there.

So the Lord turned his back on the rich man and went to the small house. He had hardly knocked when the poor man unlatched the door and asked him in. "Do spend the night in my house," he said. "You can't go any farther in this darkness." That pleased the Lord, and he went in. The poor man's wife clasped his hand in welcome and told him to make himself at home. "We haven't got much," she said, "but what little we have we will gladly share with you." She put potatoes on the fire, and while they were cooking she milked the goat, so as to have a little milk to go with them. When the meal was ready, the Lord sat down and ate with them, and he enjoyed the coarse food because of the happy faces. When they had eaten and it was time to go to bed, the wife called her husband aside and said: "Dear husband, couldn't we give the wayfarer our bed? The poor man has been walking all day and needs a good night's rest. We can pile up some straw in the corner for ourselves." "That's just what we'll do," said the poor man. So he went and told the Lord he could sleep in their bed if he wished, and give his limbs a good rest. The Lord didn't want to deprive the old people of their bed, but they insisted and he finally gave in. He lay down in their bed and they piled up straw for themselves on the floor. Next morning they got up before daybreak and made their guest the best breakfast they could. The Lord got up when the sun shone through the window. Again he ate with them. Then, after taking his leave, he turned around in the doorway and said: "Because you are so kindly and pious, I will grant you three wishes." The poor man said: "I can think of only two things to wish for: eternal salvation, and in this life good health for us both and our daily bread. What else could I wish for?" "Wouldn't you like a new house instead of this one?" the Lord asked. "Oh yes," said the man. "I'd like it very much if I could have that too." The Lord granted their wishes, turned their old house into a new one, gave them his blessing, and went his way.

The sun was high in the sky when the rich man got up. He looked out of the window and what did he see on the other side of the road but a fine new house roofed with red tiles, where an old hovel had stood the day before. For a moment he stood gaping, then he called his wife and said: "What's going on here? Look at that fine new house where only yesterday there was a ramshackle old hovel. Run over and find out how it got there." The wife went and questioned the poor man, and he explained: "Yesterday evening a wayfarer came to the door and asked us to put him up for the night. When he took leave of us this morning, he granted us three wishes: eternal salvation, good health and our daily bread in this life, and last, a fine new house instead of our old hovel." The rich man's wife hurried back and told her husband the whole story. "I could tear my hair out and kill myself!" he cried. "If I'd only known. That stranger came here first. He asked me to put him up for the night and I turned him away." "Hurry and saddle the mare," said his wife. "You can still catch up with him and get him to grant you three wishes."

The rich man took her good advice, galloped away and soon caught up with the Lord. He spoke as if butter wouldn't melt in his mouth and begged the stranger not to take it amiss that he hadn't let him in right away. "I was looking for the key," he explained, "and while I was looking you went away, but if you pass this way again you mustn't fail to spend the night with us." "So I will," said the Lord, "if I pass this way again." Whereupon the rich man asked if he could make three wishes like his neighbor. "You may," said the Lord. "But they won't do you any good, and I wouldn't advise it." "Don't worry about me," said the rich man. "Once I'm sure my wishes will come true, I'll know what to wish for." "Go home," said the Lord. "Your three wishes will come true."

Now that the rich man had what he wanted, he started for home.

On the way he pondered what he could wish for. As he was ponder-
ing, he dropped the reins and the mare began to frisk and caper so
that he couldn't collect his thoughts. He patted her neck and said:
"Easy there, Lisa," but the mare only went on capering. In the end
he lost patience and cried out: "I wish you'd break your neck!" The
words were hardly out of his mouth when *plunk!* the rich man fell to
the ground and the mare lay stone dead. His first wish had come true.
He was too miserly to abandon the horse's harness, so he cut it off,
slung it over his shoulder, and started for home on foot, consoling
himself with the thought that he still had two wishes left. As he was
plodding through the sand, the midday sun beat down and he began
to feel hot and peevish. The saddle weighed on his back, and to make
matters worse he couldn't decide what to wish for. He said to himself: "Even if I wish for all the kingdoms and treasures in the world, I
know in advance that once I get them I'm sure to think of other
things I could have wished for. I must wish in such a way that there
won't be anything left to wish for." Then he sighed and said: "If
only I were the Bavarian peasant who was granted three wishes. He
knew what to wish for: first for plenty of beer, second for as much
beer as he could drink, and third for yet another barrel." Sometimes
he thought he had the answer, but then he felt he wouldn't be asking
quite enough. Suddenly it occurred to him that his wife was too lucky
for words, sitting home in a cool room, nibbling goodies. The
thought made him angry, and before he knew it he said: "I wish she
were sitting on this saddle and couldn't get off, instead of my having
to carry it on my back." No sooner had the last word crossed his lips
than the saddle was gone from his back and he saw that his second
wish had come true. At that he began to run, for what he wanted most
in all the world was to be all alone in his room, thinking of something
splendid for his last wish. But when he got to his house and opened
the door, there was his wife on the saddle in the middle of the room,
screaming and yelling because she couldn't get off. "Stop complaining," he said. "Stay right where you are and I'll wish you all the
riches in the world." "Blockhead!" she cried. "What good will all
the riches in the world do me if I have to keep sitting on this saddle?
You wished me onto it, now you can wish me off it." Like it or not, he
had to use up his third wish getting her off the saddle, and it came

true the second he made it. So he had gained nothing but vexation, trouble, abuse, and a dead horse. As for the poor people, they lived happily, in humble piety, until they died and were rewarded with eternal salvation.

88
The Lilting, Leaping Lark

THERE WAS ONCE a man who was going on a long journey, and as he was taking leave of his three daughters he asked them what he should bring them. The eldest asked for pearls and the second asked for diamonds, but the third said: "Father dear, I should like a lilting, leaping lark." "If I can find one, you shall have it," said the father, whereupon he kissed all three of them and started out. When the time came for him to return home, he had bought pearls and diamonds for the two eldest, but though he had looked everywhere, he hadn't found a lilting, leaping lark for the youngest, and that grieved him because she was his favorite child. His way led him through a forest. In the middle of the forest there was a magnificent castle, and not far from the castle there was a tree, and in the very top of the tree he saw a lark lilting and leaping. "Oho!" he cried. "Well met!" He bade his servant climb the tree and catch the little bird, but as the servant approached, a lion, who had been lying under the tree, jumped up, shook himself, and roared so thunderously that the leaves on the trees trembled. "If anyone tries to steal my lilting, leaping lark," he cried, "I'll eat him up!" The man replied: "I didn't know the bird belonged to you. I'll gladly make amends and pay you good money if only you'll spare my life." The lion said: "Nothing can save you, unless you promise to give me whatever creature you meet first when you get home; but if you promise me that, I shall not only spare your life but also give you the bird for your daughter." The man refused. "That could be my youngest daughter," he said. "It's she who loves me best and always runs to meet me when I come home." But the servant was afraid of the lion and said: "Maybe it won't be your daughter; it could just as well be a cat or a dog." The man let himself be won over, took the lilting, leaping lark, and promised to give the lion whatever creature he met first when he got home.

When he reached home and went into the house, the first creature he met was none other than his youngest, best-beloved daughter. She came running and hugged him and kissed him, and when she saw he had brought her a lilting, leaping lark she was beside herself with joy. But her father wasn't happy at all. He burst into tears and said: "Dearest child, this little bird has cost me dear. I had to promise you to a ferocious lion, and when he gets you he'll tear you to pieces and eat you up." Then he told her the whole story and implored her not to go, come what might. But she comforted him and said: "Dearest father, if you've made a promise you must keep it. I'm sure I can calm the lion and return home safely." The next morning, after her father had shown her the way, she took her leave, and went fearlessly into the forest.

Now it so happened that this lion was an enchanted prince. He and all his courtiers were lions by day, but at night they resumed their natural human form. When she arrived, they welcomed her and took her to the castle. At nightfall the lion became a handsome man. The wedding was celebrated with splendor, and afterward they lived happily, staying up at night and sleeping in the daytime. One night he said to her: "There's to be a feast at your father's house tomorrow, for your eldest sister is being married. If you'd like to go, my lions will escort you." "Oh yes," she said. "I long to see my father." So she set out and the lions went with her. There was great rejoicing when she got home, for everyone thought the lion had torn her to pieces and that she had long been dead, but she told them what a handsome husband she had and how happy she was. She stayed there all through the wedding feast and then she went back to the forest. When the second daughter was to be married, she was again invited to the wedding. She said to the lion: "Don't make me go alone this time; I want you to come along." But the lion said that would be too dangerous, because if a ray of candlelight should strike him it would turn him into a dove and he would have to fly around with the doves for seven years. "Oh, please, please come!" she said. "I'll take good care of you and protect you from the light." So they went together and took their baby with them. When they arrived they arranged with the masons to build a room with walls so thick that no light could shine through them, and there he sat when the candles were lit for the wedding. But the door had been made of green wood that had dried and sprung a tiny crack that no one noticed. The wedding was celebrated with pomp and splendor, and when the procession with all its hundreds of torches and candles passed the room on its way back from the church a hair's breadth of light fell on the prince, and the moment it touched him he was transformed. When she came in and looked for him, he was nowhere to be seen, there was only a white dove. The dove said to her: "For seven years I shall have to fly through the world. But every seven paces I shall let fall a drop of red blood and a white feather. They will show you the way, and if you follow my track you will be able to set me free."

The dove flew out the door and she followed it, and every seven paces a drop of red blood and a white feather fell and showed her the way. Farther and farther she went into the wide world. She never looked around her and never rested, and one day the seven years were almost over. Then she was happy, for she thought they would soon be set free, but they still had a long way to go. Once as she was walking along, no feather fell and no drop of blood, and when she looked up the dove had vanished. "No human being can help me now," she said to herself, and climbed up to the sun. "You shine on every hill and hollow," she said. "Have you seen a white dove by any chance?" "No," said the sun, "I haven't, but I'll give you a little box. Open it when you're in great trouble." She thanked the sun and went on until night fell and the moon came out. "You shine all night on every field and forest," she said to the moon. "Have you seen a white dove by any chance?" "No," said the moon, "I haven't. But I'll give you this egg. Break it when you're in great trouble." She thanked the moon and went on until the night wind arose and blew on her. "You blow over every tree and under every leaf," she said to the night wind. "Have you seen a white dove by any chance?" "No, I haven't," said the night wind, "but I'll ask the other three winds. Maybe they've seen the white dove." The east wind and the west wind came and they had seen nothing, but the south wind said: "I have seen the white dove. It flew to the Red Sea, and there it became a lion again, for the seven years are over. The lion is fighting a dragon, and this dragon is an enchanted princess." And the night wind said to her: "I'll tell you what to do. Go to the Red Sea. On the right bank you'll see tall reeds growing. Count them, cut off the eleventh, and strike the dragon with it. Once you do that, the lion will be able to overpower the dragon, and both will regain their human form. Then look around and you will see the griffin on the shore of the Red Sea. Climb on its back with your dearest and it will carry you home across the sea. And now take this nut. When you're over the middle of the Red Sea, drop it. It will sprout, and a tall nut tree will spring up from the water for the griffin to rest on, because if it can't rest it won't have the strength to carry you across, and if you forget to drop the nut, it will let you fall into the sea.

So she went to the Red Sea and found everything just as the night wind had said. She counted the reeds on the bank and cut the eleventh and struck the dragon with it. The lion overpowered the dragon and both recovered their human form. But the moment the princess who had been the dragon was released from the enchantment, she picked the prince up in her arms, climbed on the griffin's back and carried him away with her. So there the poor girl stood after traveling so far, alone and forsaken again. She sat down and wept, but after a while she took heart and said: "I will keep going as far as the wind blows and as long as the cock crows, until I find him." Again she set out and traveled a long long way. Finally she came to a castle where he and the princess were living and heard they would soon be celebrating their wedding feast. She said to herself: "God will help me yet," and opened the little box the sun had given her. In it was a dress, as resplendent as the sun. She put on the dress and went to the castle, and all the courtiers and the bride herself looked at her with amazement. The bride liked the dress so much she thought it might do for her wedding dress. "Is it for sale?" she asked. "Not for silver and gold," the girl answered, "but for flesh and blood." The bride asked her what she meant by that, and she said: "Let me spend one night in the room where the bridegroom sleeps." The bride didn't want to let her, but she did want the dress, so she finally gave in, but she made the prince's manservant give him a sleeping potion. That night when the prince was asleep the girl was brought to his room. She sat down at his bedside and said: "I've followed you for seven years; I went to the sun and the moon and the four winds to ask after you, and I helped you in your fight with the dragon. Have you forgotten me entirely?" But the prince was sleeping so soundly that he only thought the fir trees were sighing in the wind. At dawn they led her away and she had to part with the golden dress.

When she saw her trick hadn't helped her, she was very sad. She sat down in a meadow and wept, and as she was sitting there she remembered the egg the moon had given her. She cracked it and out came a mother hen and twelve little golden chicks, which ran about and cheeped and crept back under their mother's wings. You couldn't have imagined a prettier sight in the whole world. She stood up and walked about the meadow, driving the hen and her brood before her until the bride looked out of the window and liked the little chicks so much that she came down and asked if they were for sale. "Not for silver and gold, but for flesh and blood. Let me spend another night in the room where the bridegroom sleeps." The bride consented, planning to cheat her as she had the night before. But when the prince went to bed, he asked his manservant about the rustling and murmuring during the night. Then the manservant told him the whole story, saying: "I was made to give you a sleeping potion because of a poor girl who secretly spent the night in your room, and I'm supposed to give you another tonight." "Empty out the potion beside my bed," said the prince. That night she was led in again and when she began to tell him what a sad time she had been having he instantly recognized his beloved wife by her voice. He jumped up and cried: "Now I am really set free! It's as if I'd been dreaming. The strange princess bewitched me and made me forget you, but God has lifted the spell before it's too late." They were afraid of the princess's father, who was a wizard, so during the night they slipped away from the castle and climbed on the griffin's back. The griffin carried them over the Red Sea. When they were in the middle, she dropped the nut and a tall nut tree sprang up. The griffin took a rest and then carried them home, where they found their child, who had grown to be tall and handsome. After that they lived happily until they died.

89

The Goose Girl

THERE WAS ONCE an old queen, whose husband had long been dead, and she had a beautiful daughter. When the princess was old enough, she was betrothed to a king's son who lived far away, and soon it was time for the marriage. The princess prepared to set out for the distant kingdom, and the queen packed all manner of precious things, jewels and goblets and gold and silver plate, in short, everything required for a royal dowry, for she loved her child with all her heart. And she also gave her a waiting maid to keep her company on the way and see to it that she reached her bridegroom safely. They were both given horses for the journey, and the princess's horse, whose name was Fallada, could talk. When it was time for them to go, the old mother went to her bedchamber, took a knife, and cut her finger till it bled. She let three drops of blood fall on a snippet of white cloth, which she gave her daughter, saying: "Take good care of this. You will need it on your journey."

After a sorrowful leavetaking the princess put the snippet of cloth in her bodice, mounted her horse, and rode away to her betrothed. When they had ridden an hour, she was thirsty and said to her waiting maid: "I'm thirsty. Get down from your horse, take the golden cup you've brought and bring me some water from the brook." The waiting maid answered: "If you're thirsty, go and serve yourself. Lie down over the brook and drink. I don't choose to wait on you." The princess was so thirsty that she dismounted, bent over the brook and drank. The maid wouldn't even let her use her golden cup. "Poor me!" she sighed. And the three drops of blood replied: "If your mother knew of this, it would break her heart." But the princess was meek. She said nothing and remounted. They rode on for a few miles, but it was a hot day, the sun was scorching, and soon she was thirsty again. They came to a stream and again she said to her waiting maid: "Get down and bring me some water in my golden cup," for she had long forgotten the girl's wicked words. But the waiting maid answered even more haughtily than before: "If you're thirsty, go and drink. I don't choose to wait on you." And again the princess was so thirsty that she dismounted. She lay down over the flowing water, wept, and said: "Poor me!" And again the drops of blood replied: "If your mother knew of this, it would break her heart." As she bent over the stream, drinking, the snippet of cloth with the three drops of blood on it fell out of her bodice and flowed away with the stream. In her great distress she didn't notice, but the waiting maid had seen the cloth fall and gloated, for now she had power over the bride who, without the drops of blood, became weak and helpless. When the princess was going to remount the horse named Fallada, the maid said: "I'll take Fallada. My nag is good enough for you." And the princess had to put up with it. Then the waiting maid spoke harshly to her, saying: "Now give me your royal garments and take these rags for yourself." After that she made her swear under the open sky never to breathe a word of all this to a living soul at court, and if she hadn't sworn, the waiting maid would have killed her on the spot. But Fallada saw it all and took good note.

Then the waiting maid mounted Fallada and the true bride mounted the wretched nag, and on they rode until they reached the royal palace. There was great rejoicing at their arrival. The prince ran out to meet them and, taking the waiting maid for his bride, lifted her down from her saddle and led her up the stairs, while the real princess was left standing down below. The old king looked out of the window and saw how delicate and lovely she was, whereupon he went straight to the royal apartments and asked the bride about the girl in the courtyard, the one who had come with her. "Oh, I picked her up on the way to keep me company. Give her some work to keep her out of mischief." But the old king had no work for her and couldn't think of any, so he said: "There's a little boy who tends the geese, she can help him." So the true bride had to help the little gooseherd, whose name was Conrad.

After a while the false bride said to the young king: "Dearest husband, I beg you, do me a favor." "I shall be glad to," he replied. "Then send for the knacker and make him cut the head off the horse that brought me here. The beast infuriated me on the way." The truth was that she was afraid the horse would tell everyone what she had done to the princess. So it was arranged, and when the true princess heard that the faithful Fallada was to die, she secretly promised the knacker some money in return for a small service. At the edge of the town there was a big dark gateway through which she passed morning and evening with the geese. Would he nail Fallada's head to the wall of the gateway, so that she could see it every day? The knacker promised to do it, and after cutting the head off, he nailed it to the wall of the dark gateway.

Early in the morning when she and little Conrad drove the geese through the gateway, she said as she passed by:

> "Oh, poor Fallada, hanging there,"

and the head answered:

> "Oh, poor princess in despair,
> If your dear mother knew,
> Her heart would break in two."

After that she didn't open her mouth, and they drove the geese out into the country. When they reached a certain meadow, she sat down and undid her hair, which was pure gold, and little Conrad looked on. He loved the way her hair glistened in the sun and tried to pull some out for himself. Whereupon she said:

> "Blow, wind, blow,
> Take Conrad's hat and make it go
> Flying here and flying there.
> And make him run until I've done
> Combing and braiding my hair
> And putting it up in a bun."

Then a wind came up that sent little Conrad's hat flying far and wide, and he had to run after it. By the time he got back she had finished her combing and braiding, and he couldn't get himself any hair. That made him angry and he stopped talking to her. And so they tended the geese until evening, and then they went home.

Next morning as they drove the geese through the dark gateway, the princess said:

> "Oh, poor Fallada, hanging there,"

and Fallada replied:

> "Oh, poor princess in despair,
>   If your dear mother knew,
>   Her heart would break in two."

When they reached the meadow, she again sat down and combed out her hair. Again Conrad ran and tried to grab at it, and again she said:

> "Blow, wind blow,
>   Take Conrad's hat and make it go
>   Flying here and flying there,
>   And make him run until I've done
>   Combing and braiding my hair
>   And putting it up in a bun."

The wind blew and lifted the hat off his head and blew it far away. Little Conrad had to run after it, and by the time he got back, she had put her hair up and he couldn't get hold of it. And so they tended the geese until evening.

When they got home that evening, little Conrad went to the old king and said: "I don't want to tend geese with that girl any more." "Why not?" the old king asked. "Because she aggravates me from morning till night." "Tell me just what she does," said the old king. "Well," said the boy, "in the morning, when we drive the geese through the dark gateway, there's a horse's head on the wall. She always speaks to it and says:

> "Oh, poor Fallada, hanging there,"

and the head answers:

> "Oh, poor princess in despair,
>   If your dear mother knew,
>   Her heart would break in two."

And little Conrad went on to tell the old king what happened in the meadow and how he had to run after his hat in the wind.

The old king ordered him to go out again with the geese next day, and in the morning he himself sat down near the dark gateway and heard the princess talking with Fallada's head. And then he followed her into the meadow and hid behind a bush. With his own eyes he soon saw the goose girl and the little gooseherd coming along with their flock. And after a while he saw her sit down and undo her glistening golden hair. Once again she said:

> "Blow, wind, blow,
>   Take Conrad's hat and make it go
>   Flying here and flying there,

And make him run until I've done
Combing and braiding my hair
And putting it up in a bun."

Then a gust of wind carried little Conrad's hat away, and he had to run and run, and meanwhile the girl quietly combed and braided her hair. The old king saw it all and went back to the palace unseen, and when the goose girl got home that evening, he called her aside and asked her why she did all those things: "I mustn't tell you that," she said. "I can't pour out my heart to anyone, because under the open sky I swore not to. I'd have been killed if I hadn't." He argued and kept at her, but he couldn't get anything out of her. So finally he said: "If you won't tell me, then pour out your heart to this cast-iron stove." With that he left her and she crawled into the cast-iron stove, and wept and wailed and poured out her heart: "Here I sit, forsaken by the whole world," she said. "And yet I'm a king's daughter. A false waiting maid forced me to give her my royal garments and took my place with my bridegroom, and now I'm a goose girl, obliged to do menial work. If my dear mother knew, her heart would break in two." The old king was standing outside with his ear to the stovepipe, and he heard everything she said. He came back in and told her to come out of the stove. They dressed her in royal garments, and she was so beautiful that it seemed a miracle. The old king called his son and told him he had the wrong bride, that she was only a waiting maid, and that the one standing there, who had been the goose girl, was the right one. The young king was overjoyed when he saw how beautiful and virtuous she was. A great banquet was made ready, and all the courtiers and good friends were invited. At the head of the table sat the bridegroom. The princess was on one side of him and the waiting maid on the other, but the waiting maid was dazzled by the princess and didn't recognize her in her sparkling jewels. When they had finished eating and drinking and were all in good spirits, the old king put a riddle to the waiting maid: What, he asked, would a woman deserve who had deceived her master in such and such a way? He went on to tell the whole story and ended by asking: "What punishment does such a woman deserve?" The false bride replied: "She deserves no better than to have her clothes taken off and to be shut up stark naked in a barrel studded with sharp nails on the inside. And two white horses should be harnessed to it and made to drag her up street and down until she is dead." "You are that woman!" said the old king. "You have pronounced your own sentence, and that is what will be done to you." When the sentence had been carried out, the young king married the right bride, and they ruled the kingdom together in peace and happiness.

90
The Young Giant

A PEASANT HAD A SON the size of a thumb, who got no bigger and for quite a few years didn't grow so much as a hair's breadth. Once when the peasant was going out to the fields to plow, the child said: "Father, I want to go with you." "You want to go with me, do you?" said the father. "You just stay here. You'd be no use to me out in the fields and you could get lost." At that the little fellow began to cry, so to keep him quiet his father put him in his pocket, took him along, and, when he got to the field, set him down in a fresh furrow. As he was sitting there, an enormous giant came striding over the hill. "See the big bogeyman?" said the father, just to frighten the child and make him behave. "He's going to carry you away." A few steps of the giant's long legs took him to the furrow. He picked the little fellow up, holding him carefully between thumb and forefinger, examined him, and without saying so much as a single word walked away with him. The father stood there too frightened to make a sound. He thought the child was lost forever and he'd never see him again as long as he lived.

The giant took the child home and suckled him, and the little fellow shot up and grew big and strong as a giant. When two years had passed, the old giant took him to the woods to test his strength, and said: "Pull up a stick for yourself." The boy was already pretty strong: he pulled up a young tree, roots and all. But the giant said: "We'll have to do better than that," and took him home again, and suckled him for another two years. The next time he was tested the boy had grown so strong that he was able to tear an old tree out of

the ground. But the giant wasn't satisfied yet. He suckled him for another two years, and the next time he took him to the woods he said:
"Now pull up a healthy stick for yourself." The boy took hold of
the thickest oak tree in sight and without even trying he pulled it out
of the ground and broke it in two. "That's fine," said the giant.
"You're a full-fledged giant now." And he took the boy back to the
field where he had found him. His father was busy plowing. The
young giant went up to him and said: "Father, look what a big man
your son has grown up to be." The peasant was terrified. "No!" he
said. "You're not my son! I don't want you! Go away!" "But I am
your son. Let me do the work. I can plow as well as you or better."
"No, no, you're not my son, and you don't know how to plow. Go
away." But being afraid of the big man, he dropped the plow, went
off to one side and sat down. The boy took the plow and pressed
with only one hand, but so powerful was his grip that the plow dug
deep into the ground. The sight was more than the peasant could
bear. "If you must plow, don't press so hard. Look what you're doing
to my field." Whereupon the boy unhitched the horses, harnessed
himself to the plow, and said: "Just go home, father, and tell mother
to cook me a big dish of food. I'll turn your field over for you in the
meantime." The peasant went home and told his wife to prepare
food, and the boy plowed the field, all two acres of it, by himself.
Then he harnessed himself to the harrows, and harrowed the whole
field, using two harrows at once. When he had finished, he went to
the woods, pulled up two oak trees and laid them over his shoulders.
He hung the harrows on the front and back of one, and the horses on
the front and back of the other, and carried the whole lot home as
easily as if it had been a bundle of straw.

When he appeared in the yard, his mother didn't recognize him.
"Who's that horrible big man?" she asked, and the peasant answered:
"He's our son." "Oh no!" she said. "That can't be our son. We never
had a big son like that. Our son was a little thing." And she cried out:
"Go away! We don't want you." The boy said nothing, took the
horses to the barn, gave them hay and oats, and put down fresh straw
for them. When he had finished, he went into the house, sat down on
the bench, and said: "Mother, now I'd like something to eat. Will it
be ready soon?" "Yes," she said, and brought him two enormous
bowls of food that would have lasted her and her husband a week.

But the boy emptied them all by himself and asked if she couldn't give him something more. "No," she said. "That's all we have." "That was only a taste," he said. "I've got to have more." She was afraid to thwart him, so she filled a big wash boiler with food and put it on the fire, and when it was done she brought it in. "At last!" he said. "At last I see a few crumbs of food." He shoveled it all in, but he was still hungry. "Father," he said, "I see I'll never get enough to eat in this house, so if you'll just get me a sturdy iron staff that I can't break over my knee, I'll leave you and go out into the world." The peasant was glad to hear it. He hitched two horses to his wagon, went to the blacksmith's, and brought back an iron staff so big and thick that the two horses could barely drag it. The boy put it over his knee and, *crack!*, broke it as easily as if it had been a bean pole, and threw it away. His father hitched four horses to the wagon and brought back a staff so big and thick that four horses could barely drag it. Again the boy broke it over his knee and said: "Father, this one's no good to me either. You'll have to harness more horses and bring me something stronger." The father hitched eight horses to the wagon and brought back a staff so big and thick that the eight horses could barely drag it. No sooner had the boy taken hold of it than a piece broke off the top. "Father," he said, "I see you can't get me the kind of staff I need, so I'll be leaving you."

He went from place to place, passing himself off as a journeyman blacksmith. Finally he came to a village where there was a miserly blacksmith, who couldn't bear to give anybody anything because he wanted to keep it all for himself. The young giant went to his smithy and asked him if he could use a journeyman. "Yes," said the black-smith, looking him over. "There's a strong young fellow," he thought, "who will do well with the sledgehammer and earn his keep." And he asked him: "How much pay do you want?" "None at all," said the giant. "But every two weeks when the other jour-neymen get paid, you must let me give you two taps." The miser was delighted, because he thought this would save him a lot of money. Next morning he let the new journeyman strike the first blow. The blacksmith held the red-hot bar in front of the giant and the giant struck it. The bar was broken in two, and the anvil sank so deep into the ground that they couldn't get it out again. The miser didn't like that at all. "Hey!" he said. "I can't use you, you hit too hard. How much pay do you ask for that one blow?" He replied: "I just want to give you one little pat, that's all." Whereupon he lifted his foot and gave the blacksmith a kick that sent him flying over four cartloads of hay. Then he picked out the thickest iron rod in the smithy and, using it as a stick, went his way.

Soon he came to a big farm and asked the bailiff if he needed a foreman. "Yes," said the bailiff, "I can use one. You look like a good worker. What pay do you want?" Again he replied that he wanted no pay at all, but: "Just once a year you must let me give you three taps." That suited the bailiff, for he too was a miser. The next morning the hired hands were all ready to ride out to the forest to cut wood, but the foreman was still in bed. One of the hands called out: "Get up, it's time. We're going out to the forest and you've got to come too." He answered rudely: "Go on ahead. I'll be back before the whole lot of you anyway." The hired hands went to the bailiff and told him the foreman was still in bed and wouldn't go to the forest with them. The bailiff told them to wake him again and tell him to harness the horses. But the foreman said the same as before: "Go on ahead. I'll be back before the whole lot of you anyway." So he lay in bed for another two hours and then finally he got up. But before doing anything else he brought two bushels of peas down from the loft and cooked them up into a porridge, which he took his time about eating. Only then did he go and harness the horses and set out.

Not far from the forest there was a ravine that he had to pass through. First he drove his wagon through it; then he walked back, gathered trees and brushwood, and made a barricade that horses couldn't pass. When he got to the forest, the others were just leaving with their loaded wagons. "Go on ahead," he said to them. "I'll be home before you anyway." He didn't drive far into the forest but just tore two of the biggest trees out of the ground, tossed them onto the wagon, and turned around. When he got to the barricade, the others were still there, for they couldn't get through. "You see," he said, "if you'd stayed with me, you'd have got home just as soon, and you'd have been able to sleep an hour more." Then he tried to drive through, but his horses couldn't manage it, so he unharnessed them, put them on top of the wagon, took hold of the shafts and pulled the wagon through as easily as if it had been loaded with feathers. Once on the other side, he said to the hired hands: "You see, I've got through quicker than you." And he drove on, leaving them stuck there. When he got back to the farm, he picked up one of the trees, showed it to the bailiff, and said: "How's this for a stick of wood?" The bailiff said to his wife: "That's a good man. He may sleep more than the others, but he gets back sooner."

So he served the bailiff for a year. When the year was over and the other hands were given their wages, he too asked for his pay. But the bailiff was afraid of the taps he had coming to him, and begged the giant to let him off. "I'll tell you what," he said, "let's change places instead. You'll be the bailiff and I'll be the foreman." "No," said the giant. "I don't want to be a bailiff. A foreman I am and a foreman I stay, but I want the pay we agreed on." The bailiff offered to give him anything he asked, but to all his suggestions the giant said, "No." The bailiff didn't know what to do, so he asked for two weeks' grace, hoping that something would occur to him in the meantime. When the foreman granted the two weeks, the bailiff called his clerks together and asked them to put their brains to work and come up with some advice. The clerks thought and thought. Finally they said that this foreman could strike a man dead as easily as he could a gnat and that with him around no one could be sure of his life. So the bailiff should order him to go down into the well and clean it, and while he was down there the men should roll up one of the big millstones that were lying around and throw it down on his head. If that were done, they said, he'd never see the light of day again. The idea appealed to the bailiff, and the foreman was willing to go down into the well. When he got to the bottom, they rolled the biggest of the millstones down. They thought they'd smashed his head, but he cried out: "Get the chickens away from the well, they're scrabbling around in the sand and throwing dust in my eyes. I can't see." The bailiff went "Shoo! Shoo!" and pretended to chase the chickens away. When the giant was finished with his work, he climbed up and said: "Look at the nice necklace I've got," meaning the millstone, which he was wearing around his neck. Then the foreman wanted his pay, but again the bailiff asked him for two weeks' grace.

The clerks met and advised him to send the foreman to the haunted mill to make flour at night. So far no one had ever spent the night there and come out alive. The suggestion appealed to the bailiff. He sent for the foreman that same evening and told him to cart a

hundred bushels of grain to the mill and grind it during the night, because the flour was needed. The foreman went up to the loft, tucked
twenty-five bushels in his right pocket and twenty-five bushels in his
left pocket, and put the rest in a sack that he hoisted up on his shoulder. When he got to the haunted mill with his load, the miller told
him he could easily grind all that grain by day, but not at night, because the mill was haunted, and anyone who went in at night would
be found dead in the morning. "Don't worry about me," said the
giant. "Just go home and go to bed." Thereupon he went into the
mill and poured the grain into the hopper. At about eleven o'clock he
went to the miller's room and sat down on the bench. When he'd
been sitting there awhile, the door suddenly opened and a big table
came in. Next wine and roast meat and all sorts of good food appeared—all by themselves, for there was no one to carry them—and
chairs moved in, but no people, except that all of a sudden he saw
fingers handling the knives and forks and putting food on the plates.
Since he was hungry and the food was right there, he sat down at the
table and ate with relish. When he had eaten his fill and the others
had also emptied their dishes, the lights were suddenly snuffed out—
he could hear the sound distinctly—and in the pitch darkness he felt
something on the order of a punch in the nose. "If I get another one
of those," he said, "I'm going to give it back." When a second punch
came his way, he too started punching. And so it went on all night,
with him giving as good as he received. Promptly at daybreak the
battle stopped. When the miller got up, he looked in to see what had
become of the foreman and was amazed to find him alive. "I had a
good meal," said the giant. "Then I got punched in the nose, but I
gave as good as I received." The miller was delighted. "You've broken the spell on my mill," he said, and offered the giant a large sum
of money. But the giant said: "I don't need money, I've got plenty."
Thereupon he hoisted his flour onto his back, went home, and said to
the bailiff: "I've done my little chore and now I want the pay we
agreed on." The bailiff was frightened to death. He kept walking up
and down the room. The sweat was running down his forehead and
he wanted to cool off, so he opened the window. Before he knew it
the foreman gave him such a kick that he flew out of the window and
rose higher and higher into the air until no one could see him. Then
the foreman said to the bailiff's wife: "If he doesn't come back, you'll

have to take the second tap." "No! No!" she cried. "It would kill me!" Whereupon she opened the other window because the sweat was running down her forehead, and he gave her a kick that sent her too flying out of the window, but she was lighter than her husband, so she flew even higher. "Come here!" the husband cried. But she answered: "I can't. You come here!" So they flew through the air, and they couldn't get together. Whether they're still flying, I don't know, but I do know that the young giant took his iron bar and went his way.

91
The Gnome

THERE WAS ONCE a rich king whose three daughters went walking in the palace garden every day. Now this king loved trees of every kind, and there was one particular tree which he loved so much that he put a curse on anyone who should ever pick an apple from it and wished that person a thousand fathoms underground. When autumn came, the apples on that tree were as red as blood. Every day the three daughters went to the tree and looked to see if the wind had blown one down, but they never found one, though the tree was so full it was groaning under the weight and the branches hung down to the ground. The youngest princess was overcome with longing. She said to her sisters: "Our father loves us too much to include us in his curse. I'm sure he meant it only for strangers." Whereupon she picked a big fat apple and ran to her sisters, saying: "Taste it, dear sisters. Never in all my life have I tasted anything so good." The two other princesses bit into the apple, and in an instant all three sank deep under the ground, and no one knew what had become of them.

At midday the king wanted to call them to table and they were nowhere to be found. He searched the palace and he searched the garden, but he couldn't find them. He was very unhappy, and he made it known throughout the country that whoever brought back his daughters would have one of them for his wife. The girls were friendly to all, and beautiful besides. Everyone loved them, so hundreds of young men went looking for them. Three young hunters went too. After searching for about a week, they came to a great castle, full of beautiful rooms. In one room a table had been set, and on it there were dishes full of delicious steaming-hot food, but there wasn't a living soul to be seen or heard in the whole castle. The hunters waited for half a day. The dishes were still steaming hot, and by then they were so hungry that they sat down and ate. After their meal they decided they would live in the castle and that each day one would stay home while the other two went looking for the princesses. They drew lots to see who would stay home the next day, and the lot fell to the eldest. When morning came, the two youngest went searching and the eldest stayed home. At midday a wee little man came in and asked for a piece of bread. The hunter took a loaf of the bread he had found there and cut off a slice. He handed it to the little man, but the little man dropped it and said: "Would you kindly pick it up for me?" The hunter stooped to pick it up and at that moment the little man took a stick, grabbed him by the hair, and gave him a sound thrashing. The next day the second hunter stayed home and didn't come off any better. When the other two came home in the evening, the eldest asked: "Well, how was it?" "Terrible!" So they told each other their tales of woe, but didn't breathe a word to the youngest, whom they disliked and called Stupid Hans, because he wasn't really of this world.

The third day the youngest stayed home, and the little man came again and asked for a piece of bread. When the youngest brother had given him his slice of bread, the little man dropped it and said: "Would you kindly pick it up for me?" "What!" cried Stupid Hans. "Why can't you pick it up for yourself? If you won't go to that much trouble for your daily bread, you don't deserve to eat it." The little man was furious. "Pick it up! Pick it up!" he screamed. But quick as a flash the young hunter grabbed hold of him and gave him a sound thrashing. "Stop! Stop!" the little man cried out. "Let me go and I'll tell you where the king's daughters are." When he heard that, he stopped hitting him, and the little man told him he was a gnome and lived under the ground. "There are more than a thousand like me," he said. "And if you'll come with me, I'll show you where the king's daughters are." Whereupon he pointed out a deep well without any water in it. "But if you want to save the king's daughters," he said, "you'll have to do it alone, because your brothers are no friends of yours. They wouldn't mind finding the king's daughters, but they won't go to any trouble or face any danger. So here's what you must do: take a big basket and sit in it with your hunting knife and a bell and get them to let you down. At the bottom you'll find three rooms and in each room you'll find one of the king's daughters picking the lice out of the heads of a many-headed dragon, and what you've got to do is cut the dragon's heads off." After saying all that, the gnome disappeared.

When the other two brothers came home that evening, they asked Hans: "How was it?" "Not bad," he replied. "I didn't see a living soul until midday. Then a little man came in and asked for a piece of bread. When I gave it to him he dropped it and asked me to pick it up. I refused and he began to yell at me, so I gave him a good thrashing and he told me where the king's daughters were." When they heard that, the other two were so angry they turned green and yellow. Next morning they all went to the well together and drew lots to see who would go down in the basket first. Again the lot fell to the eldest, so he took the bell and sat down in the basket. As they were starting to lower him he said: "When I ring, pull me up, and be quick about it." Less than halfway down he rang the bell and they pulled him up again. Then the second brother went down in the basket and exactly the same thing happened. Finally it was the turn of the youngest, and he let them lower him all the way to the bottom. When he got out of the basket, he took his hunting knife and went to the first door and listened and heard the dragon snoring loudly. He opened the door slowly and there sat one of the king's daughters with nine dragon's heads in her lap, and she was picking the lice out of them. Whereupon he drew his hunting knife and cut the nine heads off. The king's daughter jumped up and threw her arms around him and kissed him over and over again and took off her gold necklace and hung it around his neck. Then he went to the second daughter, who was also picking the lice out of a dragon's heads—hers had seven of them. He rescued her too, and went on to the youngest, whose dragon had four heads, and she too was picking the lice out of them. The princesses were all very happy and couldn't hug him and kiss him enough. Then he rang his bell till they heard him up top, and he put the king's daughters, one at a time, into the basket and they were pulled up. When it was his turn to be pulled up, he remembered what the gnome had said about his brothers being no friends of his. So he took a big stone that was lying there and put it in the basket, and when the basket was about halfway up the false brothers cut the rope. The basket with the stone in it fell to the bottom and the two wicked brothers, thinking he was dead, ran off with the king's three daughters and made them promise to tell their father that they were the ones who had saved them. Then the two elder brothers went to the king and asked to marry his daughters.

Meanwhile the youngest hunter was going from room to room in great distress, thinking he was doomed to die. But then he saw a flute hanging on the wall. "Why are you hanging there?" he asked. "Nobody could make merry in a place like this." Then he looked at the dragons' heads and said: "You can't help me either." And he walked back and forth, back and forth so often that the ground was worn smooth. Then he began to think of other things, and took the flute down from the wall and played a tune. Suddenly lots and lots of gnomes appeared, one more with each note he played. And he kept on playing until the room was packed with them. They all asked him what he desired, and he said he desired to be on top of the earth, in the daylight. So they all grabbed him, each holding on to a hair of his head, and they flew up to earth with him. When he got there, he went straight to the palace, where one of the king's daughters was just about to be married, and went up to the room where the king was sitting with the three girls. When the girls saw him, they fell into a faint. The king was furious, thinking he'd harmed the princesses, and had him thrown into prison. But when the girls revived they begged him to set the young man free. When the king asked them why, they said they weren't allowed to tell a living soul. "In that case," he said, "tell the stove." So he left the room and listened at the door. When he had heard the story, he had the two elder brothers hanged on the gallows and gave the youngest his youngest daughter. I wore a pair of glass shoes to the wedding and I bumped into a stone. My shoes said "clink" and smashed to pieces.

92

The King of the Golden Mountain

A MERCHANT HAD TWO CHILDREN, a boy and a girl, who were too young to walk. Two richly laden ships belonging to him were crossing the sea, and his whole fortune was in them. Then, just as he was thinking about all the money they would bring in, news came that they had gone down. Instead of being rich, he was now a poor man, with nothing left but a field just outside the town. One day, to take his mind off his trouble, he went out to his field, and as he was walking back and forth a black dwarf suddenly appeared and asked why he was so sad and what had happened to make him so miserable. "I'd gladly tell you," said the merchant, "if I thought you could help me." "You never can tell," said the black dwarf. "Maybe I can help you." So the merchant told him that his whole fortune had been lost at sea and that he had nothing left but this field. "Don't worry," said the dwarf. "You shall have all the money you want if you just give me your promise that whatever first brushes against your leg when you get home, you will bring it here to me in this same place in exactly twelve years." The merchant thought: "What else could it be but my dog?" He didn't think of his little boy. So he said yes, gave the dwarf his promise, signed and sealed, and went home.

When he got there, his little boy was so glad to see him that, keeping his balance by holding on to chairs, he toddled over to him and hugged his legs. The father was horrified, for he remembered his promise, and now he knew what he had made over to the dwarf. But then, finding no money in his chests and boxes, he comforted himself with the thought that the dwarf had been joking. A month later he went up to the attic for some old tinware he wanted to sell, and there was a big pile of money in the middle of the floor. He cheered up, bought goods, got to be a bigger merchant than before, and thought that everything was for the best. The child grew to be a strong, clever boy, but on his twelfth year the merchant grew more and more anxious, and his worry could be seen in his face. One day his son asked him what was wrong. He didn't want to tell him, but the boy kept at him and finally the merchant told him how without knowing what he was doing he had promised him to a black dwarf and received a great deal of money in return. "I set my hand and seal to the promise," he said. "And now the twelve years have almost passed, and I shall have to hand you over." The boy said: "Don't worry, father, everything will be all right. The black dwarf has no power over me."

The boy got a priest to bless him and when the time came he went out to the field with his father. The son made a circle and they stood inside it together. Soon the black dwarf appeared and said to the merchant: "Have you brought what you promised me?" The merchant made no reply, but the son asked: "What have you come here for?" The black dwarf said: "My business is with your father, not with you." The son answered: "You tempted my father and cheated him. Give back the paper." "No," said the black dwarf, "I stand on my rights." They argued a long time and finally agreed that because the boy belonged neither to his father nor to the fiend, he should get into a boat on the riverbank and his father would push the boat off with his foot and abandon him to the river. The boy took leave of his father and got into the boat, and the father pushed it off with his own foot. The boat turned over, the bottom was uppermost and the top underwater, and the father, thinking his son was lost, went back home and grieved for him.

But the boat didn't sink, it floated gently down the river with the boy safely inside, until at last it stopped in a strange place. The boy went ashore and soon came to a magnificent castle, but when he went in, he saw it was bewitched. He went from room to room, and they were all empty except for the last, and there he saw a coiled snake. The snake was a bewitched maiden. She was glad to see him and said: "Have you come at last, my savior? I've been waiting for you for twelve years. This kingdom is bewitched, and you must save it." "How can I do that?" he asked. "Tonight twelve black men covered with chains will come and ask you what you are doing here. Don't answer. Don't say a word, but let them do what they want with you.

They will torment you, beat you and stick knives into you. Let them, but don't open your mouth. At twelve o'clock they will have to go away. The second night twelve others will come and the third night twenty-four, and this time they will cut off your head. But at twelve o'clock they will lose their power, and then, if you've borne it all and you haven't said a word, I shall be saved. I will go to where you are lying. I have a bottle filled with the Water of Life, I'll rub you with it, and that will bring you back from the dead, as fresh and strong as ever." He replied: "I shall be glad to save you," and everything happened just as she had said. The black men couldn't get a word out of him, and on the third night the snake turned into a beautiful princess, rubbed him with the Water of Life and brought him back from the dead. Then she threw her arms around him and kissed him, and there was rejoicing all over the castle. Soon the wedding was celebrated, and he became King of the Golden Mountain.

They lived together happily and the queen bore him a handsome boy. When eight years had passed, he thought of his father. His heart was moved and he yearned to go and see him. But the queen didn't want him to go. "It will bring me misfortune," she said. "I know it." But he gave her no peace and finally she consented. In leavetaking, she gave him a wishing ring and said: "Take this ring and put it on your finger. You will be carried instantly to wherever you wish to be, but you must promise me one thing: don't use it to wish me from here to your father's house." He promised, put the ring on his finger, and wished himself at the gate of the town where his father lived. In a flash he was there, but the sentries wouldn't let him in, because his dress, though rich and splendid, struck them as outlandish. So he climbed a hill where a shepherd was tending his sheep, changed clothes with him, and, wearing the shepherd's old coat, passed through the gate unmolested. Then he went to his father and told him who he was, but his father wouldn't believe him and said: "Yes, I did have a son, but he has been dead for years." Nevertheless, feeling sorry for the poor, ragged shepherd, he offered him a dish of something to eat. But the shepherd said to his parents: "I really am your son. Isn't there some birthmark you'd know me by?" "Yes," said his mother, "our son had a strawberry mark under his right arm." He pushed back his sleeve, they saw the strawberry mark under his right arm, and after that they had no doubt about his being their son. Then he told them he was King of the Golden Mountain, that he'd married a king's daughter and had a handsome seven-year-old boy. The father said: "That can't be true. What sort of king would go running around in a ragged shepherd's coat?" That made the son angry. Forgetting his promise, he turned the ring around and wished his wife and child to be there. In that same moment there they were, but the queen wept and lamented and said he'd broken his promise and destroyed her happiness. "I did it without thinking," he said. "I meant no harm." He did his best to appease her and she pretended to give in, but she was plotting wickedness.

He took her outside the town to the field and showed her the place on the riverbank where the boat had been pushed off. Then he said: "I'm tired. Sit down. Let me rest my head awhile." He rested his head on her lap and she loused him until he fell asleep. Then she took the ring off his finger and pulled her legs out from under him, leaving only one slipper, picked up the child in her arms and wished herself back in her kingdom. When he woke up, he was lying there all alone. His wife and child were gone, and so was the ring from his finger. Only the slipper was there as a reminder. "I can't go home to my parents," he thought. "They would take me for a wizard. I'll just pack up and walk until I get back to my kingdom."

So he started out and finally came to a mountain. At the foot of the mountain three giants were arguing because their father had just died and they couldn't decide how to divide their inheritance. When they saw him passing, they called out to him. "Little men have sharp wits," they said, and asked him to divide their inheritance for them. It consisted of a very special kind of sword—if you held it in your hand and said: "All heads off except mine," everybody else's head would be lying on the ground before you knew it; second, a cloak that made anyone who put it on invisible; and third, a pair of very special boots —if you put them on and wished yourself somewhere, you'd be there that same moment. "Very well," he said. "Hand me the three articles so I can see if they're in good condition." They handed him the cloak and when he'd put it on he was invisible; he had turned into a fly. Then he resumed his own form and said: "The cloak is good. Now hand me the sword." "No," they said. "We can't do that. If you said: 'All heads off except mine,' our heads would all be off, and only you would still have yours." But after a while they gave it to him on condition that he should test it on a tree. This he did, and the sword cut a tree trunk in two like a blade of straw. Next he wanted the boots, but they said: "No, we won't let them out of our hands, because if you put them on and wished yourself up on the mountain we'd be left down here, and we wouldn't have anything." "Oh, no," he said. "I wouldn't do that." So they gave him the boots. When he had all three, he thought of nothing but his wife and child, and muttered to himself: "Oh, if only I were on the Golden Mountain!" That instant he vanished from the giants' sight, and they didn't have to worry about their inheritance any more.

As he approached the castle, he heard flutes and violins and cries of merriment, and the courtiers told him his wife was getting married to someone else. He flew into a rage and cried: "False woman, deceiving me and deserting me while I slept!" He put on his cloak and went into the castle without being seen. When he entered the hall, he saw a large table spread with choice dishes, and the guests were eating and drinking and laughing and joking. The queen was sitting in a royal chair at the end of the table, dressed in queenly garments and wearing a crown. He went and stood behind her and no one saw him. When they put a piece of meat on her plate, he snatched it away and ate it; and when they poured her a glass of wine, he snatched it away and drank it. They kept serving her, but she got nothing to eat or drink, for plate and glass vanished instantly. Shamed and distressed, she left the table, went to her room and wept, and he followed her. "Has the devil got me in his power?" she said. "Or did my savior never come?" At that he slapped her face and said: "Did your savior never come? False woman, it's your savior who has you in his power. Have I deserved such treatment at your hands?" Whereupon he made himself visible, went into the hall and cried: "The wedding is over, the true king is here!" The kings, princes, and councilors who were gathered there jeered and laughed at him. He replied in few words: "Get out!" They pressed in on him and tried to catch him, but he drew his sword and said: "All heads off except mine!" All their heads rolled to the ground, and he alone was master. Once again he was King of the Golden Mountain.

93

The Raven

A QUEEN ONCE HAD a daughter who was only a baby and hadn't
learned to walk. One day the child was naughty and nothing the
mother said could make her behave. The queen's patience was at an
end. She looked at the ravens that were flying around the castle,
opened the window and said: "I wish you'd turn into a raven and fly
away; then I'd have some peace and quiet." The words were hardly
out of her mouth when the child turned into a raven and flew
straight out of the window. She flew into a dark forest and stayed
there a long time and her parents had no news of her. Then one day a
man was going through the forest, and he heard a raven calling and
followed the voice. When he came closer, the raven said: "I'm a
king's daughter by birth and I've been bewitched, but you can set me
free." "What should I do?" he asked. "Go farther into the forest,"
she said, "and you'll come to a house. An old woman lives there.
She'll offer you food and drink, but you mustn't take any. If you eat
or drink the least thing, you'll fall into a deep sleep and you won't be
able to set me free. In the garden behind the house you'll see a big
pile of tanbark. You must stand on it and wait for me. I shall come
three days in a row at two o'clock in the afternoon. The first day my
carriage will be drawn by four white stallions, the second day by
four roan stallions, and the third day by four black ones. You must
stay awake, because if you fall asleep I won't be set free."

The man promised to do everything she had told him. But the raven
said: "Alas, I know it in advance; you won't set me free, you'll take
something from the woman." Again the man promised: "No, no! I
will touch neither food nor drink!" When he reached the house, the
old woman came out to meet him. "Poor man," she said, "you're all
tired out. Come and refresh yourself. Have something to eat and
drink." "No," said the man. "I won't eat and I won't drink." But she
gave him no peace. "If you won't eat," she said, "just take a sip from

this glass. One little sip doesn't count." And he let himself be tempted and drank. Shortly before two o'clock he went out to the pile of tanbark in the garden to wait for the raven. As he was standing there, he suddenly felt so tired that he couldn't resist the temptation to lie down. He was determined not to fall asleep, but no sooner had he stretched out than his eyes closed of their own accord and he fell into a sleep so sound that nothing in the world could have awakened him.

At two o'clock the raven came driving up in a carriage drawn by four white stallions, but already her heart was bowed with sadness and she said to herself: "I know he's asleep." And indeed, when she came into the garden, he was lying on the pile of tanbark, fast asleep. She alighted from her carriage, went over to him, shook him and called him, but he didn't wake up. At noon the next day the old woman came again, bringing him food and drink. He wouldn't touch them. But she kept at him and gave him no peace until he took another sip from the glass.

Just before two o'clock he went to the pile of tanbark in the garden to wait for the raven. Suddenly he felt so tired that his legs refused to carry him. He couldn't help it, he had to lie down, and a moment later he fell into a deep sleep. The raven drove up in a carriage drawn by four roan stallions. Already her heart was bowed with grief and she said to herself: "I know he's asleep." She went over to him, but he was fast asleep and there was no waking him. The next day the old woman said to him: "What's the matter? You don't eat and you don't drink. Do you want to die?" He replied: "I must not and will not eat or drink." But she set a dish of food and a glass of wine down before him, and when the smell rose up to him he couldn't resist the temptation and took a deep draft of wine.

When the time came, he went out to the pile of tanbark in the garden and waited for the king's daughter. But soon he felt even more tired than he had on the preceding days, and lay down and slept like a log. At two o'clock the raven came; this time she had four black stallions and the carriage and all the trappings were black. Already her heart was bowed with sadness and she said to herself: "I know he's asleep and won't be able to set me free." When she went over to him, he lay there fast asleep. She shook him and called him, but she couldn't wake him. Then she put three things down beside him, a loaf of bread, a piece of meat, and a bottle of wine, and no matter how much of them he took there would be no less. Next she took the gold ring from her finger and slipped it on his, and the ring had her name engraved on it. Last, she left him a letter telling him that the things she had given him could never be used up, and ending: "I see you can never set me free in this place, but if you still want to, then go to the Golden Castle of Stromberg. It is within your power, I am sure of that." When she had given him all those things, she got into her carriage and drove to the Golden Castle of Stromberg.

When the man woke up and saw he had slept, he was very sad. He said to himself: "She has surely driven by, and I haven't set her free." Then he caught sight of the things she had left, and read the letter telling him what had happened. So he rose to his feet and set out for the Golden Castle of Stromberg, but he didn't know where it was. After wandering for a long, long time, he came to a dark forest. He walked for fourteen days, but he couldn't find his way out. Another day passed, and in the evening he was so tired that he lay down under a bush and fell asleep. In the morning he went on and that evening, as he was about to lie down again under a bush, he heard such howling and wailing that he couldn't fall asleep. Then at the time when people light candles he saw one glimmering, so he got up and went toward it.

Soon he came to a house that looked tiny because an enormous giant was standing in front of it. The man thought to himself: "If I go in and the giant sees me, he'll probably kill me." Finally he plucked up courage and stepped up to him. When the giant saw him, he said: "It's good you've come; I haven't had anything to eat for days and days. I'll gobble you up for supper." "I wish you wouldn't," said the man. "I don't like being gobbled up. If it's food you want, I have enough to fill your belly." "In that case," said the giant, "you have nothing to worry about. I was only going to eat you because I had nothing else." So they went in and sat down to table together and the man brought out the bread, wine, and meat, and no matter how much they took, no less was left. "This is perfect," said the giant, and ate to his heart's content. When he had finished eating, the man asked: "You wouldn't happen to know where the Golden Castle of Stromberg is?" The giant said: "I'll look on my map. It's got every town, village, and house on it." He brought in the map that he kept in his room and looked for the castle, but it wasn't there. "It doesn't matter," he said. "I've got an even bigger map in the cupboard upstairs; we'll look again." But again they looked in vain. The man wanted to continue his journey, but the giant suggested that he wait a few days till his brother, who had gone to get provisions, should come home.

When the brother arrived, they asked him about the Golden Castle of Stromberg. He replied: "Wait till I've finished eating. Then I'll look for it on my map." When he had finished eating, they went up to his room and looked for it on his map, but they couldn't find it. He brought some more old maps and they looked and looked until at last they found the Golden Castle of Stromberg, but it was thousands of miles away. "How will I ever get there?" the man asked. The giant said: "I've got two hours to spare. I'll carry you to the neighborhood of the castle, but then I have to come home and nurse our baby." The giant carried the man to a place about a hundred leagues from the castle and said: "You can go the rest of the way yourself." Then he turned back, and the man walked on by day and by night until at last he came to the Golden Castle of Stromberg. But the castle was on the top of a glass mountain. The bewitched maiden was driving around the castle in her carriage and after a while she went in. He was overjoyed to see her and tried to climb up to her, but whichever way he went about it he kept slipping down on the glass. When he saw he couldn't reach her, he was very sad. He said to himself: "I'll stay down here and wait for her," and he built himself a hut, and stayed there for a whole year. Every day he saw the king's daughter driving around on top of the mountain, but he couldn't go up to her.

One day he looked out of his hut and saw three robbers fighting. "God be with you!" he cried out. At the sound of his voice, they stopped fighting, but when they saw no one they started in again, most ferociously. Again he cried out: "God be with you!" Again they stopped and looked around, but seeing no one, they started to fight again. For the third time he cried out: "God be with you!" and said to himself: "I've got to find out what those three are up to." So he went over to them and asked why they were fighting. The first said he had found a stick, and if he knocked on a door with it the door opened; the second said he had found a cloak, and if he put it on, it made him invisible, and the third said he had found a horse that could carry a man anywhere, even up the glass mountain. The trouble was they couldn't decide whether to share their three treasures or to go their separate ways. The man said: "I'll buy them from you. It's true that I have no money, but I can pay you with other things that are worth more than money. Only first I must test your treasures to make sure you're telling the truth." They let him mount the horse, put the cloak over his shoulder, and handed him the stick, after which they couldn't see him any more. He gave them a good beating, and cried out: "There, you good-for-nothings! You've got what was coming to you. Are you satisfied?" And he rode up the glass mountain.

When he got to the castle, the gate was locked, but he knocked at it with the stick and it opened. He went in and climbed the stairs. In the hall sat the king's daughter with a golden cup of wine in front of her. She couldn't see him, because he was wearing the cloak. He went up to her, pulled off the ring she had given him and tossed it into her cup, *clink!* "That's my ring!" she cried. "The man who is going to set me free must be here." The courtiers looked all over the castle and they didn't find him. He had gone outside, mounted the horse, and thrown off the cloak. When they came out through the gate, they saw him and cried for joy. Thereupon he dismounted and took the king's daughter in his arms. She kissed him and said: "Now you have set me free. We shall celebrate our wedding tomorrow."

94

The Peasant's Clever Daughter

THERE WAS ONCE a poor peasant who had no land, just a small house and an only daughter. One day his daughter said: "We ought to ask the king for a piece of newly cleared land." When the king heard how poor they were, he gave them a piece of grassland, which she and her father spaded, meaning to sow a little wheat and other grain. When they had almost finished spading their field, they found a mortar of pure gold. "Look here," said the father. "The king was kind enough to give us our field. Why not give him this mortar in re-turn?" The daughter was dead against it. "Father," she said, "if we give him a mortar and no pestle, he'll want a pestle. We'd better keep quiet about it." But the father wouldn't listen. He brought the mortar to the king, said he had found it in his field, and asked if the king would accept it as a gift. After accepting the mortar, the king asked the peasant if he hadn't found anything else. "No," said the peasant. "What about the pestle?" said the king. "Bring me the pestle." The peasant said they hadn't found any pestle, but he might have been talking to the wall. He was thrown into prison and the king told him he'd stay there until he produced the pestle.

When the servants brought him his bread and water—that's what they give you in prison—they hear him sighing: "Oh, if I had only lis-tened to my daughter! Oh, oh, if I had only listened to my daughter!" The servants went to the king and told him how the prisoner kept sighing: "Oh, if I had only listened to my daughter," and how he wouldn't eat and wouldn't drink. The king had the servants bring him the prisoner and asked him why he kept sighing: "If I had only lis-tened to my daughter!" "What did your daughter tell you?" "Well, she told me not to give you the mortar, because if I did you'd want the pestle too." "If you have such a clever daughter, tell her to come and see me." So she appeared before the king, who asked her if she were really so clever, and said: "I'll tell you what. I've got a riddle for you. If you can guess the answer, I'll marry you." "I'll guess it," she said. "All right," said the king, "come to me not clothed, not naked, not riding, not walking, not on the road, not off the road. If you can do all that, I'll marry you." She went home and took off all her clothes so then she was unclothed, sat down on a big fish net and wrapped it around her, so then she was not naked. Then she hired a donkey and tied the fish net to the donkey's tail, and the donkey dragged her along, which was neither riding nor walking. And the donkey had to drag her along the wagon track, so that only her big toe touched the ground and she was neither on the road nor off the road. When she came bumping along, the king said she had guessed the riddle and met all the requirements. He let her father out of prison, took her as his wife, and gave all the royal possessions into her care.

Some years passed, and then one day as the king was inspecting his troops, some peasants, who had been selling wood, stopped their wagons outside the palace. Some of the wagons were drawn by oxen and some by horses. One peasant had three horses, one of them foaled, and the foal ran off and lay down between two oxen that were harnessed to another peasant's wagon. The two peasants started to argue and fight, because the one with the oxen wanted to keep the foal and claimed the oxen had had it. The other peasant said no, his mare had had it, and it belonged to him. The dispute came before the king. His decision was that where the foal had lain there it should stay, and so it was given to the peasant with the oxen, who had no right to it. The other peasant went away weeping and wailing about his foal. But he had heard that the queen was kindhearted, because she came of a poor peasant family. So he went to her and asked if she could help him to get his foal back. "Yes," she said. "If you promise not to give me away, I'll tell you what to do. Tomorrow morning when the king goes out to inspect the guard, take a fish net, stand in the middle of the road where he has to pass, and pretend to be fishing. Shake out the net now and then as if it were full and go on fishing." And she also told him what to say when the king questioned him.

Next day the peasant stood there fishing on dry land. As the king was passing by, he saw him and sent his orderly to ask the fool what he was doing. "I'm fishing," was the answer. The orderly asked him how he could fish when there was no water. The peasant replied: "There's just as much chance of my catching fish on dry land as there is of an ox having a foal." The orderly took the man's answer back to the king, whereupon the king summoned the peasant. "You didn't think up that answer," he said. "Where did you get it? Tell me this minute." The peasant wouldn't tell him. "So help me," he said, "I thought of it myself." But they laid him down on a bundle of straw and beat him and tortured him until at last he confessed that the queen had given him the idea. When the king got home, he said to his wife: "Why have you played me false? I won't have you for my wife any longer, your time is up, go back to the peasant's hovel you came from." But he granted her one mercy, leave to take the best and dearest thing she knew of with her. That would be her farewell present. "Yes, dear husband," she said. "If that is your command, I will obey it." She threw her arms around him and kissed him and asked him to drink a farewell glass with her. Thereupon she sent for a strong sleeping potion. The king took a deep draft, but she herself drank only a little. When he had fallen into a deep sleep, she called a servant and took a fine white sheet and wrapped it around the king. The servant carried him to a carriage that was waiting at the door and she drove him home to her little house, where she put him into her bed. He slept a day and a night without waking. When he finally woke up, he looked around and said: "Good God, where am I?" He called his servants, but there weren't any servants. At last his wife came to his bedside and said: "Dear king and husband, you told me to take what was best and dearest with me from the palace. Nothing is better or dearer in my eyes than you, so I took you with me." The king's eyes filled with tears. "Dearest wife," he said, "never again shall we part." He took her back to the royal palace and married her again, and I imagine they are still alive.

95
Old Hildebrand

THERE WAS ONCE a peasant who had a wife, and the village priest was sweet on this wife and wanted very much to spend a whole day alone with her having a good time. She was willing too and one day he said to her: "Look. I've thought up a way we can spend a whole day having a good time together. This is what you must do: take to your bed next Wednesday and tell your husband you're sick; you'll moan and you'll groan, and you'll keep it up until Sunday when it's time for my sermon. In my sermon I'll say that anyone with a sick child, a sick husband, a sick wife, a sick father, a sick mother, a sick sister, brother, or whatever, should make a pilgrimage to Mount Göckerli in Italy, where you can buy a peck of laurel leaves for a kreuzer, and then his sick child, sick husband, sick wife, sick father, sick mother, sick sister, brother, or whatever will get well right away."

"I'll do it," said the woman. So on Wednesday she took to her bed. She moaned and she groaned for all she was worth, and her husband brought her every medicine he could think of, but nothing helped.

When Sunday came, the woman said: "I feel terrible, as if I were like to die any minute, but there's one thing I want to do before I pass away: hear the father's Sunday sermon." "Don't do that, pussycat," said the peasant. "Getting up might make you worse. I'll tell you what. I'll go to church and listen carefully to the sermon, and tell you everything the priest says." "All right," said the woman. "You go and listen carefully and tell me everything you hear." So the peasant went to church, and the priest stood up in the pulpit, and said that if anyone had a sick child, a sick husband, a sick wife, a sick father, a sick mother, a sick sister, brother, or whatever, he should make a pilgrimage to Mount Göckerli in Italy, where a peck of laurel leaves costs only a kreuzer, and the sick child, sick husband, sick wife, sick father, sick mother, sick sister, brother, or whatever would get well right away. And he ended up by saying: "If there's anyone wanting to take the trip he should come and see me after Mass, and I'll give him a kreuzer and a sack for the laurel leaves." The peasant was in seventh heaven. He went to the priest right after Mass, and the priest gave him the kreuzer and the sack for the laurel leaves. Then he went home, and before he had even got through the door he cried out: "Hurrah, dear wife, you're as good as cured. The priest said in his sermon today that anyone with a sick child, a sick husband, a sick wife, a sick father, a sick mother, a sick sister, brother, or whatever, should make a pilgrimage to Mount Göckerli in Italy, where a peck of laurel leaves costs only a kreuzer, and the sick child, the sick husband, the sick wife, the sick father, the sick mother, the sick sister, brother, or whatever, will get well right away. See, I've gotten the kreuzer and the sack for the laurel leaves from the priest, and I'm starting this minute, so you'll get well that much sooner."

Away he went, and he was hardly out of the house when the woman got up and soon the priest arrived. But suppose we leave those two to themselves, and go with the peasant. He wanted to get to Mount Göckerli as soon as possible, so he kept up a good steady pace, and as he was walking along, he met his cousin the egg man, who had just come from the market after selling his eggs. "God bless you, cousin," said the egg man. "Where are you going in such a hurry?" "For all eternity, cousin," said the peasant. "My wife is sick, and I heard the priest preach today, and he said that if anyone had a sick child, a sick husband, a sick wife, a sick father, a sick mother, a

sick sister, brother, or whatever, he should make a pilgrimage to
Mount Göckerli in Italy, where a peck of laurel leaves costs only a
kreuzer, and the sick child, the sick husband, the sick wife, the sick
father, the sick mother, the sick sister, brother, or whatever will get
well right away. So I got the kreuzer and the sack for the laurel
leaves from the priest, and now I'm making my pilgrimage." "Cousin,
cousin," said the egg man. "Are you really simple enough to believe
that? Listen to me! The priest wanted to spend a whole day having a
good time with your wife, so they thought up this trick to get rid of
you." "My goodness!" said the peasant. "I'd sure like to know if
that's true!" "All right," said the egg man. "Here's what we'll do.
Get into my egg basket and I'll carry you home and you'll see for
yourself." So that's what they did. The egg man settled the peasant in
his egg basket and carried him home on his back. When they got to
the house, oh my, oh my, what goings on! The woman had killed and
cooked practically everything they had in the barnyard and she'd
made pancakes, and the priest was already there and he'd brought his
fiddle. The egg man knocked and the woman asked who was there.
"It's me," said the egg man. "Can you put me up for the night? I
haven't sold my eggs, so now I've got to carry them home again, and
they're so heavy, I can't go another step and it's getting dark."
"Cousin," said the peasant woman, "you've come at a bad time. But if
you're here, you're here, so come in and sit yourself over there on the
bench behind the stove." So the egg man with his basket settled down
on the bench behind the stove. The priest and the peasant woman
were having a fine time. After a while the priest said: "You've got
such a fine voice. Sing me a song." "Oh, I couldn't," she said. "I can't
sing any more. I could when I was young, but that's a thing of the
past." "Please!" said the priest. "Just sing me a little something." So
the woman sang:

> "I sent my husband far away,
> He's gone to Göckerli to pray."

The priest responded:

> "I wish he'd stay a year or more,
> He can keep the sack for all I care.
> Hallelujah!"

Then the egg man behind the stove began to sing (but here I have
to tell you that the peasant's name was Hildebrand):

> "Oh, Hildebrand, oh, heavens above!
> What are you doing behind the stove?
> Hallelujah!"

And then the peasant in the basket sang:

> "That's all the singing I can stand,
> It's time for me to take a hand."

Whereupon he stepped out of the basket, took a stick to the priest and drove him out of the house.

96

The Three Little Birds

MAYBE A THOUSAND YEARS AGO or more, there were lots of petty kings in this country, and one of them, who lived on a hill called the Keuterberg, was very fond of hunting. Once when he rode out of the castle with his huntsmen, three girls were tending their cows on the hillside. When they saw the king and his men, the eldest girl pointed at the king and called out to the other girls: "Halloo, halloo, if I can't have that one, I don't want any." The second, on the other side of the hill, pointed at the man on the king's right and cried out: "Halloo, halloo, if I can't have that one, I don't want any." And the youngest pointed at the man on the king's left and cried out: "Halloo, halloo, if I can't have that one, I don't want any." The two men with the king were his ministers. The king had heard what the girls said. When he got back from the hunt, he sent for them and asked what they had said the day before on the hillside. They wouldn't tell him, so the king asked the eldest if she would take him for her husband. She said yes, and the ministers married her two sisters, for all three girls were beautiful, especially the queen, who had hair like flax.

The two sisters bore no children, and once when the king went off on a journey, he asked them to visit the queen to cheer her up, for she was with child. She gave birth to a little boy and a bright red star came into the world with him. The two sisters said to each other: "Let's throw that pretty little boy into the river." When they had thrown him in (I think it was the Weser), a little bird flew up into the air and sang:

> "Destined to cruel death,
> Farewell and adieu,
> Reprieved to draw new breath,
> Brave little boy, is it you?"

When the two sisters heard that, they were scared out of their wits and hurried back to the castle. When the king came home, they told him the queen had given birth to a dog, and the king said: "God's will be done."

Now a fisherman lived by the river, and he fished the little boy out of the water while he was still alive. The fisherman's wife had borne him no children, so they kept the little boy and cared for him. A year later the king went on another journey and the queen gave birth to another little boy. The two false sisters took that one away too and threw him into the river, and again the little bird flew up and sang:

> "Destined to cruel death,
> Farewell and adieu,
> Reprieved to draw new breath,
> Brave little boy, is it you?"

When the king came back, they told him the queen had given birth to another dog, and again he said: "God's will be done." And the fisherman fished that one out of the river too, and kept him.

Once again the king set out on a journey. This time the queen gave birth to a little girl and the false sisters threw her into the river too. Again the little bird flew up into the air and sang:

> "Destined to cruel death,
> Farewell and adieu,
> Reprieved to draw new breath,
> Brave little girl, is it you?"

When the king got home, they told him the queen had given birth to a cat. The king was so angry he had his wife thrown into the dungeon, and there she lay for many years.

Meanwhile the children grew up. One day the eldest went fishing with some boys, who didn't want him along. "Go away, you foundling," they said. That made him very sad, and he asked that old fisherman if it was true. "Yes," said the fisherman. "One day when I was fishing, I pulled you out of the water." "Then," said the boy, "let me go and look for my father." The fisherman begged the boy to stay with him, but the boy kept pleading, and in the end the fisherman gave in. The boy set out and walked for several days. Finally he came to a great river, and an old woman sat on the bank fishing. "Good day to you, grandmother," said the boy. "Thank you kindly." "You'll sit there a long time before you catch anything." "And you will look a long while before you find your father," the old woman replied. "How are you going to cross this river?" "God only knows." Thereupon she picked him up and carried him across on her back.

He searched and searched and he couldn't find his father. When a year had passed, the second son set out to look for his brother. He came to the river, and the same thing happened as with his brother. The daughter was now all alone in the house, and she missed her brothers so much that she finally begged the fisherman to let her go looking for them. When she too came to the great river, she said to the old woman: "A good day to you, grandmother." "Thank you kindly." "God help you with your fishing." When the old woman heard that, she was all smiles. She carried the girl over the river, gave her a willow switch, and said to her: "Child, take this path and go straight ahead. When you come to a big black dog, don't be afraid, just pass it in silence, without laughing and without looking at it. Then you will come to a great high castle. Drop the willow switch on the threshold and go straight through the castle and out the other side. There you will find an old well. A big tree will be growing out of the well, and on the tree you'll find a cage hanging with a bird in it. Take the cage, fill a glass with water at the well, and go back as you came. When you reach the threshold, pick up the willow switch, and when you come to the dog, strike it in the face, but make sure you don't miss. Then come back here to me." Off she went and everything was just as the old woman had said. On the way back she found her two brothers, who had searched half the world for each other. They went on together until they came to the black dog. When they struck it in the face, it turned into a handsome prince, who went along with them until they reached the river. The old woman was still there, and she was delighted to see the four of them. She carried them across the water, and then she went away, for she too had been set free. The others went to the old fisherman's house, and they were glad to be all together again. They hung the bird in its cage on the wall.

But the second son was restless at home. He took his bow and went hunting. When he was tired, he played a tune on his flute. The king, who was hunting that day, heard the sound and went toward it. When he saw the boy, he asked him: "Who gave you permission to hunt here?" "No one." "Whom do you belong to?" "I'm the fisherman's son." "That can't be. He has no children." "If you don't believe me, come with me." The king went and asked the fisherman, who told him the whole story, and the little bird in the cage began to sing:

> "In the dungeon keep
> The mother sits alone.
> Oh, good and noble king,
> These children are your own.
> Their mother's wicked sisters
> Took them from her bed,
> And surely they'd have drowned
> If not for the fisherman's net."

When they heard that, they were all seized with horror. The king took the bird, the fisherman, and the three children back to his castle with him, opened up the dungeon and brought his wife out, but she had grown sick and feeble. Her daughter gave her some of the water from the well, and that restored her health. The two false sisters were burned, and the daughter married the prince.

97

The Water of Life

THERE WAS ONCE a king who was sick, and no one thought he would live. His three sons were very sad. They went down into the palace garden and wept, and there they met an old man, who asked them what the trouble was. They told him their father was very sick and would surely die, for nothing seemed to do him any good. The old man said: "I know of a remedy: the Water of Life. If he drinks of it, he will get well, but it's hard to find." "I'll find it," said the eldest, and he went to the sick king and asked him for leave to search for the Water of Life, since that alone could cure him. "No," said the king, "the danger is too great. I would rather die." But the son begged and pleaded until the king finally consented. The prince thought in his heart: "If I bring him the Water of Life, my father will love me the best, and I shall inherit the kingdom."

So he started out and when he had ridden awhile, a dwarf, who was standing on the road, called out to him: "Where are you going so fast?" "You stupid runt," said the prince haughtily, "what business is it of yours?" And he rode on. The dwarf was furious and cursed him. The prince soon came to a ravine. The farther he rode the closer the mountains came together, and in the end the path was so narrow that his horse couldn't take another step. The prince could neither turn his horse around nor dismount, and all he could do was sit there, wedged tight in his saddle. The sick king waited in vain for his eldest son to return, and then one day the second son said: "Father, let me go and look for the Water." He thought to himself: "If my brother is dead, the kingdom will fall to me." At first the king didn't want to let him go, but in the end he gave in. So the prince set out, taking the same road as his brother, and he too met the dwarf, who stopped him and asked where he was going so fast. "You little runt," said the prince, "what business is it of yours?" And he rode on without so much as looking around. Whereupon the dwarf cursed him, and like his brother he rode deep into a ravine until he got wedged in and was unable to go forward or backward. That's what happens to haughty people.

When the second son also failed to return, the youngest son asked leave to search for the Water, and the king finally had to let him go. When he met the dwarf and the dwarf asked him where he was going in such a hurry, he stopped and answered him: "I'm looking for the Water of Life, because my father is deathly sick." "Do you know where to find it?" "No," said the prince. "Since you've spoken kindly and haven't been haughty like your two wicked brothers, I'll tell you where the Water of Life is and how to get there. It springs from a fountain in the courtyard of an enchanted castle, but you'll never get in unless I give you an iron wand and two loaves of bread. Strike the castle gate three times with the wand and it will open. Inside, there will be two lions with gaping jaws, but if you throw a loaf to each of them, they will calm down. Then you must hurry and take the Water of Life before the clock strikes twelve, because otherwise the gate will close and you will be locked in." The prince thanked him, took the wand and the bread, and went his way. When he reached the castle, everything was just as the dwarf had said. The gate opened at the third stroke of the wand, and when he had calmed the lions with the bread, he went into the castle and came to a big, beautiful hall, full of enchanted princes. He drew the rings from their fingers and also took a sword and a loaf of bread that he found in the great hall. Farther on he came to a room, where a beautiful maiden was standing. She was overjoyed to see him, kissed him and told him he had set her free. "My whole kingdom will be yours," she said. "If you come back in a year's time we shall celebrate our wedding." Then she told him where to find the fountain with the Water of Life and bade him hurry and draw the water before the clock struck twelve. He went on and came at last to a room with a beautiful, freshly made bed in it. As he was tired, he thought he would rest awhile. He lay down and fell asleep, and when he awoke the clock was striking a quarter to twelve. He jumped up in a fright, ran to the fountain, drew the water in a cup that he found nearby, and hurried away. Just as he was passing through the iron gate, the clock struck twelve, and the gate slammed with such force that it took off a piece of his heel.

All the same, he was glad to have found the Water of Life, and started for home. On the way he came to the dwarf and when the dwarf saw the sword and the loaf, he said: "Those are great treasures you've come by. With that sword you can defeat whole armies, and that loaf will always be the same size no matter how much is eaten from it." But the prince didn't want to go home to his father without his brothers, and he said: "Dear dwarf, could you tell me where my two brothers are? They set out in search of the Water of Life before I did, and they never came back." "They're wedged in between mountains," said the dwarf. "I wished them there because they were haughty." The prince pleaded and at length the dwarf released them, though he warned him, saying: "Don't trust them. They have wicked hearts."

When his brothers appeared, he was glad to see them. He told them of his adventures, how he had found the Water of Life and brought back a cupful of it, and how he had saved a beautiful princess, who was going to wait a year for him and then they were going to be married and he would be king over a great kingdom. The brothers rode on together and came to a country where war and famine were raging and the misery was so great that the king of the country thought he would perish. The prince went to the king and gave him the loaf, whereupon the king fed all his people, and stilled their hunger. Next the prince gave the king his sword, the king destroyed the enemy armies, and after that he was able to live in peace. Then the prince took back his loaf and his sword, and the three brothers rode on. They passed through two more countries where war and famine were raging, and in both the prince lent the kings his loaf and his sword, so, all in all, he saved three kingdoms. Then they boarded a ship and sailed across the sea. During the voyage the two elder brothers went aside and said: "Our young brother has found the Water of Life and we haven't found anything. Our father will reward him by giving him the kingdom, which should properly be ours, and he will rob us of our birthright." They longed for revenge and decided on a way to destroy him. They waited until he was fast asleep, and then they poured the Water of Life out of his cup, took it away, and filled the cup with bitter sea water.

When they got home, the youngest brother brought the sick king his cup, expecting him to drink and be cured. But the king had barely tasted the bitter sea water when he became sicker than ever. As he was lamenting, his two elder sons came in and accused the youngest of wanting to poison him. Then they brought in the real Water of Life and handed it to him. The moment he drank of it he felt his sickness leaving him, and was as strong and healthy as in the days of his youth. The two deceivers went to the youngest brother and jeered at him: "Oh yes," they said, "you found the Water of Life, but much good it has done you. Yours the hardship and ours the reward. You should have been smarter and kept your eyes open. We took it away from you on the ship, while you were sleeping, and a year from now one of us will go and claim the beautiful princess. But whatever you do, don't tell our father about this. He wouldn't believe you, and if you say so much as a single word you will die, but if you keep silent your life will be spared."

The old king was very angry, for he thought his youngest had

wanted to kill him. He summoned his council and had them sentence
the boy to be secretly shot. One day the prince, who suspected no
evil, went hunting, and the king's huntsman rode along with him.
When they were all alone in the forest, the huntsman looked so sad
that the prince asked him: "Dear huntsman, what's the matter?" "I
can't tell you," said the huntsman, "and yet I should." "Speak up,"
said the prince. "Whatever it is, I'll forgive you." "Well," said the
huntsman, "I'm supposed to kill you. The king ordered me to." The
prince was aghast. "Dear huntsman," he said, "let me live! I'll give
you my royal garments. Give me your lowly ones in exchange."
"Gladly," said the hunter. "I wouldn't have been able to shoot you in
any case." Whereupon they changed clothes. Then the huntsman
went home and the prince went deeper into the forest.

Some time later three wagonloads of gold and precious stones came
to the king for his youngest son. They had been sent in token of
gratitude by the three kings who had destroyed their enemies with
the prince's sword and fed their people with his loaf. The old king
thought to himself: "Can my son have been innocent?" And he said
aloud: "If only he were alive! I can't forgive myself for having him
killed." At that the huntsman spoke up: "He is alive. I couldn't bring
myself to carry out your order." And then he told the king what had
happened. A weight fell from the king's heart and he had it proclaimed in all the kingdoms that his son was free to come home and
would be welcomed with open arms.

Meanwhile the princess had a golden road built leading to her castle, and said to her guards: "The man who comes riding straight up
to me in the middle of the road will be the right one and you must let
him in. If anyone rides alongside the road, he will not be the right
man, and you are not to let him in." When the year had almost
passed, the eldest son thought he would hurry to the princess and
pass himself off as her savior. He fully expected to win her as his wife
and become master over her kingdom as well. He started out, and
when he came to the castle and saw the beautiful golden road, he
thought: "It would be a pity to ride on such a beautiful road." So he
veered off and went on to the right of it. When he reached the gate,
the guards said to him: "You are not the right man. Go away." A little later the second prince started out, and when he came to the
golden road and his horse had only set one foot on it, he thought: "It

would be a pity. What if the hoofbeats should crack it!" So he veered off and went on to the left of the road. When he reached the gate, the guards said: "You are not the right man. Go away." When the year had wholly passed, the third prince decided to leave his forest, ride away to his beloved, and forget his sorrows with her. Throughout his journey he thought of her and wished he were already with her, so when he got to the golden road he didn't even see it. His horse galloped right up the middle of it, and when he reached the gate it was opened. The princess welcomed him joyfully and said: "You are my savior and the lord of my kingdom." The marriage was celebrated with great rejoicing, and when it was over she told him that his father had sent for him and had forgiven him. Thereupon he rode home and told his father how his brothers had cheated him and how he had kept silent. The king wanted to punish them, but they had boarded a ship and sailed away, and they never came back as long as they lived.

98

Dr. Know-it-all

ONCE A POOR PEASANT by the name of Crabbe hauled a cord of wood to town in a wagon drawn by two oxen, and sold his wood to a doctor for two talers. When he came in to get his money, the doctor was sitting at the table. The peasant saw what lovely things he had to eat and drink, and he longed to be a doctor. After standing there awhile, he asked: "Is there any way of my getting to be a doctor?" "Why not?" said the doctor. "It's easy." "What would I have to do?" asked the peasant. "First, buy yourself an ABC book, the kind with a rooster in it; second, sell your wagon and your two oxen, take the money and buy clothes and the other things a doctor needs; third, have the words 'I am Dr. Know-it-all' painted on a sign, and hang it over the door of your house."

The peasant did everything he had been told. When he had doctored awhile but not for so very long, some money was stolen from a rich nobleman. Someone told him about Dr. Know-it-all, who lived in such and such a village and would be sure to know what had become of the money. So the nobleman had them harness his carriage, drove to the village, went to the peasant's house and asked: "Are you Dr. Know-it-all?" "That's me." "Then come with me and find the money that was stolen from me." "All right. But my wife Greta must come along." The nobleman had no objection. He seated them in his carriage, and away they drove together. When they got to the manor, dinner was on the table, and the peasant was asked to sit down. "Gladly," he said, "but my wife Greta must sit with us." So they sat down, and when the first servant came in with a platter of fine food, the peasant nudged his wife and said: "Greta, that's the first," meaning the servant with the first course. But the servant thought he had meant to say: "That's the first thief." And since that's just what he was, he took fright and said to his comrades in the kitchen: "The doctor knows it all, we're in trouble. He said I was the first." The second didn't even want to go in, but he had to. When he appeared with his platter, the peasant nudged his wife: "Greta," he said, "that's the second," and the second servant hurried out of the room, as frightened as the first. The third fared no better. The peasant nudged his wife again and said: "Greta, that's the third." The fourth brought in a covered dish, and the nobleman said: "Now show your skill. Tell me what's under the cover." It was a crab. The peasant looked at the dish. He hadn't the faintest idea what was in it. "Poor Crabbe!" he cried out. When the nobleman heard that, he said: "If he knows that, he must know who has the money."

The servant was frightened to death. He signaled to the doctor to come outside for a minute. When he met them outside, all four servants confessed they had stolen the money. They offered to hand it over and give him a tidy sum in addition, if only he didn't tell anyone who had taken it, for if he did they would be hanged. Then they led him to the place where the money was hidden, and that was good enough for the doctor. He went back in, sat down at the table, and said: "Your lordship, now I will look in my book and find out where the money is." At that, the fifth servant crawled into the stove, wanting to find out how much the doctor actually knew. The doctor opened his ABC book and leafed backward and forward, looking for the rooster. When he couldn't find it, he said: "I know you're there, so what's the good of hiding?" The servant in the stove thought the doctor was speaking of him and popped out in a fright, shouting: "He knows it all! He knows it all!" Then Dr. Know-it-all showed the nobleman where the money was, but didn't tell him who had stolen it. He was richly rewarded by both parties and became a famous man.

99

The Spirit in the Bottle

THERE WAS ONCE a poor woodcutter who worked from early morning till late at night. When he had finally saved a little money, he said to his son: "You're my only child. I've made a little money by the sweat of my brow, and I'm going to spend it on your education. If you learn some decent trade, you'll be able to keep me in my old age, when my limbs have gone stiff, and I have to sit at home." The boy went away to a university and studied hard. His teachers praised him and he stayed awhile. When he had completed a few courses but wasn't quite perfect in everything, his father's meager savings were used up, and he had to return home. "It's a shame," said the father sadly. "I have no more to give you, and in these hard times I can barely earn what's needed for our daily bread." "Dear father," said the son, "don't worry. I'll get used to this life, and maybe I'll be the better for it in the end." As the father was preparing to go out and earn some money cutting and piling cordwood, the son said: "I'll come along and help you." "I don't know, son," said the father. "It might be hard on you, you're not used to heavy work. I doubt if you could stand it. Besides, I have only one ax and no money to buy another with." "Go and ask our neighbor," said the son. "He'll let you have an ax till I've earned enough to buy one."

The father borrowed an ax from his neighbor, and next morning at daybreak they went to the forest together. The young fellow helped the father, and was as cheerful as could be. When the sun was high in the sky, the father said: "Let's rest now and have something to eat. The work will go twice as well afterward." The son took his bread and said: "You rest, father. I'm not tired. I'm going to take a little walk and look for birds' nests." "Don't be a fool," said the father. "What's the good of running around? Afterward you'll be too tired to move. Stay here and sit down."

But the son went deeper into the forest and ate his bread. He felt light and gay and looked up into the green branches, to see if he could find a nest. Back and forth he walked and came at last to a big angry-looking oak tree, that must have been hundreds of years old and was so thick that five men couldn't have girdled it with their arms. He stopped still, looked at the tree, and thought: "Lots of birds must have built nests in that tree." Suddenly he seemed to hear someone calling. Pricking up his ears he heard a muffled voice, crying: "Let me out, let me out." When he looked around, he couldn't see a thing, and it seemed to him that the voice came out of the ground. "Who are you?" he cried. The voice answered: "I'm in among the roots of the oak tree. Let me out. Let me out." The student cleared away the dead leaves and looked among the roots, until finally he uncovered a small hollow and in it found a glass bottle. When he held the bottle up to the light, he saw something inside that was shaped like a frog and jumping up and down. "Let me out, let me out," it kept crying. Suspecting no harm, the student pulled the cork out of the bottle. In a flash a spirit slipped out and began to grow, and it grew so fast that in a few seconds a monstrous fellow half as big as the tree was standing there. And he said in a thundering voice: "Do you know what your reward will be for letting me out?" "No," said the student fearlessly. "How could I?" "Then I'll tell you!" cried the spirit. "I'm going to have to break your neck. That's your reward." "You should have told me that before," said the student. "I'd have left you in your bottle. But I'll keep my head on my shoulders all the same. You'll have to consult a few more people before I let you tamper with my neck." "More people, indeed!" said the spirit. "You've earned your reward and you shall have it. Do you think they've kept me shut up all this time out of kindness? Far from it. They did it to punish me. I am the mighty Mercurius, and when somebody sets me free it's my duty to break his neck." "Not so fast!" said the student. "First I've got to know that you were really in that little bottle, then I'll believe you and you can do what you please with me." "Nothing could be simpler," the spirit replied haughtily. Whereupon he pulled himself in and made himself as thin and small as he had been to begin with, and crawled right through the bottle neck. No sooner was he inside than the student shoved the cork back in and tossed the bottle into its old place among the roots of the oak tree. The spirit had been outsmarted.

The student started back to his father, but the spirit cried pitifully: "Oh, please let me out, please let me out." "No," said the student. "You can't fool me twice. When I catch somebody who has threatened my life, I don't let him go so easily." "If you set me free," said the spirit, "I'll give you enough to last you as long as you live." "No," said the student. "You'd only cheat me again." "You're turning your back on your good fortune," said the spirit. "I won't hurt you, you'll be richly rewarded." The student thought to himself: "I'll take a chance. Maybe he'll keep his word, and, besides, he can't hurt me." So he pulled the cork, the spirit came out as he had the first time, and he stretched and spread until he was as big as a giant. He handed the student a piece of cloth very much like a poultice and said: "This is your reward. If you put one end of it on a wound, the wound will be healed, and if you rub iron or steel with the other end, it will turn to silver." "I'll have to try that," said the student. He went to a tree, gashed the bark with his ax and rubbed the gash with one end of the poultice. The bark grew together and the wound was healed. "It's all right," said the student. "Now we can part." The spirit thanked him for setting him free, and the student thanked the spirit for his gift and went back to his father.

"Where have you been all this time?" asked the father. "You've forgotten all about your work. I told you you wouldn't get anything done." "Don't worry, father. I'll catch up." "Catch up!" said the father indignantly. "You don't know what you're talking about." "Just watch me, father. I'll have that tree felled before you know it." He took his poultice, rubbed the ax with it, and struck a powerful blow. But the iron had turned to silver, and the blade bent. "Father, look at this wretched ax you've given me. It's all bent." The father was horrified. "I knew it!" he said. "Now I'll have to pay for the ax, and where will I get the money? You've been a big help to me." "Don't be angry," said the son. "I'll pay for the ax." "You blockhead," said the father. "What with? Can you tell me that? You have nothing except what I give you. You may be full of book learning, but you certainly don't know anything about cutting down trees."

After a while the student said: "Father, there's nothing more I can do now, so let's call it a day." "Nonsense," said the father. "Do you expect me to sit with my hands folded like you? You can go home. I've still got work to do." "Father, I've never been in these woods before, I could never get out by myself. Come and show me the way." The father's anger had died down and he finally gave in. They went home together, and the father said to the son: "Go and sell that ruined ax. See what you can get for it. I'll have to earn the rest, so as to pay our neighbor." The son took the ax to town and brought it to the goldsmith, who tested it, put it on his scales, and said: "It's worth four hundred talers, but I haven't got that much in ready money." The student said: "Give me what you have. You can owe me the rest." The goldsmith gave him three hundred talers and owed him one hundred. The student went home and said: "Father, I've got money. Go and ask our neighbor how much he wants for his ax." "I know that already," said the father. "One taler and six groschen." "Then give him twice as much, two talers and twelve groschen. That's plenty. Look, father, I've got more money than we need." He gave his father a hundred talers, and said: "From now on you shall live at your ease and never want for anything." "Good Lord," said his father, "how did you come by all that money?" The student told him exactly what had happened, and what a prize he had won by trusting in his luck. With the rest of the money he returned to the university and went on studying, and seeing as he was able to heal all kinds of wounds with his poultice, he became the most famous doctor in the whole world.

100

The Devil's Grimy Brother

A DISCHARGED SOLDIER had nothing to live on and didn't know where to turn. So he went out into the forest and after a while he met a little man. This little man was the Devil, and he said to the soldier: "What's wrong? You look so unhappy." The soldier answered: "I'm hungry and I haven't any money." The Devil said: "If you'll hire yourself out to me and be my servant, I'll give you enough to last you the rest of your life. You'll have to serve me for seven years, and then you'll be free. But there's one thing I have to tell you. During those seven years you mustn't wash, or comb, or cut your hair, or trim your beard, or pare your nails, or wipe your eyes. "If it can't be helped," said the soldier, "I may as well get started." And off he went with the little man, who led him straight to hell and told him what he had to do: tend the fires under the caldrons where the damned souls were cooking, clean the house, carry the sweepings behind the back door, and in general keep order. "But," said the Devil, "don't look into those caldrons! Not even once, or you'll be in trouble." "I understand," said the soldier. "Everything will be all right." The old Devil went off on his travels and the soldier took up his duties, tended the fire, swept, carried the sweepings behind the back door— everything just as he'd been told. When the old Devil came back, he looked to see if his man had done his work, said, "Well done," and went away again. This time the soldier took a good look around. In every corner of hell the caldrons were boiling and bubbling, with furious fires under them. He'd have loved to look into them if the Devil hadn't expressly forbidden it. But then the temptation was too much for him, and he lifted the lid of the first caldron just a little. He peeped in and who was inside but his old sergeant. "Aha, you dog!" he said. "You here? You made it hot for me, now I'll make it hot for you." Whereupon he dropped the lid, stirred up the fire, and put on some more wood. He went to the second caldron, lifted the lid a little, and looked in. His lieutenant was inside. "Aha, you dog!" he said. "You here? You made it hot for me, now I'll make it hot for you."

And so he performed his duties in hell for seven years: he didn't wash, he didn't comb or cut his hair, he didn't pare his nails or wipe his eyes. The seven years passed so quickly he thought he hadn't been there for more than half a year, and when his time was up, the Devil came and said: "Well, Hans, what have you been doing all this time?" "I've tended the fires under the caldrons, I've swept and carried the sweepings behind the door." "But you've also looked into the caldrons. Luckily for you, you put on more wood or you'd have lost your life. Now your time is up. Do you want to go back home?" "Oh, yes," said the soldier. "I want to see how my father is getting along." "You've earned your reward," said the Devil. "Here's how to get it: go and fill your knapsack with sweepings and take them home with you. And you must also go unwashed and uncombed, with long hair and a long beard, with uncut nails and bleary eyes, and if anyone asks you where you've come from you must say: 'From hell.' And if they ask you who you are, you must say: 'The Devil's grimy brother and my king as well!' " The soldier did as the Devil had said and made no complaint, but he wasn't at all pleased with his reward.

As soon as he was back in the woods up above, he took his knapsack off his back and was going to throw the sweepings away, but when he opened the knapsack, they had turned to pure gold. "This is a pleasant surprise," he said to himself, and went to the nearest town. An innkeeper was standing in the doorway of his inn, and when he saw Hans coming along, he was frightened to death because Hans looked terrible, worse than a scarecrow. "Where have you come from?" "From hell." "Who are you?" "The Devil's grimy brother, and my king as well." The innkeeper didn't want to let him in, but when Hans showed him his gold, he himself unlatched the door. Hans demanded the best room and the finest service and ate and drank his fill, but he followed the Devil's instructions and didn't wash and didn't comb his hair. Finally he went to bed. The innkeeper hadn't been able to get that knapsack full of gold out of his mind. The thought of it gave him no peace and finally, late that night, he crept in and stole it.

When Hans got up next morning and prepared to pay the innkeeper and leave, his knapsack was gone. He thought to himself: "I'm in trouble through no fault of my own," and quickly decided what to do. He retraced his steps, went straight back to hell, told the Devil his tale of woe and asked for his help. The Devil said: "Sit down. I'll wash you, comb your hair, cut your hair and nails, and wipe your eyes." When he had finished with him, he gave him back his knapsack full of sweepings and said: "Go and tell the innkeeper to return your gold. Tell him if he doesn't I'll come and take him away and he'll have to tend the fires in your place." Hans went up and said to the innkeeper: "You stole my money. If you don't give it back, you'll go to hell in my place, and you'll look every bit as horrible as I did." The innkeeper gave him the money and some more besides, but begged him not to tell anybody. So now Hans was a rich man.

He started on the way home to his father, bought himself a coarse white coat, and went about playing music, for he had learned how from the Devil in hell. There happened to be an old king in that country, and Hans played for him, and the king was so pleased that he promised Hans his eldest daughter. But when she heard she was to marry a lowborn fellow in a coarse white coat, she said: "Before I do that, I'll jump into the deepest river." So the king gave him the youngest, who was willing for her father's sake. And so the Devil's grimy brother married the princess, and when the old king died, he became king over the whole country.

101

Bearskin

THERE WAS ONCE a young fellow who enlisted as a soldier, fought bravely, and was always foremost when the bullets were flying thick and fast. As long as the war lasted, he was well off, but when peace was made, he was given his discharge and his captain told him he could go wherever he pleased. His parents were dead and he had no home, so he went to his brothers and asked them to take him in until the war started up again. But his brothers were hardhearted men. "Why should we?" they said. "What use can you be to us? Go and shift for yourself." The soldier had nothing but his gun. He slung it over his shoulder and started out. Soon he came to a great heath, where all he could see was a circle of trees. Feeling very sad, he sat down under the trees and thought about his dismal fate. "I have no money," he said to himself. "The only trade I've ever learned is soldiering, and now that peace has been made they don't need me any more. I can see I'm going to starve." Suddenly he heard a rustling, and when he looked around a stranger was standing there. He was wearing a green coat and was very handsome, but he had a horrid-looking cloven hoof. "I know what your trouble is," said the man. "I'll give you as much money and wealth as you can possibly use, but first I must know that you're not afraid, because I don't want to spend my money for nothing." "Would I be a soldier if I were afraid?" said the soldier. "Put me to the test." "All right," said the man. "Look behind you." When the soldier turned around, a big growling bear was coming toward him. "Oho!" cried the soldier. "When I get through tickling your nose, you won't feel like growling any more." Whereupon he took aim and shot the bear in the muzzle. The bear fell down and lay still, and the stranger said: "I can see you've got plenty of courage, but there's one more condition you'll have to meet." "If it won't harm my immortal soul," said the soldier, who knew perfectly well whom he was dealing with. "If it does, I won't have anything to do with it." "You'll judge that for yourself," said Greencoat. "In the next seven years you mustn't wash or comb your beard or hair, or cut your nails, or say so much as a single paternoster. I'm going to give you a coat and a clock, and you must wear them all that time. If you die before the seven years are out you'll be mine, but if you live you'll be free for the rest of your life, and rich to boot." The soldier thought of his dire poverty, remembered how often he had faced death, and decided to risk it. The Devil took off his green coat, handed it to the soldier, and said: "If you reach into your pocket when you're wearing this coat, your hand will always be full of money." Then he stripped off the bear's skin and said: "This will be your cloak and your bed. Because of it, people will call you Bearskin." And with that, the Devil vanished.

The soldier put the coat on, reached into his pocket, and found that the Devil had been telling the truth. Then he threw the bearskin over his shoulders, went out into the world and enjoyed himself, neglecting nothing that gave him pleasure and cost money. It wasn't so bad during the first year, but by the second he was looking like a monster. His face was almost entirely covered with hair, his beard was matted like felt, his fingernails were claws, there was so much dirt on his face that if cress had been sown in it, it would have sprouted. Everyone who caught sight of him ran away, but since wherever he went he gave money to the poor to pray that he wouldn't die before the seven years were out, and since he always paid well, he could count on finding lodgings. In the fourth year he came to an inn and the innkeeper didn't want to take him in or even let him sleep in the stable, because he was afraid the sight of him would make the horses skittish. When Bearskin reached into his pocket and brought out a handful of ducats, the innkeeper took pity on him and gave him a room at the back of the house, but, for fear of bringing the inn into ill repute, made him promise not to show his face.

As he was sitting there alone, wishing with all his heart that the seven years were over, he heard someone lamenting in the next room. Now Bearskin had a kind heart. He opened the door and there was an old man, weeping bitterly and wringing his hands. At the sight of Bearskin, the old man jumped up and started to run away, but when he heard a human voice he stopped and listened and finally, in answer to Bearskin's soft words, told him the reason for his despair. Little by little his fortune had dwindled, he and his daughters were reduced to starvation, he was too poor to pay the innkeeper, and he was going to be thrown into prison. "If that's all it is," said Bearskin, "you can stop worrying. I have plenty of money." He sent for the innkeeper, paid him, and put a purse full of gold into the unhappy man's pocket.

When the old man saw that his troubles were over, he didn't know how to show his gratitude. "Come with me," he said. "My daughters are miracles of beauty. Choose one of them for your wife. When she hears what you've done for me, she won't refuse. It's true, you look rather weird, but she'll set you to rights." The idea appealed to Bearskin and he went with the old man. When the eldest daughter saw him, she was so horrified that she screamed and ran away. The second stood still and examined him from top to toe, but then she said: "How can I marry a man who doesn't even look human? I'd sooner have taken the shaved bear who was here once, passing himself off as a man. He at least was wearing a hussar's uniform and white gloves. If it were only his ugliness, I could get used to it." But the youngest said: "Dear father, he must be a good man, to have helped you in your need. If you've promised him a wife in return, your promise must be kept." Unfortunately Bearskin's face was covered with dirt and hair, or you'd have seen how his heart leaped for joy when he heard those words. He took a ring from his finger, broke it in two, gave her one half, and kept the other half for himself. On her half he wrote his name and on his half he wrote her name, and he asked her to take good care of her half. Then he bade her farewell saying: "I shall have to wander for another three years. If I don't come back then, you will be free, for I shall be dead. But pray God to keep me alive."

The poor girl dressed all in black, and the tears came to her eyes when she thought of her betrothed. All she got from her sisters was mockery. "Better be careful," said the eldest. "If you hold out your hand, he'll crush it in his paw." "Watch out," said the second, "bears love sweets. If he likes you, he'll eat you up." "Be sure to do what he wants," said the eldest, "or he'll start to growl." And the second: "The wedding will be merry, though. Bears are such good dancers." But the bride made no answer and nothing they said could ruffle her. Meanwhile Bearskin wandered from place to place, helping people as much as he could, and giving generously to the poor so they would pray for him. Finally, when the last day of the seven years dawned, he went back to the heath and sat down inside the circle of trees. Soon the wind whistled and the Devil stood before him. He gave Bearskin a glum look, tossed him his old coat and asked to have his green one back. "Not so fast," said Bearskin. "First you must clean me up." Like it or not, the Devil had to bring water, give Bearskin a good scrubbing, comb his hair and cut his nails. When that was done, he looked like a dashing soldier and was much more handsome than before.

When the Devil had left him, Bearskin felt light of heart. He went to the town, bought a splendid velvet coat, seated himself in a carriage drawn by four white horses, and rode to the house of his betrothed. No one recognized him. The father took him for a general, led him to the room where his daughters were sitting, and showed him to a place between his two elder daughters. They poured wine for him, put the tastiest morsels before him, and thought they had never in all their lives seen a handsomer man. His betrothed, who was sitting across from him in her black dress, didn't raise her eyes or say a word. When at last he asked the father if he would give him one of his daughters for a wife, the two eldest jumped up, ran to their rooms and put on their best clothes, for each of them thought she was the chosen one. As soon as he was alone with his betrothed, the stranger took out his half ring, dropped it into a glass of wine and passed it across the table to her. She took the wine and drank it, and when she found the half ring at the bottom of her glass, her heart leaped. She took the other half, which she had been wearing on a ribbon round her neck, put the two together, and saw that the two parts fitted together perfectly. Whereupon he said: "I am your betrothed. I was

Bearskin when you saw me last, but by the grace of God I have regained my human form and been made clean again." He went over to her, took her in his arms and kissed her. Just then the two sisters came back in all their finery, and when they saw that the handsome man had chosen the youngest and heard that he was Bearskin, they ran out of the house in a rage. The eldest drowned herself in the well, the other hanged herself from a tree. That evening there was a knock at the door, and when the bridegroom opened, it was the Devil in his green coat. "You see," he said, "now I've got two souls in exchange for your one."

102

The Kinglet and the Bear

ONE SUMMER'S DAY as the bear and the wolf were taking a walk in the forest, the bear heard a bird singing so beautifully that he said: "Brother Wolf, what kind of bird is it that's singing so beautifully?" "That's the king of the birds," said the wolf. "We must bow down to him." Actually it was the kinglet. "In that case, I'd like to see his royal palace. Would you take me there?" "It's not as easy as you think," said the wolf. "You'll have to wait until the queen comes home." The queen soon arrived with food in her bill; the king was with her, and they began to feed their young ones. The bear wanted to go right in after them, but the wolf held him by the sleeve and said: "No, you must wait till their majesties leave." So they took note of the hollow where the nest was and ambled away. But the bear was dying to see the royal palace, he couldn't stop thinking about it, and after a while he went back. The king and the queen had flown away. He looked in and saw five or six young birds lying there. "Call this a royal palace!" the bear cried out. "It doesn't look like a palace to me. And you're not royal children either. You're nasty children." When the young kinglets heard that, they were very angry. "No, no!" they cried. "We are not. Our parents are nice people. Bear, you'll pay for this." The bear and the wolf were afraid. They went home and skulked in their dens. But the little kinglets went on screaming and yelling, and when their parents came back with food, they said: "We won't touch so much as a fly's leg until this thing is settled. Are we or aren't we nice children? The bear was here and he insulted us." The old king said: "Don't worry. The matter will be settled forthwith." The king and the queen flew to the bear's den, stopped outside and called in: "You old growler, why did you insult our children? You'll be sorry. There's only one answer to a thing like this: bloody war!" So war was declared on the bear, who summoned all the four-footed animals, the ox, the donkey, the cow, the deer, and whatever else is found on earth. And the kinglet summoned all those that fly through the air: not only the birds great and small, but also the gnats, hornets, bees, and flies reported for duty.

When it was time for the war to start, the kinglet sent out spies to find out who the enemy's commanding general was. The gnat was the craftiest of all; he flew into the forest where the enemy had assembled, found the tree under which the password was being given out, and hid under a leaf. The bear was standing right there. He bade the fox step forward, and said to him: "Fox, you're the slyest of all the animals. You shall be our general and lead us." "Very well," said the fox. "But first let's decide on our signals. What shall they be?" No one had any ideas, so the fox said: "I've got a long, bushy tail that looks almost like a red plume. If I lift up my tail, it means that all's well and you must charge; but if I let it droop, then you must run for dear life." When the gnat heard that, he flew straight back to headquarters and made a detailed report to the kinglet.

When the day of the battle dawned, my oh my, the four-footed animals came running with such a drumming of feet that the earth trembled. The kinglet and his army came flying through the air, with a buzzing and whistling and swarming and fluttering that struck terror into the hearts of everyone for miles around. Just as the two armies were about to clash, the kinglet sent the hornet down with orders to settle under the fox's tail and sting with all his might. At the first sting, the fox gave a start and one leg quivered, but he bore it and kept his tail up. At the second sting, he lowered his tail for just a moment. But at the third he lost all control over himself, bellowed, and let his tail droop. When the animals saw that, they thought all was lost and began to run, each to his own home. The birds had won the battle.

The king and the queen flew home to their children and cried out: "Children, rejoice! Eat, drink, and be merry, for we've won the war!" But the young kinglets said: "Oh no! We won't eat until the bear comes and apologizes and says we're nice children." The kinglet flew to the bear's den and called out: "Growler, you must come to our nest and apologize to our children and tell them they're nice children. If you don't, you'll have your ribs kicked in." In terror the bear crept to the kinglet's nest and apologized. At last the young kinglets were satisfied. They sat down together, and ate, drank, and made merry until late into the night.

103
The Sweet Porridge

THERE WAS ONCE a good little girl who lived alone with her mother, and they were so poor they had nothing left to eat. One day when the child was walking in the forest she met an old woman, who, knowing how poor she was, gave her a little pot and told her what to do with it: "If you say, 'Cook, little pot,' it will make good, sweet millet porridge, and if you say, 'Cease, little pot,' it will stop cooking." The child brought the pot home to her mother, and after that they had no further need to worry about poverty and hunger, for they could eat sweet porridge as often as they liked. One day when the little girl was out, the mother said: "Cook, little pot." The pot cooked and she ate her fill, but when she wanted the pot to stop cooking, she didn't know the right words. The pot went on cooking, the porridge overflowed and still it went on cooking. Soon the kitchen and the whole house were full, and then the house next door and the whole street, and the pot went right on cooking as if it wanted to feed the whole world. The distress was great and no one knew what to do. Finally, when there was only a single house left without any porridge in it, the child came home and said: "Cease, little pot." It stopped cooking, but anyone who wanted to go back to town had to eat his way through.

104
Wise Folk

ONE DAY A PEASANT took his hardwood stick from the corner and said to his wife: "Trina, I'm going away and I won't be back for three days. If the cattle dealer turns up while I'm gone and wants to buy our three cows, go ahead and sell them, but don't take less than two hundred talers. Two hundred, mind you, and no less!" "You needn't worry," said his wife. "You can count on me." "Hmm," said the peasant. "You fell on your head when you were little, and you never got over it. But let me tell you this: if you do anything stupid I'll color your back for you, and not with paint, just with this stick I have here, and the color will last a whole year, you can be sure of that." With that the peasant started off.

The next morning the cattle dealer arrived, and the woman didn't have to do much talking. When he had looked the cows over and heard the price, he said: "I'll pay that gladly. Frankly, they're worth that much. I'll take them with me." He took them off the chain and drove them out of the barn, but as he was passing through the gate, the woman held him by the sleeve and said: "You'll have to give me the two hundred talers first, or I can't let you go." "Right you are," said the man. "Trouble is, I forgot to put on my money belt. But don't worry, I'll leave you a deposit. I'll only take two cows with me and leave you the third. That will be good security for you." That struck the woman as perfectly reasonable, and she let the man go with the two cows. She thought to herself: "Won't Hans be pleased when he sees how cleverly I've handled this!" The peasant came home on the third day, just as he had said, and the first thing he did was to ask if the cows had been sold. "Oh yes, dear Hans," said his wife, "and just as you said, for two hundred talers. They're not really worth that much, but the man didn't argue, he just took them." "Where's the money?" the peasant asked. "I haven't got the money," said the woman. "You see he'd forgotten his money belt, but he'll bring it soon. He left good security." "What kind of security?" "One of the cows. We won't give it to him until he's paid for the others. I was clever. I kept back the smallest. She eats less than the others." The peasant was furious. He raised his stick and was going to give her the promised beating, but then suddenly he lowered his arm and said: "You're the silliest goose that ever waddled on the face of the earth, but I feel sorry for you. I'm going out on the highway and I'm going to sit there for three days. If anyone stupider than you comes my way, I won't hurt you. If not, you'll get what you deserve, with full measure."

He went out on the highway, sat down on a stone, and waited to see what would happen. After a while an open wagon came along, and a woman was standing right in the middle of it, instead of sitting on the bundle of straw that was lying at her feet or walking beside the oxen and guiding them. The man thought: "This must be one of the kind I'm looking for." Whereupon he jumped up and ran from side to side of the road in front of the wagon, as if he'd taken leave of his wits. "Hey!" cried the woman. "What do you want? I don't know you, where are you from?" "I've fallen from heaven," he replied, "and I don't know how to get back. Could you drive me up?" "No," said the woman. "I don't know the way. But if you've come from heaven, maybe you can tell me how my husband is getting along. He's been up there for three years now. You must have seen him." "Of course I've seen him. But you can't expect everybody to be well off. He's the shepherd up there, and the sheep have been giving him a lot of trouble. They scamper up the hills, they get lost in the woods, and he has to go chasing after them. The poor man's clothes are all worn out, they're falling to pieces. There aren't any tailors up there, St. Peter won't let them in, you know that from the fairy tale." "Goodness gracious!" cried the woman. "I tell you what I'll do. I'll go and get his Sunday coat that's still hanging in the closet. He can wear it up there, then he won't be ashamed to show himself. You'll take it to him, won't you?" "I can't," said the peasant. "It's forbidden to bring clothes into heaven. They take them away from you at the gate." "I'll tell you what," said the woman. "Yesterday I sold my best wheat for a nice bit of money. I'll send him that. If you just slip the pouch into your pocket, no one will see it." "If you insist," said the peasant. "I don't mind doing you the favor." "Stay here," she said. "I'll drive home and get the money. I'll be right back. I won't sit on the straw. When I stand, it makes the wagon lighter for the oxen." Away she drove, goading the oxen, and the peasant thought: "Now there's a candidate for the nuthouse. If she really comes back with the money, my wife can say she's in luck, because she won't get a beating." It wasn't long before the woman came running with the money and thrust it into his pocket. Before she left him, she thanked him a thousand times for his kindness.

When she got home again, she found her son, who had just come in from the fields, and told him about the unexpected news she had had. "And just think," she said. "Isn't it wonderful to be able to send your poor father something? Who'd have thought he'd be suffering want in heaven?" The son was amazed. "Mother," he said, "it's not every day that a man comes down from heaven. I think I'll go and see if he's still there. Maybe he can tell me what it's like up in heaven and how the work is going." He saddled the horse and galloped away. He found the peasant sitting under a willow tree, counting the money in the pouch. The young fellow called out to him: "Have you seen the man who came down from heaven?" "Oh yes," said the peasant. "He's started back. He's just starting up the hill there. It's nearer that way. You can catch him if you ride fast." "No," said the young fellow. "I've been working hard all day, and the ride here has worn me out. You know the man, so do me a favor. Take my horse, catch up with him and persuade him to come back here." "Aha," thought the peasant, "here's another without any wick to his lamp." "Only too glad to!" he said. Whereupon he mounted the horse and rode away at a brisk trot. The young fellow sat there until nightfall, but the peasant didn't come back. The young fellow thought to himself: "The man from heaven must have been in too much of a hurry to turn back, so I suppose the peasant gave him my horse to deliver to my father." He went home, told his mother what had happened, and explained that he had sent his father the horse so he wouldn't have to go about on foot. "You did right," she said. "With your young legs it won't hurt you to walk."

When the peasant got home, he put the horse in the barn along with the security cow. Then he went to his wife and said: "Trina, you're in luck. I found two who were even bigger fools than you are. So you won't get your beating, I'll save it for next time." Then he lit his pipe, sat down in his grandfather chair, and said to himself: "Good business, I call it. A fine horse and a pouch full of money in exchange for two skinny cows. If stupidity were always so profitable, I'd be all for it." That's what the peasant thought, but I'm sure you like the simple folk better.

105

Friendly Animals
Three Tales

I

ONCE THERE WAS a little girl whose mother gave her a bowl of bread and milk every afternoon, and the child sat down in the yard with it. When she began to eat, a grass snake came creeping out of a crack in the wall, dipped its head in the milk, and had a nice little meal. The child was delighted, and sometimes when she had sat down with her bowl and the snake wasn't there yet, she cried out:

> "Little snake, come here to me,
> Share my bread and milk with me."

Then the snake came quickly and lapped up its share of the milk. It was grateful, and showed its gratitude by bringing the child all sorts of pretty things from its secret treasure, precious stones, pearls, and golden playthings. Now it so happened that the snake only drank the milk and never touched the bread. One day the little girl gave the snake a tap on the head with her spoon and said: "You must eat the bread too, little snake." Her mother, who was in the kitchen, heard her talking to someone, and when she saw her hitting a snake with her spoon, she rushed out with a log and killed the good little animal.

From then on a change came over the child. As long as the snake had eaten with her, she had grown bigger and stronger by the day, but now her rosy cheeks faded and she became thinner and thinner. The little owl started hooting its death knell in the night, the robin began to gather twigs and leaves for a funeral wreath, and soon the little girl lay in her coffin.

I I

A LITTLE ORPHAN GIRL sat spinning at the foot of the ramparts, when suddenly a grass snake crawled out of a crack in the wall. Quickly she spread out her blue kerchief beside her, the kind that snakes love to sit on. When the snake saw that, it turned around and vanished, but soon came back, carrying a tiny golden crown, put the crown on the kerchief, and went away.

The little girl picked up the glittering crown, which was made of finely spun gold. After a while the snake came a second time. When it saw that the crown wasn't there any more, it crept back to the wall. Stricken with grief, it beat its head against the stone as long as its strength held out, and finally lay there dead. If the little girl had left the crown lying on the kerchief, the snake would probably have brought her more treasures from its hole.

I I I

TOAD CRIES: "Hoo-hoo!" Child says: "Come on out." The toad comes out and the child asks about her little sister. "Have you seen Red-stockings?" Toad says: "No, not I. No more than you. Hoo-hoo, hoo-hoo, hoo-hoo."

106

The Miller's Drudge
and the Cat

THERE WAS ONCE an old miller who lived in a mill and had neither wife nor children, but only three helpers. One day, when the helpers had been with him for some years, he said to them: "I'm getting old, it's time for me to stop work and sit in the chimney corner. Go out into the world. I've decided to give my mill to the one of you who comes back with the best horse, and let him take care of me until I die." The youngest of the three was the household drudge, and the other two thought he was stupid. "What would he do with a mill?" they said, and the fact is that when the time came he didn't even want it. All three started out together, and when they came to the next village, the two said to stupid Hans: "Why don't you stop here? You'll never find a horse." But Hans stayed with them. At nightfall they came to a cave and lay down to sleep. The two clever ones waited until Hans had fallen asleep. Then they climbed out of the cave and left him lying there. They thought they'd been pretty smart, but don't gloat, my boys, you won't come off so well.

So when the sun rose and Hans awoke, he was lying in a deep cave. He looked around and cried: "Good God, where am I?" He got up, climbed out of the cave, and went into the forest, thinking: "Here I am, alone and forsaken. How will I ever find a horse?" While he was walking, deep in thought, a little tabby cat came along and said with a friendly smile: "Good morning, Hans. Where are you off to?" "Oh, you can't help me." "I know what you're looking for," said the cat. "You're looking for a fine horse. Come with me, serve me faithfully for seven years, and I'll give you the finest horse you ever laid eyes on." "This is a very peculiar cat," thought Hans. "But her proposition seems worth looking into. Maybe she's telling the truth." So he followed the cat to her enchanted castle. All her servants were kittens. Upstairs and downstairs they bounded, always happy and gay. When the miller's drudge and the tabby cat sat down to dinner that evening, three of the servants made music for them. The first played the double bass, the second played the fiddle, the third set a trumpet to his lips and puffed up his cheeks and blew for dear life. When they had finished eating, the table was carried away, and the cat said: "Now, Hans, come and dance with me." "No," he said, "I don't dance with pussycats. I never have." "In that case," she said to the kittens, "show him up to bed." Thereupon one kitten lighted his way to his bedroom, one took his shoes off, one took his stockings off, and one blew his light out. In the morning they came back and helped him to get up. One put his stockings on, one tied his garters, one brought him his shoes, one washed him, and one dried his face with her tail. "How deliciously soft!" he said. But he also had to serve the tabby cat. Every day he was given a silver ax and saw, silver wedges, and a copper mallet, and made to cut firewood.

All this time he lived in the castle and ate well and drank well, but he never saw a living soul except for the tabby cat and her servants. One day she said to him: "Go and mow my meadow and bring in the hay when it's dry." She gave him a silver scythe and a gold whetstone, to be returned when the work was done. Hans did just as he was told, returned the scythe and whetstone, and brought the hay in. When he had finished, he asked: "But isn't it time for you to give me my reward?" "No," said the cat. "You must do one more thing for me. Here you have silver boards, a carpenter's ax, a try square, and everything else you'll need, all of silver. Take them, and build me a little house." Hans built the little house, and when it was finished he said: "Now I've done everything you wanted and I still have no horse." By then his seven years had passed, though he felt as if he hadn't been there more than six months. "Would you like to see my horses?" the tabby cat asked. "Oh yes!" said Hans. The cat opened the door of the little house and there stood twelve horses, and what fine horses they were! So sleek and glossy that his heart leaped for joy. Then she gave him food and drink and said: "Go home. I won't give you your horse to take with you, I'll bring it to you in three days." With that, she showed him the way to the mill and he started out. She hadn't even given him new clothes. He had to wear the things he had come in and had worn the whole seven years, and by then they were all ragged and much too small. When he reached the mill, the two other helpers were there too. They had both brought back horses, but one horse was blind and the other was lame. "Well, Hans," they said, "where's your horse?" "He'll be here in three days," he replied. They laughed and said: "Hans, you're a funny one. Where is this horse coming from? Some horse he'll turn out to be!" Hans went inside, but the miller said he was too filthy and ragged to sit at the table, he'd disgrace them if anyone dropped in. So he had to stay outside and they brought him a bit of food. That night when it was time to sleep the two others wouldn't give him a bed and he had to crawl into the goosehouse and lie down on the hard straw.

When he woke up in the morning, the three days had passed. A carriage drawn by six magnificent, glistening horses pulled up at the gate, and a servant brought in a seventh, which was for the miller's drudge. A beautiful princess stepped out of the carriage and went into the mill, and this princess was the tabby cat Hans had served for seven years. She asked the miller where his youngest helper was, and the miller said: "Him? We can't have him indoors, he's too dirty and ragged. He's out in the goosehouse." "Bring him here this minute!" said the princess. As they were bringing him in, he had to hold his rags together in front so as to keep more or less covered. The servant brought splendid clothes from the carriage and washed him and dressed him, and when he had finished, no king could have been more resplendent. The princess asked to see the horses the miller's other helpers had brought home, and one was blind and one was lame. Whereupon she told the servant to bring in the seventh horse. When the miller saw it, he said such a horse had never been seen in his mill. "It's for your third helper," she said. "In that case," said the miller, "the mill must go to him." But the princess said: "The horse is yours, and you can keep your mill as well." She took her faithful Hans by the hand and led him to the carriage. They drove away together and went straight to the little house Hans had built with the silver tools. It was a big castle now, and everything in it was silver and gold. Then she married him, and he was rich, so rich that he had enough to last him the rest of his life. So don't ever say that a stupid person can't get anywhere in this world.

107
The Two Traveling Companions

HILL AND DALE never meet, but among the sons of man the good and the bad sometimes do. And so it once came about that a traveling tailor fell in with a traveling shoemaker. The tailor was a nice-looking little fellow, always happy and cheerful. He saw the shoemaker coming along in the opposite direction, and recognizing his trade by the shape of his knapsack, greeted him with a song:

> "Sew the seam
> draw the thread,
> rub it right and left with pitch,
> hit the nail right on the head."

But this particular shoemaker couldn't take a joke. He screwed up his face as if he'd been drinking vinegar and it looked as if he were going to bite the tailor's head off. But the little fellow began to laugh, handed him his bottle, and said: "I meant no harm. Take a drink and swallow down your gall." The shoemaker took a good long drink and the storm on his face began to blow over. He gave back the bottle and said: "That was quite a swig. People talk about heavy drinking, but do they know how thirsty a man can get? What would you say to our traveling together?" "Suits me," said the tailor, "if you don't mind heading for a big town where there's plenty of work." "That was just my idea," said the shoemaker. "There's no money to be made in the villages, and in the country the people would just as soon go barefoot." So they went on together, putting one foot in front of the other as weasels do in the snow.

They had plenty of time but very little to eat. When they came to a town, they went to see their fellow craftsmen. Everyone was glad to give the tailor a little something because he looked so bright and cheerful and had such rosy red cheeks, and on his lucky days a master tailor's daughter might stop in the doorway with him and give him a kiss for the road. When he rejoined his traveling companion, he always had more in his pack than the shoemaker. The cranky shoemaker made a sour face and said: "The bigger the rascal the better his luck." But the tailor only laughed and sang and shared with his friend whatever the people had given him. Whenever he had a few groschen in his pocket, he ordered something good, and in his joy thumped the table so hard the glasses danced. His motto was: "Easy come, easy go."

After traveling for some time, they came to a great forest. There were two paths through it and both led to the capital city, but one took seven days and the other only two, and the travelers didn't know which was which. They sat down under an oak tree to decide what preparations to make and how much bread they would need. The shoemaker said: "A man should think ahead. I mean to take enough bread for seven days." "What!" said the tailor. "Weigh myself down like a mule so I can't even see to left or right? I trust in God and let Him do the worrying. The money in my pocket is as good in summer as in winter, but bread gets dry and moldy in hot weather. The longest coat has to stop at the feet. Why wouldn't we find the right way? A two days' supply of bread is plenty, say I." So each bought his own supply of bread, and they started out.

The forest was as still as a church. Not a breeze stirred, not a brook murmured, not a bird sang, and not a ray of sunshine found its way through the dense leaves. The shoemaker didn't say a word, his bread supply weighed heavy on his back, and the sweat ran down his sulky, peevish face. But the tailor was as cheerful as usual, hopping and skipping, whistling with a blade of grass, or singing a song. "The Lord must be pleased to see me so merry," he thought. That's how it was for the first two days. On the third day, when the forest showed no sign of coming to an end and the tailor had eaten all his bread, he wasn't quite as chipper as he had been, but he didn't lose heart and he went on trusting in God and his luck. At the end of the third day he lay down hungry at the foot of a tree, and he rose up hungry the next morning. By the end of the fourth day he was even hungrier, and when the shoemaker sat down on a fallen tree to eat his bread, the tailor could only look on. When he asked for a piece of bread, the other laughed scornfully and said: "You've always been so cheerful. Now you can see what it's like to be gloomy. Birds that sing too early in the morning get clawed by the hawk before nightfall." In short, he was merciless. On the fifth morning the poor tailor was too weak to get up and couldn't utter a word. His cheeks were white and his eyes were red. "I'll give you a piece of bread," said the shoemaker. "But to make up for it I'm going to put your right eye out." The poor tailor wanted to live, so he couldn't say no. For the last time he wept with both eyes and then the shoemaker, who had a heart of stone, cut out his right eye with a sharp knife. The tailor remembered what his mother had said when she had caught him nibbling in the pantry: "Eat as you will, suffer as you must." After eating his hard-earned bread, he started off again, forgot his misfortune, and consoled himself with the thought that he could still see pretty well with his one eye. But on the sixth day his hunger gnawed at his heart and that night he collapsed under a tree. On the seventh morning he was too weak to get up, and death was breathing down his neck. "All right," said the shoemaker. "I'll take pity on you. I'll give you another piece of bread, but I'm going to put out your other eye to make up for it." At these words the tailor saw the folly of his ways, begged God for forgiveness, and said: "Do what you must. I'll suffer as I must. But remember this: the Lord judges in His own good time. Some day your wickedness will be punished, for I've given you no cause to treat me like this. When things went well with me, I shared what I had with you. My trade calls for even stitches. Without eyes I won't be able to sew and I'll have to beg. But at least, when you've blinded me, don't leave me here alone to starve." The shoemaker, who had banished God from his heart, took his knife and cut the tailor's left eye out. Then he gave him a piece of bread, put a stick into his hand, and led him away.

As the sun was setting, they came out of the forest, and there in a field stood a gallows. The shoemaker left the blind tailor at the foot of the gallows, and continued on his way. Racked with pain and hunger, the poor tailor lay down and slept all night. When he awoke in the gray of dawn, he didn't know where he was. Two corpses were hanging there, each with a crow perched on his head. "Brother," said the first corpse. "Are you awake?" "Yes," said the second. "I'm awake." "Then," said the first, "I've got something to tell you. If a blind man bathes in the dew that fell on us tonight, he'll get his eyes back. If they only knew it, many a blind man, who never dared hope, would recover his eyesight." When the tailor heard that, he took his handkerchief and pressed it against the grass. When it was wet with dew, he bathed his eye sockets and what the hanged man had said came true—instantly a pair of sound new eyes grew into the sockets. Soon the tailor saw the sun rising over the mountains, and before him on the plain lay the capital city with its magnificent gates and its hundred towers, and the golden balls and crosses atop the church spires began to glisten. He was able to distinguish every leaf on the trees, he saw birds flying by and gnats dancing in the air. He took a needle out of his pocket and when he succeeded in threading it as well as ever, his heart leaped for joy. He fell down on his knees, thanked God for His mercy and said his morning prayers. He didn't even forget to pray for the poor sinners who were hanging there like bell clappers, jangling in the wind. Then he picked up his bundle, forgot the misery he had endured, and went his way singing and whistling.

The first living thing he came across was a brown foal running loose in a field. He caught the foal by the mane, meaning to climb on and ride to town. But the foal begged for his freedom, saying: "I'm too young. Even a skinny little tailor like you would break my back. Leave me be until I grow strong. A time may come when I can repay you." "Frisk away," said the tailor. "I can see you're a gadabout like me." He flicked him on the back with a switch, the foal kicked up his heels and ran away, leaping over hedges and ditches.

The little tailor hadn't eaten a thing since the day before. "My eyes are full of sunlight," he said. "But what's to fill my belly? The first halfway edible creature that crosses my path is in for it." Just then a stork came striding solemnly across the meadow. "Stop!" cried the tailor, grabbing him by the leg. "I don't know how good to eat you are, but my hunger leaves me no choice. I'll just have to cut your head off and cook you." "Oh no," said the stork. "You mustn't do that. I'm a sacred bird and a friend to man. No one ever harms me. If you spare my life, I'll repay you some day." "All right, Cousin Longlegs," said the tailor. "Get moving." The stork rose into the air and flew majestically away, letting his long legs trail behind him.

"What's to become of me?" said the tailor to himself. "My hunger gets greater and greater and my stomach emptier and emptier. Any creature that comes along now is lost." Just then he saw some duck-lings swimming on a pond. "Well met!" he cried, and quickly caught one of them. He was just going to wring its neck when the mother duck, who had been hidden by the rushes, let out a scream, swam over to him and implored him to spare her darling children. "Try and imagine," she said, "how your mother would feel if someone were to pick you up and do away with you." "Calm yourself," said the kind-hearted tailor. "I wouldn't think of harming any of your children." And he put his captive back in the water.

When he turned around he saw an old tree that was partly hollow. The wild bees were flying in and out. "Here's my reward for my good deed," he said. "The honey will still my hunger." At that moment the queen bee flew out and threatened him, saying: "If you lay hands on my swarm and destroy my nest, our stings will pierce you like ten thousand red-hot needles. But if you leave us in peace and go your way, we shall do you a favor one of these days."

Again the tailor saw there was no help for it, and said to himself: "Three empty dishes and nothing in the fourth is a poor meal." He dragged himself into the town with his ravening stomach, and since the clock had just struck twelve, his meal was ready when he got to the inn. He sat right down to eat, and when he had finished, he said: "Now let's get to work." He explored the town, looking for a master tailor, and soon found one who was ready to employ him. As the little tailor knew all the ins and outs of his trade, it wasn't long before he became famous and everyone wanted to order a new coat from him. His reputation grew and grew. "My work is no better than it was," he said to himself. "Yet business keeps improving." In the end the king appointed him court tailor.

But what a small world it is! On the very same day his former comrade the shoemaker became court shoemaker. When he caught sight of the tailor and saw that he had two sound eyes, his conscience troubled him, and he thought: "I'd better set a trap for him before he takes his revenge on me." But whosoever sets a trap for others is likely to fall into it himself. At nightfall that same day when the shoemaker had finished his work, he crept secretly to the king and said: "Your Majesty, that tailor is a boastful fellow. He claims he can bring back the golden crown that was lost in olden times." "That would be most welcome," said the king. Next morning he sent for the tailor and ordered him to bring back the crown or leave the town forever. "Oho!" thought the tailor. "Only a rogue gives more than he's got. If that cranky old king expects me to do something that no human being can do, why wait until tomorrow? I'll just leave town this minute." So he packed up his bundle and started out, but as he passed through the town gate, he couldn't help feeling sorry that he was leaving his good fortune behind him and turning his back on a place where he had been doing so well. He soon came to the pond where he had made the acquaintance of the ducks. The old mother duck, whose young ones he had spared, was sitting on the bank preening herself with her bill. She recognized him right away and asked why he was looking so woebegone. "You'll understand," said the tailor, "when I tell you what has happened to me." And he told her the whole story. "If that's all," said the duck, "we can help you. The crown fell in the water and it's lying on the bottom of the pond. We'll bring it up for you in no time. Just spread out your handkerchief on the bank." She dived under with her twelve ducklings and in five minutes they all came up again. The mother duck was inside the crown; it rested on her wings and the twelve ducklings had formed a circle around it, holding it up with their bills and helping her support it. They all swam ashore and laid the crown on the handkerchief. You can't imagine how beautiful that crown was. When the sun shone on it, it glittered like a thousand rubies. The tailor gathered up the four corners of the handkerchief and took the crown to the king, who was overjoyed and hung a golden chain around the tailor's neck.

When the shoemaker saw that his trick had come to nothing, he thought up another. He went to the king and said: "Your Majesty, that tailor has been boasting again. He says he can make a wax replica of the whole royal palace with everything in it, furniture and all." The king sent for the tailor and ordered him to make a wax replica of the whole royal palace with everything in it, furniture and all, and if he failed to do it or if so much as a nail on the wall should be missing, he'd be shut up in an underground dungeon for the rest of his life. The tailor thought: "This is getting worse and worse. It's more than anyone could bear." So he slung his bundle over his shoulder and left town. When he came to the hollow tree, he sat down and hung his head. The bees came flying out, and the queen asked him: "Why are you holding your head in that strange way? Have you got a stiff neck?" "Oh no," said the tailor. "I've got a different kind of trouble." And he told her what the king had asked of him. The bees started to hum and buzz among themselves, and the queen bee said: "Just go home now, but come back tomorrow at the same time and bring a large cloth. Everything will be all right." So he went home and the bees flew straight to the royal palace. They swarmed through the open windows and crawled into every nook and cranny, taking note of everything they saw. Then they flew back home and built a wax replica of the royal palace so quickly you'd have thought it was growing before your eyes. It was finished that same evening. When the tailor came back in the morning, there was the whole splendid palace, and not a nail on the wall or a tile on the roof was missing. What's more, it was snowy-white and wonderfully delicate, and it smelled like honey. The tailor wrapped it carefully in his cloth and brought it to the king, who couldn't get over his amazement, displayed the wax replica in his largest hall, and rewarded the tailor with a big stone house.

But the shoemaker didn't give up. He went to the king a third time and said: "Your Majesty, someone has told the tailor that no one has ever struck water in the palace courtyard, and now he claims he can make a fountain right in the middle of it that will send up a man-high column of crystal-clear water." The king sent for the tailor and said: "If by tomorrow there's not a fountain such as you promised in my courtyard, my executioner will shorten you by a head in that same courtyard." The poor tailor didn't waste much time thinking. He hurried out through the town gate, and seeing as this time his life was at stake, the tears ran down his cheeks. As he was walking along so deep in gloom, the foal he had once set free came bounding up to him. He had grown up to be a fine chestnut horse. "The time has come," he said, "for me to repay you for your kindness. I know what your trouble is, and I can help you. Climb up on my back, I could carry two like you now." The tailor took heart. He jumped up on the horse's back and the horse galloped through the town gate and straight to the palace courtyard. Quick as lightning, he circled the courtyard three times, and after the third time he fell to the ground. A terrible crash was heard, a clod of earth rose into the air like a cannonball and passed over the palace. It was followed by a stream of water that rose as high as a man on horseback. The water was as clear as crystal and the sunbeams danced in it. When the king saw that, he jumped up in amazement and went and embraced the little tailor in front of his whole court.

But the tailor's good fortune was short-lived. The king had plenty of daughters, one more beautiful than the next, but no son. The wicked shoemaker went to the king for the fourth time and said: "Your Majesty, that tailor is still as boastful as ever. Now he says that if he wanted to he could arrange for a son to be brought to Your Majesty through the air." The king sent for the tailor and said: "If you have a son brought to me within nine days, you shall marry my eldest daughter." "The reward is great," thought the little tailor. "I'd do a good deal for it. But the fruit is too high for me. If I reach out for it, the bough will break under me and I'll fall to the ground." He went home, sat down cross-legged on his work table and pondered. What was he to do? At length he cried out: "No! This is impossible. There's no peace for me here, I'm leaving." He packed up his bundle and hurried out through the town gate. When he reached the meadows, he caught sight of his old friend the stork, who was pacing the ground as solemnly as a philosopher, stopping now and then to scrutinize a frog and, after satisfying his curiosity, gobble it up. The stork came up to him and bade him good day. "I see you've got your knapsack on your back," he said. "Why have you decided to leave town?" The tailor told him what the king had demanded of him, and bewailed his misfortune. "Don't grow any gray hairs over that," said the stork. "I'll help you out. I've been bringing babies to this town longer than I can remember. Why shouldn't I get a little prince out of the well for a change? Go home and don't worry. Be at the royal palace in nine days and wait for me." The little tailor did just as the stork had said. He went to the palace on the ninth day and hadn't long to wait before the stork tapped at the window. When the tailor opened it, Cousin Longlegs came in very gingerly and strode gravely across the smooth marble floor. In his beak he held a baby, who was as beautiful as an angel and held out his little arms to the queen. The stork set the little boy down on her lap, and she hugged him and kissed him and was beside herself with joy. Before flying away, the stork took his knapsack and handed it to the queen. In it there were little bags full of colored candies. These were divided among the princesses, but the eldest didn't get any. She got the merry tailor for a husband. "I feel as if I'd drawn the winning ticket," said the tailor.

"My mother was right when she said: 'If you trust in God and your luck is good, you'll want for nothing.'"

The shoemaker had to make the shoes the tailor danced in at the wedding. Then he was ordered to leave the town forever. On his way to the forest he came to the gallows. Exhausted with rage and the heat of the day, he threw himself on the ground. When he closed his eyes and tried to sleep, the two crows swooped down from the heads of the hanged men with loud cries and pecked his eyes out. Maddened with pain, he ran off into the forest, and there he must have vanished, for he was never seen or heard of again.

108
Hans My Hedgehog

THERE WAS ONCE a farmer who had plenty of money and land. Yet despite all his wealth, his happiness was not complete, for his wife had borne him no children. Sometimes, when he went to town with the other peasants, they made fun of him and asked him why he had no children. That finally made him angry and one day when he got home he said: "I must have a child, even if it's a hedgehog." So then his wife had a son, who was part hedgehog, the upper half hedgehog, the lower half human. She was aghast when she saw him, and said: "Look what you've done with your wishing." "It can't be helped now," said the husband. "It's time to think about the christening. But we'll never find a godfather." "The only thing we can call him is Hans My Hedgehog," said the wife. After the christening, the priest said: "You can't put him in a bed because of his quills." So they strewed a few handfuls of straw behind the stove and laid Hans My Hedgehog on it. His mother couldn't nurse him because he'd have pricked her with his quills. So he lay behind the stove for eight years. His father grew sick of him and thought: "If only he'd die." But he didn't die, he just lay there.

One day the farmer thought he'd go to market and asked his wife what he should bring back. "A little meat and a few buns," she said.

Then he asked the servant girl, and she wanted a pair of slippers and some stockings with clocks. And last he asked: "Hans My Hedgehog, what would you like?" "Father dear," he said, "could you bring me a set of bagpipes?" When the farmer came home, he gave his wife the meat and the buns he had bought for her, and he gave the servant girl the slippers and the stockings with clocks. Last he went behind the stove and gave Hans My Hedgehog his bagpipes, whereupon Hans My Hedgehog said: "Father dear, could you go to the blacksmith and get him to shoe my rooster? Then I'll ride away and never come back." The father was glad at the thought of getting rid of him and had the rooster shod. Hans My Hedgehog climbed on the rooster's back and rode away, taking with him some pigs and donkeys he was planning to keep in the forest. When he got there, he had the rooster carry him to the top of a tall tree, and there he stayed for many years, tending the pigs and donkeys until he had a large herd. His father had no idea what had become of him. As he sat in his tree, he played his bagpipes and made beautiful music.

One day the king got lost in the same forest. He was surprised to hear the sound of music and sent his servant to look around and see where it came from. The servant looked around but all he could see was an animal that looked to him like a rooster with a hedgehog on its back, and this animal was perched in a tree, making music. The king told his servant to ask why he was sitting there and whether he knew the way back to his kingdom. Hans My Hedgehog came down from his tree and said: "I'll show you the way if you'll write out a promise to give me the first living creature you meet in the palace courtyard when you get home." The king thought to himself: "No harm in that. I can write what I like, because Hans My Hedgehog won't know what I've written." So the king took pen and ink and wrote something. Whereupon Hans My Hedgehog showed him the way and he reached home safely. When his daughter saw him coming in the distance, she was so happy she ran out to meet him and hugged and kissed him. Then he remembered Hans My Hedgehog and told her what had happened. "I couldn't help myself," he said. "I was forced to promise the first living creature I met when I got home to a strange animal that rode on a rooster and played beautiful music. But then I wrote that I would *not* give him what he had asked, because, you see, this Hans My Hedgehog couldn't read." The princess was glad of that. "You did right," she said, "I'd never have gone with him anyway."

Hans My Hedgehog went on taking care of his pigs and donkeys. He sat in the tree, playing his bagpipes, and he was always cheerful. After a while, another king came riding through the forest with his servants and heralds. He was lost and he didn't know the way home, because the forest was so big. He too heard the beautiful music in the distance, and told his herald to go and see what it was. The herald went to the tree, saw the rooster perched on a branch with Hans My Hedgehog on his back, and asked him what he was doing up there. "I'm tending my pigs and donkeys. What can I do for you?" "We're lost," said the herald. "We shall never get back to our kingdom unless you can show us the way." Then Hans My Hedgehog flew down on his rooster and said to the aged king: "I'll show you the way if you'll give me for my own the first living creature you meet outside your royal palace." The king agreed, and when he had signed a paper with his promise, Hans My Hedgehog rode ahead on his rooster and showed him the way. The king arrived safely in his kingdom and when he entered the courtyard of his palace there was great rejoicing. Now this king had only one daughter, and she was very beautiful. She was so glad to see her father that she ran to meet him, threw her arms around him and kissed him. When she asked him where in the world he had been for so long, he replied: "I was lost in a great forest and might never have got home if I hadn't met a strange creature, half hedgehog and half man, who was sitting on the back of a rooster at the top of a tall tree, making beautiful music. He helped me and showed me the way, but in return I had to promise him the first living creature I met when I got back to my royal palace. It turned out to be you, and now I'm sorry." But the princess told her old father that for his sake she would gladly go away with the strange creature if he should come and claim her.

Meanwhile Hans My Hedghog tended his pigs, and the pigs made more pigs, and there got to be so many that the whole forest was full of them. Hans My Hedgehog decided he didn't want to live in the forest any longer, so he sent word to his father to have all the pigsties in the village cleared and made ready, because he would soon be arriving with such an enormous herd that anyone who wanted to butcher could do so. His father was dismayed at the news, for he

thought Hans My Hedgehog had long been dead. Hans My Hedgehog mounted his rooster, drove his pigs into the village, and the
butchering began. My, what a slashing and chopping! You could
hear it five miles away. When it was over, Hans My Hedgehog said:
"Father dear, get the blacksmith to shoe my rooster once again and
I'll ride away and never come back as long as I live." The father had
the rooster shod. He was glad to hear that Hans My Hedgehog
wasn't coming back.

Hans My Hedgehog rode to the first kingdom. The king had given
orders that if anyone with bagpipes came riding up on a rooster, he
should be attacked with guns and swords and battleaxes and kept out
of the palace. When Hans My Hedgehog arrived, the soldiers rushed
at him with their bayonets, but he put the spurs to his rooster, which
rose in the air, flew over the gate to the king's window, and alighted
on the window ledge. "Give me what you promised," Hans My
Hedgehog cried out, "or I'll take your life and your daughter's as
well." When he heard that, the king implored his daughter to save his
life and her own by going out to Hans My Hedgehog. She dressed
herself all in white, and her father gave her a carriage with six horses,
resplendent servants, money and treasure. She got into the carriage
and Hans My Hedgehog got in beside her with his rooster and his
bagpipes. They said good-bye and drove away and the king thought
he would never see his daughter again. But there he was mistaken, for
when they had gone a little way Hans My Hedghog took off her fine
clothes and stuck her with his quills until she was all bloody, and
said: "That's what you get for being false. Go home, I don't want
you." Then he drove her away, and she was disgraced forever.

After that Hans My Hedgehog mounted his rooster and rode on
with his bagpipes till he came to the second kingdom, whose king he
had also guided. This king had given orders that if anyone looking
like Hans My Hedgehog should appear, they should present arms,
welcome him with cheers, and escort him to the royal palace. When
the king's daughter saw him, she was horrified, for he did look most
peculiar, but she said to herself that it couldn't be helped, since she
had promised her father. So she welcomed Hans My Hedgehog and
they were married. He sat down at the king's table and she sat down
beside him, and they ate and drank. When night came and it was
time to go to bed, she was mortally afraid of his quills. But he said to

her: "Don't be afraid, I'm not going to hurt you." And to the aged king he said: "Tell four men to keep watch at the door of our room and to make a big fire. Before going to bed, I shall crawl out of my hedgehog's skin and drop it on the floor. The men must run in, throw it in the fire, and stay there until it's all burned up." When the clock struck eleven, he went into the room, stripped off his hedgehog's skin, and left it on the floor. The men rushed in, picked it up, and threw it in the fire. When the fire had consumed it, he was free. He lay in the bed, human from top to toe, but coal-black as though charred. The king sent for his doctor, who rubbed him with precious balms and ointments. These made him white, and there he was, a handsome young man. When the king's daughter saw him, she was overjoyed. The next morning they arose happily, and ate and drank. Then they had a real wedding, and the aged king made his kingdom over to Hans My Hedgehog.

When some years had passed, he took his wife to see his father. "Father," he said, "I'm your son." The father replied: "I have no son. I had one, but he was born with quills like a hedgehog and he went away." When Hans My Hedgehog had succeeded in making himself recognized, his old father was glad to see him and went with him to his kingdom.

> My story is done,
> To Bessie's house let it run.

109

The Shroud

A MOTHER ONCE HAD a little seven-year-old boy with such a sweet, beautiful face that no one could look at him without loving him, and she loved him more than anything in the world. Suddenly the child fell sick, and God took him. The mother was inconsolable and wept day and night. Soon after he was buried, the child began to appear in places where he had sat playing in his lifetime. When his mother wept, he too wept, and when morning came he vanished. Then when the mother could not stop crying, he appeared one night wrapped in the little white shroud he had been buried in and wearing a wreath of flowers on his head. He sat down at her feet and said: "Oh, mother, if you don't stop crying I won't be able to sleep in my coffin, for my shroud is wet with all the tears that fall on it." When she heard that, the mother was horrified, and from then on she shed no tears. The next night the child came again. He held a candle in his hand and said: "You see, my shroud is almost dry. Now I can rest in my grave." After that, the mother gave her grief into God's keeping and bore it silently and patiently. The child never came again, but slept in his little bed under the ground.

110
The Jew in the Brambles

A RICH MAN ONCE HAD a servant who did his work honestly and faithfully, was the first out of bed in the morning and the last into bed at night, and was always on hand to do unpleasant chores that no one else would touch. He didn't complain and whatever happened he took it cheerfully. When a year had passed, his master gave him no wages, for he thought: "This is the best policy. I save money and, besides, it keeps him from leaving me." The servant said nothing. He went on working all through the second year as he had the first, and when that year was over and he again received no wages, he made no complaint but stayed on. When the third year, too, had passed, the master thought it over, put his hand in his pocket, but took it out empty. Then at last the servant spoke up: "Master," he said, "I've served you faithfully for three years. Would you kindly pay me what's owing to me, for I should like to travel and see something of the world." The old skinflint replied: "Yes, my good man, you have served me well and you shall be generously rewarded." Again he reached into his pocket, counted out three pennies, and said to the servant: "Here you have a penny for each year. That is good and ample pay, such as few masters would give you." The servant, who didn't know much about money, pocketed his capital, thinking: "Now that my pocket is full, I won't have to worry or wear myself out with hard work."

So away he went, uphill and downhill, hopping and skipping, singing and whistling to his heart's content. As he was passing a copse, a little man stepped out and spoke to him: "Where are you going so light and gay? If you have any troubles, they don't seem to bother you very much." "What have I got to be gloomy about?" said the servant. "I've got all the money I need. That's three years' wages tinkling in my pocket." "How much does your treasure come to?" the little man asked. "How much? Three pennies, neither more nor less." "Look," said the dwarf, "I'm poor and needy. Give me your three pennies. I can't work any more, and you're young, you can easily make a living." The servant had a kind heart, so, feeling sorry for the little man, he gave him his three pennies, saying: "Take them by all means. I'll manage without them." Whereupon the little man said: "I see you have a kind heart, so I'll grant you three wishes, one for each penny, and they will all come true." "Aha," said the servant, "so you're one of these wonder workers? Well, if that's the lay of the land, here are my three wishes: first, a bird gun that will hit everything I aim at; second, a fiddle that will make everyone dance when I play it, and third, that if I ask a favor of anyone he won't be able to refuse me." "All your wishes are granted," said the little man. He reached into the bushes, and, just imagine, the fiddle and the bird gun were right there. He gave them to the servant and said: "Whatever favor you may ask, no one will ever refuse it."

"My boy," said the servant to himself, "what more could you want?" And he went his way as happy as could be. Soon he met a Jew with a long goatee who was listening to the song of a bird that was perched high on the top of a tree. "Goodness gracious!" the Jew cried out. "How can such a little creature have such a big, powerful voice! Oh, if only I could have that bird! If only someone could sprinkle salt on its tail!" "If that's all that's worrying you," said the servant, "we'll bring him down in no time." Whereupon he aimed his gun and hit the bird dead center, and it fell into the brambles. "All right, you dog," said the servant, "go in and get it if you want it." "I will," said the Jew. "The young gentleman has spoken and the dog will come running. You've hit the bird and I'll retrieve it." With that he went down on all fours and worked his way into the bramble-bushes. When he was right in the middle, the servant had a mischievous thought. He took down his fiddle and began to play. The Jew picked up his feet and leaped and jumped and the longer the servant played the wilder the dance became. The brambles tore his shiny coat, combed his beard, and cut and scratched him all over. "My goodness!" cried the Jew. "What's the good of all that fiddling! Stop it, young sir, I don't want to dance." But the servant wouldn't listen. "You've skinned plenty of people," he thought. "Now the brambles can skin you." He kept on playing, the Jew jumped higher and higher, and the tatters of his coat were left hanging on the thorns. "Oh my, oh my!" he cried. "I'll give the young gentleman anything he asks if he'll only stop fiddling. A whole bag of money I'll give him." "Since you're feeling so generous," said the servant, "I'll stop playing. But I have to admit there's style in your dancing." With that he took the bag of gold and went his way.

The Jew stood looking after the servant until he was far away and out of sight. Then he screeched at the top of his lungs: "You wretched musician, you beer-hall fiddler, wait till I catch you alone, I'll chase you till the soles drop off your shoes. You tramp, put a nickel in your mouth and you'll be worth five pennies!" Every insult he could think of poured out of him. When he had got that off his chest and felt a little better, he went to town and ran to the judge. "Oh, my Lord Judge, a bad man has robbed me on the highway, and look what he's done to me. A stone would take pity. My clothes are torn, I'm cut and scratched all over, and everything I own has been stolen, bag and all, oh, my precious ducats, each one shinier than the last. For God's sake, throw the man into prison." The judge replied: "Did a soldier slash you with his sword?" "God forbid!" cried the Jew. "He had no sword. He had a gun slung over his back, and a fiddle hanging from his neck. Anybody would recognize the villain."

The judge sent out his men. They found the good servant, who had gone on very slowly, and on him they found the bag with the gold in it. When they brought him into court, he said: "I didn't touch the Jew, and I didn't take his money. He offered it to me of his own free will to make me stop playing the fiddle, because he couldn't stand my music." "God forbid!" said the Jew. "He lies in his teeth." The judge didn't believe the servant either, and he said: "That's a likely story.

No Jew would do that." And he sentenced the good servant to be hanged for highway robbery. As the servant was being led away, the Jew cried out: "You tramp, you no-good musician, now you'll get what's coming to you." The servant went calmly up the ladder with the hangman, but on the last rung he turned around and said to the judge: "Grant me one last favor before I die." "I will," said the judge, "as long as you don't ask me for your life." "Not for my life," said the servant. "Just let me play my fiddle one last time." The Jew began to scream like a stuck pig: "Don't let him, for God's sake, don't let him!" But the judge said: "Why shouldn't I grant him his brief pleasure? His favor is granted, and that's that." The truth is that he couldn't refuse because of the gift the little man had bestowed on the servant. The Jew cried out: "Oh no! Oh no! Tie me up, tie me up!"

The good servant took his fiddle from around his neck and tucked it under his chin. At the very first stroke of the bow, the judge, the clerks, and the beadles all began to shiver and shake, and the rope fell out of the hands of the beadle who was going to tie the Jew. At the second stroke they all picked up their feet. The executioner let go of the good servant and got ready to dance. At the third stroke they all jumped up and began to dance. The judge and the Jew were in front, and they were the best dancers of the lot. It wasn't long before all the people whose curiosity had made them gather in the marketplace joined in the dancing, old and young, fat and skinny. Even the dogs stood up on their hind legs and hopped about. The longer the servant played, the higher the dancers jumped, with the result that they hit their heads together and began to scream pitifully. At length the judge, who was completely exhausted and out of breath, cried out: "I give you your life. Just so you stop fiddling." The good servant took pity, stopped playing, hung the fiddle round his neck, and climbed down the ladder. Then he went over to the Jew, who was lying on the ground gasping for breath, and said: "You rascal. Now confess where you got that money, or I'll take my fiddle and start playing again." "I stole it, I stole it!" he screamed. "And you came by it honestly." So then the judge had the Jew taken to the gallows and hanged as a thief.

111
The Hunter

THERE WAS ONCE a young fellow who had learned the locksmith's trade. He said to his father: "I think I'll go out into the world and try my luck." "Glad to hear it," said the father, and gave him some money for his travels. The young fellow went from place to place looking for work. Then after a while, he lost interest in the locksmith's trade and decided to drop it and take up hunting. One day on the road he met a hunter dressed all in green, who asked him where he came from and where he was going. "I'm a journeyman locksmith," said the young fellow, "but I've lost interest in that trade and I'd like to take up hunting. Could you use me as an apprentice?" "Yes, I could, if you'll come with me." So the young fellow went with the hunter, served him for several years, and learned to hunt.

After that he wanted to try his luck somewhere else. The hunter gave him no other payment than an air gun, but this was a very special kind of air gun, that would hit the mark whenever he shot it off. So he started out and soon came to a great forest, too large to cross in one day. At nightfall he climbed a tall tree to keep from being attacked by wild beasts. Toward midnight he thought he saw a light glimmering in the distance. He peered at it through the branches, took good note of where it was, and threw his hat in that direction, so as to use it as a pointer when he came down. Then he climbed down, walked to his hat, put it on, and went straight ahead. The farther he went, the bigger the light grew. When he came close to it, he saw it was an enormous fire and that three giants were sitting there, roasting an ox on a spit. One of them said: "I wonder if this meat will soon be ready to eat. I'd better taste it and see." Whereupon he tore off a chunk and was just putting it into his mouth when the hunter shot it out of his hand. "Well, what do you know!" said the giant. "The wind blew that meat right out of my hand!" He took another chunk and was just going to bite into it when again the hunter shot it away. At that the giant gave the giant next to him a slap in the face and cried out angrily: "What's the idea of grabbing my meat!" "I didn't do anything of the kind," said the other. "A sharpshooter must have shot it away." The giant took a third chunk, but the hunter was too quick for him and he couldn't hold on to it. At that the giants said: "Anyone who can shoot the food from a man's lips must be a good shot. We could use someone like that. Hey, sharpshooter!" they shouted. "Come and sit by the fire with us and eat as much as you like. We won't hurt you. But if you don't and we have to chase after you, you're lost." The young fellow stepped up to the fire and said: "I'm a hunter, and whatever I aim at with my gun I'm sure to hit." They replied: "Come with us and you'll be well treated. At the end of the forest there's a wide river. On the other side of it there's a tower, and in the tower there's a beautiful princess. We want to carry her away." "Why not?" he said. "I'll soon get her for you." "That's good," they said. "But one more thing: there's a little dog over there that starts barking the moment anyone goes near him, and when he barks the whole royal court wakes up. That's why we can't get in. Could you shoot that little dog dead?" "Of course I could. Nothing to it."

When they came to the river, he stepped into a boat and crossed over. As he approached the bank, the little dog came running out and was going to bark, but the hunter took his air gun and shot it dead. When the giants saw that, they were glad, for now they felt sure of getting the princess. But first the hunter wanted to see what was going on in the castle and he told them to stay outside until he called them. Then he went in, and there wasn't a sound to be heard, everyone was asleep. When he opened the first room, a sword was hanging on the wall. It was pure silver with a golden star and the king's name on it. Beside it on the table lay a sealed letter. He tore it open and it said that whoever had the sword could kill anyone who crossed his path. He took the sword from the wall and buckled it on. Next he came to the room where the princess lay asleep. She was so beautiful that he stood still, held his breath and gazed at her. He thought to himself: "How can I give up an innocent maiden to those ferocious giants, who surely have wicked designs." He looked around. Under the bed there was a pair of slippers. The right slipper was marked with her father's name and a star, and the left one with her own name and a star. She was wearing a large silk kerchief, embroidered with gold, her father's name on the right side, her own on the left, all in gold letters. The hunter took a pair of scissors, cut off the right corner and put it in his knapsack. Then he took her right slipper with the king's name on it and put that in. The princess lay sleeping, and she was all sewn into her nightgown. He cut off a piece of the night-gown and put that in with the other things, and when he had done all this without touching her or disturbing her sleep, he left her. When he reached the gate, the giants were still outside, waiting for him to come and bring the princess out to them. "Come in!" he cried. "The princess is in my power. I can't open the door for you, but there's a hole. You'll have to crawl through." When the first giant put his head in, the hunter took hold of his hair, wound it around his own hand, held the giant's head, cut it off with one stroke of his sword, and pulled the body through the hole. Then he called the second and cut off his head, and then the third. Glad to have saved the beau-tiful princess from her enemies, he cut their tongues out and put them in his knapsack. He thought to himself: "Now I'll go home to my father and show him what I've already accomplished. Then I'll travel around some more; the good fortune God has in store for me is bound to catch up with me one of these days."

When the king woke up in his castle, he saw the three giants lying there dead. He went to his daughter's bedroom, woke her up and asked who had been there and killed the giants. "Father dear," she said, "I don't know. I was asleep." When she got up and wanted to put on her slippers, the right one was gone. When she looked at her kerchief, she saw it had been cut and the right corner was missing, and when she examined her nightgown she saw that a piece had been taken out of it. The king called his whole court together, the soldiers and all the rest, and asked who had set his daughter free and killed the giants. Now among the king's soldiers there was an ugly one-eyed captain, and he said he had done it. "If you've done that," said the old king, "you shall marry my daughter." But the princess replied: "Father dear, sooner than marry him I'd leave home and go away as far as my legs would carry me." The king replied: "If you won't marry him, take off your royal raiment, put on peasant's clothes, and go away. Go to a potter and arrange to sell his wares." She took off her royal raiment, went to a potter, borrowed some earthenware pots and promised to pay for them at the end of the day if she had sold them. Then the king bade her sit in a corner of the marketplace with her pots and sell them, and when she had them all set out he ordered some peasants to drive their wagons straight over them and smash them into a thousand pieces. So when the princess had set out her pots on the street, the wagons came along and turned them all into shards. She burst into tears and said: "Heavens above, how will I pay the potter?" The king had done it to make her marry the captain, but instead she went back to the potter and asked him to lend her some more pots. "No," he said, "not until you've paid for the last lot." At that she went weeping and wailing to her father and told him she wanted to leave home. "All right," he said. "I'll have a hut built for you out in the forest. There you will stay for the rest of your life and cook for everyone who comes along, but you mustn't take money for it." When the hut was ready, a sign was hung over the door, and on it was written: "Free today, tomorrow pay."

She lived in the hut for a long time and word went round that a maiden was staying there, serving free meals, and that a sign on the door said so. The hunter heard about it and thought: "That's something for a man like me, who's poor and hasn't any money." He took his air gun and his knapsack, which still had all the tokens he had brought from the castle in it, went to the forest and found the hut with the sign: "Free today, tomorrow pay." Wearing the sword he had used to cut the three giants' heads off, he went into the hut and asked for something to eat. He was charmed by the lovely girl, for she was indeed as pretty as a picture. She asked him where he came from and where he was going, and he said: "I'm going from place to place." Then she asked where he had got the sword with her father's name on it, and he asked her if she were the king's daughter. "Yes," she said. "With this sword," he said, "I cut off the heads of three giants." To prove it he took their tongues out of his knapsack, and then he showed her the slipper, the corner of her kerchief, and the piece he had cut from her nightgown. She was overjoyed, for she saw it was he who had saved her. Together they went to the old king and brought him back to the hut. She took the king to her room and told him it was the hunter who had really saved her from the giants, and when the old king saw all the tokens, he couldn't doubt any longer. He said he was glad to hear the truth at last and told the hunter he should have the princess for his wife. The princess was as happy as could be.

Then they dressed the hunter up to look like a foreign lord, and the king ordered a banquet. When they went to the table, the captain came and sat on the left side of the princess, and the hunter on her right side. The captain thought he was a foreign lord who had come for a visit. When they had finished eating and drinking, the king said to the captain: "I've got a riddle for you. Suppose a man said he had killed three giants. Suppose someone asked him where the giants' tongues were, and suppose, when he looked, there were no tongues in their heads, what would he say?" "He'd say they had no tongues." "That won't do," said the king. "Everybody has a tongue." Then the king asked the captain another question. "What would the man who made such an answer deserve?" And the captain answered: "He'd deserve to be torn to pieces." Said the king: "You've pronounced your own sentence." The captain was seized and torn into four pieces, and the princess was married to the hunter. After the wedding he went home and brought back his father and mother. They lived happily with their son and after the old king's death he inherited the kingdom.

112
The Flail from Heaven

ONCE A PEASANT went out to plow with a yoke of oxen. When he got to his field, the horns of the oxen began to grow. They grew and they grew, and by the time he started for home, they were so big that he couldn't drive through his barn door. Luckily a butcher came along just then and he was willing to buy the oxen. It was agreed that the peasant should bring the butcher a measure of turnip seeds, and that the butcher should pay him a Brabant taler for each seed. I call that a good price! The peasant went home and loaded a measure of turnip seeds into a sack, but on his way back one little seed fell out.

The butcher counted out the money as agreed, but if the peasant hadn't lost that one little seed he'd have had one more Brabant taler.

When the peasant started for home again, the seed had grown up into a tree that reached all the way to heaven. The peasant thought to himself: "Now that I've got the chance, I think I'll go up and see what the angels are doing." So he climbed up and when he got to heaven he saw that the angels were threshing oats. He stopped to watch them, and as he was watching, he noticed that the tree he was standing on was beginning to wobble, and when he looked down he saw that someone was chopping it down. "Wouldn't it be an awful thing," he thought, "if I were to fall from way up here!" He could think of no better way out of his difficulty than to plait a rope from the oat straw that was scattered all about. When he had finished, he picked up a mattock and a flail that someone had left lying on the floor of heaven, and let himself down by his rope. But it so happened that he landed in a deep, deep hole, and it was really lucky that he had the mattock, for he used it to cut out steps. So he climbed out of the hole, and took the flail with him to prove that his story was true, so that no one would ever doubt it.

113
The Prince and the Princess

A KING ONCE HAD a little boy, and the fortunetellers predicted he would be killed by a stag when he was sixteen. One day, after he had turned sixteen, the hutsmen took him out hunting. In the forest the prince got separated from the others. Suddenly he saw a big stag and tried to shoot it but he kept missing. The stag ran a long, long way and the prince followed until they had left the forest behind them. All at once a big, tall man was standing there instead of the stag. "A good thing I've caught you!" said the man. "I've worn out six pairs of glass skates chasing you." He took the prince with him and dragged him through a big lake to a big castle, where they sat down to table together. When they had eaten, the king said: "I have three daughters. Tonight you must stay with the eldest from nine in the evening until six in the morning, but you must keep awake. Every time the clock strikes I will come and call you, and if you don't answer me you'll be killed in the morning, but if you do answer me each time, you shall have her for your wife." When the young people went into the bedchamber, a stone St. Christopher was standing there and the princess said to him: "My father will come at nine o'clock and every hour on the hour till the stroke of three. When he calls, you must answer him in the prince's stead." The stone St. Christopher nodded his head very quickly and then more and more slowly until it finally stopped moving.

The next morning the king said to the young prince: "You have done your task well, but I can't give you my daughter. Tonight you must watch over my second daughter. Then I'll see if you can have the eldest for your wife. I'll come every hour on the hour, and when I call you must answer me. If you don't answer, your blood will flow." The two of them went to the bedchamber. There stood a still bigger St. Christopher, and the princess said to him: "When my father calls, you must answer." The big stone St. Christopher nodded his head very quickly and then more and more slowly until it finally stopped moving. Then the prince lay down on the threshold, slipped one hand under his head, and fell asleep. Next morning the king said to him: "You have done your task well, but I can't give you my daughter. Tonight you must watch over my youngest daughter. Then I'll see if you can have the second for your wife. I'll come every hour, and when I call you must answer me. If I call and you don't answer, your blood will flow." Again they went to the bedchamber together, and there stood a St. Christopher much bigger and taller than the other two. The king's daughter said to him: "If my father calls, you must answer," and the big, tall stone St. Christopher nodded his head for a good half hour before it finally stopped moving. Then the prince lay down on the threshold and fell asleep. Next morning the king said to him: "You have watched well, but I can't give you my daughter yet. I have a big forest. If you cut it down for me tomorrow between six in the morning and six in the evening, I'll see." Then he gave him a glass ax, a glass wedge, and a glass mallet. When the prince got to the forest, he started to chop and the ax smashed into bits. He took the wedge, but when he struck it with the mallet, it shivered into pieces no bigger than grains of sand. He was sick at heart, for he thought he would die, and he sat down and wept.

At noon the king said: "One of you girls must bring him something to eat." "No," said the two eldest, "we won't bring him a thing. The one he watched over last night can bring him something." So the youngest had to go and bring him something to eat. When she got to the forest, she asked him how he was getting along. "Oh," he said, "very badly." "Don't worry," she said. "Come here and have a bite to eat." "No," he said. "I can't. I'm doomed to die, so what's the good of eating?" At that she spoke kindly to him and begged him to try, so he went over and ate a little something. When he had eaten, she said: "Now I'll louse you a little and you'll feel better." As she loused him, he grew drowsy and fell asleep. Then she took her handkerchief and tied it into a knot and struck the ground with it three times, crying: "Earwigs, come out!" Before you knew it, a whole crowd of elves appeared and asked what the princess desired. She replied: "In three hours, this whole big forest has to be cut down and the wood all laid out in piles." The elves went and called all their friends and relatives to come and help them with the work. Then they started in and when the three hours were up, the work was done. They came back to the princess and told her so, and again she took out her white handkerchief and said: "Earwigs, go home!" And they all vanished. When the prince woke up, he was delighted, and she said: "Wait till the clock strikes six, then come home." He did as she had said, and the king asked: "Have you cut down the forest?" "Yes," said the prince. When they were sitting at the table, the king said: "I can't give you my daughter for your wife yet. To win her, you must do something more." He asked the king what it was, and the king said: "I have a big pond. Tomorrow morning you must go and clean it out till it sparkles like a mirror, and fill it with all kinds of fish." The next morning the king gave him a glass shovel and a glass pickax and said: "By six o'clock the pond must be ready."

So the prince left the palace and when he got to the pond, he thrust the shovel into the muck and the blade broke off. When he thrust the pickax into the muck, it broke too, and he was sick at heart. At noon the youngest daughter brought him something to eat and asked him how he was getting along. "Very badly," he replied. "I'm sure to lose my head. My tools are all broken again." "Don't worry," she said. "Come here and have a bite to eat and you'll feel better." "No," he said, "I can't eat. I'm much too unhappy." She spoke kindly to him until he went over and ate, and then she loused him again and he fell asleep. Again she took her handkerchief, tied it into a knot, and struck the ground with it three times, crying: "Earwigs, come out!" Before you knew it, a big crowd of elves came out and asked her what she desired. "Within three hours," she said, "you must clean out this pond till it sparkles like a mirror and fill it with all kinds of fish." The elves went and called all their friends and relatives to come and help them, and in two hours the work was done. They came back to the princess and said: "We have carried out your command." The princess took her handkerchief, struck the ground three times with it, and said: "Earwigs, go home!" And they all vanished. When the prince woke up, the pond was ready. Then the princess left him, telling him to come home at six o'clock. When he got there, the king asked: "Have you finished with the pond?" "Yes," said the prince, "and it's beautiful." When they were again seated at the table, the king said: "You've cleaned out the pond, but I can't give you my daughter yet, there's one more thing you'll have to do." "What's that?" asked the prince. "I have a big mountain," said the king, "and it's all covered with thornbushes. You must cut them all down, and then you must build a castle, as big and beautiful as anyone could imagine, and everything that's supposed to be in a castle must be in it."

When the prince got up the next morning, the king gave him a glass ax and a glass gimlet, and told him the castle had to be finished by six o'clock. When he struck the first thornbush with the ax it shivered into pieces so tiny they went flying round and round, and the gimlet was no use to him either. Sick at heart, he waited for his beloved, wondering if she were ever coming to help him in his need. At noon she came, bringing him something to eat. He ran to her, told her what had happened and ate a little. Then he let her louse him and fell asleep. Again she took out her knot, struck the ground with it, and cried: "Earwigs, come out!" Again a whole crowd of elves came out, and asked her what she desired. She replied: "Within three hours you must cut down all these thornbushes and build a castle as big and beautiful as anyone could imagine, and everything that's supposed to be in a castle must be in it." So then the elves went and called all their friends and relatives to come and help them with the work, and when the time was up, it was all finished. They came back to the princess and told her so, and the princess took the handkerchief and struck the ground three times with it. "Earwigs, go home!" she said, and they all vanished. When the prince woke up and saw it all, he was as happy as a bird in the air. When the clock struck six, the two of them went home together, and the king asked: "Is the castle finished?" "Yes," said the prince. When they were seated at the table the king said: "I can't give away my youngest daughter until the two eldest are married." The prince and the princess were sick at heart, and the prince had no idea what to do. Then one night he went and woke the princess and they ran away together.

When they had gone a way, the princess looked around and saw her father coming. "Oh," she said, "what shall we do? My father is coming to take us back home. I know. I'll turn you into a rosebush and I'll be a rose. I'll put myself in the middle of the bush and the thorns will protect me." When her father reached the place, nothing was there but a rosebush with a rose on it. He tried to pluck the rose, but the thorns pricked his fingers and he had to go home. His wife asked him why he hadn't brought the princess back, and he said: "I nearly overtook her, but then I lost sight of her, and there was nothing to be seen but a rosebush with a rose on it." "If you had just plucked the rose," said the queen, "the bush would have come along." So back he went to get the rose, but in the meantime the two had gone a long way. The king ran after them and again the princess looked around. When she saw her father coming, she said: "Oh, whatever shall we do? I know. I'll turn you into a church and I'll be the pastor and I'll go up into the pulpit and preach." When the king reached the place, a church was standing there, and in the pulpit stood a pastor preaching. So he listened to the sermon and went home. When the queen asked him why he hadn't brought the princess back, he said: "I followed her a long way, and when I thought I'd caught up with her a church was standing there, and a pastor was in the pulpit preaching." "You should have brought the pastor back," said the queen. "The church would have come along. It's no use sending you, I'll have to go myself." When she had gone a way and saw the two in the distance, the princess looked around and said: "This time we're lost, this time my mother is coming. I know. I'll turn you into a pond and I'll be a fish." When the mother reached the place, there was a big pond, and in the middle of the pond a fish was leaping and frisking and sticking its head out of the water to look around. She tried to catch the fish but she couldn't. She was very angry, so she thought she'd catch the fish by drinking up the whole pond, but that made her so sick she had to vomit and she vomited the whole pond up again. At that she said: "I see there's no help for it. Come here. You have nothing more to fear from me." So they went to her and the queen gave her daughter three walnuts and said: "These will help you in your greatest need."

The young people started off together, and when they had walked for ten hours, they arrived at the castle the prince came from, and there was a village nearby. They stopped in the village and the prince said: "Stay here, my dearest. I'll go to the castle first, and then I'll come back for you with a carriage and servants." When he got to the castle they were all overjoyed to see him again, and he told them he had a bride, who was now in the village, and they should drive there in the carriage to get her. So they hitched up the carriage, and lots of servants climbed up behind. Just as the prince was getting in, his mother gave him a kiss, and he forgot everything that had happened and everything he had meant to do. His mother ordered them to unhitch the carriage, and they all went back to the castle. Meanwhile the poor girl was in the village, waiting and waiting, thinking he'd come for her, but no one came. In the end she found work in the mill that belonged to the castle, and every afternoon she had to sit by the river washing the dishes. One day the queen came out of the castle. As she was walking along the river she saw the lovely young girl sitting there, and she said: "What a lovely girl that is! I like her." Then everyone stopped to look at her, but no one recognized her.

For a long time the girl served the miller honestly and faithfully. In the meantime the queen had found her son a bride, who came from far away. They were to be married as soon as the bride got there. A large crowd gathered to look on at the wedding, and the girl asked the miller if she could go too. "Yes," said the miller, "you may go." When the time came, she opened one of the three walnuts. There was a beautiful dress inside. She put it on and went to church and stood by the altar. The bride and bridegroom came in and sat near the altar. Just as the priest was going to marry them, the bride looked to one side, saw the girl standing there, stood up and said: "I won't be married until I have a dress as beautiful as that lady's." They all went back home and sent to ask the lady if she would sell her dress. "No," she said. "I won't sell it, but maybe the bride can earn it." "How?" asked the bride, and she answered: "If you'll let me spend the night outside the prince's door, you can have the dress." "Very well," said the bride, "I'll let you." But the servants were ordered to give the prince a sleeping potion. The princess lay down on the threshold and whimpered all night. "I cut down the forest for you," she moaned. "I cleaned out the pond for you, I built the castle for you, I turned you into a rosebush, I turned you into a church, and last of all into a pond. Have you forgotten me so soon?" The prince hadn't heard a thing, but the servants had waked and listened, and they didn't know what to make of it. Next morning when everybody was up, the bride put on the dress and went to church with the groom. Meanwhile the brave girl opened the second walnut, and inside it there was an even more beautiful dress. She put it on and went to the church again and stood by the altar, and the same thing happened as the first time. Again that night the girl lay on the threshold of the prince's room, and again the servants were supposed to give him a sleeping potion. But instead they gave him something to keep him awake. Then the prince went to bed, and again the princess lay on the threshold and moaned and spoke of everything she had done. The prince heard it all and it made him very sad, and everything he had forgotten came back to him. He wanted to go to her but his mother had locked the door. But in the morning he went straight to his beloved and told her everything that had happened to him and begged her not to be angry with him for forgetting her so long. Then the princess opened the third walnut, and the dress inside was much more beautiful than the others. She put it on and went to the church with her bridegroom, and a whole crowd of children came and threw flowers and bright-colored ribbons at their feet, and so they were married and had a merry wedding. The false mother and the bride she had chosen were sent away. And the mouth of the person who last told this story is still warm.

114

The Clever Little Tailor

THERE WAS ONCE a princess who was very proud. When a suitor presented himself, she asked him a riddle and if he couldn't answer it, she scoffed at him and sent him away. She had made it known that anyone who answered her riddle would become her husband, regardless of who he might be, and one day three tailors set out to court the princess. Because of all the difficult jobs they had already managed to sew up, the two oldest were confident of success in this undertaking as well. The third was a useless young scamp, who didn't even know his trade properly, but he thought to himself: "This thing is sure to bring me luck. Where else would I find any?" The other two said to him: "Better stay home. You'll never get anywhere with that bird brain of yours." But the little tailor refused to be discouraged. "I've set my heart on it," he said. "Don't worry, I'll know how to take care of myself." And he walked along as gaily as if the whole world belonged to him.

All three appeared before the princess and bade her ask her riddle. "We're just the men for this kind of thing," they said. "Why, our wit is so fine you could thread a needle with it." The princess said: "I have two kinds of hair on my head. What colors are they?" "Nothing to it," said the first. "They must be black and white like the cloth called pepper-and-salt." "Wrong," said the princess. "Let the second answer." "If it's not black and white," said the second, "it's brown and red like my father's frock coat." "Wrong," said the princess. "Let the third answer. I can see by the look on his face that he knows." The little tailor stepped boldly forward and said: "The princess has silver and golden hair on her head. Those are the two colors." When the princess heard that, she turned pale and almost fainted, for the little tailor had given the right answer, and she had been certain that no one in all the world would hit on it. When she recovered from her shock, she said: "You haven't won me yet. You must do one more thing. Downstairs in the stable there's a bear. You must spend the night with him. If you're still alive when I get up tomorrow morning, I'll marry you." "That will get rid of the little tailor," she thought, for no one the bear had got his paws on had ever lived to tell the tale. But the little tailor wasn't the least bit frightened. He smiled happily and said: "Faint heart never won fair lady."

At nightfall our little tailor was taken down to the bear. The bear was all set to welcome the little fellow with a good, big hug, but the tailor said: "Easy does it! Look, I've got something that will calm you down." And as nonchalantly as if he hadn't a care in the world he took some walnuts out of his pocket, cracked them with his teeth, and ate the kernels. When the bear saw that, he suddenly felt hungry for nuts. The tailor reached into his pocket and gave him a handful, only what he gave him wasn't nuts, it was pebbles. The bear put them in his mouth, but hard as he tried he couldn't crack them. "My goodness," he thought, "what a blockhead I am! I can't even crack a nut!" And to the tailor he said: "Crack them for me, will you?" "You see what a stupid brute you are," said the tailor. "Such a big mouth and you can't even crack a tiny nut!" Thereupon he took the stones, deftly put a nut in his mouth instead, and one-two-three it was cracked. "I'll have to try that again," said the bear. "When I see you do it, it looks so easy." Again the little tailor gave him pebbles. The bear set to work and bit with all his might, but you don't suppose he cracked them, do you? When he'd given up trying, the little tailor took a fiddle from under his coat and played a tune. When the bear heard the music, he couldn't help it, he began to dance, and after he'd danced awhile, he was so pleased that he said to the tailor: "Tell me, is it hard to play the fiddle?" "Easy as pie. Watch me. I put the fingers of my left hand up here and with my right hand I move the bow over the strings, merrily merrily, nothing to it." "I do wish I could play like you," said the bear. "Then I'd be able to dance whenever I felt like it. What do you say? Would you teach me?" "Gladly," said the little tailor, "if you've got the talent for it. But let's see those paws of yours. They're awfully long. I'll have to cut your nails down a little." A vise was brought in, and the bear put his paws into it. The little tailor tightened the vise and said: "Now wait till I get the scissors." Whereupon he let the bear growl to this heart's content, lay down on a bundle of straw in the corner and fell asleep.

That evening when the princess heard the bear growling, she thought he had done the tailor in and was growling for joy. When she got up in the morning, she was perfectly easy in her mind, but when she looked out toward the stable, there stood the tailor in perfect health, as spry as a fish in water. After that there wasn't another thing she could say, because she'd given her promise in the presence of the whole court. The king sent for a carriage, and she and the tailor set out for the church to be married. The moment they left, the two other tailors, who were false-hearted and begrudged him his happiness, went to the stable and let the bear lose, and he ran after the carriage in a terrible rage. The princess heard him puffing and growling and cried out in terror: "Oh, the bear is behind us! He's come to get you!" The tailor knew just what to do. He stood on his head, stuck his legs out the window, and shouted: "See the vise? Run along home or I'll put you right back in." At that the bear turned around and ran away, and our little tailor rode calmly to church. He married the princess and lived with her as happily as a woodlark. If you don't believe me, it will cost you a taler.

115
The Bright Sun Will Bring It to Light

A JOURNEYMAN TAILOR was traveling from place to place, plying his trade. For a time, he could find no work and was utterly destitute. One day when he didn't have a single penny for food, he saw a Jew coming down the road. Thinking the Jew was sure to be well supplied with money, the tailor banished God from his heart, went up to the Jew, and said: "Hand over your money or I'll strike you dead." "Oh, spare my life," said the Jew. "I haven't got any money, no more than eight pennies." The tailor replied: "You've got money all right, and I'm going to get it out of you." Whereupon he struck out and beat the Jew till he was almost dead. As he was dying, the Jew said these last words: "The bright sun will bring it to light." And then he died. The tailor searched the Jew's pockets for money, but found only the eight pennies he had spoken of. Then he picked up the body, carried it behind a clump of bushes, and went his way. After long journeying he came to a town and found work with a master tailor who had a beautiful daughter. He fell in love with her and married her, and they had a happy marriage.

Years later, after two children had been born to them, the mother-in-law and father-in-law died, and the young people had the house to themselves. One morning as the tailor was sitting on the table by the window, his wife brought him his coffee. He poured it into his saucer and was about to drink when the sun shone on the coffee, casting a reflection on the wall that danced about and made rings. The tailor looked up and said: "The sun is trying to bring it to light, but it can't." His wife cried out: "Heavens, dear husband, what are you talking about? What do you mean?" "I can't tell you," he said. But she replied: "If you love me, you must tell me." She spoke ever so sweetly, promised not to tell a living soul, and gave him no peace. And so he told her his story: how years before on his travels, at a time when he was hungry and penniless, he had beaten a Jew to death, and just before he died the Jew had spoken the words: "The bright sun will bring it to light." "Just now," the tailor went on, "the sun was trying to bring it to light. It danced on the wall and made rings, but that's as far as it got." Once again he implored her not to tell a soul, and she promised. But after he had started to work, she went to see her special friend, and told her the story in the strictest confidence. But before three days had passed the whole town knew it, and the tailor was haled into court and sentenced to death. So the bright sun had brought it to light after all.

116
The Blue Light

THERE WAS ONCE a soldier who had served the king faithfully for many years, but when the war was over and he could serve no longer because of his many wounds, the king said to him: "You can go home. I don't need you any more. You won't be getting any more money, because when I pay wages I expect something in return." The soldier was very sad, for he couldn't see how he was going to keep body and soul together. With a heavy heart he left the king and walked all day until he came to a forest. As night was falling, he saw a light and headed for it. Soon he came to a house that belonged to a witch. "Give me a night's lodging and something to eat and drink," he said, "or I shall die." "Oho!" said she. "Who gives a runaway soldier anything? But I'll be merciful and take you in, if you'll do what I tell you." "And what may that be?" "To spade up my garden tomorrow." The soldier accepted her proposition and worked hard all the next day, but by the time he had finished, night was falling. "Hmm," said the witch. "I see that you can't start out today. I'll keep you another night, but in return you must chop and split a cord of wood for me." That took the soldier all day and at nightfall the witch asked him to stay the night. "I have only a little thing to ask of you tomorrow," she said. "There's an old dry well behind the house. My light has fallen into it. It burns blue and never goes out. I want you to go down and get it for me." Next day the old woman took him to the well and let him down in a basket. He found the blue light and gave the signal for her to pull him up. She pulled him up all right, but when he was just below the rim she held out her hand and wanted him to give her the blue light. "Oh no," he said, for he read her wicked thoughts. "I won't give you the light until I have both my feet on the ground." At that the witch flew into a rage, let him drop to the bottom, and went away.

The ground at the bottom was moist and the poor soldier's fall didn't hurt him. The blue light was still burning, but what was the good of that? He was doomed to die, and he knew it. For a while he just sat there, feeling very dejected. Then he happened to put his hand in his pocket and felt his pipe, which was still half full of tobacco. "My last pleasure on earth!" he said to himself, took out the pipe, lit it with the blue light and began to smoke. The smoke rose in a ring and suddenly a black dwarf stood before him. "Master," said the dwarf, "what do you command?" The soldier was amazed. "What am I supposed to command?" he asked. "I must do whatever you ask," said the dwarf. "That's fine," said the soldier. "Then first of all, help me out of this well." The dwarf took him by the hand and led him through an underground passage, and the soldier didn't forget to take the blue light with him. On the way the dwarf showed him all the treasures the witch had amassed and hidden there, and the soldier took as much gold as he could carry. When he was back aboveground, he said to the dwarf: "Now go and tie up the old witch and take her to jail." A second later bloodcurdling screams were heard. She rode past as quick as the wind on the back of a wildcat, and a short while later the dwarf came back. "Your orders have been carried out," he announced. "She's already hanging on the gallows. What else do you command, master?" "Nothing right now. You can go home, but be ready when I call you." "All you have to do," said the dwarf, "is light your pipe with the blue light. I'll be there before you know it." And at that he vanished.

The soldier went back to the town he had come from. He stopped at the best inn, had fine clothes made, and ordered the innkeeper to furnish his room as splendidly as possible. When the room was ready and the soldier had moved in, he called the black dwarf and said: "I served the king faithfully, but he sent me away and let me go hungry. Now I'm going to get even." "What should I do?" asked the dwarf. "Late tonight, when the king's daughter is asleep in her bed, bring her here without waking her. I'm going to make her work as my slavey." "That will be easy for me, but dangerous for you," said the dwarf. "If you're discovered, you'll be in hot water." At the stroke of twelve the door opened and the dwarf carried the king's daughter in. "Aha!" said the soldier. "So there you are. Well, get to work. Go get the broom and sweep the place out." When she had finished, he called her over to where he was sitting, stretched out his legs, and said: "Pull my boots off." When she had pulled them off, he threw them in her face, and she had to pick them up, clean them, and polish them until they shone. Only half-opening her eyes, she obeyed his commands without a murmur. At first cockcrow the dwarf carried her back to her bed in the royal palace.

When the king's daughter got up in the morning, she went to her father and told him she had had a strange dream. "I was carried through the streets with the speed of lightning and taken to the room of a soldier. I had to be his slavey and do all the nasty work and sweep the room and clean his boots. It was only a dream, but I'm as tired as if I'd really done it all." "Your dream may have been true," said the king. "Here's my advice. Fill your pocket with peas and make a little hole in it. If they carry you off again, the peas will fall out and leave a trail on the street." When the king said this, the dwarf, who had made himself invisible, was standing right there and he heard it all. That night when he carried the king's daughter through the streets again, some peas did indeed fall out of her pocket, but they couldn't make a trail, because the crafty dwarf had strewn peas in all the streets beforehand. And again the king's daughter had to do slavey's work until cockcrow.

Next morning the king sent his men out to look for the trail, but they couldn't find it because in every street, all over town, children were picking up peas and saying: "Last night it rained peas." "We'll have to think of something else," said the king. "Keep your shoes on when you go to bed. And before you come back from that place, hide one of them. Never fear, I'll find it." The black dwarf heard the king's plan and that night when the soldier asked him once again to go and get the king's daughter, he advised against it. "I don't know of any way to thwart that scheme. If the shoe is found in your room, you'll really be in for it." "Do as you're told," said the soldier. And for the third time the king's daughter had to work as his slavey. But before the dwarf carried her back to the palace, she hid one of her shoes under the bed.

Next morning the king had the whole town searched for his daughter's shoe, and it was found in the soldier's room. The dwarf had implored the soldier to save himself, and he had left town in haste, but was soon caught and thrown into prison. In his hurry to escape he had forgotten his most precious possessions, the blue light and his gold, and all he had in his pocket was one ducat. As he was standing loaded with chains at the window of his prison cell, he saw an old friend passing, and tapped on the windowpane. When his friend came over to him, he said: "Do me a favor. Get me the little bundle I left at the inn. I'll give you a ducat." His friend ran to the inn and brought him his bundle. As soon as the soldier was alone, he lit his pipe with the light and the dwarf appeared. "Don't be afraid," said the dwarf. "Go where they take you, and let them do as they please. Just be sure to take the blue light with you." The next day the soldier was brought to trial and though he had done no evil the judge sentenced him to death. When he was led out to die, he asked the king for a last kindness. "What sort of kindness?" the king asked. "Let me smoke one last pipe on the way," said the soldier. "You can smoke three," said the king, "but don't expect me to spare your life." The soldier took out his pipe and lit it with the blue light. When a few rings of smoke had gone up, the dwarf appeared, holding a little cudgel. "What does my master command?" he asked. "Strike down those false judges and their henchmen, and don't spare the king who has treated me so badly." The dwarf raced back and forth like forked lightning and everybody his cudgel so much as touched fell to the ground and didn't dare to move. The king was so terrified that he begged for mercy and to preserve his bare life made over his kingdom to the soldier and gave him his daughter for his wife.

117

The Naughty Child

ONCE THERE WAS a naughty child who didn't do what his mother told him. God was displeased with him and made him fall sick. No doctor could help him and soon he lay on his deathbed. After he was lowered into the grave and covered over with earth, his arm suddenly came out and stood upright. They pushed it down and shoveled fresh earth over it, but that didn't help; it kept coming out again. The child's mother had to go to the grave and whip the arm with a switch. When she had done that, the child pulled in his arm and at last he had peace under the ground.

118
The Three Surgeons

THREE SURGEONS, who thought they had nothing more to learn about their art, were traveling from place to place. One night they stopped at an inn and the innkeeper asked them where they had come from and where they were going. "We are traveling surgeons," they said. "Show me what you can do," said the innkeeper. The first said he would cut off his hand and put it back on again in the morning, the second said he would tear out his heart and put it back again in the morning, and the third said he would cut out his eyes and put them back again in the morning. "If you can do that," said the innkeeper, "you have nothing more to learn." The fact is, they had an ointment which healed any wound they smeared with it and made the parts grow together, and wherever they went they carried this ointment with them. So they took a knife and the first surgeon cut off his hand, the second cut out his heart and the third his eyes just as they had said. Then they put them on a plate and gave them to the innkeeper, who told the servant girl to put them in the larder for safekeeping. Now the servant girl was secretly in love with a soldier, who came in when the innkeeper, the three surgeons, and everybody else in the house had gone to sleep, and asked for something to eat. The girl opened the larder and brought him something, but she was so befuddled with love that she forgot to close the door.

She sat down at the table with her sweetheart, and as they were sitting there, chatting away and suspecting no harm, the cat came creeping in, found the larder open, and made off with the hand, heart, and eyes of the three surgeons. When the soldier had finished eating and the girl thought she'd clear away the dishes and lock the larder, she saw that the plate the innkeeper had entrusted to her care was empty. She was frightened to death. "Lordy!" she cried. "What will I do now? The hand is gone, the heart and the eyes are gone too. What will they do to me tomorrow!" "Don't worry," said the soldier. "I know just what to do. There's a thief hanging on the gallows. I'll cut off his hand. Which hand was it?" "The right hand." The girl gave him a sharp knife and he went out, cut the hanged man's right hand off, and brought it in. Then he caught the cat and cut its eyes out. Only the heart was lacking. "Didn't you just butcher some pigs?" he asked. "Isn't the meat in the cellar?" "Yes," said the girl. "Then everything's fine and dandy," said the soldier, went down to the cellar and came back with a pig's heart. The girl laid all the things on a plate and put the plate in the larder. When her sweetheart had left her, she went calmly to bed.

When the surgeons got up in the morning, they asked the servant girl for the plate with the hand, heart, and eyes on it. She took it out of the larder and brought it to them. Whereupon the first put the thief's hand in place and rubbed it with the ointment, and instantly it grew onto his wrist. The second took the cat's eyes and fitted them into his eye sockets, and the third made the pig's heart fast. The innkeeper looked on and marveled at their skill. He said he'd never seen anything like it and promised to praise them and recommend them to everyone he met. Then they paid for their bed and board and started off.

Instead of walking with the others, the one with the pig's heart kept running into corners and rooting about like a pig. His comrades tried to hold him back by his coattails, but he persisted in breaking loose and running to the places where the garbage was deepest. The second was also behaving very oddly, rubbing his eyes and saying to the third: "Comrade, what's going on? These aren't my eyes, I can't see a thing. Lead me, one of you, or I'll fall." They dragged him painfully on until evening, and then they came to another inn. They went to the public room together, and there in a corner sat a rich gentleman counting money. The surgeon with the thief's hand circled round him, and his hand kept twitching. Finally, when the gentleman was looking the other way, the surgeon reached into the pile and took a handful of money. One of his friends saw him and said: "Hey, what are you doing? Stealing's not allowed. You ought to be ashamed!" "I can't help it," he said. "My hand twitches and in spite of myself I have to grab." Then they went to bed and it was so dark in their room that you couldn't see your hand before your face. Suddenly the one with the cat's eyes woke up, woke the other two, and said: "Hey, brothers, look. Do you see those white mice running around?" The two of them sat up, but they couldn't see a thing. Then the one with the cat's eyes said: "There's something wrong with us. These aren't our organs. We'll have to go back to that innkeeper. He cheated us."

So next morning they started out and when they got there they told the innkeeper that they hadn't got their right organs back, that one had a thief's hand, the second a pig's heart, and the third cat's eyes. The innkeeper said only the servant girl could be to blame. He called her, but she wasn't there. She had seen the three surgeons coming and had run out the back door. The three said to the innkeeper: "Give us money and plenty of it, or we'll set fire to your house." He gave them as much as he could lay hands on, and they went their way. It was enough to last them the rest of their lives, but they'd sooner have had their proper organs.

119
The Seven Swabians

ONCE THERE WERE seven Swabians: the first was the burgomaster, the second was Jackli, the third was Marli, the fourth was Jergli, the fifth was Michal, the sixth was Hans, and the seventh was Veitli. All seven had resolved to go forth in search of adventures and to do great deeds. Knowing that safety lay in good armament, they had the blacksmith make them a single spear, but a very long and strong one, and all seven took hold of it at once. Firste went the boldest and bravest: that was the burgomaster, of course. Then came the others, each in his turn, and Veitli was the last.

Now it so happened that one day in the haymaking season, when they had gone a long way and it was still quite a distance to the village where they were meaning to spend the night, they came to a meadow, and there in the twilight a big dung beetle, or maybe a hornet, flew out from behind a bush with a hostile buzzing sound. The burgomaster was so scared he broke out in a cold sweat and almost dropped the spear. "Hark!" he cried. "Oh, my God! I hear a drum!" Jackli, who was holding the spear behind him, got a whiff of something or other in the air, and said: "Something's afoot. I smell powder and match cord." At those words the burgomaster took flight. With the speed of lightning he jumped over a fence and landed on the prongs of a hay rake someone had left lying there. The handle shot up and gave him a mighty blow on the head. "Oh dear! Oh dear!" cried the burgomaster. "Take me prisoner, I surrender, I surrender!" The other six leaped to his side, each quicker than the last, saying: "If you surrender, I surrender." Finally, when no enemy came to bind them and lead them away, they saw they had been fooled, and for fear the story would get around and everyone would laugh at them, they swore to each other to keep silent until one of them shot off his mouth by mistake.

Then they proceeded on their way. The second danger they confronted was incomparably greater than the first. Some days later, as they were plodding through a fallow field, who should be sitting there sound asleep in the sun, with his ears pointing upward and his big glassy eyes wide open, but a hare. All seven Swabians quailed at the sight of this cruel and savage beast, and held council. "What," they asked one another, "would be the least dangerous thing to do?" For if they took to their heels, there was reason to fear that the monster would pursue them and gobble them up. Finally they said: "Our only recourse is a great and perilous battle. Nothing ventured, nothing won!" All seven grabbed hold of the spear, the burgomaster in front and Veitli at the end of the line. The burgomaster was still trying to hold the spear back, but Veitli in the rear guard suddenly felt full of courage and wanted to press forward. "Attack!" he cried.

"Attack in all brave Swabians' name,
Let him who wavers die of shame."

But Hans knew his weak point and said:

> "Ho, ho, harumph, look who's talking!
> You're always last at dragon-stalking."

Michal cried out:

> "Pointed ears and glassy eyes,
> It's the Devil in disguise."

Next it was Jergli's turn:

> "If not the Devil, then his mother,
> Or the Devil's foster brother."

At that point Marli had a good idea and said to Veitli:

> "Briskly, Veitli, to the fray,
> And I'll advance the other way."

But Veitli wasn't listening, and Jackli said:

> "The burgomaster must lead us on.
> Such honor falls to him alone."

At that the burgomaster took heart and said gravely:

> "Boldly, my hearties, to the war,
> And show the world how brave we are."

All together they advanced on the dragon. The burgomaster crossed himself and called on God for succor. But when all his prayers were in vain and his steps brought him closer and closer to the enemy, he cried out in terror: "Eek! Eek! Hoo hoo!" The noise woke the hare, who ran away in a fright, and when the burgomaster saw his headlong flight, he cried out in his joy:

> "Look, Veitli, look. Look over there!
> The monster's nothing but a hare!"

After that the Swabian League went looking for further adventures, and came to the Moselle, a mossy, deep, and tranquil river, spanned by few bridges and in many places crossable only by boat. As the seven Swabians were unaware of this, they hailed a man who was working on the opposite bank and asked him how they could get across. Because of the distance and their Swabian accent, he didn't understand them and asked in his Moselle dialect: "Wat? Wat?" The burgomaster thought he was saying: "Wade, wade. Wade across." So being first in line, he started forward and walked into the Moselle. It wasn't long before he sank into the muck and under the deep rolling waves, but the wind carried his hat to the opposite bank, and a frog settled on it. "Wat, wat, wat," croaked the frog. The six others heard it and said: "Our leader the burgomaster is calling. If he can wade across, why can't we?" So they all jumped in the water and were drowned. Six men had been done in by a frog, and not one member of the Swabian League ever came home again.

120
The Three Journeymen

THERE WERE THREE JOURNEYMEN who had agreed to stay together on their travels and always work in the same town. But a time came when their masters had no work for them and they were all penniless and in rags. One of them said: "What shall we do? We can't stay here any longer. Let's go on the road again. Then if we don't find work in the next town we come to, we'll arrange with the innkeeper to write and let him know where we are, so as to keep in touch with each other. Then we'll all go our separate ways."

That struck the others as a good idea and they started out. On their way, they met a richly dressed man, who asked them who they were. "We're journeymen looking for work. So far we've kept together, but if we don't find any work, we're going to break up." "No need of that," said the man. "If you do as I tell you, you'll have plenty of money and work. In fact, you'll soon be fine gentlemen, riding in carriages." "If it's no risk to our immortal souls," said one of the journeymen, "we'll do it." "No risk at all," said the man. "I'll have no claim on you." But the second journeyman had been looking at the ground, and when he saw that the stranger had one horse's hoof and one human foot, he thought they'd better steer clear of him. But the Devil said: "Don't worry. I'm not interested in you. I'm out for another soul, who's half mine already and who will soon be ripe for the plucking." Thus reassured, they consented, and the Devil told them what he wanted them to do. In answer to all questions, he wanted the first to say: "All three of us," the second: "For money," and the third: "And that's as it should be." Apart from these answers, which they were always to make in the same order, they were not to say another word. If they broke this rule, all their money would vanish instantly, but if they observed it their pockets would always be full. To start them off, he gave them all the money they could carry, and told them to stop at such and such an inn in the next town.

When they got there, the innkeeper came out to meet them and asked if they wanted something to eat. The first replied: "All three of us." "Naturally," said the innkeeper. The second said: "For money." "I should hope so," said the innkeeper. The third said: "And that's as it should be." And the innkeeper said: "You've hit the nail on the head." The best of food and drink was set before them, and they had no complaint about the service. When they had finished their meal and it was time to pay, the innkeeper handed them the bill. "All three of us," said the first. "For money," said the second. "And that's as it should be," said the third. "Right you are," said the innkeeper. "All three of you will pay. I can't serve anyone without payment." After all this, they paid more than the innkeeper had asked. The other guests looked on and said: "Those fellows must be crazy." "You took the words out of my mouth," said the innkeeper. "They're not right in the head."

The journeymen stayed on at the inn for a while and all they ever said was: "All three of us," "For money," "And that's as it should be." But they kept their eyes open and saw everything that went on. One day a rich merchant came to the inn. He had a great deal of money with him and he said to the innkeeper: "Would you kindly keep my money for me, I'm afraid those crazy journeymen will steal it." The innkeeper took the moneybag to his room, and as he was carrying it he felt the weight of the gold inside. Thereupon he decided to lodge the three journeymen on the ground floor and to give the merchant a room of his own upstairs. At midnight, when the innkeeper thought everyone was asleep, he and his wife went to the merchant's room with an ax and struck him dead. After the murder they went back to bed. Next morning there was a great outcry when the merchant was found lying in a pool of blood. The guests all came running, and the innkeeper said: "The three crazy journeymen did this." The guests agreed: "It can't have been anyone else," they said. The innkeeper sent for the journeymen and asked them: "Did you kill the merchant?" "All three of us," said the first. "For money," said the second. "And that's as it should be," said the third. "There you have it!" said the innkeeper. "They've confessed." So they were thrown into prison and their trial was set for the next day.

When they saw that things were getting serious, they began to be worried, but the Devil came to them at night and said: "Stick it out just one day more and don't throw your luck away. Nobody's going to touch a hair of your head." Next morning they were taken to court. The judge asked them: "Are you the murderers?" "All three of us." "Why did you kill the merchant?" "For money." "You villains!" said the judge. "Doesn't your conscience trouble you?" "That's as it should be." "They have confessed and I see no sign of remorse," said the judge. "Take them straight to the scaffold." So they were led to the scaffold and the innkeeper was obliged to stand with the witnesses. The executioner's helpers grabbed hold of the journeymen and were leading them up to the block where the headsman was waiting with his naked sword, when a carriage drawn by four blood-red chestnut horses came driving up so fast that sparks flew from the cobbles. A man leaned out of the window, waving a white handkerchief. "That's a reprieve," said the executioner, and from the carriage came cries of: "Reprieve, reprieve!" Out stepped the Devil disguised as a fine gentleman, and said: "You three are innocent. You may speak now. Tell us what you've seen and heard." Said the eldest: "We didn't kill the merchant. The murderer is right there in the circle." And he pointed at the innkeeper. "If you want proof, go to his cellar. You'll find the bodies of many others he has murdered hanging there." The judge sent the executioner's helpers, and they found that the journeyman's story was true. They told the judge, who ordered them to take the innkeeper up to the block, and the executioner cut off his head. When that was done, the Devil said to the three journeymen: "Now I've got the soul I wanted. You're free, and you've got money enough to last you the rest of your lives."

121

The Prince Who Feared Nothing

THERE WAS ONCE a prince who was sick of living in his father's house, and as he was afraid of nothing he thought: "I'll go out into the wide world. Then the time won't hang heavy on my hands, and I'll see all sorts of strange things." So he took leave of his parents and started out. On and on he went, from morning to night, not caring at all where his road led him. One day he came to a giant's house, and as he was tired he sat down outside to rest. Looking around him, this way and that he saw the giant's playthings, a set of ninepins as big as a man and several enormous balls. After a while, he had an itch to bowl, so he set the ninepins up and started rolling the balls at them. He was in high spirits and shouted when the ninepins fell. The giant heard the noise, leaned his head out of the window, and saw a human who, though no bigger than the usual, was playing with his ninepins. "Hey, you worm!" he cried out. "How can you bowl with my balls? Where did you get the strength?" The prince raised his eyes, looked the giant straight in the face, and said: "You big lug, do you think you're the only one with strong arms? I can do anything I feel like doing." The giant came down, looked on with amazement as the prince bowled, and said: "If that's the kind of human you are, go and get me an apple from the Tree of Life." "What do you want with it?" asked the prince. "I don't want it for myself," said the giant, "but I have a ladylove who keeps asking for one. I've been all over the world and I can't find the tree." "I'll find it," said the prince, "and I don't see what's to stop me from picking the apple." "It's not as easy as you seem to think," said the giant. "The garden where the tree is has an iron fence around it, and outside the fence there's a circle of wild beasts keeping watch, and they won't let anyone in." "They'll let me in," said the prince. "Maybe so, but even if you get into the garden and see the apple hanging on the tree, it won't be yours yet. There's a ring hanging in front of it. To get at the apple you'll have to put your hand through the ring, and no one has ever succeeded in doing that." "I'll succeed," said the prince.

He took leave of the giant and journeyed over hill and dale, through forests and across plains, until at last he came to the miraculous garden. The beasts were lying all around it, but their heads were down and they were asleep. They didn't wake at his approach, so he stepped over them, climbed the fence, and went into the garden. In the middle of it stood the Tree of Life, and its branches were full of glistening red apples. He climbed up the trunk, and as he was reaching for an apple he saw a ring hanging in front of it, but he had no trouble putting his hand through it, and he picked the apple. The ring closed tight around his arm, and all at once he felt enormous power flowing through his veins. After coming down with the apple, he didn't feel like climbing the fence. Instead, he took hold of the big gate, shook it just once, and it opened with a crash. When he went out, the lion who was lying there woke up and bounded after him, but the lion wasn't fierce and he wasn't angry. Not at all. He accepted the prince as his master and followed him meekly.

The prince brought the giant the promised apple and said: "You see, I had no trouble getting it." The giant was delighted to have the apple so quickly and ran to give it to his ladylove. She was not only beautiful, but wise as well. When she saw no ring on the giant's arm, she said: "I won't believe it was you who brought back the apple until I see the ring on your arm." "I'll just go home and get it," said the giant, who thought it would be easy to take it from the weak human by force if he wouldn't part with it of his own free will. So he asked the prince for the ring, but the prince refused. "The ring goes with the apple," said the giant. "If you won't give it to me of your own free will, I'm going to fight you for it."

For a long time they wrestled, but the giant couldn't get the better of the prince, for the magic ring had given him extra strength. Then the giant thought up a trick and said: "Fighting has made me hot, and you too. Let's take a bath in the river before we start in again." The prince, who knew nothing of trickery, went down to the river with the giant. In undressing, he stripped the ring off his arm. When he jumped in the water, the giant picked up the ring and ran away, but the lion, who had seen him steal it, followed him, tore the ring out of his hand and brought it back to his master. Then the giant hid behind an oak tree, and while the prince was busy putting his clothes on, the giant rushed him and put out both his eyes.

As the prince stood there, blind and helpless, the giant came back, took him by the hand as if to show him the way, and led him to the top of a high cliff, where he left him, thinking: "Just a few steps more and he'll fall to his death. Then I'll go and take the ring." But the faithful lion hadn't forsaken his master. He kept a hold on his coat and little by little led him back down. When the giant came to rob the dead, he saw that his trick had failed, and said to himself in a rage: "There must be some way of destroying this puny human!" Thereupon he took the prince by his arm and led him back to the cliff by a different path. But the lion, who saw what the wicked giant was planning, was on hand to help his master. When the giant had led the blind man close to the edge, he let go his hand, meaning to leave him there alone. At that moment the lion pushed the giant, who fell off the cliff and was dashed to pieces.

Again the faithful animal drew his master away from the precipice and led him to a tree beside a clear flowing brook. The prince sat down and with his paw the lion sprinkled water on his face. No sooner had a few drops fallen on his eye sockets than he was able to see a little. After a while he noticed a little bird, that flew past him and bumped into a tree trunk. Then it fluttered down to the brook and bathed in it. A moment later it took flight and darted off between the trees without bumping into any of them. It was clear to the prince that the bird had recovered its eyesight, and realizing that God had given him a sign, he bent down over the water and bathed his face in it. When he stood up, he had his eyes back again, as bright and clear as they had ever been.

After thanking God for his great mercy, the prince resumed his travels with the lion. One day he came to an enchanted castle. In the gateway stood a maiden who was beautiful in face and form, but pitch-black. She stopped him and said: "Ah, if you could only set me free from the evil spell that has been cast on me!" "What should I do?" asked the prince. The maiden replied: "You must spend three nights in the great hall of the enchanted castle, and no trace of fear must enter your heart. They will do all they can to torment you, but if you bear it without so much as a murmur, I shall be free. They won't be allowed to take your life." "I'm not afraid," said the prince.

"With God's help I'll try." So he went cheerfully into the castle, and at nightfall he sat down in the great hall and waited. All was quiet until midnight, but then he heard a terrible noise, and little devils came crawling from every nook and cranny. They took no notice of him, sat down in the middle of the hall, made a fire, and began to throw dice. When one of them lost, he said: "Something's wrong. There's someone here who isn't one of us. It's his fault that I'm losing." "Hey, you behind the stove!" cried another. "Just wait, I'm coming." The screams grew louder and louder, anyone would have been afraid. The prince kept perfectly calm, and no fear touched his heart, but then finally the devils jumped up from the floor and fell upon him. There were so many that he couldn't defend himself. They dragged him around, pinched him, pricked him, beat him, and tormented him in every way, but not a murmur escaped him. Toward morning they vanished, and he was so worn out he could hardly move. At daybreak the black maiden came in. In her hand she held a small bottle containing the Water of Life, and she sprinkled him with it. Instantly all his pain was gone and he felt new strength flowing through his veins. "You've handled the first night very well," she said, "but you've got two more ahead of you." Then she left the hall and as she was walking away from him he noticed that her feet had turned white. The next night the devils came back. Again they threw dice, and again they fell upon the prince. This time they beat him much harder than the night before and his whole body was covered with wounds. But since he bore it in silence, they had to stop after a while, and at dawn the maiden came and healed him with the Water of Life. As she was leaving the room, he was overjoyed to see that she was all white down to her fingertips. After that he had only one more night to endure, but that night was the worst of all. The devils came back again. "You still here?" they cried. "You're going to be tortured till you can't see straight!" They pricked him and beat him, they flung him this way and that way, they tugged at his arms and legs as though to tear him apart. But he stuck it out and not so much as a murmur escaped him. Finally the devils vanished, but he lay there helpless, unable to move or even to open his eyes when the maiden came in with the Water of Life. But the moment she sprinkled him with it, his pain was gone, and he felt as fresh and rested as after a good night's sleep. When he opened his eyes, he saw the maiden standing beside him, and she was as white as snow and as beautiful as the day. "Stand up," she said. "Swing your sword three times over the staircase, then the whole castle will be set free." When he had done that, the whole castle was delivered from the spell, and the maiden turned out to be a rich princess. Servants came and announced that the table had been laid in the great hall and that dinner was ready. So they sat down and ate and drank together, and that night the wedding was celebrated amid great rejoicing.

122

The Donkey Lettuce

THERE WAS ONCE a young hunter, who went to a blind in the forest. He was joyful and lighthearted, and as he strode along, whistling on a blade of grass, he met an ugly cold crone, who spoke to him saying: "Good day, young hunter, you seem so happy and content, but as for me, I'm hungry and thirsty. Could you give me a few pennies?" The hunter felt sorry for the poor old woman, reached into his pocket, and gave her as much as he could afford. As he was starting off again, the old woman held him back, saying: "Listen to me, my dear young hunter. Because of your good heart I'm going to make you a present. Just keep on your way now, and in a little while you'll come to a tree with nine birds perched on it. They'll be holding a cloak in their claws and fighting over it. Take your gun and shoot into the midst of them. They'll drop the cloak, and one of the birds will be hit and fall down dead. Take the cloak. It's a wishing cloak. Once you throw it over your shoulders, you need only wish yourself somewhere, and there you'll be in a flash. And if you take the heart out of the dead bird and swallow it whole, you'll find a gold piece under your pillow each and every morning of your life."

The hunter thanked the Wise Woman, and thought to himself: "Those are fine things she's promised me. If only they come true." When he had gone about a hundred paces, he heard a screeching and a squawking in the branches. He looked up and saw a whole flock of birds, all tearing at a piece of cloth with their beaks and claws, screaming and tugging and fighting as if each one wanted it all to himself. "Well, well," said the hunter. "This *is* strange. It's just as the old woman said." He took his gun, fired into the midst of the flock and sent the feathers flying. The birds scattered with loud cries, but one fell to the ground dead, and the cloak came fluttering down. The hunter did what the old woman had told him. He cut the bird open, found the heart and swallowed it whole. As for the cloak, he took it home with him.

When he woke up the next morning, he remembered the old woman's promise and looked under his pillow to see if she had told the truth. A shiny gold piece sparkled up at him, and the next day he found another, and another and another every time he got up in the morning. He soon had a large pile of gold, but in the end he thought: "What good is all this gold to me if I stay home? I think I'll go and see the world."

He took leave of his parents, slung his knapsack and his gun over his shoulders, and went out into the world. One day he passed through a dense forest, and in the open country at the end of it was a beautiful castle. An old woman and a lovely girl were standing at one of the windows, looking down. The old woman was a witch, and she said to the girl: "See that man coming out of the forest? He's got a wonderful treasure. We must relieve him of it, my dear, because we can make much better use of it than he ever could. This treasure of his is a bird's heart, and thanks to it he finds a gold piece under his pillow every morning." She went on to tell the girl how the hunter had come by his treasure and what she must do to get it. In the end the witch threatened her and said with flaming eyes: "You'll be sorry if you don't obey me." When the hunter came closer, he saw the girl and said to himself: "I've been wandering about for so long. I've got plenty of money, so why wouldn't I stop and rest in this beautiful castle?" But the real reason was that he had cast an eye on the lovely girl.

He went into the castle, where he was well received and entertained. Soon he was so much in love with the witch's daughter that he could think of nothing else. He lived by the light of her eyes and gladly did whatever she asked. One day the old woman said: "We must get that bird's heart. He won't even notice it's missing." They brewed up a potion and when it was ready the old witch poured it into a cup. The girl gave it to the hunter, saying: "My dearest, now you must drink my health." He took the cup, drank the potion, and vomited up the bird's heart. The girl carried it off in secret and then swallowed it herself, for that was what the old witch wanted. From then on the hunter found no more gold under his pillow. Instead, it was under the girl's pillow, and the old witch took it. But he was so madly in love that he had no other thought than to while away the time with the girl.

Then the old witch said: "Now we've got the bird's heart, but we must also take his wishing cloak." The girl replied: "Couldn't we let the poor man keep his cloak, now that he has lost his wealth?" At that the old witch grew angry and said: "A cloak like that is a wonderful thing. There aren't many like it in the world, and I must and will have it." She told the girl what to do and said she'd be sorry if she didn't. So the girl did as her mother told her, and stood at the window looking out over the countryside as though she were very sad. "Why are you standing there looking so sad?" the hunter asked her. "Oh, my dearest," she said, "over there across the valley lies the Garnet Mountain, where the precious stones grow. I long for them so. But who can get at them? Only the birds that fly through the air. A human being, never. That's why I'm so sad." "If that's all you've got to be sad about," said the hunter, "it won't take me long to cheer you up." Taking her under his cloak, he wished himself on the Garnet Mountain, and one-two-three they were both there. The precious stones that sparkled all about them were a joy to behold. When they had gathered up the most beautiful and costly of them, the old witch cast a spell that made the hunter drowsy. He said to the girl: "Let's sit down and rest awhile. I'm so tired I'm falling off my feet." They sat down and, resting his head in her lap, he fell asleep. While he slept, she took the cloak from his shoulders, threw it over her own, picked up the garnets and precious stones, and wished herself back home.

When the hunter had had his sleep out and woke up, he saw that his loved one had betrayed him and left him alone on the wild mountain. "Oh," he sighed. "Oh, what treachery there is in the world!" He sat there grieving, and didn't know what to do. The mountain belonged to some great ferocious giants, who made their home on it, and it wasn't long before he saw three of them coming. He lay down as though he had fallen into a deep sleep. When the giants caught sight of him, the first one prodded him with his foot and said: "Who's this earthworm lying here gazing at his inner thoughts?" The second said: "Step on him, crush the life out of him." But the third said contemptuously: "Why bother? Let him live. He can't stay here, and if he climbs to the summit the clouds will pick him up and carry him away." With that they left him, but the hunter had heard what they said, and as soon as they had gone, he stood up and climbed to the summit. When he had sat there awhile, a cloud came drifting along, picked him up and carried him away. For some time it floated around the sky, then it settled on a big walled kitchen garden, and he landed gently among the vegetables.

He looked around and said to himself: "If only I had something to eat! I'm so hungry I'd have a hard time going anywhere. But here I see no apples or pears or fruit of any kind, nothing but vegetables." Finally he thought: "In a pinch I could eat some of that lettuce. I doubt if it tastes very good, but it ought to be refreshing." So he picked out a nice-looking head and bit into it, but after the first few bites he had a very strange feeling and something told him he had changed completely. He had four legs, an enormous head, and two long ears, and he saw to his horror that he had turned into a donkey. But since he was still very hungry and since, now that he was a donkey, the fresh, juicy lettuce was very much to his taste, he ate and ate. Finally he came to a bed of a different kind of lettuce, and no sooner had he eaten a few leaves of it than he felt himself changing again and his human form came back to him.

After that he lay down and slept away his weariness. When he woke up in the morning, he picked a head of the bad and a head of the good lettuce and thought: "This will help me to get my treasures back and to punish the treachery of those women." He put the salad in his knapsack, climbed the wall, and set out in search of his sweetheart's castle. After wandering around for a few days, he found it. Before going in, he dyed his face brown so his own mother wouldn't have known him. Then he went to the door and asked for a night's lodging, saying: "I'm too tired to go any farther." "Who are you, my friend?" asked the witch, "and what is your business?" "I'm the king's messenger," he replied. "The king sent me in search of the most delicious lettuce in the world. I was lucky enough to find it and I've got some with me, but the sun is so hot I'm afraid the tender leaves will wilt, and I don't know if I can carry it any farther."

When the old witch heard about the delicious lettuce, her mouth watered for it and she said: "Dear friend, let me taste your wonderful lettuce." "Why not?" he replied. "I've brought two heads, and I'll give you one." He opened his knapsack and handed her the bad lettuce. The witch, who suspected nothing, was so eager to taste the strange new lettuce that she went to the kitchen herself to prepare it. When it was ready, she couldn't wait till it was on the table, took a few leaves and put them in her mouth. The moment she swallowed them she lost her human form, became a donkey, and ran out into the yard. Just then the servant came in, saw the lettuce all ready in the bowl and thought she'd serve it. She carried it to the table, but, as usual, she couldn't resist her desire to taste it. She ate a few leaves and the magic worked instantly: she too was turned into a donkey. The salad bowl fell to the floor and she ran out to join the old witch. Meanwhile the king's messenger was sitting with the lovely girl, and when no one came in with the lettuce, she too began to long for it. "I wonder what's become of that lettuce?" she said. "Aha!" thought the hunter. "It must have worked." And he said to her: "I'll go to the kitchen and see." When he got down to the kitchen, he saw the two donkeys running around in the yard and the lettuce lying on the floor. "So far so good," he said. "Those two have got what was coming to them." He picked up the rest of the lettuce leaves, put them in the bowl and took them to the girl. "I've brought you the delicacy myself," he said, "so you won't have to wait any longer." She ate some, and like the other two she became a donkey and ran out into the yard.

When the hunter had washed his face so that the donkey women could recognize him, he went out to the yard and said: "Now you're going to get what you deserve for your treachery." He fastened all three to a rope and drove them down the road till he came to a mill. He tapped on the window and the miller stuck his head out and asked him what he wanted. "I've got three ugly-tempered beasts here," he said, "and I'm good and sick of them. If you'll take them and feed them and treat them just as I tell you, I'll pay you whatever you ask." "Why not?" said the miller. "But how do you want me to treat them?" The hunter explained: "Beat the oldest (that was the witch) three times a day and feed her once. Beat the middle one (that was the servant) once a day and feed her three times. As for the youngest (that was the girl), feed her three times and don't beat her at all." For he couldn't find it in his heart to have the girl beaten. Then he went back to the castle, where he found everything he needed.

A few days later the miller came to him and said: "I'm sorry to tell you this, but the old donkey, the one that got beaten three times a day and fed only once, is dead. The other two have been getting fed three times a day and they're still alive, but they're so sad they can't be expected to last much longer." At that, the hunter took pity, forgot his anger, and told the miller to bring them back to the castle. As soon as they arrived, he gave them some of the good lettuce to eat, and they resumed their human form. The girl went down on her knees to him and said: "Oh, my dearest, forgive my wickedness, my mother made me do it. I didn't want to, for I love you with all my heart. Your wishing cloak is hanging in the cupboard and I'll take a vomitive to make me bring up the bird's heart." But he wouldn't let her do that. "Keep it," he said. "It makes no difference who has it, for I mean to take you as my trusted wife."

Then the wedding was held and they lived happily together until they died.

123

The Old Woman in the Forest

ONCE A POOR SERVANT GIRL was riding through a great forest with her masters, and when they were right in the middle of it, some robbers came out of the thicket and murdered everyone they could lay hands on. The whole party was killed except for the girl, who in her fright had jumped out of the carriage and hidden behind a tree. When the robbers had gone away with their spoils, she came out and saw the terrible thing they had done. She wept bitterly and said: "Poor me.

What can I do? I'll never find my way out of this forest and nobody lives here. I'm sure to starve." She wandered around looking for a way out but she couldn't find one. At nightfall she sat down under a tree, said a prayer, and decided to stay right where she was forever, no matter what happened. When she had sat there awhile, a white dove came flying down to her with a little golden key in its beak. It put the key into her hand and said: "Do you see that big tree? There's a lock on it. If you open it up with this key, you'll find plenty of food and you won't go hungry." So she went to the tree and opened it up and found a bowl of milk and some white bread to crumble into it. When she had had enough to eat, she said: "Now is the time when at home the hens go to roost. Oh, I'm so tired. If only I could lie down to sleep in my bed." Just then the dove came back with another little key in its beak and said: "Open that tree over there, and you'll find a bed." She opened it up and found a lovely white bed, whereupon she prayed God to keep her during the night, lay down and fell asleep. In the morning the dove came a third time, bringing still another key, and said: "Open that tree over there and you'll find clothes." When she opened it up, she found clothes adorned with gold and diamonds, more splendid than any princess can boast of. And so she lived for a while. The dove came every day and provided her with everything she needed. It was a good, quiet life.

Then one day the dove came to her and asked: "Would you do something to please me?" "Gladly," said the girl. The dove said: "I shall lead you to a hut. Go in. An old woman will be sitting by the stove, and she will bid you good day. But don't give her any answer, don't pay attention to anything she does. Go around her on the right side, and you'll see a door. Open it. You'll find yourself in another room, and there you'll see rings of all kinds spread out on a table. Some of them are magnificent, set with sparkling jewels, but don't touch them. Look for a plain one, it's sure to be there, and bring it here to me as fast as you can." The girl went to the hut and opened the door. There sat an old woman who stared when she saw her and said: "Good day, my child." But the girl made no answer and went toward the door. "Where are you going?" cried the old woman, grabbing her by the skirt and trying to hold her back. "This is my house! Nobody can go in there without my permission." But the girl said nothing, broke away from her, and went straight into the other room. There on the table lay more rings than she could count, and they glittered and sparkled before her eyes. She pushed them this way and that, looking for the plain one, but she couldn't find it. As she was looking, she saw the old woman creeping about, holding a birdcage and trying to slip away with it. The girl ran over to her and snatched the cage out of her hand. There was a bird inside and the bird had the plain ring in its beak. She took the ring and ran out of the house. She was very happy, she thought the white dove would come and get the ring, but it didn't. She waited and waited, leaning against a tree, and as she stood there it seemed to her that the tree became soft and yielding, and lowered its branches. Suddenly the branches twined around her, and they were two arms. When she turned to look, the tree was a handsome young man, who held her in his arms, kissed her tenderly, and said: "You have delivered me from that old woman. She's a wicked witch. She changed me into a tree, but for a few hours every day I was a white dove. As long as she had the ring, I couldn't recover my human form." His servants and horses had also been freed from the spell that had changed them into trees, and they were all standing beside him. Then they rode away to his kingdom, for he was a king's son, and they were married and lived happily.

124

The Three Brothers

THERE WAS ONCE a man who had three sons and nothing else but the house he lived in. Each of the three hoped to own the house after their father's death, and the father, who loved them all equally and had no desire to wrong any of them, didn't know what to do. He couldn't bear to sell the house, because it had been in the family for many generations; otherwise he'd have divided the money among them. Then finally he had an idea and he said to his sons: "Go out into the world and see what you can make of yourselves. Learn a

GRIMMS' TALES FOR YOUNG AND OLD

trade, each one of you, and when you come back, the one who gives the best demonstration of his skill shall have the house."

The sons were delighted. The eldest decided to become a blacksmith, the second a barber, and the third a swordsman, and after setting a time for their return home, they started out. In the course of time all three found excellent masters, who really taught them something. After a while, the young blacksmith was sent to shoe the king's horses, and he thought: "After this I can't fail. I'm sure to get the house." The young barber shaved only noble lords, and he too thought the house was already his. The young swordsman took quite a few cuts and bruises, but he gritted his teeth and stuck it out, for he thought to himself: "I'll never get the house if I let a few wounds frighten me."

At the appointed time, they all returned to their father's house. None of them knew when he'd get a chance to show his skill, and they were sitting together, talking it over, when a hare came bounding over the meadow. "Hey," said the barber. "That's just what I wanted!" He took his soap and his shaving bowl and whipped up a lather until the hare was close by. Then, running alongside the hare, he lathered and shaved him, leaving a neat little beard and neither cutting him nor hurting him in any way. "Marvelous!" cried the father. "Your brothers will have a hard time bettering that." It wasn't long before a nobleman's carriage came dashing down the road. "All right, father," said the blacksmith. "Now you'll see what I can do." Whereupon he ran after the carriage, tore the four shoes off the galloping horse, and put on four new ones while the horse kept right on going. "Not bad!" said the father. "You've learned your trade as well as your brother. I can't decide which of you should have the house." At that the third spoke up: "Father, give me a chance too." Just then it began to rain. The swordsman drew his sword and swung it over his head so fast that not a drop fell on him. The rain got worse and worse, it came down in buckets, but he swung his sword faster and faster and kept as dry as if he'd been safely indoors. When the father saw that, he couldn't get over his amazement. "You've given the best demonstration," he said. "The house is yours."

The other two accepted their father's choice as they had all agreed to do. They loved each other so dearly that all three kept living in the house, plying their trades. Since they had learned so well and were so very skillful, they made plenty of money. And so they lived happily until their old age, and when one of them fell sick and died, the two others were so heartbroken that they fell ill and soon died. And because they had all been so clever and loved one another so dearly, they were all buried in the same grave.

125

The Devil and His Grandmother

A GREAT WAR was being fought and the king had many soldiers, but he paid them too little to live on. Three of these soldiers got together and decided to desert. "If we're caught," said one of them, "they'll string us up on the gallows. So how shall we go about it?" "See that big wheat field?" said the second. "If we hide there, no one will find us. The troops aren't allowed in it, and tomorrow they'll be moving on." The three deserters crept into the wheat, but the troops didn't move on, they stayed right there, camped on all sides of the field. The deserters spend two days and two nights in the wheat, and they got so hungry they almost died. But to come out was certain death. "What's the good of deserting," they said, "if we're going to die here like dogs?" Just then a fiery dragon came flying through the air, stopped in the wheat field, and asked them why they were hiding there. "We're three soldiers," they said, "and we've deserted because the pay was too low. And now we'll die of hunger if we stay here, and die on the gallows if we come out." "If you promise to serve me for seven years," said the dragon, "I'll carry you right over the army and no one will catch you." "We have no choice," they said. "It's a deal." Thereupon the dragon picked them up in its claws, carried them over the army, and put them down on the ground far away.

Now this dragon was none other than the Devil. He gave each of them a little whip and said: "Just swish it and snap it, and all the money you could wish for will come popping out of the ground, and you'll only have to pick it up. You'll be able to live like lords, keep horses, and ride in carriages. But at the end of seven years you'll belong to me." Then he held a book in front of them, and all three had to sign. "But before I take you away," he added, "I'll give you a last chance. I'll ask you a riddle. If you guess the answer, you'll be free, and I'll have no further power over you." With that, the dragon flew away, and they started off with their little whips. There was plenty of money now, so they went about seeing the world, had their clothes made by the best tailors, lived in comfort and luxury, rode horses, kept carriages, ate and drank. But they did nothing wicked.

The time passed quickly for the three soldiers, and as the seven years were drawing to a close, a black fear came over two of them, but the third took it lightly. "Don't worry, brothers," he said. "I know a thing or two. I'll guess the riddle." They went out into the fields and sat there, two of them looking very gloomy. An old woman came along and, seeing two of them so dejected, asked them what was wrong. "What do you care?" they said. "You can't help us." "Who knows?" she said. "Tell me all about it." So they told her how they had served the Devil for almost seven years, how they had money to burn because they'd sold themselves to him, and how, when the seven years were over, he was coming to get them and would take them away unless they could answer a riddle. "There's only one way," said the old woman. "One of you must go into the forest. You will come to a fallen rock that looks like a hut. If you go in, you will find help." "A lot of good that will do us," thought the two dejected ones, and stayed where they were, but the cheerful one stood up and went to the rock hut. An old, old woman was sitting inside. She was the Devil's grandmother, and she asked him where he came from and what he wanted. He told her the whole story, and because she liked him she was moved to pity and promised to help him. Lifting a big stone that sealed off the cellar, she said: "Hide in there. You'll hear everything that's said. Just sit still and don't move. When the dragon comes home, I'll ask him about the riddle. He tells me everything. Listen carefully to his answer." At midnight the dragon came flying in and asked for his dinner. His grandmother set the table and brought food and drink. That put him in a good humor and they ate and drank together. She asked him if he'd had a good day and how many souls he'd snared. "Not so many," was his answer. "But I caught three soldiers. At least I'm sure of them." "Oh, three soldiers," she said. "Don't be too sure. They may still give you the slip."

"Don't make me laugh!" said the Devil. "Tomorrow I'll give them a last chance, I'll ask them a riddle, but they'll never guess the answer." "What is this riddle?" "Listen and I'll tell you. In the great North Sea there's a dead rabbit-fish—that will be their roast. And a whale's rib—that will be their silver spoon. And a hollow horse's hoof—that will be their wineglass." When the Devil had gone to bed, his grandmother lifted up the stone and let the soldier out. "Did you pay close attention?" she asked him. "Oh yes," he said. "I heard every bit of it and I'll know what to do." She let him out through the window, and he hurried back to his friends by a different path. When he told them how the Devil's grandmother had hoodwinked the Devil into blabbing out the answer to his riddle, the others cheered up and all three were in the best of spirits. They took their whips and whipped up so much money that the coins went bouncing about on the ground.

When the seven years were completely over, the Devil came to them with his book, showed them their signatures, and said: "Now I'm going to take you away with me to hell. When you get there, you're going to have a meal. If you can guess what kind of roast you'll get to eat, you'll be free. What's more, I'll let you keep your little whips." The first soldier replied: "In the great North Sea there's a dead rabbit-fish—that will be the roast." The Devil was furious. "Hmm, hmm, hmm," he grumbled. Then he asked the second soldier: "And what will be your spoon?" "The rib of a whale will be our silver spoon." The Devil made a sour face and again grumbled: "Hmm, hmm, hmm." Then he asked the third soldier: "Do you also know what will be your wineglass?" "An old horse's hoof will be our wineglass." At that, the Devil flew away with a loud cry, for he had lost his power over them. They kept their little whips and whipped up as much money as they wanted and lived happily until they died.

126

Faithful Ferdinand and
Faithless Ferdinand

ONCE THERE WERE a man and his wife who had no children as long as they were rich, but when they lost their money a little boy was born to them. They couldn't find a godfather for the child, so the husband went to see if he could find one in the next village. On the way he met a beggar who asked him where he was going, and he said he was trying to find a godfather, because he was poor and no one wanted to stand godfather to his child. "Well," said the beggar, "you're poor and I'm poor, so I'll be the godfather. But I'm so poor I won't be able to give the child anything. Go home and tell the midwife to bring the child to the church." When they all got to the church, the beggar was already there, and he named the child Faithful Ferdinand.

As they were leaving the church, the beggar said: "Now go home. I can't make you any presents, and you mustn't make me any either." But he handed the midwife a key, saying: "Give it to the child's father and tell him to keep it till the boy is fourteen. Then send the boy out on the heath. There he will find a castle. The key will fit the castle gate and everything that's inside will belong to him."

When the boy was seven and had grown to be quite big, he went out to play with some children. The others all bragged about the presents their godfathers had given them, but he couldn't say a thing. He went home in tears and asked his father: "Didn't I get anything from my godfather?" "Oh yes," said the father. "He gave you a key. If there's a castle on the heath, go and open it." So he went to the heath, but there was no sign of a castle. After seven more years, when he was fourteen, he went again, and this time there was a castle on the heath. When he opened the door, there was nothing inside but a white horse. The boy was so glad to have a horse that he swung himself up on the horse's back and galloped home to his father. "Look!" he cried. "I've got a white horse. I'm going to travel."

So he started out and when he had gone a little way he saw a pen lying in the road. At first he was going to pick it up, but then he thought to himself: "What's the use? I'm sure to find a pen where I'm going, if I need one." As he was riding away, a voice from behind him called: "Faithful Ferdinand, take it with you." He looked around and couldn't see anyone, but he went back and picked up the pen. When he had ridden another little while, he came to the sea. A fish was lying on the shore, panting and gasping for air. "Wait a second, dear fish," said Faithful Ferdinand, "and I'll come and help you." Whereupon he picked him up by the tail and threw him back into the water. A moment later the fish stuck his head out and said: "For helping me out of the mud, I'm going to give you a flute. If ever you're in trouble, play it and I'll come to your help, and if you ever drop anything in this sea, play the flute and I'll hand it out to you." The boy rode on, and soon a man came along who asked him where he was going. "To the next town." "What's your name?" "Faithful Ferdinand." "Then we have almost the same name. Mine is Faithless Ferdinand." So they rode to the next town together and stopped at an inn.

Now the trouble was that Faithless Ferdinand knew everything the other Ferdinand thought and everything he was planning to do. He knew because he was skilled in all the black arts. There happened to be a lovely young girl working at the inn, and she had a bright face and a fine bearing. She fell in love with Faithful Ferdinand, for he was very handsome, and asked him where he was going. "Oh, I'm just traveling around." "Why not stay here?" she suggested. "The king of this country wants to engage a servant or an outrider. You could go to work for him." Faithful Ferdinand said he couldn't bring himself to ask for employment, but the girl replied: "Oh, I'll attend to that." And true enough, she went straight to the king and told him she knew of a perfect servant for him. The king was delighted. He sent for Faithful Ferdinand and wanted to take him on as a servant. But Ferdinand preferred to serve as an outrider, because he couldn't bear to be parted from his horse, so the king took him on as an outrider. When Faithless Ferdinand heard the news, he said to the girl: "What's this? Helping him and not me?" "Not at all," said the girl,

"I'll help you too." She thought to herself: "I'd better not get that man down on me, for he's not to be trusted." So she went to the king and said she had a servant for him, and the king engaged him.

Every morning when Faithless Ferdinand dressed the king, the king moaned: "Oh, if only my beloved could be here with me!" Faithless Ferdinand had a grudge against Faithful Ferdinand, so when he heard the king's moaning, he said: "You've got an outrider. Send him in search of her, and if he doesn't bring her back to you, cut his head off." The king sent for Faithful Ferdinand and said: "In such and such a place there's a princess, whom I love. I want you to bring her here. If you don't, you must die."

Faithful Ferdinand went to the stable where he kept his white horse, and he wept and lamented: "Oh, how unhappy I am!" Then someone spoke behind him: "Why are you crying, Faithful Ferdinand?" He looked around, but there was no one there, and he kept on lamenting: "Oh, my dear little white horse, I shall have to leave you, for I'm surely going to die." The voice spoke again: "Why are you crying, Faithful Ferdinand?" And he saw it was the white horse speaking to him. "Is that you, my little white horse?" he asked. "You can talk?" And he told him the story: "I have to go to such and such a place, and bring back the princess the king loves. But how am I to do it? Can you tell me?" The white horse replied: "Go to the king and tell him you can do it if he gives you what you need, a ship full of meat and a ship full of bread. There are big giants on the sea, and they'll trample you unless you bring them meat. And there are big birds that will peck your eyes out unless you bring them bread.

The king commanded all the butchers in the country to slaughter and all the bakers to bake until the ships were full. When they were loaded, the little white horse said to Faithful Ferdinand: "Now climb up on my back and take me on board with you. When you see the giants you must say:

> 'Gently, gently, my dear giants!
> Don't go thinking I forgot you.
> Look and see what I have brought you.'

And when you see the birds, you must say:

> 'Gently, gently, my dear birds,
> Don't go thinking I forgot you.
> Look and see what I have brought you.'

Then they won't hurt you, and the giants will be very helpful. Take a few of them with you to the castle. The princess will be lying there asleep, but you mustn't wake her. Have the giants pick up her bed with her in it and carry her to the ship."

Everything happened just as the little white horse had said: Faithful Ferdinand gave the giants and the birds what he had brought along for them. The giants were friendly after that, and they carried the princess in her bed to the king. But when she woke up she said she couldn't live without her writings, which had been left behind in the castle. Again at the instigation of Faithless Ferdinand the king sent for Faithful Ferdinand and said: "You must go and get the writings from the castle. If you don't, you will die."

Faithful Ferdinand went to the stable and wept: "Oh, my dear little white horse," he said. "I have to go away again. What shall we do?" The white horse told him to have the ships loaded the same as before and everything happened as it had the first time. The meat and the bread stilled the hunger of the giants and the birds, and calmed them down. When they reached the castle, the white horse told him to go in. "The writings are on the table in the princess's bedchamber," he said. Faithful Ferdinand went in and took them. As they were crossing the sea, he dropped his pen in the water, and the white horse said: "This time I can't help you." But Faithful Ferdinand remembered the flute and began to play, and the fish came up with the pen in its mouth and held it out to him. Then he brought the writings to the castle and the wedding was celebrated.

But the queen didn't love the king, for he had no nose. She loved Faithful Ferdinand. One day when all the courtiers were gathered together, she told them she knew some tricks. For instance, she could cut somebody's head off and put it back on again. Would one of them like to try it? Nobody wanted to be first, but once more at the instigation of Faithless Ferdinand, Faithful Ferdinand was chosen. She cut his head off and put it back on. It healed up right away, and nothing was any different except for his neck, which looked as if it had a red thread around it. "Where did you learn that, my dear?" the king asked. "Oh," she said. "It's just a little trick. Shall I try it on you?" "Oh yes!" he cried. So she cut off his head, but she didn't put it back on. She pretended there was something wrong with it and it wouldn't stick. So the king was buried and she married Faithful Ferdinand.

Once when Faithful Ferdinand was out riding his white horse—for he never rode any other—the horse told him to go to such and such a heath and gallop around it three times. When he had done that, the white horse stood up on its hind legs and turned into a prince.

127

The Cast-iron Stove

IN THE DAYS when wishing still helped, an old witch with her magic imprisoned a prince in a cast-iron stove deep in the forest. There he stayed for many years and no one could set him free. One day a princess got lost in the forest and couldn't find the way back to her father's kingdom. After wandering about for nine days, she caught sight of the cast-iron stove and a voice from inside it asked her: "Where have you come from and where are you going?" She replied: "I'm lost and I can't find the way back to my father's kingdom." The voice from the stove said: "I'll see that you get home in no time if you promise to do what I ask. My father is a greater king than yours, and I want you to marry me."

That gave her a turn. "Good Lord," she thought, "what will I do with a cast-iron stove?" But she wanted very much to go home to her father, so she promised to do as he asked, and he said: "You must come back with a knife and scrape a hole in the iron." Then he gave her a companion who said nothing, but walked beside her and brought her home in two hours. There was great rejoicing in the palace when the princess got back. The old king fell on her neck and kissed her, but she was very sad. "Dear father," she said, "what a time I've had! I'd never have got out of that big wild forest if I hadn't come across a cast-iron stove and promised to go back and set it free and marry it." The king was so horrified he almost fainted, for he had only one daughter. They talked it over and finally decided to send the miller's beautiful daughter instead. They took her to the place, gave her a knife, and told her to scrape at the cast-iron stove. She scraped for twenty-four hours, but none of the iron came off. At dawn a voice came from the stove: "I think the day is breaking." And she replied: "I think so too. That clatter must be my father's mill." "In that case, you're a miller's daughter. Go straight home and tell them to send the king's daughter here." She went back to the palace and told the king that whoever it was out there didn't want her, he wanted the king's daughter.

The old king was horrified and his daughter burst into tears. But they still had a swineherd's daughter, who was even more beautiful than the miller's daughter, and they decided to pay her to go out to the cast-iron stove instead of the king's daughter. So she was taken to the place, and she too scraped for twenty-four hours, but none of the iron came off. At dawn a voice came from the stove: "I think the day is breaking." And she replied: "I think so too. That must be my father blowing his horn." "Then you're a swineherd's daughter. Go straight home and tell them to send the king's daughter here. Tell her I'll do as I promised, but if she doesn't come the whole kingdom will be destroyed and no stone will be left standing on another."

When the king's daughter heard that, she began to cry. There was no help for it, she had to keep her promise. She took leave of her father, put a knife in her pocket, and went to the cast-iron stove in the forest. When she got there, she began to scrape. The iron gave way, and in two hours she had scraped a small hole. She looked in and saw a beautiful young man, heavens above! so radiant with gold and jewels that her soul delighted in him. She went on scraping until the hole was big enough for him to get through, and then he came out. "You are mine and I am yours," he said. "You are my betrothed and you have set me free." He wanted to take her home with him to his kingdom, but she asked leave to say good-bye to her father, and he granted it, but said: "You must say no more than three words to your father, then you must come back." She went home, but she said more than three words to her father. Instantly, the cast-iron stove vanished and was carried far away, over glass mountains and sharp swords, but the prince had been set free, and he wasn't shut up in it any more.

Then she said good-bye to her father and took some money with her, but not much. She went back to the forest and looked for the cast-iron stove, but it was nowhere to be found. Nine days she searched, and by then she was so hungry she didn't know what to do, for she had nothing left to eat. When evening came, she climbed a small tree, meaning to spend the night there, for she was afraid of the wild beasts. At midnight she saw a little light in the distance and thought: "Oh, perhaps I'm saved." She climbed down from the tree and walked in the direction of the light, praying as she went. Finally she came to a little old house with a lot of grass growing around it and a little pile of wood out in front. "My goodness," she thought to herself. "What kind of place have I come to now?" She looked through the window and there was no one inside except a fat toad with some little ones, but there was also a table spread with wine and roast meat, and the plates and cups were of silver. She took heart and knocked at the door. The fat toad cried out:

> "Little green maid
> Perched on a log,
> Hobgoblin's dog,
> Wobblin' goblin,
> Quick, go and see
> What that knocking can be."

At that a little toad came and opened the door for her. When she went in, they all bade her welcome and made her sit down. "Where have you come from and where are you going?" they asked. She told them everything that had happened and how, because she had disobeyed the prince's orders to say no more than three words, the stove was gone and the prince too. "And now," she said, "I'm going to journey over hill and dale and search until I find him." At that the fat old toad said:

> "Little green maid
> Perched on a log,
> Hobgoblin's dog,
> Wobblin' goblin,
> That box you see,
> Bring it here to me."

When the little toad had brought her the box, they gave the princess food and drink and took her to a lovely made-up bed, as soft as silk and satin, and she lay down and slept the sleep of the just. When she got up next morning, the old toad gave her three needles out of the big box. "You'll need them," it said, "for you will have to cross a high glass mountain and three sharp swords and a great water, and if you manage to do all that you will get your loved one back again." And it gave her three big needles, a plow wheel, and three nuts.

The princess started on her journey, and when she got to the smooth glass mountain she stuck the three needles into the glass, first behind her feet and then, on the downward slope, ahead of them. That way she managed to get across and when she came to the other side she hid them in a place she took good note of. When she came to the three swords, she got up on her plow wheel and rolled over them. Last she came to the great water, and after sailing across it, arrived at a big, beautiful castle. She went in and introduced herself as a poor girl in need of work, for she knew that the prince she had freed from the cast-iron stove in the great forest was inside. So she was taken on as a kitchen maid at a low wage.

Now the prince had already chosen another girl and he was going to marry her, for he thought the princess had long been dead. In the evening, when the kitchen maid had finished washing up, she put her hand in her pocket and found the three nuts the old toad have given her. She cracked one with her teeth, meaning to eat the kernel, but what do you know!—there was a magnificent queenly dress inside. When the bride heard about it, she came and asked for the dress and offered to buy it and said a kitchen maid had no need for such a dress. "No," she replied. "I won't sell it, but you can have it on one condition, that you let me spend a night in the bridegroom's bed-chamber." The bride consented, because the dress was so beautiful and she had none like it. That evening she said to her betrothed: "That stupid girl wants to spend the night in your room." "If you don't mind," he said, "neither do I." But she gave him a glass of wine into which she had mixed a sleeping potion. So the kitchen maid and the prince went into the bedchamber and he slept so soundly she couldn't wake him. She wept all night and lamented: "I rescued you from the great wild forest and the cast-iron stove. I searched for you and crossed a glass mountain, three sharp swords, and a great water before I found you, and now you won't listen to me." The servants were sitting outside the door. They heard her weep all night and told their master about it in the morning. Next evening when she had finished washing up, she cracked the second nut with her teeth, and the dress inside was more beautiful than the first. When the bride saw it, she wanted to buy it, but the kitchen maid wouldn't take money and asked leave to spend a second night in the bridegroom's bedchamber. But the bride gave him a sleeping potion and he slept so soundly he couldn't hear a thing. The kitchen maid wept all night and lamented: "I rescued you from a forest and a cast-iron stove. I searched for you and crossed a glass mountain, three sharp swords, and a great water before I found you, and now you won't listen to me." The servants were sitting outside the door. They heard her weep all night and told their master about it in the morning. The third evening when she had finished washing up, she cracked the third nut with her teeth and there was a still more beautiful dress inside, woven of pure gold. When the bride saw it, she wanted it, but the kitchen maid said no, not unless she could spend a third night in the prince's bedchamber. This time the prince took good care to pour the sleeping potion away. When she began to weep and lament: "O my dearest, I saved you from the cruel wild forest and the cast-iron stove," the prince jumped up and said: "You are the right bride. You are mine and I am yours." That same night he got into a carriage with her, and they took the false bride's clothes away so she couldn't get up out of bed. When they came to the great water, they sailed across, and when they came to the three sharp swords they rode over them on the plow wheel, and when they came to the glass mountain they stuck the three needles into it. Finally they reached the little old house, but when they went in, it was a big castle. The toads had been set free, they were all princes and princesses now, and they were very happy. The wedding feast was held and they stayed in the castle, which was much bigger than her father's. But the old man complained about living alone, so they drove to his castle and brought him back to stay with them. So then they had two kingdoms and lived in happy matrimony.

> There's a mouse. Now it's gone.
> And my story's done.

128
The Lazy Spinner

ONCE THERE WAS a man who lived in a village with his wife, and the wife was so lazy she never wanted to work. When her husband gave her some spinning to do, she never finished it, and if she did spin some yarn, she didn't wind it, but left it all in a tangle. When her husband scolded her, she always had an answer ready. "How can I wind it without a reel?" she cried. "Go and get some wood in the forest and make me one." "If that's all that's bothering you," said the husband, "I'll go right out to the forest and you'll soon have your reel." At that she took fright. Why, once he had the wood, he'd make a reel and then she'd have to wind off her yarn and start spinning again. She thought it over, and soon she had a good idea. She secretly followed her husband to the forest, and when he climbed a tree to choose the wood and cut it, she crept into the bushes at the foot of the tree, where he couldn't see her, and cried out:

> "He who cuts wood for reels shall die,
>   And she who winds shall perish."

When he heard that, the man lowered his ax for a while. He didn't know what to think. "Rubbish!" he said finally. "What can it have been? It must have been a ringing in my ears. Nothing to worry about." Again he raised his ax and was going to strike, and again he heard the voice from below:

> "He who cuts wood for reels shall die,
>   And she who winds shall perish."

He stopped in terror and pondered some more. But after a while he took courage and for the third time raised his ax. He was just going to chop when for the third time he heard the voice from below, now louder than ever:

> "He who cuts wood for reels shall die,
>   And she who winds shall perish."

With that he had had enough, the heart had gone out of him. He climbed down in haste and started for home. His wife took a different path and ran as fast as she could, so as to get there before him. When he came in, she pretended nothing had happened, and asked innocently: "Well, have you brought a nice piece of wood to make me a reel?" "No," he said. "I'm afraid there won't be any winding." He told her what had happened in the forest and after that he never asked her to wind any yarn.

Nevertheless, the husband was soon complaining again about the disorder in the house. "Wife," he said one day, "it's a shame to have all that spun yarn lying there in a tangle." "All right," she said. "Here's what we'll do. Seeing we can't get a reel, you go up in the loft and I'll stay down here. I'll throw the tangle up to you and you throw it back. That way we'll get skeins." "Good idea," said the husband. So they tossed the yarn back and forth, and when they had finished, he said: "Now the yarn is in skeins, but it still needs to be boiled." That had her worried again. "Oh yes," she said, "we'll boil it first thing in the morning." But secretly she was planning a new trick. Early in the morning she got up, made a fire and put the caldron on, but instead of the yarn she threw in a ball of flax and let it boil. Then she went to her husband, who was still lying in bed, and said: "I have to go out. Get up and attend to the yarn that's in the caldron on the fire. But be quick about it, because if you're not down there attending to it when the cock crows, the yarn will turn into flax." The man was wide awake and he didn't want anything to go wrong, so he got up as fast as he could and went to the kitchen. But when he looked into the caldron, he saw to his horror that there was nothing in it but a big ball of flax. The poor man didn't say a word to his wife. He thought he was to blame for being too slow, and from that time on he never mentioned yarn or spinning again. You'll have to admit that she was a hateful woman.

129
The Four Artful Brothers

THERE WAS ONCE a poor man who had four sons, and when they were grown to manhood he said to them: "You will have to go out into the world, for I have nothing to give you. Be on your way, travel to foreign parts, learn a trade each one of you, and see what you can make of yourselves." The four brothers took leave of their father and went out the town gate together. When they had gone a little way, they came to a crossing, with roads leading in four different directions. "Here we must part," said the eldest. "But let us meet again on this spot exactly four years from today, and in the meantime try our luck."

So off they went, each in a different direction. The eldest met a man who asked him where he was going and what his plans were. "I'm going to learn a trade," he replied. "Come with me," said the man, "and learn to be a thief." "No," he said. "That doesn't pass as an honest trade nowadays. I'd only find myself dangling from the end of a rope." "Oh, you needn't worry about the gallows," said the man. "I'll only teach you how to take things that no one else can get hold of and how to do it without ever being found out." That convinced him. He went with the man and became a skilled thief, so adroit that nothing he wanted was safe from him. The second brother met a man who also asked him what trade he had in mind. "I haven't decided yet," he replied. "Then come with me and learn to be a stargazer. There's no better trade, for nothing remains hidden from you." That appealed to him and he became so proficient a stargazer that when his apprenticeship was over and he was about to move on, his master gave him a telescope, saying: "With this you will be able to see everything that happens on earth or in the heavens; nothing can remain hidden from you." A hunter took the third brother on as an apprentice and taught him all the tricks of the trade so thoroughly that he became a skilled hunter. As a farewell gift his master gave him a gun, saying: "It never misses. You will be sure to hit whatever you aim at."

The youngest brother also met a man who questioned him about his plans and asked him: "Wouldn't you like to become a tailor?" "I doubt it," said the boy. "Who wants to sit stooped over from morning to night, plying the needle and flatiron day in and day out?" "You're only showing your ignorance," said the man. "With me you would learn tailoring of a different kind, which, in addition to being pleasant and dignified, may bring you great honor." That convinced him, so he went with the man and learned his craft from A to Z. As a farewell present, the man gave him a needle, saying: "With this you will be able to mend anything whatsoever, even it it's as soft as an egg or as hard as steel; two pieces will become as one, and no seam will be visible."

When the four years were over, the four brothers met at the crossroads, hugged and kissed each other, and went home to their father. "Well, well," said the father happily, "so the wind has blown you back to me." They told him about their lives and how each of them had learned a particular trade. "All right," said the father, "suppose I put you to the test and see what you can do." It so happened that they were sitting under a big tree in front of the house. He looked up and said to his second son: "There's a chaffinch's nest up there in a fork of that tree. Tell me how many eggs are in it." The stargazer took his telescope, looked up, and said: "Five." Then the father said to the eldest son: "Bring down the eggs without disturbing the mother bird that's hatching them." The artful thief climbed up and took the five eggs out from under the mother bird, who noticed nothing and went on calmly sitting there. Then he brought them to his father, who set them down on the table, one in each corner and the fifth in the middle, and said to the hunter: "Now I want you to break all five eggs in two with one shot." The hunter took aim, and he must have had some of that gunpowder that shoots around corners, for just as his father had demanded, he broke all five eggs in two with one shot. "Now it's your turn," said the father to the fourth son. "I want you to mend the eggs and the chicks inside so the shot won't have harmed them." The tailor took his needle and repaired the damage just as his father had demanded. When he had finished, the thief had to carry the eggs up the tree and put them back under the mother hen without her noticing. The mother bird finished hatching them and a few days later the chicks came crawling out of their shells. Each one of them had a red line around its neck where the tailor had sewn it together. "Amazing!" said the old man. "You've certainly made good use of your time and learned some fine things. I don't know which of you deserves the most praise. We'll see about that when you get a chance to apply your skills."

A few weeks later, the king's daughter was carried off by a dragon and the whole country was thrown into a turmoil. The king worried day and night and made it known that the man who rescued his daughter and brought her back should have her for his wife. The four brothers said to one another: "This is our chance to show what we can do," and they decided to go and rescue the king's daughter. "I'll soon know where she is," said the stargazer. He looked through his telescope and said, "I see her. She's sitting on a rock in the sea, far far away, and the dragon is right there guarding her." So he went to the king and asked for a ship for himself and his brothers, and they sailed across the sea until they came to the rock. There sat the king's daughter, and the dragon was lying asleep with his head in her lap. "I can't shoot," said the hunter, "for I'd kill the beautiful princess at the same time." "Then I'll see what I can do," said the thief. He crept up and stole her out from under the dragon, and he did it so deftly and quietly that the monster didn't notice a thing and went on snoring. Joyfully they ran back to the ship with her and headed for the open sea. But the dragon, who had waked up and found the king's daughter gone, pursued them and came flying through the air, fuming and snorting. He hovered over the ship and was just getting ready to swoop down, when the hunter took his gun and shot him straight through the heart. The dragon fell down dead, but his body was so big and heavy that it smashed the whole ship to pieces. Luckily the brothers managed to grab hold of a few planks, which kept them and the princess afloat on the endless waters. They were in bad trouble, but without wasting a minute the tailor took his miraculous needle and sewed the planks together with a few big stitches. Then he sat down on his raft, collected the remaining parts of the ship and sewed them together so skillfully that the ship was soon ready for use and they could all sail safely home.

When the king saw his daughter again, he was overjoyed and said to the four brothers: "One of you shall have her for his wife, but you will have to decide among yourselves which it is to be." At that a furious quarrel broke out, for each had his claim. The stargazer said: "If I hadn't seen the king's daughter, all your skills would have been useless. Therefore she's mine." The thief said: "A lot of good your seeing her would have done if I hadn't stolen her out from under the dragon. Therefore she's mine." The hunter said: "The monster would have torn you all to pieces and the king's daughter with you, if my bullet hadn't killed it. Therefore she's mine." The tailor said: "And if I hadn't repaired the ship with my needle, you'd all have been miserably drowned. Therefore she's mine." The king replied: "You all have equal claims, but since you can't all marry my daughter, none of you shall have her, but I will reward you each with half a kingdom." That suited the brothers, and they said: "At least we shall have nothing to quarrel about." So each of them received half a kingdom and they lived happily with their father as long as it pleased God.

130

One-eye, Two-eyes, and Three-eyes

THERE WAS ONCE a woman who had three daughters, the eldest of whom was called One-eye, because she had only a single eye in the middle of her forehead, the second Two-eyes, because she had two eyes like other girls, and the youngest Three-eyes, because she had three eyes, two on the sides and the third in the middle of her forehead. As Two-eyes looked no different from other people, her sisters and her mother hated her. They said to her: "You with your two

eyes are no better than the common herd. You're not one of us."
They pushed her around, gave her raggedy old hand-me-downs to
wear and nothing but their leavings to eat, and did everything they
could to make her miserable.

One day Two-eyes was sent out to the meadow to look after the
goat, though her sisters hadn't given her enough to eat and she was
still very hungry. She sat down on a tuft of grass and began to cry,
and she cried so hard that two little rivulets ran down her cheeks.
When she looked up in her misery, a woman was standing there.
"Why are you crying, Two-eyes?" she asked. "How can I help it?"
said Two-eyes. "My mother and my two sisters hate me because I
have two eyes like other people. They make me stand in the corner,
they give me raggedy old hand-me-downs to wear and nothing but
their leavings to eat. They gave me so little today that I'm still starving." The wise woman said: "Two-eyes, wipe your tears. I'm going
to tell you something that will stop you from ever being hungry
again. All you have to do is say these words to your goat:

> 'Little goat, bleat,
> Bring me a table
> With good things to eat,'

and a neatly set table will appear with the finest food on it and you'll
be able to eat as much as you like. Then when you've had enough
and you don't need the table any more, just say:

> 'Little goat, bleat,
> Take the table away,
> I've had all I can eat,'

and the table will vanish." With that, the Wise Woman left her, and
Two-eyes thought: "I'll try it out this minute and see if she was telling the truth, for I'm so dreadfully hungry." So she said:

> "Little goat, bleat,
> Bring me a table
> With good things to eat."

And no sooner had she spoken than a table laid with a white tablecloth was standing there, and on it there was a plate, with a knife and
a fork and a silver spoon, and the finest dishes were set on it, all hot
and steaming, as if they had just come from the kitchen. Two-eyes
said the shortest prayer she knew: "Dear God, be with us always.

Amen," and fell to. She enjoyed every mouthful, and when she had
had enough, she said the words the Wise Woman had taught her:

> "Little goat, bleat,
> Take the table away,
> I've had all I can eat."

The table and everything on it vanished instantly. Two-eyes was
very happy. "My," she said, "what a lovely table!"

That evening when she got home with her goat, she found some
food in an earthenware bowl that her sisters had set out for her, but
she didn't touch it. The next day she went out again with her goat
and didn't touch the few crumbs her sisters gave her. The first time
and the second time they paid no attention, but when the same thing
happened every day they couldn't help noticing. "There's something
strange going on," they said. "Two-eyes always used to eat up everything we gave her, and now she leaves her food untouched. She must
have found some other way." Bent on discovering the truth, they decided that when Two-eyes took the goat to pasture One-eye should
go along and watch to see what she did and whether anyone brought
her food and drink.

As Two-eyes was starting out, One-eye stepped up to her and said:
"I think I'll go out to the meadow with you to make sure the goat is
well grazed and properly taken care of." But Two-eyes knew what
One-eye had in mind. She drove the goat into the tall grass and said:
"Come, One-eye, let's sit down and I'll sing you a song." One-eye
sat down. The unaccustomed walk and the heat of the sun had made
her tired, and Two-eyes sang over and over again:

> "One-eye, are you awake?
> One-eye, are you asleep?"

One-eye closed her one eye and fell asleep. When Two-eyes saw that
One-eye was asleep and couldn't spy on her, she said:

> "Little goat, bleat,
> Bring me a table
> With good things to eat,"

and sat down at her table, and ate and drank till she had enough, and
then she cried out:

> "Little goat, bleat,
> Take the table away,
> I've had all I can eat,"

and in an instant everything had vanished. Then Two-eyes woke One-eye, and said: "One-eye, you were going to take care of the goat, and look how you do it. You fall asleep. Why, the goat could have run God knows where. Come, let's go home." And home they went. Again Two-eyes left her bowl untouched, but One-eye couldn't tell her mother why she didn't eat, and the only excuse she could make for herself was: "I fell asleep out there."

The next day the mother said to Three-eyes: "This time I want you to go and see if Two-eyes eats anything out there and if someone brings her food and drink, because she must be eating and drinking in secret." So Three-eyes went over to Two-eyes and said: "I think I'll go with you to make sure the goat is well grazed and properly taken care of." But Two-eyes knew what Three-eyes had in mind. She drove the goat into the tall grass and said: "Come, Three-eyes, let's go and sit down. I'll sing you a song." Three-eyes sat down. The walk and the heat of the sun had made her tired, and Two-eyes began to sing the same song as before:

"Three-eyes, are you awake?"

But instead of singing

"Three-eyes, are you asleep?"

as she should have, she was careless and sang:

"Two-eyes, are you asleep?"

So that what she kept singing was:

"Three-eyes, are you awake?
Two-eyes, are you asleep?"

So two of Three-eyes' eyes closed and fell asleep, but the third didn't, because it wasn't mentioned in the song. Three-eyes closed her third eye as if it too were asleep, but that was only a trick, and it blinked and saw everything that went on.

When Two-eyes thought Three-eyes was sound asleep, she said her little rhyme:

"Little goat, bleat."
Bring me a table
With good things to eat."

And when she had eaten and drunk to her heart's content, she sent the table away again, saying:

> "Little goat, bleat,
> Take the table away,
> I've had all I can eat."

And Three-eyes had seen it all. Then Two-eyes went and woke her up and said: "Goodness, Three-eyes, have you been asleep? Is that how you take care of the goat? Come, let's go home." Home they went, and again Two-eyes ate nothing, and Three-eyes said to her mother: "Now I know why the haughty thing doesn't eat. She says to the goat:

> 'Little goat, bleat,
> Bring me a table
> With good things to eat,'

and before you know it a table is standing there spread with the finest food, much better than we have here, and when she's had enough, she says:

> 'Little goat, bleat,
> Take the table away,
> I've had all I can eat,'

and then everything disappears. I saw it all. She put two of my eyes asleep with magic words, but luckily the one in the middle of my forehead stayed awake." At that the envious mother cried out: "What's this! You think you can have it better than we do? Well, you won't think so much longer." And she took the butcher knife and thrust it into the goat's heart, and it fell dead.

Two-eyes was overcome with grief. She went out to the meadow, sat down on her tuft of grass and wept bitter tears. Suddenly the Wise Woman was standing beside her. "Why are you crying, Two-eyes?" she asked. "Haven't I reason to cry?" she replied. "My mother has slaughtered the goat that brought me such nice things to eat, and now I'll be hungry and miserable again." The Wise Woman said: "Two-eyes, I will give you a piece of good advice. Get your sisters to give you the dead goat's entrails, then bury them outside the front door. They will bring you good fortune." Then she vanished. Two-eyes went home and said to her sisters: "Dear sisters, would you give me some of my goat? I won't ask you for any of the good parts. Just let me have the entrails." They laughed and said: "If the entrails are all you want, take them." Two-eyes took the entrails and that evening she quietly buried them outside the front door, just as the Wise Woman had advised her.

Next morning when they all woke up and went outside, a marvelous tree was growing there. It had silver leaves and golden fruit, and nothing in all the world could have been more splendid or more beautiful. They couldn't imagine how the tree had got there during the night. Only Two-eyes knew it had grown from the goat's entrails, because it was growing in the exact place where she had buried them. "Climb up, child," said the mother to One-eye, "and pick us some of the fruit." One-eye climbed the tree, but when she tried to pick a golden apple, the branch slipped out of her grasp. Time and time again the same thing happened, and try as she might she couldn't manage to pick a single apple. "Three-eyes," said the mother, "you climb up. You with your three eyes are sure to be more keen-sighted than your sister." One-eye slid down and Three-eyes climbed the tree. But she was no more nimble, and for all her keen sight, the golden apples escaped her. Finally the mother lost patience and climbed the tree herself, but she was no more able to grasp the fruit than One-eye and Three-eyes, and her hands kept clutching at the air. After a while Two-eyes spoke up: "Suppose I try. Maybe I'll have better luck." The sisters cried out: "You with your two eyes! How perfectly silly!" Nevertheless, Two-eyes climbed the tree, and far from recoiling from her, the golden apples met her hand halfway. She was able to pick as many as she pleased and when she climbed down her apron was full of them. Her mother took them, but instead of treating her better she and One-eye and Three-eyes were made so envious by Two-eyes' success in picking the fruit, that they dealt with her more harshly than ever.

It so happened that one day as they were standing at the foot of the tree, a young knight came by. "Two-eyes!" cried the sisters. "Hide or you'll disgrace us." Quick as a flash they picked up an empty barrel that happened to be standing near the tree and threw it over her, and they shoved the golden apples she had just picked under it too. When the knight came closer, he proved to be very handsome. He stopped to admire the splendid gold and silver tree and said to the two sisters: "Whom does this beautiful tree belong to? If anyone were to give me a branch from it, I'd give that person anything they wished in return." One-eye and Three-eyes said the tree belonged to them and undertook to break off a branch for him. They tried and tried, but in vain, for the branches and fruit shrank back from them every time they approached. At that the knight said: "If the tree belongs to you, it seems strange that you can't break off a part of it." They said again that the tree was theirs. But as they were speaking, Two-eyes, who was angry at One-eye and Three-eyes for not telling the truth, pushed a few of the golden apples out from under the barrel, and they rolled to the knight's feet. He was astonished at the sight and asked where they came from. One-eye and Three-eyes replied that there was another sister, who wasn't allowed to show herself because she had two eyes like ordinary people. But the knight insisted on seeing her and cried: "Two-eyes, come out!" Confidently, Two-eyes came out from under the barrel. The knight was amazed at her great beauty and said: "You, Two-eyes, I'm sure, can break off a branch of the tree for me." "Yes," said Two-eyes, "I believe I can, because it's my tree." She climbed up and had no trouble at all in breaking off a branch covered with fine silver leaves and golden fruit. She handed it to the knight, and said: "What shall I give you for it, Two-eyes?" "Dear me," said Two-eyes, "I've been suffering hunger and thirst, misery and privation from early morning to late at night. If you take me away with you and save me from all that, I shall be very happy." The knight lifted her up on his saddle and carried her off to his father's castle, where he gave her fine clothes and food and drink to her heart's content. He loved her so much that he married her, and the wedding was celebrated with great rejoicing.

When the handsome knight rode away with Two-eyes, the sisters envied her in bitter earnest. "But at least," they thought, "we still have the wonderful tree. Even if we can't pick the fruit, everyone will stop to look at it, and come in to see us, and sing its praises. Who knows what good fortune may lie in wait for us?" But next morning the tree had vanished and their hopes were dashed. And when Two-eyes looked out of her window, there to her great joy was the tree, for it had followed her.

Two-eyes lived happily for many years. One day two poor women came to the castle, begging for alms. Two-eyes looked into their faces and recognized her sisters One-eye and Three-eyes, who had become so poor they were obliged to wander from door to door, begging their daily bread. Two-eyes welcomed them and treated them kindly and cared for them, and with all their hearts they regretted the evil they had done their sister in their youth.

131

The Fair Katrinelya and Pif Paf Poltree

"GOOD DAY, FATHER HOLLOWTREE." "Thank you kindly, Pif Paf Poltree." "Could I marry your daughter?" "Oh yes, if Mother Milko, Brother Stiff-and-proud, Sister Cheesaleeze, and the fair Katrinelya are willing, then you may have her."

"But where is Mother Milko?"
"She's in the cow barn, milking the cow."

"Good day, Mother Milko." "Thank you kindly, Pif Paf Poltree." "Could I marry your daughter?" "Oh yes, if Father Hollowtree, Brother Stiff-and-proud, Sister Cheesaleeze, and the fair Katrinelya are willing, then you may have her."

"But where is Brother Stiff-and-proud?"
"He's in the woodshed, chopping wood."

"Good day, Brother Stiff-and-proud." "Thank you kindly, Pif Paf Poltree." "Could I marry your sister?" "Oh yes, if Father Hollowtree, Mother Milko, Sister Cheesaleeze, and the fair Katrinelya are willing, you may have her."

"But where is Sister Cheesaleeze?"
"She's in the garden picking peas."

"Good day, Sister Cheesaleeze." "Thank you kindly, Pif Paf Poltree." "Could I marry your sister?" "Oh yes, if Father Hollowtree,

Mother Milko, Brother Stiff-and-proud, and the fair Katrinelya are willing, then you may have her."

"But where is the fair Katrinelya?"
"She's in the parlor counting her pennies."

"Good day, fair Katrinelya." "Thank you kindly, Pif Paf Poltree." "Will you be my sweetheart?" "Oh yes, if Father Hollow Tree, Mother Milko, Brother Stiff-and-proud, and Sister Cheesaleeze are willing, then you may have me."

"Fair Katrinelya, how much dowry have you got?" "Fourteen pfennigs in cash, two and a half groschen in debts, half a pound of dried fruits, a handful of roots, and a handful of shoots.

"Isn't that a pretty plenty?
Isn't that a handsome dowry?

"Pif Paf Poltree, what is your trade? Are you a tailor?" "Better still." "A shoemaker?" "Better still." "A farmer?" "Better still." "A carpenter?" "Better still." "A blacksmith?" "Better still." "A miller?" "Better still." "Are you by any chance a broommaker?" "That's it. Now tell me, isn't that a fine trade?"

132

The Fox and the Horse

A PEASANT ONCE HAD a faithful horse, who had grown too old to work, and his master didn't want to feed him any more. "I really have no further use for you," he said, "but all the same I wish you well. If you have enough strength left to bring me a lion, I'll keep you, but for the time being, get out of my barn." With that he chased him out into the open. Sadly the horse went to the forest, looking for some measure of shelter from the weather, and there he met the fox, who asked him: "Why are you hanging your head and wandering around all alone?" "Alas," said the horse, "avarice and loyalty can't live under one roof. My master has forgotten all the services I've rendered him over the years, and now that I can't pull the plow he doesn't want to feed me any longer and he has sent me away." "Without a word of comfort?" asked the fox. "Cold comfort. He said he would keep me if I had enough strength left to bring him a lion. He knows I could never do that." "If that's the way it is," said the fox, "I'll help you. Just lie down, stretch out, and keep perfectly still, as if you were dead." The horse did as the fox bade him, and the fox went to the lion, who had his den not far away. "I know where there's a dead horse," he said. "Come with me and you'll have a fine meal." The lion followed him, and when they came to the horse, the fox said: "You wouldn't be very comfortable here. I've got an idea. I'll tie the horse to your tail. Then you can drag him to your den and eat him at your ease." The lion liked the idea. He went over to the horse and stood motionless to let the fox make the horse fast to him. But the fox tied the lion's legs together with the horse's tail, and he twisted and tied it so firmly that with all the strength in the world the lion couldn't have broken his bonds. When the fox had finished his work, he tapped the horse on the shoulder and said: "Pull, horse, pull." Quick as a flash the horse jumped up and dragged the lion away with him. The lion roared so loudly that all the birds in the forest fluttered into the air in terror, but the horse let him roar, and dragged him over field and furrow to his master's door. When the master saw that, he had a change of heart and said to the horse: "You shall stay here with me and be well treated." And he gave him as much as he wanted to eat until the day he died.

133

The Shoes That Were
Danced Through

THERE WAS ONCE a king who had twelve daughters, each more beautiful than the next. Their beds stood side by side, all in the same room, and after they went to bed the king locked and bolted the door. But in the morning when he opened the door, he saw that their shoes had been danced through, and no one was able to find out how this was possible. So the king made it known that anyone who found out where they went dancing could choose one of them for his wife and inherit the kingdom when he himself died, but that if anyone came forward and had not found out at the end of three days and three nights, he would lose his life. It wasn't long before a young prince presented himself and asked to try his luck. He was well received and that evening they led him to a room adjoining the princesses' bedchamber. There his bed was set up, and he was told to keep watch and find out where they went dancing. To make sure the princesses did nothing in secret and didn't go out some other way, the door of their room was left open. But the prince's eyelids became as heavy as lead, he fell asleep, and when he woke up in the morning all twelve princesses had been dancing, for their shoes were right there and the soles were worn thin. The same thing happened the second night and the third, and then the king had the prince's head cut off without mercy. And many more came and tried their luck, but they all lost their lives.

Now it so happened that a poor soldier, who because of his wounds could serve no longer, was going to the city where the king lived. On the way he met an old woman who asked him where he was going. "I hardly know myself," he said, and added in jest: "I wouldn't mind discovering where the king's daughters danced their shoes through, and getting to be king." "That's not very difficult," said the old woman. "Just don't drink the wine they bring you in the evening, and then pretend to be fast asleep." Then she gave him a cloak and said: "When you put this on, you will be invisible and you'll be able to follow the twelve princesses." Once he had this good advice, the soldier began to take the matter seriously. He screwed up his courage and went to the king, presenting himself as a suitor. He was received as well as the others and dressed in kingly clothes. That night he was taken to the room adjoining the princesses', and just as he was getting ready for bed, the eldest princess brought him a goblet of wine. But he had tied a sponge under his chin, and he let the wine run into it and didn't drink a single drop. Then he lay down, and after a little while he began to snore as if he were sound asleep. When the twelve princesses heard him, they laughed, and the eldest said: "There's another who could have done something better with his life." Thereupon they got up, opened cupboards and chests and boxes and took out splendid clothes. They went to their looking glasses and dressed, and hopped and skipped about, looking forward to the ball. Only the youngest said: "You're all so gay, but I don't know, I have a strange feeling, I'm sure something terrible is going to happen." "You're a silly goose," said the eldest. "You're always afraid. Have you forgotten how many princes have tried in vain? We wouldn't even have had to give this soldier a sleeping potion; he'd never have waked up, the clod." When they were all ready, they took a look at the soldier, but his eyes were closed tight, he didn't stir, and they felt perfectly safe. The eldest went to her bed and tapped on it. It sank into the ground, and they went down through the opening, one after another, the eldest in the lead. The soldier, who had seen everything, lost no time. He threw his cloak over his shoulders and went down behind the youngest. Halfway down the stairs he stepped on her dress just a little and she was frightened to death. "What's going on?" she cried. "Who's tugging at my dress?" "Don't be a fool," said the eldest. "You caught your dress on a nail." They all went down, and when they got to the bottom they were in a splendid avenue of trees. The leaves were all silver and they glittered and sparkled. The soldier thought to himself: "I'd better take some evidence." He broke off a branch and the tree let out a roar.

Again the youngest princess cried out: "Something's wrong! What was that noise?" But the eldest said: "They were firing a gun salute because we shall soon have set our princes free." Next they came to an avenue of trees where the leaves were of gold, and finally to a third, where they were pure diamond. He broke a branch from each kind, and both times there was such a roar that the youngest quaked with fear, but the eldest insisted it was gun salutes. On they went until they came to a great river. Twelve boats were drawn up at the bank, and in each boat sat a handsome prince, and they were all waiting for the twelve princesses. Each prince took a princess, and the soldier went on board with the youngest. "I don't know why," said the prince, "but the boat is much heavier today. I have to row with all my strength to make it move." "What can it be but the heat?" said the youngest princess. "I'm suffocating, myself."

On the other side of the river there was a beautiful, brightly lit palace, and from it lively drum and trumpet music could be heard. Once across the river they all went in, and every prince danced with his sweetheart. The invisible soldier danced too. Whenever one of the princesses picked up a goblet of wine, he drained it, and by the time she set her goblet to her lips, it was empty. At this the youngest princess took fright, but the eldest always managed to quiet her. They danced until three in the morning. Then all their shoes were worn through and they had to stop. The princes rowed them back across the river and this time the soldier sat in the front boat with the eldest. On the bank the princesses took leave of their princes and promised to come again the next night. When they reached the stairs, the soldier ran up ahead and got into his bed. By the time the twelve came dragging wearily in, he was snoring so loud that they could all hear him, and they said: "No need to worry about him." They took off their fine clothes and put them away, set their worn-out shoes under their beds, and lay down.

Next morning the soldier decided not to say anything, but to take another look at the strange goings-on, so he followed the princesses again on the second and third nights. Everything was the same as before. Both times they danced until their shoes were worn through. But the third time he took a goblet as evidence. When it came time for him to answer, he took the three branches and the goblet and went to the king. The twelve princesses stood behind the door and listened to hear what he would say. "Where," the king asked, "have my daughters been dancing their shoes through at night?" And he replied: "With twelve princes in an underground palace." And he told the king everything that had happened, and produced the evidence. The king sent for his daughters and asked them whether the soldier had told the truth, and seeing they were betrayed and that denying wouldn't help, they admitted everything. Then the king asked the soldier which princess he wished for his wife, and he answered: "I'm not young any more, so give me the eldest." The wedding was held that same day and the king promised that when he died the soldier would inherit the kingdom. As for the princes, the spell they were under was prolonged for as many nights as they had danced with the twelve girls.

134
The Six Servants

Long, long ago there lived an old queen who was a sorceress, and her daughter was the most beautiful girl under the sun. The old queen could think of nothing but ways of luring men to their doom. When a suitor came to her court, she said that anyone wanting to marry her daughter must first perform a task and that his life would be forfeited if he failed. Dazzled by the daughter's beauty, many young men tried their luck, but when they proved unable to perform the task the old woman set them, no mercy was shown: they had to kneel down and their heads were struck off. A prince heard of the maiden's great beauty and said to his father: "Let me go and sue for her hand." "Never!" said the king. "You would only be going to your death." At that the prince fell deathly ill and took to his bed. For seven years he lay there and no doctor could help him. When his father saw there was no hope, he was sad at heart. "Go and try your luck," he said to him. "I know of no other way to help you." When the son heard that, he rose from his bed. His health was restored, and he started happily on his way.

It so happened that as he was riding across a heath, he looked into the distance and saw something that looked like a big haystack. When he came closer, he saw it was the belly of a man who was lying on the ground, and now it looked like a small mountain. When the stout man caught sight of the traveler, he stood up and said: "If you need a servant, take me." The prince replied: "What can I do with a big lummox like you?" "Ho ho," said Stout, "you haven't seen a thing. When I really expand, I'm three thousand times bigger." "If that's the case," said the prince, "I can use you. Come with me." So Stout followed the prince, and after a while they saw a man lying on the ground with his ear to the turf. "What are you doing?" the prince asked him. "Listening," said the man. "And what are you listening to so intently?" "I'm listening to find out what's going on in the world, for nothing escapes my ears. I can even hear the grass grow." "Tell me," said the prince, "what's going on at the court of the old queen with the beautiful daughter?" "A suitor's head is being struck off. I hear the sword whistling through the air." "I can use you," said the prince. "Come with me." On they went, and after a while they saw a pair of feet. They saw a pair of legs too, but they couldn't see where they ended. When they had gone quite a distance, they came to the trunk, and finally to the head. "My goodness!" said the prince. "What a beanpole you are!" "Ho-ho," said the tall man, "you haven't seen a thing. When I really stretch, I'm three thousand times taller, taller than the highest mountain on earth. I'll be glad to serve you if you wish to take me on." "Come with me," said the prince. "I can use you." On they went and soon they saw a blind-folded man sitting beside the road. "Are your eyes so weak they can't stand the light?" the prince asked. "No," said the man. "I have to keep blindfolded because of my glance. It's so powerful that whatever I look at bursts into pieces. If I can be of any use to you, I'll be glad to serve you." "Come with me," said the prince. "I can use you." On they went and after a while they saw a man who was lying with the hot sun beating down on him, but he was shivering and shaking so that there wasn't a quiet spot on his whole body. "How can you shiver like that in the hot sun?" the prince asked. "Alas," said the man, "I have a contrary nature. The hotter it is the more I shiver, the frost goes right through my bones, and the colder it is the hotter I feel. In snow and ice I can't bear the heat, and in the middle of the fire I can't bear the cold." "You're a strange fellow," said the prince, "but if you'd like to serve me, come along." On they went, and soon they saw a man who was craning his long neck, peering in all directions and looking over mountains. "What are you looking for so intently?" the prince asked. The man replied: "My eyes are so sharp I can see beyond all the forests and fields and hills and valleys in the world." The prince replied: "Then come with me if you like. Someone like you was the one thing I lacked."

After a while the prince and his six servants came to the town where the old queen lived. He didn't tell her who he was, but he said: "I'm ready to perform any task you set me if you'll give me your beautiful daughter." The sorceress was glad to have snared such a handsome young man, and she said: "I have three tasks to set you. If you perform them all, you shall be my daughter's lord and master." "What's the first?" he asked. "To bring me a ring I once dropped in the Red Sea." The prince went home to his servants and said: "The first task is not an easy one. A ring must be recovered from the Red Sea. How's that to be done?" Sharp-eyes replied: "I'll find out where it is." He looked down into the sea and said: "There it is, caught on a sharp stone." Tall carried them to the spot and said: "I'd get it if only I could see it." "Is that all that's stopping you?" cried Stout. He lay down with his mouth to the water, and the waves poured into it as into a bottomless pit. He drank up the whole sea until its bed was as dry as a meadow, and Tall stooped a little and picked up the ring. The prince was delighted. He brought the ring to the old queen, who was amazed and said: "Yes, it's the right ring. You've performed the first task, but now comes the second. Look over there. In the meadow outside my palace three hundred fat oxen are grazing. You must eat them up with their skin and bones, their hair and their horns. And that's not all. Down in the cellar there are three hundred barrels of wine. You must drink them all up. And if one hair of the oxen or one drop of the wine is left, you can say good-bye to your life." "May I invite some guests?" the prince asked. "A meal doesn't taste right without company." The old queen laughed cruelly and said: "You may invite one guest to keep you company, but no more."

The prince went to his servants and said to Stout: "Come and be my guest. For once in your life you'll get enough to eat." Stout expanded and ate the three hundred oxen. When not a single hair was left, he asked if breakfast was all they were serving. Then he drank the wine without a glass, straight out of the barrels, and licked the last drop from the last tap. When the meal was over, the prince went to the old queen and told her the second task was done. She was amazed and said: "No one has ever got this far, but there's still one more." And she thought to herself: "He won't escape me. He won't keep his head on his shoulders." "Tonight," she said, "I'll bring my daughter to your room. You're to throw your arms around her and hold her, but while you're sitting there with her you must take care not to fall asleep. I'll be there at the stroke of twelve, and if she's not in your arms, you'll lose your life." "That's easy," the prince thought. "Of course I can keep my eyes open." But even so he called his servants, told them what the old queen had said, and added: "The Lord only knows what trickery she has up her sleeve. We'd better be on our guard. Keep watch, and take care not to let the princess leave my room." At nightfall the old queen brought her daughter in and the prince took her in his arms. Tall wound himself around the two of them, and Stout posted himself in front of the door so that no living soul could have passed. The prince and the princess sat there together, and the princess didn't say a word, but the moon shone through the window and lit up her face, and the prince was able to see her great beauty. He looked and looked at her, he was filled with love and happiness, and his eyes never wearied. But then, at eleven o'clock, the old queen cast a spell on them all. They fell asleep and in that moment the princess was carried off.

They slept soundly until a quarter to twelve. At that moment the spell lost its power and they all woke up. "Oh misery, misery!" cried the prince. "Now I am lost!" The faithful servants began to lament, but Listener said: "Be still and let me listen." After listening a moment he said: "She's shut up in a rock three hundred hours' journey from here and she's bewailing her fate. Tall, you're the only one who can help us. Give yourself a good stretch and you'll be there in a few steps." "All right," said Tall, "but Blindfold must come along, for we'll have to smash the rock." Tall picked up Blindfold on his back, and in a twinkling they were on the enchanted rock. Tall uncovered his passenger's eyes, and the rock shivered into a thousand pieces. Then Tall picked up the princess in his arms, carried her back in no time, brought back his comrade just as quickly, and before the clock struck twelve they were all sitting as before, as cheerfully as could be. At the stroke of twelve the sorceress came creeping in with a scornful look on her face, as though to say: "Now he's mine," for she thought her daughter was three hundred hours' journey away, shut up in a great rock. When she saw her in the prince's arms, she gave a start and said: "That man is too much for me." But there was nothing she could do about it. She had to give him the princess. She whispered into her ear: "What a disgrace, your having to obey this lout instead of choosing a husband as you see fit!"

At that the girl's proud heart was filled with rage and she plotted revenge. Next morning she had three hundred cords of wood gathered together, and she said to the prince: "You've performed the three tasks, but I will not be your wife until someone consents to sit on that woodpile and brave the fire." Her calculation was that none of his servants would consent to be burned alive for his sake, that he himself would mount the pyre for love of her, and then she would be free. But the servants said: "We've all of us done something except Frosty. Now it's his turn." They sat him down in the middle of the woodpile, and lit the fire. The flames flared up and the fire burned for three days until all the wood was consumed, and when the blaze died down Frosty was standing in the ashes, trembling like an aspen leaf. "I've never been so cold in all my life," he said. "Another few minutes and I'd have been frozen stiff."

The beautiful princess couldn't think up any more excuses, so she had to take the young stranger for her husband. But when they rode away to church, the old queen said: "The disgrace of it is more than I can bear." And she sent soldiers after them with orders to cut down anyone who resisted and to bring back her daughter. But Listener had pricked up his ears and heard the old queen's secret words. "What shall we do?" he asked Stout, and Stout knew the answer. Once or twice he vomited up a part of the sea water he had drunk, and a big lake formed behind the carriage. The soldiers were stopped in their tracks, and they were all drowned. When the sorceress heard about that, she sent her heavy cavalry, but Listener heard the clanking of armor and he took the covering from Blindfold's eyes. Blindfold gave the enemy troops a somewhat piercing look, and they all shattered like glass. The wedding party proceeded unmolested, and after the two of them were married in church, the six servants took their leave. "You've got what you wanted," they said to their master. "You don't need us any more, so we'll go and try our luck somewhere else."

A mile or two from the palace there was a village, and outside it a swineherd was tending his swine. When they got there, the prince said to his wife: "Do you know who I really am? I'm not a prince, I'm a swineherd, and that man with the swine is my father. Now the two of us will have to join in and help him." Then he took her to the inn and secretly told the innkeeper and his wife to take away her royal clothing during the night. When she woke up in the morning, she had nothing to put on. The innkeeper's wife gave her an old skirt and a pair of old woolen stockings, and even pretended to be doing her a great favor. "If it weren't for your husband," she said, "I wouldn't give you anything at all." After that she really believed he was a swineherd. She tended the swine with him and thought: "I've only got what I deserved for being so haughty and proud." This went on for a week, and by then she couldn't bear it any more, for her feet were all sore and bleeding. Some people came and asked if she knew who her husband was. "Oh yes," she said, "he's a swineherd. He's just gone out to see if he can sell some ribbons and lace." But they said to her: "Come with us, we'll take you to him." They took her to the castle, and when they entered the great hall, her husband was standing there in kingly raiment. She didn't recognize him until he took her in his arms and kissed her and said: "I suffered so much for you, it was only right that you should suffer for me." Then at last the wedding was celebrated, and the teller of this story wishes he had been there too.

135

The White Bride and the Black Bride

ONCE WHEN A WOMAN was out in the fields cutting fodder with her daughter and stepdaughter, God came up to them disguised as a poor man and asked: "Where is the path to the village?" The mother replied: "If you want to know, go and look for it." And her daughter added: "If you're afraid of missing it, take a signpost with you." But the stepdaughter said: "Poor man, I will lead you. Come with me." God was angry with the mother and daughter. He turned his back on them and cursed them, saying: "May you become as black as night and as ugly as sin." But the poor stepdaughter had found favor in his eyes. He went with her, and when they came close to the village, he gave her his blessing, and said: "Make three wishes, and I will grant them." The girl replied: "I would like to be as beautiful and as pure as the sun." And in a twinkling she was as white and beautiful as the day. "Next, I would like to have a purse that's never empty." God gave her that too, but said: "Don't forget the best thing of all." And she replied: "I would like to live in the kingdom of heaven after my death. That is my third wish." God granted her that too, and then he left her.

When the stepmother and her daughter came home, they saw that they were both pitch-black and ugly, while the stepdaughter was white and beautiful. At that their hearts grew wickeder than ever and all they could think of was how they might harm her. Now the stepdaughter had a brother by the name of Raynald. She loved him dearly and told him what had happened. One day Raynald said to her: "I'm going to paint your picture, because I love you so much that I want to be able to look at you." "But I beg you," she replied, "don't let anyone see it." So he painted a portrait of his sister and hung it up in his room, which was in the royal palace, because he was the king's coachman. Every day he stood before it and thanked God for his dear sister's good fortune.

It so happened that the king, his master, had just lost his wife, who had been so beautiful that none could be found to compare with her, and for that reason the king's heart was bowed with grief. Now the servants saw the coachman stopping day after day to look at a beautiful picture, and they were envious and told the king. The king sent for the picture, and when he saw that it resembled his dead wife in every way, but was even more beautiful, he fell mortally in love with it, sent for the coachman and asked whose picture it was. "It's my sister," said the coachman, and the king, resolving on the spot to take no other for his wife, gave him a carriage and horses and splendid golden clothes, and sent him to bring the chosen bride. When Raynald arrived with the message, his sister was very happy, but the black girl was jealous of her good fortune, flew into a towering rage, and said to her mother: "What good are your arts if you can't give me such happiness?" "Hush," said her mother. "I'll make it come your way." With her witch's arts she so clouded the coachman's eyes that he became half-blind and so stopped the white stepdaughter's ears that she became half-deaf. They all got into the carriage, first the bride in her splendid royal raiment, then the stepmother and her daughter. Raynald, the coachman, sat on the box. When they had gone a little way, the coachman cried out:

> "Keep yourself covered, sister dear,
> Don't let the raindrops splatter you,
> Guard your skin from the dusty wind,
> For when you go before the king
> You must look your lovely best."

"What does my dear brother say?" asked the bride. And the old woman answered: "He says you should take off your golden dress and give it to your sister." So she took it off and put it on her sister, who gave her a wretched gray smock in exchange. On they drove, and a little later the coachman cried out again:

> "Keep yourself covered, sister dear,
> Don't let the raindrops splatter you,
> Guard your skin from the dusty wind,
> For when you go before the king
> You must look your lovely best."

"What does my dear brother say?" asked the bride. And the old woman answered: "He says you should take off your golden bonnet and give it to your sister." So she took off her bonnet and put it on her sister, leaving herself bareheaded. On they drove and after a while the coachman cried out again:

> "Keep yourself covered, sister dear,
> Don't let the raindrops splatter you,
> Guard your skin from the dusty wind,
> For when you go before the king
> You must look your lovely best."

"What does my dear brother say?" the bride asked. And the old woman answered: "He says you should look outside." Now it so happened that they were crossing a bridge over a deep river. When the bride stood up to look out, the two of them gave her a push and she fell into the water. She sank at once, and in that same moment a snow-white duck rose to the surface of the water and went swimming down the river. The brother, who hadn't noticed a thing, drove on till they came to the royal palace. There he brought the black girl to the king and introduced her as his sister. Indeed, he thought she was his sister, for his eyes were clouded but he could still see the golden glitter of her raiment. When the king looked at his supposed bride and saw how abysmally ugly she was, he was very angry and had the coachman thrown into a pit full of adders and snakes. But the old witch so beguiled the king and so deceived his eyes with her arts, that he let her stay and her daughter as well. In the end he decided that the daughter wasn't half bad and actually married her.

One evening as the black bride was sitting on the king's lap, a white duck came swimming up the drainage runnel to the kitchen and said to the kitchen boy:

> "Make a fire, kitchen boy,
> For me to warm my feathers by."

The kitchen boy did as he was asked and made a fire on the hearth. The duck came and sat beside it, and shook herself, and straightened her feathers with her bill. As she was sitting there basking in the warmth, she asked:

> "What is my brother Raynald doing?"

And the kitchen boy answered:

> "Poor fellow, he's condemned to sit
> With snakes and adders in the pit."

Then the duck asked:

> "And what's the horrid black witch doing?"

The kitchen boy replied:

> "She's sitting warm
> In the young king's arms."

And the duck said:

> "God shelter us from harm,"

and went swimming away down the runnel.

The next evening she came again and asked the same questions, and again the third evening. After that the kitchen boy could contain himself no longer. He went to the king and told him the whole story. The king wanted to see for himself and the next evening he went to the kitchen. When the duck swam up the runnel and stuck her head in, he took his sword and severed her neck. Instantly she turned into the most beautiful girl, the exact likeness of the portrait her brother had painted of her. The king was overjoyed. Seeing she was standing there sopping wet, he sent for fine clothes and had them put on her. She told him how she had been betrayed by guile and wickedness and thrown into the river, and the first thing she asked him was to have her brother freed from the snakepit. When that was done, the king went to the room where the old witch was sitting and asked her: "What does a woman deserve who has done thus and so?" And he told her what had happened. She was so befuddled she didn't know what he was getting at and replied: "She deserves to be stripped naked and put into a barrel full of nails, and then the barrel should be harnessed to a horse and the horse driven far and wide." Just that was done to her and her black daughter. Then the king married the beautiful white bride and rewarded her faithful brother by making him a rich and respected lord.

136
Iron Hans

THERE WAS ONCE a king who had a great forest near his palace. There was game of all kinds in the forest, and one day he sent a huntsman to shoot a roe, but the huntsman didn't come back. "Something must have happened to him," said the king, and the next day he sent two other huntsmen to look for him, but they didn't come back either. The third day he sent for all the rest of his hunstmen and said: "Search the whole forest, don't stop till you've found all three of them." But neither they nor any of the dogs they had taken with them were ever seen again. From that time on, everyone was afraid to go near the forest, which lay silent and forsaken, though now and then an eagle or a hawk could be seen flying over it. This went on for years, and then one day a strange hunstman appeared before the king, asking for employment and offering to go into the perilous forest. But the king wouldn't let him. "The place is haunted," he said. "I'm afraid you would fare no better than the others and would never come back." "Sire," said the huntsman, "I'll go at my own risk. I know nothing of fear."

The huntsman took his dog and went into the forest. The dog soon picked up a scent and started to follow it, but after running a few steps he came to a deep pool and had to stop. A bare arm rose from the water, grabbed hold of him and pulled him under. When the huntsman saw what had happened, he went back and brought three men with buckets, who emptied the water out of the pool. When they could see to the bottom, a wild man was lying there. His body was as brown as rusty iron, and his hair covered his face and hung down to his knees. They bound him with cords and carried him to the palace, where everyone was amazed at the sight of him, and the king had him shut up in an iron cage in the courtyard. All were forbidden on pain of death to open the door of the cage, and the key was entrusted to the queen herself. From that day on, it was safe to walk in the forest.

The king had an eight-year-old son who was playing in the court-yard one day, and as he was playing his golden ball fell into the cage. The little boy ran to the cage and said: "Give me my golden ball." "Not till you open the door for me," said the wild man. "No," said the boy, "I won't do that, the king has forbidden it." And he ran away. Next day he came again and asked for his ball. The wild man said: "Open my door," but the little boy wouldn't do it. On the third day the king was out hunting. The boy went back to the cage and said: "I couldn't open the door even if I wanted to, because I haven't got the key." "It's under your mother's pillow," said the wild man. "You can get it." The child, who desperately wanted his ball, threw caution to the winds, and went and got the key. He had trouble opening the door and caught his finger. When the door was open, the wild man came out, gave him the ball, and ran away. The child took fright and screamed and yelled: "Wild man, wild man, don't go away, they'll give me a whipping!" The wild man turned back, picked the child up, set him on his shoulders, and hurried away to the forest with long strides. When the king came home, he saw the empty cage and asked the queen what had happened. She didn't know a thing, and when she looked for the key it was gone. She called the little boy, but no one answered. The king sent men to look for him in the fields, but they didn't find him. He had no trouble guessing what had happened, and the palace was filled with mourning.

When the wild man got back to the dark forest, he took the child down from his shoulders, put him on the ground, and said: "You'll never see your father and mother again, but I'll keep you with me because you set me free and I feel sorry for you. If you do exactly as I tell you, you'll be all right. I have plenty of gold and treasure, more than anyone in the world." He made the child a bed of moss to sleep on, and in the morning led him to a spring. "You see this golden spring?" he said. "It's as bright and clear as crystal. I want you to sit beside it and make sure nothing falls into it, for then the spring would be defiled. I'll come to you every evening to see if you've obeyed my order." The child sat down at the edge of the spring.

Now and then he saw a golden fish or a golden snake in the water, and he was careful not to let anything fall in. Once, as he was sitting there, his finger hurt him so badly that without meaning to he dipped it in the water. Though he pulled it right out again, he saw the finger had turned to gold, and try as he might he couldn't wipe the gold off. When Iron Hans came back that evening, he looked at the boy and said: "What has happened to the spring?" "Nothing. Nothing," he replied, holding his finger behind his back to keep Iron Hans from seeing it. But the wild man said: "You've dipped your finger in the water. I'll let it pass this once, but it mustn't happen again." Bright and early next morning he was sitting by the spring, keeping watch. His finger hurt him again, he ran it over his head, and as ill luck would have it, one of his hairs fell into the spring. He quickly pulled it out, but it was all gold. The moment Iron Hans got there he knew what had happened. "You've dropped a hair in the spring," he said. "I'll let it pass this once, but if it happens again the spring will be defiled, and you won't be able to stay with me any longer." The third day the boy was sitting beside the spring, and much as his finger hurt him, he didn't move it. But the time hung heavy on his hands and he began to look at the reflection of his face in the water. He wanted to look himself straight in the eye and bent down farther and farther. All at once his long hair tumbled over his shoulders and fell into the water. Quickly he raised his head, but his hair had all been turned to gold and it glittered like the sun. You can imagine how terrified the poor boy was. He took his handkerchief and tied it around his head to keep the wild man from seeing it. But the moment the wild man got there he knew what had happened, and said: "Take off that handkerchief." The golden hair came flowing out, and nothing the boy could say was of any use. "You can't stay here any longer, for you haven't stood the test. Go out into the world. You'll find out what it is to be poor. But there's no wickedness in your heart and I wish you well, so I'll grant you one favor: if you're in trouble, come to the edge of the forest and shout: 'Iron Hans!' Then I'll come and help you. My power is great, greater than you think, and I have vast stores of gold and silver."

The prince left the forest and journeyed over beaten and unbeaten paths, until at last he came to a great city. There he looked for work but found none, for he had never learned anything that might have helped him earn his keep. In the end he went to the royal palace and asked for employment. The courtiers didn't know what to do with him, but they liked him and said he could stay. In the end the cook put him to work hauling wood and water and sweeping up the ashes. Once when no one else was available, the cook bade him carry the food platters to the royal table, and the boy kept his hat on because he didn't want anyone to see his golden hair. The king had never seen such behavior, and he said: "When you come to the royal table, you must take your hat off." "Oh, sire," he replied, "I can't do that. My head is covered with ugly scurf." The king summoned the cook and scolded him. "How could you ever take on a boy like that?" he cried. "Get rid of him immediately!" But the cook was sorry for the youngster and traded him for the gardener's boy.

Now he had to sow and plant, water the garden, and spade and hoe in good weather and bad. One summer day when he was working in the garden alone, the heat was so oppressive that he took off his hat to cool his head in the breeze. When the sunlight fell on his hair, it sparkled so bright that the glint reached the princess's bedchamber and the princess jumped up to see what it was. She caught sight of the boy and cried out: "Boy, go and get me a bunch of flowers!" Quickly he put on his hat, picked a bunch of wildflowers and tied a string around them. On his way up the stairs he passed the gardener, who said: "How can you bring the princess such common flowers? Quick, get different ones! Choose the rarest and most beautiful." "Oh, no," said the boy. "Wildflowers are more fragrant, she'll like these better." When he went in, the princess said: "Take your hat off. It's not proper for you to keep it on in my presence." "I can't," he said. "I've got scurf all over my head." But she took hold of his hat and snatched it off. His golden hair tumbled down over his shoulders, a beautiful sight. He tried to run away, but she held him by the arm and gave him a handful of ducats. He took them, but he cared nothing for gold and gave them to the gardener, saying: "Here's a present for your children, something for them to play with." Next day the princess called to him again and asked him to get her a bunch of wildflowers. The moment he came in, she snatched at his hat and tried to take it off, but he held it fast with both hands. Again she gave him a handful of ducats, but he didn't want to keep them, so he gave them to the gardener for his children to play with. The third day the same thing happened. She couldn't take his hat off, and he wouldn't keep her gold.

A short while later, the land was overrun by war. The king mustered his troops, though he didn't know if they could stand up against the enemy, who was very powerful and had a large army. The gardener's boy said: "I'm grown up now, and I'm going to war. Just give me a horse." The others said: "Go and take one while we're away. We'll leave one in the stable for you." When they were gone, he went to the stable and took the horse. It was lame in one leg and limped, clippety clop, clippety clop, but he mounted all the same and rode away to the dark forest. When he got to the edge of it, he shouted three times: "Iron Hans!" so loudly that the sound went echoing through the trees. A moment later the wild man appeared, and said: "What do you want?" "I want a sturdy horse, for I'm riding off to war." "That you shall have and more," said the wild man. He went back into the forest, and in next to no time a groom appeared, leading a horse that was snorting and prancing and could hardly be held in check. Behind him came a squadron of iron-clad riders, and their swords flashed in the sunlight. The youth gave the groom his three-legged nag, mounted the charger, and rode off at the head of his troops. When he reached the battlefield, a good part of the king's army had fallen, and those who remained would soon have had to give way. The youth and his iron squadron fell on the enemy like a whirlwind, striking down everyone in their path. The enemy turned and fled, but the youth pursued them and kept at it until not a man of them was left. Then, instead of returning to the king, he led his men over byways to the forest, and there he shouted for Iron Hans. "What do you want?" the wild man asked. "Take back your horse and your soldiers and give me my three-legged nag." All this was done, and he rode his three-legged nag back to the stable. When the king returned to his palace, his daughter came to meet him and congratulated him on his victory. "The victory was none of my doing," said the king. "It was won by a strange knight who came to my help with his squadron." The daughter asked who the strange knight was, but the king didn't know. All he could say was: "He rode off in pursuit of the enemy and I never saw him again." She asked the gardener about his boy, but he laughed and said: "He's just come home on his three-legged nag. The others all made fun of him. 'Here's our clippety-clop come home again,' they said. Then they asked him: 'Which hedge have you been sleeping under?' And he answered: 'I did all right. Things would have gone badly if it hadn't been for me.' And they laughed harder than ever."

The king said to his daughter: "I shall proclaim a great festival, to last three days, and you'll toss a golden apple. Maybe the unknown knight will take part." When the festival was proclaimed, the youth went out to the forest and called Iron Hans. "What do you want?" he asked. "I want to catch the princess's golden apple." "You've as good as got it right now," said Iron Hans. "You'll have red armor for the occasion and ride a proud chestnut horse." When the day came, the youth came galloping into the courtyard and took his place among the knights. No one recognized him. The princess stepped forward and tossed a golden apple to the knights. He alone caught it, he and nobody else, but as soon as he had it he galloped away. The next day Iron Hans provided him with white armor and a white horse. Again he caught the apple and again he galloped away, without staying for so much as a moment. The king flew into a rage and said: "That's forbidden! He's obliged to appear before me and state his name." He gave orders that if the knight who had caught the apple should again run away, his men should pursue him, and strike him with their swords if he didn't come back of his own free will. The third day Iron Hans gave him black armor and a black horse, and again he caught the apple. But as he was galloping away, the king's men pursued him and one came so close as to wound his leg with the tip of his sword. Nevertheless, he escaped, but his horse reared so brusquely that his helmet fell off and his golden hair could be seen. The men rode back and told the king everything that had happened.

The next day the princess asked the gardener about his boy. "He's working in the garden. What a queer duck he is! He went to the festival and only came back yesterday evening. He showed the children three golden apples he had won." The king sent for the boy and when he came he was wearing his hat again. But the princess went up to him and took it off, his golden hair fell down over his shoulders, and it was so beautiful they all marveled. "Were you the knight," the king asked, "who came to the festival each day, each time in a different color, and caught the three golden apples?" "Yes," he said, "and here are the apples." He took them out of his pocket and handed them to the king. "If you wish for more proof, I'll show you the wound your men gave me when they were pursuing me. And I'm also the knight who helped you defeat your enemy." "If you can do such deeds, you're not a gardener's boy. Tell me: who is your father?" "My father is a mighty king, and I have plenty of gold, as much as I choose to ask for." "I see that I owe you a debt of gratitude," said the king. "Is there anything I can do for you?" "Yes," he said. "Indeed there is. You can give me your daughter for my wife." At that the princess laughed and said: "He doesn't beat about the bush! But I knew by his golden hair that he wasn't a gardener's boy." Whereupon she went over and kissed him. His father and mother came to the wedding, and they were very happy, for they had given up hope of ever seeing their beloved son again. And as they were sitting at the wedding board, the music suddenly fell silent, the doors opened, and a proud king came in with a great retinue. He went up to the youth, embraced him, and said: "I am Iron Hans. A spell turned me into a wild man, but you have set me free. All my treasures shall be yours."

137

The Three Black Princesses

EAST INDIA WAS being besieged by an enemy who refused to leave the city unless he was paid a ransom of six hundred talers. They had the town crier beat his drum and proclaim that whoever brought in the money would be mayor. There happened to be a poor fisherman who fished in the sea with his son, and the enemy came and took the son prisoner and gave the father six hundred talers for him. So the father gave the aldermen the money, and the enemy went away and the fisherman got to be mayor. And the town crier beat his drum and proclaimed that anyone who didn't address him as "my Lord Mayor" would be hanged on the gallows.

The son escaped from the enemy and ended up in a big forest on top of a high mountain. The mountain opened and he came to a big enchanted castle, where all the chairs, tables, and benches were draped in black. Three princesses came in and they were all black and dressed in black, but there was a bit of white on their faces. "Don't be afraid," they said. "We won't hurt you, and you can set us free if you like." "I'd be glad to," he said, "if I knew how to go about it." They told him: "You must go a whole year without speaking to us or looking at us. If you need anything you must say so, and we'll answer you if it's not forbidden." When he had been there awhile, he asked if he could go and see his father. They said he could and added: "Take this purse full of money, put on these clothes, and be back in a week."

He was lifted up and in less than a moment he was in East India. When he didn't find his father in the fisherman's hut, he asked the neighbors what had become of the poor fisherman, and they said: "Don't say that or they'll hang you on the gallows." Then he went to his father and said: "Fisherman, how did you get here?" "You mustn't say that," said his father. "If the aldermen heard you, they'd hang you on the gallows." But he kept right on, so they led him to the gallows, and when he got there, he said: "Oh, my lords, let me go to the fisherman's hut." In the hut he put on his old fisherman's clothes and came back to the aldermen and said: "Now do you see that I'm the poor fisherman's son? These are the clothes I wore to earn bread for my father and mother." At that, they recognized him, begged his pardon, and took him home with them. The boy told them everything that had happened, how he had got to a forest on the top of a high mountain, how the mountain had opened and he had come to an enchanted castle where everything was black, and three princesses had come in, and they had been black too, except for a bit of white on their faces, and how the princesses had said: "Don't be afraid. You can set us free if you like." His mother said that mightn't be a good thing to do, and advised him to take a consecrated wax candle with him and let some blazing hot wax drip on their faces.

He went back again and he was full of dread. He let the wax drip on their faces while they slept. All three princesses turned half-white and jumped up. "You accursed dog," they cried, "our blood shall cry out for vengeance. Now there is no man born, nor ever will be, who can set us free. But we have three brothers who are bound in seven-fold chains and they will tear you to pieces." Then there were loud cries all over the castle, and he jumped out of the window and broke his leg and the castle sank into the earth and the mountain closed and no one knew where it had been.

138
Knoist and His Three Sons

THERE WAS ONCE a man by the name of Knoist who lived between Werrel and Soist, and he had three sons. The first was blind, the second lame, and the third stark-naked. Once when they were walking through the fields, they saw a hare. The blind one shot it, the second caught it, and the naked one put it in his pocket. After that they came to a huge big river with three ships on it. The first ship leaked, the second sank, and the third had no bottom. They all went aboard the one with no bottom. Soon they came to a huge big forest, with a huge big tree in it, and inside the tree there was a huge big chapel, and inside the chapel there was an ironwood sexton and an ironwood priest, who dispensed holy water with cudgels.

> Blessed is he who runs away
> From the holy water's spray.

139

The Girl from Brakel

A YOUNG GIRL WENT from Brakel to the chapel of St. Anne at the foot of the Hinnenberg. She wanted a husband and thought there was no one else in the chapel, so she sang:

> "Oh, holy St. Anne,
> Do get me that man,
> You know who I mean.
> He's got bright yellow hair
> And he lives by the weir.
> You know who I mean."

The sexton was standing behind the altar. When he heard her song, he cried in a shrill voice: "You'll never get him! You'll never get him!" The girl thought the child Mary, who was standing there with her mother St. Anne, had spoken. That made her angry and she cried out: "Ibbity-bibbity, you stupid brat. Shut your trap and let your mother talk!"

140

Two Families

"WHERE ARE YOU GOING?"

"To Walpe."

"You to Walpe, me to Walpe. Fine and dandy, let's be going."

"Got a husband? What d'you call 'im?"

"Willem."

"Your man Willem, my man Willem, you to Walpe, me to Walpe. Fine and dandy, let's be going."

"Got a child? What's he called?"

"Bald."

"Your child Bald, my child Bald, your man Willem, my man Willem, you to Walpe, me to Walpe. Fine and dandy, let's be going."

"Got a housemaid? What's her label?"

"Mabel."

"Your maid Mabel, my maid Mabel, your child Bald, my child Bald, your man Willem, my man Willem, you to Walpe, me to Walpe. Fine and dandy, let's be going."

"Got a farm hand? What's his name?"

"Knock-kneed-pigeon-toed-and-lame."

"My farm hand is called the same. Your maid Mabel, my maid Mabel, your child Bald, my child Bald, your man Willem, my man Willem, you to Walpe, me to Walpe. Fine and dandy, let's be going."

141

The Lamb and the Fish

THERE WERE ONCE a brother and sister who loved each other dearly. But their real mother was dead and they had a stepmother who hated them and secretly did everything she could to harm them. One day the two of them were playing with other children in a meadow outside the house, and alongside the meadow there was a pond that reached as far as one end of the house. So the children were running around, chasing each other and playing a counting-out game.

> "Enneke, Benneke, let me live
> My little bird to you I'll give.
> Little bird will pick up straw
> And I'll give it to the cow.
> Nice fresh milk the cow will make
> Which the baker man will take
> To bake a basketful of cake.

> I'll feed the cake to Mrs. Cat,
> She will catch me mice for that.
> I'll hang the mice in the chimney to smoke—
> And cut off a slice."

The children all stood in a circle, and the one the word "slice" fell to had to run away and the others chased him till they caught him. The stepmother was watching from her window, and it made her angry to see them running happily about, so she cast a spell on the two children, for she knew the arts of witchcraft, and she turned the little boy into a fish and the little girl into a lamb. The fish swam about in the pond and he was very sad, and the lamb ran about in the meadow, and she was so sad she didn't eat so much as a single blade of grass. A long time went by and guests came to the castle. The wicked stepmother thought: "This is my chance," and she called the cook and said: "Go and get the lamb from the meadow and kill it, we have nothing else to give our guests." The cook went and got the lamb and took her to the kitchen and tied her feet. The lamb bore it all patiently. The cook took out his knife to kill her and just as he was beginning to sharpen it on the doorstep, she saw a little fish swimming back and forth in the drainage runnel and looking up at her. The fish was her little brother, for when he saw the cook leading the lamb away, he had swum right up to the house. The lamb called down:

> "Oh brother in the pond so deep,
> My heart is sore, salt tears I weep.
> The cook is sharpening his knife
> To pierce my heart and take my life."

The little fish replied:

> "Oh sister on the high dry land,
> I feel so sad in this deep pond."

When the cook heard that the lamb could speak and heard her speaking so mournfully to the little fish, he was horrified. "This can't be a real lamb," he thought. "She must have been bewitched by the wicked woman of the house." And he said: "Don't worry, I won't kill you." He butchered another animal, prepared it for the guests, took the lamb to a good peasant woman, and told her everything he had seen and heard. It so happened that this peasant woman had been the little girl's wet nurse. She guessed right away who the lamb must be and took her to a Wise Woman. The Wise Woman said a blessing over the lamb and the fish, and they recovered their human form. Then she took them to a hut in a great forest, and there they lived all by themselves, but they were happy and content.

142

Simeli Mountain

THERE WERE ONCE two brothers, the one rich, the other poor. The rich one never gave anything to the poor one, who scraped along as best he could, carting grain. Often money was so scarce that his wife and children had nothing to eat. Once as he was driving his wagon through the forest he saw a big bald mountain on one side of the road. He stopped and looked at it with amazement, for he had never seen it before. While he was standing there, he saw twelve big ugly-looking men coming along. Thinking they must be robbers, he hid his wagon in the bushes, climbed a tree, and waited to see what would happen. The twelve men went up to the mountain and cried out: "Semsi Mountain, Semsi Mountain, open up." Instantly, the bald mountain opened in the middle. The twelve went in and once they were inside, the mountain closed. After a while, the mountain opened again, and the men came out carrying heavy sacks. When they had all come out, they said: "Semsi Mountain, Semsi Mountain, close up." The mountain closed, there was no longer any sign of an entrance, and the twelve men went away.

When they were out of sight, the poor man climbed down from the tree. He was curious to know what mysteries could be hidden in the mountain, so he went up to it and said: "Semsi Mountain, Semsi Mountain, open up," and the mountain opened. He went in and the whole mountain was a cave full of silver and gold, and deep inside there were big mounds of pearls and sparkling jewels, piled like grain. The poor man didn't know what to do and he wondered whether he ought to take any of the treasure. In the end, he filled his pockets with gold, but he left the pearls and jewels alone. When he came out, he said: "Semsi Mountain, Semsi Mountain, close up." The mountain closed and he drove his wagon home.

After that he had nothing to worry about. With his gold he was able to provide his wife and children with wine as well as bread, he lived happily and honestly, gave to the poor and was kind to everyone. When his money was gone, he went to his brother, borrowed a bushel measure, and got himself some more gold, but again he left the precious jewels alone. When he wanted some gold for the third time, he again borrowed the bushel measure from his brother. But the rich man had long been envious of his brother's good fortune and of the pleasant life he had been leading, and he couldn't see how his brother had come by such wealth or what he wanted with the bushel measure. So he thought up a trick: he smeared the bottom of the measure with pitch, and when he got it back there was a gold piece stuck to it. He went to his brother and asked him: "What have you been measuring with my bushel measure?" "Wheat and barley," said the poor man. The rich man showed him the gold piece and threatened to have the law on him unless he told him the truth. Then he told him the whole story. Without a moment's delay the rich man had a wagon harnessed and drove to the place, determined to make better use of this golden opportunity than his brother had done and to bring back very different treasures. When he got to the mountain, he cried out: "Semsi Mountain, Semsi Mountain, open up." The mountain opened and he went in. There lay the treasure before him, and for a long time he didn't know what to grab first, but in the end he took as many jewels as he could carry. He was going to leave with his burden, but his heart and mind were so full of treasure that he forgot the name of the mountain and cried out: "Simeli Mountain, Simeli Mountain, open up." But that wasn't the right name. The mountain stayed closed and didn't budge. He was seized with fear and the longer he racked his brains the more muddled his thoughts became. His treasure was no use to him at all. That evening the mountain opened and the twelve robbers came in. They laughed when they saw him and cried: "Well, well, little bird, we've caught you at last!

Do you think we didn't know you'd been here three times before? We couldn't catch you then, but you won't escape us a third time." "It wasn't me!" he screamed. "It was my brother." But nothing he could say helped him. Plead as he might for his life, they cut his head off.

143

Traveling

A POOR WOMAN ONCE had a son who was dying to travel, and his mother said: "How can you travel? We haven't any money to give you." The son replied: "I'll manage all right. I'll just keep saying: 'Not much, not much.'"

He walked for some time and wherever he went he said: "Not much, not much, not much." At last he happened on some fishermen, "God keep you," he said. "Not much, not much, not much." "Not much, not much," they said. "What are you saying that for?" And indeed, when they pulled in their net, there was not much fish in it. So they took a stick to the boy, saying: "You've never seen us thresh, have you?" "What should I say?" he asked. "You should say: 'Better catch! Better catch!'"

He walked along for quite a while, saying: "Better catch, better catch." After a while he came to the gallows, and they had brought a poor devil there to hang him. "Good morning," he said. "Better catch, better catch." "Why do you say 'better catch'? As though there weren't enough wicked people in the world. Do you think we need more?" And he got another drubbing. "What should I say?" "You should say: 'God have mercy on the poor soul.'"

The boy went on for quite a while, saying: "God have mercy on the poor soul." At last he came to a pit where a knacker was killing a horse. "Good morning," said the boy. "God have mercy on the poor soul." "What are you saying, you wicked man?" And he hit him over the head with his knacker's hook so hard that he saw stars. "What should I say?" "You should say: 'Stinking beast, lie down in the pit where you belong!'"

He walked along, saying: "Stinking beast, lie down in the pit where you belong." Pretty soon he met a wagonload of people. "Good morning," he said. "Stinking beast, lie down in the pit where you belong." The wagon fell into the ditch, and the driver took a whip and gave the boy such a beating that he had to limp home to his mother. He never went traveling again as long as he lived.

144

The Donkey

THERE ONCE LIVED a king and queen who were rich and had everything they could have wished for, but no children. The queen grieved day and night, saying: "I'm like a field that nothing grows on." At last God heard her prayers, but when the baby was born, it didn't look like a human child. It was a little donkey. When the mother saw it, she screamed and wailed more than ever. She'd sooner have had no child at all than a donkey, and she told the servants to throw it in the river and let the fish eat it. But the king said: "No. Since God has given us this child, he shall be my son and heir, and when I die he shall mount my throne and bear the royal crown." So the baby donkey was reared and got bigger and stronger, and his ears grew beautifully tall and straight. Apart from that, he frisked and played and had a cheerful disposition. He was especially fond of music, so he went to a famous minstrel and said: "Give me lessons until I play the lute as well as you." "Ah, my dear young master," said the minstrel, "I believe you'll find that rather difficult. Your fingers aren't made for it, they're much too big. I'm afraid you'd break the strings." But the little donkey was determined to play the lute and nothing the minstrel could say discouraged him. He worked hard and practiced regularly, and in the end he played as well as his master.

One day when the young prince was in a pensive mood he went for a walk. He came to a spring and when he looked into the mirror-bright water he saw himself reflected as a donkey. He was so distressed at the sight that he went out into the world, taking no one with him but one faithful servant. They traveled about and at last they came to a kingdom ruled over by an old king who had only one daughter, but she was very, very beautiful. "This is where we'll stop," said the donkey. He knocked at the gate and shouted: "There's a guest out here. Open up and let him in." When no one opened, he sat down, took his lute, and played it delightfully with his two forefeet. The gatekeeper's eyes almost popped out of his head. He ran to the king and said: "There's a young donkey at the gate who plays the lute like a real master." "Bring the musician in," said the king. But when the lute-playing donkey came in, the courtiers laughed at him and took him downstairs to sup with the servants. That nettled him and he cried out: "I'm no common stable donkey, I'm a noble." "In that case," they said, "go and sit with the knights." "No," he replied, "I want to sit with the king." The king laughed and said good-naturedly: "Very well, it shall be as you say. Come here and sit beside me." Then he asked: "Friend donkey, how do you like my daughter?" The donkey turned his head, looked at her, and nodded. "Beyond measure," he said. "Never have I seen anyone so beautiful." "Then you shall sit beside her too," said the king. "Delighted," said the donkey. He sat down beside her and ate and drank, and his table manners were as dainty and neat as could be. When the noble beast had been at the king's court for some time, he thought: "What's the good of all this? I'll just have to go home." Hanging his head sadly, he went to the king and asked leave to depart. But the king, who had grown fond of him, replied: "Dear little donkey, what's the matter? You look as gloomy as an empty wine barrel. Stay with me. I'll give you anything you ask. Do you want gold?" "No," said the donkey and shook his head. "Do you want jewels and treasure?" "No." "Do you want half my kingdom?" "Oh no." "If only I knew what would cheer you up," said the king. "Do you want my daughter for your wife?" "Oh yes," said the donkey. "I'd like that very much." All at once he was happy and gay, for that was just what he had been longing for.

A big, splendid wedding was held, and that night when the bride and bridegroom were taken to their bedchamber, the king wanted to make sure the donkey conducted himself gently and courteously, so he ordered a servant to hide there. When the two were inside, the bridegroom pushed the bolt of the door and looked around. When he felt sure they were alone, he threw off his donkey's skin and all at once a handsome young prince was standing there. "Now you see who I am," he said, "and you also see that I'm not unworthy of you." The bride was very happy. She kissed him and loved him with all her heart. In the morning, he jumped up and put his animal's skin on again. No one would have known what sort of person was under it. After a while, the old king came in. "Well, well!" he cried. "Is our young donkey up so soon?" And to his daughter he said: "Would you rather have had a man for your husband? Are you sad?" "Oh no, dear father, I love him as if he were the handsomest man in the world, and I'll stay with him as long as I live." The king was surprised, but the servant who had been hiding came out and told him everything. "That can't be true," said the king. The servant replied: "If you yourself watch tonight, you'll see it with your own eyes. And sire, my advice is to take his skin and throw it in the fire. Then he will have to show himself in his true form." "That's good advice," said the king. That night when they were sleeping he crept into the room and saw a fine young man lying in the bed. The stripped-off skin lay on the floor beside him. The king took it, had a big fire made outside, threw the skin into it, and watched until it had burned to ashes. Then, wanting to see what the young man would do, he stayed awake all night and listened. At the crack of dawn, when the young man had had his sleep out, he got up. He wanted to put on the donkey skin, but it was nowhere to be found. At that he took fright and was overcome with sadness. "Now," he said to himself, "all I can do is try to escape." But when he left the room, the king stood before him and said: "My son, where are you going so fast? What's on your mind? Stay here. You're such a handsome young man, I don't want you to go away. I'll give you half my kingdom now and you'll have it all when I die." "If that's how it is," said the prince, "I hope that what has begun so well will end just as well. I'll stay with you." The old man gave him half the kingdom, and when the king died a year later he had all of it. When his own father died, he received yet another kingdom, and so he lived in splendor.

145

The Ungrateful Son

ONCE A MAN AND HIS WIFE were sitting outside their house. They had a roast chicken in front of them and were just going to eat it when the husband saw his old father coming along and quickly hid the chicken, for he didn't want to give him any. The old man stopped, took a drink of water, and went away. The son wanted to put the roast chicken back on the table, but when he reached for it, it had turned into a big toad, which jumped on to his face and sat there and wouldn't go away. If anyone tried to take it off, the toad gave him a poisonous look as though it were going to jump on *his* face, so no one dared go near it. The ungrateful son had to feed the toad every day, because if he hadn't it would have fed off his face. And so he became a wanderer on the face of the earth, with never a moment's peace.

146

The Turnip

THERE WERE ONCE two brothers who were both serving as soldiers, and one was rich and the other poor. The poor one was sick of being poor and wanted to do something about it, so he hung up his uniform and turned peasant. He spaded and hoed his bit of field and sowed turnip seeds. The seed sprouted, a turnip sprang up, and it got bigger and stronger and fatter by the minute and looked as if it would never stop growing. You could have called it the king of turnips, for such a turnip had never been seen before and will never be seen again. In the end it got so big that it filled a whole wagon all by itself, and two oxen were needed to pull it. The peasant didn't know what to do with it and wondered if it meant good luck or bad. Finally he said to himself: "If I sell it, I won't get anything much for it, and there's no sense in eating it myself because small turnips will serve the same purpose. The best thing I can do is take it to the king and make him a present of it."

So he loaded the turnip on his wagon, harnessed two oxen, hauled it to the royal palace, and gave it to the king. "Do my eyes deceive me?" cried the king. "I've seen many strange things, but never such a monstrosity as this. What kind of seed did it grow from? Or can it be that you were born lucky and that such things happen only to you?" "Oh no," said the peasant, "I wasn't born lucky at all. I'm a poor soldier, I hung up my uniform because I couldn't keep body and soul together, and took to tilling the soil. I have a brother who's rich, I'm sure you know him, sire, but as for me, I have nothing and everyone has forgotten me." The king felt sorry for him and said: "I will relieve you of your poverty and give you gifts that will make you fully the equal of your rich brother." And true enough, he gave him lots and lots of gold, and fields, and meadows, and herds, until he was incomparably richer than his brother.

When the rich man heard what his brother had gained with a single turnip, he envied him and racked his brains for a way of getting such luck for himself. At last he had an idea: oh, he'd be much cleverer than his brother. He brought the king gold and horses and expected something staggering in return, for if his brother had got so much for a turnip, what couldn't he hope to get for such fine gifts. The king accepted the gifts and said he could think of nothing rarer or more precious to give him in return than the big turnip. So the rich man had to have his brother's turnip loaded onto his wagon and driven home. When he got back, he didn't know whom to vent his rage on, but in the end evil thoughts came to him and he decided to kill his brother. He hired murderers and showed them a hiding place. Then he went to his brother and said: "Dear brother, I know of a secret treasure. Come. We'll dig it up together and share it." The brother liked the idea and suspected nothing. As they were leaving the village, the murderers fell on him and bound him. They were going to hang him on a tree when loud singing and hoofbeats were heard in the distance. At that they took fright, crammed their prisoner into a sack, hoisted it up on a branch, and fled. But the prisoner wasn't idle and it wasn't long before he had made a hole in the sack big enough to stick his head through. The person coming proved to be a wandering scholar, who was riding through the forest singing merrily. When the man in the tree saw that someone was passing below, he cried out: "Hey there! You've come at the right time!" The scholar looked around and couldn't see where the voice came from. Finally he shouted: "Who's calling?" The man in the treetop answered: "Look up. I'm up here in the Sack of Wisdom. In next to no time, I've learned great things, beside which all the schools in the world don't amount to a row of pins. I'll soon have completed my studies, then I'll come down and I'll be wiser than all other men. I know all about the stars and the signs of the zodiac, the winds of heaven and the sands of the sea, about birds and stones, the healing of sickness and the properties of herbs. If ever you were in it, you'd know what wonders emanate from the Sack of Wisdom." When the student heard that, he was amazed. "We've met in a blessed hour," he said. "Could I come in for a little while?" The man in the tree replied as though begrudgingly: "All right. I'll let you in for a little while, but you'll have to wait an hour because I still have a little something to learn." After waiting only a few minutes, the scholar was overcome with impatience and begged to be let in because his thirst for wisdom was more than he could bear. The man in the tree pretended to be doing him a favor and said: "Very well. But if I'm to leave the House of Wisdom, you'll have to take the rope and let the sack down. Then you can come in." The scholar let the sack down, untied it, and set him free. Then he cried: "Quick now! Pull me up." He wanted to get into the sack right side up, but the other said: "Stop! Not like that!" And he grabbed him by the head, crammed him into the sack upside down, tied it up, and hoisted the seeker after wisdom to the top of the tree. After swinging him through the air a few times, he called out: "How goes it, friend? I bet you can already feel the wisdom pouring into you. You're getting valuable experience, so just sit still and you'll soon be wiser." With that he mounted the scholar's horse and rode away. But an hour later he sent someone to let him down.

147

The Fires of Youth

IN THE DAYS WHEN OUR LORD still walked the earth, he and St. Peter once stopped at the house of a blacksmith, who gladly agreed to lodge them for the night. That evening a beggar, bent with age and infirmity, came to the house and asked the blacksmith for alms. St. Peter was moved by pity and said: "Lord and master, I pray you, make this man well again, so he can earn his own bread." The Lord said gently: "Blacksmith, lend me your forge, put some coal on the fire, and I will make this ailing old man young again." The blacksmith was willing and St. Peter plied the bellows. When the sparks flew and the fire blazed high, the Lord picked the little old man up and thrust him right into the middle of the forge fire until he glowed like a rosebush and praised God in a loud voice. Then the Lord went to the quenching tub and plunged the red-hot man into it. The water covered him, and when he was thoroughly cooled, the Lord gave him his blessing. Lo and behold, the little man jumped out as sound and straight and youthful as a boy of twenty. The blacksmith, who had watched the Lord closely, invited them all to supper. It so happened that he had a half-blind, hunchbacked old mother-in-law. She went over to the young fellow and asked him if the fire had been very painful, and he said the flames had felt as cool as the morning dew.

All night the old woman's ears rang with the young fellow's words, and early in the morning when the Lord had thanked the blacksmith and gone his way, the blacksmith thought he would be able to make his old mother-in-law young again, because he had watched the Lord closely and everything he had done was related to the blacksmith's trade. So he called her and asked if she'd like to go skipping about like a girl of eighteen. "I certainly would," she said, because the young fellow had had such an easy time of it. So the blacksmith made a big fire and pushed the old woman in, and she wriggled and writhed and yelled blue murder. "Sit still," he said. "What are you wriggling and screaming for? Wait, I'll work the bellows harder." So he plied the bellows until all her rags caught on fire. The old woman screeched and yelled, and the blacksmith thought to himself: "I haven't got it quite right." So he pulled her out and threw her into the quenching tub. At that she screamed so loud that the blacksmith's wife and daughter-in-law heard her from the upper story. They ran down the stairs and saw the old woman lying doubled up in the quenching tub, yelling for all she was worth, with her face all wrinkled and shriveled and shapeless. The two women, who were both with child, were so horrified that they gave birth that same night, but their babies weren't human, they were apes. They ran off into the forest, and that was the beginning of the apes.

148

The Lord's Animals and the Devil's

THE LORD GOD HAD CREATED all the animals and had chosen the wolves as his dogs. The only animal he had forgotten was the goat. Then the Devil sat up and thought he'd like to create something too, and he made goats with fine long tails. But when these goats went to pasture, their tails had a way of getting stuck on thornbushes, and the Devil had to go out and disentangle them, which gave him a lot of trouble. He soon got good and sick of it, so he went and bit the tails off all the goats, as you can see to this day by the stumps.

After that he let them graze by themselves, but the Lord God watched them and saw how they gnawed at the bark of the fruit trees or damaged the noble vines when they weren't destroying other tender plants. That distressed him and in his mercy and loving-kindness he let loose his wolves, which went and tore the goats to pieces. When the Devil heard about it, he went to the Lord and said: "Your creatures have torn mine to pieces." The Lord replied: "Why did you create them to do harm?" The Devil said: "I couldn't help it. My own thoughts turn to evil, and whatever I create is bound to have the same nature. You'll have to pay me dearly for this." "I'll pay you as soon as the oak leaves fall. Come to me then and I'll have your money all counted out for you." When the oak leaves had fallen, the Devil came and demanded his due. But the Lord said: "In the church at Constantinople there is a tall oak tree that still has all its leaves." Cursing and fuming, the Devil left the Lord and went looking for the oak tree. For six months he wandered in the wilderness before he found it, and by the time he got back, all the other oak trees were covered with green leaves again. So he was obliged to write the debt off, and in his rage he put out the eyes of all the remaining goats and gave them his own.

That's why all goats have Devil's eyes and bitten-off tails, and why the Devil likes to take their shape.

149

The Beam

THERE WAS ONCE a magician who was doing his marvelous tricks in the midst of a big crowd. One of them was to make a rooster pick up a heavy beam and carry it as if it were as light as a feather. Now there was a young girl in the crowd who had found a four-leaf clover, and that made her wits so sharp she could see through any flummery. One look and she knew that the beam was nothing but a straw. "Folks," she cried out, "can't you see that the rooster is only carrying a straw and not any beam?" Instantly the magic was broken, the people saw what was what, and drove the magician away in disgrace. Seething with rage, he said to himself: "I'll get even."

A little later the girl was going to be married. She had her wedding dress on and was walking through the fields in a big procession on her way to the village where the church was. All at once they came to a swollen brook and there was no bridge or plank across it. Quick as a wink, the bride picked up her skirts and started to wade. When she was right in the middle, a man near her—it was the magician— cried out: "Ha ha! Do you think this is a brook? Where are your eyes?" That woke her up and she saw she had picked up her skirts to wade through a blue-flowering field of flax. The wedding guests saw it too, and drove her away with jeers and laughter.

150

The Old Beggarwoman

THERE WAS ONCE an old woman. You must have seen an old woman begging? Well, this woman begged, and when she was given something, she said: "God reward you." She came to the door of a house where a kindly young scamp was standing by the fire warming himself. As she stood shivering by the door, he spoke gently to her and said: "Come in, old woman, come in and warm yourself." She went in, but then she stood too close to the fire and her rags began to burn, and she didn't know it. The young fellow stood there and watched. He should have put out the fire, don't you agree? And if he had no water, he should have wept so hard that all the water in his body flowed out of his eyes. Then he'd have had two nice little brooks to put the fire out with.

151

The Three Lazy Sons

A KING HAD THREE SONS whom he loved equally, and he didn't know which of them he should choose to be king after his death. When it came time for him to die, he called them to his bedside and said: "Dear children, I've come to a decision which I will now reveal to you: whichever one of you is the laziest shall become king after me." The eldest said: "Father, then the kingdom is mine, because I'm so lazy that when I'm lying on my back all ready to fall asleep and the rain starts falling in my eyes, I'd sooner stay awake than close them." The second said: "Father, the kingdom is mine, because I'm so lazy that when I sit warming myself by the fire, I'd sooner burn my heels than pull my legs in." The third said: "Father, the kingdom is mine, because I'm so lazy that if I were going to be hanged and the noose were already around my neck, and somebody handed me a sharp knife and said I could cut the rope with it, I'd sooner let them hang me than raise my hand to the rope." When the father heard that, he said: "You're the laziest of all. You shall be king."

151*

The Twelve Lazy Servants

TWELVE SERVANTS, who hadn't lifted a finger all day, were in no mood to exert themselves when evening came. Instead, they lay down in the grass and boasted of their laziness.

The first said: "What's your laziness to me? I'm too busy with my own. My main occupation is looking after my body. I eat plenty and drink more. When I've had four meals, I fast a little while until I'm hungry again. That's the life for me. I don't go in for early rising. Toward noon I start looking for a good place to rest. If the master calls, I pretend not to hear him. If he calls again, I take my time about getting up and move very slowly. These are the little things that make life bearable."

The second said: "I have a horse to look after, but I never take the bit out of his mouth. When I'm not in the mood I don't feed him, I say he's already eaten. By then I'm so tired I lie down in the oat box and sleep for four hours. Then I stretch out one foot and pass it over the horse's flank once or twice, and call it rubbing down and combing. Why bother to do more? But even so, the work is too much for me."

The third said: "Why bother with work? It doesn't get you anywhere. I lay down in the sun and slept. It began to drizzle, but why get up? I just let it rain. Finally there was a cloudburst. The rain came down so hard it tore my hair out, washed it away, and made a hole in my skull. I covered the hole with a plaster and that was that. I've had quite a few injuries of that sort."

The fourth said: "When I'm told to do some work, I first laze around for an hour to save my strength. Then I start in very slowly, all the while looking for other people to help me, and if I find any I let them do most of the work. To tell the truth, I just watch, but even that is too much for me."

The fifth said: "That's nothing. Listen to me. They tell me to clean the manure out of the stable and load it onto the wagon. I start slowly. Maybe I pick up a little something on my pitchfork, but I only lift halfway, and I rest fifteen minutes before pitching it. A wagonload a day is plenty for me. Do they expect me to work myself to death?"

The sixth said: "You ought to be ashamed. Work doesn't frighten me. But I go to bed for three weeks at a time without even undressing. Why have buckles on my shoes? Who cares if my shoes fall off? When I want to climb a flight of stairs, I drag one foot after the other to the top of the first step, then I count the remaining steps so I'll know where to rest."

The seventh said: "That wouldn't do for me. My master keeps an eye on my work, only he's out all day. But I never neglect a duty and

I run as fast as it's possible to crawl. To make me move faster, four strong men would have to push me with all their might. I came to a place where six men were lying side by side on a bed sleeping. I lay down beside them and slept too. They couldn't wake me, and when they wanted to get me home they had to carry me."

The eighth said: "I see I'm the only chipper one of the lot. If there's a stone in front of me, I don't take the trouble to lift my feet and step over it. I lie down on the ground, and if I get wet and muddy, I lie there till the sun comes out and dries me. At the most, I shift my position a little, so as to get the full warmth of it."

The ninth said: "Listen to this. Today I had a piece of bread in front of me, but I was too lazy to reach for it and I almost starved. There was a pitcher there too, but it was so big and heavy I couldn't bring myself to lift it and preferred to suffer thirst. Just to turn around was too much for me and I spent the whole day lying flat on my back."

The tenth said: "Laziness has brought me a broken leg and swollen calves. Three of us were lying by the roadside and I stretched out my legs. Someone came along in a wagon and the wheels passed over my legs. Of course I could have pulled them in, but I didn't hear the wagon coming, because the gnats were buzzing in my ears and crawling into my nose and out of my mouth. Do you think I bothered to shoo them away?"

The eleventh said: "Yesterday I gave my master notice. I was good and sick of bringing him his big heavy books and taking them away again. It went on all day. But to tell you the honest truth, he dismissed me, because I left his clothes lying in the dust and the moths devoured them. It was all right with me."

The twelfth said: "Today I had to drive the wagon to the next village. I made myself a bed of straw in it and fell fast asleep. The reins slipped out of my hands, and when I woke up the horse had almost broken loose, the harness was gone, backband, collar, bridle and bit. Some passer-by had made off with it. To make matters worse, the wagon was stuck in the mud. I didn't try to move it, I just lay down again in the straw. Finally the master himself came and pulled the wagon out. If he hadn't, I wouldn't be lying here, I'd still be there, sleeping peacefully."

152

The Shepherd Boy

THERE WAS ONCE a shepherd boy who was famous far and wide for the wise answers he gave when anyone asked him a question. The king of the country heard about him and didn't believe what he heard, so he sent for the boy and said to him: "If you can answer the three questions I'm going to ask you, I will look upon you as my own child and take you to live with me in my royal palace." "What are the questions?" the boy asked. Said the king: "The first question is: How many drops of water are there in the ocean?" The shepherd boy replied: "Sire, dam up all the rivers on earth so not a single drop of water can flow into the ocean until I've had a chance to count it. Then I'll tell you how many drops of water there are in the ocean." Said the king: "The second question is: How many stars are there in the sky?" The shepherd boy said: "Give me a big sheet of white paper." When he had the paper, he made so many dots on it with a pen point that it was hard to tell them apart, and impossible to count them all, and it made your head swim to look at them. Then he said: "There are as many stars in the sky as there are dots on this sheet of paper. Just count them." But no one was able to do it. Said the king: "The third question is: How many seconds are there in eternity?" The shepherd boy replied: "In Farther Pomerania there's a mountain known as the Diamond Mountain. It's three miles high and three miles long and three miles wide. Every hundred years a bird comes and sharpens its beak on it. When the mountain is worn away, the first second of eternity will have passed."

Said the king: "You have answered the three questions like a wise man. From now on you shall live in my royal palace and I will look upon you as my own child."

153

The Star Talers

THERE WAS ONCE a little girl whose father and mother had died and she was so poor she had no room to live in or bed to sleep in, and in the end there was nothing she could call her own but the clothes she had on and a piece of bread that some kind soul had given her. But she was a good, pious child, and when all the world forsook her, she put her trust in God and went out into the fields. There she met a poor man who said: "Oh, give me something to eat. I'm so hungry." She handed him her whole piece of bread, saying: "The Lord bless it to your use," and went on. Then came a child who moaned and said: "My head is so cold. Give me something to cover it with." She took her bonnet off and gave it to the child. When she had gone a little way, another child came along who had no bodice and was cold, so she gave it hers. Farther on, another child asked for a blouse, and she gave that away too. At last she came to a forest. It was dark by then and when still another child came and asked for a shift, the kind-hearted girl thought: "It's dark night. No one will see me. I can give my shift away." She took it off and gave it away, and as she stood there with nothing whatever left, stars began to fall from the sky, and they were shiny talers. Though she had given her shift away, she had a new one on, and it was made of the finest linen. She gathered the talers in it and was rich for the rest of her life.

154

The Stolen Pennies

ONE DAY A MAN was sitting at the dinner table with his wife and children and a good friend who had come to visit them. As they were sitting there, the clock struck twelve. Just then the visitor saw the door open and a pale child in snow-white clothes came in. The child didn't look around and didn't speak but went straight into the next room. After a while it came back, passed through the room as silently as before, and went away. The second and third day the child came and went again. Finally the visitor asked the father whose child it was that went into the next room at noon every day. "I didn't see it," he said. "I have no idea whose child it might be." When the child came again the next day, the visitor tried to point it out to the father, but he didn't see it, and the mother and children didn't see anything either. The visitor stood up, went to the door of the next room, opened it a little and looked in. He saw the child sitting on the ground, digging its fingers into the cracks between the floor boards and looking for something. But when the child caught sight of the visitor, it vanished. The visitor told the others what he had seen and described the child. Then the mother knew who it was, and said: "Oh dear, it's my darling child who died four weeks ago." They ripped up the floor boards and found two pennies the mother had once given the child for a poor man, but the child had thought: "I'll buy myself a piece of cake instead," and had kept the pennies and hidden them under the floor boards. But it had known no peace in its grave and had come back every day at noon to look for the pennies. The parents gave the money to a poor man and after that the child never came back.

155
Choosing a Bride

THERE WAS ONCE a young shepherd who wanted to get married and knew three sisters, one as beautiful as the next. That made it hard to choose and he couldn't decide which of them to ask. He went to his mother for advice, and she said: "Invite all three to our house, serve them cheese, and watch them to see how they eat it." The young shepherd took her advice. The first bolted the cheese rind and all, the second cut the rind off but she was in such a hurry that she left a good deal of cheese on it and threw that away too, while the third cut the rind off neatly, not too much and not too little. The shepherd told his mother what he had seen, and she said: "Take the third for your wife." He did, and lived a happy life with her.

156
The Odds and Ends

THERE WAS ONCE a girl who was pretty, but lazy and slovenly. Spinning put her in such a temper that if she found the tiniest knot in the flax she'd pull out a whole handful with it and scatter it on the floor around her. She had a serving maid who was a good hard worker. She gathered the flax her mistress had thrown away, cleaned it, spun it fine, and had it woven into a beautiful dress. A young man came courting the lazy girl and they were going to be married. A ball was held the night before the wedding, and the hard-working serving maid was there dancing merrily in her beautiful dress. The bride cried out:

> "Look at how she bows and bends,
> Decked out in my odds and ends."

The bridegroom heard her and asked her what she meant, and she told him how the girl was wearing a dress made from flax she had thrown away. When the bridegroom heard that and realized what a lazybones he had chosen and what a good worker the serving maid was, he left his bride standing, went over to the other and asked her to be his wife.

157

A Sparrow and His Four Sons

A SPARROW HAD four young ones in a swallow's nest. When they were fledged, some bad boys broke up the nest, but luckily all four of the young ones were carried off by the wind. The father sparrow was grieved that his sons had gone out into the world before he'd had time to warn them of its many dangers and inculcate wise precepts for dealing with them.

That fall a great many sparrows gathered in a wheat field, and there, to his great satisfaction, the old father ran into his four sons. He took them home with him and said: "Ah, my dear sons, how worried I've been about you all summer, ever since you left home without my teachings. Listen to me now, mark your father's words, and be very careful in the future. Small birds face great dangers."

Then he asked the eldest where he had spent the summer and what he had fed on. "I lived in gardens and fed on worms and caterpillars until the cherries were ripe." "Ah, my son, such delicacies are not to be sneezed at, but the risks are great. Always be on your guard, especially when you see men going about the orchards with long green poles that are hollow inside and have a hole at the end." "Oh yes, father," said the son, "and sometimes they take wax and fasten a green leaf over the hole." "Where did you see that?" "In a merchant's orchard," said the young sparrow. "Oh, my son," said the father, "merchants are full of guile. If you've been living among that kind, you've learned all the plotting and scheming you need. Just take care to make good use of it and don't be too sure of yourself."

Next he asked the second: "Where have you been keeping yourself?" "At court," said the son. "The palace," said the father, "is full of gold and velvet and silk, armor and harness, sparrowhawks, screech owls, and falcons. That's no place for sparrows and suchlike silly little birds. Stick to the stables where they winnow and thresh oats. There, if fortune smiles, you can pick up your daily measure of grain in safety." "Oh yes, father," said the son, "but if the stable boys make traps and set their gins and snares in the straw, many a little bird will be caught." "Where did you see that?" asked the father. "At court, among the stable boys." "Oh, my son, palace boys are bad boys. If you've been at court and lived among the high and mighty without leaving any feathers, you've learned a good deal and you'll get by in the world, but keep your eyes open, for wolves have been known to eat the cleverest puppies."

The father questioned the third son: "Where have you been pursuing your happiness?" "I searched the highways and byways and occasionally found a grain of wheat and barley." "Excellent fare," said the father, "but keep an eye on the embankment and look sharp. If someone bends down to pick up a stone, it's time for you to be moving on." "That's true," said the son. "But what if someone has hidden a stone or pebble under his shirt or in his pocket beforehand?" "Where did you see that?" "Among the miners, dear father. Most of them carry stones on their way home from the pit." "Miners are resourceful and hard-working," said the father. "If you've been among miners, you've seen and learned something.

> "Fly to the mines, but mind your skin and bones,
> For miner boys kill sparrows with their stones."

At last the father came to the youngest son. "Now, my chirping little nestling. You were always the stupidest and weakest. Stay home with me. The world is full of wicked, ruthless birds with crooked beaks and long claws that spend their days lurking in wait for poor little birds and gobbling them up. Stick to your own kind, gather spiders and caterpillars from trees and houses. Then you'll live long and happily." "Oh, my dear father, he who feeds himself without harming others will go far. No sparrowhawk, vulture, eagle, or kite can hurt him if morning and evening he faithfully commends himself and his rightful food to God, who is the creator and keeper of all the birds of forest and village, who heareth the cries and prayers of the young ravens, for no sparrow or wren falleth to the ground except by His will." "Where did you learn that?" The son replied: "When the wind carried me away from you, I ended up in a church. There I stayed, picking flies and spiders from the windows in the summertime. I learned these words of wisdom by listening to the preacher. All through the summer the Father of all sparrows fed me and preserved me from all misfortune and rapacious birds." "Faith, my dear son!" said the father, "if you take refuge in churches, and help to clean out the spiders and buzzing flies, and chirp to God like the young ravens, and commend yourself to the eternal Creator, you will prosper, though the whole world be full of savage and cruel birds.

> "For he who trusts his safety to the Lord,
> Who suffers meekly, devout in act and word,
> Who keeps his faith and conscience pure—
> The Lord will guard him safe and sure."

158

The Tale of Cock-a-doodle

IN THE DAYS OF COCK-A-DOODLE I went and saw Rome and the Lateran hanging from a silk thread. I saw a man without feet outrunning a swift horse and a sharp, sharp sword cutting a bridge in two. I saw a young donkey with a silver nose, chasing two fleet hares and I saw a broad lime tree with hot pancakes growing on it. I saw a scrawny old goat whose body contained a hundred cartloads of lard and sixty cartloads of salt. Isn't that lies enough for you? I saw a plow cutting the ground without horse or ox. A one-year-old child threw four millstones from Regensburg to Trier and from Trier to Strassburg, and a hawk swam across the Rhine, which he had a perfect right to do. I heard some fishes making such a hubbub that it echoed to high heaven, and saw sweet honey flowing like water from a deep valley to the top of a high mountain. All very strange. Two cranes were mowing a meadow, two gnats were building a bridge, two pigeons were tearing a wolf to pieces, two children were delivered of two lambs, and two frogs were threshing grain. I saw two mice consecrating a bishop and two cats scratching a bear's tongue out. A snail came running and killed two ferocious lions. A barber stood shaving a woman's beard off, and two sucking babes told their mother to be still. I saw two greyhounds dragging a mill out of the river. An old workhorse looked on and said it was a good thing to do. In the farm-yard four horses were threshing with might and main, two goats were firing the stove, and a red cow was shoving bread into the oven. Then a cock sang: "Cock-a-doodle-doo, that's my story, cock-a-doodle-doo."

159

The Ditmarsh Tale of Lies

I'M GOING TO TELL YOU something. I saw two roast chickens flying, they flew swiftly with their breasts turned heavenward and their backs hellward. An anvil and a millstone swam across the Rhine, as slowly and quietly as you please, and a frog was sitting on the ice at Whitsuntide, eating a plowshare. Three young fellows on crutches and stilts were trying to catch a hare. The first was deaf, the second was blind, the third was dumb, and the fourth couldn't move his feet. Do you want to know what happened? The blind one saw the hare running across the fields, the dumb one shouted to the lame one, and the lame one caught the hare by the collar. Some men wanted to sail on dry land. They set their sails in the wind and sailed across great fields. In the end they sailed over a high mountain and were misera-bly drowned. A crab was chasing a hare, and high up on the roof lay a cow, which had got there by climbing. In that country the flies are as big as the goats in this country. Open the window and let the lies out.

160
A Riddling Tale

THREE WOMEN had been turned into flowers that grew in the meadow, but one of them was allowed to go home at night. Once, just before daybreak, when she would soon have to go back to her friends in the field, she said to her husband: "If you come and pick me this morning, I shall be set free and then I shall stay with you always." And that is just what happened. The riddle is: Considering that the three flowers were exactly alike, without the slightest difference between them, how did her husband recognize her? Answer: Since she had spent the night in the house and not in the meadow, the dew had not fallen on her as it had on the other two. That's how her husband recognized her.

161
Snow White and Rose Red

A POOR WIDOW LIVED all alone in a hut and in front of the hut there was a garden with two rosebushes growing in it, one bearing white roses and the other red roses. She had two children, who resembled the two rosebushes, and one was called Snow White, the other Rose Red. No two children in all the world had ever been so good and kind, so willing and cheerful. Snow White was quieter and gentler than Rose Red. Rose Red liked best to run about the fields, looking for flowers and catching butterflies, while Snow White stayed home with her mother, helping with the housework, or reading to her when there was no work to be done.

The two children loved each other so dearly that they always held hands when they went out together, and when Snow White said: "We will never leave each other," Rose Red replied: "Never as long as we live," and their mother added: "What one of you has, she must share with the other." They often roamed the forest alone, picking red berries, and the animals made friends with them and never harmed them. The hare ate a cabbage leaf out of their hands, the roe grazed beside them, the stag came along, bounding merrily, and the birds sat still on their branches, singing all the songs they knew. No harm ever came to the little girls. When they stayed in the forest too long and night overtook them, they lay down side by side on the moss and slept till morning. Their mother knew what they were doing and didn't worry.

Once when they had spent the night in the forest and the dawn woke them, they saw a beautiful child dressed in glittering white sitting near them. The child arose, gave them a friendly look but said nothing, and went off into the forest. When they looked around, they saw they had been sleeping near a precipice and would certainly have fallen off if they had gone a few steps farther in the darkness. Their mother told them it must have been the angel who watches over good little children.

Snow White and Rose Red kept their mother's hut so neat and clean it was a pleasure to look at. Rose Red took care of the house in the summertime. Every morning before her mother woke up the little girl brought two flowers, a rose from each of the rosebushes, to her bedside. In the winter, Snow White lit the fire and hung the kettle over the hearth. The kettle was brass, but it was scoured so clean that it glistened like gold. In the evening when the snowflakes were falling, the mother would say: "Snow White, go and bolt the door." Then they would sit by the hearth, the mother would take her spectacles and read to them out of the big book and the two little girls would spin as they listened. A lamb lay on the floor beside them, and behind them on a perch sat a white dove with its head under its wing.

One evening as they were sitting quietly together, there was a knock at the door as though someone wished to be let in. The mother said: "Quick, Rose Red, open the door. It must be a wayfarer in need of shelter." Rose Red went and pushed back the bolt. She thought it would be a poor man, but it wasn't. It was a bear who thrust his big black head through the doorway. Rose Red screamed and leaped back. The lamb bleated, the dove fluttered into the air, and Snow White hid behind her mother's bed. But the bear spoke and said: "Don't be afraid. I won't hurt you, I'm half-frozen. All I want is to warm myself a little." "Poor bear," said the mother, "lie down by the hearth. Only take care your fur doesn't catch fire." Then she cried: "Snow White, Rose Red, come out, the bear won't hurt you, he means no harm." The two girls came out and little by little the lamb and the dove moved closer and weren't afraid of him any more. The bear said: "Children, beat my fur a little, it's full of snow." They brought the broom and swept the snow out of his coat, after which he stretched out by the fire and rumbled contentedly. Soon the children were used to him and the poor awkward guest had to put up with all sorts of mischief. They tugged at his fur, walked on him, and rolled him back and forth, or else they beat him with a hazel switch and laughed when he growled. The bear took it in good part, but when they went too far, he cried: "Children, children, let me live:

> "Snow White and Rose Red,
> You'll beat your suitor till he's dead."

When bedtime came, the others retired, and the mother said to the bear: "You're very welcome to spend the night by our hearth. Then you'll be safe against the cold and the harsh weather." At daybreak the children let him out and he trotted over the snow and into the forest. From then on he came every evening at the same time, lay down by the hearth and let the children tease him as much as they pleased. They grew so fond of their black friend that the door was never bolted until he got there.

One morning when spring had come and the whole countryside was green, the bear said to Snow White: "I must leave you now. I won't be able to visit you all summer." "Where are you going, dear bear?" she asked. "I must go to the forest to guard my treasures from the wicked dwarfs. In the winter when the ground is frozen hard, they have to stay in their caves because they can't work their way through, but now that the sun has warmed the ground and thawed it out, they break through and come up and ferret around and steal. And when they get their hands on something and carry it away to their caves, it's not very likely to see the light of day again." Snow White was sad to hear that he was going. When she opened the door for him and the bear pushed through, his coat caught on the latch, which tore it just a little, and Snow White thought she saw gold shining through, but she wasn't sure. The bear hurried away and soon vanished into the woods.

Some time after that the mother sent the girls to the forest to gather brushwood. They found a big felled tree trunk and near it something was jumping up and down in the grass, but they couldn't make out what it was. When they came closer, they saw a dwarf with a wizened old face and a long snow-white beard. The end of his beard was caught in a cleft of the tree trunk, and the little man was at his wits' end and jumping about like a dog on a chain. He glared at the girls out of his fiery red eyes and screamed: "Why are you standing there? Can't you come here and help me?" "How did it happen?" Rose Red asked. "Stupid nosey goose," said the dwarf. "I was trying to split this tree trunk to make firewood for the kitchen. The small portions of food we dwarfs eat get burned if we use big logs. We don't gobble and bolt like you crude greedy people. I drove the wedge in all right and there wouldn't have been any trouble, but the damned wood was so smooth it popped right out again and the cleft clapped shut on my beautiful white beard. Now it's caught and so am I. And you with your silly milk-fed faces, all you can do is laugh. Pooh! How nasty you are!" The girls tried hard, but his beard was stuck tight and they couldn't pull it out. "I'll run and get somebody," said Rose Red. "You crazy blockheads," the dwarf snarled. "Somebody indeed! There are two of you already, and that's too many. Is that all you can think of?" "Don't be so impatient," said Snow White. "Wait. I have an idea." Whereupon she took her little scissors out of her pocket and cut off the tip of his beard. As soon as the dwarf felt that he was free, he reached for a sack, which lay among the roots of the tree and had gold in it, and lifted it out, muttering: "Uncouth brats! Cutting a piece off my lovely beard. The Devil take you!" With that he heaved the sack over his shoulder and went away without another glance at the children.

Some time later Snow White and Rose Red thought they'd catch some fish for dinner. As they approached the brook, they saw something that looked like a big grasshopper hopping toward the water as if to jump in. When they came closer, they recognized the dwarf. "Where are you going?" asked Rose Red. "Not into the water, I hope." "I'm not such a fool," said the dwarf. "Can't you see? That damned fish is trying to pull me in." The little man had been sitting there fishing, and unluckily the wind had tangled his beard in his line. Then a big fish had bitten and the puny little fellow hadn't been strong enough to land it. The fish was getting the better of the struggle and was dragging him into the water. He kept clutching at the grass and rushes, but it didn't help him much. He had to follow the fish's movements, and might have toppled into the water at any moment. The little girls had got there in the nick of time. They held him fast and tried to separate the beard from the line, but in vain, for they were hopelessly tangled. There was nothing for it but to take out the scissors and cut through the snarl. A small part of the beard was lost, and when the dwarf saw that, he cried out: "You nasty toads! What a thing to do! You've disfigured me. You weren't satisfied with clipping the end of my beard, now you've cut away the best part of it. I won't be able to show myself at home. I hope you have to walk a hundred miles and lose the soles off your shoes first." With that, he picked up a sack of pearls that was hidden in the rushes. Then without another word he dragged it away and disappeared behind a stone.

One day the mother sent the two little girls to town to buy needles and thread and laces and ribbons. Their way led across a heath that had big rocks scattered about on it. All at once they caught sight of a big bird high above them. It circled slowly downward, then suddenly swooped down on a big rock not far away. A moment later they heard a heart-rending scream. They ran to the spot and saw to their horror that the eagle had seized hold of their old friend the dwarf and was about to carry him away. The kindly children held the little man fast and tugged at him until the eagle finally let go. When the dwarf recovered from his fright, he screamed at them with his shrill voice: "Did you have to be so rough? My poor little jacket! You've practically pulled it to pieces. Clumsy clods!" Then he picked up a sack full of jewels and slipped back into his cave under the rocks. The little girls were used to his ingratitude. They continued on to town and did their errands. When they came to the heath on the way back, they surprised the dwarf, who hadn't supposed that anyone would be passing so late and had emptied a sack of jewels on the bare ground. The evening sun shone on the stones, and they sparkled and glittered so beautifully in all colors that the children stopped to look. "Why are you standing there gaping?" cried the dwarf. His ash-gray face went scarlet with rage, and he was thinking up fresh insults when a loud growl was heard and a black bear came trotting out of the forest. The dwarf jumped up in a fright, but the bear was already too near and he hadn't time to slip away into his hole. The dwarf cried out in terror: "Oh, dear Mr. Bear, spare me, I'll give you all my treasures, all these beautiful jewels. Don't eat me. What would you get out of a wee little fellow like me? You wouldn't even know you had me between your teeth. Eat these wicked girls, they're as fat as young quails, tasty morsels, eat them in good health." The bear wasn't even listening. He struck out just once with his paw, and after that the wicked creature didn't move.

The girls had fled, but the bear called out to them: "Snow White and Rose Red, don't be afraid. Wait, I'll go with you." They recognized his voice and stopped. When the bear caught up with them, his bear skin suddenly fell off, and there stood a handsome man, dressed all in gold. "I am a king's son," he said. "That wicked dwarf stole my treasures. Then with his magic he turned me into a bear, and I had to roam the forest until his death set me free. Now he has got his well-earned punishment."

Snow White was married to him and Rose Red to his brother, and they shared the enormous treasures the dwarf had heaped up in his cave. The old mother lived for many years peacefully and happily with her daughters. She took the two rosebushes with her and planted them outside her window, and every year they bore the most beautiful white and red roses.

162

The Wise Servant

How FORTUNATE A MASTER IS, and how his household prospers when he has a wise servant who listens patiently to his instructions but rather than follow them prefers to act on his own wisdom. Hans was just such a wise servant. His master once sent him to look for a lost cow, and after he had been gone a long while, the master thought: "No effort is too great for my faithful Hans." But as time passed and Hans didn't come home, the master feared he had had an accident and went looking for him. He had to look a long time. At length he saw his servant running back and forth in a big field. "Well, my dear Hans," said the master when he had caught up with him, "have you found the cow I sent you to look for?" "Oh no, master," he replied, "I haven't found the cow, but then I haven't been looking for her." "What have you been looking for, Hans?" "Something better, and I've found it, too." "What's that, Hans?" "Three blackbirds," said the servant. "And where are they?" asked the master. The wise servant replied: "I see one, I hear one, and I'm chasing the third."

Let that be an example to you. Don't worry about your master and his orders. Do whatever enters your head, whatever you feel like. Then you'll be acting as wisely as wise Hans.

163
The Glass Coffin

DON'T EVER SAY a poor tailor can't rise in the world and win great honors. All he has to do is get to the right place at the right time and, most important of all, have good luck. Once in the course of his wanderings a sprightly young tailor's apprentice came to a great forest, and there he got lost, for he didn't know the way. Night fell and there was nothing else for him to do but look for a place to sleep in the grisly wilds. He could have made a nice bed on the soft moss, but he was too much afraid of wild animals, and he finally decided to spend the night in a tree. So he climbed to the top of a tall oak and gave thanks to God that he had his flatiron with him, because otherwise the wind that was blowing through the treetops would have carried him away.

When he had spent a few hours in the darkness, scared half out of his wits, he saw a light shining not far away, and guessing it came from a human habitation where he could be more comfortable than in the branches of a tree, he climbed cautiously down and made for the light. It led him to a hut plaited from reeds and rushes. He knocked boldly, the door opened, and a shaft of light from inside fell on a little gray-haired old man dressed in a coat of many-colored patches. "Who are you and what do you want?" he grumbled. "I'm a poor tailor and night has overtaken me in the forest. I implore you to let me stay in your hut until morning." "Go away," said the old man peevishly. "I want no truck with tramps. Get yourself a lodging somewhere else." After saying these words he was going to slip back into his hut, but the tailor held him by the coattails and pleaded so heart-rendingly that the little man, who wasn't as unfriendly as he appeared, finally relented and let him in. After giving him something to eat, he showed him a comfortable place to sleep in the corner.

The weary tailor had no need of a lullaby. He slept peacefully until morning, and even then he'd have had no thought of getting up if he hadn't been startled by a loud noise. Through the thin walls of the hut a fierce roaring and bellowing could be heard. Fired with un-accustomed courage, the tailor leaped out of bed, threw his clothes on, and ran outside. Not far away a big black bull and a beautiful stag were fighting desperately, charging each other with such fury that the ground trembled under their hoofbeats and the air resounded with their bellowing. For a long time the outcome seemed uncertain, but in the end the stag thrust his antlers into his enemy. The bull fell to the ground with a frightful roar, and the stag finished him off with a few more blows.

The tailor, who had been looking on with amazement, was still standing motionless. Suddenly the stag came bounding toward him and, before he could run away, picked him up on his big antlers. He hadn't much time to think, for the stag ran headlong over hill and dale, through bush and brake, forest and meadow. The tailor clutched the ends of the antlers with both hands and abandoned him-self to his fate. He felt as if he were flying away. Finally the stag stopped at the foot of a cliff and let the tailor down gently. More dead than alive, the tailor needed some time to collect his wits. When he had more or less recovered, the stag, who had been standing beside him, butted a door at the base of the cliff so hard with his horns that it sprang open. Flames poured from the doorway, followed by clouds

of smoke that hid the stag from sight. The tailor was utterly bewildered and couldn't imagine how he would ever escape from this wilderness and get back to the world of men. As he stood thus per-
plexed, he heard a voice from inside the cliff, saying: "Come in, don't
be afraid, you will suffer no harm." He hesitated, but then, impelled
by a mysterious force, he obeyed the voice and passed through the
iron door into a large and spacious room. The ceiling, walls, and floor
were made of freestone blocks, polished till they shone. Signs unknown to him were carved on each of the blocks. He gaped for a
while in amazement and was going to leave, when again he heard the
voice. It said to him: "Step on the stone in the center of the room.
Great good fortune awaits you."

His courage had grown steadily, and he obeyed. The stone gave
beneath his feet and sank slowly. When it stopped moving and the
tailor looked around, he was in a room of the same size as the one
above. But here there was more to wonder at. Recesses had been
carved in the walls, and in them stood vessels of transparent glass,
filled with colored vapor or bluish smoke. On the floor, facing each
other, were two glass cases. These aroused his curiosity. He went
closer to one of them and saw inside it a magnificent castle, surrounded by farmhouses, stables, barns, and many other beautiful
things, all very tiny, but ever so delicately wrought, as though carved
with the utmost care by a skilled and practiced hand.

He would never have taken his eyes off these marvels, if the voice
hadn't spoken again, commanding him to turn around and look at the
glass case on the opposite side. He was more amazed than ever when
he looked inside it and saw a wonderfully beautiful maiden. She lay
as though asleep, her long golden hair wrapped around her like a precious cloak. Her eyes were closed tight but the freshness of her face
and a ribbon that moved to and fro as she breathed left no doubt that
she was alive. The tailor was gazing at her with pounding heart when
all at once she opened her eyes and started with joy at the sight of
him. "Merciful heavens!" she cried. "I shall soon be set free. Quick,
quick! Help me out of my prison. Push back the bolt on this glass
coffin and I shall be saved." Without delay the tailor pushed back the
bolt and she lifted the glass lid. After climbing out, she hurried to the
corner of the room and wrapped herself in a wide cloak. Then, sitting down on a stone, she bade the young man approach, kissed him

lovingly on the lips, and said: "You are the savior I have longed for. God in His mercy has led you to me and put an end to my sufferings. On this same day your happiness shall begin. You are my heaven-sent husband, and you shall spend the rest of your life in unbroken joy, loved by me and showered with earthly possessions of every kind. Sit down and listen to my story.

"I am the daughter of a wealthy count. My parents died when I was very young, having entrusted me in their will to my elder brother, who brought me up. We loved each other so tenderly, we were so much alike in our thoughts and inclinations, that we decided never to marry, but to stay together to the end of our lives. There was always plenty of company in our house. Neighbors and friends often came visiting, and we showed them all the fullest measure of hospitality. So it came about that one evening a stranger came riding into our castle, and asked for a night's lodging on the pretext that the nearest town was too far away. We granted his plea with the greatest courtesy, and at dinner he entertained us delightfully with his conversation and tales. My brother liked him so well that he asked him to stay a few days, and the stranger, after refusing for some time, consented. It was late that night when we left the table. The stranger was shown to a room, and I was so tired I couldn't wait to slip into my downy bed. I had barely dropped off to sleep when I was awakened by the sound of soft sweet music. I couldn't imagine where it came from, and I wanted to call my lady's maid, who slept in the next room, but to my consternation some strange power had deprived me of speech. I couldn't make the least sound and I felt as if I had a heavy weight on my chest. Then by the light of my night lamp I saw the stranger coming into my room, though it was closed off from outside by two locked doors. He came close to me and told me how with the help of magic arts he had made the sweet music in order to wake me and how he had passed through the locked doors in the intention of offering me his hand and heart. His magic arts inspired me with such loathing that I didn't even answer him. He stood there awhile, no doubt hoping for a favorable reply, but when I kept silent, he grew angry and cried out that he would avenge himself and punish me for my pride. Then he left the room. I spent an anguished night and only fell asleep toward morning. When I woke up, I ran to tell my brother what had happened, but he wasn't in his room, and his servant told me he had gone hunting with the stranger at daybreak.

"Fearing the worst, I dressed quickly, had my palfrey saddled, and, taking only one servant with me, rode full tilt into the forest. My servant's horse fell and broke its leg, and I was obliged to leave him behind. I went my way without stopping, and in a few minutes I saw the stranger coming toward me, leading a beautiful stag by a rope. I asked him where he had left my brother and how he had come by this stag, whose big eyes were full of tears. His only answer was a loud laugh. I flew into a rage, drew a pistol, and fired it at the monster, but the bullet bounced back from his chest and into my horse's head. I fell to the ground, and the stranger mumbled a few words that made me lose consciousness.

When I came to, I was in a glass coffin in this underground vault. The magician came to me again and told me what he had done. He had turned my brother into a stag and had shut up my castle and all its outbuildings in a glass case after making them very, very small. As for my courtiers and servants, he had transformed them all into vapor and put them into glass bottles. If I did as he wished, he said, he could easily set everything to rights, and he would only have to open the cases and bottles for everyone and everything to recover their natural form. I didn't answer him any more than I had the first time. He vanished and left me lying in my prison. A deep sleep overcame me, and among the visions that passed across my mind, there was one that comforted me: in it a young man came and set me free. And today when I opened my eyes, I saw you and knew my dream had come true. But still other things happened in my vision. Help me to do what remains to be done! First we must lift the glass case with my castle in it, and put it on that big stone."

Once the weight was on the stone, the stone rose, carrying the maiden and the young man through the opening in the ceiling. From the upper room the two of them easily made their way into the open, and there the maiden took off the lid. It was marvelous to see the castle, the outbuildings, and farmhouses expand and quickly grow to their natural size. Then the young man and the maiden went back to the underground cave and made the stone carry up the smoke-filled bottles. No sooner had the maiden opened them than the blue smoke poured out and was transformed into living people, whom the maiden recognized as her servants and courtiers. Her joy was even greater when her brother, who had killed the magician in the form of a bull, came out of the forest in human form. And that same day, as she had promised, the maiden gave the lucky tailor her hand at the altar.

164

Lazy Heinz

HEINZ WAS LAZY, and though he had nothing else to do but take his goat to pasture, he groaned when he came home at night after his day's work. "It's a heavy burden and a bitter trial," he said, "taking a goat to the meadow day in, day out, until late in the fall. If only I could lie down and sleep! But no, I have to keep my eyes open or she'll damage the young trees, squeeze through the hedge into the garden, or even run away. How, under such conditions, can I hope for any peace or enjoyment of life?" He sat down, mustered his thoughts, and cast about for a way of getting this burden off his shoulders. For a time he searched in vain. Then suddenly the scales seemed to fall from his eyes. "I know what I'll do!" he cried out. "I'll marry Fat Trina. She has a goat too, she'll take them both out together, and I won't have to wear myself out any more."

Heinz stood up, set his weary limbs in motion, crossed the road, for that was as far as he had to go to get to the house where Fat Trina's parents lived, and asked for the hand of their virtuous, hardworking daughter. Her parents were quick to grant it, for they held that "birds of a feather flock together." So Fat Trina became Heinz's wife and took both goats to pasture. Heinz had pleasant days, with no need to recuperate from anything more strenuous than his own idleness. He went along with her only very occasionally, and then he explained: "I'm only doing it because rest will be all the sweeter afterward. Otherwise I might lose my feeling for it."

But Fat Trina was just as lazy as he was. "Dear Heinz," she said one day, "why should we poison our lives needlessly and ruin the best days of our youth? Morning after morning these two goats of ours wake us out of our sweetest slumbers with their bleating. Wouldn't it be a good idea to trade them with our neighbor for a beehive? We'll put the beehive in a sunny place behind the house, and that will be the end of our troubles. Bees don't have to be tended or taken out to pasture. They fly to their feeding ground, they find their own way home, and they make honey without the slightest effort on our part." "You speak like a wise woman," said Hans. "We'll carry out your plan without delay. Honey tastes better than goat's milk anyway. And besides, it's more nourishing and it keeps longer."

Their neighbor was glad to give them a beehive for their two goats. The bees flew in and out from early morning till late afternoon, and filled the hive with the finest honey. That fall Heinz was able to take out a whole jugful.

They put the jug on a shelf fastened to the wall of their bedroom and, fearing it might be stolen or that mice might get into it, Trina brought in a sturdy hazel rod and put it beside the bed, where, if uninvited guests should put in an appearance, she could reach it without getting up.

Lazy Heinz didn't like to leave his bed before noon. "Early riser, none the wiser," he would say. One morning when he was lying abed in broad daylight, resting from his long slumbers, he said to his wife: "Women have a sweet tooth. You're always into the honey. Before it's all gone we'd better trade it for a goose and a young gander." "But not until we have a child to tend them," said Fat Trina. "Do you want me to wear myself out and needlessly sap my strength taking care of the goslings?" "What makes you think our son will look after the geese?" asked Heinz. "Children don't obey their parents any more. They do as they please because they think they're smarter, just like that servant who went chasing three blackbirds when he was supposed to be looking for a cow." "Well well," said Trina. "This one had better do what I tell him, or I'll show him the reason why. I'll take a stick and the blows will fall like rain." She picked up the stick she'd been planning to use on the mice, and cried out in her enthusiasm: "See, Heinz? Like this. This is what I'll do." She wound up and swung, but unfortunately the stick landed on the honey jug over the bed. The jug was dashed against the wall and broken to bits, and the lovely honey dripped down on the floor. "There go the goose and the young gander," said Heinz. "They'll need no tending now. And isn't it lucky the jug didn't fall on my head! We both have reason to be thankful." He saw a bit of honey in one of the shards and said cheerfully: "Let's enjoy the little bit that's left, and then suppose we rest up from our fright. Who cares if we get up a little later than usual? The day will still be long enough." "Yes indeed," said Trina. "Why hurry? Remember the story? The snail was once invited to a wedding. He started promptly and arrived in time for the child's christening. And as he dropped from the top of the fence outside the house, he cried: 'There never was any point in hurrying.'"

165

The Griffin

THERE WAS ONCE A KING, but I don't know where he ruled or what his name was. He had no son, just an only daughter who'd always been sick, and no doctor could cure her. A fortuneteller told the king his daughter would get well by eating apples. So he made it known all over the country that anyone who brought his daughter apples that made her well would have her for his wife and become king. A peasant with three sons heard about it, and he said to the eldest: "Go out in the garden and pick a basketful of those beautiful apples with the red cheeks and take them to the palace. Maybe the king's daughter will eat them and get well. Then you'll marry her and get to be king." The young fellow did what his father had told him and started out.

When he had gone a little way, he met an iron dwarf, who asked him what he had in the basket. "Frog's legs," said Uele, for that was his name. "So be it!" said the dwarf, and went his way. When Uele got to the palace, he told the gatekeeper he had apples that would make the king's daughter well if she ate them. The king was mighty glad to hear it and had Uele brought in, but oh, calamity! when he took the lid off there were frog's legs instead of apples in the basket, and they were still twitching. The king was very angry and had him driven out of the house.

When he got home, he told his father what had happened to him. Then the old man sent his second son, whose name was Saeme, but the same thing happened to him. He too met the iron dwarf, who asked him what he had in the basket. "Pig's bristles," said Saeme, and the dwarf said: "So be it!" When he got to the palace and said he had apples that could make the king's daughter well, they didn't want to let him in and said another fellow had been there and tried to make fools out of them. But Saeme said he most certainly had apples and insisted they should let him in. In the end they believed him and took him to the king, but when he opened the basket, it had pig's bristles in it. The king was very angry and had Saeme whipped out of the house.

When he got home, he told them what had happened to him. So then the youngest son, whom they called Stupid Hans, asked the old man to let him take some apples and go to the palace. "Wouldn't you just be the one for it!" said the father. "If the smart ones fail, what can you expect?" But the boy was stubborn. "Father," he said, "I want to go too." "Don't bother me, you stupid fool," said the father. "You'll just have to wait till you're smarter." With that the old man turned his back, but Hans plucked at his coat and said: "Father, I want to go too." "All right!" cried the old man impatiently. "Go for all I care. You'll be back soon enough." The boy was so happy he started to hop, skip, and jump. "There you go," said the old man, "playing the fool. You get stupider every day." That didn't bother Hans, nothing could spoil his pleasure. But since it was almost dark, he thought he'd wait until morning, for he couldn't have reached the palace that same day. So he went to bed but he couldn't sleep, and when he did doze off for a while, he dreamed of beautiful maidens and castles and gold and silver and things like that.

Early in the morning he started out, and in a little while he met the dirty little man in the iron clothes, who asked him what he had in his basket. Hans said he had apples and hoped the king's daughter would eat them and get well. "Then so be it!" said the little man. But when Hans reached the palace, they were dead set against letting him in, for they said two others had already been there claiming to have apples, and one had had frog's legs and the other pig's bristles. Hans insisted that he didn't have frog's legs, but the finest apples in the whole kingdom. He had such a nice way of talking that the gate-keeper thought he couldn't be lying and let him in. And he was right, for when Hans took the lid off the basket in the king's presence, golden-yellow apples came tumbling out. The king was delighted. He sent a few to his daughter and waited anxiously for someone to come and tell him what effect they had had. He hadn't long to wait. And who do you think it was that came to tell him? It was his daughter in person. She'd hardly taken a bite out of an apple when she jumped out of bed in perfect health. The king's joy was greater that anyone could describe, but he refused to give Hans his daughter for his wife, and said he'd first have to make a boat that would go faster on dry land than on water. Hans agreed to that and went home and told them what had happened.

The old man sent Uele to the forest to make the boat, and he worked hard, whistling all the while. At noon, when the sun was at its highest, the iron dwarf came and asked him what he was making. "Wooden spoons," said Uele, and the dwarf replied: "So be it!" At the end of the day Uele thought he had made a boat, but when he wanted to get into it, all he had was wooden spoons. The next day Saeme went to the woods, but the same thing happened to him. The third day, Stupid Hans went. He worked so hard that the whole forest rang with his powerful blows, and all the while he sang and whistled merrily. At noon, when the sun was at its hottest, the dwarf came and asked him what he was making. He replied: "A boat that will go faster on dry land than on water. And when it's finished I'll get the king's daughter for my wife." "In that case," said the little man, "so be it."

At the end of the day when the sun had turned to gold, Hans had finished his boat, oars and all. He got in and rowed to the palace. The boat went as fast as the wind and the king saw it coming in the distance. But he still wouldn't give Hans his daughter and said he'd first have to take a hundred hares out to pasture and tend them from morning to night, and if a single one got away he couldn't have his daughter. Again Hans agreed, and that same day he went to the pasture with his herd. He watched them so closely that not a one got away, but before many hours had passed, a maid came from the pal-

ace and said: "You must give me a hare this minute, because some vis-
itors have arrived." Hans knew perfectly well what she was up to
and refused, saying: "If the king wants to set jugged hare before his
guests, he can do it tomorrow." The maid, who couldn't see the
reason for his refusal, began to get angry. So then Hans said that if
the king's daughter came out in person, he'd give her a hare. The
maid went back with his message and the king's daughter said she'd
go. In the meantime the dwarf came to Hans and asked him what
he was doing: "I'm watching a hundred hares. If none of them gets
away, the king will give me his daughter for my wife and I'll be
king." "Good," said the little man. "Take this whistle. If one of the
hares runs away, just whistle and he'll come back." When the king's
daughter got there, Hans put a hare in her apron. But when she had
gone a hundred paces, Hans whistled, the hare jumped out of her
apron, and quick as a flash went back to the herd. At the end of the
day Hans whistled again, looked to make sure his hares were all
there, and drove them to the palace.

The king was amazed that Hans had managed to keep a hundred
hares all day without any of them running away. But he still
wouldn't give him his daughter unless he brought him a feather out
of the Griffin's tail. Hans started off right away and strode along at a
good clip. At nightfall he came to a castle and asked for lodging, because in those days there were no inns. The lord of the castle gave
him a hearty welcome and asked him where he was going. "To see
the Griffin," said Hans. "Oh, to see the Griffin! I'm told he knows
everything, and I've lost the key to the iron treasure chest. Would
you be kind enough to ask him where it is?" "Of course," said Hans.
"Of course I will." Early in the morning he went his way. That evening he came to another castle and there too he spent the night.
When the castle folk heard he was going to see the Griffin, they told
him the daughter of the house was sick, and that they had tried every
remedy but none had helped her. And then they asked him if he
would kindly find out from the Griffin what would make her well
again. "I'll be glad to," said Hans, and went his way. After a while he
came to a river. Instead of a ferry there was a big tall man who had
to carry everyone across. The man asked Hans where he was going.
"To see the Griffin," said Hans. "Fine!" said the man. "When you
see him, would you ask him why I have to carry everybody across

this river?" "Oh yes," Hans replied. "Heavens yes, I will, I will." So then the man picked him up and carried him across on his shoulders.

Finally Hans came to the Griffin's house, but only his wife was home, the Griffin himself was out. The wife asked him what he wanted, and Hans told her the whole story, how he had to get a feather out of the Griffin's tail, how there was a castle where they'd lost the key to a treasure chest and they wanted him to ask the Griffin where it was, how in another castle the daughter was sick, and they wanted him to ask what would make her well again, and how not far from the Griffin's house there was a river and a man who had to carry people across it, and how this man had asked him to ask the Griffin why he had to carry people across. "Look here, my young friend," said the woman, "no Christian can talk to the Griffin. He eats them all up. But if you like, you can lie under his bed, and during the night when he's sound asleep, you can pull a feather out of his tail. And about the things you want to know, I'll ask him myself." That was good enough for Hans, and he crept under the bed.

At nightfall the Griffin came home, and the moment he set foot in the house he said: "Wife, I smell a Christian." "Oh yes," said his wife. "A Christian was here today, but he left." After that the Griffin didn't say another word. In the middle of the night, when the Griffin had settled down to a steady snore, Hans reached up and pulled a feather out of his tail. The Griffin woke up and said: "Wife, I smell a Christian, and it seems to me that someone's been pulling my tail." "You must have dreamed that," said the wife. "I've told you a Christian was here, but he went away. He told me all sorts of things. He said there's a castle where they've lost the key to a treasure chest and they can't find it." "Oh, the fools!" said the Griffin. "It's behind the door of the woodshed, under a log." "And then he told me about a castle where they have a sick daughter and they don't know how to make her well again." "Oh, the fools!" said the Griffin. "A toad has taken some of her hair and made a nest out of it under the cellar stairs. If she got her hair back, she'd be well." "And then he told me about a man who had to carry people across a river." "Oh, the fool!" said the Griffin. "If he put somebody down in the middle just once, he'd never have to carry anyone across again."

Early in the morning the Griffin got up and left the house. Then Hans came out from under the bed. Besides having a lovely feather,

he knew what the Griffin had said about the key and the daughter
and the man. But the Griffin's wife repeated it all to make sure Hans
wouldn't forget, and then he started for home. First, he came to the
man by the river, who asked him right away what the Griffin had
said. "First, carry me across," said Hans, "and then I'll tell you."
When the man had carried him across, Hans told him that all he had
to do was put someone down in the middle of the river and then he'd
never have to carry anybody across again. The man was mighty glad
to hear it. "To show my gratitude," he said, "I'll give you another
ride back and forth." "Oh no," said Hans. "I wouldn't put you to so
much trouble. You've done quite enough for me as it is." And away
he went. When he got to the castle where the daughter was sick, he
picked her up on his shoulders because she couldn't walk, and carried
her down the cellar stairs. Then he took the toad's nest out from
under the first step and put it in her hand. In a flash she jumped off
his shoulders and ran up the stairs ahead of him in perfect health. The
father and mother were mighty happy and gave him gold and silver
and anything else he wanted. When he got to the other castle, he
went straight to the woodshed, and sure enough he found the key
under the log behind the door, and brought it to the lord of the castle. He was very happy too and rewarded Hans with a good deal of
the gold that was in the chest, and a lot of other things, such as cows
and sheep and goats. When Hans came back to the king with all that
money and gold and silver and cows and sheep and goats, the king
asked him how he'd come by it all, and Hans told him the Griffin
gave people anything they asked for. Thinking such treasures would
be just the thing for him, the king set out to visit the Griffin. But
when he came to the river, it turned out that he was the first person
to get there since Hans. The man put him down in the middle and
went away, and the king was drowned. So then Hans married his
daughter and got to be king.

166

Hefty Hans

THERE WERE ONCE a man and his wife who had only one child and lived all alone in a remote valley. One day the mother went to the woods to pick up kindling, and she took little Hans, who was only two years old with her. It was springtime, the child delighted in the bright-colored flowers, and she led him farther and farther into the woods. Suddenly two robbers jumped out of a thicket, seized the mother and child, and took them deep into a dark forest to places where from year's end to year's end nobody every went. The poor woman implored the robbers to let her and her child go, but the robbers' hearts were of stone and, deaf to all her prayers, they made her go on. After struggling through brambles and briers for several hours, they came to a rock wall with a door in it. The robbers knocked on the door and, when it opened, made their way through a long dark passage to a big cave, lit by a hearth fire. On the wall, flashing in the light, hung swords, sabers, and other murderous weapons, and in the middle of the cave there was a black table at which four other robbers sat playing dice. The robber captain was sitting at the head of the table, and when he saw the woman he came over and spoke to her. "Don't be afraid," he said. "We won't hurt you. All you'll have to do is keep house for us. If you keep the place neat and clean, you'll be well treated." Then he gave her something to eat and showed her a bed that she and the child could sleep in.

The woman stayed with the robbers for many years, and Hans grew to be big and strong. His mother told him stories and taught him to read out of an old book of chivalry that she found in the cave. When Hans was nine, he made himself a sturdy club out of a fir branch and hid it behind the bed. Then he went to his mother and said: "Dear mother, it's time you told me who my father is. I must and will know." His mother didn't answer. She was afraid he'd be homesick if she told him. And besides, she knew the wicked robbers would never let him out of the cave. But it almost broke her heart to think that Hans couldn't go to his father. That night, when the robbers came home from one of their expeditions, Hans took out his club, went up to the captain, and said: "I want to know who my father is, and if you don't tell me right this minute, I'm going to knock you dead." The captain laughed and gave Hans a clout on the ear that sent him tumbling under the table. Hans picked himself up but didn't say a word. "I'll wait another year," he thought, "and then I'll try again. Maybe I'll do better next time."

When a year had passed, he took out his club again, wiped the dust off, looked it over, and said: "It's a good strong club." That night the robbers came home and when they had drained several jugs of wine, their heads began to droop. Then Hans took his club, went up to the captain and asked him again who his father was. Again the captain clouted him over the ear so hard that he rolled under the table, but a moment later he was back on his feet, and gave the captain and the robbers such a drubbing with his club that they lay flat on their backs unable to stir a muscle. His mother stood in a corner and marveled at his strength and courage. Once the robbers were disposed of, Hans went to his mother and said: "This time I mean it. I want to know who my father is." "Dear Hans," said his mother, "come with me. We'll search until we find him." She took the door key from the robber captain and Hans filled a big flour sack with gold, silver, and any other valuables he could find. He slung the sack over his shoulder, and they left the cave. How amazed Hans was when he stepped out of the darkness into the daylight and saw the green woods, the flowers, the birds, and the morning sun! He stood there gaping as if he had taken leave of his senses. His mother managed to find the right path, and after walking a few hours they came to their remote valley and their little house. The father was sitting in the doorway. He wept for joy when he recognized his wife and heard that Hans was his son, for he had long thought them both dead. Though Hans was just twelve, he was a head taller than his father. They went inside together. When Hans put his sack down on the bench by the stove, the whole house began to creak and groan, the bench collapsed, the floor gave way, and the heavy sack fell through into the cellar. "The Lord protect us!" cried the father. "Now look what you've done. You've smashed our whole house to pieces." "Don't let that worry you, father," said Hans. "There's more in that sack than we need for a new house." And sure enough, father and son set to work building a new house, bought cattle and land, and started to farm it. Hans plowed the fields, and when he walked behind the plow, pushing it through the soil, the oxen hardly had to pull.

The following spring Hans said: "Father, you keep all the money and have a hundred-pound staff made for me, because I'm going out into the world." When the staff was ready, he left his father's house and soon came to a deep, dark forest. There he heard a sound of tearing and cracking and, when he looked around, saw a fir tree that was twisted like a rope from top to bottom. Raising his eyes, he saw a big man who had taken hold of the tree and was twisting it round and round like a willow switch. "Hey!" Hans shouted. "What are you doing up there?" The man replied: "I cut a few faggots yesterday and I'm twisting a rope to tie them with." "There's a man after my own heart," said Hans to himself. "He's no weakling." And he called out to him: "Forget your faggots and come with me." When the fellow climbed down, he turned out to be a head taller than Hans, and Hans wasn't small. "From now on," said Hans, "your name will be Fir Twister." They went on together and after a while they heard somebody pounding and hammering so hard that the earth trembled at every blow. Soon they came to a big cliff, and a giant was standing beside it, knocking off big chunks of it with his fist. When Hans asked him what he was doing, he said: "When I try to sleep at night, bears and wolves and suchlike vermin come sniffing at me and keep me awake. So I'm building a house where I can lie down in peace." "Perfect," thought Hans, "here's another man I can use." And he said to him: "Forget your house and come with me. From now on your name will be Cliff Smasher." The man agreed and the three of them strode through the forest, and wherever they went the wild animals fled in terror.

At nightfall they came to a deserted castle, climbed the steps and lay down to sleep in the main hall. Next morning Hans went down into the garden, which was overgrown with weeds and brambles. As he was strolling about, a wild boar charged him, but he gave it such a blow with his staff that it fell down dead. He threw the carcass over his shoulders and carried it upstairs. There they put it on a spit, roasted it, and had a feast. After that they agreed to take turns: each day two would go hunting, while the third would stay home and cook meat for them—nine pounds each. The first day Fir Twister stayed home, while Hans and Cliff Smasher went hunting. While Fir Twister was busy cooking, a shriveled little old man came in and asked for some meat. "Beat it, you little sneak," said Fir Twister. "You don't need any meat." But to Fir Twister's amazement the little man, who looked as if he couldn't lift a feather, jumped up on him and battered him so furiously with his fists that he couldn't defend himself and fell to the floor, gasping for air. The little man didn't go away until he had worked off all his rage. When the two others came home from hunting, Fir Twister didn't breathe a word about the little man or the beating he'd had. He thought to himself: "When it's their turn to stay home, they'll see how they make out with the old prickly pear." It tickled him just to think about it.

Next day Cliff Smasher stayed home, and what had happened to Fir Twister happened to him: he wouldn't give the little man any meat, and the little man thrashed him. When the others came home that night, one look at him told Fir Twister what had happened, but neither of them said a word, for they wanted Hans to get a taste of the same medicine. Next day it was Hans's turn to stay home and work in the kitchen. As he was standing high up, skimming the broth, the little man came in. He didn't beat about the bush but asked for a piece of meat right away. "He's a poor devil," Hans thought to himself. "I'll give him some of my share, then the others won't lose by it." He passed him a piece of meat, and when the dwarf had eaten it up, he asked for more. Good-natured Hans gave him another piece, saying: "Here's a nice big piece. That ought to be enough for you." But the dwarf asked a third time. "Now you're overdoing it," said Hans, and wouldn't give any more. The wicked dwarf tried to jump up on him and punish him as he had Fir Twister and Cliff Smasher, but he'd picked the wrong man. Without even exerting himself, Hans gave him a couple of blows that sent him running down the castle steps. Hans ran after him, but slipped and fell full length, passing the dwarf in his fall. By the time he had picked himself up, the dwarf was in the lead again. Hans chased him into the forest, saw him slip into a hole, and went back to the castle, after taking good note of the place.

When the two others got home, they were surprised to find Hans so chipper. He told them what had happened and they too came out with their stories. Hans laughed and said: "It served you right. Why were you so stingy with the meat? And aren't you ashamed, big fellows like you, letting a dwarf make hash of you?" They took a basket and a rope, went back to the dwarf's cave, and let Hans, with his staff, down in the basket. At the bottom he found a door, and when he opened it he saw a beautiful maiden, more beautiful than anyone can say. Beside her sat the dwarf, and when he saw Hans he grinned at him like a baboon. The maiden was chained and fettered, and she looked at Hans so sadly that he was moved to pity. "I've got to free her from the power of this wicked dwarf," he thought, and struck him with his staff. The dwarf fell dead and that second the maiden's chains fell from her. Hans was entranced by her beauty. "I am a king's daughter," she said. "A ferocious count carried me away from my home and shut me up in this cave, because I wouldn't have anything to do with him. He made the dwarf guard me, and I can't tell you what pain and anguish he gave me." Hans put the maiden in the basket and told them to pull her up. The basket came down again, but Hans didn't trust his companions. He thought to himself: "They've shown how false they were by not telling me about the dwarf. The Lord only knows what they're plotting against me." So he put his staff in the basket and that was a good thing, because when the basket was halfway up, they let it drop, and if Hans had really been in it, he'd have been killed. But how was he going to get out of the cave? He racked his brains but could think of nothing. "What a dismal fate," he thought, "to perish in a place like this." As he was pacing back and forth, he came back to the little room where the maiden had been, and on the dwarf's finger he saw a ring that glittered and sparkled. He pulled it off and slipped it on his own finger. When he turned it, he suddenly heard a whirring above him and looking up, he saw the spirits of the air hovering overhead. "You are our master," they said. "What is your command?" At first Hans was struck dumb, but then he spoke up and said: "Carry me up." They obeyed instantly and he felt as if he were flying. At the top, there was no one in sight, and when he went into the castle there was no one there either. Fir Twister and Cliff Smasher had hurried away, taking the beautiful maiden with them. But when Hans turned the ring, the spirits of the air came and told him they were on the sea. Hans ran without stopping until he reached the seashore. Far out on the water he saw a boat with his faithless companions in it. Too furious to think, he jumped into the sea with his hundred-pound staff, which dragged him deep under the water and he almost drowned. In the nick of time he turned the ring. Instantly the spirits of the air came and carried him quick as lightning to the ship. He brandished his staff, gave his wicked companions their just reward, and threw their carcasses into the water. The beautiful maiden was half-dead with fright. Now he saved her for the second time and rowed her home to her mother and father. When they got there, he married her and they were all as happy as could be.

167

The Poor Peasant in Heaven

ONCE A POOR AND PIOUS PEASANT died and arrived at the gates of heaven. A big rich lord got there at the same time and he too wanted to get in. St. Peter took his key, opened up, and let the rich man in. Then he locked the gate again, as though he hadn't seen the poor peasant. From outside, the peasant could hear them welcoming the rich man with joy, and making music and singing. Finally, when it was quiet again, St. Peter came and opened the gate. The peasant thought there would be music and singing for him too. Not a bit of it. Oh yes, he was welcomed with every mark of love, and the angels came to meet him, but no singing. So he asked St. Peter why they had sung for the rich man and not for him. "It seems to me," the peasant said, "that there's as much favoritism up here as there is on earth." "Not at all," said St. Peter. "We love you as much as anyone else, and you'll get your fair share of heavenly joys just the same as the rich man, but look at it this way: poor peasants like you pour in here every day. A rich man like him gets admitted once in a hundred years."

168
Skinny Lisa

SKINNY LISA HAD very different ideas from lazy Heinz and Fat Trina, who never let anything interfere with their rest. She scoured and scrubbed from morning to night, and foisted so much work on Long Lenz her husband that he was worse off than a donkey with three sacks to carry. But their labors didn't do them a bit of good. They had nothing and nothing came their way. One night as she was lying in bed, so tired she could hardly move, her thoughts kept her awake. She poked her husband in the ribs and said: "Listen to me, Long Lenz. Listen to what I've been thinking. If I found a gulden and somebody gave me another, I'd borrow a third, and then I'd expect you to give me one. Once I've got my four gulden, I mean to buy a young cow." Not a bad idea, her husband thought. "It's true," he said, "that I don't know where the gulden you expect me to give you is coming from, but if you do get the money together, and if a cow can be had at that price, you'll be wise to buy one." And he added: "I'll be glad if the cow gets a calf, because then I'll be able to refresh myself now and then with a cup of milk." "The milk isn't for you," said the wife. "If we let the calf suck, it'll get big and fat and we'll sell it for good money." "Of course," said the man. "But that won't stop us from enjoying a bit of milk. Where's the harm in that?" "What do you know about taking care of cows?" said the wife. "Harm or not, I won't have it. You don't get a single drop of that milk, not if you stand on your head. Just because your stomach is a bottomless pit, Long Lenz, you think you can gobble up my hard earnings." "Woman," he said, "shut up or I'll smack your ears down." "What!" she cried. "You dare to threaten me, you glutton, you scoundrel, you lazy good-for-nothing!" She tried to grab hold of his hair, but Long Lenz sat up, grasped Skinny Lisa's withered arms in one hand, and with the other hand pressed her head into the pillow. He let her fume and held her there until she fell asleep from sheer exhaustion. Whether she went on quarreling when she woke up the next morning, or whether she went out looking for the gulden she hoped to find, I don't know.

169

The House in the Forest

A POOR WOODCUTTER lived with his wife and three daughters in a small hut at the edge of a lonely forest. One morning before going out to work, he said to his wife: "Have our eldest daughter bring me my noonday meal. If I come home, I'll never get done with my work." And he added: "To make sure she doesn't get lost, I'll take a bag of millet with me and strew the grains on the path." When the sun stood high over the forest, the girl started out with a pot of soup. But the sparrows and starlings, the larks and finches, the blackbirds and linnets had eaten up the millet hours before, and she couldn't find the way. Trusting to luck, she went on and on, until the sun set and night fell. The trees murmured in the darkness, the owls hooted, and she began to be afraid. After a while she saw a light glimmering between the trees in the distance and thought: "There must be people living there who will let me stay the night." She headed for the light and it wasn't long before she came to a house with lighted windows. She knocked and a gruff voice cried out: "Come in." The girl stepped into a dark hallway and knocked at the inner door. "Come on in!" cried the voice, and when she opened the door she saw a gray-haired old man sitting at the table. He was holding his head propped on both hands, and his white beard hung down over the table and almost touched the floor. Three animals were lying near the stove, a hen, a rooster, and a speckled cow. The girl told the old man what had happened to her and asked leave to say the night. The man said:

> "Pretty hen,
> Pretty rooster,
> And pretty speckled cow,
> What do you say now?"

"Dooks," said the animals, and that must have meant: "It's all right with us," for the old man said: "We want for nothing here. Go out to the hearth and cook us our supper." The girl found plenty of everything in the kitchen and cooked up a nice meal, but she didn't give the animals a thought. She brought the full bowl to the table, sat down across from the gray-haired old man, and ate as much as she pleased. When she had had enough, she said: "Now I'm tired. Where is there a bed, so I can lie down and sleep?" The animals replied:

> "You've eaten with him,
> You've drunk with him,
> You haven't given us a bite.
> So find out for yourself
> Where you will spend the night."

The old man said: "Just go up the stairs, and you'll find a room with two beds in it. Shake them up and put on white linen sheets. Then I'll come up and go to bed too." The girl climbed the stairs, and when she had shaken up the beds and put on fresh sheets, she lay down in one of them and didn't wait for the old man. After a while he came up, looked at the girl by the light of his candle, and shook his head. When he saw she was fast asleep, he opened a trap door and let her drop into the cellar.

Late that night the woodcutter came home and upbraided his wife for letting him go hungry all day. "It's not my fault," she said. "I sent her out with your food. She must have got lost. Don't worry. She'll be home tomorrow." The woodcutter got up before dawn, and before leaving for the forest told his wife to send his second daughter with his noonday meal. "I'll take a bag of lentils," he said. "Lentils are bigger than millet grains. She's sure to see them and find her way." At noon the girl set out with his meal, but the lentils had vanished. The birds of the forest had eaten them the same as the day before and none were left. She wandered about in the forest until nightfall. Then she too came to the old man's house, and asked to come in, and begged for food and shelter. Again the man with the white beard asked the animals:

> "Pretty hen,
> Pretty rooster,
> And pretty speckled cow,
> What do you say now?"

Again the animals answered: "Dooks," and everything happened the same as the day before. The girl cooked a nice meal, ate and drank with the old man, and gave no thought to the animals. When she asked about a place to sleep, they said:

> "You've eaten with him,
> You've drunk with him,
> You haven't given us a bite.
> So find out for yourself
> Where you will spend the night."

After she'd fallen asleep, the old man came up, looked at her, shook his head, and let her down into the cellar.

On the third morning, the woodcutter said to his wife: "Send our youngest child with my meal this time. She has always been good and obedient. She'll find the right way and won't go wandering around like her sisters, who are no better than wild bees." Her mother didn't want her to go. "Must I lose my dearest child along with the others?" she asked. "Don't worry," he said. "She won't get lost. She's got too much sense. And besides, I'll take peas with me and strew them on the ground. They're even bigger than lentils. They'll show her the way." But by the time the girl went out with her basket over her arm, the wood pigeons had the peas in their crops, and she didn't know which way to go. She worried and fretted, thinking how hungry her father must be and how her mother would grieve if she didn't come home. At last, as night was falling, she saw the light and came to the house in the forest. She asked in a sweet, gentle voice if they could put her up for the night, and once again the man with the white beard said to his animals:

> "Pretty hen,
> Pretty rooster,
> And pretty speckled cow,
> What do you say now?"

"Dooks," they replied. The girl went over beside the stove where the animals were lying, and stroked the smooth feathers of the hen and the rooster, while with the other hand she scratched the spotted cow between the horns. At the old man's bidding she made some nice soup, and when the bowl was on the table, she said: "You wouldn't want me to sit down and eat when these dear animals have nothing. There's plenty of everything outside, I'll attend to them first." So she went out and took some barley and strewed it in front of the hen and the rooster and brought the cow a whole armful of sweet-smelling hay. "Have a good meal, dear animals," she said. "And in case you're thirsty I'll get you a drink of water." She filled the bucket and brought it in. The hen and the rooster jumped up on the rim, dipped their beaks, then held up their heads, as birds do when they drink, and the speckled cow took a good long swallow. When the animals had been fed, the girl sat down at the table with the old man, and ate what he had left her. It wasn't long before the hen and the rooster hid their heads under their wings and the speckled cow began to blink. At that the girl said: "Shouldn't we all go to sleep?

> Pretty hen,
> Pretty rooster,
> And pretty speckled cow,
> What do you say now?"

The animals replied: "Dooks,

> You've eaten with us,
> You've drunk with us,
> You've given all of us a bite,
> So all of us wish you good night."

The girl went upstairs, shook the featherbeds and put on fresh sheets. When she had finished, the old man came up and got into his bed, and his white beard reached to his feet. The girl got into the other bed, said her prayers, and fell asleep.

She slept peacefully until midnight. Then there was such a hubbub in the house that she woke up. All around her she heard a cracking and crashing, the door sprang open and hit the wall, the beams groaned as if they had been wrenched loose from their pinnings, the staircase seemed to be collapsing, and in the end there was a rumbling as though the whole roof were falling in. But she herself was unhurt, and when the noise stopped, she lay still and fell back asleep. When she woke up in the morning, the sun was shining bright, and what did she see? She was lying in a great hall, and everything around her glittered in royal splendor. The walls were of green silk covered with long golden flowers, the bed was ivory with a red-velvet coverlet, and on a chair beside it she saw a pair of slippers embroidered with pearls. She thought she was dreaming, but three richly dressed servants came in and asked for her orders. "I don't need you," she replied. "I'll get up right away and make soup for the old man. Then I'll feed pretty hen, pretty rooster, and pretty speckled cow." Wondering if the old man were already up, she looked around, but a stranger was lying in his bed. When she had looked at him for quite some time and seen that he was young and handsome, he opened his eyes, sat up, and said: "I am a king's son. A wicked witch turned me into an old man and forced me to live in the forest. No one was allowed to stay with me except for three servants, and they were changed into a hen, a rooster, and a speckled cow. The spell could only be broken by the coming of a girl with such a kind heart that there was room in it for animals as well as humans. That was you. At midnight you set us free and the old forest house was changed back into my royal palace." Then they got up out of bed, and the king's son sent the three servants to bring back the girl's father and mother for the wedding. "But where are my two sisters?" the girl asked. "I've locked them up in the cellar. Tomorrow they'll be taken to a charcoal burner's hut in the forest. There they will stay as his servants until they've grown kinder and learned not to let poor animals go hungry."

170

Sharing Joys and Sorrows

THERE WAS ONCE a cantankerous tailor, and try as she might, his wife, who was a good, pious, hard-working woman, could never please him. Whatever she did, he grumbled and scolded and cuffed and beat her. When the authorities finally got wind of it, they haled him into court and put him in jail, hoping he'd mend his ways. He stayed there awhile on bread and water, and when they let him out, they made him promise not to beat his wife any more. "You must live at peace with her," they said, "sharing your joys and sorrows, as a married pair should." All went well for a time, but then he fell back into his evil ways, and became his cantankerous, quarrelsome self again. Since beating her was now forbidden, he tried to pull her hair. She broke loose and escaped into the garden, but he ran after her with his yardstick and his scissors and chased her round and round, throwing the yardstick and scissors and everything else he could lay hands on at her. When something hit her, he laughed; when something missed her he bellowed with rage. And he kept it up until the neighbors came to the woman's help. Again the tailor was haled into court and reminded of his promise. "Your honor," he said, "I've kept my promise. I haven't beaten her, and I've shared my joys and sorrows with her." "How can that be," asked a judge, "when she has brought such grave charges against you?" "I didn't beat her, I just wanted to comb her hair with my fingers because she looked so outlandish. But she ran away from me, she maliciously deserted me. I ran after her and, wishing to bring her back to the path of duty, I threw whatever I could lay hands on at her as a well-meant reminder. And I have indeed shared my joys and sorrows with her. When I threw something and hit her, it was a joy to me and a sorrow to her. When I missed her, it was a joy to her and a sorrow to me." This explanation did not satisfy the judges, and they meted out the punishment he deserved.

171
The Hedge King*

IN OLDEN TIMES every sound carried its message and meaning. When the smith's hammer rang out, it was saying: "Strike the iron! Strike the iron!" When the carpenter's plane rasped, it was saying: "There you have it! There. There you have it!" When the mill wheels rattled, they were praying: "Help, O Lord! Help, O Lord!" And if the miller who set the mill in motion was a swindler, it started off slowly, asking: "Who's there? Who's there?" Then answered quickly: "The miller, the miller!" And then very very quickly: "Steals bravely, steals bravely, from a bushel three pecks."

In those days the birds also had their own language that everyone understood. Now it only sounds like twittering, screeching, or whistling, or in some cases like music without words. One day the birds took it into their heads that they needed someone to rule over them and decided to elect one of their number as king. Only one bird, the peewit, was opposed. He had always lived free and he wanted to die free. He flew back and forth, crying out in anguish: "Where to sit? Where to sit?" Then he flew off to a lonely marsh and was never seen again among the birds.

The birds resolved to talk the matter over, and one fine May morning they came flying in from every field and forest—the eagle and the chaffinch, the owl and the crow, the lark and the sparrow, you can't expect me to name them all. Even the cuckoo was there and the hoopoe, his sexton, so-called because he always makes himself heard a few days sooner. And in among the crowd there was also a very small bird who still had no name. Somehow the hen had heard nothing, and she didn't know what to make of this enormous crowd. "What, what? What's going on?" she clucked, but the rooster com-

---
* *Zaunkönig* (literally Hedge King)=Wren.

forted his darling hen by saying: "They're all rich!" And told her what they had come for.

It was decided that the one among them who could fly highest should be king. When he heard that, a tree frog who was sitting in the bushes nearby suspected that no good would come of it and cried out in warning: "No, no, no!" But the crow said: "Caw caw," meaning that everything would be all right.

The assembly's next decision was that they should all take off at once on this fine May morning. Then, it was thought, no one would be able to say afterward: "I could have flown higher, but night overtook me." The signal was given and they all shot into the air. Dust rose from the field, an enormous flapping and fluttering and beating of wings was heard, and if you'd seen it you'd have thought a black cloud was flying into the air. The small birds were soon left behind. Unable to fly any higher, they returned to the ground. The big ones held out longer, but none could equal the eagle, who flew so high he could have poked the sun's eyes out. When he saw that he'd left the others behind, he thought: "I win. I'll be the king. Why fly higher?" And he began to glide down. The birds below him all cried out: "You shall be our king! None has flown higher than you." "Except me!" cried the little fellow without a name, who had crawled into the eagle's breast feathers. And since he wasn't tired, he flew upward and flew so high he could see God sitting on his throne. When he had got that far, he came down and called out in his shrill, piercing voice: "I'm the king here! I'm the king here!"

"You our king?" cried the birds angrily. "You did it by fraud and trickery." Then they made a new rule, that the one who could go deepest underground should be king. How the broad-breasted goose beat the ground! How quickly the rooster scraped out a hole! The duck had the worst time of all: she sprained her ankle jumping into a ditch, and waddled off to the nearby pond, quacking: "Humbug! Humbug!" The little fellow without a name found a mousehole, slipped into it, and cried out in his shrill voice: "I'm the king here! I'm the king here!"

"You our king?" cried the birds still more angrily. "Do you think you can get away with a cheap trick like that?" They decided to keep him prisoner in his hole and starve him. The owl was posted as sentry and told that if he valued his life he wasn't to let the scoundrel out of the hole. The birds, who were very tired after flying so strenuously, all went to bed at nightfall with their wives and children. Only the owl stood by the mousehole, staring into it with his big eyes. But he too was tired. "It seems to me," he thought, "that I could close one eye and watch with the other. Then the little villain won't escape." So he shut one eye and stared at the mousehole with the other. The little fellow stuck his head out and thought he'd sneak away, but the owl took a step forward, and he pulled his head back in. Again the owl opened one eye and closed the other. He thought he'd change off all night. But the next time he closed the one eye, he forgot to open the other, and the moment both eyes were closed, he fell asleep. The little fellow was quick to take notice and slip away.

Since then the owl hasn't dared show himself in the daytime, because if he did, all the other birds would go chasing after him and give his feathers a good mussing. He only goes out at night, and he hates mice and hunts them down, because they make such nasty holes. The little bird isn't very eager to show himself either. He's afraid he won't have long to live if he's caught. He hides in hedges, and sometimes when he feels perfectly safe he cries out: "I'm the king here!" That's why the other birds make fun of him by calling him the hedge king.

No one was happier than the lark at not having to obey the hedge king. Whenever the sun comes out, he rises into the air and cries: "Oh, how lovely it all is, how very lovely, lovely, lovely, oh, how lovely it all is!"

172
The Flounder

THE FISHES HAD LONG been dissatisfied with the lack of order in their kingdom. No one turned aside to let others pass, everyone swam on the right or left as he pleased, darted between people who were trying to stay together, or blocked their way, and the strong pushed the weak aside with a flip of their tails, or gobbled them up without bat-ting an eyelash. "How lovely it would be if we had a king to enforce law and order!" they said, and met to elect the one among them who could cleave the waters most quickly to bring help to the weak.

When they had lined up by the shore, the pike gave a sign with his tail, and they all started off together. The pike darted like an arrow and with him the herring, the gudgeon, the bass, the carp, and all the rest of them. The flounder was there too, and he too had hopes of winning.

Suddenly the cry rang out: "The herring's ahead! The herring's ahead!" The flat, resentful flounder, who had been left far behind, cried angrily: "Who's ahead?" "The herring, the herring!" was the answer. "The naked herring?" cried the envious flounder, "the naked herring?" The flounder has been down in the mouth ever since. That was his punishment.

173

The Bittern and the Hoopoe

"WHERE DO YOU BEST like to graze your herd?" someone asked an old cowherd. "Here, sir, where the grass is neither too lush nor too thin. Otherwise there's trouble." "What do you mean?" the man asked. The cowherd said: "Do you hear that gloomy cry from the meadow? That's the bittern. He used to be a cowherd, and so was the hoopoe. I'll tell you the story.

"The bittern used to graze his herd on lush green meadows full of flowers. That made the cows wild and unmanageable. The hoopoe pastured his beasts on high, barren mountain slopes, where the wind plays with the sand, and the cows got skinny and never built up any strength. In the evening, when it came time to drive the herds home, the bittern couldn't get his cows together. They larked and frolicked and ran away. "C'mon, c'mon," he cried out, but it was useless. They wouldn't listen. As for the hoopoe, his cows were so weak and listless

he couldn't make them move. "Up, up, up!" he cried, but it didn't do
a bit of good, they just lay there in the sand. That's what happens
when you go to extremes. Nowadays the bittern and the hoopoe
haven't got any herds. But they still cry, 'C'mon, c'mon,' and 'Up,
up, up.'"

174
The Owl

A FEW HUNDRED YEARS AGO when people weren't nearly as clever as
they are today, a strange incident occurred in a small town. One
night a horned owl from the nearby forest somehow got into a barn
belonging to one of the townspeople. When day came, he was afraid
to come out, because he knew the other birds would raise a terrible
howl if he showed himself. When the hired man went to the barn for
straw, he saw the owl in the corner and was so frightened he ran and
told his master that a monster, the like of which he had never laid
eyes on, a monster which could certainly devour a man with no trouble at all, was sitting in the barn rolling its eyes. "I know you like a
book," said the master. "You're brave enough to chase a blackbird in
an open field, but if you see a dead chicken lying on the ground you
pick up a club before venturing too close. I'd better go and look at
this monster with my own eyes." Bravely the master entered the barn
and looked around. But when he caught sight of the strange, eerie-
looking bird, he was no less terrified than his servant. In two jumps
he was out of the barn, and a moment later he was running next door
to implore the help of his neighbors against a dangerous, unknown
animal. "Why," he cried out, "if that beast were to break out of my
barn, the whole town would be in danger!" The alarm spread from
street to street, the townspeople came running with pikes and pitch-
forks and scythes and axes, as though to attack an enemy army. Last
came the town council with the mayor in the lead. After forming
ranks in the marketplace, they moved in on the barn from all sides.

One of the bravest stepped forward and went in with lowered pike, but in next to no time a scream was heard and he was rushing out, as pale as death and unable to utter a word. Two more ventured in, but fared no better. Finally a big strong man, famed for his warlike deeds, stepped forward and said: "You won't drive the monster away by looking at him. I see you've all turned into women. But this is a serious matter and somebody has to take the bull by the horns." He sent for armor, a sword, and a pike, and made ready for battle. All praised his courage, though many feared for his life. The two barn doors were opened, and the whole crowd could see the owl, who in the meantime had settled on a big crossbeam. The hero asked for a ladder. They brought one and put it in place. As he prepared to climb up, they all cried out, telling him to bear himself like a man and commending him to St. George, the dragon-slayer. When he had nearly reached the top, the owl, suspecting his intentions, confused by the shouts of the crowd, and seeing no way out, rolled its eyes, puffed up its feathers, gnashed its beak, and hooted *tu-whit tu-whoo* in a harsh, rasping voice. The townspeople egged the intrepid hero on. "Strike home! Strike home!" they cried. "If you were standing where I'm standing," he said, "you wouldn't be shouting: 'Strike home!'" After that—you've got to give him credit—the hero set his foot one rung higher, but then he began to tremble and in a near faint started back down again.

None of the others was willing to brave the danger. "Just by gnashing its beak and breathing out fumes," they said, "the monster has poisoned and mortally wounded the strongest man in town. Why then should the rest of us risk our lives?" They took counsel: What could they do to prevent the whole town from being destroyed? For a long time nothing occurred to them, but in the end the mayor found the answer. "In my opinion," he said, "there is only one thing to do: indemnify the owner of this barn by purchasing it out of municipal funds—allowance being made for the grain, straw, and hay stored therein—and burn it along with that dreadful animal. Then no one will have to risk his life. This is no time for penny-pinching and false economy." The proposal was voted unanimously. They set fire to the four corners of the barn and the owl perished miserably in the flames. If you don't believe me, go and ask them.

175

The Moon

LONG, LONG AGO, there was a country where the night was always dark. The sky was spread over it like a black cloth, for in that country the moon never rose and there were no stars twinkling in the darkness. At the time of the Creation the night glow had been sufficient. One day four young fellows from this country set out on a journey and came to another kingdom where, when the sun sank behind the mountains at night, a glittering ball at the top of an oak tree cast a soft light far and wide. It wasn't as bright as the sun, but you could see pretty well by it and distinguish one thing from another. The travelers stopped and asked a peasant who was passing in his wagon what this light was. "It's the moon," the peasant told them. "Our mayor bought it for three talers and put it up in the oak tree. He fills it with oil every day and keeps it clean and trims the wick. We pay him a taler a week for his pains."

When the peasant had driven away, one of the friends said: "We could use that lamp. We've got an oak tree at home to hang it on that's just as big as this one. Wouldn't it be wonderful if we didn't have to grope in the darkness at night?" "I'll tell you what," said the second, "we'll get a wagon and horses and cart the moon away. These people can buy themselves another." "I'm good at climbing trees," said the third. "I'll climb up and get it." The fourth brought a wagon and horses, the third climbed the tree, bored a hole in the moon, slipped a rope through it, and let it down. When they had the glittering ball in the wagon, they covered it with a piece of cloth to keep people from seeing they'd stolen it. Then they carried it off to their own country and put it up in a tall oak tree. Old and young rejoiced when the new lamp cast its light on field and meadow and shone into people's windows. The dwarfs came out of their caves and the elves danced their rounds in the meadows.

The four friends kept the moon filled with oil, cleaned the wick, and received their taler a week. But they grew old, and when one of them fell sick and foresaw his end, he said in his will that one quarter of the moon, being his property, would have to be lowered into the grave with him. When he died, the mayor took his hedge-clippers, climbed the tree, and cut off the quarter that was to be buried. The light of the moon diminished, but so far not very noticeably. When the second friend died, the second quarter was buried with him and the light diminished a little more. It became still feebler at the death of the third, who also took his share, and after the fourth was buried, the old darkness set in again. People who went out at night without lanterns were always bumping their heads together.

When the quarters of the moon were reunited in the underworld, where darkness had always prevailed, the dead got restless and woke from their sleep.. They were amazed at being able to see again. The moonlight was quite enough for them, because their eyes had grown so weak they couldn't have stood the bright sun. They got up, came to life, and went back to their old habits. Some gambled and danced, some ran to the taverns, where they ordered wine, got drunk, bellowed and quarreled, and finally picked up their cudgels and lambasted one another. The uproar got worse and worse and was finally heard in heaven.

St. Peter, who guards the gate of heaven, thought a revolution had broken out down below, summoned the heavenly hosts, and ordered them to throw back the Fiend if he and his henchmen should try to storm the abode of the blessed. But when the rebels didn't appear, he mounted his charger, rode through the gates of heaven, and descended to the underworld. After subduing the dead and making them lie back down in their graves, he took the moon away with him and hung it up in the sky.

176

Three Score and Ten

AFTER CREATING THE WORLD, God decided to fix the life span of each of His creatures. The donkey came to him and asked: "How long shall I live, O Lord?" "Thirty years," said God. "Does that suit you?" "Oh, Lord," replied the donkey, "that's a long time. Think of the hard life I lead, carrying heavy loads from morning to night, hauling sacks of grain to the mill so others can eat bread, with nothing to encourage and refresh me but kicks and blows. I beg you, remit some part of my term." God took pity on him and struck off eighteen years, whereupon the donkey went away comforted and the dog appeared. "How long would you like to live?" God asked him. "Thirty years were too many for the donkey, but I should think they'd be just right for you." "Lord," said the dog, "is that your will? Think of all the running I have to do. My feet couldn't stand it that long. And when I have no more voice to bark with or teeth to bite with, what will I be able to do but limp from corner to corner and growl?" God saw he was right and struck off twelve years. Then came the monkey. "You, I trust, will be glad to live thirty years," said the Lord. "You don't have to work like the donkey and the dog, and you're always cheerful." "Ah, Lord," he replied, "it may look that way, but the truth is something else again. Even when it rains porridge, I have no spoon. People are always expecting me to amuse them by making faces and cutting capers. If they give me an apple and I bite into it, it always turns out to be sour. How often a grin conceals a sad heart! I could never put up with such a life for thirty years." God was merciful, and took off ten.

Last came the man. He was cheerful, bursting with health and vigor, and he asked God to fix his life span. "Thirty years," said the Lord. "Will that be enough for you?" "Too short!" the man cried. "Just when I've built my house and lit a fire in my own hearth, just when the trees I've planted are beginning to flower and bear fruit, just as I'm settling down to enjoy life, you want me to die. O Lord, give me an extension." "I'll add the donkey's eighteen years," said God. "Not enough!" the man replied. "Very well," said God, "you can have the dog's twelve years as well." "Still too little." "All right," said God, "I'll throw in the monkey's ten years, but no more. That's all you get." The man went away, but he wasn't satisfied.

So the years of a man's life are three score and ten. The first thirty are his human years. They pass quickly. His health and spirits are good, he enjoys his work and is glad to be alive. Next come the donkey's eighteen years. Burden after burden is put on him: he has to carry the grain that feeds others, and kicks and blows are his reward for his faithful services. Then come the dog's twelve years: he lies in the corner and growls, but he has no teeth left to bite with. And last of all come the monkey's ten years, when the man goes soft in the head, does foolish things, and becomes a laughingstock of children.

177

The Messengers of Death

ONE DAY IN OLDEN TIMES a giant was walking down the high road when suddenly a stranger appeared before him and cried out: "Stop! Not another step!" "What's this?" said the giant. "A weakling I could crush between my fingers trying to stop me! Who are you to speak so boldly?" "I am Death," said the other. "No one can resist me. And you too will have to obey my orders." But the giant refused and the two of them fought. It was a long, hard fight. In the end the giant won out. He struck Death down with his fist, and Death fell by the roadside. The giant went his way, and Death lay there defeated, too weak to get up. "What will become of the world," he said, "if I'm left lying here? No one will die. The place will be so full of people there won't be room enough to turn around in." Just then a sprightly young man came along, singing a song and darting his eyes this way and that. When he saw the helpless figure lying beside the road, he was moved to pity. He went over to him, propped him up, revived him with a drink from his flask, and waited till he recovered his strength. "Tell me," said Death, rising to his feet, "do you know who I am? Do you know whom you have helped up?" "No," said the young man, "I don't know you." "I am Death," he said. "I spare no one and I can't make an exception for you. But to show my gratitude, I promise not to take you by surprise. I'll send you my messengers before I come for you." "Glad to hear it," said the young man. "At least I'll feel safe until I hear you're coming." He went his way, and after that he made merry and enjoyed himself and lived with no thought for the morrow. But his youth and good health were short-lived. Soon sickness and pain were tormenting him by day and troubling his sleep at night. "I'm not going to die," he said to himself, "because Death will send his messengers first. But I do wish these terrible days of sickness were over." As soon as he felt well again, he went back to his life of pleasure. Then one day someone tapped him on the shoulder. He looked around and Death was standing behind him. "Follow me," said Death. "It's time for you to take leave of this world." "What!" said the man. "Are you going to break your word? Didn't you promise me you would send your messengers before coming to take me? I haven't seen any messengers." "Be still!" said Death. "Haven't I sent you one messenger after another? Didn't fever come and strike you and shake you and lay you low? Didn't your head spin with dizziness? Didn't gout come and rack your limbs? Didn't your ears ring? Weren't your cheeks swollen and sore from toothache? Didn't the world go black before your eyes? And hasn't my very own brother Sleep reminded you of me every single night? Didn't you lie in your bed as still as if you were already dead?" The man had no answer. Resigning himself to his fate, he went with Death.

178
Master Stitchum

MASTER STITCHUM WAS a short, thin, but active man, who never sat still for a second. His face, in which the only prominent feature was his turned-up nose, was pockmarked and deathly pale, his hair gray and shaggy. His eyes were small, but they never stopped peering about in all directions. He noticed everything, found fault with everything, and always knew best. When he walked in the street, he flailed about with both arms, and once when a girl carrying water was in his path he sent her pail flying so high that he himself got sopping wet. "You bonehead!" he cried out as he shook himself. "Couldn't you see I was coming along behind you?" By trade he was a shoemaker, and when he was working, he pulled his thread so vigorously that his fist was sure to land on anyone who didn't keep a safe distance. No apprentice ever stayed with him for more than a month, because no matter how good the work was he always found fault: the stitches were uneven, one shoe was longer than the other, one heel was too high, the other too low, or the leather hadn't been beaten long enough. "Wait a minute!" he would cry out. "I'll show you how to soften a hide." Whereupon he'd take a strap and beat the apprentice over the back with it. In his opinion, all apprentices were lazy good-for-nothings. He himself didn't get much work done, because he couldn't sit still for ten minutes. If his wife had got up early and lit the fire, he'd jump out of bed and run into the kitchen in his bare feet. "Are you trying to burn my house down?" he would shout. "That fire's big enough to roast an ox on! Didn't anyone ever tell you that wood costs money?" When the maids were standing at the wash trough, laughing and passing the time of day, he would scream at them: "Silly geese, cackling and gossiping and neglecting your work. Why all that soap? Sinful waste and shameful laziness, that's what it is! Afraid a little rubbing might make your hands red!"

With that he'd leave them, but on his way out he'd upset a bucket full of suds and flood the whole washhouse. If someone was building a house, he'd run to the window and watch. "There they are again, building with that red sandstone that never dries out. No one will draw a healthy breath in that house. And look at the way those masons lay blocks. And that mortar's no good anyway. It ought to have gravel in it, not sand. I'll live to see that house collapse right on the occupants' heads." He'd sit down and sew a few stitches, but then he'd jump up again, unbuckle his leather apron, and cry: "It's my duty to go over there and give those men a talking to." He'd start in on the carpenters. "What do you think you're doing? You're not hewing to the line. How can you expect to get straight beams? The whole house will fall apart." He grabbed the ax out of a carpenter's hand and was going to show him how to do it, but just then he caught sight of a wagon loaded with clay and ran over to the peasant who was leading the horses. "You must be out of your mind," he cried, "using young horses for such a heavy load. The poor beasts will fall down dead before you know it." The peasant didn't even answer, and that made Master Stitchum so angry he ran back to his workshop. As he was sitting down to work, an apprentice handed him a shoe. "What's this again?" he cried. "Didn't I tell you not to cut them so low? Who's going to buy a shoe that's practically all sole? I want my orders carried out to the letter!" "Master," said the apprentice, "you may be right in saying the shoe's no good, but it's the one you yourself cut out and started to work on. When you jumped up just now, you pushed it off the table. All I did was pick it up. But an angel from heaven couldn't do anything to please you."

One night Master Stitchum dreamed he had died and was on his way to heaven. When he reached the gate, he knocked and knocked. "You'd think they'd have a knocker," he said to himself. "My knuckles are raw and bleeding." The Apostle Peter opened and looked to see who was knocking so obstreperously. "Oh, it's you, Master Stitchum," he said. "Well, I'll let you in, but I'm warning you, you'll have to get over that bad habit of yours, because if you start finding fault with the things you see in heaven, you could easily get into trouble." "I don't need you to tell me that," said Master Stitchum. "I know what's fitting and proper, and up here, thank the

Lord, everything is perfect. There's nothing to find fault with as there is on earth." So he went in and started roaming around in the vast reaches of heaven. He looked to the right, he looked to the left, occasionally shaking his head or muttering to himself. After a while he saw two angels carrying a beam. It was the beam someone had had in his eye while he was looking for the mote in his neighbor's. But instead of carrying it lengthwise, they were carrying it crosswise. "Did you ever see anything so stupid?" thought Master Stitchum, but he said nothing and pretended nothing was wrong. "After all, what difference does it make whether they carry the beam lengthwise or crosswise, as long as they get through? And I have to admit they're not bumping into anything." A little while later, he saw two angels drawing water from a well and pouring it into a barrel. At the same time he noticed that the bottom of the barrel was full of holes and that the water was running out in all directions. They were watering the earth with rain. "Blast them!" he burst out, but luckily he remembered where he was and restrained himself. "Maybe it's just a game," he thought. "People often amuse themselves doing useless things. What would you expect up here in heaven where, as I've already noticed, all they do is loll around?" Farther on he saw a wagon that had got stuck in a deep hole. "No wonder," he said to the man who was standing beside it. "What a stupid way to load a wagon! What have you got there?" "Pious wishes," said the man. "I missed the right path but managed to push my cart up here all the same. Don't worry, somebody'll pull me out." And sure enough, an angel came along and hitched two horses to the wagon. "That's all very well," said Master Stitchum, "but you'll never get that wagon out with two horses. You'll need at least four." Another angel arrived with two more horses, but he hitched them to the back of the wagon. That was too much for Master Stitchum. "You fool!" he burst out. "What are you doing? Has anyone ever pulled a wagon out of a hole like that since the world was created? But these people are so conceited, they always think they know best." He would have said more, but one of the inhabitants of heaven grabbed him by the collar and heaved him out with irresistible force. In the gateway Master Stitchum looked back and saw the wagon being lifted by four winged horses.

At that moment Master Stitchum woke up. "Of course," he said to himself, "conditions aren't exactly the same in heaven as they are here on earth, and we have to make allowances for certain things, but could anyone see horses being hitched front and back at the same time without losing patience? Yes, yes, they had wings, but how was I to know that? And anyway, what damn foolishness sticking a pair of wings on a horse that already has four legs to run with! But now I'd better get up or everything will go wrong in the house here. It sure is lucky that I'm not really dead!"

179

The Goose Girl
at the Spring

AN OLD, OLD WOMAN once lived with her flock of geese in a lonely spot in the mountains, and there she had a little house surrounded by a big forest. Every morning she took her crutch and hobbled off to the woods, where she was very busy, busier than you'd have thought possible for anyone so old. She would gather grass for her geese, pick as much wild fruit as she could reach, and load it all on her back. You'd have expected her to collapse under the heavy load, but she always got safely home with it. When she met someone, she always had a friendly greeting: "Good day, my dear neighbor, fine weather we're having. It may surprise you to see me carrying this grass, but we must all of us bear our burdens." Nevertheless, people disliked meeting her. They took a different path when they could, and when a father chanced to pass with his little boy, the father would whisper: "Watch out for that old woman. She looks harmless enough, but if you ask me, she's a witch."

One morning a handsome young man came walking through the forest. The sun was shining bright, the birds were singing, a cool breeze was playing through the leaves, and he was happy and gay.

He hadn't met a living soul yet, and then suddenly he saw the old witch down on her knees cutting grass with a sickle. She had already put quite a load on a large cloth, and beside the cloth lay two baskets of wild pears and apples. "You poor thing," he said. "How can you possibly carry all that?" "I have to, my dear sir," she replied. "The children of the rich don't need to do these things, but the peasant folk have a saying: 'Never look around. You'll only see how bent your back is.'" When the young man stopped beside her, she said: "Would you care to help me? You've still got a straight back and young legs. For you it will be no trouble at all. My house isn't very far from here. It's on a heath behind that mountain. You'll be there before you know it." The young man felt sorry for the old woman. "It's true," he said. "My father is a rich count and not a peasant, and just to show you that a man can carry a load without being a peasant, I'll take your bundle." "That would be very kind of you," she said. "It's an hour's walk, but what's that to you? You'll have to take those apples and pears too." The young count began to have second thoughts when he heard about the hour's walk, but the old woman wouldn't let him go. She lifted the cloth full of grass onto his back and hung the two baskets on his arms. "You see how easy it is," she said. "I see nothing of the kind," said the count with a look of pain. "Your bundle might just as well be full of stones, and your apples and pears are as heavy as lead. I can hardly breathe." He wanted to put it all down, but the old woman wouldn't let him. "My word!" she scoffed. "The young gentleman is afraid of a load that an old woman carries every day. Oh, they're always on hand with fine words, but if you actually ask them to do something, they want to leave you flat." And she went on: "What are you standing there for? Pick up your feet. You're stuck with that bundle, and no one's going to take it away from you." As long as the ground was level, it was bearable, but when they came to the mountain, when he had to climb with the stones rolling out from under his feet as if they were alive, it was too much. Beads of sweat stood out on his forehead and ran hot and cold down his back. "I can't go on," he said. "I'll have to rest a while." "Nothing doing," said the old woman. "You can rest when we get home, but now you'll have to go on. You never can tell. Maybe you stand to gain by it." "This is too much!" cried the count, and tried to throw off the bundle, but in vain. It clung to his back as if it had grown there. He twisted and turned, but he couldn't get rid of it. The old woman laughed and jumped up and down on her crutch. "Don't lose your temper, dear young sir. You're as red in the face as a turkey cock. Bear your burden with patience. I'll give you a nice little present when we get home."

What could he do? He could only resign himself and plod along patiently behind the old woman. She seemed to get nimbler and nimbler as his burden grew heavier. All of a sudden she jumped up in the air, landed on the bundle, and sat down. Though she was as thin as a rail, she weighed more than the plumpest peasant girl. The young count's knees were trembling, but if he stopped moving she lashed his legs with a switch and a bunch of nettles. Moaning and groaning, he climbed the slope and finally, just as he was about to collapse, they came to the old woman's hut. When the geese saw her, they flapped their wings and craned their necks and ran cackling to meet her. Behind the flock, holding a switch, came a peasant wench, tall and sturdy, but no longer young and as ugly as sin. "Oh mother," she said to the old woman, "you've been so long. Has anything happened to you?" "God forbid, my daughter," she replied. "I've had no trouble at all. Far from it. This kind gentleman has carried my bundle for me —and just imagine, when I was tired, he let me ride on his back. It seemed like no distance at all. We've been having a lovely time, chatting and joking." Finally the old woman slid down, took the bundle from the young man's back and the baskets from his arms, gave him a friendly look, and said: "Now sit down on the bench and rest. You've earned your reward honestly, and you shall have it." And to the goose girl she said: "Go inside, my daughter. It wouldn't be proper for you to be alone with a young gentleman. We mustn't tempt fate. He might fall in love with you." The count didn't know whether to laugh or cry. "She could be thirty years younger," he thought, "and I still wouldn't want her for a sweetheart." Then the old woman, who had been stroking and fondling her geese as if they had been children, went into the house with her daughter, and the young man stretched out on the bench, under a wild apple tree. The air was soft and balmy. All around him lay a green meadow, covered with primroses, wild thyme, and a thousand other flowers; through it flowed a clear brook, glittering in the sunlight, and the white geese paraded back and forth or paddled about in the water. "What a lovely place!" he said to himself. "But I'm so tired I can't keep my eyes open. I'll sleep awhile. If only a gust of wind doesn't come along and blow my legs away. All the strength has gone out of them."

When he had slept a little while, the old woman came and shook him awake. "Get up," she said. "You can't stay here. I know I've given you a hard time, but it hasn't cost you your life, and I'll give you your reward. You don't need money or riches. Here you have something else." With that she handed him a little box carved out of an emerald. "Take good care of it," she added. "It will bring you luck." The count jumped up, and feeling he had got his strength back and wasn't tired any more, he thanked the old woman for the gift and went his way, without so much as looking around at the beautiful daughter. After going quite a distance, he could still hear the glad cries of the geese.

The count wandered about in the wilderness for three days before finding his way out. Then he came to a large town. Since no one knew him, he was taken to the royal palace, where the king and queen were sitting on their thrones. The count went down on one knee, took the emerald box out of his pocket, and set it at the queen's feet. She bade him rise, and he handed her the box. The moment she opened it and looked in, she fell down as though dead. The king's servants seized the count and were going to carry him off to prison when the queen opened her eyes. "Set him free!" she cried out, "and leave us alone. I must speak to this young man."

When the king and all the courtiers had left the room, the queen began to weep bitterly and said: "What good is all this splendor to me? Each new day brings me nothing but care. I had three daughters. The youngest was so beautiful that everyone looked upon her as a miracle. She was as white as snow and as pink as apple blossoms, and her eyes shone like sunbeams. When she wept, not tears, but pearls and precious stones fell from her eyes. When she was fifteen, the king called all three sisters before his throne. How the courtiers stared when the youngest came in; it was as though the sun had risen. 'My daughters,' said the king, 'since I have no way of knowing when my last day will dawn, I'm going to decide right now what each of you is to receive after my death. You all love me, but the one who loves me most shall have the best part.' Each said she loved him most. 'But couldn't you tell me how much you love me?' the king asked.

'Then I shall know what you feel.' The eldest spoke up and said: 'I love my father as much as the sweetest sugar.' The second said: 'I love my father as much as my most beautiful dress.' But the youngest said nothing. Her father asked her: 'And you, my dearest child, how much do you love me?' 'I don't know,' she replied. 'I can't compare my love with anything.' But her father insisted that she name something, and finally she said: 'The best food is tasteless without salt. I love my father as much as salt.' When the king heard that, he flew into a rage. 'If you love me like salt,' he cried, 'your love shall be rewarded with salt.' He divided the kingdom between the two eldest and ordered two servants to take the youngest out into the forest with a bag of salt tied to her back. We all begged and pleaded for her," said the queen, "but nothing could calm the king's anger. How she wept when she had to leave us! The whole path was covered with pearls that had flowed from her eyes. Soon the king was sorry for what he had done, and had the forest searched for the poor child, but no one could find her. When I think that the wild animals must have devoured her, it makes me so sad I can hardly bear it. Sometimes I comfort myself with the hope that she's still alive, that she's hiding in a cave or that some kindly people have taken her in. And now think of it! When I opened your little emerald box, there was a pearl in it exactly like the ones that flowed from my daughter's eyes. You can imagine what a turn it gave me. You must tell me how you came by that pearl." The count told her how it had been given him in the forest by an old woman who had aroused his suspicions and who was undoubtedly a witch, but that he had seen no sign of her daughter and heard no news of her.

The king and queen decided to go and see the old woman, for they thought that where the pearl had been they were sure to hear some word of their daughter.

The old woman sat spinning in her house on the lonely heath. Night had fallen and a pine knot burning on the hearth gave off a feeble light. Suddenly there were loud cries outside. The geese were coming home from pasture. A moment later the daughter came in, but the old woman hardly took notice and only nodded her head a little. The daughter sat down, took her spinning wheel, and twisted her thread as deftly as a young girl. The two of them sat there for two hours without exchanging a word. Finally there was a whirring at the window and two fiery eyes looked in. It was a night owl, and three times it cried: "Tu-whit tu-whoo!" The old woman only looked up for a moment, then she said: "Daughter, it's time for you to go out and do your work."

She stood up and went. But where did she go? Across the meadows and down down into the valley. At last she came to a spring with three oak trees beside it. The moon had risen big and round over the mountain, and it was so light you could have found a pin. She removed a skin from her face, bent down over the spring and began to wash herself. When she had finished, she dipped the skin in the water as well. Then she laid it down in the meadow to bleach and dry in the moonlight. How the girl had changed! You've never seen anything like it. Once her gray wig was off, golden hair came bursting out like sunbeams, and spread over her body like a cloak. Only her eyes shone through, as bright as stars in the sky, and her cheeks, flushed with the pink of apple blossoms.

But for all her beauty she was sad. She sat down and wept bitterly. Tear after tear fell from her eyes and rolled over her long hair to the ground. So she sat, and would have sat a long time if she hadn't heard a crackling and rustling in the branches of a tree nearby. She jumped up like a roe that has heard a hunter's shot. Just then a dark cloud covered the moon. In that moment she slipped into her old skin and vanished like a light the wind has blown out.

Trembling like an aspen leaf, she ran back to her house. The old woman was standing at the door, and the girl wanted to tell her what had happened, but the old woman laughed gently and said: "I know. I know." She took her into the house and lit a fresh pine knot. But the old woman didn't sit down at the spinning wheel; she picked up the broom and began to sweep and scrub. "Everything must be spick and span," she said. "But mother," said the girl, "why start working so late? What have you in mind?" "Do you know what time it is?" asked the old woman. "Not yet midnight but past eleven," said the girl. "Hasn't it occurred to you," the old woman asked, "that you came to me exactly three years ago today? Your time is up, we can't stay together any longer." The girl was dismayed. "Oh, mother dear," she said, "are you going to send me away? Where can I go? I have no home and no friends to turn to. I've done everything you've asked of me, you've always been pleased with me. Don't send me away." The old woman didn't want to tell the girl what was in store for her. "This is the end of my stay here," she said, "but when I go, the house must be clean. So don't interfere with my work. As for yourself, don't worry. You'll find a good-enough roof to live under, and you'll be quite satisfied with the wages I'm going to give you." "But tell me, tell me what's going to happen," the girl pleaded. "I've said it once, and I say it again. Don't interfere with my work. Not another word. Go to your room, take the skin off your face, and put on the silk dress you were wearing when you came to me. Then stay in your room until I call you."

But now I must go back to the king and the queen, who had gone with the count to look for the old woman in the forest. During the night the count strayed away from them and had to go on by himself. The next day he felt he was on the right path and plodded on until it began to get dark. Then, for fear of getting lost, he climbed a tree and decided to spend the night there. When the moon lit up the woods, he saw a figure coming down the mountain. She wasn't carrying a switch, yet he knew she was the goose girl he had seen at the old woman's house. "Ha!" he cried. "There she comes! And once I get my hands on one of those witches, the other won't escape me." But imagine his amazement when she went to the spring, threw off her skin and washed herself, when her golden hair tumbled down over her shoulders and she stood there more beautiful than anyone he had ever seen. He hardly dared breathe, but he stretched his head through the leaves as far as he could and stared at her. Either he leaned out too far or something else went wrong; anyway, a branch suddenly snapped, and in that moment the girl slipped into her skin and fled like a roe. Just then a cloud covered the moon and he lost sight of her.

No sooner had she vanished than the count came down from his tree and hurried after her. He hadn't gone far when he saw two figures moving across the meadow in the moonlight. It was the king and queen. They were heading for the light in the old woman's house, which they had seen in the distance. The count told them what strange things he had seen by the spring, and they had no doubt of the girl's being their lost daughter. They went joyfully on and soon came to the house. The geese were all asleep with their heads under their wings, and not a one of them stirred. The king and queen looked through the window. The old woman was sitting there perfectly still, nodding her head as she spun, but never looking around. The room was as neat as a pin, as though the little fog men, who carry no dust on their feet, had lived there. But they didn't see their daughter. For some time they stood there looking in; then finally they took courage and tapped softly on the window. The old woman seemed to be expecting them. She stood up and said in the friendliest tone: "Do come in. I know you." As they entered the room, she said: "You could have spared yourselves the long journey if you hadn't sent your good sweet child away so unjustly three years ago. It has done her no harm. She has tended my geese for three years and learned no evil by doing it; her heart is as pure as ever. As for you, you've been punished enough by the anguish you've suffered." She went to the door and cried: "Come out, dear daughter." The door opened and the princess appeared in her silk dress, with her golden hair and sparkling eyes. It was as though an angel from heaven had come into the room.

She went to her father and mother and hugged them and kissed them. They all wept for joy. The young count was standing beside them, and when she saw him her cheeks turned as red as a moss rose, she herself didn't know why. "Dear child," said the king. "I've given my kindgdom away. What shall I give you?" "She needs nothing," said the old woman. "I am making her a present of the tears she wept for you. They are pearls, every one of them more precious than those found in the sea, and worth more than your whole kingdom. And as a reward for her services, I'm letting her have my house." With these words the old woman vanished. For a moment the walls shook and rattled, and when they looked around, the hut had turned into a splendid palace, a royal table had been set, and servants were running this way and that.

There's still more to the story, but my grandmother who told it to me was losing her memory and she forgot the rest. All the same, I believe the beautiful princess married the count and I'm pretty sure they stayed in the palace together and lived happily as long as God wanted them to. I wouldn't swear that the snow-white geese the goose girl tended were girls (don't anybody take offense now) whom the old woman had taken to live with her, or that they got back their human forms and stayed on as maids-in-waiting for the young queen. But it seems likely. This much I do know: the old woman wasn't a witch, as people thought. She was a Wise Woman. I imagine she was present when the princess was born and that she was the one who gave her the gift of weeping pearls instead of tears. That kind of thing doesn't happen any more. If it did, the poor would get rich in no time.

180

Eve's Unequal Children

WHEN ADAM AND EVE were driven out of Paradise, they had to build themselves a house on barren soil and eat their bread in the sweat of their faces. Adam delved and Eve span. Each year Eve brought a child into the world, but the children were not alike; some were handsome and some ugly. When a good bit of time had passed, God sent an angel to tell them he was coming to take a look at their household. Eve was pleased at the Lord's kindness. She gave the house a thorough cleaning, decorated it with flowers, and strewed rushes on the floor. Then she brought in her children, but only the handsome ones. She washed and bathed them, combed their hair, put freshly washed shirts on them, and warned them to behave properly in the Lord's presence, to bow politely and hold out their hands, and answer his questions modestly and thoughtfully. As for the ugly children, they were not to show themselves. The first she hid in the hay, the second in the attic, the third under the straw, the fourth behind the stove, the fifth in the cellar, the sixth under a tub, the seventh under a wine barrel, the eighth under an old pelt, the ninth and tenth under the cloth from which she made their clothes, the eleventh and twelfth under the leather out of which she cut their shoes. She had barely finished when someone knocked at the door. Adam peeped through a crack and saw it was the Lord. He opened respectfully and the Heavenly Father came in. The handsome children stood there in a row, bowed, held out their hands, and went down on their knees. The Lord began to bless them. He laid his hands on the first, saying: "You will be a mighty king." To the second he said: "You, a prince," to the third, "You, a count," to the fourth, "You, a knight," to the fifth, "You, a gentleman," to the sixth, "You, a burgher," to the seventh, "You, a merchant," and to the eighth, "You, a scholar."

When Eve saw that the Lord was so merciful and kind and had bestowed rich blessings on them all, she thought: "I'll go and get my ugly children. Perhaps he will give them too his blessing." She ran and retrieved them from the hay, the straw, the stove, and all the other hiding places, and the whole filthy, grubby, scabby, sooty crew came in. The Lord smiled, looked them all over, and said: "I will give these too my blessing." He laid his hands on the first and said: "You will be a peasant." To the second he said: "You, a fisherman," to the third, "You, a blacksmith," to the fourth, "You, a tanner," to the fifth, "You, a weaver," to the sixth, "You, a shoemaker," to the seventh, "You, a tailor," to the eighth, "You, a potter," to the ninth, "You a carter," to the tenth, "You, a sailor," to the eleventh, "You, a messenger," and to the twelfth: "You, a domestic servant all the days of your life."

When Eve had heard all that, she asked: "Lord, how can you give out such unequal blessings? They're all my children, I brought them all into the world. Your favors should be equal for all." But the Lord replied: "Eve, you don't understand. Your children are all I've got to people the whole world with. If they were all princes and nobles, who would grow grain and thresh it, who would grind flour and bake bread? Where would the blacksmiths and weavers, the carpenters, builders, and ditchdiggers, the tailors and shoemakers come from? Each man in his place. This way one will sustain the other and all will be fed, just as the parts of the body sustain one another." And Eve replied: "Forgive me, O Lord. I was in too much of a hurry to find fault. Your divine will be done, even if they are my children."

181

The Nixie of the Pond

THERE WAS ONCE a miller who lived happily with his wife. They had money and property, and their wealth increased from year to year. But misfortune comes overnight. Just as their wealth had increased, so it dwindled from year to year, and a time came when the miller could hardly call the mill where he lived his own. He was bowed with care and when he went to bed after the day's work, he tossed and turned and found no rest. One morning he got up before daybreak and went out, hoping to find some relief out of doors. As he was crossing the mill dam, the first rays of sun appeared on the horizon. Just then he heard a sound in the pond, and turning around he saw a beautiful woman rise slowly from the water. With her delicate, well-shaped hands she was holding her long hair close to her shoulders, and it poured down over both sides of her pale white body. He saw it was the nixie of the pond, and he was so frightened he didn't know whether to stay or run. But the nixie spoke to him in a soft voice, called him by name, and asked him why he was so sad. At first the miller was struck dumb, but she sounded so friendly that he took heart and told her how he had once been rich but was now so poor he didn't know what to do. "Cheer up," said the nixie. "I'll make you richer than you ever were, but you must promise to give me what has just been born in your house." "What could that be but a puppy or a kitten?" thought the miller, and promised to give her what she had asked. The nixie slipped back into the water, and he went home to his mill with a light heart. He was almost at the door when the serving maid came out and said: "Congratulations! Your wife has just given birth to a baby boy." The miller stood as though thunderstruck. He realized that the sly nixie had known it all along and had tricked him. Deep in gloom, he went to his wife's bedside, and when she said:

"Isn't it a fine little boy? Why aren't you happy?" he told her about his meeting with the nixie and the promise he had made. "Riches will mean nothing to me," he said, "if I am to lose my child. But what can I do?" And the relatives who came to congratulate them had no suggestions to offer.

Prosperity returned to the miller's house. All his undertakings were successful, his chests and coffers seemed to fill themselves, and the money in his strongbox increased overnight. Soon he was richer than ever before. But he couldn't enjoy his wealth, for the promise he had given the nixie never ceased to torment him. Every time he passed the pond he was afraid she would appear to remind him of his debt. He never let the little boy go near the water. "Watch out," he said. "If you touch the water, a hand will come out and grab you and pull you under." But as year after year passed and the nixie didn't show herself, the miller began to feel easier in his mind.

The child grew to be a young man and was apprenticed to a hunter. When he had completed his apprenticeship and become an expert hunter, the lord of the village took him into his service. In the village there was a beautiful, truehearted girl, and the hunter took a liking to her. When his master saw that, he gave him a small house and they were married. They loved each other with all their hearts and lived together in quiet happiness.

One day the hunter was chasing a deer. When the deer left the woods and came out into the open, he followed it and killed it with a single shot. He didn't notice that he was near the dangerous pond. After gutting the deer, he went to the water to wash his bloodstained hands, and he had scarcely dipped them in the water when the nixie rose up laughing, clasped him in her dripping arms, and pulled him down so quickly that the water rose up in waves.

When dusk fell and the hunter hadn't come home, his wife began to be worried and went looking for him. She half-suspected what had happened, for he had often told her about the nixie and how he kept away from the pond, and when she found his gamebag lying on the bank she could have no further doubt. Wailing and wringing her hands, she called her darling's name, but in vain. She ran to the other side of the water and called again; she shouted angry words at the nixie, but there was no answer. The surface of the water remained unruffled, and only the face of the half moon looked up at her.

The poor woman didn't leave the pond. She walked quickly round and round it, sometimes in silence, sometimes screaming, sometimes whimpering softly. Finally, when her strength gave out, she sank to the ground and fell into a deep sleep. Soon a dream came to her.

Stricken with fear, she was climbing a rocky mountain slope. Thornbushes and creepers clung to her feet, the rain beat down on her face, and the wind ruffled her long hair. When she reached the top, everything changed. The sky was blue, the air soft, the ground sloped gently downward, and in the midst of a green meadow strewn with bright-colored flowers she saw a clean little hut. She went and opened the door, and there sat a white-haired old crone, who gave her a friendly smile. At that moment the poor woman woke up. The day had already dawned, and she immediately decided to do what she had done in her dream. She had a hard time climbing the mountain, and everything was just as she had seen it in her dream. The old crone welcomed her kindly and showed her a chair to sit in. "Only some misfortune," she said, "can have brought you to my lonely hut." In tears the hunter's wife told her what had happened. "Dry your tears," said the old crone. "I will help you. Here you have a golden comb. Wait till the full moon rises. Then go to the pond, sit down at the edge, and comb your long black hair with this comb. When you have finished, lie down on the bank, and you'll see what happens."

The woman went home, but the days till the full moon were slow in passing. At last the glowing disk appeared in the sky. She went out to the pond, sat down, and combed her long black hair with the golden comb. When she had finished, she put the comb down at the edge of the water. Soon there was a gurgling from the depths, a wave arose, rolled to the bank, and carried the comb away. In no more time than the comb needed to sink to the bottom, the surface of the water parted and the hunter's head rose up. He didn't speak, but he gazed sadly at his wife. At that same moment a second wave came along and covered his head. He vanished, the pond lay as still as before, and there was nothing to be seen on its surface but the face of the full moon.

Sick at heart, the woman went home. But that night she saw the old crone's hut in her dream. Next morning she went to see her again, and poured out her heart. The old crone gave her a golden flute and said: "Wait until the full moon comes again. Then take this flute, sit down on the bank, and play a pretty tune on it. When you've finished, lie down on the sand. You'll see what happens."

She did as the old woman had told her. No sooner had she laid the flute on the sand than a gurgling was heard from the depths. A wave arose, rolled to the bank, and carried the flute away. A moment later the water parted and not only the head rose up, but with it half the man's body. Full of yearning, he opened his arms to her, but a second wave came rolling, covered him, and carried him down again.

"Ah," the poor woman sighed, "what good does it do me to glimpse my darling only to lose him again!" Again she was sick at heart, but for the third time her dream showed her the old crone's house. She went to her, and the wise woman gave her a golden spinning wheel, comforted her, and said: "The end is not yet. Wait till the full moon rises, then take this spinning wheel, sit down on the bank and spin until the spindle is full. When you have finished, leave the spinning wheel near the water, and you'll see what happens."

The woman did exactly as she had been told. As soon as the full moon appeared, she took the golden spinning wheel to the bank and spun without stopping until her flax was gone and the spindle was full of thread. No sooner had she set the spinning wheel down on the bank than a gurgling, more violent than before, was heard from the depths of the pond and a great wave came rolling and carried the spinning wheel away. A moment later the hunter's head and his whole body rose up in a waterspout. He jumped up on the bank, took his wife by the hand, and fled. But they had only gone a little way when the whole pond rose up with a terrible gushing and roaring, and overflowed the fields with irresistible force. The fugitives thought they would surely die, but in her terror the woman called on the old crone for help, and in that moment they were transformed, she into a toad, he into a frog. When the flood overtook them, it couldn't kill them, but it carried them far away and separated them.

When the waters subsided and they touched dry land again, their human forms came back to them. But neither knew where the other was and they were both among strange people who had never heard of their country. High mountains and deep valleys lay between them. For their livelihood both had to tend sheep. Full of grief and yearning, they drove their flocks through fields and forests for long years.

One day when spring had once more burst forth from the earth, they both went out with their flocks, and as luck would have it, they headed for the same place. Catching sight of a flock on a distant mountain slope, he headed for it with his sheep. They met in the valley below, but they didn't recognize each other. Nevertheless they were glad, for they weren't alone any longer. Every day from then on, they drove their flocks side by side. They didn't talk much, but they felt comforted. One night when the full moon was shining in the sky and the sheep had lain down to rest, the shepherd took the flute from his pocket and played a lovely but mournful tune. When he had finished, he saw the shepherdess was weeping bitterly. "Why are you weeping?" he asked. "Ah," she replied, "the full moon was shining just like this when I last played that tune on the flute and my darling's head rose out of the pond." He looked at her, and it seemed to him that a veil had fallen from his eyes. He recognized his dearest wife, and when she looked at his face in the moonlight, she also recognized him. They hugged and kissed each other, and there's no need to ask if they were happy.

182
The Gifts of the Little Folk

A TAILOR AND A GOLDSMITH were traveling together, and one evening when the sun had fallen behind the mountains, they heard distant music, growing clearer and clearer. It sounded strange, but so pleasant that they forgot how tired they were and strode rapidly ahead and soon came to a hill. By then the moon had risen and they could see a crowd of little men and women, holding hands and dancing happily round and round. As they danced, they sang beautifully, and that was the music the travelers had heard. In the middle sat an old man, who was slightly bigger than the others. He was wearing a coat of many colors and a hoary gray beard flowed down over his chest.

The travelers stopped and stood watching the dance in amazement. The old man beckoned them to enter the circle, and the little folk graciously made an opening for them. The goldsmith, who had a hump and like all hunchbacks was perky and bold, stepped right in. The tailor was rather uneasy and hung back at first, but when he saw how happy and cheerful they all were, he took courage and followed. The circle closed and the little folk went on dancing with the wildest leaps, and singing. The old man drew a knife with a broad blade from his belt, whetted it, and when he thought it was sharp enough looked around at the strangers. They were terrified, but there was no time to think. The old man grabbed the goldsmith and quick as a flash cut off his hair and beard. A moment later it was the tailor's turn. But their terror vanished when the little old man, once his work was done, gave them each a friendly pat on the shoulder, as though to say they had done well to take their shearing so cheerfully and not to resist. He pointed at a pile of coal that lay off to one side and motioned them to fill their pockets with it. They both obeyed, though they couldn't imagine what they'd ever do with the coal. After that they went on to look for an inn. When they got to the bottom of the hill, the clock of the nearby cloister struck twelve. Instantly the singers fell silent, everything vanished, and the hill lay deserted in the moonlight.

The two travelers found an inn. They lay down in the straw and covered themselves with their coats, but they were so tired they forgot to take the coal out of their pockets. The heavy weight on their limbs woke them earlier than usual. They reached into their pockets and couldn't believe their eyes when they saw that what they had taken out wasn't coal at all, but pure gold. And to complete their happiness, their beards and hair were back again, as abundant as ever. They were both rich, but the goldsmith, who was greedy by nature, had put more coal in his pocket, and was twice as rich as the tailor.

Now greedy people always want more, so the goldsmith suggested that they stay another day and go back to the little old man that night for still greater treasure. The tailor shook his head. "No," he said. "This is enough for me. Now I'll set myself up as a master tailor and marry my little chickadee (as he called his sweetheart). I'll be a happy man." But to oblige the goldsmith, he consented to stay on. That evening the goldsmith slung some bags over his shoulders, so as to be able to help himself generously, and set out for the hill. Again he found the little folk dancing and singing. Again the little old man cut off his hair and beard and motioned him to take some coal. Without delay he took as much as his pockets and bags would hold, went back to the inn overjoyed, and covered himself with his coat. "No matter how much that gold weighs," he said to himself, "I'll bear it gladly." At last he fell asleep in the sweet anticipation of waking up as rich as Croesus.

The moment his eyes opened, he jumped up to examine his pockets, but much to his amazement all he could get out of them, though he reached in again and again, was black coal. "I still have the gold I took the night before," he thought, and went to get it, but to his horror he saw it had been turned back to coal. He clapped his dusty black hand to his forehead and felt that his head was shorn smooth, as was his chin. But that wasn't the end of his misfortunes. Only then did he notice that, as a companion piece to the hump on his back, another, just as big, had cropped up on his chest. He realized then that he had been punished for his greed, and wept aloud. The sound awoke the good tailor, who did his best to comfort the unhappy man and said: "You've been with me in all my travels; you shall stay with me and share my treasure." The tailor kept his word, but the poor goldsmith had to put up with his two humps as long as he lived, and wear a cap over his bald head.

183

The Giant and the Tailor

A TAILOR, WHOSE WORDS spoke louder than his actions, took it into his head to leave home for a while and see what he could see in the forest. At the first opportunity he left his workshop,

> and went his way
> up hill and down,
> this way, that way
> and on and on.

After a while he looked into the blue distance and saw a steep hill, and behind the hill, rising from a dark, wild forest, he saw a tower that reached to the sky. "Good God!" he cried. "What's that?" And goaded by curiosity, he headed for it at a good clip. How he gaped and stared when he came closer, for the tower had legs and jumped right over the steep hill. Who should be standing before the tailor a moment later but an enormous giant! "What are you doing here, you contemptible flyspeck?" the giant cried in a voice that sounded like thunder coming from all directions. The tailor answered in a whisper: "I just came out here to see if I couldn't earn a little something in the forest." "If that's what you want," said the giant, "you can work for me." "If it can't be helped, why not?" said the tailor. "What will my wages be?" "Your wages? I'll tell you. Every year you shall have three hundred and sixty-five days, with an extra day in leap year. What do you say to that?" "Fair enough," said the tailor, thinking: "I may as well make the best of a bad bargain. I'll clear out as soon as I can."

"All right, you little rascal," said the giant. "Go and get me a pitcher of water." "Why not take the whole well while I'm about it?" the braggart asked as he started out with the pitcher. The giant was rather slow-witted. "What! The whole well?" he grumbled into his beard, and he began to be afraid. "That fellow has something up his sleeve. I bet he's swallowed a mandrake. Watch your step, Hans old man. He's not the right kind of servant for you." When the tailor had brought the water, the giant ordered him to go out into the woods, cut a few logs and bring them back. "Why not the whole forest at one stroke,

"the entire forest
with everything in it,
with little and big,
with branch and twig?"

the tailor asked, and went off to cut the wood. "What!

"The entire forest
with everything in it,
with little and big,
with branch and twig?—

not to speak of the well!" the credulous giant grumbled into his beard and was more terrified than ever. "That fellow's got something up his sleeve. I bet he's swallowed a mandrake. Watch your step, Hans old man, he's not the right kind of servant for you." When the tailor had brought the wood, the giant ordered him to shoot two or three wild boars for supper. "Why not a thousand with one shot and bring you the whole lot of them?" asked the boastful tailor. "What!" cried the terrified giant. "Let it go for today. Lie down and sleep."

The giant was so frightened he didn't close an eye all night. He lay awake racking his brains: he had to get rid of this damned magician he'd taken on as his servant. The sooner the better. But how was he going to do it? By morning he had an idea. He took the tailor to a swamp with willow trees all around it. When they got there, the giant said: "Listen to me, tailor. Sit down on one of these willow branches. I'm curious to know if you're heavy enough to bend it." One two three, the tailor was up on the branch, holding his breath and making himself heavy, so heavy that the branch bent beneath him. But when he had to draw another breath, it sprang back and (since unfortunately he hadn't put his flatiron in his pocket) sent him flying so high that the giant, much to his delight, couldn't even see him any more. If he hasn't come down again, he must still be floating around in the air.

184

The Nail

A MERCHANT HAD DONE good business at the fair, sold all his wares and filled his moneybag with gold and silver. Wanting to get home before nightfall, he strapped the trunk with his money in it to his horse, and started out.

At noon he stopped at an inn. When he was ready to leave, the stable boy brought him his horse, but said: "Sir, a nail is missing from the left hind shoe." "That's all right," said the merchant. "The shoe will hold for the six hours I still have to go. I'm in a hurry."

That afternoon when he stopped again and had them feed his horse, the stable boy came in and said: "Sir, a shoe is missing from your horse's left hind hoof. Should I take him to the blacksmith?" "Never mind," said the merchant. "I've only an hour or two to go. He'll be all right. I'm in a hurry."

He started off, but it wasn't long before the horse began to limp. He hadn't been limping very long when he began to stumble, and he hadn't been stumbling very long when he fell and broke a leg. The merchant had to leave the horse where he was, unbuckle his trunk, take it over his shoulder and walk. It was late in the night when he got home. "It's all the fault of that damned nail," he said to himself.

Haste makes waste.

185

The Poor Boy in the Grave

ONCE THERE WAS a poor shepherd boy whose father and mother had died, and the village elders had appointed a rich farmer to lodge him, feed him, and bring him up. But this man and his wife were wicked; for all their wealth they were stingy and grudging, and they couldn't bear to see anyone taking a bite out of their bread. Try as he might to please them, they gave the poor boy very little to eat, but they were all the more generous with beatings.

One day he was told to watch a hen and her chicks. They all wandered off through a hedge and hardly a moment had passed before a hawk swooped down and carried the hen away. The boy shouted at the top of his lungs: "Stop, thief!" But do you think that made the hawk bring the hen back? The man heard the noise and came running. When he heard what had happened to his hen, he gave the boy such a beating that he couldn't move for several days. After that he had to guard the chicks without the help of the hen, and that was even harder, because they all ran in different directions. Then he took it into his head that if he tied the chicks together with a string the hawk wouldn't be able to steal any of them. That was a big mistake. A few days later his hunger and all the running about made him so tired that he fell asleep. The hawk swooped down and seized one of the chickens, but since they were all tied together, it carried off the whole lot, perched on a treetop, and gobbled them up. The farmer had just come home. When he saw the disaster, he flew into a rage and beat the boy so unmercifully that he had to lie in bed for a week.

When he was up again, the farmer said to him: "You're too stupid. I can't use you to watch the animals. You'll have to run errands instead." Thereupon he sent him to the judge with a basket of grapes and a letter. On the way, the boy was so tormented by hunger and thirst that he ate two bunches of grapes. He brought the judge the basket, and after reading the letter the judge counted the bunches of grapes. "Two bunches are missing," he said. The boy admitted truthfully that hunger and thirst had driven him to eat the two missing bunches. The judge wrote the farmer a letter asking for more grapes, twice as many bunches. Again the farmer sent a letter with the grapes. Again the boy was so fearfully hungry and thirsty that he couldn't resist and ate another two bunches. But before eating them, he took the letter out of the basket, put it under a stone, and sat down on the stone to prevent the letter from watching him and giving him away. Nevertheless, the judge called him to account for the missing bunches. "My goodness!" said the boy. "How did you ever find out? The letter couldn't have known, because I put it under a stone first." The judge had to laugh at his simplicity and wrote the farmer a letter, ordering him to take better care of the boy, give him enough to eat and drink, and teach him the difference between right and wrong.

"I'll show you the difference!" said the hard man. "If you want to eat, you'll have to work, and if you do wrong, you'll get plenty of blows to correct you." The next day, he set him a hard task: to chop up several bundles of straw for fodder. "I'll be back in five hours," said the man. "If you haven't made all this straw into chaff by then, I'll beat you till you can't move." The farmer went to the fair with his wife, his maid, and his hired man, leaving the boy nothing but a small piece of bread. The boy sat down on the chopping stool and started to work with might and main. When he began to feel warm, he took off his jacket and tossed it in the straw. He was so afraid of not getting done in time that he kept chopping and chopping, and in his frenzy he chopped up his jacket along with the straw. By the time he noticed, it was too late; there was nothing to be done. "Oh! Oh!"

he cried. "Now I'm done for! That wicked man meant every word he said; when he comes home and sees this, he'll kill me. I'd rather kill myself!"

The boy had once heard the farmer's wife say: "There's a jar of poison under my bed." Actually there was honey in the jar, and she'd only said that to discourage greedy people. The boy crawled under the bed, brought out the jar, and ate up all the honey. "I don't know," he said to himself. "People say death is bitter. It tastes sweet to me. No wonder the farmer's wife is always wishing she were dead." He sat down in a chair and was all ready to die. But instead of getting weaker, he was strengthened by the good food. "It couldn't have been poison," he said to himself. "But the farmer once said there was a bottle of fly poison in his clothes cupboard. That must be the real thing; that will make me die." But it wasn't fly poison at all, it was Hungarian wine. He brought out the bottle and drank up the wine. "This is another sweet death," he said to himself. But soon the wine rose to his head and numbed his senses and he thought his end was near. "I can feel I'm going to die," he said. "I'll go out to the churchyard and find myself a grave." He staggered out, went to the churchyard, and lay down in a freshly dug grave. He felt more and more befuddled. A wedding was being celebrated at a tavern nearby, and when he heard the music he thought he was in Paradise. In the end he lost consciousness completely. The poor boy never woke up. The heat of the strong wine and the cold dew of the night took his life, and he stayed in the grave he had laid himself down in.

When the farmer heard the news of the boy's death, he was afraid of being haled into court and was so terrified that he fell down in a faint. His wife, who was standing at the stove with a pan full of fat, ran to help him. But the flames shot into the pan, the whole house caught fire, and in a few hours there was nothing left but ashes. The two of them spent the rest of their lives in dire poverty, ravaged by the pangs of conscience.

186
The True Bride

THERE WAS ONCE a girl who was young and beautiful, but her mother had died when she was very young, and her stepmother did everything in her power to make her miserable. When the stepmother set her a task, she never complained; no matter how hard it was, she started right in and did her very best. But nothing could move the wicked woman's heart, nothing the girl did could satisfy her. The harder she worked, the more she was given to do, and all the stepmother could think of was finding still harder work for her to do and making her life more wretched in every way.

One day she said to her: "Here you have twelve pounds of feathers. I want you to strip them, and if you're not done by nightfall, you can expect a good thrashing. Did you think you could spend the whole day lolling around?" The poor girl started to work, but the tears flowed down her cheeks, for she saw it would not be possible to do all that in one day. When she sighed or beat her forehead in anguish, the feathers she had in front of her blew in all directions and she had to pick them up and start all over again. Once, when that happened, she propped her elbows on the table, held her face in both hands, and cried out: "Is there no one on God's earth to take pity on me?" A gentle voice replied: "Take heart, child. I've come to help you." The girl looked up and an old woman was standing there. She took the girl gently by the hand and said: "Just tell me what the trouble is." Encouraged by her friendliness, the girl told her about her dismal life, how she was given one crushing task after another and could never get to the end of them. "If I haven't got these feathers done by nightfall, my stepmother will beat me. She said she would and I know she'll keep her word." Again her tears began to flow, but the good old woman said: "Don't worry, child. Go and rest. Meanwhile I'll be doing your work." The girl lay down on the bed and soon fell asleep. The old woman sat down at the table. Her withered hands barely touched the quills, but my! how the feathers flew. She had soon finished the twelve pounds. When the girl woke up, she saw great heaps of snow-white down, and the whole room had been put nicely in order, but the old woman had vanished. "Thank God," said the girl, and sat quietly until nightfall. When the stepmother came in, she was amazed to see that the work was done. "Aha, you slut!" she cried. "Now you see what a little effort can do! Couldn't you have started on something else? Oh no. There you sit with your hands folded." After leaving the room she said to herself: "The creature isn't entirely useless. I'll have to find something harder for her to do."

Next morning she called the girl and said: "Here you have a spoon. I want you to take it and empty out the big pond beside the garden. If you're not finished by nightfall, you know what will happen." The girl took the spoon and saw it was full of holes, and even if it hadn't been she could never have emptied the pond with it. Without a moment's delay she went to the pond, got down on her knees, and scooped. Her tears fell into the water. But the good old woman appeared again and when she heard the reason for the girl's unhappiness, she said: "Don't worry, child. Lie down under the trees and sleep, I'll do your work." When the old woman was alone, she barely touched the pond. The water rose up in vapor and mingled with the clouds. Little by little the pond emptied, and just before nightfall, when the girl woke up and came back, all she could see where the pond had been was fishes floundering in the mud. She went to her stepmother and told her the work was finished. "You should have been done long ago," she said, going white with rage. Then she started thinking up something new.

On the third morning, she said to the girl: "I want you to build me a beautiful castle over there on the plain, and I want to see it finished by nightfall." The girl was thunderstruck. "How can I ever do that!" "Don't you dare talk back to me!" the stepmother screamed. "If you can empty a pond with a spoon full of holes, you can build a castle. I want to move in before the day is out, and if the slightest thing is missing, even from the kitchen or cellar, you know what to expect." She drove the girl out of the house, and she started walking. When she came to the valley, boulder lay piled on boulder, and though she tried with all her strength, she couldn't move the smallest of them.

She sat down and wept, but she hoped the good old woman would come and help her and she didn't have long to wait. The old woman came and comforted her. Then she said: "Lie down over there in the shade and sleep. I'll build you a castle. If you want to, you'll even be able to live in it." When the girl had gone, the old woman touched the gray boulders. Instantly they stirred, moved into place, and stood there as though giants had built a wall. On this foundation a building rose up, as though innumerable hands were working invisibly, laying stone upon stone. The earth rumbled, great columns shot up of their own accord and formed orderly ranks. Tiles laid themselves on the roof and by noon a golden Virgin in fluttering robes stood like a weathervane at the top of the tower. The interior was finished by nightfall. How the old woman managed it I don't know, but the walls of the rooms were hung with silk and velvet, there were chairs covered with colorful needlework and round the marble tables stood richly ornamented armchairs. Crystal chandeliers hung from the ceiling and their light was reflected in the polished floor. In golden cages sat green parrots and sweet-singing foreign birds. On all sides there was splendor, as though a king were going to move in. The sun was just setting when the girl awoke. The first thing she saw was the glow of a thousand lamps. She hurried toward them and passed through the open gate into the castle. The stairway was covered with red cloth and the golden balustrade adorned with flowering shrubs. When she saw the splendor of the rooms, she stood stock-still, as though turned to stone. The Lord only knows how long she would have stood there if the thought of her stepmother hadn't crossed her mind. "Oh dear!" she said to herself. "If only she'd be satisfied now and finally stop tormenting me!" She went and told her the castle was finished. "I'll move right in," said the stepmother, rising from her chair. When she stepped into the castle, the radiance was so dazzling she had to hold her hand before her eyes. "You see," she said to the girl, "you see how easy it's been for you. I ought to have given you something harder to do." She went through all the rooms, looking in every corner to see if anything was missing or unsatisfactory, but she couldn't find anything to complain of. "But now we shall go downstairs," she said with a malignant look at the girl. "I haven't inspected the kitchen and cellar yet. If you've forgotten anything, I wouldn't want to be in your shoes." But the fire was burning on the hearth, food was cooking in the pots, the tongs and shovel were leaning in the corner, and gleaming brass pots and pans were ranged on shelves along the walls. Nothing was missing, not even the coal bunker or the water buckets. "Which way to the cellar?" the stepmother asked. "If it's not amply stocked with wine, I feel sorry for you." She opened the trap herself and went down the stairs, but she had no sooner taken the two steps than the heavy trap door, which hadn't been fastened, fell. The girl heard a scream and quickly lifted the door, meaning to go to her help. But the stepmother had fallen down the stairs and she found her lying dead at the bottom.

Now the splendid castle belonged to the girl alone. At first she couldn't get used to her good fortune. There were beautiful dresses hanging in the cupboards, the chests were filled with gold and silver or pearls and precious stones, and she had no desire she couldn't satisfy. Soon the news of her beauty and wealth spread far and wide. Every day suitors presented themselves, but she didn't care for any of them. At length a prince succeeded in moving her heart, and they became engaged. There was a linden tree in the castle garden and one day when the lovers were sitting under it, the prince said to her: "I must go home and get my father's consent to our marriage. I beg of you, wait for me here under this linden tree. I shall be back in a few hours." The girl kissed him on the left cheek and said: "Be true to me. Never let anyone else kiss you on this cheek. I shall wait here under the linden tree until you come back."

The girl sat under the linden tree till the sun went down, but he didn't come back. For three days she sat waiting from morning to night, but in vain. On the fourth day, when he still didn't appear, she said to herself: "Something must have happened to him. I will go and look for him and I won't come back till I've found him." She packed three of her most beautiful dresses, the first embroidered with glittering stars, the second with silver moons, and the third with golden suns, tied a handful of jewels in a cloth, and started out. Everywhere she asked for her betrothed, but no one had seen him, no one had news of him. Far and wide she wandered, but she didn't find him. In the end she went to work as a shepherdess and buried her dresses and jewels under a stone.

After that she spent her days tending her flock. Her heart was sad and filled with longing for her loved one. She made a pet of a little lamb. It ate out of her hand, and when she said:

> "Lambkin, swear on bended knee
> You won't forget your shepherdess
> As the prince forgot the lass
> Waiting under the linden tree,"

the lamb would kneel and she would caress it.

When she had lived a few years in sorrowful loneliness, it was bruited about that the king's daughter was to be married. The road to the town passed through the village where the girl was living, and one day, as she was driving her flock to pasture, the bridegroom passed by. He sat proudly on his horse and didn't look at her, but when she looked at him, she recognized her beloved and felt as if a sharp knife had pierced her heart. "Ah," she said, "I thought he had stayed true to me, but he forgot me."

The next day he passed again. When he came close to her, she said to her lamb:

> "Lambkin, swear on bended knee
> You won't forget your shepherdess
> As the prince forgot the lass
> Waiting under the linden tree."

When he heard her voice, he looked down and reined in his horse, glanced at the shepherdess's face, and held his hand to his eyes as though trying to remember something. But then he rode on and soon disappeared. "Ah," she said to herself, "he doesn't know me any more," and her grief was greater than ever.

Not long after that a three-day feast was to be held at the king's palace, and the whole country was invited. "I'll make one last try," the girl thought, and that evening she went to the stone she had buried her treasures under. She took the dress with the golden suns, put it on, and decked herself with the jewels. She unbound her hair, which she had hidden under a kerchief, and it fell in long tresses at her sides. Then she went to the town and no one noticed her in the darkness. When she stepped into the brightly lit hall, everyone started back in amazement, and no one knew who she was. The king's son went up to her, but he didn't recognize her. He took her to dance with him and was so enchanted by her beauty that he didn't give a thought to his other bride. When the ball was over, the girl vanished in the crowd. By daybreak she was back in the village, dressed once more as a shepherdess.

The next night she took the dress with the silver moons on it and put a jeweled half moon in her hair. When she appeared at the feast, all eyes turned toward her. The king's son was so full of love that he danced with her alone and had eyes for no other. Before she left, he made her promise to come again the next night.

The third time she came, she had on the starry dress, which glittered with every step she took, and her headband and girdle were starred with jewels. The king's son, who had long been waiting for her, pushed through the crowd and went to her. "Tell me who you are," he said. "I have a feeling I've known you for a long time." And she replied: "Don't you remember what I did when you left me?" With that she stepped up to him and kissed him on the left cheek. It was as though scales had fallen from his eyes: there and then he recognized his true bride. "Come," he said to her. "I shall stay here no longer." He gave her his hand and led her down to his carriage. The horses broke into a gallop, and the carriage, as though it had been harnessed to the wind, sped away to the miraculous castle. The lighted windows shone in the distance. Countless glowworms were flitting about in the linden tree when they passed it. It shook its branches and sent down its fragrance. Flowers bloomed along the stairway, and the song of exotic birds could be heard from every room. The whole court was assembled in the great hall, and the priest was waiting to marry the bridegroom and his true bride.

187

The Hare and the Hedgehog

WELL, CHILDREN, THIS STORY sounds like a pack of lies, but it's true, because my grandfather, who told it to me, always used to say before starting to spin it out: "It must be true, son, 'cause if it weren't, it wouldn't be possible to tell it." All right. Here it is.

It happened one Sunday morning at harvest time, just as the

buckwheat was in flower. The sun was bright in the sky, a warm morning breeze was blowing over the stubble fields, the larks were singing in the air, the bees were buzzing in the buckwheat, the people were going off to church in their Sunday best, all God's creatures were happy, and so was the hedgehog.

The hedgehog was standing at his door with his arms folded, looking out into the morning breeze and humming a little tune no better and no worse than the little tunes a hedgehog is likely to hum of a fine Sunday morning. As he was quietly humming to himself, he had an idea. Why, while his wife was washing and dressing the children, wouldn't he mosey out to his field to see how his turnips were doing? These particular turnips were close to his house and he and his family were in the habit of eating them. That's why he thought of them as his own. No sooner said than done. He closed the door behind him and started out. He hadn't gone far from the house and he was just turning around the sloe bush at the edge of the turnip field, when he met the hare, who was there on the same sort of business, namely, to inspect his cabbages. When the hedgehog saw the hare, he gave him a friendly good morning. But instead of responding to the hedgehog's greeting, the hare, who was a fine gentleman in his own way and disgustingly high and mighty, just turned up his nose and said: "How do you come to be running around out here so early in the morning?" "I'm taking a walk," said the hedgehog. "A walk!" the hare guffawed. "It seems to me you could use your legs to better purpose." This response made the hedgehog very angry, for if there was one thing he couldn't abide it was remarks about his legs, which nature had made short and crooked. "I suppose you think your legs will get you farther?" said the hedgehog. "I certainly do," said the hare. "I defy you to prove it," said the hedgehog. "Let's have a race. I bet you I'll win." "You with your crooked legs!" said the hare. "Don't make me laugh. But I'm willing if you're dead set on it. What'll we bet?" "A golden loo-ee-dore [louis d'or] and a bottle of brandy," said the hedgehog. "Done," said the hare. "Let's shake hands on it. We can start right away." "Oh no," said the hedgehog. "What's the hurry? I never race on an empty stomach. Let me go home and have a bit of breakfast first. I'll be back in half an hour."

The hare was willing and the hedgehog went home. On the way he said to himself: "The hare is banking on his long legs, but I'll show

him. He may be a fine gentleman, but he's not very bright, and I'll
make him pay." When he got home, the hedgehog said to his wife:
"Wife, go and get dressed, I'm going to need you out in the field."
"How come?" asked the wife. "I've bet the hare a gold loo-ee-dore
and a bottle of brandy that I'll beat him in a race, and you've got to
be there." "Husband, husband!" cried the hedgehog's wife. "Are you
plumb crazy? Have you taken leave of your senses? How can you
run a race with the hare?" "Shut up, woman!" said the hedgehog.
"Who asked for your opinion? This is a man's business, so don't butt
in. Just put some clothes on and come along." What could the
hedgehog's wife do? Like it or not, she had to obey.

So they left the house, and on the way the hedgehog said to his
wife: "Now listen carefully. We're going to run this race in the long
field. The hare will be in one furrow and I'll be in another, and we'll
start at the upper end. All you have to do is stand in the furrow
down here at this end. When you see the hare coming, I want you to
sing out: 'I'm here already.'"

When they got to the field, the hedgehog showed his wife her
place. Then he went up the field and when he got to the other end,
the hare was ready to start. "How about it?" said the hare. "I'm
ready if you are," said the hedgehog. With that each took his place in
his furrow. The hare counted: "One, two, three, go!" and darted
down the field as fast as the wind. As for the hedgehog, he took three
steps and no more; then he ducked down in his furrow and stayed
there.

When the hare, running for all he was worth, reached the lower
end of the field, the hedgehog's wife called out to him: "I'm here already!" The hare was flabbergasted. He thought it was the hedgehog
in person, for as everyone knows, the hedgehog's wife looks exactly
like her husband. The hare thought to himself: "There's something
fishy about this." And he called out: "Let's give it another try. Back
again." And away he ran like the wind, so fast that his ears blew
straight back. The hedgehog's wife stayed quietly where she was, and
when the hare got to the other end, the hedgehog himself called out:
"I'm here already." The hare was beside himself with rage. "Another
try!" he cried. "Back again." "It's all right with me," said the
hedgehog. "As often as you like." So the hare ran seventy-three times
more, and the hedgehog always won. Every time the hare got to the

lower or upper end, the hedgehog or his wife said: "I'm here already."

The seventy-fourth time the hare didn't make it to the end. He collapsed in the middle of the field; blood flowed from his mouth and he fell down dead. The hedgehog took the loo-ee-dore and the bottle of brandy he had won, called his wife to come out of her burrow, and they went happily home together. And if they haven't died in the meantime, they're still alive.

That's the story of how the hedgehog raced the hare to death on Buxtehude Heath. Since then no hare has ever taken it into his head to race with a Buxtehude hedgehog.

The moral of the story is, in the first place, that nobody, no matter how fancy he thinks he is, should ever make fun of an inferior, even if it's only a hedgehog. In the second place, that if a man wants to get married, he should take a wife of his own kind, who looks exactly the same as he does. So in case you're a hedgehog, make sure your wife is one too, and so forth.

188

The Spindle, the Shuttle, and the Needle

THERE WAS ONCE a girl whose father and mother had died when she was very young. Her godmother, who lived by spinning, weaving, and sewing, had a little house at the end of the village. The old woman took the poor child in, kept her at work, and taught her to lead a good pious life. When the girl was fifteen, the old woman fell sick and called her to the bedside. "Dear daughter," she said, "I feel that my end is near. I'm leaving you the house, which will protect you against wind and weather, and my spindle, shuttle, and needle, which will help you to earn your bread." She laid her hands on her head, blessed her, and said: "Just keep God in your heart and all will go well." Then she closed her eyes. At her funeral the girl walked behind her coffin weeping bitterly, and prayed over her grave.

After that the girl lived all alone in the little house. She worked hard at spinning, weaving, and sewing, and the good old woman's blessing prospered everything she did. The flax in the storeroom seemed to increase of its own accord, and when she had woven a piece of cloth or a rug, or sewed a shirt, she always found a buyer who paid amply, so that she wanted for nothing and was even able to help others.

It so happened that the king's son was riding about the country looking for a bride. He had been told not to take a poor one, but he didn't want a rich one. So he said to himself: "I shall marry the one who is the poorest and at the same time the richest." When he came to the village where the girl lived, he asked about the richest girl in town and about the poorest, as he did wherever he went. First they named the richest. The poorest, they said, was the girl who lived in the little house at the end of the village. The rich girl was sitting outside her door in all her finery, and when the king's son came along she stood up, went over to him, and curtsied. He looked at her, said not a word, and rode on. When he came to the poor girl's house, she wasn't standing at the door but sitting in her room. He reined in his horse, looked through the window, and in the bright sunlight saw the girl working at her spinning wheel. She raised her eyes, and when she saw the king's son looking in, she blushed to the roots of her hair, lowered her eyes, and went on spinning. I don't know if the thread she was spinning at that particular moment was quite even, but I do know that she kept on spinning until the king's son rode away. Then she went to the window and opened it, saying to herself: "It's so hot in here," but then she looked after him as long as she could make out the white plumes on his hat.

After that she sat down again and went on spinning. All at once a little song the old woman had occasionally sung while working popped into her head and she too began to sing:

> "Spindle, spindle, speed away,
> Bring my suitor here today."

And what happened? Before you knew it, the spindle leaped from her hand and out through the door. When in her surprise she got up and looked after it, she saw it dancing merrily across the fields, drawing a shining golden thread behind it. In a very short while, it had vanished from her sight. Now that she had no spindle, she picked up the weaver's shuttle, sat down at her loom, and began to weave.

But the spindle danced on, and just as the thread was at an end, it caught up with the king's son. "What's this!" he cried. "Is this spindle trying to show me the way?" He turned his horse around and followed the golden thread back. The girl was sitting at her loom, weaving and singing:

> "Shuttle, shuttle, weave and glide,
> Bring the suitor to my side."

In a flash the shuttle leaped from her hand and out through the door. At the threshold it began to weave a carpet, more beautiful than anyone has ever seen. On both sides there were roses and lilies, and in the middle, on a golden ground, green vines; rabbits and hares bounded about in the foliage, harts and roes peered through, and bright-colored birds perched on the branches all ready to burst into song. The shuttle leaped this way and that, and the carpet seemed to grow of its own accord.

Now that the shuttle had run away, the girl had sat down to sew. She plied her needle and sang:

> "Needle, needle, sharp and thin,
> Make my chamber fit for him."

Instantly, the needle leaped from her fingers and flew about the room as quick as lightning. It was as though invisible spirits were at work. In a moment the table and benches were covered with green cloth, the chairs with velvet, and silk curtains hung at the windows. No sooner had the needle taken its last stitch than the girl saw the prince's white plumes in the window; the spindle had led him back with its golden thread. He got down from his horse and followed the carpet to the house. When he came in, the girl was standing there in her dingy old dress, but in it she was as radiant as a rose in a rosebush. "You are the poorest and also the richest," he said to her. "Come with me and be my bride." She said nothing but held out her hand. He kissed her, led her out of the house, lifted her up on his horse, and carried her away to the royal palace, where they were married amid great rejoicing. The spindle, the shuttle, and the needle were kept in the treasure room and held in great honor.

189

The Peasant and the Devil

ONCE THERE WAS a sly peasant. I could talk about his exploits all day, but the best story of the lot is how he outwitted the devil and made a fool of him.

After working in his field all day this peasant was getting ready to go home. Night was falling, and to his amazement he saw a heap of glowing coals in the middle of the field. He went over to it and a little black devil was sitting in the flames. "Are you sitting on a treasure?" the peasant asked. "I certainly am," said the devil. "There's more gold and silver in this treasure than you've seen in your whole life." "By right the treasure is mine," said the peasant, "because it's in my field. "You can have it," said the devil, "if you give me half of what your field produces for the next two years. I have plenty of money, but I'm hungry for the fruits of the soil." "Suits me," said the peasant, "but to avoid any misunderstandings later on, let's agree that everything above ground belongs to you and everything below ground to me." The devil was pleased with that, but the sly peasant had sown turnips. At harvest time, the devil came to gather his crop, but all he found was withered yellow leaves, while the peasant rubbed his hands and dug up his turnips. "You win this time," said the devil, "but next year it will be a different story. What grows above ground will be yours and what grows below it will be mine." "All right me with," said the peasant. But when the time came he didn't sow turnips, he sowed wheat. The grain ripened, the peasant went to the field and mowed the full stalks. When the devil got there, there was nothing left but stubble, and in a rage he vanished into a cleft in the rocks. "That's the way to cheat a cheat," said the peasant, as he went to dig up the treasure.

190

The Crumbs on the Table

THE ROOSTER ONCE SAID to his chicks: "Quick, come in and pick the crumbs off the table. Your mistress has gone visiting." "No, no," said the chicks. "We won't do it. The mistress would beat us." "She won't know," said the rooster. "Come on. You know she never gives you anything good." "No, no," the chicks said again. "Nothing doing, we won't do it." But the rooster gave them no peace until they finally went up on the table and started picking up breadcrumbs like mad. Just then the mistress came in, grabbed a stick and gave them a good dusting. Once they were outside, the chicks said to the rooster: "Did you see see see see see?" The rooster laughed and said: "Didn't I know know know?" Then they ran away.

191

The Mongoose

THERE WAS ONCE a princess who lived in a castle, and high up, just under the battlements, she had a hall with twelve windows pointing in all directions. When she went up and looked around, she could see her whole kingdom. Even from the first window she saw more clearly than other people; from the second still more clearly, from the third even more clearly than that, and so on to the twelfth, through which she could see everything above the surface of the earth and below it, so that nothing remained hidden from her. She was very proud; she wanted to rule all by herself and not take orders from anyone, so she made it known that she would accept no man as her husband unless he could hide so well that she couldn't find him and, moreover, that if anyone tried and she found him, his head would be cut off and mounted on a pole. There were already ninety-seven poles topped with severed heads outside the castle, and no one had come forward for quite some time. The princess was overjoyed. "I'll be free as long as I live," she thought. Then three brothers came and said they wished to try their luck. The eldest thought he'd be safe if he crept into a lime pit, but she saw him from the very first window, and had him pulled out and beheaded. The second crawled into the cellar of the castle, but him too she saw from the first window, and that was the end of him: his head was mounted on the ninety-ninth pole. Then the youngest came and asked her to grant him a day's time to think, and in addition to let him off if she found him on the first and second try, for if he failed a third time he would accept his fate. Because he was so handsome and pleaded so earnestly, she said: "Very well. Your requests are granted, but you won't succeed."

The next day he racked his brains for a good place to hide. When he could think of nothing, he took his gun and went hunting. He saw a raven, took aim, and was about to pull the trigger, when the raven cried out: "Don't shoot. I'll make it worth your while." He lowered his gun, went on, and came to a lake. Just then a big fish stuck his head out of the water. He put his gun to his shoulder, but the fish cried out: "Don't shoot. I'll make it worth your while." He let the fish go, went on, and met a fox who was limping. He fired and missed. The fox cried: "You'd be wiser to come here and pull the thorn out of my foot." He pulled out the thorn, but he was still going to kill the fox and skin him. "Let me go," said the fox, "and I'll make it worth your while." The youth let him go and went home, for by then it was getting dark.

The next day he was supposed to hide, but though he thought and thought, he didn't know where. Finally he went to see the raven in the forest and said: "I let you live. Now show me a hiding place where the king's daughter won't see me." The raven lowered his head and pondered. After a long while he croaked: "I've got it." He took an egg from his nest, broke it in two, and put the youth inside. Then he put it together again and sat on it. When the king's daughter looked out of the first window, she couldn't find him. When she couldn't see him through the next and the next, she began to be alarmed. But in the eleventh window she found him. She had the raven shot and the egg brought to her and cracked. The young man had to come out, and she said to him: "I'll let you off this first time. But if you can't do better than that, you're lost."

The next day he went to the lake, called the fish, and said: "I let you live. Now show me a hiding place where the king's daughter won't see me." The fish pondered, then finally he cried out: "I've got it. I'll shut you up in my stomach." Thereupon he swallowed him and swam down to the bottom of the lake. The king's daughter looked through her windows. When she didn't see him even in the eleventh, she was mightily upset, but in the twelfth she found him. She had the fish caught and killed, and the youth came to light. It's not hard to imagine how he felt. She said: "I'll let you off this second time, but I'm pretty sure your head will be mounted on the hundredth pole."

The last day he went out into the fields with a heavy heart and met the fox. "You know all about hiding places," he said. "I let you live. Now show me a hiding place where the king's daughter won't see me." "A difficult problem!" said the fox, looking very solemn. Finally he cried out: "I've got it!" He led him to a spring, dipped into it, and came out in the form of a peddler and dealer in animals. The youth dipped in too, and was turned into a mongoose. The peddler went to town and displayed the pretty little creature. A big crowd gathered, and at last the king's daughter came to see it. The mongoose was very much to her liking, and she gave the peddler a good deal of money for it. Before handing it to her, the vendor whispered to the mongoose: "When the princess goes to the window, quick, creep under her braids." When it came time for her to look for him, she went by turns from the first to the eleventh window without finding him. She went to the twelfth window and there too she saw no sign of him. Overcome with fear and rage, she slammed the window with such force that the glass in all her windows burst into a thousand pieces and the whole castle trembled.

Stepping back from the window, she felt the mongoose under her braids. In her anger, she grabbed hold of it and threw it on the ground, crying, "Out of my sight!" It ran to the peddler and both hurried to the spring, dipped in and recovered their true forms. The youth thanked the fox. "The raven and the fish," he said, "are just plain stupid compared to you. You certainly know all the tricks."

From there the youth went straight to the castle. The princess was expecting him, she had resigned herself to her fate. The wedding was held, and from then on he was king, lord and master over the whole kingdom. He never told her where he had hidden the third time or who had helped him. That way she looked up to him, for she thought he had done it all on his own and said to herself: "He's smarter than I am."

192

The Master Thief

ONE DAY A POOR PEASANT and his wife were sitting outside their old house, resting from their work, when a splendid carriage, drawn by four black horses, drove up and a richly dressed gentleman got out. The peasant stood up, went over to the gentleman and asked if he could be of any service to him. The stranger shook hands with the old man and said: "All I ask is a dish of plain country fare. If you'll cook me some potatoes the way you eat them, I'll sit down at your table and partake of them with pleasure." The peasant smiled and said: "You must be a baron or a count, maybe even a duke. Fine gentlemen sometimes get these whims. You shall have your country dish." The woman went into the kitchen and started washing and grating potatoes to make dumplings, such as peasants eat.

While she was working, the peasant said to the stranger: "Come into the garden with me in the meantime. I still have some work to do there." Indeed, he had dug some holes to plant trees in. "Haven't you any children to help you with your work?" the stranger asked. "No," said the peasant. But then he added: "I had a son. But he left home long ago. He was a good-for-nothing, clever and sharp, but he refused to learn anything sensible and was always up to some mischief. In the end he ran away, and I've had no news of him since." The old man took a sapling, set it in a hole and drove a pole in beside it. After filling the hole with earth and tamping it down firmly, he took three lengths of straw and tied the tree trunk to the pole at the top, in the middle, and at the bottom. "But tell me," said the gentleman. "That crooked, knotted tree over there in the corner that's bent almost to the ground—why don't you tie it to one of those poles to straighten it out?" The old man smiled and said: "You can say that, sir, because you've never done any gardening. That tree is so old and gnarled that nothing could ever straighten it. Trees have to be trained while they're young." "Like your son," said the stranger. "If you had trained him while he was still young, he wouldn't have run away. He too must be gnarled and twisted by now." "I suppose so," said the old man. "It's a long time since he went away. He's bound to have changed." "Would you know him if he turned up?" "I doubt if I'd recognize his face, but I'd know the birthmark on his shoulder—it looks like a bean." At that the stranger took off his coat, bared his shoulder, and showed the peasant the mark. "Heavens above!" the peasant cried out. "You really are my son," and his heart was stirred with love for his child. "But how can you be my son?" he asked. "You're a great lord, living in the lap of luxury. How have you managed that?" "Ah, father," said the son, "the young tree wasn't tied to a pole, so it got all twisted. Now it's too old to mend. How did I get rich? By thieving. But don't worry. I'm a master thief. Locks and bolts don't exist for me. If I want something, it's mine. You mustn't take me for a common thief, I steal only from the rich, from people who have more than they need. The poor have nothing to fear from me, I'm much more likely to give to them than to take. And another thing: if I see something I could get without deftness, imagination, and pains, I don't touch it." "Son, son," said the father, "I still don't like it. A thief is a thief. Believe me, you'll come to a bad end." He led the young man to his mother, and when she heard he was her son, she wept for joy, but when he told her he'd become a master thief, two streams flowed down her cheeks. In the end she said: "Thief or not, he's still my son, and my eyes have seen him once more."

They sat down to table and once again, after so many years, he shared his parents' simple fare. The father said: "If our lord the count over there in his castle finds out who you are and what you do, he won't pick you up in his arms and dandle you as he did when he held you over the font. He'll hang you on the gallows." "Don't worry, father. I know my trade and he won't do a thing to me. I'll go and see him of my own free will before the day is out." Toward evening the master thief got into his carriage and drove to the castle. The count took him for a nobleman and received him graciously. But when the stranger made himself known, the count turned pale, and for a time he didn't say a word. Finally he said: "Because you're my godson, I shall put mercy before justice and be lenient with you. Since you boast of being a master thief, I shall put your skill to the test. If you fail, you'll have to marry the ropemaker's daughter, and croaking ravens will make music at your wedding." "Count," said the master thief, "think up three exploits, the harder the better, and if I fail to perform them, do what you like to me." The count reflected a few moments, then he said: "Very well. First, you are to steal my favorite horse from the stable. Second, at night when my wife and I are asleep, you are to steal the sheet out from under us without our noticing, and on the same occasion steal the wedding ring from my wife's finger. Third and last, you are to steal the priest and the sexton out of the church. Make a careful note of it all, for your life depends on it."

The master thief went to the nearest village, bought an old peasant woman's clothes and put them on. He stained his skin and painted wrinkles on his face, and when he was done no one could have recognized him. Finally, he mixed a powerful sleeping potion with some old Hungarian wine, filled a keg with it, and put the keg in a basket which he slung on his back. Then with slow, reeling steps he made his way to the count's castle. Arriving in the courtyard after dark, he sat down on a stone and began to cough like a consumptive old woman and to rub his hands as though suffering from the cold. Some soldiers were lounging around a fire not far from the stable. One of them noticed the old woman and called out: "Hey, old lady, come and warm yourself by our fire. If you haven't got a bed of your own, you may as well take what you can find." The old woman came lurching over, asked the soldiers to take the basket off her back, and joined them by the fire. "What have you got in your keg, old lady?"

one of them asked. "Good wine," she replied. "I'm a peddler. For money and a kind word you can have a glass." "Let's have it," said the soldier, and when he had drained one glass he said: "When the wine is good, I always come again." He let her pour him another glass and the others followed suit. "Hey, comrades," one of them called out to the soldiers inside the stable. "There's an old woman out here with a wine that's as old as she is. Come and have a drink, it will warm you better than our fire." The old woman took her keg into the stable. The favorite horse was saddled. One soldier was sitting in the saddle, another was holding the bridle, and a third was holding the tail. She poured them as much wine as they wanted, until the source ran dry. It wasn't long before the one holding the bridle dropped it, slumped to the ground, and began to snore. The second let go the tail, lay down, and snored even louder. The one sitting in the saddle stayed where he was, but his head drooped till it almost touched the horse's neck, and soon he was fast asleep, blowing out of his mouth like a blacksmith's bellows. The soldiers outside had been asleep for some time and were lying on the ground, as still as stones. When the master thief saw everything had gone smoothly, he put a rope into the hand of the first instead of the bridle and a bundle of straw into the hand of the second who had been holding the tail. But what was he to do with the one who was sitting on the horse's back? He couldn't very well push him off, for he might have woken up and started yelling. He knew what to do, though. He unbuckled the saddle girths, tied the saddle to some ropes that were hanging from rings on the wall, and pulled the sleeping rider up in the air. Then he hitched the ropes to a post. It didn't take him long to undo the horse's chain, but if he had ridden over the stone flags in the yard, the noise would have been heard in the castle. So he wrapped the horse's hoofs in old rags and led him gingerly to the gate. There he mounted and galloped away.

At daybreak the master thief sped to the castle on the stolen horse. The count had just got up and was looking out of the window. "Good morning, count!" the thief shouted. "I've brought your horse back. The one I took from the stable. Look how blissfully your soldiers are sleeping, and if you'd care to go into the stable, you'll see how comfortable your guards have made themselves." The count couldn't help laughing, but then he said: "You've succeeded once, but you won't be so lucky next time. And I warn you, if I catch you thieving, I'll treat you as a thief." When the countess went to bed that night, she made a tight fist with the hand on which she wore her wedding ring, and the count said: "All the doors are locked and barred. I'm going to stay awake and wait for the thief. If he climbs in the window, I'll shoot him down."

In the dark of night the master thief went out to the gallows, cut a hanged man down, and carried him to the castle on his back. There he placed a ladder outside the count's bedchamber, hoisted the dead man onto his shoulders, and climbed up. When he had got so high that the dead man's head appeared in the window, the count, who had been sitting up in bed waiting, fired his pistol. The thief dropped the dead man, jumped off the ladder, and hid in a corner. The moon gave enough light for the thief to see the count climb down the ladder from his window, carry the dead man into the garden, and start digging a hole to bury him in. "Now's my chance," said the thief to himself. Nimbly popping out of his corner, he climbed the ladder to the bedchamber where, imitating the count's voice, he said to the countess: "Dear wife, the thief is dead, but he *was* my godson, and all in all he was more of a rogue than a criminal. I wouldn't want to expose him to public disgrace and besides I feel sorry for his poor parents. I've decided to bury him in the garden before daybreak and hush the matter up. So give me the sheet to wrap the body in and I'll bury him as I'd bury a dog." The countess gave him the sheet. "And another thing," the thief went on. "I'm somehow feeling magnanimous. Give me your ring. The poor fellow lost his life for it; let him take it with him to the grave." She didn't want to part with the ring, but the count's word was law, so she took it off her finger and handed it to him. The thief made off with both items and was safely home before the count had finished with his gravedigging.

What a long face the count made next morning when the master thief brought him the sheet and the ring. "Are you a wizard?" he asked. "Who got you out of the grave where I buried you with my own hands? And who brought you back to life?" "It wasn't me you buried," said the thief. "It was a hanged man I took from the gallows." He went on to tell him exactly what he had done, and the count had to admit that he was an astute and resourceful thief. "But you're not at the end of your pains. You still have the third task ahead of you, and if you fail in that, no power on earth can help you." The thief only smiled.

After nightfall, he went to the village church with a sack on his back, a bundle under his arm, and a lantern in his hand. In the sack he had crabs and in the bundle short wax candles. He sat down in the churchyard, took out a crab and stuck a wax candle on its back. That done, he lit the candle, put the crab on the ground, and let it loose. Then he took a second crab from the sack, stuck a candle on its back, lit it, and so on, until the last crab was gone from the sack. Next he put on a long black garment that looked like a monk's gown, and fastened a gray beard to his chin. When he had made himself quite unrecognizable, he took the sack the crabs had been in, went into the church, and climbed up to the pulpit. The clock in the church tower struck twelve. When the last stroke had died away, he cried out in a loud, piercing voice: "Hearken, ye sinners, the end of all things is at hand, the last judgment is near. Hearken, hearken! If anyone wants to go to heaven with me, let him crawl into this sack. I am St. Peter, who openeth and closeth the gates of heaven. Look out at the churchyard, see how the dead are going about collecting their bones. Come! Come and crawl into my sack, for the end of the world is at hand." His voice could be heard all over the village. The priest and the sexton, who lived nearest the church, were the first to hear it, and when they saw the candles moving around the churchyard, they knew something unusual was afoot and hurried to the church. After listening to the sermon for a while, the sexton nudged the priest and said: "It looks like a nice easy way of getting to heaven before the last day dawns. Maybe we ought to take him up." "Quite so," said the priest, "those were my very thoughts. If you like, we can start right now." "Yes, indeed," said the sexton. "But you go first, father. I'll follow." The priest went up to the pulpit, and the master thief held the sack open for him. First the priest crawled in, then the sexton. The thief tied the sack up tight, took hold of it by the neck and dragged it down the pulpit steps. Every time the heads of the two simpletons bumped against the stairs, he cried out: "Now we're climbing the mountains." He dragged them from end to end of the village. When they went through puddles, he said: "Now we're passing through rain clouds," and as he pulled them up the castle steps, he cried: "Now we're on the stairs of heaven, we'll soon be in the outer court." When he got to the top, he crammed the sack into the dovecote. The pigeons fluttered into the air, and he said: "Hear that? The angels are flapping their wings for joy!" Then he pushed the bolt and left them.

Next morning he went to the count and told him he had abducted the priest and the sexton from the church and the third task was done. "Where have you put them?" the count asked. "They're in a sack in the dovecote and they think they're in heaven." The count went up and convinced himself that the thief was telling the truth. After setting the priest and the sexton free, the count said: "You're the prince of thieves, and you've won your wager. This time you're getting off with a whole skin, but see to it that you leave my territory. If you ever again show your face in these parts, you can count on a prompt elevation on the gallows." The prince of thieves took leave of his parents and went back into the wide world. He hasn't been heard from since.

193

The Drummer

ONE EVENING WHILE TAKING a solitary walk in the country, a young drummer came to a lake and saw three pieces of white linen lying on the shore. "What fine linen!" he said and put one piece in his pocket. After that he went home and to bed without giving another thought to what he had found. Just as he was falling asleep, it seemed to him that someone was calling him by name. He pricked up his ears and heard a soft voice saying: "Drummer, drummer, wake up." He couldn't see anyone, for it was black night, but he had a feeling that a figure was gliding this way and that beside his bed. "What do you want?" he asked, and the voice replied: "My shift, that you took last night by the lake." "I'll give it back to you," said the drummer, "if you tell me who you are." "Ah," the voice replied, "I'm the daughter of a great king, but a witch has got me in her power and forces me to live on the glass mountain. Every day I have to bathe in the lake with my two sisters, but I can't fly away without my shift. My sisters have gone, but I had to stay behind. I beg you, give me back my shift." "Poor child, calm yourself," said the drummer. "Of course I'll give it back." He took it out of his pocket and handed it to her in the darkness. She quickly took it and was going to leave. "Wait just a moment," he said. "Maybe I can help you." "The only way you could help me would be to climb the glass mountain and set me free from the witch. But you'll never get to the glass mountain, and even if you did you'd never reach the top." "I can do anything I set out to," said the drummer. "I feel sorry for you, and I'm afraid of nothing. But I don't know the way to the glass mountain." "The way is through the great forest where the man-eating giants live," she replied. "That's as much as I'm allowed to tell you." Then he heard her whirring away.

At daybreak the drummer buckled on his drum, and started fearlessly into the forest. When he had gone quite a way without seeing any giants, he said to himself: "I'll have to wake those lazybones up." He swung his drum in front of him and beat such a tattoo that the birds flew up from the trees with loud cries. It wasn't long before a giant who had been lying in the grass asleep stood up. He was as tall as a fir tree. "You little runt!" he cried. "Why are you drumming like that? You've waked me out of my sweetest sleep." "I'm drumming," he said, "so the thousands marching behind me will know the way." "What business have they got in my forest?" the giant asked. "They're coming to wipe you out. What need has the forest of a monster like you?" "Ha ha!" cried the giant. "I'll trample them like ants." "Do you really think so?" said the drummer. "If you bend down to grab one, he'll slip away and hide. And so will the next and the next, and so on. Then, when you lie down to sleep, they'll all come crawling out of the bushes and swarm over you. Every last one of them has a steel hammer in his belt. They'll bash your skull in with those hammers." The giant was troubled. "Maybe I'd better not quarrel with these crafty humans," he thought. "I can strangle wolves and bears, but what defense have I got against such earthworms? All right, little fellow," he said. "Run along. I promise to leave you and your people in peace from now on. And if there's anything else you want, just tell me, I'll gladly do you a favor." "You've got long legs," said the drummer, "and you can walk faster than I can. If you'll carry me to the glass mountain, I'll signal my men to turn back, and they'll leave you in peace for the present." "Worm, come here," said the giant. "Sit on my shoulder and I'll carry you wherever you say." The giant picked him up and, once seated on the heights, the drummer drummed to his heart's content. "That," thought the giant, "must be a signal for the army to turn back."

After a while they came to a second giant, who took the drummer from the first and stuck him in his buttonhole. Steadying himself by holding on to the button, which was as big as a dinnerplate, the drummer looked happily around. Soon they came to a third giant, who took him out of the buttonhole and put him on the brim of his own hat. Here the drummer was able to stroll about and look over the trees. When he caught sight of a mountain in the blue distance, he thought: "That must be the glass mountain." And so it was. The giant took another few steps and set him down at the foot of the mountain. The drummer asked the giant to carry him up to the top, but the giant shook his head, mumbled something in his beard, and went back to the forest.

The poor drummer stood looking at the mountain, which was as high as if three mountains had been piled on top of one another, and to make matters worse, as smooth as a mirror. He couldn't see how he'd ever get to the top. He tried to climb but it was useless, he kept sliding down. "If only I were a bird!" he said to himself, but wishing was no help, he didn't sprout wings. As he stood there wondering what to do, he saw two men engaged in a violent quarrel not far away. Going closer, he saw they were quarreling over a saddle that was lying on the ground between them. "What fools you are!" he said. "What sense is there in fighting over a saddle when you've got no horse to go with it?" "This saddle is worth fighting over," said one of the men. "Anyone who sits on it and wishes himself somewhere, even at the end of the world, will be there before the words are out of his mouth. The saddle belongs to us both. It's my turn to ride on it now, but he won't let me have it." "I'll settle your argument in a minute," said the drummer. He went off a little way, planted a white stick in the ground, came back to them and said: "That stick is your goal. Start running. The first to reach it gets the saddle." Both started running, but no sooner had they taken a few steps than the drummer jumped on the saddle and wished himself to the top of the glass mountain. He was there in a twinkling.

On the top of the mountain there was a plain; on the plain there was an old stone house; in front of the house there was a big fishpond, and behind it a dark forest. Clouds drifted by not far above his head. He saw neither people nor animals, and there was no sound but the wind murmuring in the trees. He went to the door and knocked. After the third knock, an old woman with a brown face and red eyes opened. She gave him a piercing look through the spectacles perched on her long nose, and asked him what he wanted. The drummer replied: "Shelter, food, and a bed for the night." "You shall have them," said the old woman, "but in return you must perform three tasks." "Why not?" he said. "I'm not afraid of work." The old woman let him in, fed him, and when night came gave him a good bed. In the morning when he'd had his sleep out, she took a thimble from her withered finger, and handed it to him. "Now you must go to work. Take this thimble and empty the pond with it. I want it done before nightfall. In addition, you must gather up all the fishes that are in the pond and lay them out in rows according to kind and size." "That's a strange task," said the drummer, but he went to the pond and began to scoop. He scooped all morning, but even if you scoop a thousand years how can you expect to empty a big pond with a thimble? At noon he stopped and sat down, for he thought: "I'm not getting anywhere. It makes no difference whether I work or not."

Just then a girl came out of the house, set a basket of food before him, and said: "Why are you sitting there so sad? What's the matter?" He looked at her and saw she was very beautiful. "Ah," he sighed. "I can't even finish the first task, how will it be with the others? I've come to look for a princess who's supposed to be living here, but I haven't found her, so I'd better be on my way." "Please stay," said the girl. "I'll help you. You're tired. Lay your head in my lap and sleep. When you wake up, the task will be done." The drummer didn't have to be asked twice. The moment his eyes closed, the girl turned a wishing ring and said: "Water, up! Fishes, out!" Directly, the water rose like a white mist and drifted away with the clouds, and the fishes sputtered, jumped up on the bank, and lay down side by side, each according to its size and kind. When the drummer woke up, he saw to his amazement that the task was done. The girl said to him: "One of the fishes isn't lying with its kind. It's all by itself. This evening, when the old woman comes out and sees the task is done, she will ask: 'What's that fish doing all by itself?' Throw the fish in her face and say: 'It's for you, you old witch!'" In the evening the witch came out, and when she had asked her question he threw the fish in her face. She pretended to take no notice and said nothing, but there was a wicked look in her eyes.

The next morning she said: "You had it too easy yesterday. I'll have to give you something harder to do. Today I want you to cut down the whole forest, chop the wood into logs, and pile them cord by cord. And I want it all done by nightfall." She gave him an ax, a mallet, and two wedges. But the ax was made of lead and the mallet and wedges of tin. When he began to cut, the ax blade bent double and the mallet and wedges collapsed. He didn't know what to do, but at noon the girl came again with food and comforted him: "Lay your head in my lap and sleep," she said. "When you wake up, the task will be done." She turned her wishing ring, and in that moment the whole forest fell with a crash and the wood split itself and piled itself up cord by cord, as though invisible giants had been at work. When he woke up, the girl said: "You see, the wood is cut and piled. Only a single branch has stayed by itself. This evening, when the old woman comes out and asks what that branch is for, hit her with it and say: 'It's for you, you witch.'" The old woman came out and said: "You see how easy it was. But that branch over there. What's that for?" "For you, you witch," he said and hit her with it. But she pretended not to notice, laughed scornfully, and said: "Tomorrow morning you're to put all that wood in one pile, set fire to it and burn it."

He arose at daybreak and began to haul wood, but how can one man pile up a whole forest? The work didn't get ahead. But the girl didn't forsake him in his need. At noon she brought him food, and when he had eaten he rested his head in her lap and fell asleep. When he woke up, the whole woodpile was burning in one enormous blaze, and tongues of flame were shooting up to the sky. "Now listen to me," said the girl. "When the witch comes out, she'll tell you to do certain things. If you do what she says without fear, she won't be able to hurt you; but if you're afraid, the fire will take hold of you and burn you up. When you've finally done everything, seize her in both hands and fling her into the midst of the fire." The girl went away and the old woman came creeping out to him. "Oh, I'm so cold," she said. "But that's a good fire. It warms my old bones. How good it feels! But see the log over there that's not burning. Get it out for me. Once you've done that, you'll be free to go wherever you please. In you go!"

The drummer didn't stop to think. He jumped right into the middle of the flames, but they didn't harm him, they didn't so much as singe his hair. He took out the log and put it down. No sooner had the wood touched the ground than it was transformed: there stood the beautiful girl who had helped him in his need, and he knew she was the princess by her garments of silk and gold. The old witch laughed venomously and said: "You think you've got her. Oh no, you haven't got her yet!" She tried to grab hold of the princess and drag her away, but the drummer seized her with both hands, lifted her up and flung her into the flames, which closed over her as though they took pleasure in burning a witch.

The princess looked at the drummer, and when she saw he was handsome and considered that he had risked his life to save her, she gave him her hand. "You've risked all you had for me," she said, "and I shall do all I can for you. If you promise to be true to me, you shall be my husband. We won't be poor; the riches the witch has piled up will be quite enough for us." She led him into the house, and in it there were chests and boxes filled with the witch's treasure. They left the gold and silver and took only the jewels. The princess didn't want to stay on the glass mountain a moment longer, and he said to her: "Climb on my saddle with me, and we'll fly down like birds." "I don't like your old saddle," she said. "I have only to turn my wishing ring and we'll be home." "Good," said the drummer. "Wish us outside the town gate." They were there in a twinkling, and the drummer said: "Wait for me here while I go and tell my parents I'm safe. I won't be long." "Oh," said the princess, "I implore you. When you get home, be careful not to kiss your parents on their right cheeks, because if you do you'll forget everything, and I'll be left here alone and forsaken." "How could I possibly forget you?" said the drummer. Then he promised to be back very soon and gave her his hand on it.

When he arrived at his father's house, he was so changed that no one knew him, for the three days he had spent on the glass mountain had been three long years. When he told them who he was, his parents fell on his neck for joy, and his heart was so moved that he forgot what the princess had said and kissed them on both cheeks. The moment he kissed their right cheeks, every thought of the princess vanished from his mind. He emptied his pockets and poured whole handfuls of enormous jewels on the table. At first his parents couldn't imagine what they would do with such a fortune, but finally the father built a magnificent castle, surrounded by gardens, woods, and meadows, as though a prince were going to live there. When it was finished, the mother said: "I've found a girl for you. The wedding is to be in three days." And the drummer was content to do as his parents wished.

The poor princess had waited a long time outside the town for the drummer to return. When evening came, she said to herself: "He must have kissed his parents on their right cheeks and forgotten me." Her heart was bowed with grief and she wished herself into a lonely hut in the forest, for she didn't want to go back to her father's court. Every evening she went into the town and passed the drummer's house. He saw her now and then, but he no longer knew her. One day she heard the people saying: "He's going to be married tomorrow," and she said to herself: "I'll try and win back his heart." On the first day of the marriage feast she turned her wishing ring and said: "A dress as resplendent as the sun." Instantly, the dress lay before her, as resplendent as if it had been woven all of sunbeams. When all the guests had gathered, she stepped into the hall. Everyone marveled at the beautiful dress, most of all the bride, and since fine clothes were what she loved most in all the world, she went up to the strange girl and asked if she'd sell it to her. "Not for money," she replied. "But I'll give it to you if you let me spend the first night out-

side the door of the room where the bridegroom sleeps." The bride
wanted the dress so much that she couldn't resist. She consented, but
mixed a sleeping potion with the bridegroom's bedtime wine, so that
he fell into a deep sleep. When all was still, the princess crouched
down by the door of the bedchamber, opened it a little, and cried:

> "Drummer, drummer, won't you hear!
> Have you utterly forgotten
> How I helped you on the great glass mountain?
> How from the witch I saved your life?
> How you vowed I'd be your wife?
> Drummer, drummer, won't you hear!"

All in vain. The drummer didn't wake up, the princess accomplished
nothing, and at daybreak she had to leave. The second evening she
turned her wishing ring and said: "A dress as silvery as the moon."
When she appeared at the marriage feast in a dress as delicate as
moonlight, the bride's desire was again aroused, and the princess gave
her the dress in return for leave to spend a second night outside the
door of the bedchamber. And in the still of night she cried:

> "Drummer, drummer, won't you hear!
> Have you utterly forgotten
> How I helped you on the great glass mountain?
> How from the witch I saved your life?
> How you vowed I'd be your wife?
> Drummer, drummer, won't you hear!"

But the drummer was benumbed by the sleeping potion and she
couldn't wake him. In the morning she went sadly back to the house
in the forest. But the servants had heard the strange girl's plaint and
told the bridegroom about it. They also told him they had mixed a
sleeping potion with his wine and that that was why he hadn't heard
her.

On the third evening the princess turned her wishing ring and said:
"A dress that glitters like the stars." When she wore it to the marriage feast, the bride was beside herself with longing for it and she
said: "I must and will have that dress." The girl gave it to her, as she
had given her the others, in return for leave to spend the night outside the bridegroom's door. This time the bridegroom didn't drink his
wine, but poured it away behind his bed. And when the house had
fallen still, he heard a soft voice calling him:

"Drummer, drummer, won't you hear!
Have you utterly forgotten
How I helped you on the great glass mountain?
How from the witch I saved your life?
How you vowed I'd be your wife?
Drummer, drummer, won't you hear?"

Suddenly his memory came back. "Oh!" he cried. "How could I have been so faithless? In the joy of my heart I kissed my parents on their right cheeks. Those kisses were to blame, they dulled my senses." He jumped up, took the princess by the hand, and led her to his parents' bedside. "This is my right bride," he said. "I should be doing a great wrong if I married the other." When his parents heard how it all had happened, they consented. The candles in the hall were lit again, drums and trumpets were brought in, the friends and relatives were asked to come back, and the true wedding was celebrated with great joy. To make it up to the first bride, they let her keep the beautiful dresses, and she was satisfied.

194
The Ear of Wheat

LONG, LONG AGO, when God still walked the earth, the soil was much more fruitful than it is today. An ear of wheat contained not fifty or sixty kernels, but four or five hundred. The whole stalk from top to bottom was covered with grains, and an ear was as long as the stalk. But people will never change; in times of plenty they become heedless and indifferent and stop thinking about God's gifts. One day, as a woman was walking past a wheat field, her little daughter, who was running along beside her, fell into a puddle and soiled her dress. The mother tore off a handful of the lovely ripe ears and wiped the dress with them. When the Lord, who happened to be passing by, saw that, he was very angry. "From now on," he said, "wheat stalks will bear no more ears. The human race is no longer worthy of such divine gifts." The bystanders who heard Him were horrified. They went down on their knees and implored Him to leave some wheat on the stalk—if they themselves didn't deserve it, then for the sake of the innocent chickens, who would otherwise starve. The Lord, who foresaw the sufferings of mankind, took pity on them, granted their plea, and left the ear growing at the top of the stalk, as it does now.

195

The Grave Mound

ONE DAY A RICH FARMER was standing in his yard, looking out over his fields and gardens. His grain was growing plentifully, his fruit trees were heavy with fruit. There was so much of last year's grain piled up in the granary that the rafters groaned under the weight. He went to the barn for a look at his fatted oxen, sleek cows, and shiny-smooth horses. And finally, coming back into the house, he glanced at the iron coffers where he kept his money. As he stood surveying his wealth, he suddenly heard a violent knocking. It wasn't at the door of his house, but at the door of his heart. The door opened and he heard a voice saying: "Have you used it for the good of your family? Have you given a thought to the distress of the poor? Have you shared your bread with the hungry? Have you been content with what you had or have you coveted more and more?" His heart replied at once: "I have been hard and unfeeling. I have never shown my family the least kindness. When a poor man appealed to me, I turned away. I never troubled my head about God and thought only of piling up more wealth. Even if everything under the sun had belonged to me, I wouldn't have been satisfied."

When he heard this answer, he was seized with terror. His knees trembled and he had to sit down. Then there was another knock, but this time at the door of the house. It was his neighbor, a poor peasant with a whole tribe of children whose hunger he was unable to satisfy. The poor man thought: "I know my neighbor is as hardhearted as he is rich. I don't think he'll help me but there's no harm in asking, and my children are crying for bread." To the rich man he said: "You don't often give anything away that's yours, but the man you see before you is desperate. My children are starving. Lend me four bushels of grain." The rich man gave him a long look, and a first sunbeam of kindness began to melt the ice of his greed. "I won't lend you four bushels," he said. "I'll give you eight, but on one condition." "What must I do?" the poor man asked. "When I die, you must watch over my grave for three nights." The poor man shuddered to think of it, but his need was so great he'd have agreed to anything. He said he would do it and carried the grain home.

It was as though the rich man had had a presentiment. Three days later he suddenly fell dead. People wondered how he could have gone so quickly, but no one mourned for him. After the funeral, the poor man remembered his promise. He would gladly have been released from it, but he thought: "He showed me a kindness, I can't deny it. I fed my hungry children with his grain, and, besides, I gave him my promise and promises must be kept." As night was falling, he went to the churchyard and sat down on the grave mound. The moon shone on the tombstones, now and then an owl flitted past and broke the silence with its mournful cry. When the sun rose, the poor man went safely home, and again on the second night nothing happened. On the evening of the third day he felt a strange foreboding. Near the churchyard wall, he saw a man he didn't know. The man was no longer young, his face was seamed with scars, and his eyes darted eagerly this way and that. He was wrapped in an old cloak, and only his big riding boots could be seen. "What are you looking for?" the poor peasant asked. "Doesn't this lonely churchyard give you the shivers?" "I'm not looking for anything," the man replied, "and I'm not afraid of anything. I'm like the young fellow who left home to learn how to get the shivers. He never did learn, but he married the king's daughter and she brought him great riches. The only difference is that I'm still poor. I'm only a discharged soldier, and I've come here to spend the night, because I have nowhere else to go." "Since you're not afraid," said the peasant, "stay with me and help me watch this grave." "Guard duty is a soldier's stock in trade," he replied. "Whatever comes of it, the good and the bad, we'll share it." The peasant agreed and the two of them sat down on the grave.

All was still until midnight. Then suddenly a shrill whistling was heard, and the Evil One in person was standing before them. "What are you doing here, you no-goods?" he cried. "The man in this grave is mine, and I've come to get him. Go away, or I'll wring your necks for you." "Lord of the Red Feather," said the soldier, "you're not my captain. I don't have to obey you and I've never learned fear. Go away. We're staying right here." The Devil thought to himself: "The best way to get around these scoundrels is with gold." So he changed his tune and asked them politely if they'd consent to go home if he gave them a bag of gold. "Now you're talking," said the soldier. "But one bag of gold isn't enough. Give us as much as one of my boots will hold and the field is yours." "I haven't got that much on me," said the Devil, "but I'll go and get it. I have a moneychanger friend in the next town. He'll advance me the money." When the Devil had gone, the soldier pulled off his left boot and said: "We'll play a little trick on the old charcoal burner. Let's have your knife, comrade." He cut the sole off his boot and put the boot down in the tall grass at the edge of an overgrown pit not far from the grave. "This'll do it," he said. "Now we're ready for the chimney sweep."

They sat and waited, and it wasn't long before the Devil came back with a small sack of gold. "Just pour it in," said the soldier, lifting the boot a little. "But it won't be enough." The Devil emptied the sack, the gold passed through, and the boot remained empty. "Stupid Devil!" cried the soldier. "Didn't I tell you? It won't do. Go back and get more." The Devil shook his head, left them, and came back an hour later with a much bigger sack under his arm. "Fill her up!" cried the soldier. "But I doubt if you'll succeed." The gold jingled as it fell, but the boot was still empty. The Devil looked in with his flaming eyes and seeing was believing. "You've got legs like an elephant," said the Devil with a sneer. "Did you think I had a cloven hoof like you?" said the soldier. "Since when have you been so stingy? You'll have to bring more gold or the deal is off." Again the Evil One left them. This time he stayed away longer, and when he finally came back he was carrying an enormous sack over his shoulder and panting under its weight. He emptied it into the boot, and once again it didn't fill up. He flew into a rage and was just going to snatch the boot out of the soldier's hand when the first ray of the rising sun appeared. The Evil One fled with a loud cry and the rich man's soul was saved.

The peasant wanted to divide the gold, but the soldier said: "Give my part to the poor. I will move into your hut with you, and we'll live in peace on what's left as long as it pleases God."

196

Old Rinkrank

ONCE THERE WAS a king with an only daughter, and he had a glass mountain built and said that whoever could cross it without falling should have the daughter for his wife. There was a young man who loved the princess and he asked the king if he could have her. "Why not?" said the king. "If you can cross the mountain without falling, you shall have her." The king's daughter said she'd go with him and help him if he was going to fall. They started out together, and when they were halfway up, the king's daughter slipped and fell, and the glass mountain opened and shut her up inside. Her sweetheart couldn't see where she'd gone, because the mountain had closed up right away. He wept and wailed, and the king grieved too and had the mountain broken open. He thought he'd get her out again, but they couldn't find the place where she'd fallen in.

In the meantime, the king's daughter had ended up in a big deep cave. An old fellow with a long gray beard came up to her and said that if she'd be his maid and do everything he told her, he'd let her live and if she didn't he'd kill her. So she did everything he told her. Every morning he'd take his ladder out of his pocket and put it up against the mountain, climb to the top, and pull the ladder up after him. She had to cook his food and make his bed and do all his work, and every time he came home he brought a pile of gold and silver. When she'd been with him for a good many years and had grown very old, he took to calling her Mother Mansrot and she had to call him Old Rinkrank. One time when he was out, she made his bed and washed his dishes, and then she shut the doors and windows tight. But

there was one little window that let the light in and she left that one
open. When Old Rinkrank came back, he knocked at the door and
shouted: "Mother Mansrot, open the door!" "No!" she said. "I won't
open the door for you, Old Rinkrank." At that he said:

> "Here I stand, poor Rinkrank,
>   On my twelve legs long and lank,
>   And my one decrepit foot.
>   Wash my dishes, Mother Mansrot."

"I've already washed your dishes!" she cried. And he said:

> "Here I stand, poor Rinkrank,
>   On my twelve legs long and lank,
>   And my one decrepit foot.
>   Make my bed now, Mother Mansrot."

"I've already made your bed!" she cried. And he said:

> "Here I stand, poor Rinkrank,
>   On my twelve legs long and lank,
>   And my one decrepit foot.
>   Open the door now, Mother Mansrot."

He ran all around the house and when he saw the little window was
open, he thought: "I'll just look in and see what's she's doing and
why she won't open the door for me." So he tried to look in, but he
couldn't get his head through because of his long beard. So he put his
beard in first, but the second he had it in Mother Mansrot shut the
window with a cord she had tied to it, and his beard was stuck fast.
He began to screech and whimper, because it hurt something awful,
and beg her to let him go. "Oh no," she said. "I won't let you go until
you give me the ladder you climb out of the mountain with." And
like it or not, he had to tell her where the ladder was. She tied a long
rope to the window, set up the ladder, and climbed out of the mountain. Once she was out, she pulled the window open. Then she went
home to her father and told him everything that had happened to
her. The king was very happy and her sweetheart was still there.
They went and dug up the mountain and found Old Rinkrank inside
with all his gold and silver. The king had him put to death and took
all his gold and silver. And the princess married her sweetheart and
they lived happily, in great splendor.

197

The Crystal Ball

THERE WAS ONCE a sorceress who had three sons and they loved each other dearly. The old woman didn't trust them and thought they wanted to steal her magic. She turned the eldest into an eagle, who had to live amid rocky crags and now and then he could be seen gliding through the sky in great rising and falling circles. She turned the second into a whale, who lived deep under the ocean, and all that was ever seen of him was the great spout of water that he shot into the air from time to time. As for the third son, he slipped away in secret, for fear she'd turn him into a bear or wolf or some other ferocious animal.

He had heard that an enchanted princess was waiting for deliverance in the Castle of the Golden Sun. It was a perilous adventure, for twenty-three youths had met a cruel death, and only one more was allowed to try. But his heart was fearless and he decided to go looking for this Castle of the Golden Sun. For a long time he journeyed this way and that without finding it. Then one day he wandered into a great forest and didn't know the way out. Suddenly he saw two giants in the distance. They hailed him, and when he got to them they said: "We've been fighting over a cap, but we're equally strong and neither of us can down the other. You little folk are more intelligent, so we'll let you decide." "How can you fight over an old cap?" the youth asked. "Aha!" they said. "You don't know what kind of a cap it is. It's a wishing cap. Anybody who puts it on can wish himself wherever he pleases, and before you know it there he is!" "Give me the cap," said the youth. "I'll go off a little way. When I call you, start running, and the one who reaches me first gets the cap." He put the cap on and went off, but he was thinking about the princess so hard that he forgot the giants and just kept on walking. All at once he heaved a deep sigh and said: "Oh, if only I were at the Castle of the Golden Sun!" The words were no sooner out of his mouth than he was standing on a high mountain outside the castle gate.

He went in and walked through all the rooms. In the last he found the princess, but what was his horror when he looked at her! She had an ashen face seamed with wrinkles, bleary eyes, and red hair. "Are you the princess famed far and wide for her beauty?" he cried. "Ah," she said, "this ugliness is not my true nature, but it's the only form in which human eyes can see me. If you want to see me as I really am, look into this mirror, which cannot be deceived. It will show you the truth." She handed him the mirror and when he looked in it he saw the most beautiful maiden in the world and saw that the tears were rolling down her cheeks. "But how can you be set free?" he asked. "No danger can frighten me." She replied: "If anyone gains possession of the crystal ball and holds it up in front of the sorcerer, his magic will be broken and I shall recover my true form. But oh!" she added, "so many have gone to their death for it, and you are so young. It grieves me to see you face such perils." "Nothing can stop me," he said. "Just tell me what I must do." "I'll tell you all you need to know," said the princess. "First you must go down this mountain. At the bottom you will see a wild bull standing beside a spring. You must fight the bull. If you manage to kill it, a firebird will fly out of its body. Inside the bird there is a red-hot egg, and the yolk of that egg is the crystal ball. But the bird won't drop the egg until it has to, and then if the eggs fall to the ground it will burst into flames that will consume everything near it, the egg itself will melt and the crystal ball with it, and all your trouble will have been for nothing."

The youth went down the mountain to the spring, where the wild bull fumed and bellowed at him. After a long fight he thrust his sword into the bull's body, and it fell to the ground. Instantly the firebird rose up and tried to fly away, but the eagle, the youth's brother, who had been soaring among the clouds, swooped down, chased it to the sea, and harried it with its beak until it dropped the egg. But the egg didn't fall into the sea. It fell on top of a fisherman's hut, and the hut began to smoke and was about to burst into flames. But just then a wave as big as a mountain poured over the hut and put the fire out. The second brother, the whale, had come swimming to the spot and stirred up the water. Once the fire was out, the youth looked for the egg and fortunately found it. It hadn't melted, but the sudden cooling in the cold water had cracked the shell, and he was able to take out the crystal ball unharmed.

The youth went to the sorcerer and held up the crystal ball in front of him. The sorcerer said: "My power is destroyed. From now on you will be king of the Castle of the Golden Sun. And there is something else you can do with the crystal ball: you can give your brothers back their human form." The youth hurried to the princess, and when he entered the room she was standing there in all the radiance of her beauty. They exchanged rings and they were very happy.

198
Maid Maleen

THERE WAS ONCE a prince who courted a great king's daughter; her name was Maid Maleen and she was very beautiful. Her father wanted her to marry someone else and the prince was rejected. But they loved each other dearly and were unwilling to give each other up. Maid Maleen said to her father: "I cannot and will not take any other for my husband." The king was so angry that he ordered his builders to put up a dark tower, into which not a single ray of sunlight or moonlight would ever shine. When it was finished, he said: "You shall be shut up for seven years. Then I'll come and see if you're still so obstinate." Food and drink for seven years were brought to the tower. Then she and her waiting maid were led in and the door was walled up, sealing them off from heaven and earth. There they sat in the darkness, not knowing when the day broke or the night fell. Many times the prince walked round the tower, calling her name, but no sound reached her through the thick walls. What could they do but grieve and lament?

Nevertheless, the time passed, and they could tell by the dwindling food and drink that the seven years were drawing to a close. They expected to be set free, but no hammer stroke was heard and no stone fell from the wall. The princess's father seemed to have forgotten them. When there was only enough food for a few days left and they thought they might die wretchedly of starvation, Maid Maleen said: "Let's see if we can pierce the wall. It's our last chance." She took the bread knife and dug and scraped at the mortar, and when she was tired, her waiting maid relieved her. After long labor, they managed to loosen a stone and then a second and a third. After three days the first ray of light shone into their darkness, and finally the opening was big enough for them to look through. The sky was blue, a cool breeze was blowing, but what a dismal scene! Her father's castle lay in ruins, the town and countryside as far as the eye could see had been burned and the fields for miles around laid waste. There wasn't a living soul to be seen. When the opening in the wall was big enough for them to slip through, the waiting maid jumped down and Maid Maleen followed. But where were they to turn? The enemy had devastated the whole kingdom, driven out the king, and killed all the inhabitants. They set out in search of another country, but they found no one to offer them shelter or give them a crust of bread, and they were so hungry they had to eat nettles. After long wanderings they came to another country, where they went from door to door offering their services, but no one took pity on them and they were always turned away. Finally they came to a city and went to the royal palace. There again no one wanted them, but in the end the cook said they could stay in the kitchen and work as scullery maids.

Now it so happened that the son of the king to whose kingdom they had come was Maid Maleen's old sweetheart. His father had found him another bride, whose face was as ugly as her heart was wicked. The date of the wedding had been set and the bride had arrived, but because of her awful ugliness she shut herself up in her room where no one could see her, and Maid Maleen had to bring her her meals from the kitchen. When the day came for the bride to go to the church with the groom, she was so ashamed of her ugliness and so afraid of being laughed at if she were seen in the street that she said to Maid Maleen: "You're a very lucky girl. I've sprained my ankle and I can't walk very well. I want you to put on my bridal dress and take my place. No greater honor could possibly come your way." But Maid Maleen refused, saying: "I want no honor I'm not entitled to." The bride offered her gold, but in vain. Finally she grew angry and said: "If you don't obey me, it will cost you your life. I have only to say the word and the executioner will lay your head at your feet." She had no choice but to obey and put on the bride's magnificent dress and her jewels. When she entered the great hall, everyone marveled at her beauty, and the king said to his son: "This is the bride I chose for you." The bridegroom was amazed. "She looks like my Maid Maleen," he thought. "I'd think it was Maid Maleen herself, but if she's not shut up in the tower, she must be dead." He took her by the hand and led her to the church. On the way they passed a nettle bush and she said:

> "Oh nettle bush,
> Oh nettle bush, my own.
> Why are you all alone?
> I ate you unroasted,
> I ate you unboiled.
> Why are you all alone?"

"What did you say?" asked the prince. "Nothing," she said. "I was only thinking of Maid Maleen." He was surprised to hear she knew of her, but said nothing. When they came to the footbridge leading to the churchyard, she said:

> "Footbridge, don't break.
> I'm not the right bride."

"What did you say?" the prince asked. "Nothing," she said. "I was only thinking of Maid Maleen." "Do you know Maid Maleen?" "No," she said. "How could I know her? I've only heard of her." When they got to the church door, she said:

> "Church door, don't break.
> I'm not the right bride."

"What did you say?" he asked. "Oh," she replied, "I was only thinking of Maid Maleen." He brought out a precious necklace, put it round her neck, and fastened the clasp. Then they went into the church and stepped up to the altar, where the priest joined their hands and married them. After the ceremony the prince led her back to the palace, but she didn't say one word on the way. When they got there, she hurried to the bride's room, took off the magnificent dress and the jewels, and put on her gray kitchen dress, but she didn't take off the necklace the bridegroom had given her.

When night came and the bride was to be taken to the bride-groom's room, she veiled her face to keep him from discovering her deception. When all the courtiers had left them, he said to her: "What was it you said to the nettle bush along the way?" "What nettle bush?" she asked. "I don't talk to nettle bushes." "If you didn't," he said, "then you're not the right bride." Then she had an idea and said:

> "I'll have to go and ask my maid
> Who keeps my thoughts stored in her head."

She went and snapped at Maid Maleen: "What did you say to the nettle bush, you slut?" "I only said:

> "Nettle bush,
> Oh nettle bush, my own.
> Why are you all alone?
> I ate you unroasted,
> I ate you unboiled.
> Why are you all alone?"

The bride ran back to the bedchamber and said: "Now I know what I said to the nettle bush." And she repeated the words she had just heard. "But what," the prince asked, "did you say to the footbridge when we were crossing it?" "The footbridge?" she replied. "I don't talk to footbridges." "Then you're not the right bride." And again she said:

> "I'll have to go and ask my maid
> Who keeps my thoughts stored in her head."

She ran and snapped at Maid Maleen: "What did you say to the footbridge, you slut?" "I only said:

> "Footbridge, don't break,
> I'm not the right bride."

"That will cost you your life!" the bride screamed, but she hurried back to the bedchamber and said: "Now I know what I said to the footbridge," and she repeated the words. "But what did you say to the church door?" "To the church door?" she replied. "I don't talk to church doors." "Then you're not the right bride." She went out and snapped at Maid Maleen: "What did you say to the church door, you slut?" "I only said:

> "Church door, don't break,
> I'm not the right bride."

"That will break your neck!" the bride screamed. She was very angry, but she hurried back to the bedchamber and said: "Now I know what I said to the church door," and she repeated the words. "But what have you done with the necklace I gave you at the church door?" "What necklace?" she said. "You didn't give me any necklace." "I put it round your neck myself and fastened the clasp with my own hands. If you don't know that, you're not the right bride." He pulled the veil off her face, and when he saw her abysmal ugliness, he recoiled in horror and said: "How did you get here? Who are you?" "I'm your betrothed, but I was afraid people would scoff at me if they saw me outside, so I ordered the scullery maid to put on my dress and go to the church with you in my place." "Where is the girl?" he asked. "I want to see her. Go and bring her here." She went out and said to the servants: "That scullery maid is a cheat. Take her down to the courtyard and cut off her head." The servants seized her and were going to drag her away, but she screamed so loud for help that the prince heard her, came running from his room, and ordered the servants to release the girl at once. Lamps were brought, and on her neck he saw the gold necklace he had given her outside the church door. "You're the right bride who went to the church with me," he said. "Come with me to my bedchamber." When they were alone, he said: "On the way to church you spoke of Maid Maleen, who was once my betrothed. If it seemed possible, I'd think she was standing before me. You're like her in every way." She answered: "I am Maid Maleen. For you I was shut up in the darkness for seven years, for you I suffered hunger and thirst and lived in dire poverty. But now the sun is shining on me again. I was wedded to you in church and I'm your lawful wife." They kissed and after that they were happy as long as they lived. The false bride was punished by having her head cut off.

The tower where Maid Maleen had been imprisoned remained standing for many years. When the children passed it, they sang:

> "Ding dong gloria,
> Who's behind that dooria?
> A beautiful princess is sitting there,
> No one can get a glimpse of her.
> The tower's made of solid rock
> Without the smallest chink or crack.
> Oh Johnny with the pretty coat,
> Follow, come follow me home."

199

The Buffalo-hide Boots

NOTHING CAN WORRY a fearless soldier. One such soldier had been given his walking papers and, seeing as he'd never learned a trade and had no way of earning a living, he was going from place to place asking for handouts. An old woolen cloak hung from his shoulders, and he still had a pair of buffalo-hide boots. One day on his wanderings he strayed into a forest and didn't know where he was. After a while he saw a man in a trim green hunting coat sitting on a felled tree trunk. The soldier shook hands with the hunter, sat down in the grass beside him and stretched out his legs. "Fine boots you've got there," said the soldier. "And nicely polished too. But they wouldn't last long if you had to slog around like me. Look at mine. They're made of buffalo hide. I've worn them a long time, but they still carry me through thick and thin." After a while the soldier stood up and said: "I'll have to be going now. Hunger makes me restless. But tell me, brother Glossyboots, where does this path lead?" "I couldn't tell you," said the hunter. "I'm lost." "So am I," said the soldier. "That makes us birds of a feather. Suppose we join forces and find our way out of this forest together." The hunter smiled just a little and they went on together until nightfall. "We're still in the woods," said the soldier, "but I see a light twinkling out there in the distance. Where there's light there's food." They soon came to a stone house and knocked at the door. An old woman opened. "We're looking for a night's lodging," said the soldier, "and something to line our stomachs. Mine is as empty as an old knapsack." "You can't stay here," she said. "Robbers live here, and if you know what's good for you, you'll make yourself scarce before they get home, because if they find you here, you're done for." "It can't be as bad as all that," said the soldier. "I haven't had anything to eat in two days and it's all the same to me whether I'm killed here or die of hunger in the forest. I'm coming in." The hunter didn't want to follow, but the soldier pulled him by the sleeve. "Come on, brother," he said. "They won't be in such a hurry to kill us." The old woman felt sorry for them. "Crawl behind the stove," she said. "If there's anything left over from supper, I'll slip it to you when they go to sleep."

The two of them had scarcely crawled into the corner when twelve robbers came charging in, sat down at the table, which had already been set, and clamored for food. The old woman brought in a big roast and the robbers fell to. When the smell of the food tickled the soldier's nostrils, he said to the hunter: "I can't stand it any longer. I'm going to sit down and eat with them." "You'll get us both killed," said the hunter and held him back by the arm. But then the soldier began to cough loudly. When the robbers heard him, they dropped their knives and forks, jumped up, and discovered the two behind the stove. "Aha!" they cried. "Look who's hiding in the corner! What are you doing here? Spying on us? Just wait. We'll teach you how to dance in mid-air." "Mind your manners," said the soldier. "I'm hungry. Give me something to eat. After that you can do what you please to me." The robbers were flabbergasted, and the captain said: "You don't scare easy, do you? All right. You'll get something to eat. But when you've finished, you die." "We'll see about that," said the soldier, sitting down at the table and helping himself to a good chunk of roast. "Brother Glossyboots," he said to the hunter, "come and eat. You must be as hungry as I am, and even in your own home you won't get a better roast." But the hunter wasn't in the mood for eating. The robbers watched the soldier with amazement and cried out: "He's sure making himself at home!" "Well," said the soldier after a while, "that food was all right. But now bring me something nice to drink." The captain was in a good humor and didn't take offense. "Go down to the cellar," he said to the old woman, "and get a bottle of the best." The soldier pulled the cork with a loud *pop* and, holding the bottle in his hand, went over to the hunter. "Now keep your eyes open, brother, and you'll see something. I'm going to drink the health of the whole clan." He waved the bottle over the robbers' heads, took a deep draft, and cried: "Long life to you all, but with your mouths open and your right hands upraised!" No sooner had he spoken than they all froze fast and sat as though made of stone, with their mouths open and their right arms in the air. The hunter said to the soldier: "I'm sure you've got more tricks up your sleeve. But hadn't we better get along home?" "Brother, brother, of course not. It's too soon to leave the field. We've defeated the enemy, but what about the spoils? There they sit, gaping with amazement. They won't be able to move until I give them permission. So come on, brother, let's eat and drink." The old woman had to bring another bottle of the best, and the soldier didn't get up from the table until he had eaten enough for three days.

At daybreak he finally said: "Time to strike tents. We won't have too long a march, for the old woman will show us the shortest way to town." When they got there, he sought out his old comrades and said: "I've found a nest of gallowsbirds in the forest. Come on, we'll clean it out." The soldier led them and said to the hunter: "Come back with us and see how they flutter when we grab them by the feet." He placed his men around the robbers. Then he picked up a bottle, took a swig, waved it back and forth over their heads, and cried: "Long life to you!" Instantly the stone figures began to move, and the moment they moved the soldiers' comrades jumped on them, tied them hand and foot, and threw them into a cart like so many sacks. "Take them straight to prison," said the soldier. But the hunter took one of the soldiers aside and gave him yet another order.

"Brother Glossyboots," said the soldier, "we've routed the enemy and got ourselves a good meal. Now let's take it easy and quietly bring up the rear." As they approached the town, the soldier saw a big crowd pouring out of the town gate. The people were all cheering and waving green boughs. And then the whole royal bodyguard came marching up. "What's going on?" he asked the hunter in amazement. "Didn't you know?" said the hunter. "The king was long absent from his kingdom and today he's coming back. The people are here to meet him." "But where's the king?" the soldier asked. "I don't see him." "Here!" said the hunter. "I am the king. I sent word I was coming." He opened his hunting coat, and when the soldier saw his royal garments he fell down on his knees in consternation. "Forgive me," he cried, "for treating you as an equal in my ignorance, and giving you such a nickname." The king gave him his hand and said: "You're a good soldier and you saved my life. I shall take care of you from now on and you shall want for nothing. If you ever feel the need of some good roast meat, as good as at the robbers' house, come to my royal kitchen. But if you want to drink anyone's health, you'll have to ask my permission first."

200

The Golden Key

ONE WINTER'S DAY, when the ground lay deep in snow, a poor boy was sent to the forest with a sled to bring back wood. After gathering the wood and loading it onto the sled, he was so cold that instead of going straight home, he thought he'd make a fire and warm himself a bit. He cleared a space, and as he was scraping away the snow, he found a little golden key. "Where there's a key," he said to himself, "there's sure to be a lock." So he dug down into the ground and found an iron box. "There must be precious things in it," he thought. "If only the key fits!" At first he couldn't find a keyhole, but then at last he found one, though it was so small he could hardly see it. He tried the key and it fitted perfectly. He began to turn it—and now we'll have to wait until he turns it all the way and opens the lid. Then we'll know what marvels there were in the box.

LEGENDS FOR CHILDREN

1
St. Joseph in the Forest

THERE WAS ONCE a mother who had three daughters. The eldest was rude and wicked, the second was a good deal better, though she too had her faults, and the third was a good pious child. But the mother was strange. She loved the eldest daughter best and couldn't abide the youngest. She often sent the poor girl out into the forest to get rid of her, for she thought she'd get lost and never come back. But the guardian angel that watches over every good child always showed her the right way and never forsook her.

One day the guardian angel pretended not to be there. The little girl couldn't find her way out of the forest and she went on and on until nightfall. Then she saw a light shining in the distance and it led her to a hut. She knocked, the door opened, and, coming to a second door, she knocked again. This door was opened by a venerable-looking old man with a snow-white beard, who was none other than St. Joseph. His welcome couldn't have been friendlier. "Come in, my dear child, seat yourself on my little chair by the fire, and warm yourself. If you're thirsty, I'll get you a drink of good fresh water. But all I can offer you to eat out here in the woods is a few roots and you'll first have to scrape them and cook them." St. Joseph handed her the roots. The little girl scraped them clean. Then she took out

the bread and the piece of pancake her mother had given her, put
them into a little pot with the roots, and cooked the whole into a porridge. When it was done, St. Joseph said: "I'm so hungry. Give me
some of your porridge." The child was glad to share her food and
gave him more than she kept for herself, but her hunger was stilled,
because God's blessing was with her. When they finished eating, St.
Joseph said: "Now we shall go to sleep. But I have only one bed. You
take it. I'll put some straw on the floor for myself." "No," she said.
"Keep your bed, the straw will be soft enough for me." But St.
Joseph picked the child up in his arms and carried her to the bed,
where she said her prayers and fell asleep. When she woke up next
day, she wanted to bid St. Joseph good morning, but he was nowhere
to be seen. She got up and looked for him, but couldn't find him anywhere. At last she saw a bag of money behind the door, and it was so
heavy she could barely lift it. On it there was a message saying it was
for the child who had slept there that night. She took the bag, ran out
of the house, and found her way safely home to her mother, who
couldn't very well be displeased with her, because she gave her all the
money.

The next day the second child thought she'd like to go out into the
forest. Her mother gave her bread and a much bigger piece of pancake. The same thing happened to her as had happened to her sister.
At nightfall she came to the hut, and St. Joseph gave her roots to
make porridge out of. When it was done, St. Joseph said again: "I'm
so hungry. Give me some of your porridge." The child replied:
"Share and share alike." Afterward, when St. Joseph offered her his
bed and said he'd sleep in the straw, she replied: "No. Lie in the bed
with me. There's room enough for us both." St. Joseph picked her
up in his arms, put her down on the bed, and went to sleep in the
straw. When the child woke up in the morning and looked for St.
Joseph, he had vanished, but behind the door she found a little moneybag about the size of a fist, and on it there was a message saying it was
for the child who had slept there that night. She took the little bag
and ran home. When she got there, she gave her mother the money,
but secretly kept a few coins for herself.

The eldest daughter's curiosity was aroused, and the following
morning she too wanted to go out into the forest. Her mother gave

her cheese as well as bread, and all the pancakes she wanted. At nightfall she found St. Joseph in his hut, just as the other two had found him. When the porridge was done, St. Joseph said: "I'm so hungry, give me some of your porridge." And the girl replied: "Wait till I'm full. If I leave any, you can have it." But she ate nearly all there was and St. Joseph had to scrape the bowl. Then the good old man offered her his bed, saying he'd sleep in the straw. The girl accepted without a word, lay down in the bed and left the hard straw for the old man. When she woke up in the morning, St. Joseph was not to be found, but she didn't let that worry her. She just looked behind the door for a moneybag. Thinking she saw something on the ground, she bent down to see what it was. The something stuck to her nose, and when she straightened up she saw it was a second nose clinging fast to her own. She began to scream and yell, but that didn't help, and her nose stuck out so far that she couldn't help looking at it. She ran out of the house and never stopped running or screaming until she met St. Joseph. Whereupon she fell at his feet and pleaded until he took pity on her, removed the extra nose, and gave her two pennies. When she got home, her mother was waiting at the door. "What did he give you?" she asked. "A big bag of money," the daughter lied, "but I lost it on the way." "Lost it!" cried the mother. "Never mind, we'll soon find it again." She thought they'd look for it together, and took her by the hand. The child burst into tears and said she wouldn't go, but after a while she went. On the way so many lizards and snakes came slithering after them that they couldn't get away. In the end they stung the wicked child to death, and stung the mother in the foot for not bringing her up better.

2

The Twelve Apostles

THREE HUNDRED YEARS before the birth of the Lord Jesus Christ there lived a mother who had twelve sons and was so poor and needy she didn't see how she was going to keep them alive any longer. Every day she prayed God to let her sons be on earth along with the promised Saviour. When their misery became greater than ever, she sent one after another out into the world to seek his bread. The eldest, whose name was Peter, was first to leave home. At the end of a day's journey, he strayed into a big forest and couldn't find the way out. The farther he went, the more lost he became, and to make matters worse, he grew so hungry he could hardly stand on his feet. In the end he was so weak he had to lie down. He thought he was near death. Then all at once a little boy was standing beside him. He was gleaming bright and as beautiful and friendly as an angel. After clapping his little hands to make Peter look up, the child asked: "Why are you lying there looking so forlorn?" "Ah," said Peter. "I'm going about looking for a way to earn my keep, in the hope that I may live long enough to see the promised Saviour. That is my dearest wish." "Come with me," said the child. "Your wish shall be fulfilled." He took Peter by the hand and led him past rocks and boulders to a big cave. When they went in, everything glittered with gold and silver and crystal, and in the middle twelve cradles lay side by side. The angel said to Peter: "Lie down in the first and sleep awhile. I'll rock you." Peter did as he was bidden and the angel sang to him and rocked him until he fell asleep. As he slept, the second brother arrived, he too led by his guardian angel, and like the first he too was rocked to sleep. Then came the others, each in his turn, until all twelve lay sleeping in their golden cradles. They slept three hundred years, until the night the Saviour was born. Then they awoke and were with Him on earth, and were called the Twelve Apostles.

3
The Rosebud

THERE WAS ONCE a poor woman who had two little girls. The youngest was sent to the forest every day to gather wood. Once when she had gone a long way before finding any, a beautiful little child appeared who helped her to pick up the wood and carried it home for her. Then in a twinkling he vanished. The little girl told her mother, but the mother wouldn't believe her. Then one day she brought home a rosebud and told her mother the beautiful child had given it to her and said he would come again when the rosebud opened. The mother put the rosebud in water. One morning the little girl didn't get up out of bed. The mother went and found the child dead, but looking very lovely. The rosebud had opened that same morning.

4
Poverty and Humility Lead to Heaven

ONCE THERE WAS a king's son who went out into the countryside one day when he was sad. Deep in thought, he looked up at the sky, so pure and blue, and heaved a sigh. "How wonderful it must be up there in heaven!" Then he saw a poor old man coming along and spoke to him. "How can I get to heaven?" he asked, and the man replied: "By poverty and humility. Put on my ragged clothes, wander about for seven years and get to know the misery of the world.

Don't take any money with you. When you're hungry, ask kindly souls for a crust of bread. When you've done all that, you'll be nearer heaven." The king's son took off his splendid coat, put on the beggar's clothes, and went out into the world. He suffered great want, accepted no other gifts than a little food, spoke to no one, and prayed the Lord to receive him into heaven when the time came.

When the seven years had passed, he returned to his father's palace. But no one recognized him. He said to the servants: "Go and tell my parents I've come back." But the servants didn't believe his story. They only laughed and left him standing there. Then he said: "Go and tell my brothers to come down. I'd be so glad to see them." Again the servants ignored him. Then in the end one of them went and told the king's other sons, but they didn't believe it either, and didn't go down. Finally he wrote his mother a letter telling of his misery, but not saying he was her son. Moved by pity, the queen arranged for him to be given a place under the stairs, and bade two of the servants bring him food every day. But the first servant was a wicked man. "Why," he said to himself, "should a beggar have this good food?" So he kept it all for himself or gave it to the dogs, and gave the feeble, exhausted beggar nothing but water. The second servant was honest and faithfully gave the beggar everything intended for him. It wasn't much, but it kept him alive for a while. He bore his lot patiently, but grew weaker and weaker. When he became very sick, he asked to take Communion. Halfway through Mass that day, all the bells in the town and the whole region began to ring of their own accord. After Mass, the priest went to the poor man under the stairs. He lay dead with a rose in one hand and a lily in the other. Beside him they found a sheet of paper with his story written on it. When he was buried, a rose grew up on one side of the grave and a lily on the other.

5
God's Food

THERE WERE ONCE two sisters, one of whom had no children and was rich, while the other, a widow, had five children and was so poor she hadn't bread enough to feed them. In her distress, she went to her sister and said: "My children and I are starving. You are rich, give me a little bread." The sister was as hardhearted as she was rich. "There's nothing to eat in my house either," she said, and drove the poor woman away with harsh words. After a while, the rich sister's husband came home. He wanted a piece of bread, but when he cut into the loaf, blood came pouring out. When his wife saw that, she was stricken with horror and told him what had happened. He hurried to the poor widow's house to help her. When he went in, he found her praying. She was holding her two youngest children in her arms, and the three eldest lay dead. He offered her food, but she replied: "We have no further need of earthly food. God has already fed three of my children, and he will soon hear our prayers as well." She had hardly spoken when the two little ones drew their last breath, whereupon her heart broke and she too fell dead.

6

The Three Green Branches

THERE WAS ONCE a hermit who lived in a forest at the foot of a mountain. He spent his time in prayer and good works, and, in addition, for the greater glory of God, carried a few pails of water up the mountain every evening. Quite a few animals drank of it and quite a few plants were refreshed by it, for on the heights there is always a harsh wind that parches the air and the soil, and the wild birds, which are afraid of humans, circle high in the air, looking down with their sharp eyes for something to drink. And because this hermit was so pious, an angel of God, visible to his eyes, went up with him, counting his steps, and brought him his food when his work was done, just as the ravens at God's bidding had fed the prophet. When the hermit had lived in piety to a great age, it so happened that one day, looking into the distance, he saw a criminal being led to the gallows and said to himself: "That man is getting his just deserts." That evening, when he carried the water up the mountain, the angel who had always gone with him did not appear, nor did he bring him his food. Stricken with horror, he searched his heart, asking himself what he could have done to make God angry, but he could not find the answer. He threw himself on the ground and neither ate nor drank, but prayed day and night. One day as he lay weeping, he heard a little bird singing gloriously. That made him sadder than ever, and he said: "How happily you sing! The Lord's not angry with you. Ah, if only you could tell me what I've done to offend Him, so I can do penance and my heart will be glad again." The bird spoke and said: "It was wrong of you to condemn a poor sinner who was being led to the gallows. That's why the Lord is angry with you. God alone sits in judgment. But if you repent of your sin and do penance, He will forgive you." Then he saw the angel standing beside him with a log in his hand, and the angel said: "You must carry this log about with you until three green branches grow from it, and when you lie down to sleep at night you must put it under your head. You must beg for bread from door to door and never stay in a house more than one night. That is the penance the Lord has imposed on you."

The hermit took the log and went back into the world that he hadn't seen in so long. He ate and drank only what people gave him as he begged from door to door. But often his pleas went unheard, many a door remained closed to him, and sometimes he went whole days without eating so much as a crust of bread. Once after he had spent the whole day going from door to door and no one had given him anything to eat or offered to lodge him for the night, he went out into the forest and found a cave fitted out to live in. There was an old woman in it. "Good woman," he said, "let me spend the night in your house." "No," she replied. "I couldn't even if I wanted to. I have three sons who are fierce and wicked robbers. If they came home and found you, they'd kill us both." "Please let me stay," said the hermit. "They won't hurt you and they won't hurt me." She was a kindly soul, and at that she let him in. He lay down under the stairs and laid his head on his log. When the old woman saw that, she asked him why he did it. He told her he carried the log about with him as a penance and used it as a pillow at night. He had offended the Lord, he told her; on seeing a poor sinner on his way to the gallows he had said: "That man is getting his just deserts." The woman burst into tears and cried out: "If the Lord punishes a single word so severely, what will happen to my sons when they come to judgment?"

At midnight, ranting and roaring, the robbers came home and made a fire. When the cave was lit up and they saw a man lying under the stairs, they flew into a rage. "What's this man doing here?" they shouted. "Didn't we forbid you to let anyone in?" "Leave him alone," said the mother. "He's a poor man atoning for his guilt." "What did he do?" the robbers asked. And then to the hermit: "Old man, tell us your sins." The old man sat up and told them how with a single word he had sinned enough to make God angry, and how he was now doing penance for his sin. His story so moved the robbers' hearts that, horrified by their evil lives, they searched their consciences, repented sincerely, and began to make atonement. After converting the three sinners, the hermit lay down again under the stairs and fell asleep. In the morning he was found dead, and three green branches had sprouted from the log on which he had pillowed his head. The Lord had taken him back into favor.

7

Mary's Glass

ONCE A WAGON heavily laden with wine was stuck so deep in the mud that the wagoner, try as he might, couldn't get it out. The Virgin Mary happened to come that way, and when she saw the trouble the poor man was in, she said: "I'm tired and thirsty. Give me a glass of wine, and I'll get your wagon out for you." "Gladly," said the driver, "but I have no glass to put your wine in." Thereupon the Virgin picked a white flower with red stripes, known as cornbind, which is shaped very much like a glass, and handed it to the wagoner. He filled it with wine and the Virgin Mary drank it. In that same moment, the wagon was freed from the mud and the wagoner was able to drive on. The peasants still call that flower Mary's glass.

8

The Old Woman

AN OLD WOMAN LIVED in a big city, and one evening she sat in her room all alone, thinking how she had lost first her husband, then her two children, then little by little all her relatives, and that very day her last friend, so that she was now all alone and forsaken. She was sad at heart. Hardest of all to bear was the loss of her two sons, and in her grief she reproached God for her misfortunes. She was sitting quietly, deep in thought, when all at once she heard the bells ringing for early Mass. Surprised to find that she had sat up all night in her grief, she lit her lamp and went to church. The church was lighted, though not with candles as usual, but with a diffused glow, and it was already crowded, all the seats were taken. When the old woman came to her usual place, it too was occupied, and so indeed was the entire pew. When she looked at the people, she saw that they were all relatives who had died. There they sat in their old-fashioned clothes. Their faces were pale, they didn't speak and they didn't sing, but the church was filled with a soft buzzing murmur. An elderly aunt stood up, came over to the old woman, and said: "Look at that altar over there and you'll see your sons." The old woman looked and saw her two sons. The one was hanging on the gallows, the other tied to the wheel. "You see," said the aunt, "that's what would have happened to them if they had lived and if God hadn't called them to Him while they were innocent children." The old woman went home trembling, and thanked God on her knees for having shown her more mercy than she had been able to understand. And the third day she lay down and died.

9

The Heavenly Wedding

ONCE A POOR PEASANT BOY went to church and heard the priest say: "Anyone who wants to go to Heaven must walk straight and never turn aside." So he started out, walked straight ahead over hill and dale, and never turned aside. His path finally took him to a large town and straight into the church, where services were being held. At the sight of all that splendor, he thought he was in heaven and, overcome with happiness, sat down. When the services were over and the sexton told him to leave, he replied: "No, I've come a long way, and now that I'm in heaven, I'm not leaving." The sexton went to the priest and reported: "There's a child here who won't leave because he thinks he's in heaven." "If that's what he thinks," said the priest, "we'll let him stay." He went to the boy and asked if he'd be willing to work. "Oh yes," said the boy. "I'm used to working, but I'm not leaving heaven." So he stayed in the church, and when he saw people kneel down and pray before a wooden statue of the Madonna and Christ Child, he thought: "This must be God," and he said: "Look here, God, you're as thin as a rail. The people around here must be letting you go hungry, but don't worry, I'm going to bring you half my food every day." From then on he brought the statue half his food every day, and the statue ate it. In a few weeks the statue began to fill out, and the people didn't know what to make of it. Neither did the priest, so he stayed in the church, followed the boy around, and saw how he shared his bread with the Blessed Virgin and how she accepted it.

Some time later the boy fell sick and didn't leave his bed for a week. When he was able to get up, the first thing he did was to take his food to the Virgin. The priest followed him and heard him say: "Dear God, don't be angry with me for not bringing you anything for so long. I was sick and couldn't get up." The statue replied: "I've seen your good will and that's enough for me. Next Sunday you shall go to the wedding with me." The boy was glad to hear that and told the priest, who said: "Go and ask if I may come too." "No," said the statue. "No one but you." The priest wanted to prepare him by giving him Holy Communion, and the boy was willing. The following Sunday when it was his turn to take Communion he fell dead and went to the eternal wedding.

10

The Hazel Branch

ONE AFTERNOON the Christ Child lay down in his cradle and fell asleep. His mother came in and said: "So you've gone to sleep, child? Sweet dreams. In the meantime, I'll go out to the forest and get you a handful of strawberries. I'm sure you'll be glad to have them when you wake up." In the forest she found a place full of the finest strawberries, but when she stooped down to pick one, a viper shot out of the grass. She took fright, left the strawberry untouched, and ran away. The viper darted after her, but, as you can imagine, the Blessed Virgin knew what to do. She hid behind a hazel tree and stayed there until the viper crept away. Then she picked her berries, and on the way home she said: "As the hazel tree has protected me today, so shall it protect others in the future." That is why since the earliest times a green hazel branch has been the best protection against snakes and vipers and all other creatures that crawl on the ground.

INDEX